ARCTIC OCEAN

EUROPE

ASIA

NORTH PACIFIC
OCEAN

AFRICA

INDIAN OCEAN

AUSTRALIA

ARCHAEOLOGICA

The World's Most Significant Sites and Cultural Treasures

ARCHAEOLOGICA

The World's Most Significant Sites and Cultural Treasures

CHIEF CONSULTANT
Dr. Aedeen Cremin

F
FRANCES LINCOLN LIMITED
PUBLISHERS

Frances Lincoln Limited
4 Torriano Mews
Torriano Avenue
London NW5 2RZ
www.franceslincoln.com

Archaeologica
Produced by Global Book Publishing
Level 8, 15 Orion Road
Lane Cove, NSW 2066, Australia
Ph: (612) 9425 5800   Fax: (612) 9425 5804
Email: rightsmanager@globalpub.com.au

British Library Cataloguing in Publication Data
A catalogue record for this book is available from the
British Library.

The moral rights of all contributors have been asserted.

ISBN 13: 978-0-7112-2822-1

Printed in China by Regent Publishing Services Ltd.
Color separation Pica Digital Pte Ltd, Singapore

9 8 7 6 5 4 3 2 1

PHOTOGRAPHS
Photography credits appear on pages 398–399.
Australian Aborigines and Torres Strait Islanders should note
that this book may contain images of deceased persons.

MANAGING DIRECTOR
Chryl Campbell

PUBLISHING MANAGER
Sarah Anderson

ART DIRECTOR
Kylie Mulquin

PROJECT MANAGER
Dannielle Doggett

CHIEF CONSULTANT
Dr. Aedeen Cremin

CONTRIBUTORS
Dr. Bahram Ajorloo, Associate Professor Alison Betts, Professor
Jeffrey Blomster, Dr. Robert Bollt, Professor Sandra Bowdler,
Maree Browne, Dr. Heather Burke, Dr. David Cameron,
Dr. Michael B. Collins, Professor Robin Coningham, Lisa
Cougle, Dr. R. Alan Covey, Dr. Kate da Costa, Professor Paola
Demattè, Dr. Peter Edwell, Dr. Dorian Q. Fuller, Dr. Yosef
Garfinkel, Dr. Wolfram Grajetzki, Dr. Ömür Harmanşah,
Gary Jackson, Dr. Simon Kaner, Professor Stephen H. Lekson,
Dr. Barry Lewis, Dr. Tracey Lie Dan Lu, Mark Manuel,
Dr. Sally May, Dr. Ian McNiven, Dr. Magdalena S. Midgley,
Dr. Iain Morley, Dr. George Nash, Dr. Dougald O'Reilly,
Dr. Innocent Pikirayi, Dr. Jeffrey Quilter, Dr. Karim Sadr,
Roger Sandall, Associate Professor Claire Smith, Professor
Glenn Summerhayes, Dr. Laura Villamil, Dr. Peter White,
Dr. Pamela R. Willoughby, Duncan Wright, Louise Zarmati

EDITORS
Loretta Barnard, Monica Berton, Annette Carter, Dannielle
Doggett, Judith Simpson, Marie-Louise Taylor

COVER DESIGN
Lena Lowe, Kylie Mulquin

DESIGNERS
Stan Lamond, Lena Lowe, Avril Makula, Kylie Mulquin,
Jacqueline Richards

DESIGN CONCEPT
Lena Lowe

CARTOGRAPHER
John Frith/Flat Earth Mapping

MAP EDITORS
Monica Berton, Alan Edwards, Katie Holmes

PICTURE RESEARCH
Jo Collard, Tracey Gibson

INDEX
Jon Jermey

PRODUCTION
Ian Coles

CONTRACTS
Alan Edwards

FOREIGN RIGHTS
Kate Hill

PUBLISHING ASSISTANT
Katie Holmes

Contributors

Dr. Bahram Ajorloo was born in Tehran, Iran, in 1975. He obtained his BA, MA, and PhD degrees in Archaeology from the University of Tehran, and has been a member of the academic staff at the NAZAR Research Center for Art, Architecture, and Urbanism in Tehran since 2001. Dr. Ajorloo has participated in more than 13 excavation projects in Azerbaijan, Iran, Kurdistan, and Turkey. He has conducted, at the University of Tehran, research projects on the Ark of Alishah in Tabriz, and the Achaemenid–Sassanid site of Bistun. Dr. Ajorloo is the cultural heritage editor of the newspaper *Asr-e Azadi* in Tabriz, and archaeology editor for *Bagh-i Nazar,* the journal of the NAZAR Research Center.

Associate Professor Alison Betts is a specialist in the archaeology of nomadic peoples and Director of the University of Sydney (Australia) Central Asian Programme. She has worked extensively in the Middle East and Central Asia and directed a number of major excavations and surveys in Jordan and Uzbekistan. Her interests include rock art, game drives, the early development of pastoral societies, nomad–state relations, and long-range transmission of ideas and innovations.

Professor Jeffrey Blomster is an anthropological archaeologist specializing in social complexity, political development and change, interregional interaction, and approaches to style, ritual, and ideology. His regional and spatial research interests lie primarily in Mesoamerica, where he has focused on the Mixtec, Zapotec, and Olmec cultures. In addition to Mexico, he has also performed fieldwork throughout the United States, from the Four Corners region of the Southwest to eastern Pennsylvania. He received undergraduate training in anthropology and political science at Washington and Lee University, and graduate training in anthropology and archaeology at Yale University. He is currently an Assistant Professor at The George Washington University in the United States.

Dr. Robert Bollt (PhD, University of Hawaii at Mānoa, 2005) specializes in the archaeology of East Polynesia. His concentration is on the Austral Islands, where he found and excavated the earliest-known site to date. He has also excavated sites in Hawaii and the Marquesas. Primary interests include Polynesian material culture (mainly lithics), and patterns of long-distance exchange among islands, which is achieved by using geochemical sourcing analyses to trace stone tools to their geological source of origin. He also enjoys experimental archaeology, especially adze making. Additional interests include Polynesian subsistence strategies, human–environment relations, sociopolitical transformation, and warfare.

Professor Sandra Bowdler was born in Sydney, Australia. A graduate of the University of Sydney (BA Hons 1970) and the Australian National University (PhD 1979), she has been employed by the University of Papua New Guinea and New England University and has been Professor of Archaeology at the University of Western Australia since 1983. She has carried out archaeological research in many parts of Australia, and in Southeast Asia. Current research interests include the archaeology of northeast Tasmania, the origins and cultural meanings of the Hoabinhian stone artifact assemblages of Southeast Asia and Australia, and the origins of gender in the human species.

Maree Browne studied Classical and Near Eastern Archaeology and Prehistory at the University of Sydney, Australia. She has worked on a number of sites, principally at the University of Sydney's site at Pella in Jordan, but also on Australian Aboriginal midden and rock art sites on the New South Wales coast and on colonial sites in Sydney. Her main interest is in the archaeology of the ancient environment and the manipulation of this environment to benefit its inhabitants. She lectures in the Faculty of the Built Environment at the University of New South Wales.

Dr. David Cameron is a Visiting Fellow in the School of Archaeology and Anthropology at the Australian National University in Canberra. He has conducted archaeological–paleoanthropological excavations and surveys in Australia, India, the United Arab Emirates, Hungary, Jordan, Israel, Turkey, and Vietnam. His major academic interests include human and ape anatomical evolution.

Dr. Michael B. Collins, PhD, is a native of West Texas, where as a boy he became interested in the many archaeological sites exposed by wind erosion during a severe drought in the 1950s. He pursued this interest through BA, MA, and PhD degrees in anthropology, with a secondary emphasis in geology. His research, carried out in the Near East and Europe as well as South, Central, and North America, emphasizes Stone Age technology and the earliest peoples in the New World. He has published numerous reports, articles, and monographs, as well as a book on these topics. He is currently Research Associate at the Texas Archeological Research Laboratory, University of Texas at Austin, United States.

Professor Robin Coningham is Professor of Archaeology at Durham University in the United Kingdom. He has conducted fieldwork throughout South Asia, and has directed excavations at the Citadel of Anuradhapura in Sri Lanka, the Bala Hisar of Charsadda in Pakistan, and Tepe Pardis in Iran. Currently, he is codirecting a five-year survey of the extramural hinterland of Anuradhapura and a program of survey and excavation in the Tehran Plain of Iran.

Lisa Cougle is an archaeologist with many years' experience in excavation and archaeological illustration. She has a BA (Hons) and MA both from the University of Melbourne in Australia, and has worked on digs throughout the Middle East and Australia. Cougle's research interests include mortuary analysis, gender, and the archaeology of dress and jewelry. She is currently undertaking doctoral research at the Australian National University on Iron Age Italian burial practices.

Dr. R. Alan Covey is Assistant Professor of Anthropology at Southern Methodist University in Texas, United States. He received his PhD from the University of Michigan in 2003 and held a postdoctoral fellowship at the American Museum of Natural History. Dr. Covey has conducted archaeological research and archival studies of the Inca civilization for more than a decade. His principal research has focused on the Inca heartland, and his book *How the Incas Built Their Heartland* was published by the University of Michigan Press in 2006. In addition to ongoing work in the Cuzco region, Dr. Covey has also worked in several Inca provincial regions.

Dr. Aedeen Cremin, trained in Ireland and France, was formerly a senior lecturer at the University of Sydney, Australia, and is now a Visiting Fellow at the Australian National University in Canberra. She is a past president of the Australasian Society for Historical Archaeology and is the general editor of *Historic Environment,* the journal of the Australian Committee for ICOMOS (International Council on Monuments and Sites). She has written *The Celts in Europe* and *The Celts,* and is coauthor of *The Enduring Past, Experience Archaeology, Archaeology, 1901: Australian Life at Federation,* and *Australia's Age of Iron.* Her current research is with the Greater Angkor Project in Cambodia.

Dr. Kate da Costa studied Near Eastern and Classical Archaeology at the University of Sydney, Australia, where she currently holds an Australian Research Council Fellowship. She has also worked in Historical Archaeology in Sydney. Her research interests relate to the relationships between indigenous populations and foreign political control. She is investigating how these connections operated between the Roman Empire and long-established cultural groups in the southern Levant in the first millennium CE. Her fieldwork is in Jordan. She is also interested in local trade, and is a specialist in ceramic lamps of the Levant.

Professor Paola Demattè is Associate Professor of Chinese Art and Archaeology at the Rhode Island School of Design, Providence, United States. She holds a Laurea in Chinese Language and Literature from the Università degli Studi di Venezia, and a PhD in archaeology from the University of California, Los Angeles. She specializes in the Neolithic and Bronze Age archaeology of China. She has written on the origins of Chinese writing, predynastic urbanism, archaic jades, and funerary art as well as on East–West contacts and exchanges.

Dr. Peter Edwell is a lecturer with the Department of Ancient History at Macquarie University in Sydney, Australia. His research and teaching interests focus on the lands of the eastern Mediterranean and Mesopotamia from the conquests of Alexander to the late Roman period. Dr. Edwell completed a PhD thesis in 2005, which focused on the expansion of Roman power in the Near East. He has traveled extensively throughout Syria and the Near East and is presently writing a book on the Romans in Syria and Mesopotamia.

Dr. Dorian Q. Fuller is Lecturer in Archaeobotany at the Institute of Archaeology, University College, London (United Kingdom). He also lectures on the cultural history of Nubia. He was educated at Yale (BA) and received his PhD from Cambridge. He has carried out archaeological fieldwork in Sudan, Morocco, China, and India. He is on the committees of the Sudan Archaeological Research Society and the Society for Libyan Studies. In 2004, he directed a salvage archaeology field project in the threatened Fourth Cataract region of the Nile in Sudan.

Dr. Yosef Garfinkel is a professor of Biblical Archaeology at the Hebrew University of Jerusalem, Israel, and a curator of the museum of Yarmukian Culture at Kibbutz Sha'ar Hagolan. He specializes in the protohistoric era of the Near East, the period of time when the world's earliest village communities were established and the beginning of agriculture took place. He has excavated numerous Neolithic and Chalcolithic sites, like Gesher, Yiftahel, Ashkelon, Sha'ar Hagolan, and Tel Tsaf, and has published ten books and over 90 articles. These contributions relate both to aspects of daily life like architecture, pottery, and water supply, and to more spiritual aspects like art, culture, and dance.

Dr. Wolfram Grajetzki obtained his PhD from the Humboldt University of Berlin, Germany, and has taught Egyptology there. He has excavated in Egypt and Pakistan, and was principal archaeologist and author for the online learning project Digital Egypt for Universities (University College, London). He is preparing the catalog of Egyptian coffins for the Fitzwilliam Museum, Cambridge. His publications include *Burial Customs in Ancient Egypt* (2003) and *The Middle Kingdom in Ancient Egypt* (2006).

Dr. Ömür Harmanşah currently teaches Ancient Near Eastern archaeology, architectural history, and material culture at Brown University's Joukowsky Institute for Archaeology and the Ancient World in Providence, Rhode Island, United States. He received his PhD from the University of Pennsylvania by writing a dissertation on the topic of founding new cities in antiquity. He is currently working on a book provisionally entitled *City Stories: New Urban Foundations and Architectural Practices in the Ancient Near East.* He taught at Reed College, which gave a new direction to his research interests in the theories of the body, performance, spatiality, and social memory. His favorite place in the world is Taşkahve in Ayvalık, Turkey.

Dr. Simon Kaner is Assistant Director of the Sainsbury Institute for the Study of Japanese Arts and Cultures in Norwich, United Kingdom. He is an archaeologist specializing in the prehistory of the Japanese archipelago, and has taught and published on many aspects of East Asian archaeology. His recent publications include an adapted translation of Kobayashi Tatsuo's *Jomon Reflections* (Oxbow Books, 2004).

Professor Stephen H. Lekson is Curator of Anthropology at the Museum of Natural History, University of Colorado in Boulder, Colorado, United States. He received his PhD from the University of New Mexico. Lekson directs archaeological projects throughout the US Southwest. His publications include a dozen books, many chapters in edited volumes, and articles in journals, most recently *The Archaeology of Chaco Canyon* (SAR Press, 2006); *Archaeology of the Mimbres Region* (British Archaeological Reports, 2006); and *Salado Archaeology of the Upper Gila, New Mexico* (University of Arizona Press, 2002). His wife, Professor Catherine Cameron, is also an archaeologist teaching at the University of Colorado.

Dr. Barry Lewis received his PhD from the University of Illinois at Urbana-Champaign, where he is currently Professor of Anthropology. His teaching includes courses in archaeology, geographic information systems, quantitative and qualitative research methods, eastern United States prehistory, South Asian history, and the archaeology of warfare. He has published extensively on his archaeological investigations of prehistoric towns and villages in the eastern United States. His current research focuses on the archaeology and history of early modern kingdoms in southern India.

Dr. Tracey Lie Dan Lu is currently an associate professor in the Anthropology Department of the Chinese University of Hong Kong. She obtained her undergraduate and MPhil degree in archaeology from the Zhongshan and Beijing Universities of China respectively, and her PhD degree from the Australian National University. Her research interests from 1983 to the early 1990s were archaeology of the Qin and Han Dynasties. From 1994 onward she has been working on prehistoric archaeology of mainland China and Hong Kong, particularly on the transition from hunting and gathering to agriculture, and the impact of agriculture on prehistoric cultural developments and the human diaspora in East Asia and the Pacific. Recently, she has also worked in the field of cultural heritage management. She has published two books, and 38 papers and book chapters.

Mark Manuel is a PhD student at Durham Saninsury University in the United Kingdom, testing models of social and political organization for the Indus Valley Tradition. He received his BSc and MA in archaeology from the University of Bradford in 2001 and 2003 respectively.

Manuel has worked on excavations in Pompeii in Italy and has conducted surveys in Gujarat, India. He is currently involved in ongoing projects in the Tehran Plain in Iran and at Anuradhapura in Sri Lanka.

Dr. Magdalena S. Midgley is a Senior Lecturer in Archaeology at the University of Edinburgh, United Kingdom. Her teaching and research interests are centered on continental Europe, including the spread of early farming communities, Neolithic rituals, and the emergence of monumentality in funerary and ceremonial contexts. She is also interested in antiquarianism; the representation of prehistoric monuments, especially megaliths, in Romantic painting; and the history of archaeology as a discipline.

Dr. Iain Morley is based at the McDonald Institute for Archaeological Research, Cambridge University, United Kingdom, and is a Fellow of Darwin College. After initially studying Psychology he moved into Paleolithic and Mesolithic Archaeology, and has specialized in the evolution of human cognition. Particular areas of interest include the emergence of ritual and religion, Paleolithic imagery, and the evolutionary origins and archaeology of music, which was the subject of his PhD research at Cambridge. As well as academic writing and teaching, he has contributed to programs for BBC radio and has excavated at prehistoric sites in Britain, Croatia, Moravia, and Libya.

Dr. George Nash is a visiting fellow and lectures at the Department of Archaeology and Anthropology, University of Bristol, United Kingdom. He is also Associate Archaeologist at SLR Consulting (Shrewsbury), where he works within the private sector. He has worked in northern Europe, North America, Romania, Indonesia, and the Iberian Peninsula, researching mainly prehistoric art and Neolithic mortuary practices. He has written and edited many books, including recently *The Architecture of Death: The Neolithic Chambered Tombs of Wales* (2006), *Looking Beyond the Castle Walls* (2006), *The Archaeology of Fire* (2007), and *Art as Metaphor: The Prehistoric Rock-Art of Britain* (2007). In addition to publishing, George also writes and presents for radio and television and is currently producing five programs on European rock art for the BBC.

Dr. Dougald O'Reilly is an archaeologist researching the development of political complexity in Bronze and Iron Age Southeast Asia. He is also the founder and director of a nongovernmental organization called Heritage Watch that is dedicated to heritage preservation in Cambodia. Heritage Watch conducts grassroots training in conservation and poverty alleviation, the root cause of looting. Currently, Dr. O'Reilly is a lecturer in archaeology at the University of Sydney, Australia, and is undertaking research with the Greater Angkor Project in an effort to understand the nature of the ancient site of Angkor.

Dr. Innocent Pikirayi has researched on the Iron Age of the Zimbabwe plateau and adjacent regions. He is the author of *The Zimbabwe Culture: Origins and Decline in Southern Zambezian States* (AltaMira Press, 2001). Currently, he is investigating prehistoric urban landscape dynamics associated with the development of early second millennium CE complex societies in the middle Limpopo Valley in southern Africa. He is also working on the decline of Great Zimbabwe as a city and center of political power and influence.

Dr. Jeffrey Quilter is Deputy Director for Curatorial Affairs and Curator of Intermediate Area Archaeology at the Peabody Museum of Archaeology and Ethnology, Harvard University, United States. His research interests focus on the intersections of theory in art history, history, and anthropology. He has conducted archaeological research primarily in Peru and Costa Rica. His most recent research is the excavation of an early colonial period church and town on the north coast of Peru. He is the author of *Cobble Circles and Standing Stones: Archaeology at the Rivas Site, Costa Rica* (University of Iowa Press, 2004) and *Treasures of the Andes* (Duncan Baird, 2005).

Dr. Karim Sadr received his PhD in Anthropology from the Southern Methodist University in Dallas, Texas, United States, with a dissertation on the origins of pastoral nomadism in northeast Africa. Since 1995, he has taught archaeology at the Universities of Botswana and the Witwatersrand in South Africa. His current research interests are the origins of livestock, the herding way of life, and ceramic technology in southern Africa.

Roger Sandall was born in New Zealand, and attended Columbia University in New York, United States, where he studied fine arts, film, and anthropology. Moving to Australia, he made a number of award-winning documentaries about Australian Aboriginal life and later taught in the Department of Anthropology at the University of Sydney. He is the author of *The Culture Cult*, a critical study of romantic social thought, and has contributed to a variety of international journals including *Commentary, The New Criterion,* and *The American Interest.*

Professor Glenn Summerhayes FSA FLS is Professor and Head of the Department of Anthropology at Otago University in New Zealand. He has extensive experience in the archaeology of the western Pacific, in particular Papua New Guinea, where he is affiliated with the National Museum and Art Gallery. Although an expert in Lapita studies, Professor Summerhayes has just started a new project in the Kosipe Valley, exploring 40,000 years of archaeology in the great landmass of New Guinea.

Dr. Laura Villamil received her BA (University of California, Berkeley) and MA and PhD (University of Michigan, Ann Arbor) in anthropology, with a specialization in Maya archaeology. She has participated in archaeological projects in the United States (California and Georgia), Belize, and Mexico (Valley of Mexico, Oaxaca, and Quintana Roo). Since 1998 she has directed a regional archaeological project in central Quintana Roo, Mexico, aimed at investigating different aspects of urbanization by comparing the spatial organization and long-term development of two ancient Maya cities. She is Assistant Professor of Anthropology at the University of Wisconsin-Milwaukee in the United States.

Dr. Peter White is a prehistoric archaeologist, recently retired from the University of Sydney, Australia. His research has been primarily concerned with New Guinea, Australia, and the settlement of the Pacific. He has worked with people who grew up making and using stone tools; he has also excavated sites and analyzed pottery and animal bones. He has edited academic journals for many years, and has written several books and many articles.

Dr. Pamela R. Willoughby is Professor of Anthropology at the University of Alberta, Edmonton, Alberta, Canada. She has a BA (Honors) degree from Trent University, an MA from the University of Alberta, and a PhD from the University of California in Los Angeles (UCLA), all in anthropology. She is a specialist in human evolutionary studies and carries out Middle and Later Stone Age archaeological field research in southern Tanzania—these are the periods associated with the appearance of the first modern humans. She is also the editor of *Nyame Akuma,* the research bulletin of the Society of Africanist Archaeologists.

Louise Zarmati has had a varied career as an archaeologist and teacher. She received a BADipEd from the University of Sydney, Australia, and completed a Master's degree in archaeology at the University of Cambridge, United Kingdom. Zarmati has worked as an archaeologist in Israel, Greece, Cyprus, and Australia. She taught archaeology at schools and universities, and developed archaeology education programs for museums and archaeological excavations in Sydney. She has written a number of books and articles on archaeology, including *Experience Archaeology* (1998) and *Archaeology* (2004) with Dr. Aedeen Cremin, and *Pompeii and Herculaneum* (2005). In 2005 Zarmati was awarded a NSW Premier's History Scholarship to research archaeology in Italy. She is currently undertaking a PhD at Deakin University.

The majority of the contributions in the Australian Aborigines chapter of the Australia and the Pacific section were written by a coalition of researchers from Flinders University (Adelaide, Australia) and Monash University (Melbourne, Australia). These contributions were organized by Claire Smith, President of the World Archaeological Congress. The contributors are **Dr. Heather Burke, Gary Jackson, Dr. Sally May,** and **Associate Professor Claire Smith** from Flinders University, and **Dr. Ian McNiven** and **Duncan Wright** from Monash University.

Contents

Foreword

In archaeology, every day brings new discoveries. Archaeologists are constantly "rewriting history," building upon a body of reliable knowledge to retell the human story in its amazing diversity. This tale continually unfolds with new and intriguing twists, some of which are published here for the first time.

This book reflects what archaeology does best: it gives a voice to the people without written history, be it the tragic young Inca girls sacrificed in the *capacocha*, or the anonymous craftsmen who glazed the bricks of Susa in Iran. We can learn about and feel with our fellow humans in everyday activities to which we can all relate. It is fun to work through the book by theme—the environment, clothing, food, architecture, religion—or by time: what was happening around the world during the mid-winter solstice 4,000 years ago?

The answer is here before your very eyes. This is the first great lesson of archaeology: history is out there, you need only look for it and you will certainly find it. The past is not gone; it is here, and now. The second great lesson is that the human past is our shared story— it belongs to us all and we all have a duty of care, a duty to cherish the information and antiquities that archaeologists have worked so hard to record, analyze, and conserve.

More than 40 archaeologists, historians, and cultural anthropologists from around the world have contributed to this book, all of them active in their fields—guaranteeing that the information is as up to date as it can be. The great mysteries of the world—the Easter Island statues, the Nazca Lines, Stonehenge, the pyramids of Mexico—are not demystified; on the contrary, they are put into their context, which makes them seem even more remarkable.

Dr. Aedeen Cremin

INTRODUCTION

What is Archaeology?

The buried past has long fascinated humans; the treasures and secrets of the people and buildings that lie beneath their feet have led many to dig into this hidden world. This world and the endeavor to uncover it are the foundations of the discipline of archaeology, the study of the material remains of the cultures of the past.

As long as humans have lived on earth they have left traces of their existence. These traces may be a surface scatter of stone tools and other cultural debris, or it may be an almost perfectly preserved buried town. Whatever the deposit, it will tell those who excavate and research these remains something of the lives of the people who left them behind. This is archaeology. The range of sites studied and the enormous variations in the amount and complexity of the remains have led to great specialization in the disciplines that exist today under the general umbrella term of archaeology.

PENETRATING THE PAST
Two millennia have passed since the Romans built their city, Londinium, by the Thames River. In order to reach the Roman foundations of modern-day London in the United Kingdom, archaeologists need to dig through several centuries' worth of occupational deposits.

QUEST FOR EGYPTIAN GOLD
The most attractive and valuable treasures removed from Egyptian tombs were the gold artifacts, such as this pectoral that now resides in the Egyptian Museum of Turin, Italy. The museum was established in 1824, long before cultural property laws came into being.

WHO IS INVOLVED IN ARCHAEOLOGY?

In the past, many people have shown an interest in the lives of their ancestors; however, this interest was overshadowed by a greater one in the art of the past. This interest led to the clearing from ancient sites of all that was intrinsically valuable or beautiful, removing pieces of sculpture, wall paintings, and hoards of gold but leaving behind the more prosaic accoutrements of the people who produced them. These pieces were taken at a time before it was understood how much valuable information could be gathered by recording the details of all the material from one context, not only the major pieces. Now every piece from a site, be it a beautiful vase or the bones from a meal eaten 2,000 years ago, is recorded, analyzed, and assessed as part of the wider local environment.

The callous "treasure hunts" of the past have given way to the organized scientific excavation of ancient remains. A number of specialists are involved in an archaeological project. On-site excavators often work alongside volunteers and members of the local communities, as photographers and draftspeople record their work. In the laboratories, both on site

WHY IS ARCHAEOLOGY IMPORTANT?

All people need to know their story. Individually we want to understand where we came from, who our family is, and what our cultural inheritance is; so it is with humanity. It is archaeology that can most accurately tell us our story. It differs from the written story of the past, as it is the study of all cultures, not only those that were literate. It tells the story of all people and places—not only the powerful and important—and while it often enhances the written word, it can also contradict it.

Archaeology is far more than simply the scientific excavation, recording, and categorization of objects. It is the use of this in-depth research to plot environmental changes, trade distribution, catastrophic natural events, disease patterns, population fluctuations, and technological evolution. It shows the subtle artistic and stylistic changes that can indicate social evolution and cultural interchange. It endeavors to tell us how the people and societies of the past have lived.

WHEN A RESCUE BECOMES A REMARKABLE RECOVERY
Many archaeological discoveries are made during quickly arranged rescue digs. In 2005, workers at a construction site in Ziyang, China, watched in awe as a bronze sculpture of a Qin or Han Dynasty horse and carriage was unearthed by archaeologists before building work recommenced.

and elsewhere, conservators, archaeobotanists, paleopathologists, ceramicists, and a wide range of other specialists analyze the material. Then the findings are correlated and published.

Permits to excavate are granted through a government authority. Those applying for such permits usually come from universities, other institutes of higher education, or museums. Generally, ownership of the excavated material remains with the country of excavation, though many generously allow long-term loans of some material to the excavating institution for research purposes. Many countries are signatories to a variety of treaties that serve to protect the cultural heritage of the world and give general direction for the ethical excavation of ancient sites.

CHOICE OF SITES

A variety of factors govern the choice of a site for excavation. Today, a large number of sites excavated are what are referred to as rescue digs. These are sites that are under threat because of development. This may be a new dam, an apartment block, a highway—any area where the encroachment of human activity will destroy the evidence from the past.

Other sites are chosen because of their architectural or historical significance or because of the richness of the initial surveys. Surveys of large areas of terrain are conducted to indicate where there may be deposits of significant interest. What dictates their significance varies; it could be that a particular deposit may fill a gap in our knowledge of a particular period, it may be that it uncovers a new culture, or it may solve a long-standing archaeological problem.

THE SIGNIFICANCE FOR THE FUTURE

While the main concern of archaeology is certainly the study of the past, the important information archaeologists uncover can often help us to see something of what the future may hold. For example, where we can see the deterioration of the natural environment due to excessive irrigation in the past, we can warn of consequences for the overusage of irrigation in the future. Technologies that have become obsolete in the past may be reintroduced because they are actually superior to modern methods or because they help to conserve dwindling resources.

Archaeology tells the story of the past of all peoples; without this knowledge we are like a person without memory, floundering along the pathway to the future in search of identity, connection, and purpose.

History of Archaeology

Most people can name at least one great discovery in the history of archaeology, like the Tomb of Tutankhamun. However, the discipline of archaeology is much more than just discovering tombs, temples, and gold. Archaeology is the quest for knowledge about our human history. It is a search to find tangible links from the present to the past. Archaeology is a product of our need to know the past and to ensure our place in the present.

FABULOUS FINDS
The history of archaeology is peppered with outstanding discoveries made by archaeologists with a determination to find the truth. This unattributed engraving shows an archaeologist making notes at the site of Troy in Turkey, famously uncovered by Heinrich Schliemann during the 1870s.

PLUNDERED FOR PROFIT
Corinthian pottery, much like this vase from the seventh century BCE, became some of the world's first looted antiquities, when the Romans established a colony in Corinth and set about trading ceramic grave goods throughout the Roman Empire.

The history of archaeology is the story of our search for tangible evidence of humanity and how the processes of discovery changed over time. In comparison to many other bodies of knowledge, archaeology is a relatively new player. For a long time archaeology was considered the "handmaid of history." This meant that archaeology was only used to fill in gaps in the written record. By the late nineteenth century, archaeology became established as a proper academic discipline based on scientific methods. It soon became clear that archaeology could produce evidence which would do more than just fill in the gaps.

Some scholars began to criticize historians for drawing conclusions about the past only from written sources. Was it possible to find out about people who lived in the times *before* writing was used? Archaeology is our only source of information about prehistory, the millions of years before humans began to use writing to communicate. It is also a method of finding out about people who couldn't read and write, even after writing had been "invented."

EARLY CHRONICLERS
Greek historian and geographer Strabo of Pontus (*c.* 62 BCE–CE 24) provides one of the earliest records of digging and collecting. Strabo tells us that when the Romans colonized ancient Corinth during the time of Julius Caesar, they dug up graves and removed terracotta reliefs, bronze vessels, and pottery. These artifacts became valuable commodities because of their antiquity and rarity, and were traded around the Roman world for a high price.

The Italian Renaissance humanist considered the earliest archaeologist was Ciriaco Pizzicolli, better known as Cyriac of Ancona (*c.* 1391–1455). Cyriac was a merchant and diplomat, and adviser to Pope Eugene IV; he spent much of his spare time traveling around the Mediterranean, studying

AN HISTORICAL STUDY TEN YEARS IN THE MAKING
William Camden's work on British antiquities—the
first topographical and historical survey of
Britain—was first translated from the
original Latin into English in 1610.

many different
languages of the region as
well as the physical remains of
the ancient world. He wrote detailed descriptions of
the magnificent monuments and spectacular sites he
came across, illustrating them beautifully with his
own insightful drawings. His approach was radical
for his time: Cyriac wrote a history that questioned
the reliability of written sources and analyzed ancient
artifacts and architecture.

SIXTEENTH-CENTURY TOPOGRAPHERS

During the sixteenth century, many scholars traveled
widely and visited ancient sites. They developed the
simple method of topographical recording of sites
and monuments that lay exposed in the countryside.
They described the ruins in detail, took measurements,
and made comprehensive drawings. In Britain, one
of the first of these topographers was John Leland
(1506–1552), librarian to Henry VIII, who bestowed
on Leland the impressive title of Royal Antiquary. In
1533, Henry commissioned Leland to create a full
inventory of England's extant antiquities. Leland
developed a method that combined the study of
sources with "peregrinations" (journeys) and wrote his
Itinerary, the first record of Britain's many antiquities.
Unfortunately, Leland was struck by "madness" and
eventually abandoned his research in 1550.

John Leland's innovative recording methods were
continued in the next generation by William Camden
(1551–1623), historian and biographer of Elizabeth I.
Camden's method was to construct history, not only
from written sources, but also from the information
he gained from the study of sites, monuments, and
artifacts, such as coins. Camden's unique approach
revolutionized the knowledge of British antiquities,
and for this he is considered the founder of British
archaeology. A plate in Camden's *Britannia* (1600)
shows what is probably the earliest known illustration
of an excavation—two people digging in front of
Stonehenge, and beside them some bones and a skull
that they have recovered from the site.

SEVENTEENTH-CENTURY ANTIQUARIANS

In the early seventeenth century, most
educated Europeans knew of the ancient
Greeks and Romans from reading Latin and
Greek texts at school. This resulted in many age-old
locations becoming the focus of digging for plunder.
Inspired by the works of ancient writers like Strabo,
Pliny, Homer, Herodotus, Thucydides, and Pausanias,
wealthy amateur art collectors or dilettantes gathered
pottery, jewelry, and even pieces of buildings, like the
Parthenon, to take back home with them. The ancient
sites produced thousands of artifacts and created a
fashion in Europe for collecting.

By the end of the seventeenth century this interest
in collecting and plunder had developed into a process
of recording, describing, and analyzing sites and artifacts known as antiquarianism. Although antiquarians
were highly educated and extremely knowledgeable
about a number of different areas, such as medicine,
astronomy, geography, and Classical literature, the
study of antiquities began to evolve into a separate
and specialized discipline.

COLLECTOR OF ARTIFACTS
Antiquarian by Italian painter
Lorenzo Lotto (c. 1480–1556).
Antiquarianism—the study of
antiquities—was just beginning in
the sixteenth century CE; it wasn't
until the seventeenth century CE
that it became a passionate pastime
for many educated Europeans.

WHEN VOLCANOLOGY MEETS ARCHAEOLOGY

Produced under the supervision of Sir William Hamilton, the illustrations in *Campi Phlegraei* (1776) by Pietro Fabris focus on Italian volcanoes and their impact. The above etching shows the Temple of Isis at Pompeii being dug out from beneath the layers of ash.

While the Renaissance humanists questioned the existence of historical "truth," antiquarians of the seventeenth century questioned the reliability of written texts, and maintained that greater "security" could be gained from "reading" artifacts.

John Aubrey (1626–1697) was an antiquarian whose pioneering research on the sites and monuments of prehistoric Britain established field archaeology as a scientific study. Aubrey made accurate drawings, plans, and descriptions of monuments in the Wiltshire countryside, such as Avebury and Stonehenge. Aubrey's *Monumenta Britannica* made him a leading figure of seventeenth-century antiquarianism in Britain.

William Stukeley (1687–1765) was a medical doctor, whose interest was the study of the geography, topography, and monuments of the British landscape. Stukeley's work led to a chronological analysis of the past that challenged the accepted theory that megalithic structures like Avebury and Stonehenge were built by the Romans or Saxons. Stukeley argued that these structures were built by the Druids, the Celtic priests described by Julius Caesar. Although Stukeley's observations and descriptions were accurate, his interpretations were later proven incorrect—the Druids had not constructed these monuments; they were built much earlier during the prehistoric period. Stukeley's contribution to the study of the past was far-reaching. He became the first president of the London Society of Antiquaries, whose annual journal, *Archaeologia*, was first published in 1770, and he was also a founder of the British Museum.

Both John Aubrey and William Stukeley improved standards of fieldwork through their precise methods of data collection, description, and observation, and laid the foundations for the development of archaeology as a distinct discipline in Britain.

EIGHTEENTH-CENTURY DEVELOPMENTS

The eighteenth century saw a continuation of the method of using ancient texts to locate ancient sites. The importance placed on these texts and the perceived truths within them had a great influence on the first major archaeological excavations of that era. Scholars used descriptions in Classical texts to help them locate ancient sites where important events in history had taken place.

THE FATHER OF MODERN ARCHAEOLOGY

Johann Joachim Winckelmann was an expert on Greek art and wrote extensively on the subject, which influenced the rise of the Neoclassical period. Unfortunately, he was murdered in Trieste, Italy, before he was ever able to journey to Greece.

During the eighteenth century, many wealthy and influential people spent enormous fortunes collecting antiquities. At that time countries like Greece, Egypt, and Turkey did not have laws in place to stop people from removing antiquities from their countries and setting up private collections in their own homes. In southern Italy, the English consul at Naples, Sir William Hamilton (1730–1803), acquired hundreds of Greek pots and shipped them back to England for his personal collection.

The desire of wealthy individuals to acquire private antiquities collections caused many problems. Some of the most important archaeological sites of the time were robbed by callous thieves who were only too happy to provide collectors with artifacts. Many countries today are still in the process of trying to recover their cultural treasures.

The highly respected German art historian Johann Joachim Winckelmann (1717–1768) had a profound impact on the development of archaeology in Europe.

Winckelmann was already an established authority on art history analysis when he turned his attention to the way archaeological sites were being dug up in Italy. Winckelmann visited Pompeii and Herculaneum in the 1760s and exposed the careless methods being used to uncover buildings and retrieve artifacts. His criticisms became widely known in the scholarly community and encouraged an awareness of the importance of carefully recording and preserving buildings and artifacts for posterity.

Thomas Jefferson (1743–1826) is best known as the third president of the United States. He is perhaps less well known for his remarkable achievements as an amateur archaeologist: he conducted the first recorded excavation in North America in 1784. Jefferson set out to discover how the mounds located on his Virginia estate were constructed, and who built them. He found that they were composed of several layers, or strata, which he used to establish a sequence of deposit over time.

Attractive frescoes found at Herculaneum, such as this one dated to around 20 BCE of a girl wearing a wreath, were looted from the site by employees of the King of Naples in the 1700s.

POMPEII AND HERCULANEUM

In 1594, an Italian landowner decided to build an aqueduct to carry water from the river Sarno to his villa at the foot of Mt. Vesuvius. To the workmen's surprise they uncovered ruined buildings and an inscription. Nothing much was done about the discovery; they did not know they had been digging up the lost town of Pompeii.

The exact locations of Pompeii and Herculaneum were not discovered until over 100 years later, and quite by accident. In 1709, a peasant digging a well on his property discovered large slabs of inscribed marble. An Austrian prince deciphered the inscription and realized that the peasant had uncovered the site of ancient Herculaneum. The prince quickly bought the land and plundered large architectural pieces from the site until 1716 when he could extract no more.

In 1738, the King of Naples ordered his antiquaries to dig tunnels at Herculaneum so they could find treasures for his private collection. Hundreds of pieces of sculpture, columns, and wall paintings were removed to decorate his palace. The royal collection now forms the basis of the National Archaeological Museum in Naples.

In 1763, a block bearing an inscription was discovered at a site assumed to have been Stabiae. The inscription established conclusively that the site was not ancient Stabiae but the lost town of Pompeii. The king and his advisers quickly shifted their digging to the promising new site.

Karl Weber (1712–1764), a Swiss army officer, was commissioned to direct the recovery of Pompeii and was the first person to record what was being discovered at the site. He began by making a map of all the known buildings, and uncovered the buried areas section by section. Unfortunately, the site had already been plundered for about 50 years before any attempt was made at accurate record keeping.

UNCOVERING UR

Known in the Bible as "Ur of the Chaldees," the ancient city of Ur was one of the most prosperous and powerful cities operating in Sumeria during the third and fourth millennia BCE. The city was abandoned in the fourth century BCE and remained long forgotten, until its ruins were found and excavated in 1854 and 1855 by the British consul to Mesopotamia, J. E. Taylor. During his excavations, Taylor partly uncovered the great ziggurat dedicated to the Sumerian moon god known as Nanna, and a few baked clay cylinders that identified the city as Ur.

Taylor's work was continued by Sir Charles Leonard Woolley (1880–1960) from 1922 to 1934, when he dug up an entire city quarter in order to gain a comprehensive picture of its occupation sequence of over 5,000 years. One of Woolley's most spectacular discoveries was the graves of the Sumerian ruling family, which contained precious objects and evidence of human and animal sacrifice.

Known as "The Ram in the Thicket," this is one of the finest examples of the treasure unearthed at Ur, Iraq. It is made from gold, copper, lapis lazuli, red limestone, and shell.

NINETEENTH CENTURY: DEVELOPMENT OF EXCAVATION METHODS

In 1819, the curator of the Danish National Museum, Christian Thomsen (1788–1865), set up a new kind of museum to display prehistoric artifacts. He chose to arrange the artifacts in their showcases according to the materials from which they were made—stone, bronze, and iron—then used these terms to describe the "ages," or times, from which the materials came. Thomsen's revolutionary system of naming became known as the "Three Age System," and by the second half of the nineteenth century it was widely accepted by scholars around the world. It still forms the basis of the archaeological descriptions of cultures used today: Paleolithic (Old Stone Age), Neolithic (New Stone Age), Bronze Age, and Iron Age.

Heinrich Schliemann (1822–1890) is without a doubt one of the best-known archaeologists in history, due to his discovery of Troy. He maintained that it was his childhood passion for the dramatic stories of the Trojan War that inspired him to seek the long-lost city of Troy. Schliemann put complete faith in the written evidence, and he used Homer's *Iliad* to help him locate the site.

With the help of American archaeologist Frank Calvert, Schliemann began digging at the mound of Hisarlik in western Turkey in 1870. Eager to reach the oldest layer—which he believed to be from the

MR. SCHLIEMANN'S OPUS
Hisarlik (which means "Place of Fortresses"), was a 100-ft (30-m) high mound when Heinrich Schliemann began excavating it in the 1870s. Since then, much of the Homeric city of Troy has been uncovered, including a ramp leading to the city entrance.

period of the Trojan War—Schliemann dug a 36-ft (11-m) deep shaft, right to the bottom of the mound. Excavations in the 1930s by American archaeologist Carl Blegen proved that Schliemann had dug right through "Priam's Troy," and in the process had destroyed everything later than 2000 BCE.

In 1874, Heinrich Schliemann began excavations at Mycenae in Greece in search of the graves of Agamemnon, legendary king of Mycenae, and his royal family. Schliemann dug inside the walls and uncovered at least five graves filled with gold and precious objects. He discovered the gold "Mask of Agamemnon," so named because of the telegram Schliemann sent to the King of Greece that said, "I have gazed upon the face of Agamemnon." But at the time Schliemann sent the telegram he was not even in Mycenae; he sent it long after the excavation had finished, and Schliemann was referring not to that particular mask, but to the burials in general. Once again, later scholars proved that the shaft graves from which that particular mask came were about 300 to 400 years older than the time that Agamemnon lived.

The development of archaeology as a distinct discipline came at about the same time as the publication of Charles Darwin's theory of evolution. As a result of the theory of evolution, a whole new science—the study of the physical form of ancient

humans—developed, and many archaeologists became involved in this exciting new scientific field.

The range of archaeological methods developed by Lieutenant-General Augustus Pitt Rivers (1827–1900) were greatly influenced by two factors: Darwin's theory of evolution and Pitt Rivers's own military career. For over 20 years Pitt Rivers conducted excavations on his private properties in southern England and recovered a wealth of archaeological material from the Neolithic to the Saxon periods. Pitt Rivers's approach to recording archaeological material was innovative because he believed all artifacts, not just unique and beautiful ones, should be collected and cataloged. His excavation notebooks were meticulously detailed and systematically recorded in military fashion.

Pitt Rivers introduced a new approach to archaeological display, by arranging artifacts "typologically"— in other words, grouped by form or purpose rather than by geographic or cultural origin—to show evolutionary changes over time. Pitt Rivers's personal collection now forms the basis of the Pitt Rivers Museum in Oxford, United Kingdom.

TWENTIETH CENTURY: ARCHAEOLOGY COMES OF AGE

Like Heinrich Schliemann and others before him, Englishman Arthur Evans (1851–1941) was another archaeologist whose aims were greatly influenced by

Greek mythology, specifically the famous legend of Minos, King of Crete, who kept a half-man and half-bull monster called the Minotaur in a labyrinth in his palace. Evans first became interested in Crete in 1894 when he was shown black seal stones with writing on them, which had come from Kephala. At first he was convinced that the stones were Mycenaean, so he began digging at the site in March 1900. Immediately the excavated site revealed unusual architecture and extraordinary artifacts. Evans soon realized that this culture was quite different from that of the Mycenaeans, so he called it "Minoan" after Minos of Crete.

THE KING OF KNOSSOS
English archaeologist Arthur Evans was photographed in 1935 at the scene of his most triumphant discovery, Knossos in Crete. He was knighted in 1911 for his services to the field of archaeology.

CONTROVERSIAL ARCHAEOLOGIST AND ADVENTURER
Although generally remembered for his destructive excavation methods, and his misleading reporting of finds, Heinrich Schliemann was responsible for some of the most important archaeological digs of the 1800s, including those at Troy, Mycenae, Orchomenos, and Tiryns.

Even at the time he began digging at Knossos, Arthur Evans was criticized for reading too many of his ideas into the interpretation of the Minoans. His reconstruction of the palace is controversial. Rather than conserving the architecture so that it did not deteriorate, Evans decided to reconstruct the palace. He often made up missing features where no evidence of them remained. Today, archaeologists are able to differentiate between the products of Evans's imagination and the facts of archaeological evidence, and they still recognize the great contribution that he made to the history of mankind: his discovery of the "Minoans" of ancient Crete.

Sir William Matthew Flinders Petrie (1853–1942) made a significant contribution to the development of archaeological methods through his innovative approaches to excavation and recording. Petrie excavated a remarkable number of sites in Egypt— including Tell el-Amarna, the city created by the heretic pharaoh Akhenaton—and developed meticulous excavation and recording methods. He paid particular attention to detail, making sure that everything was recorded, measured, drawn, and described in situ. Petrie was responsible for developing the process of dating artifacts called seriation, which places types of artifacts into a sequence often based on their shape or method of manufacture. He was always quick to publish his results, and is credited with more than 1,000 publications. He eventually became the first Professor of Egyptology in Britain at University College, London.

Sir Mortimer Wheeler (1890–1976) was a war hero, serving in both World War I and World War II, and he made many great contributions to the field of archaeology. First, he developed the grid system of

excavation that divided the site into squares to be systematically excavated and recorded. This method was further developed by Dame Kathleen Kenyon, and became known as the Wheeler–Kenyon method. Wheeler used this method in his excavation of Maiden Castle in the United Kingdom.

Wheeler's second main contribution was the establishment of archaeology in India and Pakistan. As Director-General of the Archaeological Survey of India, he explored in detail the remains of the Indus Valley Civilization at Mohenjo-Daro, as well as helping to establish the Archaeological Department and National Museum of Pakistan.

Perhaps Wheeler's greatest contribution was as a "celebrity archaeologist." Wheeler believed that archaeology needed public support, and he promoted it with great wit and humor in the media. He appeared on numerous television and radio shows in the 1950s, and was well known for his popular books on archaeology, including *Archaeology from the Earth* (1954) and his autobiographical *Still Digging* (1955). Wheeler was knighted in 1952 for his services to archaeology.

Dame Kathleen Kenyon (1906–1978) is recognized as one of the greatest archaeologists of her generation. Following Sir Mortimer Wheeler's fine example, she developed the technique of laying out a carefully measured grid and digging in squares, which has become known as the Wheeler–Kenyon method. Kenyon was a competent administrator and excellent teacher, both in the lecture room and in the field. From 1948 until 1962 she was a lecturer in archaeology at the University of London. In 1952 she excavated the site of Jericho in Palestine, and from 1951 to 1963 she was the Director of the British School of Archaeology located in Jerusalem. Kathleen Kenyon is one of only a handful of female archaeologists who reached the highest level of their profession at this time. Another was Dorothy Garrod, first Professor of Archaeology at Cambridge University in the United Kingdom (1939).

HIRAM BINGHAM LOCATES MACHU PICCHU

In 1911 Hiram Bingham (1875–1956), a young lecturer at Yale University, led an expedition to the Andes and inadvertently located the "lost" Incan city of Machu Picchu. The site had been largely forgotten by everyone except the local people who guided Bingham to the area. Bingham mapped and photographed the site then returned the next year to clear and record it more thoroughly. *National Geographic*, who sponsored the expedition with Yale, described Bingham's work as "one of the most remarkable stories of exploration in South America in the past fifty years." Bingham's interpretation was that Machu Picchu was the lost city of Vilcabamba, for which he had been searching originally, or perhaps the legendary place known as Tampu Tocco. Recent research has located Tampu Tocco and Vilcabamba elsewhere, and shown that Machu Picchu was simply a royal estate that belonged to one of the Incan emperors. Today it is one of the major tourist attractions in Peru. Hiram Bingham's book, *Lost City of the Incas*, became a bestseller when it was published in 1948, and he may even have been the inspiration for the film archaeologist Indiana Jones, played by Harrison Ford.

GREAT DISCOVERIES OF THE LATE NINETEENTH AND EARLY TWENTIETH CENTURIES

Howard Carter (1874–1939) had worked as an archaeologist in Egypt for many long years before he met George Herbert, fifth Earl of Carnarvon (1866–1923), the wealthy man who became his friend

STARE INTO THE PHARAOH'S EYES
Perhaps the most famous artifact ever to be found in Egypt, the mask of Tutankhamun is made from solid gold, with decorative touches in quartz, glass, obsidian, and lapis lazuli. When the 24-lb (11-kg) mask was discovered by Howard Carter back in 1922, the ear lobes surprisingly did not have earrings—the holes were hidden by gold-foil disks.

and patron. Carter worked for Carnarvon for seven years, excavating various tombs around Egypt, but always with disappointing results. Then in 1914 Carter and Carnarvon gained permission to excavate in the Valley of the Kings. Carter was absolutely convinced that the tomb of one insignificant young pharaoh, known as Tutankhamun, remained unrobbed and undiscovered in the Valley of the Kings.

In the final season of their campaign in 1922, Carter uncovered what is perhaps the most spectacular discovery in the history of archaeology: the undisturbed tomb of Pharaoh Tutankhamun. Within weeks of opening the tomb, Lord Carnarvon died in Cairo of blood poisoning, and the legend of the "curse of Tutankhamun," invented by the press, was born. Carter himself did not actually become a victim of the "curse." He died peacefully at his London home 17 years later.

THE LEAKEY FAMILY

There is one noteworthy British family that has made an immense contribution to archaeology: the Leakeys. Louis Leakey (1903–1972) and his wife Mary Leakey (1913–1996) made a number of significant discoveries at Olduvai Gorge in Kenya that proved correct Charles Darwin's radical theory (at the time) that Africa was the homeland of humankind. Their discoveries changed the previously held belief that early humans originated somewhere in Asia.

OLD MAN OF OLDUVAI

The fragments of the *Zinjanthropus* skull that Mary Leakey found in 1959 have been fitted together, with missing pieces reconstructed, giving us a good idea of the skull structure of early man. This skull is now housed in the National Museum of Tanzania.

ARCHAEOLOGY GONE MAD

Adolf Hitler took Gustaf Kossinna's ideas on Germanic superiority and used them to stake a claim over neighboring countries of Europe. He created special units within the secret service that were devoted to excavating sites that might contain ancient "Germanic" artifacts.

In 1959, Mary Leakey discovered the skull of *Zinjanthropus* (later reclassified as *Australopithecus boisei*), then in 1978 she found a trail of clear ancient human footprints made by two adults and a child some 3.5 million years ago. They had been impressed and preserved in volcanic ash at a site in Tanzania called Laetoli. They belonged to a new species, best represented by the 3.25 million-year-old Lucy skeleton discovered in Ethiopia by Donald Johanson.

Richard Leakey (1944–) continued the family's paleontological research and discovered the complete 1.6 million-year-old skeleton of an African *Homo erectus*. As a result of the pioneering work of the Leakey family, eastern Africa came to be recognized as the cradle of modern humanity.

ARCHAEOLOGY AND TWENTIETH-CENTURY POLITICS

Evolutionists of the nineteenth century saw prehistoric culture developing uniformly at the same time and as a single whole. By the early twentieth century, archaeologists became interested in the geographic distributions of artifacts, ideas, and technologies across both time and space. This theory was called diffusionism, and it had a profound impact not only on archaeology but also on politics of the twentieth century.

Vere Gordon Childe (1892–1957) is often credited with being the most influential archaeologist of the twentieth century. Childe's most famous excavation was at Skara Brae, a 5,000-year-old village in the Orkneys, Scotland. Childe became a leader in the field of prehistory. His knowledge was encyclopedic, and his interpretations of archaeological evidence were groundbreaking. It was Childe who made popular the idea of archaeological cultures, or socially distinct groups that can be defined by characteristic artifacts.

Throughout his life, Childe believed wholeheartedly in the theory of Marxism. In 1935, especially as a reaction to fascism, he began to apply the theory to his interpretations of archaeological findings. Childe presented his Marxist view of European prehistory in a number of books, and spoke out against the way the Nazis used archaeology and history to justify their ideas of racial superiority.

Childe retired from scientific life in 1956 and returned to his homeland of Australia. The following year he took a trip to the mountains west of Sydney and ended his life by throwing himself from a cliff. He left a letter saying he did not wish to be a burden to society in his old age.

Diffusionism and the Nazis

You have probably seen the blockbuster movie *Raiders of the Lost Ark* (1981), in which Hollywood's most famous archaeologist, Indiana Jones, battles the Nazis for control of archaeological material. There is some truth to the movie because the Nazis did use archaeology to justify their plan for world domination.

Gustaf Kossinna (1858–1931) was Professor of German Prehistory at the University of Berlin. He used diffusionist theory to claim the "superiority" of the Germans, arguing that the German people had been the original inhabitants of Europe, and that all influences, ideas, and models were passed on by the more advanced Germans to the less advanced people with whom they came in contact. Kossinna set out to prove his theory by finding archaeological evidence of the prehistoric "Germanic" culture.

When Adolf Hitler came to power in 1933, he increased government funding

for German archaeological research to "prove" that the Germans were the dominant cultural group in Europe. Hitler and his Propaganda Minister, Joseph Goebbels, were often photographed viewing so-called "Germanic" artifacts. They used such "evidence" to justify their brutal invasions of Czechoslovakia and Poland, where "Germanic" artifacts and sites had purportedly been found.

Fascist Archaeology in Italy

During the fascist period of the 1920s and 1930s, archaeology thrived in Italy. Fascism propaganda promoted *romanità*, the ideal of Italian nationalism that used Roman archaeology and history to justify Benito Mussolini's imperialistic expansion into North Africa. Mussolini styled himself as the "new Augustus," and enormous amounts of money and human labor were poured into the excavation of significant archaeological sites such as the Mausoleum of Augustus, the Altar of Augustan Peace, the Roman harbor at Ostia, and Herculaneum. The message was that Rome once had a great empire and the fascists were restoring to Italy its rightful glory. Mussolini himself was often shown turning the first soil of excavations and visiting prominent sites.

MID- TO LATE TWENTIETH CENTURY: ADVANCES IN THEORY AND METHOD

In the 1960s a revolution in thinking took place in archaeology when Lewis Binford and David Clarke published articles that challenged the way scholars

interpreted archaeology. This "new" or "processual" archaeology focused on the social processes that work to produce material culture in a society. While the processual approach never dominated the discipline, it did offer a challenge to the way people interpreted archaeological evidence and led to the development of a wealth of new ideas.

In the late 1980s' climate of postmodernism, Cambridge University archaeologist Ian Hodder introduced his "postprocessual" approach as a reaction to processualism. Hodder argued that individuals and groups should be considered the agents of archaeology rather than "systems." Hodder also believed that there can and should be no single interpretation of the past, and that multiple interpretations should both be allowed and be accepted.

Scientific and technological innovations have also revolutionized archaeology. The introduction of radiocarbon dating, which measures the amount of carbon remaining in nonliving organic materials, has allowed archaeologists to assign approximate dates to sites, artifacts, and bodies such as Lindow Man and the Ice Man. Since the 1990s the application of DNA testing to the analysis of human remains has revealed the identity and family relationships of individuals and groups, such as the tragic Romanov family. Such scientific techniques have also brought new evidence to the debate on ethical issues in archaeology, such as the repatriation of cultural artifacts and human remains to groups like the indigenous people of Australia and North America.

MARXIST BELIEFS ASIDE ...

Australian archaeologist Vere Gordon Childe carried out excavations at Skara Brae in Scotland, beginning in 1928. He had many outstanding ideas about Neolithic life, but his theory that the Skara Brae site was quickly abandoned has been discounted.

Concepts and Techniques

Archaeology's extraordinary growth in the twentieth century affected every part of the discipline, but its basic concepts remain largely unchanged. The enduring fundamental questions that, when answered, enable all significant investigations of the human past are simple ones. What is it? Where was it found? What was found with it? How old is it? And, the question that fills museums, empowers teachers, and drives the curiosity of everyone from archaeologists to children around the world—what can it tell us about the past?

Before considering the wide diversity found in the discipline of archaeology, as well as the research problems, issues, and questions that motivate modern examinations of the human past, let's briefly consider how archaeologists answer these basic questions. We'll do it in two parts: first, by examining the relevance and importance of the key concepts implied by each question, and second, by exploring how archaeologists address these concepts in the field through specialized techniques.

CONCEPTS

The preserved material remains of the archaeological record are our "window on the past," but it takes a lot of hard work to ensure that the "past" created by archaeologists is more than merely a caricature of the modern world and its biases and values.

What is It?

One essential research task in the study of all ancient material remains is to answer the question "What is it?" Such a question may seem trivial at first glance, but as any field archaeologist can tell you, the answer is often elusive. Take, for example, a stone hand ax plowed up by a modern-day Belgian or French farmer. Shaped much like a teardrop and measuring about 6 in (15 cm) long, this artifact resembles tens of thousands of similar stones found in fields, riverbanks, and road cuts from England to southern Africa and parts of Asia. Many medieval European peasants knew them to be thunderbolts, a product of nature; others were equally confident that they were charmstones made by fairies. It was not widely agreed that they were ancient human tools until the mid-nineteenth

ARE THEY TOOLS OR STONES?
Even the smallest and seemingly most insignificant rock can in fact be a prehistoric tool. Archaeologists are trained to tell the difference between stones that have been hand-flaked by early humans, and those that have eroded naturally.

FUTURE OF THE PAST

Throughout their work, archaeologists also promote greater public awareness of the finite nature of the archaeological record. It is vanishing at an alarming rate in this crowded world, much faster than it can be recorded and studied. Each rock-cut Buddha blasted to bits on an Afghan mountainside, each Mayan stela smuggled in pieces out of Mesoamerica and sold to European art dealers, each prehistoric Native American village that vanishes under a new shopping mall, all destroy irreplaceable parts of our common human heritage. A certain amount of such destruction is inevitable because life must go on, but archaeologists take the position that the responsible course of action is to manage these resources in an informed way so that the maximum public and scientific benefit can be realized. The development of an archaeological conservation ethic and sense of stewardship among the public, the identification of national preservation priorities, and the increased public awareness of the many threats faced by archaeological sites and monuments can all make a difference in the heritage bequeathed to our children.

This ancient statue of Buddha, one of two carved into a rocky cliff at Bamiyan, Afghanistan, was destroyed in 2001 by the Taliban, who claimed it was a false idol.

century. And even now, with all the extraordinary accomplishments and technology of modern archaeology, researchers are still learning about how ancient people used these implements.

How Old is It?

Along with identifying archaeological materials, the researcher must also be able to situate them in their proper place within the 2.6-million-year span of the archaeological record (i.e., "How old is it?"). You cannot discover much about the past if you lack the ability to scale it in time. For example, Cyriac of Ancona, the early antiquarian introduced in the previous section, greatly admired the ancient monuments and ruins that he visited on his travels around the Mediterranean world, but to him and his contemporaries the human past was simply past. They lacked the ability to give time depth to the archaeological record, and consequently, there was little about the human past that they could discover.

Where Was It Found?

Equally important is the need to identify the locations of material remains in space (i.e., "Where was it found?"). Archaeological artifacts and features (an archaeological feature is a nonportable artifact, such as the preserved remains of an ancient house) without provenience information lose much, if not most, of their potential interpretive value and are reduced to little more than curiosities and junk. The related concepts of archaeological context and association (i.e., "What was found with it?") define the basic spatial relationships among artifacts and features in the archaeological record. Fortunately, space has been easier for archaeologists to deal with than measuring past time. The concept of a map as a graphical device for locating objects in space has been around for at least the past couple of thousand years. Antiquarians such as Cyriac of Ancona may have been ill-prepared to deal with past time, but they were extremely familiar with maps as tools for recording spatial information.

Getting the Whole Picture

By the beginning of the twentieth century, researchers finally possessed the basic conceptual understanding of time, space, and archaeological context needed to make great strides in archaeology (i.e., "What can it tell us about the past?"). The main goal in these early days was largely unraveling and comprehending cultural history; most research aimed at sorting out the chronicle of major events in world archaeology, reasoning that, until we answered the most important "what," "where," and "when" questions about the past, we would not have much success with those that asked "why" and "how."

CHARTING HISTORY

Maps were one of the first tools used to plot the location of sites, and many old maps have become archaeological treasures. This large Byzantine mosaic of the Holy Land made in *c.* CE 560 for the church at Medeba, Jordan, shows the Mediterranean at the top, and the city of Jerusalem in a large oval on the left.

Profiting greatly from these early accomplishments, twenty-first century archaeology can do considerably more than build descriptive accounts of prehistory. Many of the theories and big questions that motivate current research are drawn from anthropology and history. Some such questions demand comparative analysis across many cases (e.g., "Why did the earliest farmers emerge after the end of the last ice age?") and place extraordinary demands on our archaeological understanding of many parts of the world. At the other extreme, many research problems are grounded in specific events or periods (e.g., "What impact did

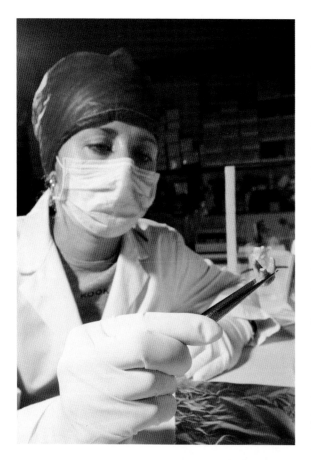

the invention of the shaduf, or pole-and-bucket lever, have on Egyptian agriculture during New Kingdom times?"). Both research extremes continue to demand that we command time, space, and context within the archaeological record.

TECHNIQUES

Although the popular image of the field archaeologist patiently excavating a site with a trowel and brush still holds true, today's diverse toolkit may also include seemingly unarchaeological things such as satellite imagery, digital elevation models, computer simulations, DNA analysis, and even heavy earthmoving equipment of the kind ordinarily seen in the construction of roads. The modern archaeologist is well prepared to deal with the technical challenges of understanding the past.

Experiments and Ethnoarchaeology

To help correctly identify an artifact or feature, archaeologists may conduct experiments that replicate the same type of tool or even the observable patterns of wear that resulted from its use by prehistoric people. For example, recalling the hand axes mentioned earlier, researchers have conducted many experiments with replicas of these tools, using them to butcher big game and throwing them like projectile weapons. Such experiments help to identify the range of tasks for which ancient hand axes were once used.

The outstanding technical advances of the past few decades are such that it is now even possible to identify tool uses from direct evidence found on the implements themselves. In Israel, soil samples collected from the tiny pores and cracks in the working surface of a grinding stone unearthed in the remains of a well-preserved Epipaleolithic hut enabled researchers to identify the type of wild cereal grass grains that were ground to a flour on it around 23,000 years ago.

INSIGHT INTO THE COPPER AGE
One of the most useful methods for understanding past societies and cultures is to replicate techniques that they had available at the time. Here, archaeologists at Shiqmim in Israel are making copper by heating the ore in a fire kept hot by constantly blowing on it.

MOLECULAR LINK TO THE PAST
The invention of DNA analysis has enabled archaeologists to learn a lot more about past humans. This researcher is carrying out a DNA test on a Peruvian mummy's tooth, which will increase the knowledge of the genetics of the pre-Hispanic population in Peru.

DIG DEEPER AND DEEPER TO REACH FURTHER INTO THE PAST
Stratigraphy is the commonsense idea that, over time, cultural and natural deposits are left on top of each other, so that the oldest material is at the bottom, while the youngest is at the top. This material can include pottery, tools, bones, wind-blown earth, charcoal from fires, clay, and organic matter, as shown in this display from Mexico's National Museum of Anthropology.

(e.g., wood from a preserved roof beam dated to 3100±75 BP [Before Present] in radiocarbon years).

The most common relative dating methods, all of which are still used today, are stratigraphy, cross-dating, and seriation. Of the three, stratigraphy is the most robust method, largely because of the principle of superpositioning, which basically asserts that the stuff on top was put there last. This principle is simple, but strong. When systematically applied in the field, it gives the archaeologist a solid basis for interpreting the relative ages of excavated strata and the materials contained within them.

Cross-dating, as the name suggests, consists of estimating the relative age of artifacts or features from one archaeological context based on distinctive attributes shared with material remains in another context, the age of which has been determined by other dating methods. Cross-dating is often used when archaeologists want to come up with a quick and inexpensive age estimate of a newly discovered site. They study a sample of cultural debris from the site's surface and compare attributes of these tools, potsherds, and other artifacts with cultural materials from well-dated, excavated sites in the same general region. Where the artifact attributes are similar between two or more sites, or strata within sites, it is inferred that the compared contexts may also be close together in time.

Seriation, the third kind of relative dating, applies a similar logic as that of cross-dating to construct a relative ordering of archaeological contexts. Seriation assumes that the cultural world in which we live changes over time in an orderly way, with the rise and fall of fad and fashion, the discarding of old technologies and the adoption of new ones, and so on. Granted this assumption for at least some classes of archaeological debris, researchers further reason that archaeological sites can be ordered according to carefully chosen attributes, say the presence or absence of selected decorative motifs on pots or the frequencies with which particular artifacts are represented in surface collections. The ranked result serves as a proxy measure of relative time differences. Experiments conducted with samples of known age demonstrate that seriation works. It has two weak points: first, its crude assumption about cultural changes, and second, you cannot tell which end of a seriated set of archaeological samples is youngest or oldest unless you have external data, such as stratigraphy, to anchor it in time.

Researchers also try to understand and explain archaeological patterning by seeking out possible analogies in ethnographic accounts that describe modern-day people who make and use similar implements or features. Where such accounts are inadequate or do not yet exist, archaeologists may undertake their own ethnographic research (often called ethnoarchaeology). For example, researchers working in many parts of the world have drawn on ethnoarchaeological research among village potters in the Philippines to understand how pottery decoration and style can encode important information about social interaction and networks.

Relative Dating

Estimating the age of ancient materials and deposits is another major archaeological activity. The main dating methods utilized today can be divided into two types: relative dating, which comprises methods that give ordinal or ranked estimates (e.g., old, older, oldest), and absolute dating methods, which are those that yield dates expressed in some fixed scale

1940s, scientists figured out how to use this to estimate the age of a sample of ancient organic materials. With appropriate calibration, these age estimates can be expressed in calendar years.

Radiocarbon dating's strengths are that potential samples are commonly available from most archaeological contexts, the processing costs are relatively cheap (they run about US$200–250 per sample these days), and the results are fairly accurate. Datable sample sizes can be as small as two thousandths of an ounce (5 milligrams), which is so small that many prehistoric cave paintings can be now dated by sampling tiny flecks of pigment.

One of radiocarbon dating's few drawbacks is arguably its effective range, which spans the past 50,000 years. While this covers many interesting millennia of our past, the archaeological record extends for hundreds of thousands and in some cases millions of years in parts of the world. Fortunately, absolute dating techniques also exist for constructing age estimates of these ancient materials. For example, the K/Ar method uses the ratio of potassium (K) to argon (Ar) in volcanic rocks to date archaeological contexts older than 1,000,000 years. This method and others like it have been used to date some of the oldest archaeological sites in eastern Africa.

Site Discovery

Dating samples, identifying artifacts, reconstructing ruins, and so on are all central activities of archaeological field research, which to most people means excavations. However, site discovery and site survey are also important field activities, which often take place long before the first trowel goes in the ground on any given project.

Site discovery is just what the name suggests—the process of identifying where sites are (and where they are not!). Even with all of today's sophisticated technological aids, most sites are still found by individuals who walk through fields or check road cuts, quarries, beaches, and other places where exposed ground can be searched for artifacts, flint chips, burials, potsherds, and other material evidence that people were there at some time in the past.

Site Survey

Once sites are found, various site survey methods provide the means to investigate the areas without excavation. The collected information ranges from basic attributes such as area, location, estimated age,

Relative dating methods were archaeology's mainstay until the middle half of the twentieth century, when the modern generation of absolute dating techniques began to revolutionize archaeologists' ability to measure past time. Although relative dating will always be part of the archaeological toolkit, absolute dating techniques are far more useful, making it possible to assess the age of archaeological deposits with measurable accuracy and precision.

Radiocarbon Dating

Radiocarbon dating is the most widely used absolute dating method in archaeology. It is based on measuring the level of radioactive decay of the C14 contained within a specimen. All living creatures, both plants and animals, ingest carbon isotopes through the food chain. Only one of these isotopes, known as C14, is radioactive. After the organism dies, the C14 in its tissues decays at a known, measurable rate. In the late site use, depositional characteristics, and preservation condition to maps showing possible buried houses, refuse-filled pits, streets, and so on. Hand-held computers with global positioning satellite (GPS) capabilities greatly ease the task of recording the field data; back in the lab, information stored in the hand-held computers can be added to the project database with the click of a button.

Modern site survey maps are also constructed by a wide range of instruments. The days when map-making equipment such as transits, alidades, and Brunton compasses were essential field gear are quickly passing. Many archaeologists now head to the field with GPS-based mapping instruments that have built-in data recorders and accuracies that can be in the order of an inch or so (a few centimeters) for mid- to high-end products.

Field investigators can also turn to a growing number of different instruments that can help map buried features, which may be undetectable from the surface evidence. Magnetometers, for example, measure the unique anomalies caused by soil disturbances in the background magnetism of the earth. These devices can be dragged across a site or even towed through water to detect and map subsurface features. Another instrument, called ground-penetrating radar, uses the reflection of electro-magnetic pulses to build up a similar picture of a buried site.

Site Excavation

In spite of the many essential contributions of modern site discovery and survey methods, archaeology will probably always mean "excavation" to most people. It is still the single most important data source that archaeologists have for reconstructing in detail both the human past and the local environments in which ancient people lived.

Excavations vary considerably according to their purpose. One common distinction is that between horizontal and vertical excavation types. Horizontal excavations expose a large site area, which facilitates making accurate interpretations about exposed features. The primary disadvantage of such excavations is encountered in deeply stratified sites, because of the immense time, money, and personnel resources needed to expose large areas of such sites.

THE EVERYDAY TASKS OF SITE SURVEY AND EXCAVATION

Archaeology is rarely as glamorous as Hollywood movies would have us believe. Much of the work involves mundane—but necessary—tasks such as recording measurements and cataloging finds. It can be cold, dirty, and tiring work, but the information gleaned from these digs is well worth it.

REMOTE-SENSING TECHNOLOGY

This has been a rich source of site discovery methods since the early twentieth century, when aerial photography first enabled archaeologists to use indirect evidence such as vegetation characteristics and topographical shadow marks to find sites. Modern satellite digital imagery delivers even more prospective site location information than aerial photos, and satellite images on the Internet have allowed even laypersons to become involved in searches for sites. Many archaeologists now employ geographical information systems (GIS) software to analyze data and predict where previously undiscovered sites should exist in a given study area.

Satellite images of the Great Wall of China. At left, the wall is shown as an orange line. At right, close-ups reveal two parts— the Ming wall as a bright white line, the Sui as a broken line.

Vertical excavations, on the other hand, are primarily designed to expose a site's depositional sequence in a reasonably quick time frame. Their main advantage is the relatively low-cost picture they give of a site's different occupation layers. Their main weakness is that they typically expose such a small horizontal area that it is hard to accurately interpret the cultural contexts of the various deposits cut through by the vertical excavation.

THE FIRST MAJOR SURVEY OF THESE MYSTERIOUS GEOGLYPHS
In the late 1990s, researchers at the Federal Institute of Technology in
Zurich, Switzerland, used more than 1,000 aerial photographs to create
three-dimensional computer representations of the ancient lines carved
into the desert at Nazca in southern Peru.

Excavation is obviously a destructive process, and
there's no archaeological counterpart to the "undo"
function in computer software. Since it has to be
done right the first time, it is archaeological practice
to thoroughly document every step of the process. In
principle, the field archaeologist will always return to
the lab with the ability to place every artifact, feature,
and stratigraphic relationship in the proper three-
dimensional context of the excavated site volume.
Computing technology makes this relatively easy
to do well using many of the same tools described
earlier. The current trend in excavation-data recording is toward GPS-enabled hand-held computers that
feed measurements and other essential information
directly into project databases. Back in the lab, the
data can be imported into CAD (computer-aided
drafting) software packages to produce measured
drawings of features exposed by the excavation, and
visualization software can take the CAD output and
use it to build three-dimensional and dynamic "virtual
reality" images of the reconstructed appearance of
ancient houses, tombs, temples, and town walls.

Analysis

Potsherds, stone tools and tool-making debris, beads,
animal bones, shellfish remains, seeds, nut shells,
carbonized wood, and all the other kinds of cultural
debris recovered during archaeological excavations
have traditionally provided the main evidence upon
which archaeologists base many inferences they make
about the past. Most artifacts bigger than, say, your
thumbnail, are carefully collected by hand during the
excavation. Many smaller items down to about the

size of the nail on your smallest finger are recovered
by screening excavated soil through wire mesh. Items
that are too small to be caught by these screens or are
too fragile to survive this rather rough method of
data collection are often found by processing soil
samples in tubs of running water. The outlets from
these tubs spill into graduated sieves that catch fish
scales, tiny seeds, wood charcoal, flint chips, and other
bits that the water releases from the soil matrix.

Molecular and microscopic evidence collected
from excavated soil samples and other debris has also
become an important information source. Recent
developments in the field of molecular genetics, combined with the discovery that minute DNA traces are
archaeologically recoverable, are beginning to have
significant impacts on many research questions, and
on the study of human evolution generally. Likewise,
research on prehistoric plant use and the origins of
agriculture have profited greatly from the discovery
that minute plant microfossils such as phytoliths are
distinctive to the kind of plant that created them and
to the plant part (e.g., seed, stem, leaf) in which they
developed. Phytoliths are inorganic, so they have the
added benefit of preserving well in contexts where

DEBATE AT GRAN DOLINA
Excavators at Gran Dolina in
northern Spain claimed to have
discovered fossilized remains of a
new species of early human, which
they named *Homo antecessor*.
Science is yet to prove their claims;
however, analysis of the material
at Gran Dolina has certainly
advanced our understanding
of human evolution.

large organic parts, such as seeds and nut shells, cannot survive. These and other minute data sources significantly aid the development of fresh perspectives on human prehistory.

Organic Remains

Regardless of their size, cultural artifacts, preserved food waste, and tool-making by-products provide many different lines of information about the lives of people who created the site under investigation. Given a large, well-preserved collection of organic food remains from an excavated village site, archaeologists can reconstruct the inhabitants' hunting patterns, how particular game animals were butchered and processed for consumption, and the seasons of the year during which the site was occupied. If human coprolites (preserved feces) are also available for analysis, they offer outstanding snapshots of the kinds of foods that were consumed at the site; it is even possible to identify the sex of the person who excreted them! All such data, combined with the measured drawings and other information about excavated features, are essential to the archaeologist's ability to reconstruct the everyday lives of the people who created the site.

Excavated organic remains and soil samples also yield the main evidence needed to reconstruct the local natural environment as it once existed around a site. Much of this information can be inferred from the habitat preferences of animals and plants that the site inhabitants ate. Less obvious data sources include the tiny shells of land snails that lived in the leaf litter and grass of the site. Many land snail species are sensitive environmental indicators due to their narrow habitat tolerances. A slight change in the forest canopy, for example, and some species die out, while others become more abundant. Another good environmental indicator is fossil pollen, or plant spores, which give a general sense of the major plant communities that existed in the immediate neighborhood of the site.

It is important to note that no one single archaeologist, however brilliant and hard working they may be, possesses all the technical skills and experience necessary to collect, process, analyze, and interpret each of the different lines of evidence that come into consideration in an archaeological research project. Throughout the world, archaeological fieldwork is inherently a collaborative, interdisciplinary undertaking that involves specialists from many different fields.

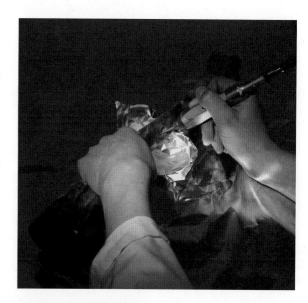

REVEALING ORGANIC REMAINS
Small shavings from a reindeer's bone can be used to determine much about the ancient animal, including its diet and genetic makeup, while marks on the bone itself may show if and how the animal was butchered.

SIFTING SHIFT IN THE SUN
A volunteer at an archaeological dig in Barton, Maryland (United States) uses a square screen to sift the dirt for artifacts. This method allows a large amount of ground material to be searched in a short period of time, but tiny artifacts can slip through the holes.

Types of Archaeology

Archaeology, especially within the past 50 years, has started to incorporate many other disciplines such as anthropology, geography, and the environmental sciences. The inclusion of these subjects into archaeology has strengthened the discipline, and has clearly shown the diverse and dynamic nature of humans.

With the introduction of chronometric dating methods—including radiocarbon dating—archaeologists can now recalibrate, construct, and secure chronologies. For example, the long-held view that the pyramids of Egypt were older than Neolithic temples was shattered following the advent of radiocarbon dating. Along with chronometric dating and science-based methods, new approaches assist in widening the various debates and enigmas that have previously existed.

ANTHROPOLOGY AND ARCHAEOLOGY

Anthropology, the study of behavior in human societies, was an approach used in the 1970s and 1980s by American archaeologist Lewis Binford and British archaeologist Ian Hodder. It was seen as a useful tool when attempting to make sense of the archaeological record, in particular the distant past. Anthropology is subdivided into physical and social anthropology.

Physical anthropology is concerned with the study of human origins and has assisted archaeologists and anatomists such as Richard Leakey and Raymond Dart to gain a greater understanding of the development of archaic humans. In 1974, the remains of an archaic human known as Lucy were discovered by the paleo-anthropologist Donald Johanson within a gully near Hadar in Ethiopia. The fossil human was dated to 3.25 million years and was in a remarkable state of preservation. The fossil remains confirmed that this archaic human was bipedal, and this discovery was not in isolation. In 1978, a number of footprints were found in volcanic ash at Laetoli in Tanzania that were dated to 3.6 million years.

Social anthropology—the study of the mechanisms and social structures that control and manipulate societies—developed in the early twentieth century. Initially, this British tradition focused solely on social organization and structural functionalism. Many of the ideas formulated by anthropologists such as

A BOUNTY OF BONES
Paleoanthropologist Donald Johanson (far left) is seen here with two other researchers. Scattered in front of them is a large collection of hominid fossils found in deposits exposed along the ravines and tributary valleys of the Hadar River in Ethiopia.

ENTERING DANGEROUS WATERS
Relating anthropological studies of contemporary non-Western societies—such as that found on the Trobriand (Kiriwina) Islands of Melanesia—to prehistoric societies can be problematic: there have been narrow evolutionary assumptions made that nonurban societies reflect an earlier way of life.

A. R. Radcliffe-Brown and Meyer Fortes were influenced by the work of French sociologist Emile Durkheim. In America, social anthropology at this time focused on the culture concept. In modern terms, social anthropology is the study of societies and cultures and is incorporated into cultural anthropology.

Archaeology and anthropology are both social sciences, but where archaeology seeks to interpret physical remains, anthropology seeks to understand why human societies behave in a particular way. Archaeologists have previously thought that by looking at contemporary societies, they could gain observable information and relate it to the past. Despite problems concerning analogy, it is clear that society both now and in the past is complex, and many of the systems controlling and manipulating present-day society are also present in past societies. However, these systems are general and do not provide all the answers.

ART AND ARCHAEOLOGY

Art is a product of human expression and creativity that has its probable origins in the Middle Paleolithic. It is one of a number of actions that involves abstract thought and that separates humans from animals.

In archaeological terms, art has been used widely to describe objects and actions that range from the purely aesthetic to the totally abstract. Therefore, the definition of art is not fixed, and the debate over what is and what is not art is definitely not settled. Within the early archaeological record, art is divided into two clear forms: portable art (also referred to as mobile or mobiliary art) and static art (also known as rock art). Both forms originated in the Paleolithic, and are probably linked to the movement of modern humans in South Africa around 75,000 years ago.

Portable Art

Portable art is present in the Upper Paleolithic and later within most areas of Europe including the United Kingdom and Scandinavia. The earliest portable art in Europe comprises small carved ivory, schist, steatite, and calcite female figurines (sometimes referred to as "Venus" figurines). These female figures,

FUNCTIONAL ART
An upside down neighing horse is clearly seen in this Upper Paleolithic spear thrower found at Mas d'Azil cave in France. Carved into a piece of reindeer antler, the image may represent the importance placed on the horse as a food source.

with their distinctive full breasts and round buttocks, have been found in France, Germany, the Czech Republic, and the Russian Federation and date to around 28,000 BCE, falling within the Gravettian and Magdalenian periods. The most famous example is the Willendorf figure, carved from limestone and discovered in Austria in 1908.

Other forms of portable art from the Upper Paleolithic and Mesolithic periods include perforated shells, and carved bone and antler animal figures; one such group of carvings is the Upper Paleolithic Magdalenian bâtons that were in use at the same time as artists were painting and carving cave walls in southwestern France. Other assemblages include the famous painted pebbles from Mas d'Azil in France; these are found in at least 35 sites throughout France, Italy, Spain, and Switzerland. The painted art comprises a variety of geometric forms including lines and dots; some pebbles are also engraved.

Throughout Europe, as more settled forms of life developed from the third to the first millennium BCE, there seems to have been a trend toward more personalized ownership of decorative items, implements, and weapons. These items were deposited in hundreds of individual tombs. While this may represent a genuine trend away from communal art to be seen by all, we should bear in mind that, apart from Skara Brae, there are no surviving dwellings from Europe beyond the Mediterranean regions. It may well be that timber buildings were painted or carved, inside and out. Attachments for woven wall-hangings are said to have been recovered from the timber walls of a sixth-century BCE tomb at Hochdorf in Germany.

PALEOLITHIC CHRONICLE
The art of Rouffignac Cave tells us much about the fauna that inhabited the surrounding region of southwestern France around 15,000 years ago. As well as a large-horned rhinoceros, there are paintings and engravings of bison, mammoths, horses, and ibex.

Static Art

Static rock art, regarded as a worldwide phenomenon, includes pictographs (drawings or paintings), petroglyphs (carvings or inscriptions), engravings (incised motifs), petroforms (rocks laid out in patterns), and geoglyphs (ground drawings).

The development of rock art has been most intensively studied in Europe, over the last 250 years. Dated to around 30,000 BCE, one of the earliest examples is Chauvet Cave in the Ardèche, southeastern France. Discovered in 1994, the cave walls contain some of the region's most vibrant animal scenes, painted mainly in red and black. Painted animals include bison, cave lion, horse, mammoth, reindeer, and rhinoceros. Other cave sites from this period include Lascaux, Pech Merle, and Rouffignac in southwestern France,

and Altamira in northern Spain. The cave art from these and other caves within this part of Europe falls within a date range of 15,000 to 20,000 years BCE.

French archaeologist André Leroi-Gourhan did much to revolutionize scientific ideas about cave art, and he came up with a series of stages in Paleolithic art (Styles I–IV), suggesting that cave art complexity evolved at a steady rate. However, initial radiocarbon dating at Chauvet Cave suggests that the evolution of cave art is far more complex. Outside Europe, cave art that is contemporary with the major caves in southwestern France and northern Spain is present in South Africa and Australia, and was produced from the hand of modern humans.

Rock art is also present during the Mesolithic and Neolithic periods and is found mainly in two areas of Europe: northern Scandinavia and Atlantic Europe. The open-air rock art of northern Europe, found mainly along the coastal fringes of Norway and southwestern Sweden, comprises mainly images of bear, elk, red deer, and reindeer. Also present is a series of uniquely carved marine mammals such as the bottlenose dolphin and sperm whale, found at sites such as Bardal and Strand in central Norway.

Located in rock shelters within the mountain areas of southeastern Spain are around 130 painted sites that display images of dancing, herding, hunting, honey collecting, and warfare. This assemblage gives a unique insight into mundane and ritual life in the region. Both the Scandinavian and Spanish rock art depicts representational imagery. However, during the Neolithic period, rock art becomes more stylized, and during the later Neolithic and Bronze Age, it becomes abstract.

Megalithic Art

By the fourth millennium BCE, artists begin to carve and paint within passage grave monuments. Megalithic art appears to be purely an Atlantic-zone phenomenon and is found in areas where passage graves are constructed, including the Iberian Peninsula, Brittany in France, Ireland, Anglesey in Wales, and northern Scotland. One of the most ornately carved passage grave interiors is at Gavrinis in Brittany, where almost every upright stone slab is carved. Within the Boyne Valley in Ireland, the well-known passage grave monuments of Newgrange, Knowth, and Dowth also have fine examples of megalithic art carved on curbstones that delineate the circumference of the mound. Interestingly, megalithic art did not extend to the passage grave tradition in southern Scandinavia.

The dominant motifs applied to the passage and chamber walls include chevrons, concentric circles, cup marks, labyrinths, lozenges, spirals, and zigzags. Many of these motifs are later included in open-air art that predominantly dates to the Bronze Age and is distributed along the Atlantic zone of Europe.

Static art, like its portable art counterpart, extends into history. Arguably, modern urban graffiti has become a living laboratory and an essential research tool in attempting to understand the mechanisms that controlled and manipulated art in our distant past.

RELIGION AND ARCHAEOLOGY

Within all periods of time and in all parts of the world, religion is archaeologically represented. Prior to the beginning of Christianity, there is evidence for burial monuments, shrines, and natural cult sites. Arguably, Paleolithic caves that contain rock art possess religious meaning. British Mesolithic sites such as Aveline's Hole in the Mendip Hills of Somerset, United Kingdom, show clear burial evidence. Excavations here revealed over 70 burials, some with grave goods including fossilized ammonites.

The Neolithic period witnessed the greatest change in European religion, with the introduction of artificial caves for burial— the chambered tomb. This unique phenomenon coincided with the agricultural revolution that swept across Europe between 10,000 and 2000 BCE. Included with Neolithic burial sites is the deposition of engendered grave goods and evidence of feasting: hearths usually found within the facade and chamber areas of the monument.

During the Bronze Age, a similar system of burial was in use. The architecture of the burial monument, however, had changed: mounds were now round, and they usually enclosed a central stone cist. Grave goods included ornately decorated ceramics referred to as beakers, as well as worked flint and jewelry. During the Iron Age and Roman periods, natural places such as bogs and rivers appear to have become religious shrines where status items were deposited.

MESMERIZING MOTIFS

The megalithic passage tomb on the island of Gavrinis in France contains a stunning array of upright stone slabs that have been carved with intricate swirls, semicircles, and wedge shapes. Of the 29 slabs, 23 are decorated.

ART AT BLOMBOS CAVE

At Blombos Cave located in South Africa, a team of archaeologists led by Christopher Henshilwood uncovered human activity within the cave stratigraphy that extended back some 140,000 years. Among the human debris were 41 perforated beads and several pieces of ocher that featured geometric patterns. These finds, dating to around 75,000 years ago—which is some 30,000 years earlier than the cave art in Europe—clearly show that *Homo sapiens* possessed abstract thought. The geometric forms possibly represent a recognizable symbolic language that was known to the cave's inhabitants. The shell beads may have once formed a necklace that was worn by someone with a special social or political status.

Measuring 2½ in (6 cm) in length, this piece of ancient ocher from Blombos Cave shows a deliberate zigzag design.

Biblical Archaeology

Biblical archaeology usually centers on the scientific investigation, excavation, recovery, and interpretation of a variety of biblical sites found within the Near Eastern countries of Egypt, Israel, Jordan, Lebanon, and Syria. In the past, and due to the often tense geo-political situation between these countries, biblical archaeology has been an extremely controversial discipline. Biblical archaeology became a popular pursuit during the late eighteenth and early nineteenth centuries following a number of expeditions across Palestine by renowned biblical scholar Edward Robinson. At this time the oldest complete Hebrew scripture was dated to the Middle Ages. Further expeditions were organized, one culminating in the publication of *The Survey of Western Palestine* (1871–1877) by Charles Warren. At about the same time Warren also undertook excavations around Temple Mount in Jerusalem, where he discovered the foundations of Herod's Temple. Also discovered was a series of ancient Israelite inscriptions that were inscribed on several jar handles.

From this point, the biblical lands of the Near East became a hive of archaeological activity that included excavations at a number of tell (settlement) sites, undertaken by F. J. Bliss and R. A. S. Macalister. However, many of these internationally important sites were pillaged, and their antiquities were sold to the highest bidder. After World War I, Palestine became a British Mandate, and antiquity laws were quickly established along with the formation of the Department of Antiquities (later to become the Israel Antiquities Authority). From this period of time, biblical sites were excavated using systematic and—where possible—scientific methods. The period was dominated by W. F. Albright and J. Garstang, who established chronologies between biblical and prehistoric archaeology. In the same period the tell sites of Beth-shean, Jericho, and Samaria were excavated.

Apart from site excavation and the subsequent interpretation of information, biblical archaeology also deals with documentary sources. This essential component has greatly assisted in the interpretation of certain sites, especially those mentioned in biblical texts. In 1945, the Gnostic Gospels were discovered near the settlement of Nag Hammadi in Upper Egypt. This 12-volume leatherbound papyrus codex was buried within a sealed jar and contained the lost Gospel of Thomas. The Dead Sea Scrolls, probably the most famous of all literal biblical sources, were discovered in 1947 in caves near Qumran in modern-day Israel. The first seven scrolls, however, were found in an antiquities market.

After the declaration of the State of Israel in 1948, biblical archaeology gained academic momentum and political interest. Following the Six-Day War in 1967, the first Israeli archaeologists undertook large

LINKS TO THE BIBLICAL PAST
The ruins of the ancient synagogue at Capernaum in Israel include decorative stonework believed to be dated to between the third and fourth century CE. In the Gospels, Jesus is said to have healed the slave of a centurion at Capernaum.

FANTASTIC FIND OR FORGERY?
Excavations at Temple Mount in Jerusalem unearthed a stone tablet featuring an ancient Hebrew inscription attributed to the biblical king Jehoash, who ruled in the ninth century BCE. Authentication of the tablet has been difficult.

excavations such as those around the Western Wall and Temple Mount in Jerusalem. Several discoveries from these and other nearby excavations were made, including two small silver scrolls (known as the Ketef Hinnom amulets) that contain biblical texts dated to the seventh century BCE—making them some four centuries older than the most ancient of the writings found on the Dead Sea Scrolls.

SOCIAL ARCHAEOLOGY, FROM A PHILOSOPHICAL PERSPECTIVE

Philosophical approaches in archaeology—what is referred to as postprocessual archaeology—became popular in American, British, and Scandinavian university departments during the early part of the 1980s. It was a direct reaction to the processual archaeology that sought to work within an analytical and scientific framework, establishing a deterministic approach to interpretation.

The postprocessual school of thought initiated by British archaeologists Ian Hodder, Michael Shanks, and Christopher Tilley introduced numerous ideas, including contextual archaeology, critical analysis, Marxist approaches, phenomenology, semiotics, and poststructuralism. Many of these specialist approaches, adapted from the fields of sociology and philosophy, radicalized archaeological thought by challenging the traditional archaeological views of the past. It was clear that science and analytical approaches could only provide some of the answers to the fundamental questions of human behavior.

Marxist approaches in archaeology formulated the notion that society is defined and shaped by the modes of production, which are based on the forces of production (human and natural resources) and the relations of production (the relationship between people and how each person interacts with the production and distribution of goods). Although the postprocessual school took up this approach vigorously, Australian archaeologist Vere Gordon Childe placed an emphasis on the forces of production when looking at how prehistoric societies functioned.

Gender and Archaeology

The discipline of gender archaeology emerged during the mid-1980s in the United Kingdom, Scandinavia, and the United States, along with other radical forms of archaeological discourse. An offshoot of gender archaeology—and very closely associated with it— is feminist archaeology.

Prior to 1985, there had been a number of misconceptions concerning gender roles within society, and this confusion had, in the past, been promoted by interpretations of archaeological finds. However, based on the anthropological and ethnographic record, it is clear that gender roles should not necessarily be based on the way Western society operates. Within the archaeological record there are many references to "man the hunter." It is now conceived that in some societies and cultures women also hunted, gathered, and fished.

Gender archaeology has played an important role in attempting to understand the roles of men and women in Danish Bronze Age society and settlement in Iron Age Holland. Gender archaeologists have also established the role of class, families, individuals, age, and religion in society. All these components are indelibly intertwined and collectively represent a complex structure within society.

THE FEMININE DIVINE
The role of women in past societies is studied with great enthusiasm by gender archaeologists. Sculptures and artifacts, such as this thirteenth-century CE statue of a female musician at Konarak's Sun Temple complex in India, assist in the examination of gender roles.

LANDSCAPE ARCHAEOLOGY

This school of thought places the site into a wider geographic and topographic context. Although landscape archaeology has become an "in vogue" topic, its roots are well established in the nineteenth century, when Danish archaeologist Jens Worsaae suggested that archaeology could only be understood when the environment was taken into consideration. This holistic view was later taken up by Robert Gradmann, who made the important link between the fertile loess soils of Central Europe and the development of the Neolithic Linearbankramik (LBK) settlement. This approach was the forerunner for formal methods such as spatial analysis and geographical information systems (GIS).

In the 1970s, landscape archaeology incorporated an historical element and included a number of projects that revolutionized medieval studies in England. Using an applied landscape-orientated methodology, archaeologists such as Trevor Rowlcy charted the development of the medieval and post-medieval landscape using fieldwork investigation supported by historic map data and documentary sources. This approach could trace the intensification of an historic and prehistoric landscape through features such as field systems, settlements, and the relationship between the economic and ritual landscape.

During the mid-1980s and with the emergence of the postprocessual school, new approaches to landscape were introduced, such as hermeneutics, phenomenology, and semiotics. These philosophical approaches allowed archaeologists to rethink landscape in terms of a human construct rather than focusing on the economic and functional components that had previously dominated landscape archaeological interpretation. Hermeneutics, originally used for the interpretation of sacred texts, has been used by British archaeologist Julian Thomas to describe the understanding of the Neolithic and Bronze Age world as a subject of human thought and action. Similarly, phenomenology, applied by Christopher Tilley to the Neolithic period in northwestern Europe, explores the experience of the self and the interaction with monuments and landscapes. In applying these philosophical discourses, both Thomas and Tilley used quantitative and qualitative approaches in order to support their ideas.

Semiotics, originally applied by Swiss linguist Ferdinand de Saussure in his quest to understand the grammar of signs, has been used by archaeologists to describe landscape and its relationships, in particular Neolithic burial monuments. By using this approach, archaeologists could see a series of spatial patterns emerging in relation to the distribution and location of Neolithic burial long mounds. It became apparent that mound orientation, shape, and topographic location were important to the builders and users of these monuments.

ENVIRONMENTAL ARCHAEOLOGY

This subdiscipline, which is an important tool in understanding past environments, became popular during the 1950s, following the introduction of new scientific advances in archaeology. Environmental archaeology includes archaeobotany, archaeozoology,

SAILOR'S NAVIGATIONAL AID?
Landscape archaeology takes into account the surroundings of the site in question. The Paracas Candelabra, a Peruvian geoglyph marked on the side of a hill at Pisco Bay, is most apparent when viewed from many miles off the coast—archaeologists are yet to determine what its purpose was.

A TIMBER TIME CAPSULE
Dendrochronology is the science of dating environmental changes in earlier times by studying the growth rings of trees. Each ring corresponds to a single year, and climatic fluctuations result in patterns of wide and narrow rings.

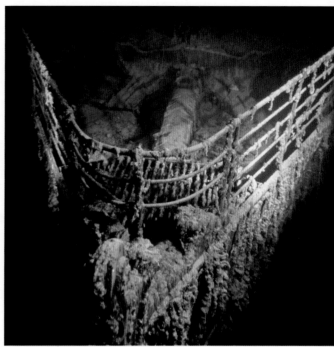

THE FINAL RESTING PLACE OF OVER 1,500 SOULS
The *Titanic* is perhaps the world's most famous shipwreck. More than 70 years after it sank, oceanographer Dr. Robert Ballard located the ship. Surprisingly, many fragile artifacts like plates were found in one piece on the ocean floor.

SALVAGE FROM THE SEA FLOOR
Divers in the Bahamas use a float to guide a heavy iron cannon from the wreck of the seventeenth-century CE Spanish galleon *Nuestra Señora de las Maravillas* to the surface. The English-made cannon bears the imprint of Henry VIII and the date 1543.

insect analysis, molluscan analysis, pollen analysis (known as palynology), paleobotany, and paleo-ethnobotany. These research methods are used in order to understand the total environment of past societies and, more importantly, the impact that humans have had on the environment. Included within this subdiscipline is the chronometric dating technique of dendrochronology (tree-ring dating).

MARITIME ARCHAEOLOGY

Maritime archaeology is the study of human activity related to the ocean and the material evidence that survives underwater. This discipline is concerned mainly with ship and boat wrecks, but can also include the study of submerged settlements, ethnography, and the historical development of coastal sites and communities. The Late Mesolithic (Ertebølle) hunter-gatherer settlement site of Tybrind Vig, located in shallow seas off the island of Fyn in Denmark, was discovered and excavated by a team led by the Danish archaeologist Søren Andersen during the early 1980s. Recovered from this site and in remarkable condition were two canoes, associated decorated paddles, shell and bone middens, and stone and bone tools that dated to *c.* 4200 BCE.

Over the past 50 years many famous wrecks have been discovered, including the large ocean-going liner *Titanic* that sank in the Atlantic Ocean in April 1912. Where possible, archaeologists have employed conventional techniques such as site planning and artifact retrieval methods when surveying and excavating shipwrecks and coastal settlements. Following the retrieval of waterlogged artifacts made from bone, leather, and wood—including the remains of boats and ships—conservation plays an essential role within this discipline.

THE RAISING OF THE *VASA*

The *Vasa* was a Swedish warship built under the patronage of King Gustavus Adolphus in 1626–1628, and was one of four ships designed by the Dutch shipbuilder Henrik Hybertsson. The ship's dimensions were radically altered following demands for new warships. As a result, the length of the ship was increased from 120 ft (36 m) to 135 ft (41 m). During its maiden voyage on August 10, 1628, Captain Söfring Hansson ordered the ship to set sail from Stockholm harbor. Within a few minutes and following a sudden gust of wind, the *Vasa* overbalanced and capsized just 330 ft (100 m) from shore and in only 100 ft (30 m) of water. Despite being so close to shore, between 30 and 50 sailors drowned.

Although the whereabouts of the wreck was known and many of the ship's cannons had been salvaged over the years, the recovery of the wreck did not start until the mid-1950s. Six sets of cables were fed underneath the hull, and the ship was moved to shallow waters where she was secured prior to the final lift on April 24, 1961. Following her successful lift, the *Vasa* was placed into dry dock where she was conserved using a specialized polyethylene glycol method. This process took over 17 years. Recovered from the wreck were more than 26,000 artifacts, including folded sails and over 700 carved wooded sculptures. The conserved wreck of the *Vasa* is now housed in a purpose-built museum in Stockholm, Sweden.

Problems and Issues

The single most important issue in modern archaeology is the question of who owns the past. All other problems—from obvious ones such as the repatriation of objects from museums or skeletons from universities, to lesser ones such as the best method of conservation or the funding of publications—stem from this central concern.

A TRIUMPHANT RETURN
In March 2007, the National Archaeological Museum of Athens, Greece, placed on display for the first time several Greek antiquities recently returned to their country of origin by the J. Paul Getty Museum in the United States.

It would be fair to say that, until the 1980s, even the most open-minded archaeologists considered themselves, if they thought about it at all, the principal or sole arbiters of what material should be excavated and how it should be studied. The only generally recognized limits on this were laws, enacted by most—but not all—modern countries, which made the excavation and export of archaeological materials illegal without prior consent.

CULTURAL PROPERTY LAWS

Most countries have brought in laws that limit the export of antiquities, although this varies in date— Greece had laws as early as 1932, and El Salvador as early as 1903. Some countries allow material that is excavated within their territories to be exported on loan for study in the archaeologist's home country, while others insist that all analysis be done within the country of origin. Others do give permits for the export of antiquities, but in recent years this has been largely limited to objects in public ownership that would ordinarily be displayed in a museum. Some countries are reluctant even to give excavation permits to foreign archaeologists.

In the past two decades, states that have identified objects on display in foreign museums as the state's looted property have been much more active—and more successful—in launching legal moves to effect their return. Turkey, Greece, and Italy in Europe, and most of the Central American countries, have been working hard to force large museums, usually in the United States, to return material that was originally looted from archaeological sites, or stolen from local museums. This process can take years.

LEGAL REQUIREMENTS FOR EXCAVATION

Even countries that do not have laws limiting the export of antiquities usually have laws that restrict excavations within their jurisdiction, and they often require permits to be issued from an antiquities or heritage department. The authorities need to be completely satisfied that the excavation is to be carried

INTERNATIONAL PROTECTION

There are three main international agreements that relate to cultural property, either sites or objects. UNESCO's Convention on the Means of Prohibiting and Preventing the Illicit Import, Export, and Transfer of Ownership of Cultural Property (April 1972) covers archaeological material, and by 2003 it had been ratified or accepted by 102 of the 192 United Nations member states. UNESCO also established the World Heritage Convention in 1972, under which monuments, places, or areas are listed by member countries. The UNIDROIT Convention on Stolen or Illegally Exported Cultural Objects (1995), which provides for court action and bluntly requires the current owner of an object proven to have been illegally exported to return it, has so far been ratified by very few countries. There are still no international agreements relating to objects removed from their country of origin either before the UNESCO 1972 Convention or the origin country's own antiquities laws.

UNESCO stepped in to rescue the Egyptian island of Philae, which was flooded due to the building of the Aswan Dam.

out by reputable scholars associated with museums, universities, archaeological institutes, or similar organizations. This even applies to rescue excavations carried out by scholars from the same country.

Responsible archaeologists include site and object conservation as well as information publication in their research timetable and budget. Generally speaking, the requirements of each country regarding the involvement of local authorities (compulsory joint projects), conservation, analysis, publications, and archiving of field notes is well known, and archaeologists can take these into consideration when designing their projects and seeking funding. However, permits may specify a different timetable, more comprehensive publication strategy, or more extensive conservation program than the archaeologist's original plan.

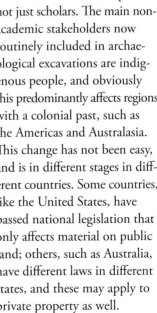

There may be a requirement to rebury finds or publish in a time frame that the archaeologist considers unfeasibly short, or authorities may specify a site conservation plan that exceeds the archaeologist's budget. If no extra funding can be raised, the archaeologist can be faced with a choice of abandoning the project or cutting short the excavation to fund the conservation. This means that the original rationale for the excavation—to solve a research problem—will have to be adjusted to take into account the needs of other stakeholders. In the case of rescue excavations, depending on the type of permit, archaeologists are often pressured by private developers to shorten the length of their excavations in order to ensure that the development project can go ahead quickly. This saves money for the developers, but often compromises the results of the dig.

STAKEHOLDERS

By far the greatest change in the practice of archaeology in the last 20 years has been the recognition that there are other owners of the past, not just scholars. The main non-academic stakeholders now routinely included in archaeological excavations are indigenous people, and obviously this predominantly affects regions with a colonial past, such as the Americas and Australasia. This change has not been easy, and is in different stages in different countries. Some countries, like the United States, have passed national legislation that only affects material on public land; others, such as Australia, have different laws in different states, and these may apply to private property as well.

COST OF PRESERVING THE PAST
Object conservation is an important part of the archaeologist's work on a site. Here, a member of an underwater archaeology expedition carefully cleans a clay jug that was found on an eleventh-century CE shipwreck off the coast of Turkey.

insisting on their equal claims. A celebrated example involves the renewed excavations at Çatal Hüyük in southern Turkey. The site has been famous since the mid-twentieth century, when James Mellaart's excavations uncovered wall paintings and statues dating to around 7400 BCE. Many of the statues and paintings depict females in association with animals, often felines. They are usually interpreted as goddess figures, although the ancient belief system at Çatal Hüyük is still unclear to researchers.

When new excavations at the site began in 1993, a loose umbrella group of people from diverse backgrounds, linked by their interest in or even devotion to the Mother Goddess, demanded of the director, Ian Hodder, that they be given direct access to all information derived from the excavations, before publication. Their demands were based on a belief that, because archaeologists tend not to be interested in understanding the Mother Goddess in the same way that devotees are, important data would be misinterpreted or left out of any publications. Their request to be given "objective data" such as the field notes and information about all finds revealed a fundamental problem for nonarchaeologists claiming rights over this type of material. Field notes are not really objective data—they reflect the subjective opinions of excavators, opinions that archaeologists try to make as scientific and factual as possible, but which, despite their best intentions, often reflect preexisting ideas and beliefs.

The only way the Mother Goddess followers could get data without the archaeologists' opinions would be to do their own excavation—but since they are not trained archaeologists, should they be allowed to do this? And if they were, would not their results also be subjective, as they might leave out data from their publications that relate to aspects of ancient life they are not interested in? In fact, an amicable arrangement was made at Çatal Hüyük, where the Mother Goddess groups accepted that there would be some initial interpretations made by archaeologists about the material, and they were allowed prepublication access to some materials.

Public Participation

In modern archaeological practice, the usual expressions of interest from nonarchaeologists are restricted to a desire to see the dig in operation—this has resulted in an increase, particularly with rescue digs in cities, in open days and interpretive posters. The natural interest of people in the material remains of their past, and an equally natural interest in seeing how their tax dollars are being spent, is usually more than adequately satisfied by this. Archaeologists have come to see that this communication and interaction with the general public is not an onerous infringement on their time (a common early response), but a reasonable

GOOD WORKING RELATIONSHIP
Professor Steve Webb from Bond University in Queensland works closely with members of the local indigenous community to study over 450 Pleistocene footprints discovered in the Lake Mungo area of New South Wales, Australia.

The background to these changes is the undeniable difference in treatment that had been given to artifacts and skeletal material of indigenous peoples, compared with that of people of European descent. In some cases, indigenous peoples have been given greater rights over material than archaeologists. Early on in the process of developing a dialog between principal stakeholders, this led to considerable friction between scholars and local peoples. In most cases a working relationship has now developed, but problems still arise from time to time, and they are particularly acute with very ancient skeletal material. Adding to the problem is the very small number of indigenous archaeologists. As their numbers rise, easier resolutions to problems of access should ensue.

The Impact of Interest Groups

Indigenous or minority ethnic groups are not the only ones who have increasingly been included in access to archaeological material. Other interest groups are method of explaining what they are doing to the ultimate funders of their work. Many laypersons, seeking a closer involvement, offer to take part as volunteers in digs, either in their own country or abroad as part of an adventure holiday.

SKELETONS

Traditionally, skeletal material was excavated and stored in boxes in institutions, and if study was undertaken, it often occurred years after the original excavation. The material was, after study, put in comparative anatomy collections; in some cases the bones were taken back and reburied in some way at or near the original site. Archaeologists made little—if any—attempt to contact the descendants of the deceased, and, in fact, with bodies more than about 200 years old, thought that there would not, nor ought, to be anybody claiming a connection with the bones. This attitude extended to all burials, as archaeologists were (and sometimes still are) notoriously blasé about bones. It is also the case that in European culture, attitudes to the dead have changed and differ from country to country. Improvements in our knowledge of anatomy, for example, in the eighteenth and nineteenth centuries involved the dissection of bodies that had been effectively robbed from graves in Europe and North America. Earlier than that, anatomists who attempted to dissect corpses risked permanent excommunication from the Church for interfering with the dead.

In some modern countries, notably Israel, religious authorities have effectively ended the excavation and study of any skeletal material at all, regardless of its age. In Islamic countries, pre-Islamic skeletons may be studied, but bones of Muslims must be reburied on the same day they are uncovered, in a recognized cemetery supervised by religious authorities. It is always assumed that all bones excavated that date to a Muslim period must be Islamic, unless there is overwhelming evidence to the contrary. In the South Pacific, where skulls are held in traditional cultures to be the source of ancestral spiritual power, local people have little interest in bones from the rest of the body, but might well refuse permission for the archaeological study of heads. This background of conflict between scientific examination and religious beliefs about the dead is part of the current dialog surrounding skeletal remains.

THE PUBLIC LENDS A HAND TO UNEARTH HISTORY
Volunteers are an important part of many digs, such as the excavation of the Miami Circle site in the United States, as they greatly assist with the bulk of the heavy or mundane work. This leaves the archaeologists free to concentrate on gathering and analyzing information about the site.

SENSITIVITY TO INDIGENOUS TRADITIONS REQUIRED
Archaeologists must deal with local customs when digging in foreign lands. For instance, skulls are revered in the South Pacific, and it is often difficult to obtain permission to study them. This is particularly relevant to the Solomon Islands, where skulls of chiefs are kept on an island in Roviana Lagoon.

DESCENDANTS DEMAND THEIR RIGHTFUL INHERITANCE
Most archaeologists now recognize and accept the need to consult descent groups when dealing with indigenous artifacts and remains. In Peru, the modern-day Quechua people are involved in preserving their Incan past.

Descent Groups

Most scholars now recognize the existence of descent groups—modern indigenous people whose culture relates fairly directly to an ancient culture that is perhaps hundreds or even thousands of years old, which existed when what is now a skeleton was buried. These descent groups often have the main role in deciding on any investigation, or whether immediate reburial or handing over for additional religious rites is appropriate. One question for archaeologists is how widely should they search for members of descent groups—do they need only to consult with those living locally, or should they try to contact families who have moved away? Perhaps the religious rites are secret, and it is not at all clear to archaeologists who should be consulted, even if legally the archaeologists are required to make these decisions. When set in the framework of indigenous stakeholders, there are cases where indigenous groups who are not descent groups have nonetheless refused permission for excavation or study. It can be a problem

DESCENDANTS DEMAND THEIR RIGHTFUL INHERITANCE
Most archaeologists now recognize and accept the need to consult descent groups when dealing with indigenous artifacts and remains. In Peru, the modern-day Quechua people are involved in preserving their Incan past.

for some Western archaeologists to acknowledge these claimed relationships because this attitude of ownership due to descent does not exist in Europe—there are no descent groups claiming a role in the excavation of dead Romans.

A much more widespread quandary within the discipline of archaeology, however, is to acknowledge descent from skeletons that are tens of thousands of years old. Overall, we still have very few skeletons anywhere in the world that date to the beginnings of the history of *Homo sapiens*, and a case can be made that any skeleton older than 20,000 years is equally important to all humans, not just those whose local culture is associated with the place in which the remains were found. Archaeologists point out that their study of very ancient remains, such as at Lake Mungo in Australia or the Kennewick Man in the United States, has proven the antiquity of indigenous cultures in those countries, and that further work on the movement of humans into these continents depends entirely on access to early skeletal material. This argument, though, imposes a Western definition

MORAL RESPONSIBILITY VERSUS SCIENTIFIC OBLIGATION
The storeroom of the National Museum of the American Indian in New York, United States, is packed with masks, baskets, and other artifacts. It has been argued that, rather than storing or displaying culturally sensitive material, museums should return these items to the traditional owners.

on the length of time that a person's cultural heritage lasts, and sets an archaeological limit on indigenous ownership of their ancestors.

CULTURAL TREASURES

Objects of sacred importance to indigenous people, which are often items that would have remained secret and hidden within their own cultures, used to be taken by archaeologists and anthropologists and openly displayed in museums. Universities and museums around the world are now engaged in a process of identifying such material and repatriating it to the proper owners. Not all objects held in these institutions are being returned, as some traditional owners or descent groups cannot be found, and some objects are not considered secret or sacred. However, a less patronizing and fairer relationship between living cultures and scholars has developed from this significant process.

Another large class of cultural treasures whose ownership is disputed is made up of those objects taken from their country of origin by European and American collectors between the seventeenth and twentieth centuries. Although origin countries accept that there is little that can be done legally to regain objects taken before their modern laws banning export came into force, there are still some

pieces that are considered of such vital national importance that their return is seen as essential. These important artifacts include the "Elgin Marbles," the Rosetta Stone, sculptures from Benin, and Montezuma's feathered headdress.

THIS LADY IS A LONG WAY FROM HOME
Many sculptures from Benin—such as this sixteenth-century CE brass head of the Queen Mother, Idia— are located at the British Museum in London, United Kingdom. The small African nation is naturally keen to see the return of its historical artifacts, but has not yet been successful in this endeavor.

LOST MARBLES AND STROLLING STONES

The "Elgin Marbles" are a collection of part of the sculptural decoration of the Parthenon Temple in Athens, assembled by Lord Elgin in the eighteenth century and subsequently purchased by the British Museum, where part of the collection is on display. At that stage, the Ottoman Empire had controlled the territory of Ancient Greece for some 300 years, and it was to Turkish authorities in Athens and Istanbul that Lord Elgin appealed for permission to export the sculptures. The British Museum also now possesses the Rosetta Stone, which has a trilingual inscription (Greek, demotic, and hieroglyphic) that allowed the decipherment of Ancient Egyptian hieroglyphic writing. The Rosetta Stone was found during Napoleon's conquest of Egypt in 1799, damaged and reused as building fill near Rashid (Rosetta) in the Delta. Within a few years, the British had

Part of the "Elgin Marbles," now controversially residing in the British Museum in London, United Kingdom, this 3½-ft (1-m) high piece was originally a section of the west frieze of the Parthenon.

defeated the French forces in Egypt, and as part of the surrender treaty, took possession of the bulk of archaeological material that Napoleon's army of scholars had amassed. Egypt then also formed part of the Ottoman Empire, and after this relatively brief Anglo-French outburst, reverted to Istanbul's control.

In both cases, the arrival of the objects in Europe caused a major sensation— Empire-style fashion derived directly from Napoleon's time in Egypt, and caused an outburst of furniture with sphinxes on the legs, gowns with high waistlines, and various other interpretations of Egyptian art. The Parthenon marbles were highly influential in swaying British public opinion toward the fledgling movement for independence in what was to become modern Greece, resulting in the British fleet being sent to support the Greeks in their war against the Ottoman Empire.

A CONTROVERSIAL QUEEN

The Egyptians have repeatedly requested that the bust of Nefertiti be returned to them from Germany. They were incensed when, in 2003, a Hungarian duo called Little Warsaw staged an "artistic" project whereby the bust was for a short time placed on top of a near-nude bronze sculpture of a female body.

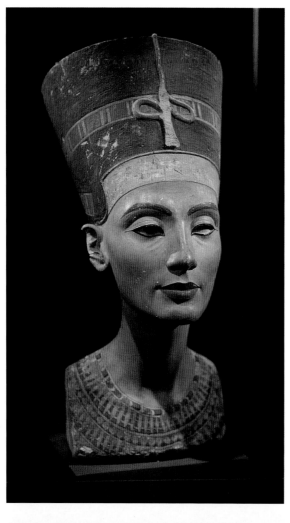

THE VALUE OF MUSEUMS

Visiting the stunning Egyptian rooms in the Musée du Louvre is a great way for both the general public and academics to see and appreciate a wealth of different artifacts from this ancient culture, particularly if they are unable to travel to Egypt themselves.

Among its many missing artifacts, modern Egypt is also demanding the return of the bust of Nefertiti from the Berlin Museum. This sculpture—widely valued for its beautiful representation of the Egyptian queen—was exported in 1912, as part of the legal division of finds from German excavations at Tell el-Amarna. It was not individually listed, but was shown to Egyptian authorities, and formed part of the collection of material exported under a general permit. Egyptian authorities assert that the excavator should have made clear what the bust was, and a permit for such a treasure would never have been issued. More controversially, they also seek the return of the bust of the Khephren pyramid builder, Ankh-khaf, which was legally exported with a special permit, and is now in the Boston Museum of Fine Arts.

Unfortunately, there is no legal basis for the return of any of these precious objects to their country of origin, mainly because modern laws postdate their export, or in the case of the bust of Ankh-khaf, the piece was exported from Egypt with a legal permit. However, a strong moral argument for their return can certainly be made, which is related back to the central issue of ownership of the past. As a guiding principle, it is accepted that objects belong to the modern state in which they are found—they form part of the heritage of that state and its people, and can be critical in the struggle to have non-European cultures valued equally.

Public Service Versus Nationalism

On the other hand, large museums like the Louvre, the British Museum, and the Metropolitan in New York provide a valuable service by displaying, in one place, a collection of important objects from throughout the world. People—including scholars—who cannot travel around the globe are able to see original artifacts, which helps the viewer to understand their own and other people's cultures. Even with improvements in technology, so that almost perfect replicas of objects can be created, we know from museum and exhibition surveys that visitors much prefer to see the actual, original object, rather than an exact copy. This leads to a dilemma for museum curators, because an obvious solution to calls for the repatriation of cultural objects is to display replicas, as suggested by the Greeks for the "Elgin Marbles."

There is also the ethical issue of the nationalism of antiquity. As an example, one of the strong moral points that Greek authorities use to claim the return of the "Elgin Marbles" to the Parthenon is that the temple they once adorned symbolizes the ancient Greek world—a culture that developed literature, the arts, democracy, and philosophical ideas, all of which underpin modern Western culture. It could be argued then, that all Europeans are the inheritors of the Greek Idea, and that such fine sculptures could equally belong in London as Athens.

ARCHAEOLOGY, POLITICS, AND NATIONALISM

Another problem archaeologists must face is the ownership of the results of their work. Both their interpretations and the sites they excavate are sometimes used by politicians or other interest groups to further ideas of ethnicity or nationalism. Archaeological work that challenges these political uses can be subject to varying degrees of interference.

Great Zimbabwe is an enormous, elaborate site with massive masonry walls and clear evidence of a highly structured society. From the time it was first rediscovered, it was usually considered to be the ruins of an Arabic trading city, because native Africans were thought to be too unsophisticated to have had a social system complex enough to have produced such a city. Archaeologists who challenged this racist view were ignored until the 1960s, when a non-African use of the site became an untenable interpretation. More benignly, before World War II, Japanese emperors used the antiquity of elaborate tombs in Japan as evidence for the longevity and stability of the Chrysanthemum Throne.

Modern territorial arguments, such as in the Balkans or the southern Levant, often resort to archaeological evidence in an attempt to prove that one ethnic group or another has prior rights to disputed land. This use of evidence ranges from political interpretations at

ONE OF AMERICA'S MOST FAMOUS ARCHAEOLOGICAL HOAXES
The Cardiff Giant, a "petrified man," was found in a farmer's field in Cardiff, New York, in 1869. Skepticism by archaeologists and paleontologists led the perpetrator, George Hull, to confess less than two months after its discovery.

variance to archaeological ideas, through to the restriction of public funding to only those projects targeting politically favored sites. It can be no coincidence, for instance, that in northern Greece, very few Thracian sites have been excavated compared to Ancient Greek colonies.

A much more volatile situation exists at Ayodhya in India, where in 1992 a group of fanatic Hindus destroyed the medieval Babri Masjid mosque, on the grounds that it was built, hundreds of years ago, over a destroyed Hindu temple. There are archaeological remains beneath the level of the mosque, although their interpretation is controversial, and the situation was so tense that it affected the 1994 World Archaeology Congress held in India. Archaeologists have little control over the political use of their work, but most professional associations' codes of ethics stipulate that members should not become involved in nationalist debates.

FAKES AND FORGERIES

By and large, forged artifacts are more of a problem for art and antiquities collectors than for archaeologists. They generally surface at a dealer's gallery, or when a museum buys an object, and rarely (if ever) in an archaeological excavation. But deciding the status of a hitherto unknown object is important for archaeologists if the piece fills a gap in existing typologies, or depicts a new or startling image.

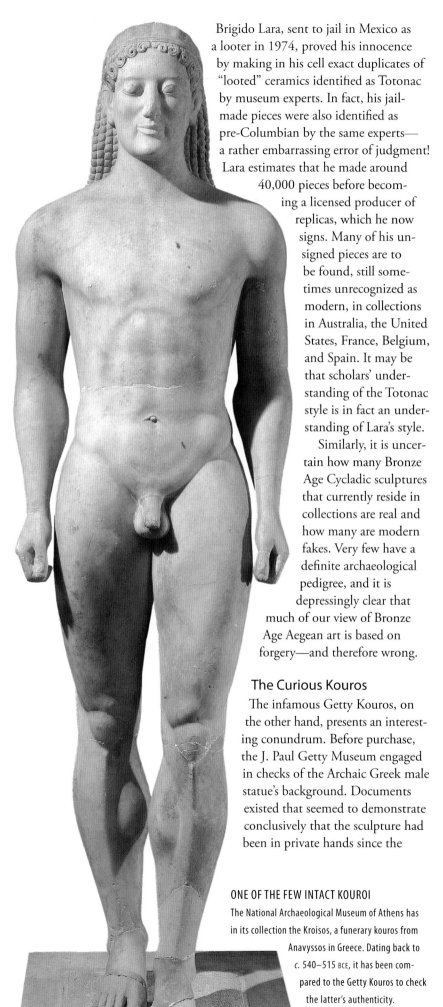

Brigido Lara, sent to jail in Mexico as a looter in 1974, proved his innocence by making in his cell exact duplicates of "looted" ceramics identified as Totonac by museum experts. In fact, his jail-made pieces were also identified as pre-Columbian by the same experts—a rather embarrassing error of judgment! Lara estimates that he made around 40,000 pieces before becoming a licensed producer of replicas, which he now signs. Many of his unsigned pieces are to be found, still sometimes unrecognized as modern, in collections in Australia, the United States, France, Belgium, and Spain. It may be that scholars' understanding of the Totonac style is in fact an understanding of Lara's style.

Similarly, it is uncertain how many Bronze Age Cycladic sculptures that currently reside in collections are real and how many are modern fakes. Very few have a definite archaeological pedigree, and it is depressingly clear that much of our view of Bronze Age Aegean art is based on forgery—and therefore wrong.

The Curious Kouros

The infamous Getty Kouros, on the other hand, presents an interesting conundrum. Before purchase, the J. Paul Getty Museum engaged in checks of the Archaic Greek male statue's background. Documents existed that seemed to demonstrate conclusively that the sculpture had been in private hands since the

ONE OF THE FEW INTACT KOUROI

The National Archaeological Museum of Athens has in its collection the Kroisos, a funerary kouros from Anavyssos in Greece. Dating back to c. 540–515 BCE, it has been compared to the Getty Kouros to check the latter's authenticity.

DOES THIS TOTONAC KNOW SOMETHING WE DON'T?

This ceramic head has been identified as an ancient Totonac artifact from Veracruz state in Mexico, but with master forger Brigido Lara's works still on show in many museums around the world, it is difficult for even the experts to know for certain whether it is real or fake.

1930s (predating antiquities laws that would have made it an illegal export from the likely countries of origin, modern Greece or Turkey), and museum authorities in Italy and Greece were consulted but did not recognize the piece as a looted item. After purchase, the patina on the marble was subject to scientific study, which concluded that it developed over a long period of time—that the statue was indeed ancient. Stylistic peculiarities meant that questions about its authenticity continued, although only 13 intact, genuine kouroi are known anyway from the entire ancient Hellenic world.

The discovery of a definite fake torso of very similar style in Switzerland in 1985, coupled with the realization that one of the provenance documents dated to 1952 had a postcode that only came into use in the 1970s, led the J. Paul Getty Museum to remove the statue from exhibition and convene a colloquium. The results were unclear—scientists are generally convinced of its age, while art historians and archaeologists are more likely to think it is a fake. It is back on display, with the "real fake" torso and an excellent discussion of the problem.

COLLECTING AND LOOTING

Estimates of the value of the global trade in antiquities vary from US$200 million to US$1 billion per year. Most public museums around the world have now adopted ethical collecting protocols, which restrict them to acquiring only objects they are sure have not been illegally exported from their country of origin.

Private collectors are under no such obligation. Since most countries have stringent laws that prohibit export, the number of objects that can be ethically acquired is shrinking yearly, and by and large now includes only a small number of pieces known to have been in genuine private collections assembled before the twentieth century. Clearly then, the huge number of objects traded in the art market must have been looted. The rate of looting is increasing every year, as the demand in the art market fuels this illegal trade. Archaeologists are forced to deal with the terrible consequences of looting and the trade in antiquities in a number of ways.

Sadly, a very real dilemma for archaeologists in art-exporting countries is that their work inevitably attracts the attention of looters. Survey or excavation of a site alerts local looters to its potential value. As soon as archaeologists leave (or in some cases, when the looters are particularly well informed, shortly before the archaeologists arrive), robbing teams move in. Usually using long lengths of reinforcing steel, they probe the ground for holes. Looters seek burials because they usually contain valuable, intact objects such as jewelry. The price obtained for stolen antiquities increases as they move up the chain, with the original looters getting the smallest amount of money, although this is often relatively well-paid work compared with local wages.

DISREGARD FOR THE DEAD
Even today, looters show no respect for human remains in their search for valuable tomb items. In 2004, archaeologists working in Egypt's Valley of the Golden Mummies found mummified limbs strewn across the sand by grave robbers.

BOGUS BONES

Probably the most famous forgery in archaeological history is the Piltdown Man. In the late nineteenth century, well before the uncovering of hominid remains in the Rift Valley of Africa, there was a tremendous search for evidence demonstrating the evolution of humans from apelike ancestors. Early hominids had been found throughout Europe (Neanderthals, Cro-Magnon) and Asia (Peking Man). British pride was salvaged when in 1912 Charles Dawson found fragments of a skull in Piltdown Quarry that had a cranial vault like *Homo sapiens*, but jawbones like an ape. Questions of national pride and scientific anxiety, especially in the face of still widespread antievolutionary feeling, meant that the find was accepted nearly without question. Any doubt was smothered by the finding of a second skull three years later. Over the years the geological dating of the quarry was queried, and increasing finds of fossil hominids elsewhere made Piltdown Man look decidedly peculiar, but the skull was not subjected to full scientific test-ing until the late 1940s. It was revealed as a fake in 1953, although to this day the conspirator has not been identified.

In 1953, Alvan T. Marston demonstrated that the Piltdown skull was actually of comparatively recent origin, and was composed of the top portion of a human skull and the jaw of an orangutan.

Important Questions That Archaeology Can Answer

For most of the Earth's history, archaeology is the only tool we have available to answer questions about what happened, when, and why. Even in the relatively recent past, when written sources are available, these writings often exist as myths or unsubstantiated documents rather than as actual history. Archaeology can help separate fact from fiction.

Archaeology is particularly good at documenting and explaining the movement of peoples. The expansion of early hominids out of Africa is not the only fascinating migration that archaeology has been able to illuminate. The colonization of the Pacific can only be understood through archaeology. At least 40,000 years ago, people began to sail over short sea stretches into New Guinea and Australia; around

4,000 years ago, people began to sail from New Guinea into the Solomons, and later as far as Hawaii, Easter Island, and New Zealand. The technology needed, the understanding of astronomy, and the supplies these intrepid Pacific explorers had can all be reconstructed through archaeological investigation of migration routes, shared tools, and the diversity of plants and animals that accompanied the travelers. But there are still a number of critical questions to answer, such as which island in East Polynesia was settled first.

ANCIENT STONE ALIGNMENTS

Some structures or objects often mystify us because their contexts are not properly known. This is where archaeology can provide some, but not always all, the answers. Stonehenge, like all the prehistoric stone monuments of Europe, is clearly arranged in some kind of systematic pattern. Before scientific study, this monument appeared mysterious, and even now,

ALAS, POOR YORICK ...
Mike Pitts, editor of *British Archaeology*, holds the skull from a skeleton excavated at Stonehenge in 1923. Recent reexamination of the skeleton by forensic scientists has determined that the person was a victim of execution—a finding that has answered some questions and raised others about Stonehenge.

FOLKLORE OR HISTORY?
This stone statue of a fertility god on Mokoia Island in Lake Rotorua is said to have been brought from the legendary Maori homeland of Hawaiki in the ancestral canoe. This myth may be based on the real-life migration of the Maori ancestors to New Zealand.

THE STONE SPHERES OF COSTA RICA

In contrast to the Egyptian pyramids and European stone patterns, the unique stone spheres of Costa Rica have almost all been removed from their original contexts. Since no written source discusses them, and none are known to have been made since the Spanish Conquest, only archaeology can hope to tell us how these granodiorite balls were made and used. We do know that the spheres are made of a stone that occurs in limited outcrops in Costa Rica. The stone flakes off like onion layers when heated, so that to modify boulders only fire and simple chisels would be needed, tools available to the indigenous populations of the Diquis Delta, where most of the spheres have been found. They seem to have been made between 200 BCE and CE 1500, and their primary usage must have involved a complex symbolism. Some are said to have been found in alignments either to the Earth's magnetic field or to astronomical features. Those particular stones have since been moved from their original locations, and so the measurements cannot be checked. While some 300 spheres are currently known, further archaeological understanding relies on locating spheres that have been left in situ.

This well-preserved example of an ancient Costa Rican stone sphere can be seen in the courtyard of the National Museum in the country's capital city, San José.

archaeological investigations have sometimes raised more questions than answers. Built in three major phases, some of the stones were brought from as far as Wales, over 240 miles (385 km) away. Although prodigious effort would have been needed to raise the sarsen stones and place the massive lintels on the five trilithons within the circle, archaeological research and experimentation has shown that this would have been possible with the technology of levers and ropes that was available at the time.

The Avenue, a set of parallel ditches leading from Stonehenge in a U-shape to the Avon River, confirms that the Henge was part of a much larger complex, one clearly important to the people who constructed and maintained it over a thousand years. Slightly to the north is the post and ditch Woodhenge, the settlement of Durrington Walls, and the rectangular 1⅘-mile (3-km) long Cursus. Clearly, Stonehenge is in the middle of a complicated landscape of particular religious importance, although its own role is still unclear. It not only aligns with the mid-summer solstice, but it can also serve as a lunar observatory. We do not yet know why these people were buried at the Henge, nor do we know of the ancient rituals associated with mid-summer at the site—archaeology may provide the answers to these questions in the future. But we can now better understand these structures within the society at that time, whose members themselves were seeking to comprehend the world in which they lived.

WRITTEN STORIES AND ARCHAEOLOGY

Archaeology is also a valuable tool for understanding historical periods. Since the nineteenth century, it has been recognized that the story of Noah's Flood in the Bible is remarkably similar to the Flood story in the Mesopotamian Epic of Gilgamesh. It is reasonable to assume that the differing written versions both derived from some oral history, a folk memory of an actual, massive flooding event. Current speculation centers on the flooding of the Black Sea shelf. Although most scholars agree that the area was inundated after the end of the last Ice Age, there is still no consensus on whether this was a gradual water rise or a sudden, catastrophic event. There is also still no firm evidence of flooded settlements, although some structures off the coast of Turkey have been investigated. It may be that the written Flood(s) and the Black Sea flood are unrelated—but only archaeology will be able to resolve this contentious issue.

DIGGING UP THE TRUTH ABOUT THE XIA

For many years, the Xia Dynasty of China was presumed to be a myth, as no archaeological evidence was found to support the oral history. Then in 1959, bronze artifacts (such as this jue, or wine vessel) and tombs began to be discovered at Erlitou, southwest of the city Yanshi—the location of the Xia Dynasty in ancient texts. The age of these finds supports the idea that they are remnants of the Xia Dynasty.

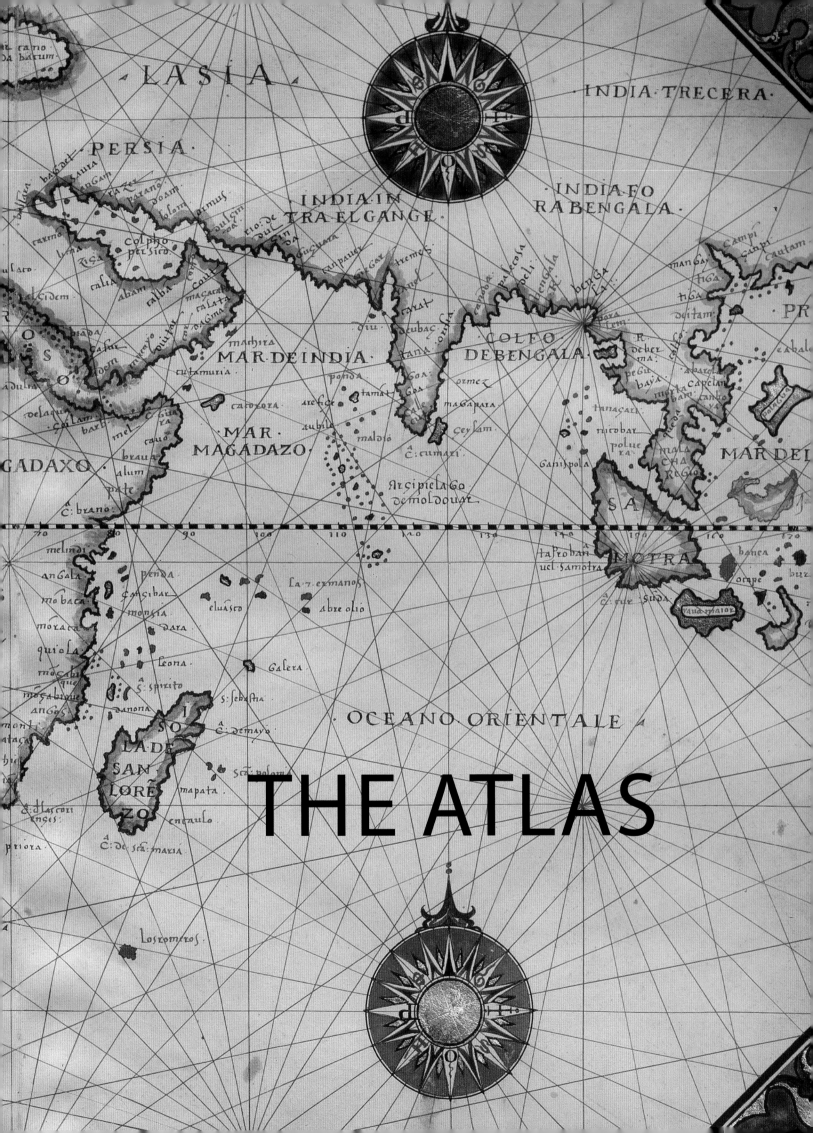

THE ATLAS

Timelines of Archaeology

The history of humankind is an epic saga of evolution, migration, and adaptation over time. Archaeology has helped to place the dramatic events of the long human record in a chronological sequence, allowing us to see the development of humans from early apelike beings to modern-day members of complex societies.

2 MILLION YEARS AGO

Australopithecus boisei roamed the East African Rift Valley 2 million years ago, leaving traces of their existence in a number of stone tools and fossilized bones *(see page 82)*.

25,000 YEARS AGO

The "Venus" of Willendorf is just one of many plump female figurines from the Gravettian period in Europe some 25,000 years ago *(see page 131)*.

AFRICA

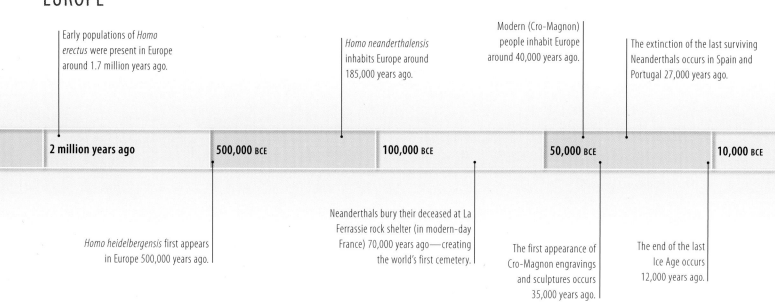

The fossil record of human evolution in Africa extends to 7 million years ago.

The earliest fossils with complete skeletons—found in Hadar, Ethiopia—date to 3.25 million years ago.

Humans with modern body proportions, called *Homo erectus* or *Homo ergaster*, appear 1.7 million years ago.

Archaic *sapiens* or *Homo heidelbergensis* appears in Africa 600,000 years ago.

| 7 million years ago | 4 million years ago | 2 million years ago | 1 million years ago | 100,000 BCE |

Human footprints are left in volcanic ash at Laetoli, Tanzania, 3.6 million years ago.

At Gona in Ethiopia, the oldest signs of material culture (in the form of stone tools) date to 2.6 million years ago.

Out of Africa 1—the first movement of early humans *(Homo erectus/Homo ergaster)* from Africa to Eurasia—occurs 1.7 million years ago.

The first anatomically modern humans appear in Africa 200,000 years ago.

EUROPE

Early populations of *Homo erectus* were present in Europe around 1.7 million years ago.

Homo neanderthalensis inhabits Europe around 185,000 years ago.

Modern (Cro-Magnon) people inhabit Europe around 40,000 years ago.

The extinction of the last surviving Neanderthals occurs in Spain and Portugal 27,000 years ago.

| 2 million years ago | 500,000 BCE | 100,000 BCE | 50,000 BCE | 10,000 BCE |

Homo heidelbergensis first appears in Europe 500,000 years ago.

Neanderthals bury their deceased at La Ferrassie rock shelter (in modern-day France) 70,000 years ago—creating the world's first cemetery.

The first appearance of Cro-Magnon engravings and sculptures occurs 35,000 years ago.

The end of the last Ice Age occurs 12,000 years ago.

2,200 YEARS AGO

Terracotta warriors have faithfully guarded the tomb of the first emperor of China's Qin Dynasty for 2,200 years, showing steely determination in the face of eternal duty *(see page 256)*.

1,800 YEARS AGO

Quetzalcoatl's serpent head has sneered menacingly at Teotihuacan in Mexico for 1,800 years, and appears in many Mesoamerican sculptures and artworks *(see page 302)*.

900 YEARS AGO

Polynesians on Easter Island carved large, stony-faced effigies called *moai* from the island's abundant volcanic rock around 900 years ago *(see page 379)*.

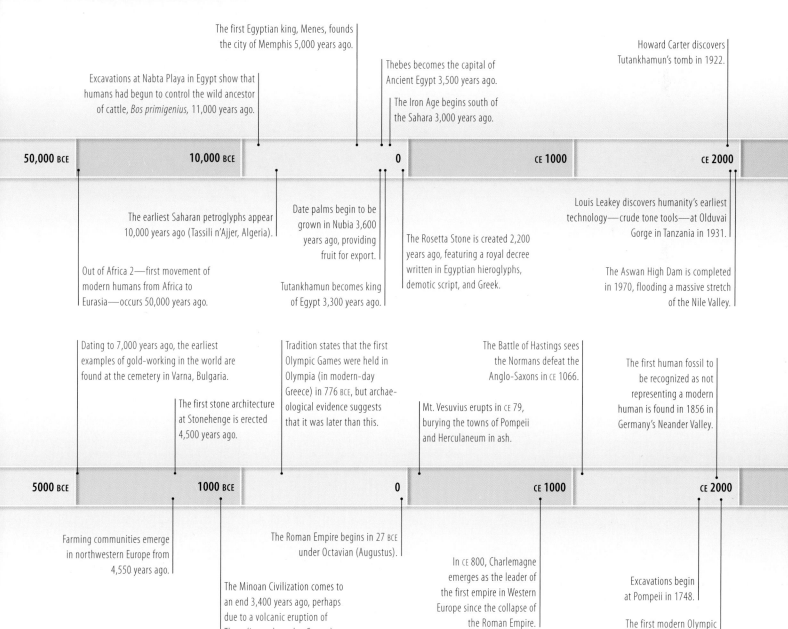

The first Egyptian king, Menes, founds the city of Memphis 5,000 years ago.

Excavations at Nabta Playa in Egypt show that humans had begun to control the wild ancestor of cattle, *Bos primigenius*, 11,000 years ago.

Thebes becomes the capital of Ancient Egypt 3,500 years ago.

The Iron Age begins south of the Sahara 3,000 years ago.

Howard Carter discovers Tutankhamun's tomb in 1922.

50,000 BCE	10,000 BCE	0	CE 1000	CE 2000

The earliest Saharan petroglyphs appear 10,000 years ago (Tassili n'Ajjer, Algeria).

Out of Africa 2—first movement of modern humans from Africa to Eurasia—occurs 50,000 years ago.

Date palms begin to be grown in Nubia 3,600 years ago, providing fruit for export.

Tutankhamun becomes king of Egypt 3,300 years ago.

The Rosetta Stone is created 2,200 years ago, featuring a royal decree written in Egyptian hieroglyphs, demotic script, and Greek.

Louis Leakey discovers humanity's earliest technology—crude tone tools—at Olduvai Gorge in Tanzania in 1931.

The Aswan High Dam is completed in 1970, flooding a massive stretch of the Nile Valley.

Dating to 7,000 years ago, the earliest examples of gold-working in the world are found at the cemetery in Varna, Bulgaria.

The first stone architecture at Stonehenge is erected 4,500 years ago.

Tradition states that the first Olympic Games were held in Olympia (in modern-day Greece) in 776 BCE, but archaeological evidence suggests that it was later than this.

The Battle of Hastings sees the Normans defeat the Anglo-Saxons in CE 1066.

Mt. Vesuvius erupts in CE 79, burying the towns of Pompeii and Herculaneum in ash.

The first human fossil to be recognized as not representing a modern human is found in 1856 in Germany's Neander Valley.

5000 BCE	1000 BCE	0	CE 1000	CE 2000

Farming communities emerge in northwestern Europe from 4,550 years ago.

The Roman Empire begins in 27 BCE under Octavian (Augustus).

The Minoan Civilization comes to an end 3,400 years ago, perhaps due to a volcanic eruption of Thera (in modern-day Greece).

In CE 800, Charlemagne emerges as the leader of the first empire in Western Europe since the collapse of the Roman Empire.

Excavations begin at Pompeii in 1748.

The first modern Olympic Games are held in 1896.

ASIA

Homo ergaster is established in the Middle East by 1.5 million years ago.

The earliest evidence for pottery manufacture in the world dates to 16,500 years ago, and was discovered at Odai Yamamoto, on the northern tip of Japan's Honshu island.

Farming villages develop in western Asia around 10,000 years ago.

The earliest wheeled vehicles (wagons) appear west of the Caspian Sea 4,900 years ago.

Rice agriculture begins in Southeast Asia as early as 5,000 years ago.

1.5 million years ago	100,000 BCE	10,000 BCE	5000 BCE	3000 BCE

Homo erectus fossils from China and Indonesia may date to as early as 500,000 years ago, but are more likely to be 200,000–300,000 years old.

The first human occupation of the Japanese archipelago occurs around 30,000 years ago (and perhaps even earlier).

The world's first village communities are established in the Levant 11,400 years ago.

The earliest writing system in the world is developed in southern Mesopotamia around 5,300 years ago.

The Indus Civilization develops 4,600 years ago, declining some 700 years later.

THE AMERICAS

Compelling evidence at Cactus Hill in Virginia, United States, shows that human occupation of the region occurred 17,000 years ago.

The earliest petroglyphs in North America are thought to date to around 13,000 years ago.

People were living in Mesoamerica from around 12,000 years ago.

A warming trend some 9,000 years ago causes many large herd animals in Mesoamerica to migrate to other areas; the inhabitants are forced to diversify their diet.

Large ceremonial complexes are built in Peru as early as 4,500 years ago.

The rise of chiefdoms in Mesoamerica occurs 3,600 years ago.

15,000 BCE	10,000 BCE	5000 BCE	2000 BCE	1000 BCE

There is evidence of the occupation of South America some 14,500 years ago at Monte Verde in Chile.

Plants are domesticated in Mesoamerica as early as 10,000 years ago.

Maize cultivation begins in Mesoamerica 9,000 years ago.

Spear points found near Clovis in modern-day New Mexico, United States, date to around 13,000 years ago; this date was long thought (incorrectly) to represent the earliest peopling of the Americas.

People are settled in villages in the Central and Southern Highlands of Mexico by 4,000 years ago.

AUSTRALIA AND THE PACIFIC

The first attempt at a major sea crossing from Indonesia to the Australian continent is likely to have been made some 60,000 years ago.

Striated pigments found at Malakunanja II in the Northern Territory have been dated to around 50,000 BP.

The oldest date for rock paintings in Australia is 40,000 BP (Carpenter's Gap, Western Australia).

By 30,000 years ago humans inhabited all of Australia, from the northern coast to the southern tip of modern-day Tasmania.

Wall markings are made in Koonalda Cave, South Australia, around 20,000 years ago.

60,000 BCE	50,000 BCE	40,000 BCE	30,000 BCE	20,000 BCE

The Australian continent may have been first reached at least 53,000 years ago, but there is no conclusive archaeological evidence of this.

Radiocarbon dates for the oldest sites show that the Australian continent was being settled 42,000 to 48,000 years ago.

Early people begin to colonize Near Oceania (mainland New Guinea, the Bismarck Archipelago, and the Solomon Islands) 40,000 years ago.

The Pleistocene colonization of New Guinea is complete by 30,000 years ago.

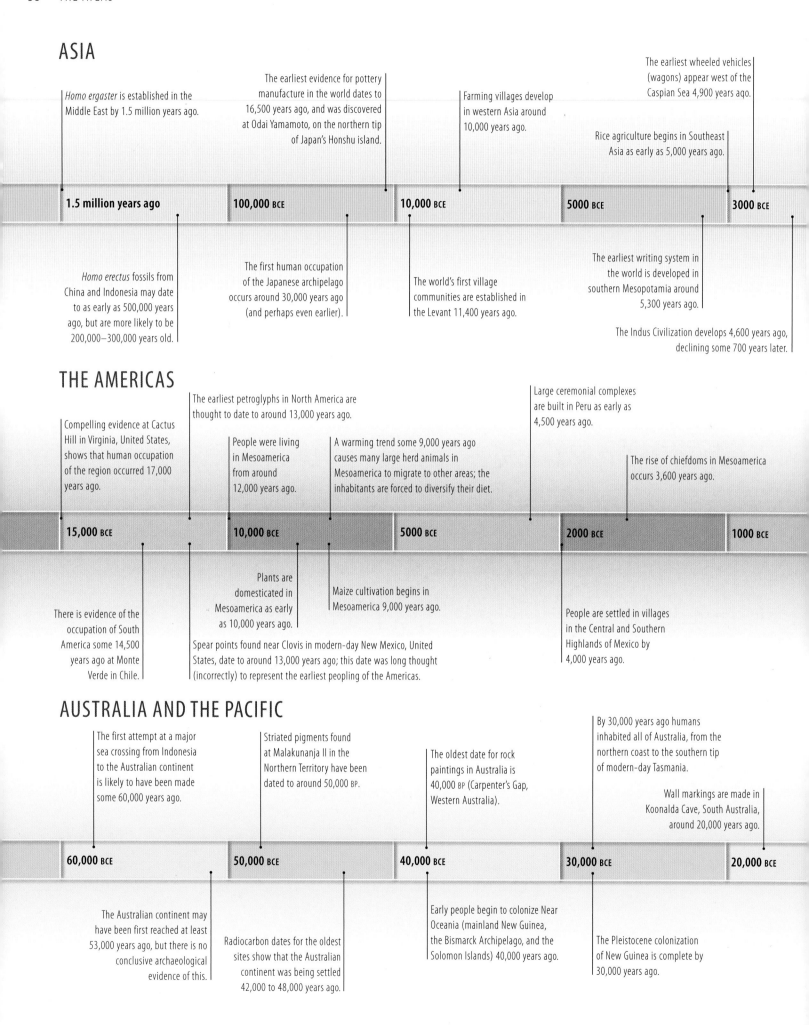

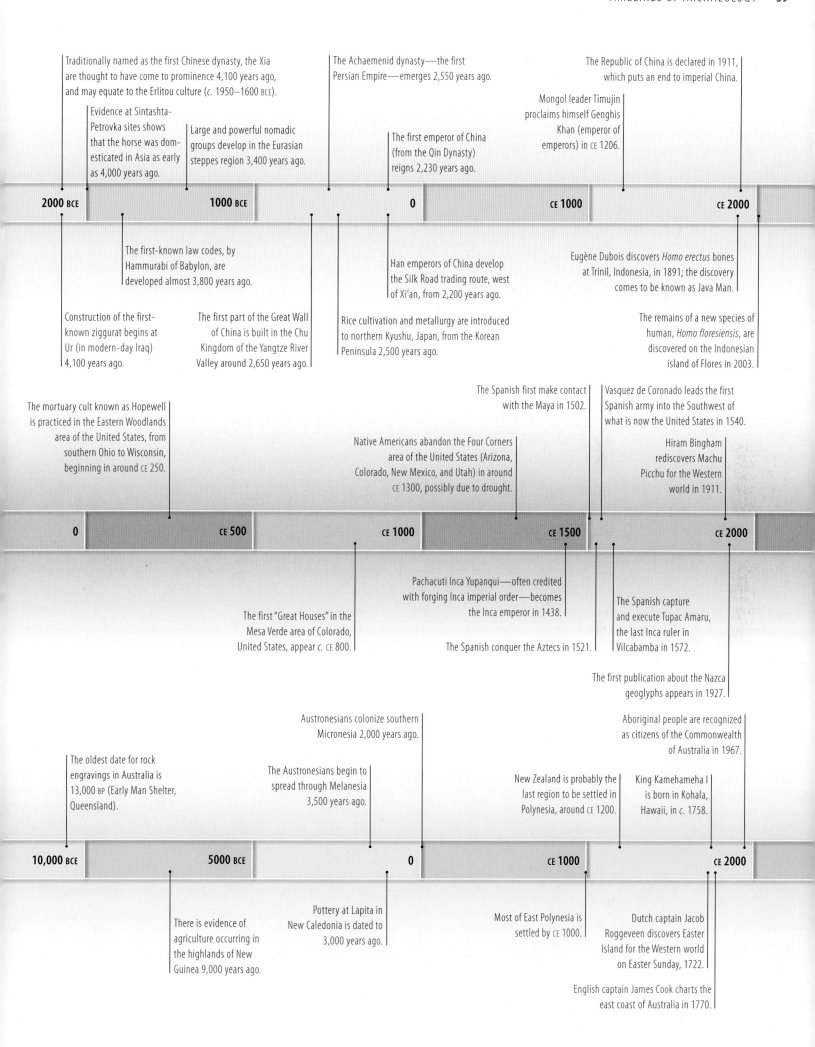

Traditionally named as the first Chinese dynasty, the Xia are thought to have come to prominence 4,100 years ago, and may equate to the Erlitou culture (c. 1950–1600 BCE).

Evidence at Sintashta-Petrovka sites shows that the horse was domesticated in Asia as early as 4,000 years ago.

Large and powerful nomadic groups develop in the Eurasian steppes region 3,400 years ago.

The Achaemenid dynasty—the first Persian Empire—emerges 2,550 years ago.

The first emperor of China (from the Qin Dynasty) reigns 2,230 years ago.

The Republic of China is declared in 1911, which puts an end to imperial China.

Mongol leader Timujin proclaims himself Genghis Khan (emperor of emperors) in CE 1206.

2000 BCE   **1000** BCE   **0**   CE **1000**   CE **2000**

The first-known law codes, by Hammurabi of Babylon, are developed almost 3,800 years ago.

Construction of the first-known ziggurat begins at Ur (in modern-day Iraq) 4,100 years ago.

The first part of the Great Wall of China is built in the Chu Kingdom of the Yangtze River Valley around 2,650 years ago.

Han emperors of China develop the Silk Road trading route, west of Xi'an, from 2,200 years ago.

Rice cultivation and metallurgy are introduced to northern Kyushu, Japan, from the Korean Peninsula 2,500 years ago.

Eugène Dubois discovers *Homo erectus* bones at Trinil, Indonesia, in 1891; the discovery comes to be known as Java Man.

The remains of a new species of human, *Homo floresiensis*, are discovered on the Indonesian island of Flores in 2003.

The mortuary cult known as Hopewell is practiced in the Eastern Woodlands area of the United States, from southern Ohio to Wisconsin, beginning in around CE 250.

The Spanish first make contact with the Maya in 1502.

Native Americans abandon the Four Corners area of the United States (Arizona, Colorado, New Mexico, and Utah) in around CE 1300, possibly due to drought.

Vasquez de Coronado leads the first Spanish army into the Southwest of what is now the United States in 1540.

Hiram Bingham rediscovers Machu Picchu for the Western world in 1911.

0   CE **500**   CE **1000**   CE **1500**   CE **2000**

The first "Great Houses" in the Mesa Verde area of Colorado, United States, appear c. CE 800.

Pachacuti Inca Yupanqui—often credited with forging Inca imperial order—becomes the Inca emperor in 1438.

The Spanish conquer the Aztecs in 1521.

The Spanish capture and execute Tupac Amaru, the last Inca ruler in Vilcabamba in 1572.

The first publication about the Nazca geoglyphs appears in 1927.

Austronesians colonize southern Micronesia 2,000 years ago.

The Austronesians begin to spread through Melanesia 3,500 years ago.

Aboriginal people are recognized as citizens of the Commonwealth of Australia in 1967.

The oldest date for rock engravings in Australia is 13,000 BP (Early Man Shelter, Queensland).

New Zealand is probably the last region to be settled in Polynesia, around CE 1200.

King Kamehameha I is born in Kohala, Hawaii, in c. 1758.

10,000 BCE   **5000** BCE   **0**   CE **1000**   CE **2000**

There is evidence of agriculture occurring in the highlands of New Guinea 9,000 years ago.

Pottery at Lapita in New Caledonia is dated to 3,000 years ago.

Most of East Polynesia is settled by CE 1000.

Dutch captain Jacob Roggeveen discovers Easter Island for the Western world on Easter Sunday, 1722.

English captain James Cook charts the east coast of Australia in 1770.

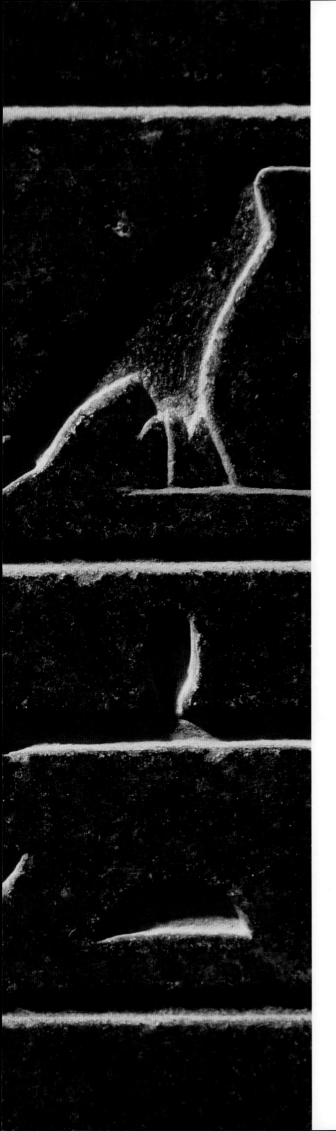

Africa

The First Humans

Most human species evolved in the African continent. The fossil record of human evolution there extends back almost seven million years. However, the first archaeological sites only appear around 2.5 million years ago. In order to be human, there must be skeletal evidence of adaptations for bipedal walking.

CAUSING A RIFT

A great rift valley, which has been forming for about 30 million years, extends from Jordan in the Middle East to Mozambique in southern Africa. Faults, such as the one below in Kenya, are caused by volcanic action. Fossils frequently appear in the disturbed earth.

I n the Early Miocene, 25 to 17 million years ago, East Africa was mostly rainforest. Fossil apes, known from sites near Lake Victoria, had a lower molar cusp pattern that is common to the superfamily Hominoidea (apes and humans), but they moved horizontally with legs of equal length, much as modern Old World monkeys do. At the start of the Middle Miocene, continental drift created the land bridge between Africa and Eurasia in the Middle East that still exists today. African apes left Africa through the almost continuous tropical forests. However, by the end of the Miocene, around five million years ago, they had disappeared from Europe completely, and their range in Asia and Africa was reduced to the areas they still inhabit today. It was at this time that the first bipedal apes appeared in Africa.

SPLITTING HUMANS FROM APES

Paleontologists generally agree on the skeletal traits that identify a member of the tribe Hominini, the highest level of classification that divides humans from apes. These include the head balanced on the S-curved vertebral column, a dish-shaped pelvis, the legs longer than the arms, knock knees, and a foot with the big toe in line with the other digits. These features are all related to the adoption of upright posture and bipedal locomotion, that is, walking on the hind legs.

There are 7 human genera and between 25 and 30 human species. The earliest genus is *Sahelanthropus tchadensis* from Chad, 6 to 7 million years ago. Other genera, named in order from the oldest to the most recent, are *Ardipithecus, Orrorin, Kenyanthropus,*

CUTTING-EDGE TECHNOLOGY
Most of the tools currently used on excavation sites in Africa are simple, inexpensive, and readily available. They have changed little since digs began, especially in remote locations. Large tins do just fine as containers for small fossils and Stone Age implements.

RE-CREATING THE PAST
Away from the fossil sites, anthropologists have many more techniques at their disposal. Here one is seen preparing a model of an *Australopithecus* skull for an appearance on television in 1987. Television has engaged the general public's interest in anthropology.

Australopithecus, Paranthropus, and our own *Homo.* Because fossils from the appropriate part of the body have not yet been found, it is not known if many of these were bipedal or not. Most early humans have apelike cranial and dental features, so fossil skulls and teeth do not help to answer the question. The earliest hominids for which almost complete skeletons are known are the famous "Lucy" dating to 3.25 million years ago in Ethiopia, and a skeleton from the South African site of Sterkfontein, which could be 4 million years old. Both of these show a surprising mixture of ape and humanlike traits, but are bipedal. Modern body proportions first appear with *Homo erectus/Homo ergaster* around 1.7 million years ago.

THE ARCHAEOLOGICAL RECORD

The oldest signs of material culture are stone tools dated to 2.6 million years ago at Gona in the Middle Awash of Ethiopia. Discoveries at other early archaeological sites—Olduvai Gorge and East Turkana in East Africa, and Sterkfontein and Swartkrans in South Africa—date to around 1.8 million years ago. These first stone tools coincided with the appearance of the genus *Homo,* defined by its larger brain relative to overall body size. In Africa, this period coincides with the onset of regular climate cycling between cold glacial and warmer interglacial periods.

In Eurasia and North Africa, archaeologists divide the record into Lower, Middle, and Upper Paleolithic periods. In Africa, south of the Sahara, researchers use the terms Early, Middle, and Later Stone Age (ESA, MSA, and LSA). The ESA is composed of the Oldowan, the Acheulean, and contemporary industries. The Oldowan is named after Olduvai Gorge, where small stones and pebbles were struck to remove flakes. These tools were probably made to prepare animal carcasses as food. In a cooler, drier environment, plant foods became much less available, and the larger *Homo* required better protein sources.

In the Acheulean period, beginning around 1.6 million years ago, cores or flakes were shaped into bifaces, pieces worked on both sides. Later in the Acheulean, smaller flake tools became important; these were produced by shaping a core to remove flakes of a predetermined form in what has become known as the Levallois technique.

In the MSA, which started around 200,000 years ago, large bifacial tools started to disappear. Smaller flake tools were manufactured by removing pieces from radial, blade, or point cores. Similar tools continued to be made from Levallois-prepared cores.

The Upper Paleolithic, dating to 40,000 years ago, was noted for its cultural innovations. Parallel-sided blade tools were made from prismatic cores, and retouched into end scrapers, points, and burins. At the same time, in sub-Saharan Africa, LSA tools tended to be smaller and were set into handles to make composite tools.

THE FORMING OF FOSSILS

Africa has the longest record of human evolution. The evidence comes predominantly from the East African Rift Valley and South Africa. Volcanic and tectonic activity over the last few million years produced highlands and valleys. The low points acted as traps in which animal carcasses were quickly buried and preserved. Subsequent uplift and erosion exposed fossil-bearing layers. In parts of South Africa, the underlying rock was dolomitic limestone. Water action carved out underground caves. If open to the surface, these caves also acted as traps to collect animal bones and sediments; over time, these became cemented into breccia and were thus preserved.

Laetoli, Tanzania

Laetoli is a paleontological site located 31 miles (50 km) south of Olduvai Gorge in northern Tanzania. Mary Leakey, who had previously worked at Olduvai, decided to reexamine Laetoli in the 1970s. This led to the discovery of a volcanic ash or tuff layer with numerous human and animal footprints.

Louis Leakey first identified Laetoli as a fossil locality when he found a human canine tooth there in 1935. German paleontologist Ludwig Kohl-Larsen carried out a general survey in the same area in 1939, calling the site Garusi after the name of a local river. More than 30 years later, Leakey's second wife, Mary, already famous for her archaeological research at Olduvai Gorge, focused on Laetoli again. Her team's research led to the discovery of a number of fossil human specimens, as well as the famous footprints preserved in volcanic tuff.

The site consists of a number of rock layers. The older units, which contain the footprint tuff as well as most of the fossil human remains, are referred to as the Laetolil Beds. Note that while the name for the site was eventually changed to Laetoli, due to formal geological rules, the name for the beds remains Laetolil. Leakey's team collected many fossil animal bones from this deposit, as well as some fragmentary human remains. These consist mainly of upper and lower jaws and single teeth. One lower jaw, LH 4 (Laetoli Hominid 4), is the reference specimen for the early human species *Australopithecus afarensis*, which is much better known from fossils collected in the Afar triangle of Ethiopia (see opposite page for information on the Lucy skeleton).

FAMOUS FOOTPRINTS

The 1978 discovery of the footprint tuff was a landmark in human evolution studies. This unique geological layer was formed when the Sadiman volcano erupted some 3.6 million years ago, blanketing the surrounding area with ash. A number of animals (including giraffe, hyenas, antelopes, and guinea fowl) and three humans walked across the fallen ash, which eventually hardened into a cement-like rock or tuff. Later, another ash fall buried and preserved the prints. The human footprints represent two people who might have walked side by side, with a third person who walked in the footsteps of one of the others, blurring the prints. Many researchers have tried to reconstruct the pattern of movement and have debated whether or not an *Australopithecus afarensis* foot, with its long, curved, toes, could have produced the prints.

Fossils and Middle Stone Age artifacts have also been recovered from the succeeding Ngaloba Beds, including the LH 18 (fossil hominid) skull, which represents an archaic *Homo heidelbergensis*. The age of this fossil is uncertain, but it is an example of the population from which anatomically modern humans developed in Africa.

FAINT FOOTPRINTS

The footprints at Laetoli are faint but unmistakable, and they all lead in the same direction. They appear to represent two adults and one child.

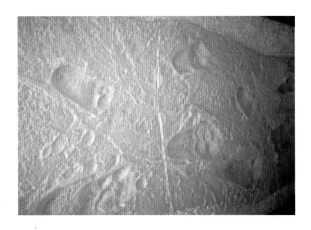

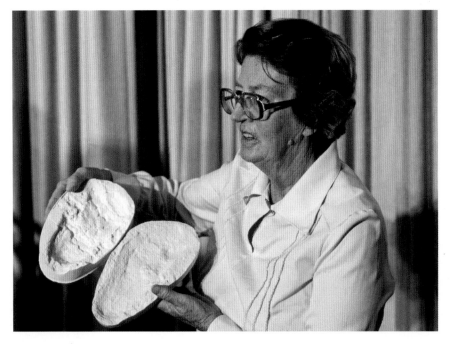

SPREADING THE WORD

An important part of an anthropologist's work is bringing their findings to the wider world—future funding may depend on it. On March 21, 1979, in Washington DC, Mary Leakey announced the discovery of a 75-ft (23-m) trail of human footprints laid in fresh volcanic ash dating to 3.6 million years ago. To illustrate the news Mary showed a plaster mold of one of the footprints from Laetoli.

Lucy Skeleton, Hadar, Ethiopia

Hadar
○Addis Ababa
ETHIOPIA

Lucy is one of a number of fossil human specimens from the Afar triangle in Ethiopia. Discovered in 1974, these remains represent about 40 percent of the bones of one individual who lived around 3.25 million years ago. Classified as *Australopithecus afarensis,* this partial skeleton shows a combination of human and apelike traits.

WHAT'S IN A NAME?

The model below suggests what a living Lucy might have looked like. After finding her bones, Donald Johanson pondered on what to call her. In the background, the radio was playing the Beatles' hit "Lucy in the Sky with Diamonds" and so the choice seemed obvious.

Lucy is the fossil human classified as AL 288-1 (Afar Locality 288, specimen 1) and is dated to around 3.25 million years ago. The bones come from the Hadar area, near the Middle Awash River in the Afar triangle of Ethiopia. Since this discovery, the Middle Awash region has produced fossilized human remains dating from around 5.5 million years ago to recent times. Another locality, the 2.6 million-year-old site of Gona, has yielded the world's oldest stone tools.

WHY IS LUCY SPECIAL?

Lucy's bones were discovered in 1974 and represent one of the earliest fossil humans known. The collection was certainly the most complete, and Lucy immediately became the most famous specimen among dozens of noteworthy finds from the Hadar region. In 1978, together with those from Laetoli, they defined the new species, *Australopithecus afarensis.*

The amazing preservation of critical bones from the body, rather than just the skull and teeth, made Lucy unique. Many vertebrae, limb bones, part of the pelvis, and bones of the

hands and feet were found, as well as the lower jaw and skull fragments. Lucy has been estimated to be between 3½ and 4 ft (1 and 1.2 m) tall, with hips and lower limbs adapted for upright bipedal walking. These features clearly place her within the human line. But the upper part of the body, skull, and teeth all retain apelike features. How bipedal was Lucy? Owen Lovejoy and Donald Johanson see her as completely bipedal. Other experts, including Jack Stern and Robert Sussman, observing her long arms and short legs, suggest that Lucy also moved through tree branches.

Specimens of *Australopithecus afarensis* vary greatly in size and form. Johanson and his colleagues interpreted this variation as sexual dimorphism, meaning there were large males and small females. This view led to Lovejoy's social model of bipedal males provisioning a female in exchange for the right to parent her offspring. But it could just as easily mean there were two separate species, one large and one small. They lived in an environment that was a mixture of forest and more open conditions, which was a long way from the grasslands portrayed in most reconstructions of early humans.

RECENT DISCOVERIES

In 2006, an Ethiopian paleoanthropologist, Zeresenay Alemseged, published a report of a remarkably complete child skeleton, about 3.3 million years old, which his research team had uncovered in the Dikika locality in the Middle Awash. Almost certainly a female and estimated to have died at three years old, it was immediately described as a "baby Lucy."

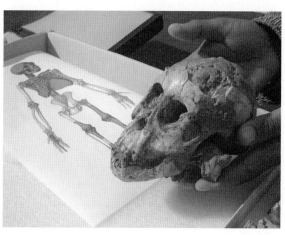

CHOICE OF NAMES

Here Zeresenay Alemseged holds the 3.3 million-year-old skull of the *Australopithecus afarensis* child, called "baby Lucy" in the popular press. Alemseged and his team of researchers named their precious discovery "Selam," which means "peace" in Amharic.

Taung Child, Norlim, South Africa

The Taung child is a fossil discovered in 1924 in South Africa. Raymond Dart classified this first truly ancient human as *Australopithecus africanus*—"southern ape from Africa." But the fossil showed a strange combination of apelike and humanlike skeletal features, leading to endless debates about its place in human evolution.

CAST OF PILTDOWN MAN

From 1912 to 1953, even experts believed in the authenticity of the "Piltdown Man," which purported to be ancient fossilized fragments of a skull and jawbone. In truth, the specimen combined the lower jaw of an orangutan with parts of the skull of a modern man.

The Taung child was the first truly ancient fossil human found in Africa. It consisted of the face, mandible, and part of the fossilized brain of a young child, and was recovered from calcium carbonate or tufa deposits at the Buxton quarry near Norlim, north of Kimberley in South Africa, in 1924. It retained its baby teeth as well as the first permanent molar. Modern children cut this tooth by about five to six years old, but given the faster maturation inferred for early humans, the Taung child might have been significantly younger.

ONGOING DEBATE

Raymond Dart, Professor of Anatomy at the University of the Witwatersrand, prepared and studied the specimen. In an article submitted to the UK journal *Nature* in 1925, he drew attention to the human affinities of *Australopithecus africanus*: a small canine, possible upright body posture, and a brain with fissures and lobes unlike those of an ape. He suggested that the child moved by upright walking on its two hind legs, thus engaging in bipedal locomotion—the hallmark of membership of the human evolutionary line.

This article set off debate about what it means to be a fossil human, a debate which still continues today. Taung had a small brain, but was supposed to be bipedal. This was totally unexpected in the 1920s. It was the opposite of conventional thinking that maintaned that expansion of the brain led the way in human evolution. This idea was based on preconceived ideas of the superiority of the human brain, cemented by the Piltdown "find" in England: a partial humanlike skull, and apelike canine and mandible. Piltdown had passed the "cerebral Rubicon" or brain size of 46 cu in (750 cc) which made a fossil human. But Taung did not. Not until Piltdown was revealed to be a fake in the 1950s did people begin to think that the australopithecines could be truly human.

The first finds of adult australopithecines began in the 1930s at Sterkfontein near Johannesburg, and they continue to be recovered from other South African sites. They are associated with fossil animals, which are between 2.5 and 3 million years old. At Taung, most of the associated animals are small, which may explain how they ended up in this limestone cave; Dart originally thought that the australopithecines were mighty hunters, but the most recent idea is that Taung was the victim of a prehistoric bird of prey, such as an eagle, because of the damage to his skull and eye sockets.

APPLYING MODERN SCIENCE

Kenneth Haines of the National Physical Research Laboratory in Pretoria, South Africa, uses lasers and fluorescences to re-create a holographic image of the Taung child's skull for the cover of the November 1985 issue of the *National Geographic* magazine.

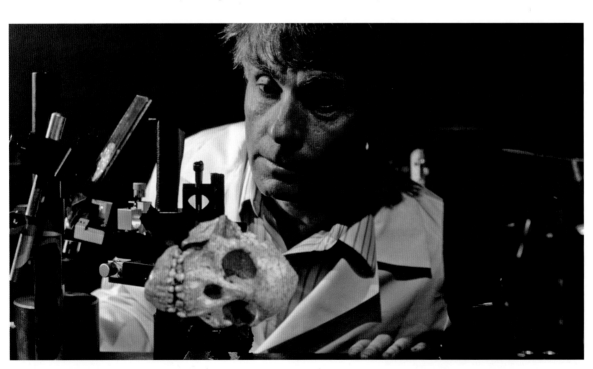

Turkana Boy, Lake Turkana, Kenya

The Nariokotome skeleton comes from the west side of Lake Turkana in northern Kenya. The Turkana boy is remarkable for his long, slender body, which is within the modern size range. It is an example of *Homo erectus* or *Homo ergaster*, the first-known human species to migrate out of Africa.

The Nariokotome specimen, KNM WT-15000 (Kenya National Museums, West Turkana, specimen 15000), is an almost complete skeleton of a teenage male human. Much paleoanthropological exploration has focused on Lake Turkana since the 1960s. Research west of the Omo River in Ethiopia in the 1960s had led to the development of the idea of paleo-anthropology: the interdisciplinary study of human evolution. Subsequent fieldwork, east of Lake Turkana, resulted in the discovery of many fossil humans, most notably the KNW ER-1470 skull (note that the fossils from the east side are cataloged as ER or East Rudolf, the former name for the lake).

NARIOKOTOME—A FOSSIL *HOMO ERECTUS*

The West Turkana specimen was found in 1984 at the Nariokotome III site on the south bank of the Nariokotome River. It was eroding out of lake sediments above the Okote Tuff, a volcanic ash dated by the potassium-argon method to 1.65 million years ago. It represented most of the body of an individual not quite fully grown. Most of the long bones or limbs were made up of separate parts; the joint ends were not yet fused to the shaft as they would be in an adult. Not all the adult teeth had yet come through. Using these skeletal measures of growth, the boy appeared to be between 10 and 15 years old. His body shape and proportions were tall and slim, as predicted by Bergmann's and Allen's rule for tropical mammals. This would allow his body temperature to remain cool even in a hot savanna environment. His height was calculated to be 5 ft 3 in (160 cm); if he had been an adult, he would have been around 6 ft (1.8 m) tall. KNM WT-15000 is the earliest specimen within the size range of living humans. But his brain size, estimated to be 54 cu in (880 cc), is still smaller than ours (averaging around 82.4 cu in/1,350 cc).

READING THE PELVIS

The shape of the pelvic bones indicate that the West Turkana specimen was male. The pelvic structure is narrower than in *Homo sapiens*, suggesting that *Homo erectus* of 1.65 million years ago ran swiftly, and could have been both the pursuer and the pursued.

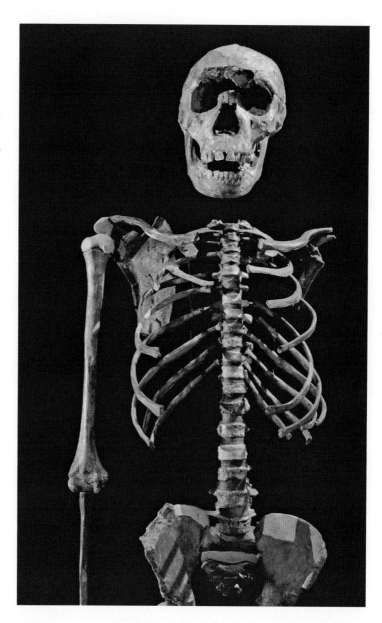

All these features represent a quantum leap over all earlier humans. The skeleton of Turkana Boy is assigned either to *Homo erectus* or *Homo ergaster*. The former is the first Asian species of human, while *Homo ergaster* is used by paleontologists who view the African specimens as a different species from the roughly contemporaneous specimens found in Asia. But, however one classifies the Nariokotome skeleton, this specimen is probably an early member of the species that moved into Eurasia around 1.7 million years ago. This migration event is popularly known as Out of Africa 1.

Earliest Modern Humans

In the last two decades, it has become clear that the first anatomically modern humans appeared in Africa around 200,000 years ago. Except for two sites in Israel, the earliest sign of similar people elsewhere is around 40,000 years ago. By this time, they had developed many new kinds of tools and a relatively complex culture.

MARITIME BOUNTY

Humans have watched the waves splash the shoreline of South Africa's Eastern Cape coast for thousands of years. The earliest peoples of the nearby Klasies River caves culture were well fed by marine mammals and shellfish; later they learned to fish.

Anatomically modern humans (like us) appeared in Africa around 200,000 years ago as the Acheulean gave way to the Middle Paleolithic/Middle Stone Age. Our models of their origins, however, are still drawn from Europe, where they only appear after 40,000 years. In Europe, the indigenous Middle Paleolithic people, the Neanderthals, are skeletally and behaviorally quite different from the anatomically modern Upper Paleolithic people who followed them. Middle Paleolithic tools are made by retouching flakes removed from radial cores, or from producing similar types using the Levallois technique. Both of these methods are holdovers from the Acheulean. But when modern humans arrive in Europe as the "Cro-Magnons," they are associated with a whole range of new technologies. These Upper Paleolithic innovations are supposed to be the sign of the first people like us.

Analysis of mitochondrial DNA in living people led to the idea that our most recent female ancestor lived in Africa between 100,000 and 200,000 years ago.

This, and more recent genetic research, confirms a relatively recent African ancestor for all of us, much younger than *Homo erectus*. There must have been more than one Out of Africa event. New dating techniques also show that modern humans preceded Neanderthals in the Middle East at two sites—Skuhl and Qafzeh— and could have lived in Africa at least 200,000 years ago. African moderns and European Neanderthals are only cousins, and African modern humans were the most likely ancestors of the Cro-Magnons.

BEHAVIORAL MODERNITY— THE ARCHAEOLOGICAL EVIDENCE

The first modern humans were not European Upper Paleolithic people, but Middle Paleolithic/Middle Stone Age Africans, whose artifacts resembled the Neanderthals. So a new model was created, one which split the appearance of anatomical modernity from the beginnings of behavioral modernity. The latter continues to be represented by innovations associated with the European Upper Paleolithic.

These include blade or bladelet tools, composite tools, organic tools (made of ivory, bone, antler, or wood), jewelry or personal adornment, and other symbolic items, such as portable (animal and human figurines) and parietal art (paintings and engravings). Other Upper Paleolithic developments are supposed to be the use of new environments (forests, northern regions, and deserts) and changes in social strategies to emphasize long-distance social networks. This might be reflected in the emergence of regional artifact styles. New food resources were exploited, such as fish and shellfish, and the intentional burial of people either began or became more complex.

A SECOND MIGRATION

The Out of Africa 2 model proposes that modern humans developed in Africa then spread out from 50,000 years ago. By this time or soon after, they developed the technologies associated with the Upper Paleolithic, which let them replace the indigenous populations of Eurasia with minimal fuss. If so, how and when did the new technologies develop? Anthropologist Richard Klein thinks that this happened late in the Middle Stone Age in Africa when people developed symbolically based language and culture. However, there is no anatomical evidence of change at this time, and the transition is associated with a decrease in numbers of archaeological sites, due to the onset of a really cold glacial episode.

Africanist archaeologists have responded to this idea in two ways. Some search for signs of innovation in the African Middle Paleolithic/Middle Stone Age, but signs remain scarce. The Klasies River site shows bladelike technology, but it is still Levallois-like.

WHAT DOES IT MEAN TO BE MODERN? THE FOSSIL AND MOLECULAR EVIDENCE

The first anatomically modern humans developed in Africa. On this continent, the earliest members of our genus *Homo* lived between 2.5 and 1.7 million years ago, and are associated with the first stone tools. By 1.7 million years ago, one sees the first people with body sizes within the modern range, *Homo erectus*, also referred to as *Homo ergaster*. They also become the first people to spread out of Africa into Eurasia. Around 600,000 years ago, archaic *sapiens* or *Homo heidelbergensis* appears. They have brain volumes within the modern range, and are only slightly different from modern humans. They become the last common ancestor of African modern humans, *Homo sapiens*, and the European Neanderthals, *Homo neanderthalensis*.

EARLY MEAT AX

This stone implement, found at Ismila in Tanzania, dates to around 60,000 BCE. The maker flaked both sides to produce a serrated cutting edge. About 10 in (25 cm) in length, its teardrop shape indicates that it was a hand ax probably used for cutting up meat.

Fish and shellfish were clearly consumed in the Middle Stone Age in many South African contexts. Blombos Cave near Cape Town has evidence of fishing, engraving with red ocher, marine shell beads, and bone tools, all in the final Middle Stone Age. Archaeologists, not convinced by this evidence, are looking for sites that will show the transition to the Later Stone Age, in order to test Klein's model. The site of Enkapune ya Muto has both periods represented, but there is a hiatus between them.

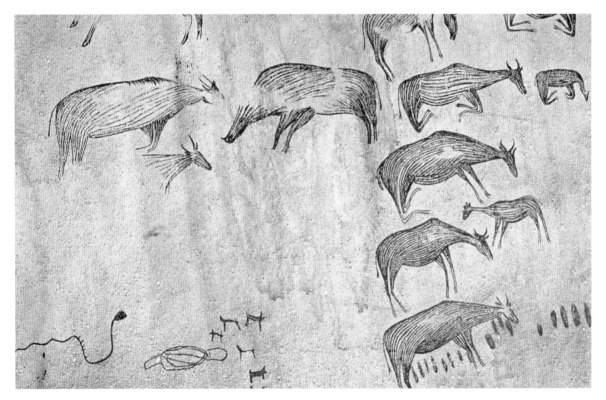

READING THE STONE AGE

These Stone Age beasts look like a species of antelope. The artist or artists were probably ancestors of the modern Tanzanian Sandawe people who still live by hunter-gathering. Were these animals favorite game or do they represent a shaman's hallucination?

Olorgesailie, Kenya

KENYA

Nairobi
Olorgesailie

The Acheulean is a Lower Paleolithic or Early Stone Age industry, which is associated with distinctive bifacial tools, including hand axes, cleavers, and picks. These tools come in a variety of sizes and shapes and are found in Europe, Africa, the Near East, and South Asia. Olorgesailie is a typical example of an African Acheulean site.

EVIDENCE EXPOSED

Exposed by infrequent gentle rain, the scattered "rocks" in the foreground of this photograph are stone hand axes, carefully shaped by a race of people who lived about 400,000 years ago. The roof, to the left, covers and protects the excavation of an intact campsite.

There are signs of technological change over the course of the Acheulean. By 500,000 years ago, more attention is being paid to smaller detached flakes rather than the large bifaces. The flakes are struck off radial (circular) cores and retouched into finished tools such as points and scrapers. Similar kinds of cores could also be worked in order to remove flakes of predetermined shapes; these Levallois pieces were used without further modification.

In Africa, bifaces are typically made on detached flakes; as a result, cleavers are common. In Eurasia, bifaces are usually made on cores. The exception is in southern France and the Iberian Peninsula where the tools resemble those made in African sites and has led some archaeologists to propose that humans could have entered Western Europe directly from North Africa. Another site, Gesher Benot Ya'acov on the border between Israel and Syria, is about 780,000 years old. It too has cleavers and other signs of Acheulean technology thought to be of direct African origin.

While Acheulean sites are abundant in Europe, the Near East, and South Asia, there are also many sites of similar age without any diagnostic Acheulean elements at all. In East Asia, these are classified as part of the chopper/chopping tool tradition. Choppers are cores which are flaked unifacially, or on one surface in one direction, whereas chopping tools are bifacial choppers. The geographic division between the Acheulean and the chopper/chopping tool tradition

was first noted by the American archaeologist Hallam Movius in the 1940s, and continues to be called the Movius line in his honor. Its cultural meaning still remains unclear.

Archaeologists stress the similarities in Acheulean technology over time and space. Their sites are described as conservative; the same kinds of tools were made there for hundreds of thousands of years. When the Acheulean ends, people continue to make flake tools, with or without Levallois-prepared core methods. The transition is said to be associated with the development of hafted point technology, and represents the beginning of the Middle Paleolithic/Middle Stone Age.

OLORGESAILIE—AFRICAN ACHEULEAN SITE

Olorgesailie is an Acheulean site in the Rift Valley of southern Kenya. Artifacts there are eroding out of sedimentary rocks labeled the Olorgesailie Formation. Research was carried out at Olorgesailie by Mary and Louis Leakey in the 1940s, by Glynn Isaac in the 1970s, and continues with the work of Richard Potts of the Smithsonian Institution. The most recent estimates have put the Acheulean occupation between approximately one million and 500,000 years ago. Early researchers concentrated on localities where many bifaces were eroding out. One is named the Catwalk Site; there thousands of Acheulean artifacts have been left in situ for visitors to observe. Another was a place where many baboon bones are associated with stone tools. For Isaac, this was a kill or butchery site.

On the other hand, Richard Potts and his team are following old soil units or paleosols, especially one dating to around 980,000 years ago. They are plotting the distribution of artifacts, raw material outcrops, and animal fossils in order to determine use of resources over time and space. This work allows them to reconstruct the behavior of the tool makers. Complementary research on the Middle Stone Age there is being done by Alison Brooks of the George Washington University and John Yellen of the National Science Foundation. A similar landscape archaeology project is in progress in the early Bed II levels at Olduvai Gorge in Tanzania, this one is directed by Rob Blumenschine of Rutgers University, New Jersey, United States.

Potts has collected some fossil fauna, and has identified what he thinks were animal butchery sites. A few years ago, the first fossil human remains were collected, in association with many bifaces. The KNM OL-45500 fossil is estimated to be between 970,000 and 900,000 years old. It consists of the frontal, left temporal, and some cranial vault fragments of an adult or a near-adult human. The KNM OL-45500 fossil, though small in size, is considered to be an example of *Homo erectus/Homo ergaster*.

ANCESTRAL ANIMALS
Ancient elephant bones have been found at Olorgesailie. They provide invaluable information about one animal species that shared the ecosystem with the early humans. Fauna also included saber-toothed tigers, hippo-sized wild pigs, and baboons as big as bears.

OLORGESAILIE'S SECRETS
Ancient stone implements and their distribution across the landscape tell us much about ancestral toolmakers. Joint excavations by the Smithsonian Institution and the National Museum of Kenya are uncovering significant evidence of early human activity.

THE ACHEULEAN AND CONTEMPORARY ARCHAEOLOGICAL INDUSTRIES

The Acheulean is an archaeological period, ranging from around 1.6 million years to approximately 200,000 years ago in Africa. It is also known in Europe, the Middle East, and South Asia (India and Pakistan). African Acheulean sites contain many large bifacial tools, along with core and flake tools similar to those from the earlier Oldowan. A biface is a stone tool flaked on two sides to produce a sinuous serrated edge. Teardrop forms are called hand axes. There are also cleavers, which exhibit a sharp, natural flake edge; the other edges are bifacially worked. Picks are thick bifaces, and are triangular in cross section. Bifaces could have been used as projectiles, for butchering, or as digging tools. Alternatively, they could just have been cores for detaching flakes, or they could have had many purposes and be the Stone Age equivalent of the Swiss army knife.

Klasies River, South Africa

Klasies River is a Middle Stone Age (MSA) site on the Tsitsikamma coast of South Africa, where more than 65 ft (20 m) of cultural deposits were produced by people who used both marine and land resources. It provides the basis for many of the arguments about the behavioral abilities of the first modern humans.

The Klasies River site lies west of the modern city of Port Elizabeth; the cultural deposits date from approximately 118,000 to 60,000 years ago.

CAVES OF DISTINCTION
The Klasies River caves, protected by the Department of Environmental Affairs and Tourism and the South African Heritage Resources Agency, are designated both as a National Monument and a Natural Heritage Area. Archaeologists are constantly working at the site.

SEDIMENTARY EVIDENCE
Bones, tools, and other matter from the 65-ft (20-m) thick layers of deposits have already shown that the Klasies River peoples gathered shellfish and plants for food, learned to hunt and fish, and used fire to roast vegetable matter and meat—seal, penguin, and antelope.

Sediments accumulated against a sheer cliff in what now appear to be caves. They include many stone artifacts, hearths, shellfish, bones of both marine and terrestrial mammals, and some fragmentary remains of near modern or modern humans. The site was first studied by Ray Inskeep, Ronald Singer, and John Wymer in the 1960s, and from 1984 by Hilary Deacon and his colleagues.

SORTING THE SEDIMENTS
The cultural sequence, from bottom to top, consists of MSA 1, MSA 2, Howieson's Poort, MSA 3, and MSA 4. The last two have since been combined.

MSA 1 artifacts are made of local quartzite; they consist of large flake-blades, struck from prepared or Levallois cores rather than prismatic ones more typical of the Upper Paleolithic. Some were retouched into points, and are associated with radial and disc cores, more typical of this period. MSA 2 levels contain more Levallois points than earlier, as well as denticulates and scrapers.

The Howieson's Poort level marks a clear break with what came before and after. It is named after the Howieson's Poort site where similar materials were first excavated by Stapleton and Hewitt in the 1920s. Blade production dominates; these parallel blanks were removed from a core with soft hammer percussion, rather than by more typical Levallois methods. They were used to produce large backed and geometric pieces, especially crescents. More non-local raw materials, such as silcrete, were used. Apart from their size, they resemble much younger Later Stone Age tools. Howieson's Poort evidence represents an unexpected, precocious industry, which could be as much as 80,000 or as recent as 40,000 years old.

MSA 3 (and MSA 4) levels show a return to local production methods and raw materials. Quartzite unifacial points are the most common tools there. After this, the site appears to have been abandoned as the sea level dropped with the beginning of cold glacial conditions. Perhaps the Middle Stone Age people might have followed the shoreline out onto the emergent continental shelf; the site is not re-occupied until around 2,000 years ago. This long sequence has been used as evidence of modern cultural practices during the Middle Stone Age.

Enkapune ya Muto, Kenya

KENYA

Enkapune ya Muto
Nairobi

Enkapune ya Muto is a cave in southwest Kenya where Stanley Ambrose has excavated an archaeological sequence spanning much of the last 50,000 years. It has a record of technological evolution from the Middle to the Later Stone Age, and sheds light on how early humans may have become behaviorally modern.

Enkapune ya Muto or Twilight Cave is located on the Mau Escarpment, west of Lake Naivasha in southwest Kenya at an elevation of 7,875 ft (2,400 m). It is near many obsidian sources; this hard volcanic glass, usually black, was highly prized as a raw material for flaked stone tools. Excavations by Stanley Ambrose of the University of Illinois in 1982 and 1987 produced an 18 ft (5.5 m) deep cultural sequence interstratified with a series of tephras or volcanic ash levels.

LAKE NAIVASHA

The highest of the Rift Valley lakes is a recreational center for modern Kenyans, and this area was known to earlier people. Enkapune ya Muto cave, west of the lake, was used as a seasonal shelter by Neolithic pastoral communities.

TWILIGHT CAVE—A RECORD OF CULTURAL EVOLUTION

At the top of the site's archaeological sequence is the Iron Age or protohistoric period. Below is a layer of the Neolithic period (a period in which animals are domesticated and people produce the earliest ceramics), as well as the Eburran period. All date to the Holocene or postglacial period.

Underneath the Eburran is the Sakutiek Industry, a Later Stone Age period industry marked by thumbnail end scrapers, *outils écaillés,* and a few backed microliths. Thumbnail scrapers are small flakes, shaped further on one end; *outils écaillés* are scalar pieces, produced through working a core by bipolar flaking; microliths are small backed tools—all are hallmarks of the Later Stone Age, at least in the Holocene. But other items, more typical of earlier periods, found at this site include small, thin, partly bifacial knives, discoids, discoidal cores, and faceted platform flakes. Ambrose interprets all of this as Later Stone Age, or possibly transitional from the Middle Stone Age.

Below the Sakutiek is the Nasampolai; this Later Stone Age industry includes large backed blades and geometric microliths, *outils écaillés,* scrapers, and burins. Then the final or basal level contains the Endingi Middle Stone Age, where there are flake tools typical of classic Levallois production methods. But the most common tools still remain *outils écaillés* and scrapers. Quartz and chert are now more common than in the Later Stone Age, where obsidian was the preferred material. Precise dates for this sequence remain uncertain, but it is possible that the Middle to Later Stone Age transition there might have occurred before 46,000 years ago.

Beads, made from ostrich eggshells, from the early levels have been used to argue that the Middle Stone Age is more complex than expected. Ambrose interprets them as possible proof of the existence of an !hxaro trade network. !Hxaro is seen in historical and modern Ju/hoansi or San populations in southern Africa. There, trading partners in neighboring settlements exchange nonfood items, such as ostrich eggshell beads, arrows, tools, and clothing: visible signs of a social safety net of obligations between people in neighboring areas.

When Did Early Humans Leave Africa?

Almost all stages of human evolution began in Africa. Over the last two million years, there have been repeated episodes of the dispersal of humans out of Africa into Eurasia. The first people who spread outside the continent were *Homo erectus*/*Homo ergaster*, somewhere around 1.7 million years ago.

This first exodus was before the beginning of the Acheulean, more than 1.6 million years ago, and is known as Out of Africa 1. It accounts for the fact that at all sites, such as Dmanisi in the Republic of Georgia, and the *Homo erectus* sites of China and Java, only cores and flakes have been found—tools that belong to the chopper/chopping toolmaking tradition.

There could have been another episode which brought the African Acheulean to places like Gesher Benot Ya'acov in Israel, as well as to the Iberian Peninsula in southwestern Europe. The former dates to just before 780,000 years ago, the latter to around 500,000 years ago. But there was already a human presence at the Gran Dolina or Trinchera Dolina, Sierra de Atapuerca site in Spain. Fossil human remains and pebble tools have been recovered there from sediments dated to around 800,000 years ago.

There is stronger evidence that people who made the Acheulean penetrated into Europe, north of the Mediterranean, around 500,000 years ago. This species, *Homo heidelbergensis,* had a body, brain size, and shape within the range of living people. The same species had appeared in Africa by 600,000 years ago. These people were the last common ancestor between the European Neanderthals and African modern humans, our direct ancestors.

OUT OF AFRICA 2

Then there is the event of interest, traditionally called Out of Africa 2, which describes the migration of anatomically modern humans out of Africa around 50,000 or 40,000 years ago. Modern human fossils date back to almost 200,000 years ago in Africa, and geneticists propose a common mitochondrial DNA ancestor there around the same time. Anthropologist Richard Klein of Stanford University thinks that before Africans could extend their environment, they needed to develop modern symbolically based language and culture, which allowed them to invent Upper Paleolithic technologies and to out-compete

JAVA MAN TWO

Paleontologist G. H. R. von Koenigswald found this *Homo erectus* skull in Sangiran, Java, in 1936. Called the second Java Man, it followed anatomist Eugène Dubois's discovery of the first Java Man in 1891. Until older human remains appeared in the Great Rift Valley in Kenya, these Indonesian skulls were the oldest hominid remains ever found.

THE MIGRATION OF MODERN HUMANS

In the Out of Africa 2 event, people walked around the top of the Red Sea and from there west into Europe and east into Asia and the Americas. From southern Asia, others moved via Indonesia to Australia and New Guinea; millennia later, migrants sailed around New Guinea to reach Oceania.

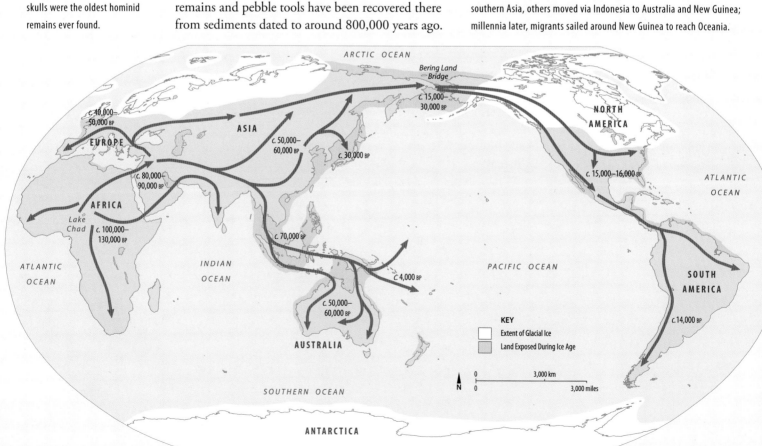

KEY
☐ Extent of Glacial Ice
▨ Land Exposed During Ice Age

SCRUTINY OF A TIBIA

The largest cluster of *Homo erectus* bones ever found at the one site comes from Dmanisi in the Republic of Georgia, where the first hominid mandible was recovered in 1991. The tibia (above), the inner large bone in the lower human leg, is a strong bone necessary for walking upright on two feet.

all other contemporary humans. Anthropologist Stanley Ambrose points to the super-eruption of Mt. Toba in Indonesia around 71,000 years ago, and suggests that it caused a near-extinction of humans in Africa, something which is still reflected in the lack of mitochondrial DNA diversity in living people worldwide. Pamela Willoughby of the University of Alberta, Canada, supports a modified version of this, suggesting that the extreme cold conditions late in the Ice Age made life extremely difficult for our ancestors.

It is hard to see archaeological evidence of routes out of Africa. The Nile River more or less disappeared at the height of the last glacial period. The Red Sea was passable, but it would have been extremely dry and cold throughout North Africa. If we want to test Klein's idea, we also need to find sites that span the Middle to Later Stone Age transition in Africa. Pamela Willoughby's field research has recently led to the discovery of such places. They are located in granite rock shelters, north of the famous Acheulean site of sandstone pillars—Isimila in the Iringa Region of southern Tanzania.

IRINGA, TANZANIA

The Isimila Stone Age site dates to the Acheulean period. Bones, tools, and other stone artifacts have been found in this landscape of sandstone pillars. The site was first known in 1951, but serious digging did not begin until 1957.

WHAT WAS NEEDED IN ORDER TO LEAVE AFRICA?

The event known as Out of Africa 1 began around 1.7 million years ago and involved *Homo erectus/Homo ergaster*. This was the first species with bodies the size of living people, but their brains were slightly smaller than ours. They must have had flexible social and cultural adaptations, which would have promoted group survival.

The migration of anatomically modern humans out of Africa began around 50,000 years ago. While present in Africa at least 200,000 years ago, there is no sign of them in Eurasia until this time. (The exception is a short, extremely warm, interval around 100,000 years ago at Qafzeh and Skuhl in Israel.) Why are people "stuck" in Africa until this time? Richard Klein thinks they needed to develop modern symbolically based language and culture first. Stanley Ambrose thinks that they had to recover from a natural disaster such as the eruption of Mt. Toba.

Early Hunters and Herders

Africa provides archaeologists with their oldest materials. It is the continent on which our most distant ancestors diverged from apes, and the only continent where all major stages of human cultural evolution can be investigated. How did people manage the transition from food extraction to food production?

Hominids, scavengers first, developed hunting, gathering, and foraging in Africa. It is also one of the places where wild cattle were first domesticated and where a myriad of pastoral economies are still practiced.

HUNTING AND GATHERING

To many readers, the phrase "African hunter-gatherer" may conjure up images of the celebrated Kalahari !Kung San. This rather simple foraging subsistence economy—practiced in a marginal environment, and based on immediate consumption enforced by strict rules of sharing whatever the individual cannot use there and then—is only one variant of a range of possible hunting, gathering, and foraging adaptations.

Geographic setting makes a difference but so does social organization. Socially and economically complex hunter-gatherers are of much interest. The acceptance of delayed consumption goes hand in hand with the nascent concept of private property: i.e., people own their savings. Just how did some hunter-gatherer societies manage to bypass the rules of sharing that keep simple hunter-gatherer bands egalitarian? This question is very important because worldwide, such complex hunting and gathering societies seem to have preceded the farming and herding way of life. Perhaps the rise of one can thus help explain the development of the other. Africa provides the right landscape for such investigations, for not only does the continent boast the longest record, but also the most diverse hunting, gathering, and foraging lifestyles, from deserts to mountains, and from tropical forests to the sand dunes overlooking the oceans.

FOOD PRODUCTION

Hunter-gatherers extract their food from what nature freely provides. At different times, however, many hunter-gatherer societies became farmers or herders when they began to produce their own food by cultivating plants and breeding animals. Africa provides a vast laboratory for examining what the archaeologist Vere Gordon Childe once referred to as the "Neolithic Revolution." It helps that in some of the more southerly parts of the continent this revolution took place relatively recently, hence the relevant archaeology is better preserved, and written or oral histories, as well as close ethnographic analogies, can assist us to understand the transition better. The archaeology of Africa may thus help elucidate such transitions in other parts of the globe.

THE SPREAD OF HERDING IN AFRICA

It seems to have been the climatic changes—which gradually created the modern arid Sahara Desert—that spread the herding way of life throughout Africa. Cattle herders began to leave the desert in the fourth millennium BCE, some going to the Nile Valley where their impact on the newly developing predynastic and Pharaonic state was significant. Saharan cattle pastoralists also headed south, reaching the Niger Valley in the West and the Kenyan Highlands in the East during the third millennium BCE. But stock diseases in forested parts effectively halted the further southward spread of cattle until climatic changes created drier, disease-free corridors out of East Africa. Through these, herds and herders eventually reached southern Africa in the first few centuries CE.

Recent research has suggested that more disease-resistant sheep slipped through earlier and reached the south of the continent a few centuries ago. Some local southern African hunter-gatherers responded by adding low intensity shepherding to their existing hunting and gathering subsistence economies, an adaptation that has very few if any surviving

AN ARID LAND
Algeria's central Saharan Hoggar Mountains no longer have a moist enough climate to support much in the way of plants and animals. Cave paintings found in the region attest to a time when humans were sustained by the flora and fauna native to the region.

SIDE BY SIDE
Louis Leakey (1903–1972) and his wife Mary (1913–1996) were partners in a successful search for ancient human cultures in East Africa. Here they are digging for the bones and tools of prehistoric humans in Tanzania.

DOMESTICATION OF PLANTS AND ANIMALS

Excavations at Nabta Playa in Egypt's Western Desert have shown that human control of the wild ancestor of cattle, the aurochs (Bos primigenius), began gradually there as early as 9000 BCE; it was fully domesticated by the seventh millennium BCE. Modern DNA analyses corroborate this by showing that a branch of modern cattle populations originated in northern Africa. Small livestock, such as sheep and goats, who have no wild African ancestors, must have been domesticated in western Asia and somehow reached Africa, perhaps with migrating herders, or perhaps in primitive trade deals between groups of herder-hunters.

Winter rainfall cereals, such as wheat and barley, may have been locally domesticated in Egypt, or perhaps arrived also through trade contacts or migrations. Summer rainfall crops, such as sorghum and millet, however, are indigenous. When, where, and how these were first domesticated in Africa are questions that archaeologists and paleobotanists continue to ask.

ethnographic analogies today. Recent archaeological evidence has suggested that the southernmost African herders encountered by European mariners exploring the region—the sixteenth-century Hottentots at the Cape—may have been, in part, descendants of the subcontinent's first hunters-with-sheep.

AFRICAN DIVERSITY
Africa thus provides in its past and present many variations on what is misleadingly oversimplified by terms in current use, such as "hunter-gatherer," "herder," and "pastoralist." As Cambridge University Professor of African Archaeology David W. Phillipson wrote in his grand synthesis of the subject: "African archaeology provides a unique view of cultural development leading to recent societies that are now appreciated, not as failures that have fallen by the wayside in the rise of industrial civilization, but as examples of different—perhaps more viable in the long term— expressions of human cultures fully adapted to their practitioners' circumstances."

TREASURY OF FOSSILS
Africa is a continent of exciting archaeological surprises. During years of patient digging, many bones and tools from Stone Age cultures have been unearthed. At sites such as Olduvai Gorge, fossil-bearing rocks, like the one below, are still being found.

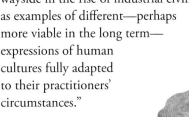

Saharan Petroglyphs

Scattered throughout the rocky massifs of the Sahara Desert are paintings and engravings that seem like ghosts of vanished cultures. Tassili n'Ajjer, a 311-mile (500-km) long sandstone mountain range in the southeast of Algeria, is rich in such images, the earliest of which are 10,000 or more years old.

Tassili n'Ajjer, well known for its natural rock arches, Saharan cypresses, and archaeological sites, was declared a National Park in 1972, a World Heritage site in 1982, and a UNESCO Biosphere Reserve some four years later.

What did these petroglyphs mean to their makers? The logistical difficulties and expense of working in the Sahara, coupled with the sparse archaeological remains and the difficulty of dating the art, make this a challenging question to answer. Ultimately, with a better understanding of the petroglyphs' stylistic diversity in space and time may come also a rudimentary understanding of the images' original meanings, although the vast stretch of time that separates us from the ancient Saharan artists may stop us from ever really decoding their art.

THE WET SAHARA

During the last Ice Age the Sahara was much drier and vaster than it is today. Around 10,000 BCE, the rapid northward shift of the monsoonal rainfall belts that are now confined to tropical West Africa brought wetter conditions to the Sahara, creating freshwater ponds and lakes in what is now one of the driest parts of the world. The spaces between the lakes and ponds were still arid, but the vegetated shorelines of the lakes attracted all kinds of animals and consequently soon became the focus of human habitation. Oscillations between wet and dry conditions have continued, but on a smaller scale, and the general trend has been toward greater aridity.

SAHARAN HUNTERS AND HERDERS

Similarities in stone tools suggest that some of the first hunters to reoccupy the Sahara after the Ice Age came from northwest Africa, while the early "round-head" style of rock art suggests some Africans had moved northward into the wet Sahara from the south. The early Holocene Saharan hunter-gatherers led relatively sedentary lives on the shores of the many lakes and ponds, exploiting aquatic resources for their subsistence. Their characteristic artifacts, aside from the ubiquitous stone tools, include bone harpoon tips, grinding stones for wild cereals, and ceramic pots that are among the earliest in the world and are densely decorated with impressed patterns, perhaps to imitate basketry. Associated with some of these early sites are the remains of small, circular

INCISED IMAGES

A nomad desert dweller examines evidence of a thriving culture that existed here when the Sahara Desert was fertile and reasonably wet. The environment is now much too arid to sustain human life on any permanent basis, and the change in the climate has made archaeological research into the petroglyphs that remain both challenging and costly.

SPECIFIC SPECIES

In many ancient petroglyphs, animal species are difficult to identify. In this one from the mountain range of Tassili n'Ajjer in Algeria, there is no mistaking the outline of a giraffe incised into the sandstone.

DATING ROCK ART

The chronological sequence of Saharan petroglyphs is based mainly on the art's style and technique of execution, as well as on the animal species represented. Engraved images of wild animals, for example, are commonly assigned to an early phase, before cattle herding became the preferred way of life. Painted images often depict long-horned cattle and humans. Those that show humans with clearly African features may be older than the ones that depict long-haired individuals, perhaps of Mediterranean type. Images of camels and horses are thought to date from the second millennium BCE onward. Given the rarity of radiocarbon-dated petroglyphs, it is clear that our understanding of the chronological sequence of Saharan rock art still has much room for improvement.

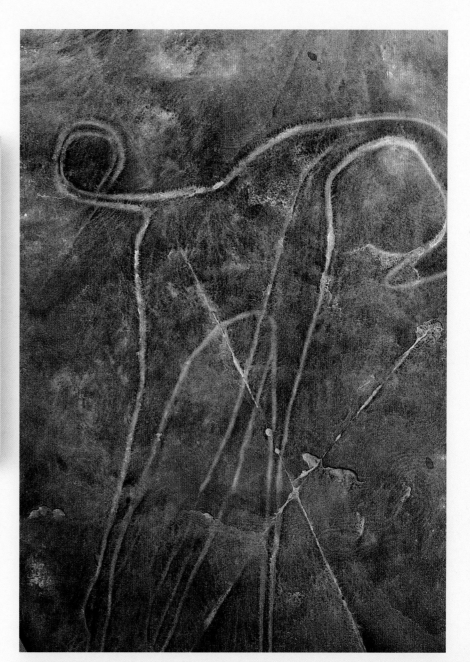

stone structures. In what is now southwestern Libya, wild Barbary sheep were corralled at the cave of Uan Afuda. Elsewhere, well-preserved petroglyphs depict tethered giraffes, and the heavy stones themselves, to which these animals were tied, are still found scattered across the Sahara Desert.

Eventually, such attempts at bringing wild animals under human control succeeded. Cattle were first domesticated in the eastern Sahara. But relatively little material change distinguishes the "pastoral" period from the preceding "hunter-gatherer" one, which indicates continuity in populations and cultures. The principal changes were a reorientation of life ways and art styles toward an emphasis on the herding of cattle, and away from hunting and fishing. By the fourth millennium BCE, cattle were held in such esteem throughout the Sahara that they are found buried in graves similar to those used for human interment. Indeed, the important role played by cattle in the religion and art of Pharaonic Egypt is now thought to be in part a legacy of the Saharans who flocked to establish settlements along the Nile river banks when the desert started to become too dry for their pastoral way of life.

CARING FOR THE CATTLE

A herdsman and long-horned cattle are testament to a time when Saharan land was green and life-supporting. Many of Libya's southern mountain ranges preserve scenes of a way of life that existed about 12,000 years ago.

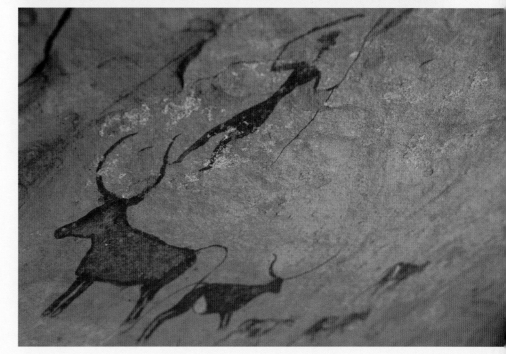

Apollo 11 Cave, Namibia

Although southern Africa is rich in ancient rock art, most of the paintings are so well-preserved that they seem quite recent. But the integrity of the art style and its sophistication suggest centuries of tradition. Apollo 11 gives a good indication of the age of that tradition.

The German archaeologist W. E. Wendt began excavating a large cave in southwestern Namibia on July 24, 1969, the day the Apollo 11 space mission ended successfully, hence the name he gave it. The excavation of the cave revealed Namibia's longest sequence of occupation during the so-called Middle Stone Age, which in southern Africa lasted roughly from 200,000 to 20,000 years ago.

This large cave has no spectacular paintings on the walls. A few handprints and zigzag lines are all that remain visible today. There are engravings in front of the cave, where many of the cobbles and boulders display animal images, some now barely visible which must be quite old. The artistic treasure of Apollo 11 came from the excavated soils. Red ocher (hematite, or iron oxide) crayons with faceted edges were found in layers dating to more than 50,000 years ago. More importantly, in the overlying levels, seven slabs of local rock were found to contain painted images.

APOLLO'S ART

These slabs are clearly not pieces that fell from the cave walls, but are true "portable" art. They are all quite small; each would fit comfortably in a man's hand. On the complete pieces, the image is centrally placed, and invariably depicts a single animal. Aside from a rhinoceros, the other images are not easily recognized. One painting, composed of two fragments found separately in 1969 and 1972, possibly depicts a felid (a member of the cat family). Another fragment shows a black and white striped body, but with legs too long for a zebra.

Of interest is the fact that all seven painted slabs were found within 6½ ft (2 m) of each other, and were lying face down. This may have been deliberate positioning or simply may mean that the paint on the exposed face has faded away. Throughout, the style of execution is fairly crude and the animals' legs are drawn unusually long.

The dates are particularly significant. There have been eight radiocarbon assays at the Cologne and Pretoria laboratories on organic materials from the same level and in the vicinity of the painted slabs. All have given results dating to between 25,500 and 27,500 years ago. These are exceptionally early dates for southern African rock art, and although the recent find of a small engraved piece of hematite at Blombos Cave on the south coast of South Africa now may qualify as the oldest image on the African continent, at the time of their discovery, the animals painted on the Apollo 11 slabs already showed that Europe was not the sole cradle of art.

QUESTIONABLE FELID

Many of the animal images from the Apollo 11 cave are difficult to identify. This one recovered in two fragments—each piece found some three years apart—is very probably a species of cat, though precisely which one is difficult to tell from the faded impression.

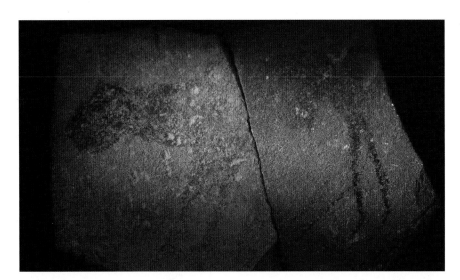

TOUCHDOWN IN APOLLO 11

This visitor to Namibia's famous rock art cave is both comfortable and well placed to scrutinize the walls. About 27,000 portable plaques have been found at this site and are the subject of intense study.

Matupi Cave, Dem. Rep. of the Congo

Matupi Cave ■

DEMOCRATIC REPUBLIC OF THE CONGO

Kinshasa

The archaeology in today's Okapi Wildlife Reserve of the Democratic Republic of the Congo suggests at first glance that Stone Age populations could survive exclusively by hunting and gathering in the rain forest. The surfaces of all rock shelters there, even the smallest and barely habitable ones, contain Stone Age archaeological remains.

Matupi Cave was discovered in 1973 by Francis Van Noten of the Royal Museum for Central Africa in Tervuren, Belgium. With deposits to a depth of well over 6½ ft (2 m), Matupi Cave contains recent and Iron Age materials in the top 10 in (25 cm), followed by an unbroken sequence of microlithic Stone Age remains, which date back to over 40,000 years ago, near the base of the deposits. The cave soil is neither extremely acidic nor wet, and organic matter is adequately preserved at least in the upper parts of the deposits.

EARLY MICROLITHS

The age of the microlithic stone tool technology at Matupi Cave is of particular interest. Microliths are tiny stone flakes and blades set into bone or wooden handles to make composite tools. Attached to a long shaft, microliths become a part of an arrow; a number of them set in a row form a long cutting edge.

This miniaturization of stone tools represents a considerable technological advance. Small, modular, multipurpose bits of sharp-edged stone lightened the load of nomadic hunter-gatherers, and extended their range by turning even the smallest pebbles into

usable raw material. Modular in design, microliths can be made into different tools simply by changing the configuration of the handle, so that repair would involve replacing the broken bit, rather than re-fashioning the entire tool from scratch.

Matupi Cave represents one of the earliest phases of this technological revolution, but does it mean that Stone Age people could live exclusively in the rain forest without agriculture and forest-clearing tools? As it turns out, the makers of the microliths at Matupi Cave occupied the site when it was not in a rain forest setting. The radiocarbon dates cluster within the last Ice Age, which ended around 12,000 years ago. The animal bones and plant remains at Matupi from that time reflect a savanna rather than a forest environment. The drier climate during the last Ice Age apparently broke the forest into a patchwork mosaic of vegetation zones from savanna to forest, which would have increased the diversity of ecotones available to the hunter-gatherers. In this setting, the microliths would have provided just the technological edge to enable people to range farther and exploit a multitude of resource zones with the same modular and adaptable toolkit.

CLIMATE CHANGE

Low clouds shroud a jungle village in the Matupi Cave region of the Democratic Republic of the Congo. Evidence has revealed that when Stone Age people lived there, it was much drier; the vegetation then was the flora of the savanna rather than rain forest species.

Olduvai Gorge, Tanzania

Olduvai Gorge is one of the most important localities for understanding our earliest history. It has yielded the remains of over 50 hominid individuals, and excellent samples of our earliest stone tools in association with butchered animal bones. Most importantly, the fossil-bearing layers are sandwiched between layers of volcanic rock that can be absolutely dated.

PREHISTORIC ANCESTORS
The skull of *Australopithecus boisei* from Bed I at Olduvai Gorge is dated to about two million years ago. Louis and Mary Leakey first named the species *Zinjanthropus boisei,* but it was not long before it became reassigned to the *Australopithecus* line of hominids.

In the East African Rift Valley, the 30-mile (48-km) long and 295-ft (90-m) deep Olduvai Gorge cuts into the eastern Serengeti Plain of Northern Tanzania. The first European to describe the gorge was German butterfly hunter Wilhelm Kattwinkel, who visited the area before World War I. In 1913, Hans Reck excavated fossil human bones there, but did not recognize any stone tools. It was Kenyan-born Louis Leakey who in 1931 discovered humanity's earliest technology: crude tools—not much more than broken pebbles with a sharp edge. There is very little standardization in shape and size, and some are so simple that they may just be naturally broken rocks. Named after the gorge, Oldowan technology—now known from several parts of Africa—is between 2.6 and 1.5 million years old.

OLDUVAI HOMINIDS
From 1935 onward, Louis Leakey and his wife Mary surveyed and excavated numerous sites in the gorge. In 1959 they discovered the nearly complete skull of a primitive humanlike creature, a hominid, that they named *Zinjanthropus boisei*. Soon after, the Leakeys

and their sons discovered another hominid type they named *Homo habilis,* "handy man," because the bones were associated with the earliest stone tools. *Zinjanthropus* was soon reassigned to the *Australopithecus* line of hominids already known from South African limestone caverns. Australopithecenes are thought to have become extinct, leaving *Homo habilis* as our most likely direct ancestor.

The oldest fossil remains of *Australopithecus boisei* and *Homo habilis* were found in Bed I, where their stone tools were often found together with the bones and teeth of animals. The animal species indicate that

"CRADLE OF MANKIND"
Olduvai Gorge is of paramount importance on a global scale for our understanding of human evolution. Embedded artifacts found there have mostly been dated by the potassium-argon method that is used on very old archaeological materials.

a semiarid environment much like that of today existed at the time. In one locality, or "floor," as the sites are called, a loose circle of lava blocks suggests crude shelter built by the early hominids. In Bed II, which dates to 1.5–1.7 million years ago, more sophisticated stone tools, such as the teardrop-shaped hand ax of a type archaeologists call Acheulean, are found. These are associated with the bones of a more evolved hominid known as *Homo ergaster*, previously referred to as *Homo erectus* (a taxonomic label now restricted to the Asian hominids). Beds III and IV contain more recent Acheulean hand axes dating from 1.15 million years ago to about 600,000 years ago. The remaining Masek, Ndutu, and Naisiusiu beds date from about 500,000 years to 15,000 years ago. In all, Olduvai Gorge has yielded the remains of over 50 hominids and a complete sequence of stone tool industries from the earliest to the latest Stone Age.

HOMINID BEHAVIOR

Much remains to be discovered about hominids in Olduvai Gorge's distant past. Recent research there has concentrated on the problems of hominid social and dietary adaptations. The floors, rather than being longer-term campsites, simply may have been places to which hominids returned from time to time to use the cached store of stone tools for processing animal carcasses. The so-called Zinjanthropus floor, for example, which is 1,238 sq ft (115 sq m) in area, revealed a pile of shattered bones that perhaps marks an area of marrow-extraction. Tools were made of different stone materials, some of which came from a distance. The bones of animals that inhabit different microenvironments were perhaps also brought to the site by the hominids.

The many bones of carnivores found on the floors suggest much competition for meat. Did the early hominids hunt or merely scavenge what the carnivores killed? This question is a difficult one to answer because the hominids were unlike us or any other known animal, so their behavior has no necessary modern analogy. Nevertheless, a famous study by anthropologist Pat Shipman of the various marks visible on the bones is helpful. She found that the cut marks made by a stone tool often lay over carnivore teeth marks, indicating that hominids were mainly scavengers who fed on the carnivores' leavings. But meat is not all that hominids ate, and it is probable that plant foods would also have been very important to them.

Unfortunately, the archaeological traces of plants have long since vanished and we cannot prove this. Proxy evidence, however, in the form of microwear on fossil hominid teeth suggests they had a diet similar to modern nonhuman primates.

LYING IN LAYERS
Olduvai Gorge is a trench hewn out of the Serengeti Plain by natural events. The walls contain exposed fossil-bearing strata dating back two million years. The site is known as the "Cradle of Mankind" for its contribution to tracing our human ancestors.

THE FORMATION OF THE GORGE

Besides archaeology, Louis Leakey was also trained in geology and he succeeded in unraveling the complex processes that led to the formation of the gorge. He suggested that long ago a lake, as large as 15½ miles (25 km) in diameter, bordered what is now Olduvai Gorge, and successive volcanic eruptions regularly covered the area in ash and lava. Then around 500,000 years ago earthquakes diverted a nearby stream, which started to cut into the accumulated sediments of successive lake beds and volcanic ash layers, eventually creating the now 295-ft (90-m) deep gorge. Its cutting has exposed seven main stratigraphic layers, of which the oldest, Bed I, rests on volcanic rocks dated by the potassium-argon method to about two million years ago.

Ancient Egypt

Around 3200 BCE a state developed with sophisticated features, including writing, a calendar, formal figurative art, and a stable administration. Ancient Egypt is a unique case for archaeology. The dry desert with minimal rainfall during the winter months has preserved many organic materials, which survive only in exceptional conditions in other parts of the world.

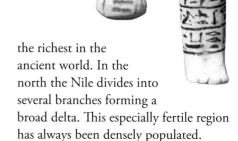

E gypt is dominated by its unique geography. The Nile River flows from south to north through the Sahara Desert, which is rich in raw materials, but hostile for settled life. Before human interference with its natural flow, the river flooded in late summer bringing fertile soil to the regions closest to its banks, and making Egypt's agriculture one of the richest in the ancient world. In the north the Nile divides into several branches forming a broad delta. This especially fertile region has always been densely populated.

The country was divided into a number of provinces usually known as nomes. Many of the towns and villages within these provinces had a local temple, which in later periods was often richly decorated with scenes showing the ruling king under whom the temple was constructed. Each town had its local main deity, some of them only worshipped at a certain place, others in several towns. The three most famous are Amun, who became state god when his local town Thebes became capital around 1500 BCE; Ra (or Re), the sun god, worshipped at Heliopolis; and Horus, the god of kingship, as the king was considered a form of Horus on earth. Horus was worshipped at several places, including Edfu and Hierakonpolis, one of the oldest cities in Ancient Egypt.

A PYRAMIDAL SOCIETY

A king stood at the head of Egyptian society; from the New Kingdom period he was often called Pharaoh, in Egyptian *per-aa*—literally "great house"; this expression referred originally to the palace, and only later to the king. Pharaoh was the absolute ruler, a god on Earth, who was seen as the son of Ra. Beneath the king were his ministers, important officials who are often well known to us from their significant monuments and beautiful tombs. Under these ministers came the great number of scribes who were responsible for the administration of the country.

Farmers and herdsmen, who lived in small villages along the banks of the Nile, formed the great bulk of the population. The annual river cycle dominated the farmers' lives. After the flood distributed rich silt during September and October, they had to plough

TIMELINE OF ANCIENT EGYPTIAN HISTORY

Time	Dynasties	Important Events
5000–3200 BCE	Prehistory	Farming communities
3200–2700 BCE	Early Dynastic Period Dynasties 1–2	Development of a state, as well as writing and formal art
2700–2200 BCE	Old Kingdom Dynasties 3–6	Pyramid age; strong central government; capital at Memphis
2200–2000 BCE	First Intermediate Period Dynasties 7–10	Country divided into several local kingdoms
2000–1650 BCE	Middle Kingdom Dynasties 11–13	Classical period for arts and literature; stable administration; conquest of Nubia; capital at Lisht
1650–1550 BCE	Second Intermediate Period Dynasties 14–17	Conquest of northern Egypt by the Hyksos from western Asia
1550–1300 BCE	New Kingdom Dynasty 18	Egypt conquered Nubia and parts of western Asia; religious reforms under King Akhenaton
1300–1070 BCE	New Kingdom (continued) Dynasties 19–20	Wars against the Hittites followed by the world's earliest peace treaty; capital at Piramesse on the Delta
1070–664 BCE	Third Intermediate Period Dynasties 21–25	Egypt separated into several political units; around 750 BCE Nubian kings conquered part of Egypt
664–525 BCE	Late Period Dynasty 26	Capital at Sais; contact with Greeks; many important monuments all around the country
525–402 BCE	First Persian Domination Dynasty 27	Persian rule
402–342 BCE	Late Dynastic Period Dynasties 28–30	Last period of indigenous Egyptian rule
343–332 BCE	Second Persian Domination	Persian rule
332–30 BCE	Ptolemaic Period	Capital at Alexandria; Greek-speaking kings from Macedon rule Egypt; many temples in Egyptian style
30 BCE–CE 395	Roman Period	Roman rule over Egypt; Egyptian-style temples and funerary art; daily life and culture becomes Classical Greco-Roman
CE 395–643	Byzantine Period	Egypt becomes Christian; period ends with Arab conquest

AN AFTERLIFE OF EASE

Mummiform funerary figurines *(shabtis)* in the image of their deceased owner were designed to do all physical work in the afterlife. This quartet, made from glazed earthenware, were from the tomb of vizier Paser of the Nineteenth Dynasty of the New Kingdom in the reign of Rameses II.

the muddy land and then sow the grain in the later winter months; most of the cereal crops were ready for harvesting around April.

PREPARING FOR AN AFTERLIFE

The Ancient Egyptians believed in an afterlife and equipped their tombs richly with goods for eternity. Although graves have frequently been plundered over the thousands of years, they still preserve many objects, such as furniture, clothes made of linen, and books and administrative documents written on papyrus, an early form of paper. These documents are the world's oldest examples of medical treatises and include a veterinary and a gynecological papyrus, both dating from around 1800 BCE; mathematical papyri; and many religious texts, most famously the *Book of the Dead* placed in tombs as a guide for the deceased. There are also many literary compositions such as the famous *Tale of Sinuhe* from about 1900 BCE.

While tombs were often in the dry desert, houses of the living were located in the fertile land. They were made of mud-brick which does not survive as well as stone-built tombs. We are therefore much better informed on the world of the deceased than on the world of the living.

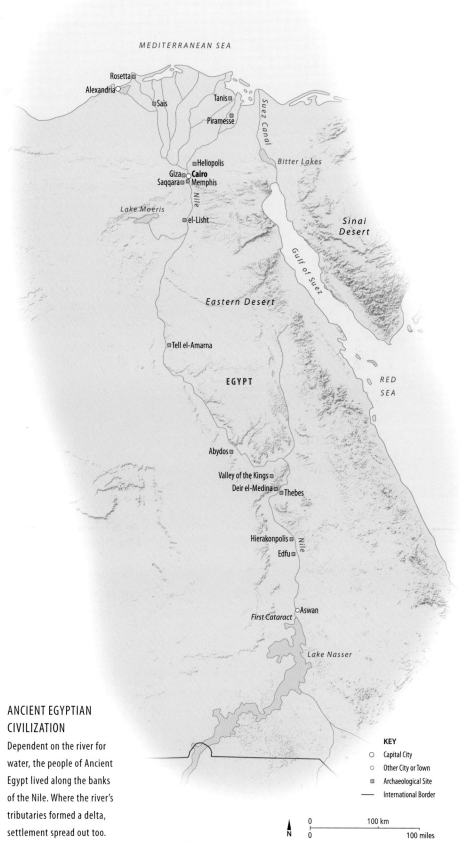

ANCIENT EGYPTIAN CIVILIZATION

Dependent on the river for water, the people of Ancient Egypt lived along the banks of the Nile. Where the river's tributaries formed a delta, settlement spread out too.

KEY
○ Capital City
○ Other City or Town
▢ Archaeological Site
— International Border

RELIGIOUS CAPITAL AT THEBES

During the annual Opet Festival, the sacred barques of the three Theban gods—Amun, Mut, and Khons—rested in this shrine dedicated to them. The shrine is in the First Courtyard added to the temple by Rameses II.

Saqqara, Egypt

Saqqara is the modern name for the cemetery of the Ancient Egyptian city of Memphis, the Old Kingdom (2700–2200 BCE) capital. Memphis lies just south of modern Cairo at the border of Upper and Lower Egypt. Third Dynasty King Djoser built Egypt's first monumental stone building at Saqqara—a Step Pyramid 195 ft (60 m) high.

The city of Memphis was founded by the first Egyptian king Menes, around 3000 BCE. From about this time the archaeological record shows that Saqqara became its main cemetery. In the Second Dynasty the kings started to build their monumental tombs there.

OLD KINGDOM COMPLEXES

The architect of King Djoser's Step Pyramid was perhaps his minister Imhotep, worshipped in later times as a god, and identified by the Greeks with Asklepios, their god of medicine. Though the pyramid and its complex have been targeted by several important expeditions, the site is still not yet fully excavated. The French Egyptologist Jean-Philippe Lauer (1902–2001) devoted most of his life to excavating this first pyramid. The pyramid was surrounded by temples for the cult of the king and possibly for the cult of different gods. A limestone wall enclosed the whole complex, almost certainly copying the walls of Memphis. The king's burial chamber lay under the pyramid. Robbed in antiquity, some bones found there might be all that remains of King Djoser's body. Long underground galleries, discovered in other parts of the complex, contained thousands of stone vessels securing the eternal food supply.

After King Djoser, many Old Kingdom kings built their pyramid complexes at Saqqara. In these earlier pyramids, the burial chambers were uninscribed. But the pyramid of King Unas, the last ruler of the Fifth Dynasty, contained extensive religious inscriptions which covered his burial chambers securing the afterlife of the king and describing how, after his death, he became one of the stars in the night sky. The *Pyramid Texts* are the first long religious

TRANSLUCENT ALABASTER
Among funerary goods recovered from King Djoser's Step Pyramid at Saqqara was the alabaster vase to the right. Alabaster, a popular stone with the Ancient Egyptians, is soft and fragile, and must be handled carefully to prevent "bruising" the surface.

STEPS TO IMMORTALITY

Djoser's Step Pyramid, the first pyramid built in Egypt, was attributed to architect Imhotep. The final measurements of this mighty monument were about 460 ft (140 m) by 385 ft (118 m) with a height of 195 ft (60 m).

texts known from Ancient Egypt. They were discovered by the French Egyptologist Gaston Maspero in 1881. In the Sixth Dynasty such texts adorned the burial chambers of all kings and some queens; the same and similar texts were later inscribed on coffins, and from the New Kingdom (1550–1070 BCE) onward written on papyrus.

SUBSERVIENT TO THE KINGS

Near the pyramids lay the tombs of the officials working under the kings. The overground chapels of richer tombs, today known by the Arabic word for bench, *mastaba*, were adorned with scenes of daily life. One of the finest of these belongs to a high court official called Ti, discovered around 1860 by Auguste Mariette. Mariette worked in Saqqara for several decades, making numerous important discoveries, and recording many tombs and their inscriptions. A large part of these are now lost and so Mariette's records continue to be of great importance for Egyptologists. The *mastaba* of Ti still bears some of the original colors. The reliefs show Ti with his wife in activities, such as overseeing workshops and hunting in the marshes, or long rows of patient offering-bearers providing his eternal food supply. The scenes and their captions provide a lively picture of Egypt in the Old Kingdom, although it is still an open question whether they are effective snapshots of ancient life or a more symbolic representation for the tomb.

NEW KINGDOM MONUMENTS

Saqqara remained an important cemetery, and a number of lavishly decorated tombs were built there. New Kingdom (1550–1070 BCE) monuments have long been known; many of their relief-decorated blocks were sold to museums all around the world, but they have been excavated systematically only over the last 30 years. The most famous tomb belonged to Haremhab, general-in-chief to King Tutankhamun, who later became king himself.

SECURING THE TOMB

In the Late Period (664–525 BCE) the capital was at Sais in the delta of the Nile River, but there are still several important tombs at Saqqara. Egyptians knew well that burials were looted, and security became ever more important. There are several gigantic Late Period shaft tombs, 60 ft (20 m) or even 90 ft (30 m) deep and about 30 ft (10 m) wide. The burial chamber was at the bottom of the shaft, and contained a huge stone sarcophagus enclosing the mummified body. The sarcophagus was decorated with long religious inscriptions for the eternal life of the deceased. At the end of the funeral rites, the shaft was filled with loose sand. To reach the burial, any potential robber had to empty the whole shaft, and prise open the massive sarcophagus. The system must have worked quite well, for at least some of these gigantic tombs have been found intact containing grave goods, many golden amulets, and the mummy of the deceased.

His tomb was rediscovered in 1975 by a British-Dutch mission; the reliefs on its walls show scenes of the general receiving honors from his king and with his soldiers, proving that he went on military campaigns for Tutankhamun. Later, sculptors added an uraeus (cobra-diadem) to the headdress of the general. This was a symbol of royal authority and demonstrated Haremhab's accession to the throne. However, when King Haremhab died, he was not interred at his Saqqara tomb; he was buried instead in a royal tomb in the Valley of the Kings at Thebes.

SHAPING A SHIP

A painted limestone relief from the Fifth Dynasty *mastaba* of Ti shows shipyard workers preparing a tree trunk. As there were no tall trees in Egypt, all the wood for ship building had to be imported. Most Ancient Egyptian industries were extremely labor intensive.

Abydos, Egypt

Since the beginning of the nineteenth century, archaeological excavations have focused on Abydos in southern Egypt, 6 miles (11 km) west of the Nile River. The first Egyptian kings were buried in this religious center, and the main temple in Upper Egypt of the Underworld god Osiris was sited there.

In 1894 the French archaeologist Emile Amelineau discovered the tombs of the first kings. These monuments were reexcavated shortly afterward by the British archaeologist Flinders Petrie, and are today the target of a German mission. Recently the tomb of a king named "Scorpion" has been found. This ancient burial site dates to about 3300 BCE and contains the earliest evidence of writing found so far in Egypt. These hieroglyphic signs were inscribed on many bone labels from boxes and incised on pottery vessels, providing information about their contents. This is useful as the tomb had been robbed.

ON A MONUMENTAL SCALE

The most visible part of the royal burials of the First Dynasty was a fortresslike mud-brick enclosure close to the cultivated area where the cult for the king was performed. The tombs themselves were ¾ mile (1 km) away in the desert. Each had an underground chamber of mud bricks, surrounded by many small tombs belonging to servants who seem to have been killed when the king died and buried with him as his eternal royal court. The royal tombs were robbed in antiquity, but still contained many objects, such as seal impressions, parts of furniture, and hundreds of stone vessels of the highest workmanship; there was even the arm of a mummy still with fine jewelry on it. Two stelae, displaying the name of the king, stood in front of each royal tomb. A single small stela inscribed with their name and sometimes a title, adorned the tombs of servants.

In the Middle Kingdom, around 2000–1650 BCE, the god Osiris became one of the most important gods of the country. The Egyptians identified an early king's tomb at Abydos as Osiris's resting place. From this period many Egyptians sought to be close to him and were buried at the site, even if they had lived in a different part of the country. Others built small chapels adorned with stelae and statues at Abydos, for if they could not be buried there, they would still have a monument with their name on it and at least be symbolically close to Osiris. The Twelfth Dynasty king Senusret III (around 1850 BCE) had a great rock-cut tomb constructed to the south, and was probably buried there, though he also had a pyramid in the north of Egypt. During the New Kingdom Abydos remained important and several kings built big temples there, the best-preserved being that of Sety I (about 1290 BCE).

PORTICO, TEMPLE OF ABYDOS

Begun by Sety I and completed by Rameses II, the substantial temple of Abydos contains seven sanctuaries, each one dedicated to a different deity. In front of these are two courtyards with porticos; the rectangular pillars are carved with sunken reliefs relating to the cult of Sety I.

Giza Pyramids, Egypt

Three awe-inspiring pyramids stand at Giza in the western desert near Cairo. They belong to kings from the Fourth Dynasty: Kheops, Khephren, and Mykerinos. The pyramid of Kheops, which Ancient Greek writers regarded as one of the seven wonders of the world, is the oldest of the three. It is the only wonder still standing.

PYRAMID COMPLEX

The workforce of a nation built the main pyramids at Giza. Smaller pyramids cluster round the big three—the monuments of Kheops (Khufu), Khephren (Khafra), and Mykerinos (Menkaura). Built to last, these edifices still dominate suburban southern Cairo.

FALCON SECURITY

King Khephren receives maximum protection from the god Horus, who sits on the back of his throne. Horus is habitually represented as a falcon—a fierce bird of prey. This time his extended wings enhance his powerful presence.

Recent excavations under Egyptologists Zahi Hawass from Egypt and Mark Lehner from the United States have unearthed the town where the workmen who built the pyramids lived. There were huge barracks where they slept, and kitchens where their food was prepared.

THE KHEOPS COMPLEX

The pyramid of Kheops (to the Egyptians Khufu or Khnum-Khufu, meaning "the god Khnum protects me") was originally 479 ft (146 m) high and contained more than two million limestone blocks, most of them quarried just next to the pyramid. It had three chambers and a complex system of corridors. The burial chamber still contained the stone sarcophagus of the king but the mummy had long since gone. In front of the pyramid were the pyramid temple, a causeway, and a valley temple—the classic arrangement of a pyramid complex from the Fourth Dynasty until the Middle Kingdom.

Around the king's pyramid were much smaller ones for the queens, and the tombs of officials and Kheops's family. In 1925 American Egyptologist George Reisner and his team discovered the intact burial chamber of the king's mother Hetepheres, still containing a fine set of gilded furniture. The wood had rotted away, but careful examination of the gold foil once covering the bed, canopy, and chairs made it possible to reconstruct them. To the excavators' great surprise, the limestone sarcophagus of the king's mother was empty.

KHEPHREN AND MYKERINOS

The next large pyramid at Giza belonged to King Khephren (Khafra), perhaps a son of Kheops; at 470 ft (143 m) high it is just a little smaller than the pyramid of Kheops. Its burial chamber was also found empty. Its pyramid temples, built of granite blocks from Aswan in southernmost Egypt, are among the best preserved. In the valley temple the French Egyptologist Auguste Mariette found a group of perfectly preserved life-size statues of Khephren showing him sitting on a throne. These rank among the greatest artworks of Ancient Egypt. The Great Sphinx of Giza crouches next to the valley temple. Most likely also sculpted under Khephren, it shows the king with a human head and a lion's body, and is one of the largest sculptures ever created.

Giza's smallest main pyramid, partly covered with red granite, belonged to Mykerinos (Menkaura), a son of Khephren. The building was once 213 ft (65 m) high, but was never completely finished. Nevertheless, in ancient times, as it is today, it must have been an impressive monument.

Deir el-Medina, Egypt

The royal tombs of the New Kingdom (about 1550–1070 BCE) were rock-cut corridors and chambers in the Valley of the Kings at Thebes. A large team of workmen and artists built and decorated these tombs. It included stone-cutters, painters, sculptors, and carpenters, and the people supplying these craftsmen with food and other important items.

These people lived in the desert in a small village at Thebes, less than a mile (just a kilometer) from the Valley of the Kings. The settlement, known in ancient times as *set-maat* ("the place of truth"), is today called Deir el-Medina, and has been excavated several times.

EARLY DISCOVERIES

Single objects and tombs were already being found at Deir el-Medina in the nineteenth century; the most important was the intact tomb of Sennedjem, famous for its beautiful ceiling and wall paintings of religious motifs. It contained the mummies of Sennedjem and his family, in total about 20 bodies, some placed in brightly painted coffins showing the deceased in the everyday dress typical for this period.

Italian Egyptologist Ernesto Schiaparelli conducted the first systematic research in Deir el-Medina from 1905 to 1909. He found the undisturbed tomb of the architect Kha, whose tomb equipment is now in the Egyptian Museum in Turin in northwest Italy. From 1917 to 1947 the French Egyptologist Bernard

SLAKING HIS THIRST

In his tomb at Deir el-Medina, the royal tomb builder Pashedu drinks from the sacred pool. The colors of this painting from the Nineteenth Dynasty (c. 1296–1186 BCE) are still surprisingly vivid, and the subject matter gives us a record of an everyday ritual.

A LIFE OF CRIME

Paneb, the adopted son of overseer Neferhotep and a head of workmen himself, is perhaps the most famous or infamous man in the history of Deir el-Medina. The surviving records accuse him of terrible crimes. If the documents are to be believed, Paneb and his gang of thieves looted the tomb of Rameses II's daughter and stole parts of Sety II's tomb equipment (around 1200 BCE). When officials discovered him, Paneb had the means to bribe them to keep his freedom. He was repeatedly accused of seducing married women, causing civil strife in the village. After several charges were made against him, he disappears from the sources and might have been put to death in year six of King Siptah's reign, as existing records show the "execution of a head of workmen" at that time.

Bruyère excavated the village, its temples, and many of the tombs; his results were published in a series of volumes richly illustrated with photographs and drawings of his finds.

VILLAGE LIFE

The village consisted of narrow, but relatively long houses fronting two main roads and surrounded by a wall. The houses were one story high and each contained several rooms: an entrance room, often with a small chapel; the main living room arranged around a central column; a back room, perhaps used as the owners' sleeping quarters; a side room that functioned as the kitchen; and sometimes a cool cellar for storing food.

Next to the village were the chapels and small temples where the workmen worshipped their gods. The main deity of the village was Meretseger, a cobra goddess, embodying the dangers of the desert. The tombs of the workmen surrounded the village, many of them finely painted. Above most tombs were chapels surmounted by small pyramids. This site provides archaeologists with the unique opportunity of studying houses, chapels, and tombs all belonging to the same people.

One exceptional discovery was a well, 656 ft (200 m) away from the village, filled with some 5,000 ostraca—inscribed potsherds and stones, used as a cheap substitute for papyrus paper—ranging from bills, administrative documents, and short

letters to literary compositions. These inscriptions told of the life of the people in amazing detail, making some better known than most Egyptian kings. There were accounts of every festival held in the village, and lists of workmen showing who was working and who stayed at home. In Deir el-Medina, at least, a week was ten days. Men worked eight days, living in small huts close to the building sites; they then returned to Deir el-Medina for the ninth and tenth days. Workers were usually paid with food—measures of grain, cakes, beer, dates, vegetables, and fish—but also with fuel and pottery. Good work earned extra food rations.

Ostraca even revealed what some objects were worth. Egyptians did not have coins at this time, but used a unit of weight, the deben "ring," as a measure of value; every object was priced in deben enabling exchange of objects of the same value. A pair of sandals was priced at 66 deben, a simple chair cost 12 to 20 deben, and a basket of emmer wheat 2 deben. The documents also reveal how prices could soar in times of political and economical crisis.

GRAIN FLOW PROBLEMS

During the reign of Rameses III the government had problems providing the grain payments for the workers at Deir el-Medina. After months without pay, the men downed tools and walked off the job, simply saying: "We are hungry!" Only the skillful intervention of vizier To calmed them; he arranged for food to be delivered without delay, although he was unable to supply the full amount. Strikes continued over the following years and the village remained in a state of unrest until it was abandoned at the end of the New Kingdom period, when kings stopped being buried in the Valley of the Kings.

STORAGE CONTAINER
This well-preserved, painted wooden box was found at Deir el-Medina in the tomb of the well-to-do architect Kha. It dates to the Eighteenth Dynasty and would have been used to store toilet articles, such as perfume bottles and jars of ointment.

WORKFORCE CONTROL
The builders of the royal tombs lived apart from the general population to help keep their labors secret. The ruins of the workers' accommodation at Deir el-Medina, mostly tiny mud-brick dwellings with common walls, show how cramped their living quarters must have been.

Tutankhamun's Tomb, Egypt

Around 1330 BCE a young boy of about nine became king of Egypt. Little is known about his reign, which is thought to have lasted less than ten years. Tutankhamun's tomb, one of the most famous archaeological discoveries of the twentieth century, was filled with valuable objects, some of solid gold.

Tutankhamun's father was Akhenaton who worshipped one god, the sun disc Aton, and made this the state religion. His mother's identity is not clear. His father's new religion may have been unpopular for, when Akhenaton died, the old religion was reintroduced. Amun again became the main god, with a host of other gods and goddesses worshipped throughout the country. Accordingly the young king changed his name from Tutankhaton ("Living image of Aton") to Tutankhamun ("Living image of Amun"), accentuating the return to the traditional religion. The king died young and was buried in a small nonroyal tomb in the Valley of the Kings opposite Thebes. Clearly his death was unexpected, as no suitable tomb had been prepared for him.

By 1920 the tomb of almost every New Kingdom (about 1550–1070 BCE) king had been identified in the Valley of the Kings, but Tutankhamun's burial place was still missing. The British Egyptologist Howard Carter worked hard in Thebes for several years searching for this elusive tomb; he dug in several parts of the valley until, in 1922, he finally located the correct site.

MEMORABLE MASK

Perhaps this is the image that springs most readily to mind when people today think of Ancient Egyptian artifacts. This golden mask covered the mummified head of the boy king Tutankhamun as he lay so well protected in his innermost coffin of solid gold.

TUTANKHAMUN'S TREASURES

Tutankhamun's tomb consisted of four small rooms. Two life-size statues of the king guarded the entrance to the burial chamber, and there was a figure of the Underworld god Anubis depicted as a jackal on a shrine, perhaps protecting the whole tomb. In the burial chamber, the only one decorated, stood four gilded shrines, one inside the other. Within the innermost shrine lay a quartzite sarcophagus, and inside this were three coffins; two were gilded, and the innermost one was made of solid gold and weighed 243 lb (110.4 kg). Inside this lay the mummy of the young king, his head covered by the famous mummy mask, beaten from thick gold plate, inlaid with blue glaze, and inscribed on the back with religious spells for his protection in the afterlife.

A set of boxes in another chamber contained gilded statues of the king and several gods. Remains of similar statues have been found in other royal tombs; they were evidently standard equipment in royal tombs in the New Kingdom, and were especially produced for kings and not found in queens' burial chambers. Several models of boats represented the state ships in which the living king had traveled through Egypt; they would allow him to sail the sky above and in the Underworld for all eternity.

Other objects found in the tomb were from the palace; clearly these had once been used in daily life. They included clothes worn by the young king, and a magnificent array of furniture, but some of the utilitarian pieces, such as a folding bed, were quite simple. There were also many plain boxes, stacked alongside other boxes richly painted—one of these was decorated with scenes of the king hunting and on a battlefield. Many pieces of furniture were richly adorned with gold, notably a throne showing the king with his wife Ankhesenamun.

CARTER'S TRIUMPH

In 1922 Howard Carter found a staircase obviously leading down to an ancient tomb. He excavated it and discovered a sealed door. From the very beginning, it was clear that this was the entrance to an undisturbed tomb. When Carter opened the first chamber, he could not believe his eyes. The whole space was crammed with well-preserved treasures, many objects of types never seen before. Indeed it was the greatest archaeological treasure ever found, and it took Carter a full ten years to empty all the chambers. He meticulously described every object, photographed them where they were found, and then packed and transported them to the Egyptian Museum in Cairo, where they are the highlight of a collection rich in marvels.

Howard Carter holds the crowbar that he had earlier used to open Tutankhamun's tomb. His companion at the entrance is Arthur Mace from New York's Metropolitan Museum of Art.

COURAGE OF A KING

A painted wooden chest from Tutankhamun's tomb shows the young king on his chariot, facing his Syrian enemies. He is wearing the blue helmet crown of war and preparing to loose an arrow from his bow. Vultures, believed to be birds of protection, fly above him.

STATE-OF-THE-ART X-RAY

In January 2005, Zahi Hawass, head of the Egyptian Supreme Council for Antiquities, supervised a CT (computerized tomography) scan of Tutankhamun's mummy in an attempt to find out what caused his early death. The scans proved inconclusive.

TRAPPINGS OF THE TOMB

A highlight of the burial equipment was a collection of wonderful alabaster vessels—the most elaborate in the form of a ship with an ibex-prow, and the figures of a dwarf and an elegant lady—perhaps once placed on a dining table. There were also gaming boards, and a large number of scepters and staffs, some of them richly decorated with figures.

In ancient times the tombs of all rich Egyptians contained funerary goods. Tutankhamun's tomb yielded a set of canopic jars containing the entrails of the mummified body and more than 400 *shabtis* (statuettes meant to serve as substitute laborers in the afterlife), as well as four magical bricks found in most tombs of this period.

MYSTERY AND INTIMACY

Among the most mysterious finds are two miniature coffins containing mummies of stillborn babies. Were these the children of the young king?

There were also some very personal objects in the tomb: a curly lock from the hair of Tutankhamun's grandmother Tiyi; a small golden statue showing his grandfather Amenophis III; and a small box, not of the highest workmanship but in itself very charming, which depicted Neferneferuaton, the sister or half-sister of the king. This is the closest we ever come to a ruler of the ancient world.

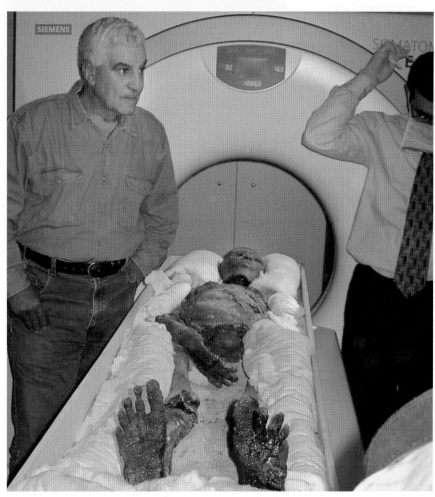

Mummies and Mummification

Several well-traveled Classical authors described the preparation of a mummy—the Greek historian Herodotus (484–c. 425 BCE) was one of them—but the process is still not fully understood by modern researchers. Mummies are perhaps the most famous product of Ancient Egyptian culture, inextricably linked with a belief in an afterlife.

GUARDIAN QUARTET
Sacred canopic vessels were used to preserve the viscera. This set from the Third Intermediate Period is made of painted wood and depicts (from left to right) falcon-headed Qebehsenuef, ape-headed Hapy, jackal-headed Duamutef, and human-headed Imsety.

The dry Egyptian climate and hyper-arid desert soil favor the preservation of organic matter. There are examples from all periods of naturally desiccated bodies preserved by the waterless desert ground in which they were buried. At first mummification was very expensive and only reserved for the richest people, while commoners buried their loved ones in the ground just wrapped in a sheet of linen. In the Late Period (664–525 BCE) mummification moved toward mass production, as more and more people were then able to afford the procedure. At this time, groups of mummies were often buried in mass graves.

A DEVELOPING PROCESS

Preservation of the body was essential for securing eternal life, and extensive efforts were made to ensure its physical survival. At the beginning of Egyptian history, around 3000 BCE, dead bodies were often just wrapped in linen and placed in a contracted position in the ground or in a coffin. The following Old Kingdom (2700–2200 BCE) was a time of experimentation. In some examples the linen wrapped around the body was covered with plaster, and the whole corpse modeled like a sculpture. In other cases the flesh of the body was removed and only the bones were wrapped in linen. However, over the centuries it must have become clear that the crucial factor was the removal of all liquid from the body. Around 2500 BCE people at the royal court started to remove the entrails from dead bodies; as the softest part, they decayed first. They were placed in special vessels, now known as canopic jars, and were often wrapped in linen and treated as miniature mummies.

In the New Kingdom (1550–1070 BCE) and Third Intermediate Period (1070–664 BCE), the process of preserving the body was finally perfected. According to Herodotus and some Egyptian sources, in the most expensive treatment, the body was stretched out in natron—a naturally occurring absorbent salt—for a total of 70 days. The brain, considered unimportant in those times, was extracted through the nose with a long thin metal tool, and discarded. The heart was wrapped in linen and then carefully returned to the body, while the other viscera were placed in a set of four sacred canopic jars, which were then put under the protection of four gods called the Sons of Horus: Qebehsenuef was responsible for the intestines, Hapy for the lungs, Duamutef for the stomach, and Imsety for the liver.

THE SLEEP OF THE DEAD
Sety I died in c. 1279 BCE and his mummy is perhaps the finest royal mummy ever made. The elderly monarch seems to be quietly sleeping. During his 15-year tenure as king, Sety I restored order and prestige to the kingdom and embarked upon an ambitious building program.

MUMMIES BY THE THOUSAND

Thousands of coffins containing mummies have been located in underground cemeteries in the vicinity of Saqqara. They belong to the numerous court officials who served under the pharaohs of the Late Period Twenty-Sixth Dynasty (664–525 BCE).

MUMMIFICATION PERFECTED

Third Intermediate Period embalmers were so proficient that they could treat the entrails and return them safely to the body. The mummy was rubbed with different ointments, wrapped in several layers of linen, and laid in one or even a set of two or three coffins. The head was covered by a mask showing an idealized image of the deceased, and sometimes inscribed with special spells for protection. Pieces of jewelry were arranged on the body; some had already been worn by the deceased in daily life, others were especially made for the burial. The heart scarab—an amulet inscribed with a special spell—was placed next to the heart. In the Third Intermediate Period parts of the body were even filled with bags of sand, which gave them a very lifelike look. Other mummies were painted to re-create a lifelike impression.

UBIQUITOUS MUMMIES

Thousands of mummies have survived, and even small museums around the world may have one. In medieval and early modern times, many were ground into powder and used as medicine—the object of a considerable trade with Europe. The belief prevailed that these mummies contained life-giving ingredients.

Mummification was not only reserved for human bodies; animal mummies abound. Pet cats and dogs were sometimes mummified, as were the sacred Apis-bull of Ptah, and Mnevis-bull of Ra. In the Late to Roman Period (about 664 BCE–CE 395), millions of animals and birds sacred to certain gods were embalmed, often killed for the purpose, and then placed as offerings in catacombs beside the temples.

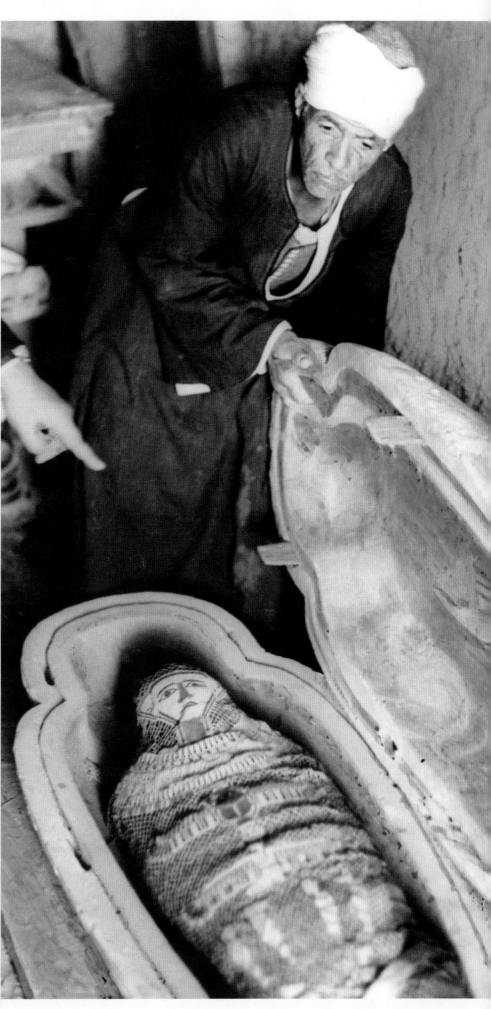

Valley of the Kings, Egypt

The Valley of the Kings was the royal burial place during the New Kingdom (about 1550–1070 BCE). Long underground galleries were cut into the rocks of the western desert, across the river opposite Thebes (today's Luxor and Karnak). Many of these tombs must once have been furnished with treasures.

ANCIENT MILK SUPPLY

A painted limestone fragment shows Eighteenth Dynasty king Amenophis II (Amenhotep II) drinking milk from Hathor's udder. Hathor, often depicted as a cow, or as a woman wearing cow's horns, was the goddess of love, fertility, happiness, and music.

Old and Middle Kingdom rulers were buried in pyramids. Not surprisingly, these conspicuous tombs were robbed in remote antiquity. This is doubtless one reason why New Kingdom kings chose to be buried in a desert valley, today known as the Valley of the Kings. Almost all the New Kingdom kings and many important officials were buried there. The first royal tombs were relatively modest in size, but they gradually increased in scale, until they became a chain of halls and corridors more than 300 ft (100 m) long.

SANCTIONED GRAVE ROBBING

At the end of the New Kingdom, when the Egyptian state needed funds, officials opened the tombs and melted down objects made of gold; many great stone sarcophagi were broken up, and the mummies of the kings were collected and buried elsewhere. Several tombs remained open and consistently attracted visitors; the site was frequently mentioned by Classical and later authors.

EXCITING EXCAVATIONS

The first tomb to be opened in the Valley of the Kings since Carter found Tutankhamun's in 1922 was entered in February 2006. Ranks of stone vessels were immediately visible. The tomb is also known to contain six sarcophagi but their occupants are as yet unidentified.

Systematic exploration of the region began in the early nineteenth century when in 1817 Italian Giovanni Battista Belzoni discovered several tombs, notably that of King Sety I, the most beautiful as well as the biggest. Belzoni's methods were rough by modern standards—he sometimes used charges of dynamite to blast open tombs—but he was the first excavator to take detailed measurements and record the inscriptions that he found.

Scientific excavations started at the end of the nineteenth century. Victor Loret discovered the tomb of Amenophis II (sometimes called Amenhotep II), and also the last resting place for several other pharaohs interred there after their tombs had been emptied. The tomb of the official Maherper containing an array of well-preserved objects was the first found intact. In 1905 the American lawyer and excavator Theodore Davies discovered the partly robbed tomb of Yuya and Tuyu, grandparents of Akhenaton and parents of Queen Tiyi, wife of Amenophis III. After Tutankhamun's tomb was found in 1922, the series of amazing discoveries ended for almost 80 years.

FUTURE REWARDS

Today many expeditions go to the valley to record the tomb decorations. However, recently a tomb was rediscovered, already known since the 1820s but its precise location lost. On reentering the tomb, it became clear that it was much bigger than hitherto thought, and contained the burials of Rameses II's many sons. Another tomb was discovered in 2005 and opened in February 2006, after coffins and embalming material were found in a small hiding place. More surprises may reward careful excavation.

Tell el-Amarna, Egypt

Tell el-Amarna is the best excavated and recorded ancient Egyptian city. It stands 190 miles (300 km) south of Cairo. Once the royal residence of King Akhenaton, where he lived with his beautiful Queen Nefertiti, this city was known then as Akhet-Aton ("horizon of Aton"). After his death, it was soon abandoned and the building materials used elsewhere.

In the sixth year of his reign King Amenhotep IV, a king of the Eighteenth Dynasty (1536–1353 BCE), changed his name to Akhenaton and moved with his wife Nefertiti to a new capital in Middle Egypt. In Akhet-Aton the king built great palaces and temples for his new religion dedicated to just one god, the sun disc Aton. Later in Akhenaton's reign the temples of Amun were closed and his image and name erased throughout the land. Aton became the only official god. King Akhenaton's reign lasted for 17 years; after he died the next king and his people reinstated the old Egyptian gods. Over the following decades the temples of Akhet-Aton were used as quarries, and this city of sun-worship was forgotten.

TELL EL-AMARNA REDISCOVERED

While the Napoleonic expedition occupied Egypt from 1798 to 1799, French scientists rediscovered and charted Tell el-Amarna. In the following years several travelers and expeditions recorded the visible monuments—such as the tombs of officials—and made small excavations. In 1891 and 1892 the famous British Egyptologist Flinders Petrie cleared several houses, glass-kilns, and parts of the palaces. Ludwig Borchardt's German expedition excavated much of the residential quarters from 1911 to 1914. Borchardt found the sculptor Thutmes's house, and

in it the famous bust of Queen Nefertiti, now in the Berlin Museum. Expeditions working on the site since then have been mainly British.

TOWN PLANNING

Great palaces and temples dominated the central city. An archive was also found there containing the international correspondence of King Akhenaton, written not in Egyptian but in Akkadian, the common language of that time. The living quarters of the population ran north and south of the town center. The ruling class lived in mansions with a columned middle hall, painted walls, and an expansive garden. The dwellings of the poorer people often clustered around these big houses, giving the impression that the servants of the powerful lived very close to their masters so they could quickly carry out orders.

A massive wall in the north of the city may mark the palace where the king and his family lived, while the palaces in the center of the city functioned more for cultic purposes and formal state visits. All palaces were richly adorned with statues made from different materials; their walls were inlaid with glass paste and colored stones. East of the city of the living lay the resting place of the privileged dead—the tombs of the king and officials—with walls all richly decorated with scenes of city life.

SWIFT CONSTRUCTION
Talatat sandstone blocks, three handspans wide, could easily be lifted by a single man. This made construction speedier, and they were used to build Tell el-Amarna during the Eighteenth Dynasty. The relief carvings designed for *talatat* blocks covered entire walls.

Tanis, Egypt

At the beginning of the Third Intermediate Period, Piramesse, the New Kingdom capital, was abandoned and a new one—Tanis—was founded nearby. This city in the eastern Delta was Egypt's capital during the Twenty-First Dynasty (around 1070–945 BCE). Though its monuments are much damaged, it boasts several intact royal tombs.

A monumental temple of Amun was soon built in the new capital; it was adorned with re-cycled sculptures from Piramesse. During this period most kings added to the new temple, and it became one of the preeminent religious centers in the country, rivaling in magnificence the main temple of Amun at Thebes. The city was not abandoned until early medieval times, when all its limestone structures were burnt for lime, or quarried for the palaces and mosques of other cities.

BENEATH THE RUINS

By the time the first European archaeologists began recording monuments in Egypt, Tanis was only a large mound scattered with loose granite fragments. The many archaeological excavations at the site revealed statues, obelisks, and blocks from temples. In 1929 the French Egyptologist Pierre Montet started more systematic work. On February 27, 1939, he came upon underground structures within the temple complex and, digging further, soon discovered several chambers that belonged to the tombs of the kings of the Twenty-First and Twenty-Second Dynasties. Some were intact and yielded an astonishing array of gold and silver objects.

The richest tomb was that of King Psusennes I, whose body was found in a set of stone coffins enclosing an inner silver one. His head was adorned with a golden mask, and numerous gold and silver pieces of jewelry and amulets were placed over his body. The mummified body of the king survived only as a skeleton. The dampness of the Delta soil had destroyed the mummy, and all other organic materials in the tomb. Of the wooden coffins in other burials, only the inlaid eyes survived. Burial customs had changed since the times of Tutankhamun; furniture and objects from daily life were no longer placed in tombs for use throughout eternity. Most of the objects found in the Tanis tombs were amulets and ritual items, from coffins and canopic jars to the hundreds of *shabti* figures who had the task of working for the deceased in the afterlife.

Building royal tombs within a temple complex is typical of the Third Intermediate Period (1070–664 BCE) and Late Period (664–525 BCE). Officials and kings must have been aware that tombs were always looted, and their placement in Tanis afforded better protection under the direct watch of the soldiers guarding the temple complex. The new security system was at least partly successful; though some of the tombs at Tanis had already been plundered, others were found still completely sealed, robbed only by natural decay.

SYMBOL OF ROYAL AUTHORITY

Psusennes I reigned and died during the Twenty-First Dynasty. A rearing cobra sits on the brow of his golden funerary mask. This royal symbol, known as an uraeus, was thought to protect the king against his enemies.

Rosetta Stone, Rosetta, Egypt

The Rosetta Stone, recording a royal decree issued in 196 BCE, is written in Egyptian hieroglyphs, demotic script, and Greek. Comparison of the three texts was the key to deciphering Egyptian hieroglyphs, as, when the stone was discovered, the demotic and hieroglyphic systems had been lost, whereas Greek was still well known.

PUZZLE IN LINGUISTICS

A decree from 196 BCE in three scripts engraved on a damaged block of black steatite, the Rosetta Stone is named after its place of discovery in the western delta of the Nile River. The slab finally gave the key to unraveling the meaning of Egyptian hieroglyphs.

I n 1799 soldiers of the Napoleonic expedition reinforcing a fort near the port of Rashid (Rosetta) found a stone inscribed in three scripts. When the French capitulated in 1801, the Treaty of Alexandria assigned the stone to Britain, and since 1802 it has been displayed in the British Museum. The stone's inscription records a decree passed by a council of priests, affirming the cult of Ptolemy V (210–180 BCE) on the first anniversary of his coronation. The best-preserved portion is in Greek, the language of his dynasty, and perhaps already the main written language in Egypt following more than 100 years of Ptolemaic rule. The central area is inscribed in demotic (from the Greek meaning "popular") script, which was then the daily handwriting script of the Egyptians. The damaged upper part is in the hieroglyph script, reserved for sacred purposes, and known only to select Egyptian officials and priests.

DECODING THE STONE

The last line of the Greek mentions that the same decree was to be carved in three scripts, making the stone a key to deciphering hieroglyphs. The most famous ancient inscription found in Egypt stimulated intense competition to decode it throughout Europe. The stone helped confirm that the names of kings and queens in the hieroglyphic text were written in an elongated oval frame, called a cartouche by Egyptologists. Comparing different sources, several signs could be identified from the Macedonian ruler-names "Ptolemaios" and "Kleopatra," between which five letters recur (p, l, o, t, a). By 1814 the British scientist Thomas Young, celebrated for work in physics, had mathematically matched the demotic and Greek sections, listing 86 demotic words, though misinterpreting the

HIEROGLYPHS UNRAVELED

At 16 Jean-François Champollion had mastered six ancient Oriental languages, as well as Latin and Greek. This accomplished linguist is credited with solving the hieroglyph puzzle that had taxed many European scholars. Champollion became curator of the Egyptian collection at the Louvre in 1826.

script as alphabetic. Like earlier researchers, Young continued to believe that hieroglyphs used sound-signs only for foreign names, just as Chinese treats European names, and assumed that hieroglyphs generally had symbolic meaning.

CHAMPOLLION'S BREAKTHROUGH

In 1822 the French scholar Jean-François Champollion, working only from variable copies, announced in his *Lettre à M. Dacier* (Dacier was the permanent secretary of the French Académie des Inscriptions) that the hieroglyphic script combined sound-signs and idea-signs; he offered a first translation with much earlier sources in support. Just two years later he wrote his inspired *Précis* of the hieroglyphic system. Champollion knew Greek and Coptic (the language of Christian Egyptians), and later went on to catalog whole collections in France and Italy; from 1828 to 1830 he codirected a Franco-Tuscan expedition to Egypt. He died very suddenly at 41, leaving behind his remarkable legacy for others to develop.

Kingdoms of the Upper Nile

Historically, Nubia has been the link between Egypt and the Mediterranean on the one hand, and sub-Saharan Africa on the other. Its peoples developed their own distinctive culture, but also participated in the larger Egyptian and East African worlds. Monuments often drew inspiration from Egyptian art, but had their own local styles.

GOLDEN JEWELRY

This hinged gold and enamel bracelet was found in the royal pyramids at Meroe in Sudan. It belonged to the wealthy and powerful Queen Amanishakheto and dates to the first century CE.

Nubia can be defined geographically as the region of the Nile between the savannas and the portion of the Nile that is Egypt. In contrast to Egypt, Nubia's opportunities for agriculture were limited, and its population was consequently much sparser. For most of Nubia's early history, the same winter crops of emmer wheat and barley were the staple foods in the floodplain area. In many areas, the rocky desert projects right into the Nile creating cataracts, which present barriers to movement by boat. Nevertheless, one of Nubia's lasting sources of wealth came through its role in trade with neighboring countries.

For most periods Nubia's trade consisted of transporting raw materials northward to Egypt. Boats carried exotica from the sub-Saharan zone in the south, such as ebony, ivory, incense, and leopard skins, but cargoes also included the products of Nubia, of which gold was prominent. Ancient Egyptian sources refer to the "Gold of Wawat," which came from the desert east of northern Nubia reached by the Wadi el-Allaqi, and the "Gold of Kush," which came from outcrops near the Nile River in the region between the Second and Third Cataracts.

NEW SOURCES OF WEALTH

In later periods, Nubians developed important sources of agricultural wealth. From about 1600 BCE, date palms began to be grown in Nubia, providing fruit for export, as they have continued to do into recent times. In the early centuries CE, cotton production and the weaving of cotton textiles developed to help supply Roman demands for cotton cloth. It was only in this later period with a new irrigation technology—the cattle-powered Persian waterwheel—that summer crops like sorghum became a major component of agriculture. Another source of exported wealth was people. This included the trafficking of slaves in many periods, but Nubians also frequently served as mercenaries and soldiers in Egypt. Nubian archers were famous throughout antiquity, from the earliest periods of Ancient Egypt when Nubia was called Ta-Sety ("the land of bows"), through to Roman times.

In the long term, the historical pattern of Nubia was marked by periods of conquest by Egypt alternating with periods of local state development.

EXTENT OF THE KINGDOMS OF THE UPPER NILE

Like Egypt, the ancient kingdoms of the Upper Nile depended on the Nile for their water supply. With its annual flood, the river was the deciding factor in creating communities.

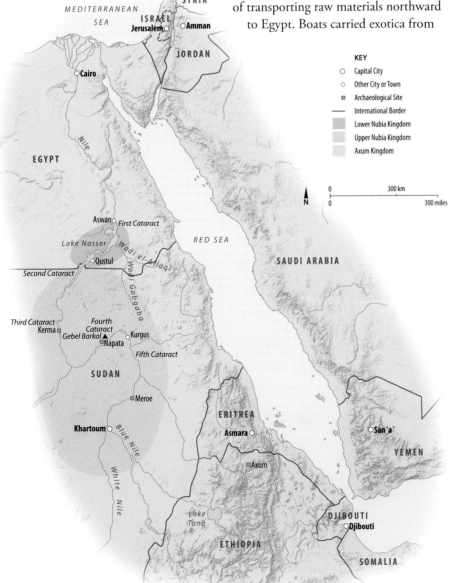

KEY
- ○ Capital City
- ○ Other City or Town
- ▫ Archaeological Site
- — International Border
- Lower Nubia Kingdom
- Upper Nubia Kingdom
- Axum Kingdom

0   300 km
0   300 miles

N

LEBANON
SYRIA
MEDITERRANEAN SEA
ISRAEL
Jerusalem   Amman
JORDAN
Cairo
Nile
EGYPT
Aswan   First Cataract
Lake Nasser   Wadi el-Allaqi
Qustul
Second Cataract
Wadi Gabgaba
RED SEA
SAUDI ARABIA
Third Cataract   Fourth Cataract
Kerma   Gebel Barkal   Kurgus
Napata
Fifth Cataract
SUDAN
Meroe
ERITREA
Khartoum   San´a´
Blue Nile   Asmara
YEMEN
Axum
White Nile
Lake Tana   DJIBOUTI
Djibouti
ETHIOPIA
SOMALIA

Just before the Egyptian state first emerged, there had been a center of local royalty at Qustul; it was brought to an end by Egyptian conquest. After a period of Nubian resurgence, Egypt reconquered Nubia at the beginning of the Middle Kingdom, around 2000 BCE, and established a series of fortresses in Nubia focused on the Second Cataract. These fortresses served as points of administration for trade and gold extraction in the surrounding region, while fortifying the Southern Egyptian frontier against the rising power at Kerma. Kerma eventually came to control these forts sometime around 1700 BCE, only to fall to another Egyptian conquest around 1570 BCE. This time Egyptian control extended to Kurgus beyond the Fourth Cataract. In the wake of declining Egyptian power, after 1100 BCE, local elites developed new centers of power that drew upon some of the religious traditions and artistic styles introduced from Egypt. These developments culminated in the rise of Napata in the eighth century BCE.

FARMING IN ETHIOPIA

The origins of agricultural communities in Ethiopia are still mysterious, although it is clear that three distinct sources of crops contributed to the economy: firstly, crops native to the African savannas at lower levels, such as sorghum; secondly, crops from the Near East, namely wheat, barley, lentils, and peas, which had been the staple foods that supported the rise of civilization in Mesopotamia, Egypt, and Nubia; and thirdly, crops native to the Ethiopian highlands, especially finger millet and tef millet, which provided straw for livestock fodder, as well as cereal grain. This combination of agricultural products, together with long-distance trade with Egypt, allowed for the growth of larger communities. Ancient Egyptian records refer to a land called Punt, from which they acquired incense, live wild animals, and other exotica. By the mid-first millennium BCE, we know of a kingdom called Daamat. Its successor was Axum.

PORTRAIT OF A NUBIAN
A painted relief on a sandstone wall in Rameses III's tomb in the Valley of the Kings in Thebes depicts the daily dress of a Nubian courtier. The long, loose robe and skullcap would have kept him cool.

PRESERVING THE RECORD

Archaeological knowledge of Nubia largely focuses on rescue archaeology in the north, and on major monuments further south. George Reisner and Raymond Firth led the first systematic survey from 1907 to 1911, before flooding by a dam at Aswan. Heightening the dam in the 1930s encouraged further survey; archaeological research in the early 1960s anticipated the building of the current Aswan High Dam, completed in 1970, which flooded a massive stretch of the Nile valley. Moving and reconstructing Egypt's Abu Simbel temple popularly represented Nubian salvage, but academic institutions from many countries ran dozens of other research excavations in both Egypt and northern Sudan. At the start of the twenty-first century, part of Nubia is threatened again with flooding. The Hamdab Dam at the Fourth Cataract is scheduled to be completed in 2008, and in recent years several research projects have been working in this threatened area.

When the Aswan High Dam reservoir threatened to flood Rameses II's temple at Abu Simbel, an international team literally moved a mountain to higher ground by cutting it into blocks. Reconstruction took more than four years and cost US$40 million.

Kerma, Sudan

Kerma lay at the lower (northern) end of the Dongola Reach. It was the important urban center of a distinctive Bronze Age civilization in a kingdom the Ancient Egyptians called Kush. At its height, *c.* 1600 BCE, Kerma was one the world's largest cities and the center of a formidable state.

LIDDED POT

This painted pot with its conical lid and distinctive zigzag decoration was found among grave goods in a tomb at Kerma. It dates to between 2040 and 1660 BCE.

A monumental temple stood at the core of the city. This massive structure of eroding mud-brick, now called the Western Deffufa, still dominates the horizon. The huge building is some three stories high and covers an area of 15,070 sq ft (1,400 sq m). In the desert to its east, there is a cemetery boasting massive royal burial monuments with funerary temples, and the remains of hundreds of sacrificed humans and animals.

The Western Deffufa and the large number of burial mounds in the desert attracted the attention of Harvard archaeologist George Reisner, who excavated there from 1913 to 1916. He uncovered massive earthen tumuli, about 263 ft (80 m) in diameter, built over mud-brick frameworks with royal burial chambers in the middle of a subterranean corridor. These monuments contained a wealth of artifacts and animal remains; the largest and latest royal burial

sites included numerous skeletons, suggesting human sacrifices were made when a ruler died. In one of the latest royal chambers Old Kingdom (2700–2200 BCE) Egyptian sculptures were discovered, which had been plundered from upper Egyptian tombs and brought to Kerma as booty by a marauding army.

SECRETS FROM THE GRAVES

Burials in this cemetery chart the development of funerary customs and the emergence of a state with increasing social hierarchy and long-distance trade. In Early Kerma burials, the body was laid out on one side in a contracted position on a cowhide, and covered with another cowhide. Offerings, mostly in pottery bowls, were placed round the deceased. After the tombs were filled in, small earthen mounds wreathed with stone slabs were raised over them.

In the subsequent Middle Kerma Period (2000–1750 BCE), burials became more elaborate and variable, implying that social hierarchy and wealth difference were well established. The larger, richer tombs contained more ceramic ware and other goods, including the bones from cuts of meat, or even whole animals. Smaller tombs revealed fewer and less costly items. From the Middle Kerma Period, bodies tended to be placed on wooden beds, some with elaborate decorations, including carved ivory inlays of winged giraffes and anthropomorphic hippopotami. Other burial chambers yielded fans of ostrich feathers.

During the Classic Kerma Period (1750–1570 BCE), richer tombs became even more grandiose; the social strata that can be recognized from them imply that Kerma was a well-developed early state. With the rise of the Egyptian New Kingdom (*c.* 1550 BCE), Kerma fell to conquest, thus bringing to an end more than 1,000 years of cultural evolution.

BEYOND THE TOMBS

Accompanying the largest tumuli were mud-brick mortuary temples. Investigations in the 1990s of one of the latest and largest of these funerary temples recovered traces of wall painting: a rare glimpse

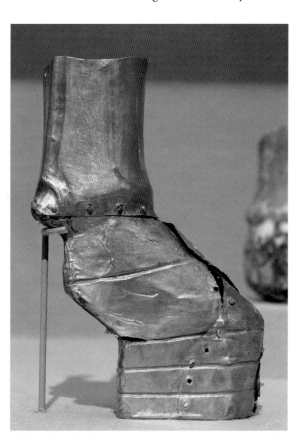

DEATHBED'S FOOT

In the Middle Kerma Period (2000–1750 BCE), the corpse of a deceased person was laid out on a bed that was often decorated with animal motifs; this photograph shows the gilded quartz leg of a funerary bed, carved in the form of a cow's hoof.

of 3,600-year-old African painting. Scenes included fauna, such as giraffe and hippopotami; fishing and cattle herding in the Kerma countryside; and various styles of boats, which were doubtless important for the role Kerma played in international trade.

Since 1977, a Swiss project led by Charles Bonnet has revealed more about the site: not only how the city and its temple grew, but also information about its prehistoric precursors. It is now clear that Kerma had Neolithic roots from before 3000 BCE. Beneath part of the main Kerma cemetery, excavators found the remains of the earliest Kerma settlement: post-holes and ditches that defined huts and other structures, as well as storage pits. By about 2500 BCE, this early village had been abandoned for the nearby new town of Kerma to the west; the abandoned area became the burial ground, and remained so until the Egyptian conquest *c.* 1550 BCE.

The main city of Kerma grew around the Deffufa temple. The temple was periodically expanded and enlarged, and around it developed a craft and trade center, which showed evidence for a bronze foundry during the Middle Kerma Period. While most buildings in the city were rectangular, a large prominent round building, that recalled more ancient traditions of hut architecture, seemed to have been a royal residence or audience hall. In the final phase, the city appeared to have had earthen ramparts. When the Deffufa temple reached it final size, it had an internal stair-case of three flights to a large open roof platform, where we can imagine public ritualized performances were staged, which must have been visible through-out the city center.

IGNORED BY PASSERSBY
Beside the dirt road at Tumbus, north of Kerma, a huge statue in Egyptian style lies toppled on its side. Standing tall, it must once have been impressive at the time when the Ancient Egyptians called this region Kush.

HALLMARKS OF A CIVILIZATION

Kerma's economy was based on trade, craft production at its urban center, and a well-developed settlement network of agricultural villages. In recent years, surveys along the Nile Valley, south of Kerma, have revealed hundreds of small cemeteries and settlement sites, which represent the population bases of farmers and herders that supported Kerma. Faience, copper objects, and fine ceramics were produced by skilled artisans in the city itself. Black-lipped, red-bellied, bell-shaped drinking beakers, formed by hand, polished to a high shine, and eggshell thin, are one of the most distinctive and widespread artifacts of the Kerma civilization.

Napata and Meroe, Sudan

Another major Nubian civilization emerged on the world stage in the eighth century BCE. This was the kingdom of Napata, also called the kingdom of Kush by the Ancient Egyptians. Piye, a Napatan ruler, invaded Egypt in 727 BCE and established himself as pharaoh over his conquest.

Egyptian history records Piye and his successors as the rulers of the Twenty-Fifth Dynasty, who dominated Egypt until 664 BCE. This civilization continued through a shift in the capital to Meroe in the fourth century BCE until the dissolution of the state around CE 350.

CENTERED ON NAPATA

The spiritual and political center of the kingdom was originally at Napata, and focused on the sacred table

VIEW FROM ABOVE

Today neat fields border the Nile River. Gebel Barkal, the mountain sacred to Napatans in ancient times, rises starkly from flat land that otherwise has no geographic protuberances to distinguish it.

BATHHOUSE RESIDENT

Taking his ease for all time, this statue of a reclining man was found in a bathhouse at Meroe. It dates to c. CE 100 and shows Hellenistic sculptural influence spread by trading contacts with Greco-Roman Egypt.

mountain of Gebel Barkal. The people thought the distinct southern pinnacle of this hill represented an uraeus—the ancient Egyptian and Nubian cobra surmounting a crown that symbolized sacred kingship. This end of Gebel Barkal was the site of temple and palace buildings. The first temple was erected there during the rule of the Egyptian Eighteenth Dynasty, but subsequent Napatan rulers rebuilt and expanded the complex, especially in the eighth and seventh centuries BCE. On the west side of Gebel Barkal, looking toward the desert, a group of six pyramids was built to house the royal dead during the fourth and third centuries BCE. Early royal pyramids were also constructed nearby at El-Kurru and then Nuri.

Karl Richard Lepsius made the first serious archaeological recordings of the area when he led a Prussian expedition up the Nile from 1842 to 1845; it produced detailed drawings of temples and inscriptions. In 1862, Egyptian army officers discovered a large granite stele commemorating Piye's conquest of Egypt. Systematic studies began in the early twentieth century (1916–1925) when George Reisner excavated the royal pyramids.

CENTERED ON MEROE

Further south at ancient Meroe, Reisner also excavated another cemetery of royal pyramids, dating from the fourth century BCE to CE 350. The large urban center of Meroe, where an indigenous script was invented, was nearby. English archaeologist John Garstang worked at the Meroe site from 1909 to 1914; he investigated the royal center of temples and palaces, and found a remarkable bathhouse. A Canadian expedition, focusing on domestic areas, excavated the site again from the late 1960s through most of the 1970s.

Meroe's economy mainly depended on extensive cattle pastoralism and summer crops such as sorghum. Cotton production and ironworking were also important. The site was famous for the production of iron; large mounds of slag from the smelting furnaces can still be seen outside the city.

The collapse of Meroe in the fourth century CE came at a time of increasing economic and military conflict in the region, which included hostilities with Axum. Meroe's demise may also be attributed to increasing aridity from climatic change.

Axum, Ethiopia

The ancient city of Axum (also known as Akusum) was located in the northern part of the Ethiopian highlands, at an elevation of more than 6,562 ft (2,000 m). It was contemporary with Meroe in Nubia, founded in CE 1, and persisted as a capital until the seventh century.

Axum has presented evidence for royal burials and urban architecture, supported by a role in long-distance trade in luxuries, and in the accumulation of agricultural surplus from the surrounding hinterland. Like Meroe, it developed its own writing system in Ge'ez, an ancient Ethiopian language using a version of the Greek alphabet. Axum was the only ancient African kingdom to produce its own coinage. Axum's important place in trade is implied by finds of its gold coins in Yemen and India, which were normally inscribed in Greek, in contrast to the silver and copper coins inscribed in the native Ge'ez and found mainly in Ethiopia.

DISCOVERING AXUM

Axum first came to the attention of Europeans when the Scottish explorer James Bruce visited the region in search of the source of the Nile in 1769. Bruce found where the Blue Nile began, and spent about two years living in Ethiopia, where he recorded regional customs, as well as local politics, flora, and fauna.

Traveling through Axum, he noted some of its most impressive archaeological monuments: a ruined temple and about 40 enormous funerary stelae.

A German expedition, led by Enno Littman in 1906, carried out the first archaeological research. Archaeologists connected with the British Institute in East Africa conducted major excavation programs from 1972 to 1974 and in the 1990s. These expeditions found the remains of an urban center and a royal burial ground, which had once been at the center of an East African empire.

STELAE AND STONE THRONES

The most recognizable archaeological monuments of Axum are its carved stone stelae associated with the royal burial ground. Some of these are among the tallest monuments ever created. The tallest standing is 75 ft (23 m), and weighs approximately 150 tons (152 tonnes). A broken example, that may have never been erected, is some 98 ft (30 m) high and weighs 517 tons (525 tonnes).

Axumite kings also erected monumental inscribed stone thrones. Fragments of one found at Meroe in Nubia support other historical evidence that during the fourth century CE Axum had, at least for a time, extended its conquests to the Nile. One king known from such monuments is King Ezana, who campaigned in Nubia, called himself the "King of Kings," and converted Axum to Christianity around the mid-fourth century. During this period the first cathedral was built at Axum; its place has since been taken by a cathedral that was rebuilt in the seventeenth century. Unlike surrounding areas, the highlands of Ethiopia persisted in Christianity from the Axumite years to modern times.

PILLARS OF STONE

Axum is notable for its tall, carved, stone stelae, which once covered the royal necropolis. A view from the air indicates the remarkable height of the ones that are still standing. On the ground lie many fallen stelae, abandoned like the kingdom they represented.

Iron Age Sub-Saharan Africa

While Saharan northern Africa witnessed technologies based on bronze and copper, the rest of the continent was dominated by iron. An Iron Age developed south of the Sahara from about 1000 BCE onward and significantly transformed the life of the food producers already based there.

IMPORTANT SITES OF IRON AGE SUB-SAHARAN AFRICA
The map below shows most of the sites where an early knowledge of ironworking flourished. South of the Sahara Desert, these Iron Age societies dominated the west and southeast; many of them have now been extensively studied by today's archaeologists.

The increasing dryness of the Sahara began to make it uninhabitable in many places, and forced farmers to move to areas with permanent supplies of water, such as the river flats beside the Nile and Niger, and the shores of Lake Chad. Iron implements transformed the exploitation of tropical rainforests and savanna wooded grasslands. Agricultural production improved remarkably once land was subjected to the more efficient ax and hoe. The emergence of permanent settlements; the rise and development of towns, cities, and kingdoms; and the growth of regional and long-distance commerce were also facilitated by iron, which enhanced African manufacturing capacities. The development of African societies, south of the Sahara, during the next 3,000 years was defined by the Iron Age.

ADVANTAGES OF IRON TECHNOLOGY

The rise and development of urban centers in the western African Sahel and savanna regions such as Jenne-jeno, Kumbi-Saleh, Niani, Timbuktu, Gao, and others was initially thought to have been a result of the trans-Saharan commerce with Islamic northern Africa. But today it is accepted that when iron replaced the stone-polished ax, western Africa saw increased regional interactions, urbanization, craft specialization, and growing political centralization. Craft specialists— ironworkers, pottery makers, weavers, brass casters, and stonemasons—provided goods and services to people in the towns and their hinterlands. The kingdoms of Ghana (c. CE 700–1100), Mali (c. CE 1230–1460), and Songhai (c. CE 1340–1530) were products of these networks of interaction and specialization. The terracotta objects from Nok and other regions of western Africa are an example of how Iron Age Africa was expressed in terms of ritual and other symbols.

A similar picture occurs on the eastern African coast. By the turn of the first millennium CE, cities engaged in Indian Ocean trade with the Near East, India, and the Far East were sprinkled along the coast of East Africa. There, too, large regional networks of hinterland settlements supported the coastal centers and enabled them to become African entrepreneurs to world markets. Towns, such as Manda, Shanga, Galu, Ungwana, Limbo, Kilwa, and Sofala, processed iron for export, as well as amber, turtle shells, rock crystal, and gold. Increasing commerce saw the steady

KEY
○ Capital City
○ Other City or Town
▫ Archaeological Site
— International Border
NOK Name of Kingdom
Sub-Saharan Africa
Saharan Africa

IRON AGE POWER

Iron Age Africa is not only about the emergence and impact of metal technology on the continent, but also about the contribution of the continent to the modern world. Discussions of the African Iron Age generally focus only on the spread of iron metallurgy and pottery manufacturing technology to the southerly parts of the continent, and most of them tend to ignore the development of African social life and how iron shaped society.

Throughout Iron Age Africa, rulers were able to increase their power bases by consolidating food production, by trading in prestige commodities, and by controlling key resources such as iron, copper, gold, salt, ivory, and cattle. Political power was symbolized by sacred objects, and many of these were made of iron. Ironworkers played important political roles as kingmakers, manipulating rituals and symbolism that centered on the production of iron.

This iron sculpture was found in an ancestral shrine in the Bandiagara Hills in the country we call Mali today. The sacred meaning of the figurative spears and bells is lost in antiquity.

development of the Swahili culture, so that by the fifteenth century, a hierarchy of settlements had spread along the coast, with some towns becoming vibrant commercial centers.

SPREADING THE KNOWLEDGE

It appears that iron production started quite early in both the central African rain forest and the adjacent equatorial savanna. How the knowledge spread to other regions remains unclear. Most probably using "slash-and-burn" methods in pursuit of nutrient-filled ash, farmers opened up much of the savanna grasslands and woodlands of eastern, central, and southern Africa. This practice dictated repetitive movement and reoccupation of the same environments, rather than migration. In this way, large tracts of southern and eastern Africa were rapidly occupied during the first millennium CE.

From around the fifth century, Iron Age societies in the Upemba Depression of central Africa laid the foundations of the Luba and other kingdoms that were to dominate the eastern savanna during the second millennium. There, kings used sacred objects of iron and copper to symbolize their power. In southern and eastern Africa, cattle played such a significant role in the ideology and economy that by the early second millennium CE those with the capacity to keep large herds attained social and political advantages over other peoples. The wealth generated by trade was invested in monumental architecture built from stone. Such buildings reflected skill and innovation in construction, labor mobilization by the elite, and a system of reward for artisans.

WALLS BUILT TO LAST

Near Gweru in Zimbabwe a wall still stands that was built around 1100 BCE. The Iron Age people of this region were masters of the art of stone-wall construction, and large parts of many of their complex structures still survive.

Mapungubwe (CE 1200–1280), Great Zimbabwe (CE 1290–1550), and the other stone-walled capitals of southern Zambezia illustrate this development. A considerable range of iron implements was required in order to quarry and shape the stones, and to work with the other building materials that were used in the construction of these capitals. These Iron Age peoples were well-qualified for the task.

TRADITIONAL TECHNIQUE

In Niger a blacksmith, possibly from the Tuareg or Songhai people, softens a piece of iron in hot coals. The tradition of blacksmithing is an ancient one; people in these parts have been practicing it for many hundreds of years.

Nok, Nigeria

NIGERIA
○Abuja
Nok ■

Nok terracotta figures are among the most famous pieces of sculpture ever found in Africa. Finely modeled, life-sized human heads, mostly broken and eroded, were recovered from disturbed soil deposits. They show details of hair, beard, dress, headgear, and personal adornment. Animal figures, such as monkeys, elephants, and snakes, were also discovered.

NOK, NOK, WHO'S THERE?

No two Nok terracotta sculptures are ever the same; there is sureness of touch and unlimited variety in the way the artists incised or affixed the features. But who the pieces represent or why they were created is likely to remain an unsolved riddle.

The figures were part of the Nok culture that appeared in Nigeria from 500 BCE to CE 200, and were created by Iron Age farmers. The largest number of terracotta heads comes from the central Jos Plateau region extending to the Middle Niger and the Lower Benue valleys, although some have been found elsewhere in western Africa. Terracotta pieces were first unearthed during the course of tin mining operations in the Jos Plateau from the late 1920s to the 1940s. By 1943, the village of Nok yielded more of these. Archaeologist Bernard Fagg, realizing their importance, collected pieces from the villagers and then decided to excavate systematically over an area much larger than the original site, where he unearthed many more.

A PUZZLE IN TERRACOTTA

This fired clay sculpture is complex in subject matter. Individual but stylized heads, slightly elongated in form, surmount scenes from everyday village life. The meaning behind such works may never be unraveled by archaeologists.

FASHIONED BY FARMERS

Archaeologists have so far excavated two sites, Samun Dukiya in the Nok valley, and Taruga some 62 miles (100 km) to the south-west. Samun Dukiya yielded pottery, iron artifacts, and fragments of terracotta in the Nok style, while Taruga was mainly an iron production site. Radiocarbon and luminescence tests from these sites give dates ranging from 2,000 to 2,500 years ago. Iron was in use in western Africa as far back as 1000 BCE; the now famous terracotta figures were made by farmers of the Iron Age.

Thousands of distinctive terracotta pieces have been unearthed; no one resembles another. Life-sized heads, male and female, carry detailed and refined hairstyles, and are decorated with sculptured jewelry. Facial features, defined by drilled holes, include triangular eyes with pupils, mouths, nostrils, and ears. The coarse-grained clay was scraped from the sculpture in much the same way as in wood carving, and the finished figure was polished smooth. Many figures are hollow inside, coil built, with a uniform body thickness to prevent thermal stress. Statuettes, up to 49 in (125 cm) tall, show a well-developed mastery of modeling techniques. The technical skill, style, precision, and finish on these figures indicate a long artistic tradition.

The purpose of these pieces is unclear; perhaps they were burial markers, charms, or monumental ornaments. The head size dominates the body, which symbolizes the African respect for intelligence. Statuettes of riders and clearly distinguished persons on horseback may demonstrate the importance of the horse in the western African savanna and the Sahel.

The Nok terracottas, especially the rare complete figures in standing, sitting, or kneeling positions, are highly prized art objects and are at the center of illicit trade, particularly in the United States. Many terracotta sites are being destroyed through illegal excavations by antique dealers. Some museums have also acquired these objects on the black market.

Great Zimbabwe, Zimbabwe

The impressive stone buildings (dzimbabwe) found in the plateau region between the Zambezi and the Limpopo Rivers were long attributed to outsiders on the assumption that Africans were incapable of erecting such monumental architecture. Archaeologists have established that these Iron Age royal palaces and residences are indeed African in origin.

Great Zimbabwe, some 186 miles (300 km) into the Limpopo Valley, rose after the decline of Mapungubwe (CE 1200–1280). Mapungubwe, whose wealth had been enhanced by trade with the Indian Ocean coast in gold, ivory, animal skins, cloth, and glass beads, declined due to increased aridity in the region. Early Karanga Iron Age farmers developed chiefdom-level societies at Chivowa and Gumanye Hills in south-central Zimbabwe. Simple communities, relying mainly on land and cattle, transformed into long-distance traders. The wealth from trade financed the first stone-walling. By about 1270, the foundations of an elaborate urban complex had been laid at Great Zimbabwe. From about 1300, sturdy stone buildings of a scale and magnitude unparalleled on the entire Zimbabwe Plateau were constructed.

A DOMINANT AUTHORITY

For the next 150 years, Great Zimbabwe became the most dominant political authority south of the Zambezi. Stone-walling extended outward, covering more than 1,730 acres (700 ha). Great Zimbabwe with its elite residences, ritual centers, public forums,

NATIONAL PRIDE

The ruins of Great Zimbabwe are a source of pride for the present inhabitants of the region. They chose the name of the abandoned city when the nation attained independence in 1980, and Southern Rhodesia became the Republic of Zimbabwe.

markets, artisans' houses, and a population of nearly 20,000, became the largest metropolis in southern Africa, exercising political and economic control over much of the region. Dzimbabwe, near the Suwa Pan in the eastern Kalahari, and Manyikeni, near the Indian Ocean coast, represent the extent of this strong political influence.

The first stone-wall structures were raised on a whaleback hill where two large enclosures and intervening smaller enclosures adjoin natural granite boulders. A ritual spearhead, iron gongs, and carved soapstone bird effigies later found there were probably ceremonial. Commoner settlements within a perimeter wall at the hill's base soon became uncomfortably overcrowded, triggering further expansion beyond. Royalty also moved downhill to the more elaborate elliptical enclosure.

The largest stone-built structure in southern Africa, representing the peak of Great Zimbabwe's development, had a girdle wall 800 ft (244 m) long, 16 ft (5 m) wide, and 33 ft (10 m) high. This wall surrounded subenclosures, parallel passages, and a conical tower marking the focus of the settlement. Five enclosure complexes to the northeast and east were subsequently added, and a second perimeter wall attests to the continuous growth of the city. Stone enclosures in the precincts indicate the increased administrative functions of the metropolis.

DECLINE OF A GREAT CITY

Why Great Zimbabwe declined from the fifteenth century CE onward is not known with any certainty. It is thought that the shift in the gold trade toward the northern Zimbabwe Plateau possibly undercut Great Zimbabwe's economic and political influence, when the Zambezi River became the preferred inland route. Coincidentally, political power shifted northward and westward, where the traditions of stone building continued until they were disrupted by Nguni incursions and the arrival of the Portuguese explorers.

Iron Metallurgy in Africa

Iron technology spread from Eurasia and Anatolia around 1500 BCE, reaching Africa between 1000 and 300 BCE. It probably diffused to sub-Saharan Africa through several routes—possibly through the central and western Sahara Desert—but explaining how this happened is not easy. Iron technology certainly skipped Egypt, where copper remained the metal of choice throughout this period.

Once iron was adopted, knowledge of how to work the metal effectively spread rapidly over western, central, eastern and southern Africa. The technological activities involved were smelting, where the naturally occurring iron oxide ores (e.g., laterite and magnetite) were reduced in a furnace, and smithing, where the metal was heated and shaped into objects, such as rings, bangles, knives, arrowheads, spearheads, axes, hoes, and fish hooks.

TRADITIONAL IRON PRODUCTION

Archaeological evidence for ancient ironworking comes from clay furnaces, clay air pipes (tuyères), and waste material (slag) from the smelting process. The ore was quarried or surface collected from rock outcrops or riverbeds and crushed into smaller fragments. Charcoal, an essential smelting and smithing ingredient, was made from suitable wood cut from trees and burnt primarily in the absence of oxygen. It was piled into the furnace, a clay structure sometimes up to 10 ft (3 m) high. The ore was fired at high temperatures—between 1,472°F (800°C) and 2,192°F (1,200° C)—for several hours or days, with air being pumped in by bellows or through natural holes drilled in the furnace base. Complex chemical processes would take place inside the firing chamber, resulting in the reduction of the ore to iron and carbon dioxide.

THE SMELTING AND SMITHING MYSTIQUE

The highly secretive methods of smelting and smithing were supported by a series of rituals and symbols. Ironworkers featured in many traditional African creation stories; they were regarded as divine persons who brought life, and were revered for their knowledge of fire and how to work heated metal (the wrought-iron figure from Mali seen at left may represent a revered blacksmith). Iron production technology was used as a mechanism for controlling society. A successful smelt was a combination of ore prospecting and preparation, charcoal preparation, construction of the furnace, firing, smithing, and the rituals that accompanied these processes. Production impacted on agriculture, social organization, and many economies of Africa south of the Sahara. The core activities of iron smelting and smithing were the specialist domains of men. Women performed other activities, such as ore mining, and the preparation of charcoal, clay, and food.

SOCIAL IMPLICATIONS OF IRON

Iron production and trade were the major specialist activities in Africa south of the Sahara, and were also important in the drive toward social differentiation, enhancing the economic and social status of the iron-worker. Iron production had the potential to centralize control of food production and political authority, such as chiefdoms and kingdoms. This did not always happen, as kingship and ironworking did not have a clear political and symbolic relationship. The only exception is that of the Luba Kingdom in central Africa, where iron features very strongly in the origins of the founders of the state. The kingdoms of Ghana, Mali, and Kongo had production centers close to their capitals, so did Kanem, Nupe, Benin, and others, implying some political control over the processes of iron production there.

SLAG HEAPS

Outside the city of Meroe, Sudan, telltale heaps of slag endorse the one-time importance of iron-working to this ancient city. Belief that a knowledge of iron smelting diffused throughout sub-Saharan Africa from this center has now been discredited.

The product of the firing process, which was called the bloom, was then removed and taken to the forge where it was reheated and worked by a smith. The smith also required prepared charcoal, a stone anvil, iron hammers, and the other tools necessary for working the bloom. Reheating the bloom softened the metal, allowing more work on it, and further helping to reduce the impurities, which might mar the final quality of the iron or steel. This part of the process was also accompanied by traditional ritual and ceremony. There remain very few ethnographic examples of traditional iron production processes for us to observe, as the modern blast furnace has completely replaced the former.

Iron production was usually carried out in the dry season, when it did not interfere with agriculture, and avoided the problems associated with rain and flooding, which could have interrupted the process. Regional trade brought specialists together, but rarely did iron production become a full-time activity in parts of western, central, and eastern Africa, as this would have necessitated trade and exchange among neighboring communities. Ironworkers were well-regarded artisans in their societies, and were normally well-rewarded for their labor with trade goods, live-stock, and agricultural produce.

Jenne-jeno, Mali

MALI

Jenne-jeno
Bamako

Caravan traders from North Africa and Europe, and from the savanna and forest regions of western Africa, crossed the Sahara at the Inland Niger Delta. According to Arabic and French written sources of the seventeenth and nineteenth centuries, the city of Jenne-jeno was pivotal in this commerce for more than 500 years.

TERRACOTTA CONTAINER

This heavy-rimmed pot excavated from a tumulus in the Jenne region has been dated to *c.* CE 1400. From the middle of the ninth century, local potters show the influence of incoming migrants.

DIGGING DEEP INTO HISTORY

This photo of Jenne-jeno shows the LX unit, a 35 × 20 × 17 ft (10 × 6 × 5 m) excavation dug in 1981. This unit was divided into two parts (LX-N and LX-S), which were separated by a 20-in (50-cm) wide balk. In the photo, the balk is being removed.

Archaeologists Susan and Roderick McIntosh identified the mound of Djoboro as ancient Jenne-jeno, and extensively investigated there from the late 1970s to the mid 1990s. They uncovered the history of a remarkable settlement dating back to 200 BCE, concealed beneath more than 17 ft (5 m) of archaeological deposits. Modern Jenne and ancient Jenne-jeno are both listed on the UNESCO World Heritage List for their contributions to the understanding of the origins and development of western African civilizations.

From the third century BCE, increased aridity in the Sahara and Sahel drove people to the Inland Niger Delta. A century later, Neolithic food producers moved southward to settle close to permanent water, a process surprisingly recalled in some oral traditions. The Inland Niger Delta, like the Nile River, provided a floodplain seasonally inundated by floods from the equatorial rain forest, rich in silt, and conducive to the growth of wild grasses and the cultivation of cereal crops such as rice, sorghum, and millet.

THE RISE OF JENNE-JENO

The earliest Jenne-jeno inhabitants lived in circular mat houses plastered with mud, worked iron imported from areas beyond the floodplain, and manufactured fine pottery. Roman or Greek glass beads indicated that they had indirect trading links with the Mediterranean world. By CE 450 Jenne-jeno, covering 62 acres (25 ha), was larger than a village in size.

From the middle of the fifth century CE, Jenne-jeno's social organization changed. Cemeteries indicated interment in large burial urns and ordinary pits. Increased building activity continuously expanded the town, which by CE 850 occupied 82 acres (33 ha). Iron, copper, and gold were imported from distant regions, and processed by well-organized guilds of craftsmen; the local painted pottery was extensively used in the town.

By the mid-ninth century CE, Jenne-jeno had developed into an urban complex distinguished by cylindrical brick architecture and a pottery style with impressed and stamped decoration. Migrating ethnic groups brought these changes, but they were adapted locally. A brick wall located inside the precincts of the town indicates the increasing social complexity of Jenne-jeno.

THE DECLINE OF JENNE-JENO

Why Jenne-jeno declined from the thirteenth century CE onward is unclear. Increased regional aridity after 1200 may well have been a contributing factor. Jenne-jeno lost economic and political ascendancy to modern Jenne nearby, and by 1400, was abandoned. Written sources show stronger Islamic influences in material culture from the eleventh century, with some local people converting to Islam. Ongoing production of artifacts, such as terracotta statuettes in large numbers, and the practice of urn burial throughout the fourteenth century probably indicated resistance to Islam and the continuation of indigenous cultural practices in the surrounding district.

Lydenburg, South Africa

In 1961 a schoolboy living on a farm near the town of Lydenburg, in what is now the Mpumalanga Province of South Africa, stumbled upon fragments of humanlike heads. The "Lydenburg heads," dated to between CE 500 and CE 800, are the earliest-known forms of African Iron Age sculpture in southern Africa.

In total there are eight fired earthenware heads from one of the early Iron Age villages in Lydenburg Valley. They were deliberately buried in pits, suggesting that they were respected enough to be interred with care. Archaeological remains associated with them included animal bones, pottery, beads, and metal objects. University of Cape Town (UCT) archaeologist, Ray Inskeep, was the first to recognize the importance of these art objects, and he conducted controlled excavations at the site. Although these heads are unique in southern Africa, other ceramic figurines found in Iron Age sites in Zimbabwe, Botswana, Mozambique, and South Africa indicate a widespread tradition of pottery sculpture. Human figurines have also been recovered at Schroda in the middle Limpopo valley.

SKILLED ARTISTRY

The heads are not identical, but share many attributes. Two are sufficiently large to be worn as helmet masks. They carry animal figures on their crowns and small clay "bobbles" which represent raised hair braids. The animals, formerly covered by a heavy slip, are now difficult to identify but have disk-shaped faces indicative of lions. Modeled facial features include thinly opened oval eyes, slightly projecting mouths, noses, and ears, and raised bands decorating the faces. The back of the heads are decorated with incised linear patterns; the necks are defined by large wide ring columns decorated with grooved incisions. The five smaller heads, too small to have been worn as helmets, resemble each other, except that one has an animal visage with a projecting snout. Tiny holes located on either side of the lowest neck rings suggest that they may have been attached to something else. Specularite, a hematite that sparkles when spun, was placed strategically on the masks in incisions and elevations, such as eyebrows.

The region's rich utilitarian arts have been neglected by outsiders because of southern Africa's infrequent use of masks, and the rarity of figurative sculpture of the sort prized by collectors. Archaeologists have speculated on the purpose of the heads. The regular inclusion of ceramic figurines in initiation rites and the secretive sourcing of hematite and graphite in traditional pottery manufacture suggest ceremonial use of these heads.

The Lydenburg heads are in the UCT collection housed in the South African Museum in Cape Town. At UCT, replicas of one of these heads are awarded to recipients of the Chancellor's Award for Oustanding Leadership in Africa. They are important in the reconstruction of pre-colonial African identities and achievements. Their dating attests to the antiquity of the Iron Age in southernmost Africa, belying the colonial belief that early European colonists arrived there almost simultaneously with native populations. Besides rock art, the heads are real proof of artistic tradition among iron-working farming communities.

LYDENBURG'S TREASURE
This example of the earliest-known sculptures from southern Africa is one of the eight terracotta heads found near the town of Lydenburg in South Africa. Archaeologists speculate that they were once used in initiation rites.

Europe

Earliest Peoples of Europe

The earliest fossil humans so far found outside of Africa are specimens from Dmanisi in the Republic of Georgia. Archaeologists digging a medieval site found the first specimen, a mandible, near some primitive stone tools. Recently three skulls have been discovered from the same locality, and most experts now consider them to represent members of a European population of the early African human species *Homo ergaster*.

NEANDERTHAL MAN

This is an artist's impression of a *Homo neanderthalensis* man. Evidence of this species in Europe has been found from Spain across to Uzbekistan. It is believed that climate change was a significant factor in the evolution of the Neanderthal populations.

The Dmanisi humans are similar to *H. ergaster* in having similar brow-ridge development, moderate height of the skullcap, and similar proportions of the facial skeleton. The Dmanisi hominids, however, have a rather small cranial capacity compared to *H. ergaster*. These fossils indicate that early populations of our genus *Homo* were present in Europe by 1.7 million years ago.

One million years later, populations of the "Asian" early human species *Homo erectus* appear to have also migrated into Europe as shown by the *H. erectus*-like skull from Ceprano in Italy, dated to around 900,000 years ago. Following on from these specimens are the specimens from Gran Dolina Cave (Atapuerca Hills of northern Spain) that date to around 800,000 years ago. Following the *H. erectus*-like humans are those allocated to the species *Homo heidelbergensis*, which

MAUER MANDIBLE

This close-up view of the 500,000-year old mandible found at Mauer in Germany was taken by specialist photographer Kenneth Garrett. The specimen is an almost complete early human jawbone that is very robust but has no chin.

first appeared in Europe around 500,000 years ago. These humans had a relatively large brain compared to their predecessors, reduction in the projection of the face from the brain case, a large "puffed out" face as a result of the brain's inflated frontal and maxillary sinuses, and a robust mandible with relatively small teeth.

The earliest undoubted appearance of *H. heidelbergensis* in Europe is the mandible from Mauer, a town near Heidelberg, Germany, found in 1907 and dating to around 500,000 years ago. A near contemporary with Mauer is the robust leg bone fragment from Boxgrove in England. Following are specimens from Arago in southern France, dated to approximately 450,000 years ago, and Petralona in Greece, perhaps 250,000 years old. The African population of this species is thought to have given rise to early modern *Homo sapiens* (Cro-Magnons) while the European population of this same species later gave rise to the Neanderthals (*Homo neanderthalensis*).

H. heidelbergensis was not restricted to using the hand-ax lithic technology, but clearly also used wood as evidenced by the Clacton spear found in Essex, which dates to approximately 450,000 years ago. Additional throwing spears have been discovered from Schöningen in Germany that are 7 ft 6 in (2.3 m) in length. There is also evidence of toolkits having been made of stone, including flakes struck on anvils from elephant and rhino long bones, and there is even a bone biface from Castel di Guido in Italy dating to around 450,000 years ago.

THE EARLIEST MEMBERS OF THE NEANDERTHAL LINEAGE?

The group of European fossil specimens that most experts believe represent the basal stock from which the Neanderthals ultimately evolved (the proto-Neanderthals) include the skull from Steinheim,

SHELTERS BUILT BY *HOMO HEIDELBERGENSIS*

There is evidence from Terra Amata, located within the city limits of Nice (dated to around 400,000 years ago), that *Homo heidelbergensis* at least had the capacity to construct shelters. This site has long been considered as a seasonal occupation site, where humans built freestanding shelters. These "huts" were very large at around 26 by 13 ft (8 by 4 m), and the construction is supposed to have been of saplings embedded into the ground and bent toward the middle where they were tied off. Inside the shelters there is evidence of hearths, with considerable numbers of broken animal bones, showing that a diverse type of animal prey was consumed.

near Stuttgart, Germany, the Sima de los Huesos specimens from Atapuerca in northern Spain, and the Swanscombe cranium from England. Most of these specimens are considered to date between 300,000 and 230,000 years ago although a strong case has been made for the Swanscombe skullcap to be around 400,000 years old.

These fossils clearly display incipient Neanderthal features, including the configuration of the brow ridges, the large size of the nasal opening, a projection from the side walls of the nasal cavity, well-developed neck musculature, and a long low skull but with a slightly more elevated forehead.

HOW CLIMATE CHANGE AFFECTED HABITAT

Climate change and its associated habitat instability are likely to have been responsible for the emergence of the Neanderthals during the Middle Pleistocene of Europe. Severe climatic oscillations were starting to dominate Europe, if not Africa. Populations of *H. heidelbergensis* persisted in warmer southern Europe (that is, Petralona), while contemporary populations of the proto-Neanderthals lived in the northern latitudes, within extremely cold conditions. One of the longest and coldest patterns of glaciation occurred between 300,000 and 240,000 years ago, just at about the time the proto-Neanderthals made their first appearance in northern and central Europe. This was quickly followed by another even colder period between 185,000 and 130,000 years ago, corresponding with the emergence of the "classic Neanderthals." As such, *H. heidelbergensis* seems to have remained a warm-climate species, and more of a generalist in terms of dietary requirements; while the proto-Neanderthals and their classic Neanderthal descendants adapted more and more to an ice-bound Europe and by necessity became less reliant on a vegetable diet, consuming more and more meat as they became increasingly adapted to local conditions, and more and more specialized.

It would be the arrival into Europe of truly modern people from Africa approximately 40,000 years ago that would lead to the decline and eventual extinction of the Neanderthals.

AN IMPORTANT SITE

In this aerial photograph we see the medieval town of Dmanisi, which is located in the Mashavera River Valley, Republic of Georgia. The remains of four early hominids were found near here.

Cro-Magnon Rock Shelter, France

The first discovery of prehistoric human skeletal remains that can be considered truly modern in appearance was made in 1868. Thought to be around 30,000 years old, these skeletons were excavated at the Cro-Magnon Rock Shelter at Les Eyzies in the Dordogne, southwestern France, which gave these people their name, "Cro-Magnon."

HOME OF CRO-MAGNON

Les Eyzies is situated in the Vézère River Valley, France. Remains of Cro-Magnon people were identified here in 1868 by the French geologist Louis Lartet, who had been working with British ethnologist Henry Christy.

CRO-MAGNON SKULL

The very significant 1868 discovery of a Cro-Magnon skull came about during the construction of railway lines. The Cro-Magnons have a different skull structure to that of the Neanderthals.

The Cro-Magnon Rock Shelter was found to contain several Upper Paleolithic human skulls and partial skeletons along with artifacts. The skeletons were stained with red ocher. They represent between five to eight individuals including a middle-aged male (known as the Old Man of Cro-Magnon), two younger adult males, a young adult female, and a very young infant. They are believed to represent burials because of their position and location within the stratigraphy of the site.

During the latter half of the nineteenth century, excavations identified 12 distinct levels of occupation at the rock shelter, which also contained the remains of Ice Age animals, including mammoths, lions, and reindeer. While the site itself has not been directly dated, a nearby site with a very similar stratigraphy has been dated to 30,000 years ago, suggesting that the Cro-Magnon burials and associated prehistoric fauna also date to this period. Subsequently all forms of European early *Homo sapiens* have been given the generalized name Cro-Magnon (even though they do not in themselves represent the earliest modern *H. sapiens* from Europe, which can currently be attributed to the Pestera cu Oase remains from Romania, dating to sometime before 32,000 years ago).

While the Cro-Magnon people were a little more anatomically robust than modern people, when compared to their contemporaries, the Neanderthals, the Cro-Magnons are remarkably different from them and more like us. They possessed higher, more domed skulls, with small brow ridges, prominent chins, and smaller teeth; they were also taller than the Neanderthals and more slender in their overall body proportions. Indeed, Cro-Magnon is now a generalized term often used to refer to long-limbed, robust, but anatomically modern people from the early Upper Paleolithic of Europe.

CRO-MAGNON CULTURE

Along with faunal remains, a large number of cultural artifacts were excavated which not only included flint tools but also stone-lined hearths, bone points, a bone fragment with notches, perforated Atlantic marine shells, perforated teeth (part of a necklace?), ivory plaques (pendants?), and carved reindeer antlers.

Cultural artifacts associated with Cro-Magnons are from the Upper Paleolithic industries, called the Aurignacian, Perigordian, Gravettian, Solutrean, and Magdalenian. Long, thin blades of stone (many of which appear to be specialized for working on bone and ivory), plus specialized knives, scrapers, piercers, and engravers help define these tool traditions. The crowning achievement of Cro-Magnons, however, was their art. Early evidence of engravings and sculptures first appear around 35,000 years ago, which eventually resulted at its high point in the painted walls and ceilings of caves like Altamira and Lascaux around 15,000 years ago.

Altamira Cave Paintings, Spain

Altamira Cave

Madrid

SPAIN

The wondrous 13,500-year-old paintings in Altamira Cave in northern Spain have been described as the "Sistine Chapel" of cave art. The paintings were first identified in 1879 and published in 1880. They represent the first glimpse that modern people had of a significant example of Ice Age cave paintings.

At the time of their publication most scholars believed that the paintings were far too sophisticated to be from the "primitive" Cro-Magnons of Ice Age Europe. It was only with the later and ongoing discoveries of "similar" examples in Europe that scholars finally accepted them to be genuine.

The paintings represent a diverse portrayal of animals, but the largest are red-and-black bison in standing and lying positions. Others include wild boars, deer, and horses. The painters did not just paint their animal on the wall haphazardly, but used the cave wall relief to help emphasize the shape of the animals. Also present are a number of human-like figures engraved into the ceiling, as well as handprints and hand outlines. These figures, along with more abstract signs, hint that the people who painted these figures and signs had a complex arrangement of beliefs, including story, myth, and perhaps even a spiritual belief system. This is emphasized when one considers that the paintings are located in the dark and dangerous recesses of a deep cave, which is almost 985 ft (300 m) long and consists of a series of twisting passages and chambers. The majority of the paintings are located in one large chamber approximately 95 ft (30 m) from the main entrance. How often did they return to examine and add to their art, using fat-burning lamps?

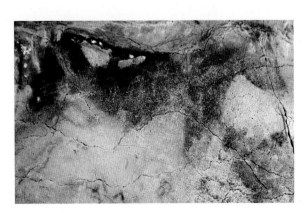

The Altamira paintings would have required a considerable investment in time; the artists clearly had a surplus in the time required to eke out a living, which enabled them to dedicate considerable thought and effort to Altamira. The rich wildlife that would have grazed in the surrounding valleys as well as the nearby coastal area likely provided the people with an abundance of food resources.

DATING AND ARCHAEOLOGICAL EXCAVATIONS

The dating of the main cave art at Altamira to the Magdalenian period (13,500 years ago) was obtained by radiocarbon dating charcoal taken from one of the bison figures. Archaeological excavations at Altamira have also shown that there were earlier phases of occupation in the cave. These include bone engravings (engraved antler rods) and wall markings, as well as animal engravings dating to the Upper Solutrean period (around 18,500 years ago) and the Lower Magdalenian period (16,500 to 14,000 years ago). These excavations have also uncovered the skeletal remains of bison, horse, boar, and deer.

POLYCHROME BISON

Bison were a common subject for the Altamira paintings. While today the cave is closed due to conservation concerns, in 2001 Altamira II, an exact replica of the original cave, was opened on the grounds of the Altamira Museum.

MAGDALENIAN ROCK ART

This painting of a horse is part of the spectacular cave art on display at Altamira. Considered to be a site of "outstanding universal value," Altamira Cave was put on UNESCO's World Heritage List In 1985.

La Ferrassie, France

La Ferrassie rock shelter in the Perigord region of France has been excavated intermittently from 1902 through to 1972. The Neanderthals buried there were found along with Mousterian tools, and the site dates to around 70,000 years ago.

RECTANGULAR BURIAL PIT

This burial pit of a Neanderthal was found near La Chapelle-aux-Saints in France. The pit had been dug into the cave floor's limestone bedrock. The adult man's skull and mandible were well-preserved.

I t is quite fascinating that these burials appear to represent the world's first cemetery; in all, seven Neanderthals were buried. The rock shelter itself runs in an east–west line, with the burials orientated in a similar direction; the only exception is an infant burial in a north–south orientation at the back of the cave wall. Recent paleopathological studies of the male adult indicate that he was most likely a victim of lung cancer. He was buried in a shallow

subrectangular pit, in a flexed posture. The female adult skeleton was more tightly flexed and must have been bound to achieve the fetal position, suggesting that Neanderthals could work with fiber or animal hide to make rope.

There were two adults, the rest being children, and the age and sex distribution is suggestive of a "family plot." Whether material culture and faunal remains associated with such burials can be considered grave goods remains an unresolved issue. Most of the "deliberate grave goods" can probably be attributed to an inadvertent deposition into the grave at the time of burial, which would have been dug through Mousterian layers and the artifacts incorporated into the grave as part of the backfilling operation. Even so, the La Ferrassie burials suggest some form of ritual and belief, which is normally only attributed to Cro-Magnons.

The adult skeletons at La Ferrassie display many of the robust characteristics of the Neanderthals including a projecting face and relatively short limbs. Also indicative of these populations is the use of their dental complex to help in working material in a horizontal axis. As such, their teeth appear to have been used for extensive working of hides and other materials. For example, in the teeth in the lower jaw it is the left molars that are most worn, while in the upper jaw the teeth on the right side have suffered corresponding heavy wear.

The upper levels of the site contain the more refined toolkits associated with modern *Homo sapiens* (Cro-Magnons) including the Châtelperronian, Aurignacian, and the Perigordian dating to less than 36,000 years ago.

NEANDERTHAL BURIALS

Throughout Europe, Neanderthal burials are not restricted to La Ferrassie: the La Chapelle-aux-Saints individual had been buried in a rectangular pit at the base of the Mousterian deposits. A similar burial pit occurs at Le Moustier, containing the remains of a young Neanderthal child. At Le Regourdou, also in France, a Neanderthal was excavated from a burial pit, which was lined with a bed of stones and covered over with a cairn containing a mixture of animal bones and artifacts, though these artifacts may merely be part of the backfill.

Feldhofer Grotto, Germany

The first human fossil to be identified as not representing a modern human was the Neanderthal specimen from Feldhofer Grotto in the Neander Valley, Germany (1856). It was found and recognized just three years before the publication of Charles Darwin's *The Origin of Species*.

Berlin○

□ Feldhofer Grotto

GERMANY

ADDING TO OUR KNOWLEDGE

This Neanderthal skull was unearthed at La Chapelle-aux-Saints, France. The finds made at La Chapelle-aux-Saints helped scholars in their interpretations of the Feldhofer fossil remains.

NEANDERTHAL DAILY LIFE

An artist's impression shows how the Neanderthals from Krapina in modern-day Croatia would have lived. The Krapina discovery was made more than 30 years after the Neanderthal specimen had been found at Feldhofer Grotto.

The Feldhofer Grotto remains are represented by a skullcap and some postcranial bones. The workmen who entered the grotto discovered the remains in about 5 ft (1.5 m) of mud on the cave floor. These quarrymen may have inadvertently discarded parts of the original skeleton, along with many associated items, perhaps including stone tools. A part owner of the quarry, Mr. Beckershoff, sent the remains to Johann Carl Fuhlrott, who immediately recognized them to represent "a typical very ancient individual of the human race."

The Feldhofer Neanderthal was not the first discovery of this human extinct species; unrecognized specimens had previously been discovered in Engis Cave in Belgium between 1829 and 1830, and Forbes Cave in Gibraltar in 1848. Not all accepted the significance of the Neander discovery. For example, some suggested that the robust nature of the specimen with its thick brow ridges merely represented an idiot who squinted a great deal.

The continuing discovery of similar fossils across Europe, including those from La Naulette and Spy in Belgium, as well as La Chapelle-aux-Saints, La Ferrassie, and La Quina in France, showed that such interpretations could not stand up to the ever-increasing evidence, especially when these fossils were found with a distinct material culture, as well as remains of extinct animals. Many of the early researchers were now beginning to place these finds within a geological and archaeological context. In 1889 the first Neanderthals were being excavated from Krapina, in Croatia, and this site would soon yield the remains of up to 36 Neanderthals. How could anyone still seriously argue that all of these remains represented a family or clan of pathological idiots? By the turn of the century most accepted that the Neanderthals were a distinct nonpathological population, clearly different from ourselves.

NEANDERTHAL DNA

DNA from a Neanderthal specimen was first retrieved from the leg bone of the Feldhofer Grotto Neanderthal in 1996 and indicated that there was around 500,000 years of divergence between the modern human and Neanderthal lineages. In 2006 a Neanderthal leg bone from Vindija cave in Croatia revealed more detail, showing that its DNA sequence is 99.95 percent identical to the modern human DNA sequence. While this sounds very similar, it must be remembered that humans and chimpanzees have a sequence that is also close at 98 percent, and that these species last shared a common ancestor around 6.5 million years ago. Using simple mathematics indicates that modern humans and Neanderthals last shared a common ancestor around 450,000 years ago, confirming the earlier result from the Feldhofer specimens. These studies indicate that Neanderthals do indeed represent a distinct human species, which is now commonly cited as *Homo neanderthalensis*.

What Happened to the Neanderthals?

BIG BRAIN CASING

This reconstructed skull shows that a Neanderthal brain was generally bigger than that of a modern *Homo sapiens*.

MOUSTERIAN CULTURE

The Mousterian (Neanderthal) occupation of the French site La Roche-Cotard is reconstructed below. An exciting find from here is "The Mask," a flat piece of flint that was changed to accentuate its resemblance to a human face.

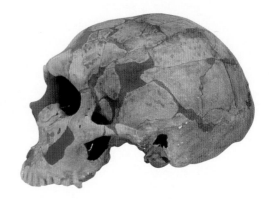

All of the available archaeological and fossil evidence supports the rapid displacement of more "primitive" European Neanderthal populations by modern humans who first arrived from Africa around 40,000 years ago. This displacement finally resulted in the extinction of the last surviving Neanderthals in Spain and Portugal around 27,000 years ago.

The correlation in western and central Europe between the disappearance of Neanderthals from both the paleontological and archaeological records, around 27,000 years ago, and the appearance of modern humans, Cro-Magnons, around 35,000 years ago (with some evidence of earlier colonization around 40,000 years ago), strongly supports the extinction of the Neanderthals, not through some prehistoric genocide but rather as a result of competition for finite resources between the endemic Neanderthal populations and the modern human populations from Africa.

Indeed, there appears to have been limited contact between the endemic Neanderthals of Europe and the modern *Homo sapiens* populations from Africa. For example, Neanderthals are believed to have never attained a high population density. As such, far-flung populations probably had to exchange individuals in order to keep up a viable population, resulting in the thin spreading of biological and cultural resources. With the emergence of *H. sapiens* (Cro-Magnons), however, we see the appearance of ever-increasing groups; as these large and dense population clusters became reproductively viable and economically self-sufficient, they also became more biologically and culturally closed. From time to time, some fossils have been claimed to be hybrids, or Neanderthals showing evidence of gene flow, or even modern humans showing evidence of gene flow. Only one such claim carries any weight: the skeleton of a child, about 25,000 years old, from Lagar Velho in Portugal.

LINKS WITH OTHER MAMMALS

Studies have also shown that the presence of human species within the fossil record is strongly correlated with the presence of principal mammalian fauna, showing that they were an integral component of mammalian communities. This is clearly the case for the Neanderthals and early modern *H. sapiens*, which were each dependent on and associated with a distinctive mammalian group. The increasing southward and eastward expansion of glacial conditions likely resulted in a retreat from these northern regions of the existing floral and faunal groups, including herds of red deer, wild horse, and roe deer. It is also likely that at least some Neanderthal populations dependent on these resources also shifted southeastward, eventually settling in the Middle East. Such dispersal patterns were probably intermittent, as shown by the early penetration into this region by the Tabun Neanderthals (Israel), who

may be the only Neanderthal population to have preceded *H. sapiens* in the Near East, with later Neanderthal populations moving into the region around 50,000 years ago. From around 40,000 years ago we see in this region a more sophisticated toolkit, similar to those documented in Europe from around 30,000 years ago. We also see, for the first time, remains of modern *H. sapiens* dating to around 40,000 years ago, and an African-like fauna.

TERRITORIAL EXPANSION AND ADAPTATION TO CLIMATIC CHANGES

While initially the Neanderthals' adaptation to the cold enabled them to occupy their distinct ecological niche, it in no way restricted them to this type of habitat. With the emergence of modern *H. sapiens* in

Africa around 200,000 years ago, we see an initial short-term territorial expansion into the Middle East by early modern humans, associated with a similar migration by other African faunal groups during the more temperate periods from around 120,000 to 70,000 years ago. Conversely, around 70,000 years ago we see the return of colder climates and the colonization or recolonization of large areas in the Middle East by Neanderthals with perhaps a remigration from Europe around 50,000 years ago. Truly modern humans arrived into these regions from around 40,000 years ago. By 30,000 years ago modern *H. sapiens* had established themselves in Europe, and the last-known Neanderthal refuge, Zafarraya Cave in the far south of Spain, dating to 27,000 years ago, witnesses the final demise and extinction of the Neanderthals.

EXTENT OF THE NEANDERTHAL POPULATION

This map shows just how far *Homo neanderthalensis* reached across Europe and Eurasia over 200,000 years. Their ability to adapt to changing climatic conditions enabled Neanderthal populations to survive and expand.

NEANDERTHAL WITH CRO-MAGNON TOOL TRADITION?

Some scholars have argued that the *Homo sapiens*-like material culture (Châtelperronian tradition) associated with the Saint-Césaire Neanderthal from France supports biological and cultural continuity between Middle and Upper Paleolithic populations. However, it is more likely that this was a local Mousterian (Neanderthal) cultural adaptation. Indeed, the Châtelperronian industry associated with the Saint-Césaire Neanderthal is recognized as closely resembling the Mousterian tradition Type B, thus likely representing a local variant of a Mousterian (Neanderthal) technology rather than a true Châtelperronian tool tradition.

NEANDERTHAL WOMAN

An artist's reconstruction shows the head of a Neanderthal woman. Evidence to date tells us that the last place Neanderthal populations lived was at Zafarraya Cave near Malaga in Spain.

Atapuerca, Spain

In the early 1980s, a major discovery was made in the Sima de los Huesos cave systems within the Atapuerca Hills of northern Spain. At the bottom of a deep, vertical shaft was a large collection of hominid bones representing at least 30 individuals: adult males and females as well as children. Also found were the remains of a number of cave bears.

A SIGNIFICANT PALEOLITHIC SITE

Archaeologists work on the Sima de los Huesos cave systems, where 30 individual bodies were found. We still don't know how the bodies ended up at the bottom of a deep shaft. One suggestion is that they may have been deliberately thrown into the cave.

The fossil humans are usually allocated to the species *Homo heidelbergensis*, which appears to have its origins in Africa, but they may also stand at the base of a different species that dominated Europe for 200,000 years, the Neanderthals.

Among the earliest European representatives of the African species *H. heidelbergensis* (which originated in Africa around 600,000 years ago) are the specimens from Atapuerca dating to approximately 300,000 years ago. The site was long known to contain a large number of bones, mostly belonging to cave bears, thus its name Sima de los Huesos (Pit of the Bones). The deep pit containing the remains was not part of a living floor or burial. The remains appear to have been deposited there through secondary processes such as mudflows and soil slides.

The Atapuerca specimens are thought by most to be proto-Neanderthals. Indeed, these specimens for the first time show the robust anatomical features that are indicative of an adaptation to a cold climate, and are observed in later Neanderthal populations. These populations likely evolved as a result of the severe climatic oscillations then starting to dominate Europe. While populations of *H. heidelbergensis* persisted in warmer southern Europe, those living in more northern latitudes found themselves in a colder climate, as demonstrated by the Ice Age fauna found at Atapuerca. These northern populations continually adapted both physically and culturally to the increasing Ice Age conditions, eventually evolving into what we call today the "classic Neanderthals" that dominated the northern parts of Europe almost 150,000 years later.

AN EVEN EARLIER HUMAN SPECIES AT ATAPUERCA?

Near the Sima de los Huesos are the earlier human specimens from Gran Dolina Cave, also in the Atapuerca Hills. These specimens are more than twice as old as the specimens from Sima de los Huesos and date to around 780,000 years ago. It has been argued that the humans from these caves evolved from the even earlier "African" *Homo ergaster* species, which was also present in Dmanisi in Georgia one million years before. In terms of their anatomy the Gran Dolina specimens are relatively gracile, and most similar to *H. ergaster* and modern *Homo sapiens*, contrasting with most of its successors, including *H. heidelbergensis* and *Homo neanderthalensis*. As such, the species was evidently not adapted to cold conditions, but, like *H. ergaster,* was adapted to the relatively warm, temperate climate that existed in the region at this time.

Lagar Velho, Portugal

Lagar Velho is a rock shelter in northern Portugal where in 1998 the burial of a partial skeleton of a four-year-old male child dating to around 24,500 years was discovered. Some claim this individual represents a "hybrid" child, indicating that Cro-Magnons and Neanderthals were members of the same species.

HOME OF A "HYBRID" CHILD?
Heated debates continue on the significance of the 1998 discovery of a four-year-old boy's remains in the Lagar Velho region of Portugal (seen below). The Lagar Velho find highlights the complexity of the emergence of modern humans.

The human remains from Lagar Velho are said to show a combination of Cro-Magnon-like and Neanderthal-like features. Unlike Neanderthals, there is a clear chin with tooth proportions that are within the modern human range. Some aspects of the pelvis (it is narrow) are also similar to modern humans and unlike Neanderthals, as are aspects of its shoulder blade and its forearm bones, as well as the configuration of muscle markings on the thumb. It does share with "classic Neanderthals" its developed pectoral muscle markings, its knee proportions, and its strong and shorter lower leg bones. However, the ends of the bones (epiphyses) are missing and if present may have indicated a relatively robust, thickset child, albeit still within modern human proportions.

Tools that were found within the grave also indicate a "modern" Cro-Magnon technology (unlike the Neanderthal Mousterian technology) and are similar to the Gravettian sites known from Wales through to Moravia at this time. It postdates the last-known Neanderthals by around 2,500 years as determined by radiocarbon dating.

The burial ritual associated with the Lagar Velho child is similar to those that have been documented in other contemporary sites associated with Cro-Magnons. The body was laid out in an extended position, slightly tilted toward the back wall of the shelter with his left foot on top of his right one. There is evidence that a single branch of pine was burned inside the shallow grave pit, along with red ocher staining that confirms the body was covered in painted red ocher. A shell pendant was found around the child's neck. Also found were four pierced, red-stained canine teeth. Similar burials have been found in the region dating to this time, including the Gruta do Caldeirão site where archaeologists discovered identical pierced periwinkle shells.

IS THE LAGAR CHILD A NEANDERTHAL–CRO-MAGNON HYBRID?

The original describers of the Lagar Velho child maintain that his short, stocky, and Neanderthal-like body proportions reflect a "hyperarctic" adaptation, and the fact that the area during this time was temperate confirms a close Neanderthal contribution to its genetic history. This is suggested to support the argument that Neanderthals and Cro-Magnons were part of the one species. However, the child's body proportions, which constitute the main argument for the proposition supporting a Neanderthal–Cro-Magnon hybrid, are within the range of Cro-Magnon's and in themselves are not entirely diagnostic of Neanderthals anyway. Also, DNA studies tend to refute this proposition. Clearly the anatomical condition of the Lagar Velho boy is intriguing, but it is far from proof of a Neanderthal–Cro-Magnon hybrid.

Côa Valley Petroglyphs, Portugal

The Côa River, in the northeastern region of Portugal, has produced a deep valley system. Along its rocky banks and upper outcrops can be seen an amazing series of concentrated engravings and painted figures, which have been described as an "outstanding example of early human artistic activity."

AN OPEN-AIR GALLERY

The Côa Valley is most unusual in that the art sites are in the open. Most European Paleolithic art is in caves or shelters. On the right we can see a finely detailed carving of a bovid.

ANCIENT ART TRIUMPHS OVER MODERN DESIRES

Visitors to Portugal's Côa Valley Archaeological Park will have the privilege of viewing the series of engravings and painted figures that altered a government's plans. Below is just one example from this magnificent gallery.

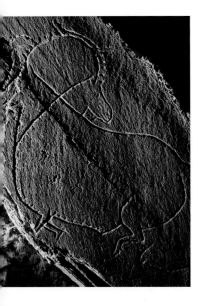

It was only in the 1990s that the significance of the Côa Valley petroglyphs gained Portuguese and international attention. In 1992 the Portuguese government planned to flood the area as part of a dam proposal. It was only after an extensive archaeological survey, along with the lowering of the river level, that many previously unknown sites were exposed. As such the original proposal to dam the river and flood the valley was rejected and the sites along the Côa River as well as the adjacent Douro River are now preserved for posterity. The Côa Valley Archaeological Park was established and it was declared a UNESCO World Heritage Site in 1998.

Themes of the Côa Valley petroglyphs are zoomorphic (animallike), with most appearing to represent large herbivores including mountain goats (ibex), horses, deer, and aurochs (wild cattle) that first frequented this region around 25,000 years ago. There are also some rare examples of engravings of fish, and an even rarer example of engravings that appear to represent human forms. It is currently thought that the engravings were made using a number of tools and techniques. Tools include the use of quartzite and flint, while techniques include fine incisions as well as pecking a succession of points hammered into the rock, along with scratching.

DATING THE ENGRAVINGS

The earliest examples of petroglyphs are suggested by some to be Solutrean in style. Overall the artistic tradition of the valley is believed to have spanned a broad period of between 20,000 and 8,000 years ago; although the earliest dating (Upper Paleolithic) has been challenged. The dating of the work to the Paleolithic has been based on three main techniques. First, finding an animal figure that depicts a species existing at a restricted period in time (that is, present during the Upper Paleolithic) but not during the later Holocene (10,000 years ago to the present). It has been suggested that this is the case for horse, deer, and ibex that were not present in this area during the Holocene. Second, finding petroglyphs below ground level and minimum-dating them via stratigraphy to associated Upper Paleolithic sites. Third, finding occupation evidence of the Upper Paleolithic period. Until radiocarbon dates from Côa Valley sites are provided, the actual dating of the Côa Valley petroglyphs remains a hot issue of debate.

Lascaux Cave, France

The prehistoric masterpiece that is the painted Lascaux Cave is located in the Dordogne region of southern France on the banks of the Vézère River. Four teenagers who in 1942 found a small entrance into the cave were the first to see the rock paintings in thousands of years.

ANCIENT ART
On the right we can see early Magdalenian rock art depicting scenes from a hunt. A human figure is shown with a bison, a bird, and two spearlike objects, in the Apse at Lascaux Cave.

LASCAUX HORSE
The walls of Lascaux Cave have a naturally formed layer of white calcite, which in places has flaked off and revealed the yellow rock of the cave walls. The artwork at Lascaux can be classified into three categories: animals, signs, and human representations.

Perhaps the most striking feature of the Lascaux Cave paintings, and others like Altamira, is that these astonishingly beautiful and complex works appear suddenly without precedent—there is nothing foreshadowing their emergence—and apparently without any trial and error. This is especially true of the earlier Mousterian period in which the Neanderthals dominated; indeed, there is very little evidence of anything that might even truly be called "art." The Lascaux paintings depict many different Paleolithic animals within the cave, including aurochs (wild cattle), horse, bison, deer, bulls, bear, a rhinoceros, as well as a scene with a wounded bison and tall thin human figure.

The first large chamber of the cave has been called the "Hall of Bulls" because it is thought to show a stampede of horses and bulls. The corridor that leads off from this chamber is called the "Corridor of Engravings" because of the many hard to interpret engravings dominating the corridor. Other parts of the cave, called the "Apse" and the "Nave," are also decorated with a huge black bull and a number of horses. Indeed, one of the most significant paintings is found in the Apse where the only depiction of a human is shown next to a wounded bison.

Lascaux Cave is also rich in engravings and signs, adding to the notion that the Cro-Magnon painters

had a form of spiritual belief. Like those discovered earlier at Altamira in Spain, these animals are not lifeless but appear to be full of movement, and the artists have used the rock surface to give the work a three-dimensional aspect. The paintings have been described as representing a classic Early Magdalenian style dating to between 17,000 and 16,000 years ago.

Father Glory, who studied the cave paintings on site from 1952 until 1963, documented over 2,000 individual depictions on the cave's walls and ceilings. Archaeological excavations have discovered numerous reindeer bones, indicating that these animals were part of the prehistoric diet of the painters.

TOURISM AND ITS IMPACT ON THE ART
Lascaux quickly became famous and people flooded into the region to view the paintings. The subsequent change in the microclimate of the cave led to algae contamination appearing on the paintings. This unintentional damage prompted the then Minister of Culture, André Malraux, to purchase the site on behalf of the French government. In 1963 he closed the cave for 14 years in order to help prevent further damage to the artwork. Although the paintings have recovered from the damage, the original cave remains closed to tourists. An exact replica of the main gallery of the cave, Lascaux II, is now open not far from the original site. Another replica gallery can be viewed in France's National Museum of Antiquities at Saint-Germain-en-Laye, near Paris.

Early Hunter-Gatherers and Farmers

This chapter explores some aspects of the activities and lifestyles of humans in Europe and western Asia during the late Pleistocene (Ice Age) and the early, prehistoric period of the Holocene (our current Interglacial age). It follows the transition from a predominantly hunter-gatherer way of life to a settled, agricultural lifestyle.

ANCIENT JEWELRY

This pendant with human facial features is one of numerous decorative objects found at Dolní Věstonice, a very important site of the Upper Paleolithic period. The site provided important details on how humans lived during one of the coldest periods in history.

EARLY HUNTER-GATHERERS

The map below provides a picture of the area of Europe and western Asia covered by the early hunter-gatherer populations. The lifestyle followed by these people allowed them to survive in a great range of environments.

Throughout all but the last 10,000 years, humans and human ancestors subsisted by hunting, gathering, and foraging food from their surrounding environment. These activities took many different forms, allowing humans to live in a wide variety of environments from arctic tundra near the ice sheets to fertile plains and river valleys further south. Some communities would have been largely nomadic, while others lived in settlements and may only have moved location when required to track the migrations of the animals they hunted. Many groups had long-distance contacts with other communities, trading raw materials and objects over large areas. In addition to dwellings and sophisticated stone and bone toolkits, the people also made a variety of personal ornaments and carved objects.

The end of the last Ice Age around 12,000 years ago ultimately had a great impact on the ways in which humans lived their lives in northern Europe and Eurasia. The melting of the ice sheets led to rises in sea levels, changing the land areas available for occupation. While some land was lost to the sea, the new, milder climatic conditions allowed humans to exploit other environments in new ways. In several regions, including western Asia and China, communities began to domesticate plants and animals more intensively than they had before, and these practices ultimately led to large settled farming communities.

THE TRANSITION TO FARMING

The adoption of agriculture is sometimes termed "the agricultural revolution"; however, although it certainly transformed many aspects of the way in which people lived, it is important not to imagine it as a sudden change. The increase in the use of agricultural practices (domestication of plants and animals) for the provision of food occurred at very different times in different places. Some populations continued their successful hunting-gathering-foraging-fishing lifestyle for thousands of years after others began to settle in agricultural communities. Of course some continue to do so today.

It is also sometimes difficult to classify a particular population as being either hunter-gatherers or agriculturalists. There is some evidence that hunter-gatherer societies of the Upper Paleolithic and Mesolithic of Europe had been horticulturally tending

KEY

- ▫ Hunter-gatherer Site
- ◇ Neolithic Site
- ◉ Bronze Age Site
- △ Iron Age Site
- — International Border

particular plants for a long period of time prior to the formal domestication of crops in the Neolithic, and that the domestication of certain animals also pre-dated Neolithic societies. Conversely, Neolithic and Bronze Age populations often continued to engage in quite intensive hunting and foraging activities to supplement their farmed foodstuffs. Eventually, however, populations began to rely on domesticated crops and animals as their principal source of food, and it was this that led to the greatest changes in social and economic organization.

CHANGES THAT CAME WITH INTENSIVE AGRICULTURE

While a hunting and gathering lifestyle tends to support groups of less than a hundred people (who may converge periodically but then disperse again), an agricultural way of life tends to encourage population growth, leading to the potential for larger communities, and greater numbers of communities. But although agricultural practices (when successful) allow for population growth, among many of the early urbanized farmers health, nutrition, sanitation, and life expectancy were often rather poorer than in the hunter-gatherer populations who preceded them and lived alongside them.

Nevertheless, the population growth that could be sustained in Neolithic populations, and thus the growth in both the size and number of groups living in this way, undoubtedly contributed to the spread and influence of the agricultural lifestyle. Whether agricultural practices spread by replacement of existing

THE CHANGING WORLD AT THE END OF THE ICE AGE

During the last Ice Age global temperatures were up to 68°F (20°C) colder than at present. After the Last Glacial Maximum at 21,000–19,000 years ago, temperatures gradually rose a little, but it was not until around 12,000 years ago that temperatures settled at close to those of the present day. During the cold periods, massive volumes of water were locked in continental ice sheets up to 2½ miles (4 km) thick, which resulted in sea levels 330 ft (100 m) lower than today and the exposure of large areas of land. For example, Britain was joined to continental Europe by a dry English Channel. This was all reversed with the onset of the Holocene Interglacial period, and over the next 6,000 years or so the coastlines as we know them today were formed by the rising sea.

hunter-gatherer populations, or by the adoption of agriculture by those populations, is a matter of great debate. Probably both of those situations occurred, in different places at different times.

The development of large-scale, permanently settled societies that eventually came about is seen as having been essential for the development of features that are considered to be fundamental to our modern society but which were either not possible, for climatic reasons, or not desirable, before this time. The accumulation and management of wealth and resources among particular groups within a hierarchical society, the construction of monumental architecture, political systems and accounting, for example, all flourished in the context of the networks of settled agricultural communities that emerged during the Holocene Interglacial period.

NEOLITHIC STONE WALL
This close-up view of a drystone wall discovered at Skara Brae on Orkney, Scotland, demonstrates the ingenuity of the early residents of this barren, windswept island.

Dolní Věstonice, Czech Republic

Located in the region of Moravia in the Czech Republic, Dolní Věstonice is one of the most significant sites of the Upper Paleolithic period of Europe, and is just one of many sites from that region that have told us a great deal about how humans lived in Europe during one of the coldest periods of the last Ice Age.

KULNA CAVE, MORAVIA

This Gravettian site not far from Dolní Věstonice would have been freezing in the depths of winter. The Paleolithic populations who lived here around 25,000 years ago would have needed fuel, shelter, and clothing to withstand the extremely low temperatures.

Discovered in 1924 and excavated almost continuously since, Dolní Věstonice (pronounced Dolny Viestonitser) is made up of three "open-air" sites that were inhabited at various times between 28,000 and 24,500 years ago. Unlike most open-air sites of this period elsewhere, the sites in Moravia have been very well preserved, because they were buried in a fine wind-blown soil called loess, which was created by the glacial ice sheets to the north.

The people who lived at Dolní Věstonice and the other nearby East Gravettian sites have sometimes been known as "The Mammoth Hunters" because these sites typically feature very large quantities of mammoth bones and ivory. Mammoth was apparently a major food source, but it is not yet clear whether people hunted the mammoths, trapped them, or scavenged them. In any case the bones were used for many things, including as fuel—because the landscape in the region was extremely cold at this time (with an average annual temperature of a few degrees above freezing), and there was very little wood vegetation, the inhabitants used mammoth bones as fuel, burning the oils that occur within them.

HOT HEARTHS AND CERAMIC KILNS

As well as the more usual finds such as animal bone and "Gravettian" stone tools, the site has revealed evidence for circular and oval dwellings constructed with stone and mammoth bones, hearths and kilns, decorative objects, and bone and mammoth ivory beads. There are several burials, including a child, and a triple burial (26,600 years old) of two teenage men and a crippled woman of the same age. As well as red ocher (iron oxide) coloring the heads and pelvises of the bodies, the two men had strings of pierced ivory beads and teeth around their heads.

Most famously, the people at Dolní Věstonice used the loess soil like a clay to make figurines, such as the "Black Venus," and other decorative objects that they then baked, making the earliest ceramic sculptures known. Until these clay objects were found it was believed that ceramics were not invented until the Neolithic period. Many of the objects seem to have been deliberately broken, and some of them preserve impressions of woven fabrics—another insight this site provides as to the great variety of activities and materials these people used, but which have been mostly lost to the passage of time.

Venus of Willendorf, Austria

Southwest of Dolní Věstonice lies the Wachau gorge, home of the site of Willendorf. Like Dolní Věstonice, Willendorf features tool types known as East Gravettian, and dates to the mid-Upper Paleolithic (28,000 to 22,000 years ago). Willendorf is famous for the female figurine that was found there in 1908.

The "Venus" of Willendorf is dated to the middle of the Gravettian period, around 25,000 years ago, and is one of a number of so-called "Venus" figurines that were produced during this period across Europe. Many of them feature large breasts, belly, and buttocks, but there are several slender examples too. The Willendorf figure has a curious mixture of detailed and accurate representation, and abstract or stylized elements. She features an elaborate hairstyle, but no facial features. Her lower arms are minimal, but she has clearly represented hands; her substantial legs only have tiny feet.

THE PUZZLE OF THE PAINTED LADY

The significance of the large build of many of these figures has been much debated. In some ways the interpretations that have been made in the past were very much a product of their times. Nineteenth-century views that they might represent an immigrant Negroid population gave way to ideas that they instead represented pregnant women and were connected with sympathetic magic, which would help ensure fertility. This idea of fertility was then connected in the 1960s and 1970s with an idea of a "mother goddess" religion that spanned Europe across thousands of years.

Some suggest they were made by men who wanted a representation of women that they could carry with them; others believe they may have been made by

women, perhaps even as self-portraits. More recently it has been proposed that the different styles of female figurines may represent women at different stages of their lives. While many of the female figurines might have had similar meanings, it is also likely that there have been different meanings for them in different areas during this long period.

In the case of the Willendorf figurine, the most pragmatic interpretation is that this represents a well-fed lady. The physiological features of the figure do not obviously represent pregnancy, but they are an accurate representation of adipose (fatty) deposits on a female form. She has rounded thighs and knees, upper arms, stomach, hips, buttocks, and breasts, and her back shows deep creases between the waist and shoulders.

The limestone used to carve the Venus was not native to the region, so must have been considered quite an exotic material. The figure is also colored with red ocher in places, which is likely to have had special significance. In many historical hunter-gatherer societies ocher has been equated with blood and power, and may have had similar meanings in the past.

A WELL-FED WOMAN?
It may be that the Willendorf Venus is a sculpture based on a living individual, but that it represents not a *portrait* of a person but an *idea* of a form of woman that was very important to her creators. At around 4 in (10 cm) high, the limestone figurine is portable.

WILLENDORF TODAY
This is where the famous "Venus" figurine was discovered in 1908 by the archaeologist Josef Szombathy, more than 20,000 years after it had been made. Szombathy showed the figurine to the Yale anthropologist George Grant MacCurdy, who published a note that year in the *American Anthropologist* journal.

Mezhirich, Ukraine

Mezhirich □ ○Kiev

UKRAINE

After the coldest period of the last Ice Age (20,000 years ago) had passed, humans with equipment and knowledge adapted to the cold environments started to move further north into the arctic tundras of central and eastern Europe. There they built some of the most impressive settlements of the Paleolithic period, such as that at Mezhirich in Ukraine.

The settlement at Mezhirich was discovered in 1965 when a farmer uncovered huge bones in the wall during the process of extending the cellar of his house. The site was excavated and revealed a settlement of at least five large shelters made from stacked mammoth bones, dating to around 15,000 years ago.

The circular or ovoid bone shelters were 13–16 ft (4–5 m) across; the bones of at least 149 individual mammoths were used in the huts' construction. Although some bones may have been from hunted animals, most probably came from accumulations in the surrounding environment. Many have carnivore marks and weathering on them showing that they had been exposed for some time before being collected; at the similar site of Mezin (also in Ukraine) the bones have been shown by radiocarbon dating to vary in age from around 14,000–22,000 years old, proving that they were not all hunted at the time of construction of the settlement.

HOUSE OF BONES

This reconstruction of a mammoth-bone hut at Mezhirich shows the form these dwellings took. More than 70 mammoth-bone huts have been discovered at similar settlements from throughout the Central Russian Plain (Russian Federation, Ukraine, Poland, and the Czech Republic), including sites such as Mezin, Krakow, Kiev, and Kostenki.

BONES AS BUILDING BLOCKS

Mammoth crania (skulls) and mandibles (jawbones), interlocked like building-bricks into a herringbone pattern, were used as the foundation circle of the huts. Other mammoth bones, including shoulder blades, pelvises, and more skulls, were built on top forming a frame, probably covered with skins, with tusks and limb bones providing a doorframe. The bones used for each hut were extremely heavy, with each mammoth skull usually weighing more than 220 lb (100 kg), and the total mass of hut No.1, for example, being around 44,000 lb (20,000 kg). Other huts vary between around 33,000 lb (15,000 kg) and 42,000 lb (19,000 kg).

DAILY LIFE AT MEZHIRICH

As was the case at Dolní Věstonice around 10,000 years earlier, fresh bone was an important fuel for fire at Mezhirich. Recent research has found charcoal at the site too, probably from burning small shrubs. It is possible that not all of the huts were used for habitation, and that at least one was a communal or meeting space. This hut has produced one of the most intriguing finds from the site: in the entrance was found a mammoth skull decorated with patterns in red ocher, which may represent flames and sparks. This bears damage marks on the top where it has apparently been repeatedly struck, and longbones of animals found nearby show similar damage to their ends, suggesting the possibility that the mammoth skull was used as a drum. Around 50 people would have resided at the settlement, returning at a certain time each year; they also either traveled or traded widely, as they had amber ornaments and fossil shells from up to 310 miles (500 km) away.

Lepenski Vir, Serbia and Montenegro

The end of the last Ice Age meant that human populations could access new resources and environments, and the successful hunter-gatherer way of life continued in Europe for several thousand years. The site of Lepenski Vir has told us much about both the way of life of these later hunter-gatherers and how they interacted with the emerging farming populations.

Belgrade
Lepenski Vir

SERBIA AND MONTENEGRO

The hunter-gatherers of the postglacial period are known in Europe as Mesolithic. Lepenski Vir, discovered in 1967, is the site of a succession of village settlements of hunter-fisher-gatherers who lived on the sandy river terrace of the Danube River between about 8,000 and 7,100 years ago.

The site has some of the best-preserved dwellings from the Mesolithic period. All are trapezoidal in shape, with the wide end, where the entrance was, facing toward the river. The huts were between 16 and 98 ft (5 and 30 m) square, with hardened limestone plaster floors, the earliest known mortar in Europe. In the center each had an elongated hearth-pit, often full of bones of fish such as carp and sturgeon. Postholes placed around the perimeter of each dwelling indicate that shelter was provided by large branches creating a tent-shaped roof, probably then covered with skins. Bone pins and obsidian and flint tools have been found, as well as a total of 85 burials, from both inside and between the houses; many of the dead were buried with a range of grave goods such as fish and antlers.

AN IDEAL PLACE TO LIVE

Cone-shaped haystacks punctuate the hillsides above the Danube River at the settlement of Lepenski Vir. The first settlers at Lepenski Vir would have found a raised terrace sheltered from harsh winds that was above the flood waters of the Danube, as well as plenty of food sources in the forest and waters.

FISH-FACED GOD

This carved stone sculpture was found at Lepenski Vir. It has been nicknamed "Danubius," and is thought to represent a creator god; it dates to around 6000–5500 BCE.

FISHERS AND SCULPTORS

Most interestingly, almost every single dwelling featured a carved limestone boulder measuring 8–24 in (20–60 cm) high. In the earliest phase of occupation these carvings were generally abstract or geometric designs; however, later the boulders were carved into an image of a fish-human hybrid. These hybrids were located outside the front of several of the houses.

Even while the Mesolithic population resided at Lepenski Vir, early farmers (Neolithic populations) lived nearby, using the fertile soils on the terraces of the river. The foragers had broad networks of contact with other groups, including with the Neolithic farmers, and traded a variety of goods. In this way, Lepenski Vir acquired pottery, toolmaking materials (flint and obsidian from far away), and beef and other foods. It was certainly not necessary for the people to engage in trade, as they had a highly successful way of life of their own, illustrating that the farmers and foragers were able, at least for a time, to live side by side cooperatively.

Eventually, it seems that the foraging communities abandoned the site, or that way of life, and it came to be occupied for its last 200 years (5100–4900 BCE) by a community of Neolithic farmers.

Çatal Hüyük, Turkey

Built in a dry lake bed on the Anatolian Plateau (Turkey), the Neolithic town of Çatal Hüyük is one of the earliest urban settlements known. Inhabited by farmer-pastoralists, it was occupied for nearly one-and-a-half thousand years, from about 9,400 years ago until 8,000 years ago.

Discovered in 1958 by James Mellaart, and then first excavated under his direction between 1961 and 1965, the mound, or "Tell," formed by the town covers an area of 32 acres (13 ha). It is also 56 ft (17 m) deep with layer upon layer of houses built on top of each other over the course of the 1,400 years that the site was occupied. Excavations recommenced in 1993, but in total only about 5 percent of the area has been excavated so far. Funding from the Global Heritage Fund in 2006 has allowed improvements to be made in conservation and site presentation. The money has paid for, among other things, a large tent shelter and fences.

LIVING IN A LAND WITH NO TOWNS

The area of the site now has the lowest rainfall in Turkey, but at the time of the settlement the former lake bed was riddled with streams and fertile soils (alluvium) washed down from the hills by the rivers that used to feed the lake. There is also evidence that swamps formed in certain areas in particular seasons, and that some areas near the settlement were regularly flooded. Wild animals such as boar, leopards, goats, wolves, and vultures would have populated the landscape of plains and trees.

The inhabitants herded sheep and grew cereals and legumes in the fertile natural terraces nearby. They also hunted animals and gathered other resources from the environment. Wood for building and fuel, reeds for thatching, raw materials to use in basketry, and fruit, nuts, and eggs for food were all collected. Cattle and deer were hunted in autumn, and scenes of this activity adorn the walls of several of the buildings.

LAYERS OF CIVILIZATION
Neolithic farmers built houses of mud-brick, in successive layers, which eventually formed the artificial mound today called a "hüyük" or "höyük."

PLASTERED SKULLS AND THE DEAD

Many of Çatal Hüyük's buildings were decorated with the skulls of animals, especially cattle, covered with plaster and built into the walls and features of the room. These plastered cattle skulls, which have huge horns, are known as "bucrania." Many houses also feature human burials in their floors; like the bucrania, skulls from these burials were sometimes exhumed, plastered with a new "skin," and placed in significant places or into new burials. The female figurines found at the site were originally attributed to a matriarchal "mother goddess" religion (Çatal Hüyük is visited by many people who believe the site is important in the emergence of the goddess). However, although the figures seem sometimes to have been treated in special ways, men and women themselves were treated in remarkably similar ways in burial. In fact, there is evidence for a great diversity of beliefs—about various aspects of life, death, animals, and food—represented in the various stages of the town.

LIVING IN A TOWN WITH NO STREETS

The town evidently grew out of a number of smaller settlements in the area. There are no streets and alleys separating buildings and allowing access via doors; instead, the inhabitants would have traveled over the flat rooftops and accessed their houses via a trapdoor in the roof. Most of the houses are built up against each other and surrounded on all four sides, but there are also some spaces between buildings that were used for corralling animals.

A wooden staircase or ladder led from the trapdoor to the floor of the house. The houses themselves are rectangular with remarkably consistent layouts, usually of two rooms, one a "living room" and the other a side room for storage. The main room typically features an ovenlike hearth under the stairs (allowing the trapdoor entrance to double as a chimney), and around this area a number of raised platforms. The floors were usually painted red, while the walls were covered repeatedly with layers of white plaster, which was often painted with geometric patterns and representations of animals in red, white, and black. These very often feature leopards and cattle, as well as goats, deer, and horses. There is also one wall painting which may constitute a representation of the town from above, in which case it could be the earliest known map.

In addition to the paintings and plasterwork, the site has yielded many other remarkable material goods. There is evidence of weaving of mats and baskets from plant fibers, tools, and even polished mirrors made from obsidian (volcanic glass). As well as being used for containers, clay was sculpted into "stamp seals," small patterned blocks that may have been used for marking skins, clothes, or the human body; there were also many figurines of large females.

Each mud-brick house would have been occupied by probably five to ten people, and the settlement as a whole would have housed several thousand people at any given time. A house was used for around 70 years (three generations) before the top halves of the walls would be demolished and the lower half of the house filled in with earth, sometimes with specific items placed in particular places. Finally, new walls and a floor would be built on the base of the old, creating the many layers that we find today.

CAPTURING A DEER

As part of the current excavation and research work being carried out at Çatal Hüyük, local people have been trained by conservators to help remove wall plaster to reveal wall paintings. Some wall paintings are conserved and removed for future display in the local Konya Museum, while others are conserved for on-site display.

MOTHER GODDESS

This Neolithic clay sculpture of the "mother goddess" seated on her throne was unearthed at Çatal Hüyük. She is flanked by two leopards whose tails curl up and over her shoulders, perhaps suggesting she has a protective strength and power. Some say her naked, abundant body represents her nurturing qualities.

Varna, Bulgaria

The cemetery at Varna has produced the earliest collection of gold-working in the world, with more than 280 graves dating to the Chalcolithic (Copper Age) nearly 7,000 years ago. It indicates changes not only in metal-working skills but also in social organization and the treatment of the dead.

VARNA GOLD

At right is a gold appliqué plate from Varna. More than half of the gold objects were found in graves without bodies; for example, three cenotaph graves and three mask graves were comparably rich in gold artifacts. Below is a reconstruction of a chieftain's grave at Varna, complete with gold jewelry and other items.

Cemeteries are known from a few Paleolithic sites (such as Predmosti in Moravia and Taforalt in northeastern Africa), but burials inside houses seem to have been popular among many of the early settled societies, as at Lepenski Vir and Çatal Hüyük. Varna constitutes a stark contrast: there we see a preference for burying (certain) people collectively, outside the main settlement. To date, 211 of the graves have been excavated intact, and these included both males and females, all more than 12 years of age. There are also graves with no body but with grave goods laid out as if around a corpse ("cenotaphs"), as well as graves that contained a clay mask instead of a body ("mask graves").

DISPLAY OF THE EXOTIC: NETWORKS AND KNOWLEDGE

The majority (170) of the graves at Varna contained ten or fewer items, but 18 of them were particularly richly equipped with grave goods, apparently indicating a marked differentiation of wealth among individuals. A variety of important items were placed in the graves, including copper tools such as axes, chisels, and awls. These replicated practical items in what was then a precious metal. There were beads made of copper, bone, shells, limestone, and marble. Marble was used for dishes, drinking vessels, and figurines, and some graves contained spectacular 16 inch (40 cm) blades made of obsidian and flint.

It was the astounding quantity of gold at the site that first made it famous, however. Grave 14 (also known as Tomb 43) contained the body of a male in his forties, accompanied by over 1,000 items, including copper axes, flint tools, pottery, and more than 980 gold objects. These include gold disks pierced to be sewn onto clothes, beads, wire work, a penis sheath, bracelets, and a gold-plated ax-shaft. Curiously, however, 60 percent of the gold objects from the site came from the graves that had no bodies. These may well have celebrated individuals buried elsewhere, or may have symbolized ownership not by individuals but collectives.

It is worth remembering that in this period equal (or even greater) prestige could be associated with a number of other materials and objects besides gold. Rarity and aesthetic qualities, both natural and as a product of craftsmanship, gave many different objects potential for display and as status symbols. Many of the items at Varna came from far away (shells came from the Aegean, for example) and would have been exotic and valuable as a consequence. In addition to their exotic nature, these objects had the potential to indicate an individual's wide knowledge and influence over networks of exchange throughout eastern Europe.

The Iceman, Italy

One of the most important finds for helping to reconstruct details of Neolithic life in Europe is the very well-preserved "Iceman," nicknamed Ötzi. He was found by two mountaineers in 1991 in a glaciated mountain pass near the border of Italy and Austria, where he died between 5,000 and 5,300 years ago.

His nickname is derived from the Ötzthal (Ötz Valley) on the Austrian side of the pass in which he was found (he was 330 ft [100 m] inside the Italian border), although this was most likely his intended destination rather than his home. Pollen, along with isotopes in his tooth enamel, suggest that he came from a small village in the Val Senales near where he was found, but that he grew up in the Velturno area to the south of the region. He was probably aged between 40 and 50 when he died.

AN EXPERT TRAVELER

His clothes and equipment show that he was very well equipped for his journey. He had a grass cape, a tunic made of strips of light and dark animal skins, fur leggings, shoes lined with insulating grass, and he wore a bearskin hat. His clothes were finely sewn but had also been repaired less expertly, possibly on his journey.

He had a flint knife and copper ax, both with wooden handles, and an unfinished bow. He also had two arrows with flint points and 12 unfinished arrows plus some antler, which might have been used for arrowheads, all in a fur quiver. He carried fire-making equipment (flint, pyrite, and plant tinder) and two containers of birch bark, one of which apparently contained embers. He also had a frame

rucksack, and two types of fungus, one of which was tinder in his fire-making kit and the other is known today to have antibacterial properties.

Detailed examination of the skin, nails, and hair has helped provide information on his health. He had evidence of osteoarthritis in his legs and lower back (although this would not necessarily have caused him pain). Copper and arsenic levels in his hair suggest that he carried out copper-smithing during his life. His stomach contents showed that he had recently eaten chamois and venison meat, einkorn wheat, and sloe berries.

Did Iceman die just from exposure on his perilous journey over the mountains, or did he die from other injuries? Scholars believe it was likely a combination of both. He had an arrowhead embedded in his back, and this wound had apparently not healed, suggesting that he had recently been shot. On the other hand, his clothes and equipment suggest that this was not a hastily planned journey. He was well equipped for a journey in the early spring, which is when he died, as indicated by the fresh hop-hornbeam pollen grains that were found on his clothing. This would mean that the snowstorm in which he was caught—and so well preserved—was unusual, and quite probably unexpected.

A MAN CAUGHT OUT BY UNSEASONABLE WEATHER

The remains of Iceman are seen here laid out so scientists could examine them. These experts determined that Iceman had blue eyes, dark hair, was 5 ft 5 in (about 1.65 m) tall, and probably weighed about 112 lb (50 kg).

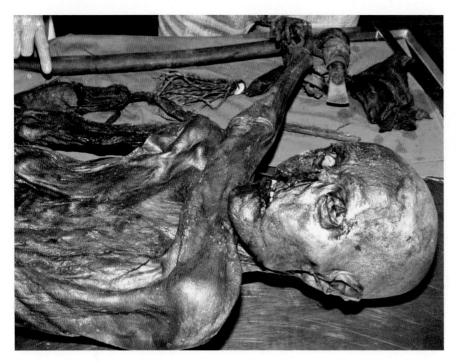

SHOES ADAPTED FOR TRAVEL OVER HARSH TERRAIN

For his long journey, Iceman wore shoes lined with grass. This insulation would have protected his feet from the effects of walking for hours on end over the mountain pass. The soles of the shoes were made of bearskin, the upper panels of deerskin. A leather thong was used to stitch the soles and uppers together. The woven netting that formed the back of the shoes was constructed using alpine grass. The replicas of the shoes pictured here were made using boiled liver and pigs' brains.

Bog Bodies

WINDEBY GIRL

In 1952, workers on Windeby Estate near Schleswig, Germany, were shocked to discover the body of a 14-year-old girl. She was found on her back, her head turned to one side, and her eyes covered with a cloth bandage. Scientists later concluded that she had been deliberately drowned.

BOG BURIAL

This is the peat bog in Denmark where Tollund Man was found in May 1950. Two brothers were digging for peat to use as fuel when they came across the body with a rope around its neck. They thought the man must have been killed recently because his body was so well-preserved.

Extremely hot or very cold conditions can lead to the preservation of bodies because the organic matter dries out before it can start to decay. Another form of preservation can occur where there is no air present at all (an anaerobic environment) or when certain chemicals are present. Both of these conditions prevent the growth of the microbes that normally cause the decay of organic matter.

In the peat bogs of northern Europe, which have formed since the end of the Pleistocene, exactly these conditions exist, and this has resulted in the quite remarkable preservation of nearly 2,000 human bodies. Sometimes the bone matter is dissolved by the acidic peat environment; however, skin, hair, internal organs, and accompanying plant matter can be preserved extremely well.

Around a hundred of these bodies have been radiocarbon dated, showing that they vary greatly in age, from prehistory to the medieval period. The oldest body dated so far is a woman in her early twenties from the early Mesolithic, 10,000 years ago, found in Denmark. There are several from the Neolithic of Britain and Denmark, and others from the Bronze Age. Most of those that have been dated are between 2,500 and 1,500 years old, from the late Bronze Age through the Iron Age to the late Roman period (500 BCE–500 CE). The most famous and well-preserved Iron Age bog body is that of Tollund Man.

HOW AND WHY DID THEY DIE?

Some of the bodies show no sign of injury at their death and these may simply have been conventional burials. It is possible that a few were accidental deaths of travelers getting lost and mired in the dangerous waterlogged peat bogs. However, several of the bodies show signs of violent death. Some may have been the victims of murder who were unceremoniously dumped where they wouldn't be found; however, some careful investigation has shown that many were not straightforward murders but more complicated deaths, perhaps sacrifices or executions.

The bodies, their deaths, and depositions are very varied, as might be expected when dealing with a large geographic area and time span, but there are some trends that emerge in the different periods. A surprisingly large number of the bodies

from throughout the Neolithic to Iron Age were of young people, in their teens to early twenties. Neolithic examples were often accompanied by, or close to, deposits of other valuable goods such as pottery, weapons, amber, and domestic animals. One young Neolithic woman (from Østrup, Denmark) was deposited with a swan. Many were naked, or virtually naked (such as the famous Tollund Man, also from Denmark, who wore only a hat and belt), while others have been found fully clothed and sometimes accompanied by valuable possessions.

Few of the individuals who suffered violent deaths were killed simply. In the Iron Age in particular, a combination of strangulation, throat-slitting, and bone-breaking strikes to the head and limbs dispatched the individuals. In some cases the individual was deliberately subdued or rendered unconscious through gentle strangulation, a strike over the head, or eating a particular food, before being finally killed by a cut to the throat, stabbing, or heavy blow to the skull.

SPECIAL INDIVIDUALS?

The proportions of men and women represented are not significantly different, but a relatively high number show deformities, perhaps suggesting that these persons were considered to be special in some

way. Others show little sign on their hands of hard labor in the months leading up to their deaths, suggesting that they may have been considered to be elite individuals, or that they were treated specially for a long period in advance of their impending death.

FINAL MEALS

The preserving qualities of the peat have allowed archaeologists to find out what several of the people deposited there ate in the time leading up to their deaths. The stomach contents of the Iron Age man from Tollund (Denmark) showed he had eaten a gruel of mixed seeds, grain, and moss, as had several other Iron Age individuals. Lindow Man (England) ate unleavened bread of wheat, barley, oats, and seeds, with some meat. His stomach also contained the pollen of mistletoe, a plant with a long history of religious significance but which can also act as a sedative. Similarly, the bog body now known as Grauballe Man (Denmark) had eaten ergot, a poisonous and hallucinogenic fungus that grows on damp grain. This may have been on the grain in his gruel, but he had consumed enough ergot to put him into a coma before his death.

TOLLUND MAN

Unlike the near-naked Tollund Man, many bog bodies were found fully clothed. The preservation of such garments has allowed archaeologists to learn much about the manufacture of fabrics and material goods during the Neolithic, Bronze, and Iron Ages.

Skara Brae, United Kingdom

Skara Brae, on the West Mainland island of Orkney, Scotland, is a settlement of subterranean stone houses occupied 5,100 to 4,500 years ago. It is the most complete Neolithic settlement in Europe, and is one of a number of famous stone structures on Orkney from this period, including stone circles at Brodgar and Stenness.

SCOTTISH STONE HOUSES

The later, rectangular, buildings at Skara Brae are still virtually intact. The stones of some of the buildings were decorated with incised and pecked patterns of lozenges, triangles, chevrons, and zigzags.

The Skara Brae settlement is so well preserved because it was covered with drifting sand after it was abandoned, locking the buildings and their contents in place and protecting them. A violent storm in 1850 first started to expose the settlement again, and it was partially excavated by William Watt, the local landowner. Major excavation was then carried out by Vere Gordon Childe in the 1930s.

The buildings were dug into low midden mounds, which provided insulation and protection, and then walled in stone. The site seems to have been occupied continuously for around 600 years, but with two main phases of building. The earliest dwellings were roughly circular, while the later ones are more rectangular. As it is preserved today it consists of eight buildings linked by alleyways.

SHELTER UNDERGROUND

The alleyways were roofed with stone, which was then also covered with midden deposits, and the buildings were probably roofed with turf supported by driftwood or whalebone. The doorway of each of the buildings plus the main entrance to the settlement's alleyways were closed with a block of stone that could be held in place with a bar. Seven of the buildings have virtually identical layouts, and were clearly dwellings. The eighth has a number of chambers, and may have been used as a toolmaking area, for winnowing and threshing wheat and barley, and possibly for brewing.

The houses have an average area of around 14 sq ft (36 sq m), with a fireplace in the center (on which the inhabitants burned peat), a bed on each side, and stone shelves opposite the entranceway. The beds on the right (upon entering the house) are typically larger than those on the left, which may indicate usage by males and females, or adults and children. Because there was (and still is) little wood on Orkney, all the internal furniture of the houses such as beds, cupboards, and storage shelves were also made of stone, so were very well preserved.

As well as grooved-ware pottery, the middens have provided a great deal of evidence of the subsistence activities of the inhabitants. As with many Neolithic populations, they subsisted by a mixture of arable farming, animal husbandry, hunting, and foraging. They farmed barley and wheat, and sheep and cattle; fished and foraged for fish and shellfish; and hunted red deer and wild boar on the island.

Swiss Lake Dwellings, Switzerland

Unusually low water levels at Meilen, Lake Zurich, in January 1854 exposed wooden piles, artifacts, and bones that had lain undisturbed on the lake bed for thousands of years, the remains of Neolithic and Bronze Age settlements. These produced much public interest, and the following years saw the discovery of many more "Lake Villages" with remarkable levels of preservation.

Lake dwellings (also referred to as lacustrine settlements) have since been found at the edges of lakes throughout Switzerland, as well as in Austria, Germany, Italy, Slovenia, France, and Britain. This form of settlement seems to have begun in the Neolithic, over 6,000 years ago, with some locations still being used in the late Bronze Age, more than 3,000 years later. Occupation would not have been continuous over this time; many settlements were periodically flooded and then reoccupied at later times, the people repairing or building on top of the previous settlement. Dating can be remarkably accurate, thanks to tree-ring dating (dendrochronology) in combination with radiocarbon dating of bones, wood, and other plants.

DETAILS OF DAILY LIFE

Such finds show that the inhabitants undertook a mixture of pastoral, agricultural, fishing, and hunting activities. They grew a variety of cereals, flax (linen), and opium poppies—some containers containing seeds have been discovered. These people kept animals such as sheep, goats, pigs, cattle, and dogs, hunted red deer and boar, and fished from the lakes. They also foraged nuts and root plants, such as turnip, from the surrounding environment.

The sites have preserved clothing and a range of tools. Archaeologists have found more than 2,600 axes and 160 arrows. The axes (used during battle as well as for peaceful purposes) were mostly made from serpentine and diorite, although some were made of flint and jade. The oldest known evidence for wheeled vehicles in Europe comes from a Swiss lake settlement at Seefeld, in the form of a wheel dating to around 5,150 years ago. Domesticated horses are also known from this time.

VILLAGES IN THE LAKE, OR BY THE LAKE?

The houses are typically made of logs or planks, sometimes with clay-covered walls and a thatched roof, and settlements are surrounded by palisades of stakes. One of the key debates has concerned whether they were dwellings near the lake-edge, or on stilts in the water. For many years it was thought that the dwellings were all built on stilts in the water; however, careful investigations of new evidence have

demonstrated that in many cases fire hearths had been built on the soils that formed the lake bed—proving that in at least some cases the settlements had been built on dry land at the edges of the lakes. However, other sites, such as Böschen (Lake Geneva), have recently provided evidence that in some cases and in some periods the houses must actually have stood in the water. Others were built on short stilts on land that was dry much of the time but periodically flooded.

As is the case with many questions in the discipline of archaeology, when dealing with thousands of years worth of evidence there are likely to be several correct explanations. Only careful excavation and increasingly sophisticated analysis allow us to find these answers.

ACCURATE DATING

Tree-ring dating of the original Swiss lake dwellings is possible because of the superb preservation of the wooden structures. The reconstruction seen here is one of many that have been made of such houses found beside Swiss lakes.

Sacred Landscapes

From the mid-sixth millennium BCE onward, farming communities began to emerge in northwestern Europe. Although their agricultural practices altered the natural environment around them—forests were cut to create fields and meadows—the most powerful and lasting legacy of the farmers was the creation of sacred ceremonial landscapes.

While the preceding hunter-gatherers undoubtedly recognized places in the landscape to which they attributed special meaning, the life of the Neolithic farmers—in addition to daily activities—was punctuated by ritual and ceremonial acts performed at many different places. The most dramatic aspect of these sacred landscapes manifests itself in the construction, throughout the fifth and early fourth millennia BCE, of megalithic tombs. Less tangibly, votive offerings bear witness to the heavily ritualized consumption of commodities. At the beginning of the third millennium BCE significant social transformations were taking place and new monuments—stone and timber circles—emerged. These sites are a testimony to the changing view of the world in which new beliefs and new gods replaced the older ones.

MONUMENTAL FUNERARY ARCHITECTURE

The megalithic tombs (from the Greek word *megas*, meaning great, and *lithos*, meaning stone) represent the most dramatic remains of the Neolithic sacred landscapes from Iberia in the south to southern Scandinavia in the north and the British Isles in the west. However, monumental burial structures, the so-called long barrows, were also constructed in timber and earth. Today completely eroded through ploughing, such monuments, in groups of a dozen or more barrows, some reaching up to 985 ft (300 m) in length, formed veritable cemeteries in areas from Kujavia in Poland through to the Paris Basin. They

usually covered one or two timber-built graves that contained single individuals, privileged dead to be remembered by future generations.

Megalithic tombs equally dominated the landscape inhabited by Neolithic farmers and were often placed in relation to prominent landmarks. The earliest were built along the Atlantic coastline from the mid-sixth millennium BCE (Iberia and western France), and by the beginning of the fourth millennium BCE megaliths were being constructed all over northwestern Europe. There are many types of megalith, from small closed chambers (dolmens) intended for single burials to passage graves whose massive and elaborate chambers, sometimes decorated with carvings, were accessed along narrow passages. Some were true houses of the dead, not only serving as burial chambers but also providing theatrical settings for other rituals.

The elaborateness of megalithic architecture was complemented by the complexity of the funerary ritual. The accessibility of chambers permitted repeated use of the interior: some tombs are today empty, with human bones either having decayed or else been removed in prehistory; while in other tombs remains from as many as two hundred individuals have been found. The piles of bones reveal an ordered deposition, which speaks strongly in favor of ancestor cults. Associated rituals are expressed in the deposition and destruction of ceramics and stone tools at the entrances to the tombs, a practice most widely seen in Scandinavia but known from other regions as well.

CEREMONIAL ENCLOSURES

Investment in the sacred landscape was not limited to the construction and maintenance of burial monuments and the tombs were complemented by central ceremonial sites. The enclosing of an area by means of banks, segmented ditches, and palisades created places with their own architectural identity, devoted to communal activities for a scattered population. The sites frequently occupy prominent hilltops and provided venues for larger public gatherings, bringing communities together for thanksgiving, worship, feasting, forming alliances, and possibly even facilitating social and economic encounters with strangers. Significantly, partial human remains have also been found in the ditches,

CARVED TOMB

These carved stone slabs are part of a tomb found at Kivik in Skane, Sweden. The Bronze Age tomb is in a cairn 245 ft (75 m) in diameter, with a chamber 13 by 3 ft (4 by 0.9 m), made of eight stones carved with symbols and narrative scenes.

and the enclosures may have served as places for exposure of the dead prior to their placement in the ancestral tomb, thereby extending the ancestral influence further into the world of the living.

EVIDENCE OF VOTIVE OFFERINGS AND HUMAN SACRIFICE

Votive offerings placed at the edges of lakes and deep in marshy and boggy areas are best documented in Scandinavia, where such deposits make ritual use of pottery, foodstuffs, and thousands of flint axes. Similar deposits could be made at the foot of menhirs (large, single, upright standing stones), or in other places in the landscape, which need not have been specifically marked. Human sacrifices were also part of these rituals, and at least some of the Neolithic bodies found in bogs represent individuals who had met with a violent death. What led people to dispose of material goods, animals, and humans in lakes and rivers is unknown—they may have been offerings to appease gods and spirits—but such practices demonstrate that material culture was an important symbolic resource used in mediation between people and their natural environment.

PENTRE IFAN, WALES

The megalithic mound and stones of Pentre Ifan (Ivan's Village) date to around 3500 BCE. The capstone is delicately balanced on three upright stones. Some believe the original portal dolmen tomb may have been built first and later embellished by a cairn and facade.

NEW GODS AND BELIEFS

During the third millennium BCE, profound changes were taking place among the farming communities in northwestern Europe. Competition led some groups to become dominant and new ideologies emerged. The ancestors, previously so powerfully invoked by the living, lost their importance and instead, new monuments emerged: stone and timber circles. The scale of some of these undertakings, the time, effort, and coordination required, speak strongly in favor of powerful leadership, challenging the old traditions and creating a new order in which individual authority could be drawn from a special relationship with the gods.

A healing megalith in England called Men-an-Tol is in the form of male and female genitalia. Some believe the earth's vibrations pass through the megalith, giving it curative properties.

Bougon, France

The cemetery at Bougon offers one of the earliest examples of megalithic architecture in Western Europe. From its very beginning, around 4700 BCE, it formed a focus of funerary and ceremonial activities, with each of its five spectacular monuments redesigned and enlarged to reflect the changing architectural and ritual traditions over a period that spanned nearly two millennia.

COVERED TUMULUS ENTRANCE
Visitors to the Bougon site can follow a discovery trail that meanders across 30 acres (12 ha) of parkland from the nearby Bougon Museum to the necropolis, passing by the entrance to each of the tumuli.

In 1840 a sensational discovery, of over 200 skeletons in the chamber of tumulus A, confirmed the prehistoric and funerary nature of these monuments. Purchased by the Department of Deux-Sèvres soon afterward, the site was designated a national historic monument. Reconstruction of the tumuli (barrows) following modern excavations (1968–1986), together with displays of finds in the nearby Bougon Muscum, offer a unique experience at this remarkable megalithic cemetery.

THE FUNERARY ARCHITECTURE

The cemetery began modestly with relatively simple, round, and rectangular drystone-walled structures (F0, E1, and E2) in small mounds culminating, in the fourth millennium BCE, in elaborate orthostatic rectangular chambers (A and F2). The latter were built using large slabs quarried at various locations within a radius of 6 miles (10 km), emphasizing a link betwccn the sanctuary and outlying communities. Chamber A in particular is an excellent example of technological accomplishment. Its exceptional size—26 ft (7.8 m) long, 16 ft (5 m) wide, and 7 ft (2.2 m) high—is matched by the skill with which the large slabs were arranged together to support a massive capstone, estimated to weigh about 99 tons (90 tonnes).

The most remarkable feature of the cemetery, reflecting the changing architectural styles, is the successive remodeling and enlargement. One of the oldest circular chambers was converted into a rectangular form; the two easternmost chambers were joined by means of a long mound of stone and earth resulting in a 262-ft (80-m) long and 9-ft (3-m) tall tumulus, while another mound was enlarged twice, eventually reaching 187 ft (57 m) in diameter. The juxtaposition of elongated and circular mounds, with multilevel stone revetment walls, reveals the social importance of elaborate external architecture.

THE BURIALS

Those living around Bougon always remembered their dead. Initially only a few adults and children were buried in each chamber. When the bodies decomposed, the bones were ordered inside the chambers to create a community of ancestors. Skulls, arranged along the chamber walls, became objects of veneration; other bones were removed to circulate as relics among the living, and ceremonies outside the tombs ensured continuous contact between the living and the dead.

However, just as architecture was changing, so were attitudes toward the dead: the chambers were reused in the fourth millennium BCE. The accumulation of skeletons suggests that the ancestors lost their importance in favor of new divine powers—their mediation was no longer required, and they were left to rest inside the chambers in peace.

Hill of Tara, Ireland

The Hill of Tara captivates the imagination of archaeologists and poets alike. By early medieval times this already ancient landscape was the place of coronation for the High Kings of Ireland. From the sixth century CE onward there are references to Tara in poems, records, king-lists, and accounts of saints' lives. St. Patrick himself is credited with converting King Lóegaire to Christianity on this site.

The history of Tara stretches far back in time. The name "Tara" derives from the word Temair, which refers to a sacred or special place. The panorama over the plain, which is commanded by the low ridge, may explain why this site attracted attention four and a half thousand years ago. There were three major periods of activity: from Neolithic to Bronze Age, during the Iron Age when Tara was a royal center, and during the early medieval period when Tara entered Irish literature.

EARLY TARA

The earliest monument is a large, palisaded, circular enclosure whose northern circuit was later overlain by a passage grave. A white granite stone stood in front of the entrance to the tomb, and many cremations were placed in the interior. In turn the passage grave was surrounded by a henge, and a processional way—a cursus—led up from the north. Over the following centuries several round barrows were built, most respecting the axis of the cursus and passage tomb. Fine artifacts (gold torcs, earrings, and a bronze rapier) found on the hill indicate rich Bronze Age burials.

THE ROYAL SITE

During the Iron Age, the Hill of Tara became a royal site, described in later medieval accounts such as *Echtra mac nEchdach Mugmedóin (The Adventures*

CONCENTRIC DESIGNS

This carved stone was found inside the passage grave known as Mound of the Hostages, which was given this title because Irish kings of the time often took "important" people hostage.

MOUND OF THE HOSTAGES

There are several versions of a particular legend that relates to the standing stone Lia Fáil (Stone of Destiny), which once sat outside the tomb. Some say that the stone shrieked in the presence of any king; others believe that it roared whenever it was touched by the true king of Tara.

of the Sons of Eochaid Mugmedón). A large earthwork (Ráith na Ríg) encircled the earlier monuments, and a smaller circular earthwork (Ráith Lóegaire) was built to the south of Ráith na Ríg, while a more complex monument containing four concentric earthworks and timber buildings (Ráith of the Synods) was constructed to the north. Within the center of Ráith na Ríg a prominent mound was formed over several of the prehistoric barrows.

The prehistoric monuments at the Hill of Tara entered medieval legends and accounts of kingship such as the *Leabhar Gabála (Book of Invasions)*. The passage grave became known as the "Mound of the Hostages," and the standing stone Lia Fáil was moved from outside the tomb. The great respect with which the prehistoric monuments were incorporated within much later sites suggests that the kings of Tara derived some of their power from this link to the distant past; that is, the power of harnessing ancient traditions.

Newgrange, Ireland

Newgrange is one of three massive tombs in the Brugh na Bóinne area, which was an important ritual center for Neolithic communities. It was described in 1699 by the antiquarian Edward Lhwyd and is regarded by archaeologists as one of the great national monuments of Ireland. It was systematically excavated and reconstructed by Professor Michael O'Kelly.

In 1993, UNESCO designated the area a World Heritage Site. With about 200,000 visitors each year, Newgrange is the most visited archaeological site in Ireland.

The Newgrange passage grave is a great marvel of engineering: 450 slabs were needed to build the passage and chamber, and 97 large boulders form the curb surrounding the mound. The latter is 280 ft (85 m) across and contains 220,000 tons (200,000 tonnes) of stone and earth. The reconstructed white marble and granite vertical facade is controversial, and it is possible that the quartz and granite fragments formed a platform in the vicinity of the entrance. Such arrangements are known from many northern European megalithic tombs where platforms served as a base for votive offerings to the ancestors. A 62-ft (19-m) long passage leads to a cruciform chamber that is roofed with a corbeled vault, with the closing capstone 20 ft (6 m) above the floor. The chamber was rendered dry by the sophisticated structure of the mound and by the provision of rain grooves in the roof of the passage.

The chamber has three recesses that contained exquisitely carved stone basins. Human remains, cremated as well as unburnt, belonging to at least five individuals were found close to the basins and elsewhere on the chamber floor. Fragments of marble, bone pins, and pendants represent what is left of the original grave goods.

ENTRY TO A DARK WORLD

The Newgrange entrance stone features dramatic spiral carvings. Archaeologists continue to search for ways of interpreting these abstract symbols. Newgrange was inscribed on the World Heritage List in 1993, as part of the Archaeological Ensemble of the Bend of the Boyne.

A SACRED PLACE

Several features, some without parallel elsewhere, demonstrate that Newgrange was a sacred building. Exotic materials from other parts of Ireland, such as white quartz from the Wicklow Mountains and granite from Dundalk Bay, used together with local materials, emphasize the scale of social relations among the Boyne communities and suggest that the tombs in the Brugh na Bóinne area may have been a ceremonial center of significance in the wider world.

A deliberate orientation executed by the builders over 4,000 years ago (curiously surviving in the vernacular tradition) was proved in 1967, when it was shown that a decorated aperture above the entrance, known as the roof box, allows the light of the rising sun at the winter solstice to reach deep into the chamber. A place of the dead, cold, and dark is for a time dramatically illuminated at this fixed point

THE THREE TOMBS OF BRUGH NA BÓINNE

Newgrange is one of three megalithic tombs that form the Brugh na Bóinne prehistoric cemetery in Ireland's County Meath. Dowth was partially investigated in the nineteenth century, and the third mound, Knowth, has been excavated and reconstructed under the direction of Professor George Eogan. Knowth is unusual in being surrounded by 17 smaller satellite tombs, and two megalithic chambers are hidden under its massive mound. The eastern chamber featured a very fine carved-stone basin; an elegant mace-head of flint, carved with lozenge and spiral designs, was found near the entrance to one of the recesses of the chamber.

in the annual cycle—a recurrent astronomical ritual which brings the dead and the living together. A laser simulation permits modern visitors to experience this truly wondrous event.

MEGALITHIC ART

While the chambers were being built, master carvers were at work, decorating many of the stones. Indeed, the Brugh na Bóinne region contains the highest concentration of decorated stones anywhere in

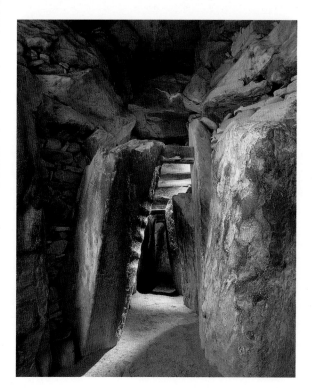

Europe. Ninety of the 123 curbstones at Knowth (see the feature box opposite) were decorated, while at Newgrange the number is 31, although the whole perimeter of the curb has not been fully exposed there. Twelve of the satellite tombs also have decorated stones along the curbs and in the interior. While most stones were carved in advance of their placement, the Newgrange entrance stone was carved after it was put in place. Many decorated stones were placed in prominent positions: private art accessible to the privileged few entering the passage and chambers, and public art to be seen by all at the entrance and on the curbstones. Decoration on other stones is curiously hidden from view, as if to suggest that the process of carving was important in itself, irrespective of where the stone was placed.

All of the designs are abstract, which provides an interesting contrast to other areas with megalithic art, such as Brittany and the Iberian Peninsula where representational designs are also known. The study of Irish megalithic art suggests two principal categories of motif: curvilinear (circles, dots, cup marks, and spirals) and rectilinear (short lines, chevrons, zigzags, lozenges, and triangles). Geometric forms such as circles, lozenges, and chevrons are most common, and triple spirals famously feature on the entrance stone and in the chamber of Newgrange. It is quite difficult to interpret these abstract designs, but they clearly had significance in the context of burial ritual and may have played a role in the passing of knowledge, with only a privileged few understanding the precise significance of such symbols.

AN ENGINEERING FEAT

The awe-inspiring passage tomb at Newgrange was rediscovered just over 300 years ago, when workers were looking for building materials to use in a road they were constructing.

A MAGICAL EVENT

Admission to the chamber of the tomb for the winter solstice sunrise is by lottery only. A select, lucky, group of people can witness the first rays of sunlight pass through the roof box to illuminate the chamber.

Avebury and Stonehenge, United Kingdom

Avebury and Stonehenge, 40 miles (65 km) apart, are Britain's most famous prehistoric monuments. Avebury is exceptional for its sheer size, while Stonehenge is unique in its design and longevity of use. In 1986 Avebury, Stonehenge, and surrounding monuments became a UNESCO World Heritage Site.

The Hyperborean temple, described by the Greek historian Hecataeus of Abdera in 330 BCE, may well refer to Stonehenge. However, the most famous account—of a legend crediting the wizard Merlin with the supernatural move of the Giants' Dance from Ireland—was given in CE 1136 by Geoffrey of Monmouth.

SILBURY HILL

This large artificial mound with a flat top was part of an elaborate landscape focused on Avebury. The mound of chalk and earth was built in three stages, beginning around 2660 BCE.

PURITAN VANDALS

Part of the Avebury monument encircles the village. Many of the original stones were destroyed several centuries ago by those who were suspicious of the pagan rituals associated with the site.

ANCIENT LANDSCAPES

Both Avebury and Stonehenge were built in ceremonial landscapes that were already a millennium old. The Neolithic long barrows, megalithic tombs, and causewayed enclosures provided a focus for rituals involving communal gatherings, celebrations, feasting, and ancestor worship. Construction at both sites began around 3000 BCE, although Stonehenge continued in use long after Avebury lost its importance.

AVEBURY: A GIANT OF A HENGE

The mighty size of Avebury is best illustrated by the fact that it has half a modern village sprawling inside it. The ditch, up to 46 ft (14 m) deep and 69 ft (21 m) wide, with spoil piled up into a bank originally 20 ft (6 m) high, encircles an area 1,150 ft (350 m) in diameter. Massive sarsen stones, weighing more than 44 tons (40 tonnes), were brought from the Marlborough Down and set up in a series of circles: the outer, originally of 100 rough stones, is by far the largest in Britain (1,150 ft [350 m]) while the pair of inner rings, each made up of 30 stones, is smaller only by comparison (over 330 ft [100 m] each). One of the pair has a "cove," a gigantic three-stone portal, while the other has a tall stone pillar, the "obelisk."

CEREMONY AND RITUAL

While the nature of ceremonies is speculative, Avebury's size suggests a great many people assembling for communal gatherings, the worship of divine spirits, and the celebration of harvests; strangers would arrive with gifts, goods to trade, and news from afar. Stonehenge became grander and more elaborate with each rebuilding, but would accommodate fewer people inside. The sarsen and bluestone circles determined the order of rituals, and solar–lunar alignments indicated propitious times for consulting the gods in this temple. Pilgrimages from afar are tantalizingly suggested by rich barrow burials in the vicinity. Some perhaps desired a final resting place at a sacred location, while others may have come in search of cures for their ailments. The so-called "Amesbury Archer," for example, had lived part of his life in the Alps, he was crippled, and many of his possessions were made on the continent. Many such individuals were drawn to Stonehenge.

Avebury was joined to another ceremonial site, the Sanctuary, via a processional route, the West Kennet Avenue, defined over one and a third miles (2 km) by a double row of alternating tall and squat stone pillars. As people walked along the avenue they passed important landmarks: Silbury Hill, the largest mound ever built in prehistoric Britain; and the timber enclosures at West Kennet, where sumptuous feasts took place. From a distance the West Kennet burial mound was a reminder of the ancestral presence watching over the living.

STONEHENGE: A TEMPLE FOR THE GODS

Beginning as an architecturally inconspicuous monument, Stonehenge was defined by a segmented ditch, an inner bank, and a ring of 56 timber posts. Cattle and deer bones, already centuries old, were placed in the ditch while the timber uprights, in cavities known today as the Aubrey Holes after their seventeenth-century discoverer, heralded a new tradition of timber circles; cremations were also deposited in various parts of the site.

ARRIVAL OF THE STONES

The first stone architecture appears at Stonehenge around 2500 BCE, initiating a half-millennium long program of redesign and alteration. Four sarsen "station stones," set in a rectangle, mark astronomical alignments and were perpetuated and enhanced in subsequent phases. They define the position of the sunrise at mid-summer and sunset at midwinter, and make a reference to the 18.6-year cycle of the moon. Eighty-two blue-stones, a gift or tribute from the Presceli Mountains in Wales, defined a double oval within the ditch. They set Stonehenge apart from other monuments on Salisbury Plain, connecting it to the wider world; their reuse in later designs reflects these distant "ancestral" links. The monument was now formally approached from the River Avon along a banked avenue.

A UNIQUE LAYOUT

The trilithon horseshoe within Stonehenge's great sarsen circle is unique. The closely set vertical stones are expertly arranged in such a way that they direct light into the central space.

BIRD'S-EYE VIEW

Unlike the inhabitants of many thousands of years ago, modern tourists have the benefit of being able to see Stonehenge from above. Around the stones are the remains of the earlier earthen ditch-and-bank enclosure.

A few centuries later, a dramatic new structure was desired. To achieve this, massive sarsen blocks from Marlborough Down, 27 tons (25 tonnes) in weight, were expertly worked into shape. A circle of 30 pillars, joined horizontally by 30 lintels, preserved the wood-working mortice and tenon techniques of contemporary timber circles. It enclosed a horseshoe arrangement, open to the northeast, of five trilithons (two uprights joined atop by a horizontal block) of even larger sarsens. This was replicated on a smaller scale reusing the ancient bluestones: a ring of 40 within the sarsen circle and an oval inside the trilithons, eventually remodeled into a horseshoe. The construction was an immense under-taking overseen by some centralizing power, and this final design, even if incomplete, must have been a truly spectacular and awe-inspiring sight both for the participants in ceremonies and for distant spectators.

Archaeologists have recently discovered evidence of a large Neolithic village just 2 miles (3.2 km) away from the monuments at Stonehenge.

Stone Circles

Stone circles and standing stones (menhirs) are among the most enduring Neolithic and Bronze Age monuments in northwestern Europe. The British Isles, with a record of well over 2,000 circles, boast by far the densest distribution, though 1,200 standing stones are known in northwestern France alone, with many more such stones scattered throughout Atlantic Europe.

Legends surrounding the stones abound, evoking maidens turned to stone for dancing on the Sabbath or witches holding court beneath the stones. The fact that many of the circles survive is due to popular superstitions and beliefs in the supernatural power of the stones.

Standing stones were raised in Brittany as early as 5000 BCE, and erected in many parts of Europe during the subsequent two and a half millennia. They stand powerfully in the landscape, dwarfing humans with their height: at 33 ft (10 m) tall, the Kerloas menhir is the tallest still standing in Brittany, while Rudston monolith in Yorkshire stands 26 ft (8 m) above ground. The stones are considered to be boundary markers or monuments expressing space, time, and social identity. Most are plain stones but others, known as statues-menhirs, are engraved with anthropomorphic designs that may represent ancestors, clan founders, or deities.

Stone circles either are freestanding settings of rough stones placed at intervals, or they form components of a monument that incorporates other features. A monument known as a henge, exclusive to the British Isles, often includes a stone circle enclosed by a ditch and an external bank. Sometimes the entrance is marked by larger stones, and outlying uprights or stone avenues lead away from the circle.

SCOTTISH MENHIR
Towering over the landscape, this standing stone is part of Scotland's very rich Neolithic archaeology. Sometimes in Scotland, groups of menhirs are referred to as "cat stones" (the Gaelic word *cath* means "a battle").

RING OF BRODGAR
Part of the Heart of Neolithic Orkney World Heritage Site, the Ring of Brodgar measures 340 ft (104 m) across. The standing stones vary in height from 7 ft (2.1 m) to 15 ft 3 in (4.7 m). Of the original 60 stones, only 27 remain today.

A MASSIVE UNDERTAKING

The labor involved in building circles was considerable, and the cooperation of many people was needed. At Almendres, the largest monument in the Iberian Peninsula, nearly a hundred stones were set up in a huge horseshoe on an east-facing slope overlooking the plain of Évora, while at the Ring of Brodgar, on the Orkney Islands, 60 stones were placed 6 degrees apart in a perfect circle within the inner perimeter of a massive rock-cut ditch, on a promontory joining two lochs. At such large sites many people could come together for ceremonies, although at the small, intimate circles such as Callanish only a few families would participate.

FROM TIMBER TO STONE

The stone circles are the surviving counterparts of wooden originals, known from ephemeral postholes at Sarn-y-bryn-caled in Wales, and Durrington Walls and Woodhenge in Wiltshire. A timber circle, built in 2049 BCE, was dramatically revealed by the low tide in 1998 on Holme Beach in Norfolk and, together with the submerged circle at Er Lannic in Brittany, suggests that the boundary between land and sea was especially significant. Elsewhere, at Balfarg in Scotland or the Sanctuary near Avebury in Wiltshire, southern England, the original timber circles were later replaced by stone.

ASTRONOMY AND RITUAL

Neolithic and Bronze Age people keenly observed the sky. They knew the movement of the sun and moon, and orientations toward these heavenly bodies are obvious in many circles. Not explicable in modern scientific terms, they were nevertheless important in embodying the sense of time and place, satisfying spiritual needs, and confirming religious beliefs. The circle shape structured the nature of rituals—dancing, singing, recounting of myths and deeds of ancestral heroes—and the orientation marked the times within the annual cycle at which ceremonies took place.

WHERE LAND MEETS SEA

Also known as "Seahenge," the timber circle at Holme Beach in Norfolk, England, is around 4,000 years old. In the center of the circle is a very large upturned oak tree stump. After extensive conservation work has been done on the timber posts, they will be displayed at the Lynn Museum.

THE RECUMBENT STONE CIRCLES

A very distinctive tradition is known in Aberdeenshire, Scotland. The circles are small, with an average diameter of 65 ft (20 m), composed of between eight and 13 stones graded in height. They display the curious architectural device of a massive prostrate block in the southwest quadrant—the recumbent—flanked by the two tallest uprights. The stones were carefully selected for their different shapes, colors, and textures. Often this segment offers a wide vista toward the distant horizon, featuring conspicuous landmarks. The orientation of these circles is closely linked to the moon, which at certain times would "glide" horizontally over the recumbent at night. This may have been the principal time for ceremonies, the burning fires offering a spectacle for distant onlookers while the participants, in the light of the moon reflected on the stones, deposited cremated human bones and evoked gods and ancestral spirits.

Carnac, France

The area of Carnac, in Brittany, is the most important megalithic center in Europe. For centuries the tombs and stone alignments inspired legends—most notably the one that credits the local St. Cornelius with petrifying an army of his pursuers into stones—and aroused the curiosity of antiquarians, travelers, writers, and painters.

DECEPTIVE DESIGN

In all the alignments at Carnac, the stones increase in height toward the enclosures, creating an optical illusion of progressing uphill and of shortening the real distance. The enclosures are of different sizes and shapes, from oval or barrel-shaped to the rare quadrangular shape.

While the name Carnac most obviously evokes the multiple avenues of miraculously balanced stones that traverse the landscape for hundreds of feet, the stone architecture at this site began with other monuments. Soon after 5000 BCE, the farmers who lived along this littoral buried their dead in small cists (chambers) that were then covered by earthen mounds.

Standing stones, singly or in short rows, marked some of the mounds; many were engraved with symbolic images. The famous Grand Menhir Brisé, 65 ft (20 m) tall and close to 330 tons (300 tonnes) in weight, is a magnificent feat of stone extraction and transportation. Now lying broken near the mound of Er Grah, it would originally have been the tallest in a row of 19 stones.

In time the architecture of the dead became more elaborate, culminating in the dolmens and passage graves. The carved stones lost their importance and were broken down, but the ancestral value of decorated fragments caused them to be reused, as seen in the capstones of La Table des Marchands and Gavrinis (also in France), in these spectacular new abodes for the dead.

THE STONE ALIGNMENTS

The landscape of the dead was intimately linked with that of the living. Stone enclosures, constructed in the elevated parts of the terrain, provided sanctuaries for the deities who were venerated by these Atlantic communities, and may also have served as important places where pilgrims from near and far met to recount myths and to celebrate with feasts, songs, and dance. These sacred locations needed formal approaches, initially perhaps a simple processional avenue marked by two rows of rough, standing stones. Over the centuries, additional lines of stones were added on either side to create the famous Carnac stone alignments, of which four groups still survive.

While there are many stone alignments in Brittany, the Carnac rows are the most impressive. The Le Ménec lines, of 1,099 stones in 12 rows stretching over a third of a mile (1 km), provide a processional route between two enclosures. The Kermario lines run roughly parallel over a similar distance, negotiating land elevations and climbing over the earlier Le Manio burial mound, while the Kerlescan alignments fan out from 9 to 13 rows by the time they reach the square enclosure in the west.

ARMORICAN NEOLITHIC BESTIARY

The decorated menhirs expressed the worldview of the communities living around Carnac. The images include animals and objects: horned cattle, sperm whales, birds, and snakes, as well as axes and crosiers. Such motifs were deeply symbolic, reflecting concern with the sky, sea, and land as well as relationships between people and nature.

Bush Barrow, United Kingdom

Constructed between 1750 and 1550 BCE, Bush Barrow is one of many barrows that have been found on Normanton Down, south of Stonehenge. It appears as a large inverted bowl, 130 ft (40 m) in diameter and 10 ft (3 m) tall.

GOLD MASTERPIECES

The three gold objects from Bush Barrow—the large lozenge found on the chest of the skeleton, the small lozenge, and the almost square-shaped belt hook—are Bronze Age masterpieces.

AN IMPRESSIVE PART OF THE STONEHENGE LANDSCAPE

The barrow cemeteries of colorful Normanton Down are located just a third of a mile (1 km) from the monuments at Stonehenge.

B ush Barrow covered one of the most richly furnished burials of a Wessex chieftain, who lived and was buried near Stonehenge in the early second millennium BCE. In 1808 Sir Richard Colt Hoare (1758–1838) and William Cunnington (1754–1810), pioneers of Wiltshire archaeology, excavated a barrow within sight of Stonehenge, the so-called Bush Barrow. Here they discovered the skeleton of "a stout and tall man" accompanied by a wealth of objects displaying an exquisite level of craftsmanship and denoting the power and prestige of the deceased.

The man was buried on his back, head to the south and rich artifacts arranged around his body. Bronze rivets and thin fragments of bronze by his head suggest he was wearing a helmet. A large ax wrapped in cloth had been placed above his right shoulder, two daggers by his right arm, and a third in his hand. The wooden hilt of one of the daggers was ornately decorated with hundreds of tiny gold pins; the weapon may already have been of considerable antiquity when buried. A macehead from polished fossil stromatoporoid *(Amphipora ramosa)* was laid by the right side of the body; only a few bone fragments

survive from the handle. The craftsmanship and the beauty of the stone imply that the macehead was a symbol of power, like a scepter.

However, the most potent symbols of power are the gold objects. A lozenge-shaped gold plate was found over the breast of the dead man, and other smaller items—a lozenge and a belt hook—were found to the right of the body. These works of a master craftsman are intricately decorated with diamond-shaped linear designs, but their thinness implies they were worn only on ceremonial occasions. It has been suggested that the larger of the lozenges may have functioned as a solar or lunar calendar, although this has not been proven.

OTHER BARROWS ON NORMANTON DOWN

Many similar mounds were built in this area from 2600 BCE onward—some while Stonehenge was in use, others when it became a relic from a bygone era, albeit awesome enough for memories of its significance to linger on. Some other barrows in the vicinity of Stonehenge also contained rich burials, with bronze weapons, gold and amber jewelry, and fine decorated gold and shale cups; many of the items were clearly of continental provenance. They demonstrate that the Wessex elite had sufficient status and prestige to engage in competition and exchange on an equal footing with contemporary continental groups.

Mediterranean Worlds

For centuries the cultures of the ancient Mediterranean have attracted treasure hunters, romantics, and scholars. It is sometimes difficult to separate myth from history; however, archaeology is still illuminating the immense cultural, intellectual, political, and artistic legacy of this region. The building blocks of Western civilization can be found here.

PALACE OF MINOS

All we can see today are the ruins of the once magnificent Hypostyle Hall in the Palace of Minos at Knossos, Crete. During the golden age of the Minoan civilization, the "palace" was most likely the people's political and religious center.

THE MEDITERRANEAN WORLD

Archaeologists continue to uncover evidence of the enormous wealth of art and ideas bequeathed to us by the ancient peoples who lived in the Mediterranean region. Trade was a significant factor in cultural and intellectual exchange.

The Mediterranean Sea links three culturally distinct continents: Africa, Asia, and Europe. The empire-builders of Greece and Rome, the Phoenicians and Canaanites of the Levant, the Hittites of Anatolia, and the Minoans of Crete are some of the diverse ancient peoples that have contributed to the melting pot of Mediterranean history and culture. A mild climate, fertile landscape, abundant natural resources, and easily navigable waters provided ideal conditions for the development and prosperity of the Mediterranean world.

Ancient Mediterranean cultures are characterized by diverse religious, political, and social customs. These did not develop in isolation. Archaeological evidence and historical sources tell us that Egypt's ties with Levantine sites like Byblos were already strong in the third millennium BCE. Centuries later, a shipwreck discovered off the Turkish coast at Uluburun attests to complex ancient trading networks that linked the eastern Mediterranean with places as far flung as Egypt and the Baltic

region. These relationships were well established by the thirteenth century BCE.

Trade and intellectual exchange have enriched the Mediterranean cultural landscape since the Bronze Age (around 3000–1200 BCE). Vast natural disasters like the volcanic eruption of Thera around 1600 BCE provided opportunities for movement of cultural groups seeking to exploit and resettle weakened cities. Throughout history travelers seeking adventure or trade have helped spread innovations that are now the foundation of Western political, cultural, social, and intellectual life.

THE BIRTH OF WESTERN CIVILIZATION

Archaeology has allowed us to trace the beginnings of many defining characteristics of Western civilization to the ancient Mediterranean. The importance of books and writing in shaping the modern world cannot be overstated. The humble inscription using the first known alphabet, discovered at Byblos in modern Lebanon, is for most archaeologists a more exciting discovery than the spectacular gold of Troy or Mycenae. By the second millennium BCE there was already well-organized trade in Egyptian papyrus throughout

KEY
- ○ Capital City
- ○ Other City or Town
- ▣ Archaeological Site
- — International Border

0   250 km
0   250 miles
N

CULTURAL HERITAGE
After 1921, the Roman theater at Byblos in modern Lebanon was relocated to a site with a commanding view out over the sea. The Ancient Greeks adopted and transmitted the Phoenician alphabet used in Byblos.

THE GIFT OF DEMOCRACY
Democratic rule was evident in Ancient Greece from the sixth century BCE. An allotment machine known as a *kleroterion* was used by Athenians to select their jurors. Here we see just a fragment of a *kleroterion* that was found in the Athenian Agora. Only male citizens aged 30 or over could volunteer to be selected to go on a jury panel.

the Mediterranean, which allowed the written alphabet to spread. And the subsequent invention of parchment at Pergamon in modern Turkey paved the way for modern book-based communication and learning.

One of the most important contributions of the ancient Mediterranean to Western civilization is democracy. The form of democracy with which we are familiar has evolved significantly from that known by Ancient Greeks, but both were born of similar ideals. Excavation of the Agora in Athens has shown us how the earliest concept of democratic rule was translated into practice in the sixth century BCE.

In addition to politics, the Greek world has made a substantial contribution to Western cultural life. Perhaps one of its most significant contributions has been in the sporting arena. Artistic evidence suggests that sporting activities may have played a part in social and religious life since the heyday of Minoan civilization in the middle of the second millennium BCE. While the earliest boxing and bull-jumping scenes from Crete and Akrotiri appear to have illustrated primarily cultic activities, by the time the first Olympic Games were held in approximately 700 BCE sport had evolved into a more familiar form. The Olympic ideals of friendly competition, excellence, and harmony are celebrated today in the modern revival of this ancient festival.

A RICH TAPESTRY
Civilizations of the ancient Mediterranean world endured many challenges: from volcanic eruptions and earthquakes in the middle of the second millennium BCE, to devastating invasions of so-called "Sea Peoples" around three hundred years later. The

Minoan and Mycenaean civilizations eventually collapsed under circumstances that are still debated by scholars. Others, such as the Hellenistic city of Pergamon in Turkey, maintained a degree of cultural independence in spite of their eventual incorporation into the Roman province of Asia.

With the rise of the Roman Empire throughout the Mediterranean there was some degree of cultural homogenization, but cities falling under the wing of the empire still maintained varying degrees of cultural uniqueness. The great diversity of the Mediterranean region endures today; there are 21 modern countries that border its shores.

TREASURE HUNTERS AND SCHOLARS

The passion with which the excavation of the ancient Mediterranean world has been undertaken has not always been accompanied by rigorous scientific standards. In fact, many archaeologists can be characterized as little more than treasure hunters. Heinrich Schliemann professed not to seek riches but was driven to prove the myths of Homer. In his quest to establish the historical reality of the Trojan War, he destroyed valuable archaeological evidence in a hastily conducted dig. Other sites have been compromised by a public fondness for ancient artifacts. A great deal of important historical information has been lost through the pillages of black-market antiquity traders. Despite this, many rigorous and scientific digs conducted since the late nineteenth century have increased our understanding of the region. The establishment of specialized institutes, collaborating with the state and local authorities, ensures that our knowledge of the earliest days of Mediterranean civilization continues to grow.

Temples of Tarxien, Malta

The megalithic structures of the Tarxien temple complex in eastern Malta are among the earliest and most spectacular examples of Mediterranean Copper Age architecture. Finely executed stone carvings, advanced construction techniques, and abundant evidence of animal sacrifice are features of this cult site from the late fourth millennium BCE.

MEGALITHIC PORTAL
This entrance to one of the Tarxien temples shows pairs of orthostats used as door jambs, to be topped with a stone lintel (still visible on the inner pair).

The fertile soil covering the site of Tarxien had been farmed for centuries before the site's discovery in 1913. A farmer recognized the potential importance of the large stone blocks that had been exposed by his plough, and immediately alerted the director of the National Museum, Sir Themistocles Zammit. With the enthusiastic help of local villagers and farmers, Zammit commenced three years of excavations in 1915. He eventually identified the remains of three monumental temples that had been progressively constructed to form a single complex linked by a square court. The temples date to the Copper Age (around 3600–2500 BCE), with the earliest construction thought to have begun somewhere around 3100 BCE.

HOW WERE THE TEMPLES CONSTRUCTED?

The Tarxien temples are built from stones ranging in size from rubble to enormous dressed slabs known as orthostats. These were ornately decorated with carvings and painted plaster inside the temples, but the outside appearance was surprisingly plain. Gaps between the orthostats are extremely narrow, and it is not fully understood how such precision was achieved. Limestone spheres still visible underneath some walls were used to roll huge slabs of stone into position. The temples were not roofed in stone, but archaeologists believe the walls may originally have supported a roof of wooden beams thatched in wattle and daub or animal skin.

The three temples are laid out as joined pairs of semicircular apses. Access to the innermost apses was probably restricted to important religious officials.

ANIMAL SACRIFICE

The builders of the temples were farmers who raised livestock and grew cereal crops. Both fertility and prosperity of the land would have been an important focus of their religious rituals, and this is reinforced by symbolic wall decorations. Relief carvings of a pig with thirteen piglets, a bull, and numerous female figurines with abundant thighs and breasts are all powerful symbols of fertility and reproduction.

Animal sacrifice was an important element of religion at Tarxien. Bones of the sheep, goats, pigs, and cattle represented in carvings in the temples have been recovered from niches behind the altars. One hollow altar contained a long flint knife, which may have been used to sacrifice these animals. Holes drilled into stone slabs were probably used to tether animals before they were led to sacrifice on the altars inside. There is no evidence of human sacrifice.

All Maltese temples were abandoned after around 2500 BCE, but Tarxien was later transformed into a Bronze Age cremation cemetery that remained in use until approximately 1500 BCE.

Knossos, Greece

The spectacular multistoried complex discovered at Knossos (Knossus, Cnossus) is thought to have been the political and religious center of the Minoan civilization. Despite the administrative and ritual uses identified by modern scholars, the imaginations of visitors to the site are still sparked by the mythic connections that excited the earliest archaeologists.

BULL'S HEAD VESSEL
Found at Knossos and dating to around 1500 BCE, this exquisite carved stone artifact was either a *rhyton* (drinking horn) or a libation vessel. It features inlaid jasper, crystal, and mother-of-pearl. The gilded horns have been restored.

REVEALING THE PAST
This detail of a restored fresco depicting dolphins and fish is from the Queen's Megaron (Apartments) at Knossos. It is just one of many beautifully colored frescoes that illustrate various aspects of Minoan daily life.

The most famous archaeological remains at Knossos (pronounced kuh-NOSS-oss) date to the Minoan period (around 1900–1400 BCE), but the site was occupied continuously from around 7000 BCE until Roman times.

The so-called "Palace of Minos" was partially excavated in 1878 by Minos Kalokairinos, who was a Cretan merchant. His discoveries excited Heinrich Schliemann, the excavator of Troy, who sought to purchase the site and carry out his own excavations. However, the price demanded by local landholders was so great he was unable to reach agreement. Lengthy negotiations eventually led to the purchase of the site by wealthy Englishman Arthur Evans who excavated and undertook controversial restorations between 1900 and 1931.

"THE PALACE OF MINOS"
Evans identified the site as "The Palace of Minos," but it is uncertain whether this complex of over 1,000 rooms was ever a royal residence. It housed workshops, archives, and wine presses, and is probably better described as an administrative and religious complex. Numerous storerooms contained gigantic ceramic jars called pithoi, which stored food items such as peas, oil, olives, and grains.

The original building, dating to around 1900 BCE, was destroyed by an earthquake in 1700 BCE, after which it was rebuilt on a grander scale. The second structure had a more intricate layout, with a vast network of labyrinthine corridors. A catastrophic fire destroyed this complex around 1400 BCE, and it was left in ruins until Evans rebuilt the sections that still stand today.

The architectural complexity of the second building is most impressive. Archaeologists have discovered that some sections would have been up to five stories high. A sophisticated drainage network formed part of an intricate sanitation system that included a bathroom with a toilet that could be flushed using jugs of water.

A wealth of colorful frescoes provide a fascinating view of Minoan dress, rituals, and sports. However, many frescoes were reconstructed from tiny fragments, and their accuracy is debated by scholars.

THE LABYRINTH
Connection of the complex at Knossos to the mythical labyrinth of King Minos seems to have been made in Roman times. Legend tells that Daedalus (Daidalos) constructed the labyrinth to imprison the Minotaur, a terrifying half-man, half-bull creature. The hero Theseus eventually killed the Minotaur with help from the king's daughter, Ariadne. The word "labyrinth" derives from "labrys," a double-headed ax that was a protective symbol in the Greek world. Carvings of these axes on a number of walls at Knossos strengthened the site's mythical connections for early archaeologists. Some scholars believe the complex was known as "The Labyrinth" to the Minoans.

Palaikastro, Greece

The Bay of Palaikastro in eastern Crete was the site of the most important Minoan city. Excavations have uncovered a large cosmopolitan commercial center near the coast that provided the island's main base for maritime trade. The city's rebirth after a devastating fire around 1400 BCE demonstrates its enduring importance.

The modest ruins visible today offer few clues about the importance of Palaikastro to Minoan Crete. Plundered stones have strengthened village walls for centuries at the expense of once-grand houses and shops. Nowadays, even the name of this imposing ancient city is lost.

By around 1900 BCE a fairly large settlement on the site already had trading links with Egypt and Anatolia. It was largely destroyed by a powerful earthquake around 1700 BCE. The city that rose from the ruins was rich and prosperous, characterized by impressive houses and a large population. Wealth from maritime trade was supplemented with income from olives and sheep farming.

This city was in turn destroyed in the catastrophe that overwhelmed Crete in the fifteenth century BCE. The cause of widespread burning and destruction is debated, but it probably resulted from either a massive volcanic eruption of Thera, on modern Santorini, or invading Mycenaeans from the Greek mainland. Palaikastro was one of only a few Cretan cities to be rebuilt after this calamity.

URBAN LIVING

Palaikastro is the largest excavated Minoan town. At its peak, it probably extended over 17 sq miles (45 sq km). Houses lined cobbled streets, from which ground-floor workshops were easily accessed. Above these, sleeping and living quarters were entered via stairs. (Plaques found at Knossos made from a ceramic material called faience show us what these houses would have looked like.) A building identified as a shop contained weights, storage jars, a sink, and a drain. Outside, stone drains bordering the city's main road are a legacy of the Minoans' impressive engineering skills.

To the south of the town of Palaikastro, a sanctuary excavated on the peak of Petsophas has yielded many clay votive figurines. These provide us with valuable information regarding the dress and hairstyles of the Minoans.

THE PALAIKASTRO KOUROS

Remains of the so-called Palaikastro Kouros were found scattered in a sanctuary among the debris of the fifteenth-century BCE destruction. This male figure was made of hippopotamus ivory, and also included elements of serpentine, rock crystal, wood, Egyptian blue, and gold. It originally stood around 20 in (50 cm) tall. The skilled workmanship and naturalistic rendering of the statuette's features make this the most important piece of Minoan art that has yet been discovered. Some scholars believe the kouros represents the youthful god Zeus Diktaios, who came from the underworld to mark the beginning of the harvest. There was an important shrine to Zeus Diktaios at Palaikastro in the third century BCE (in what is known as the Hellenistic period).

SACRED DANCE

These Bronze Age clay votive figurines were discovered at the sanctuary south of Palaikastro. The numerous small clay figurines of men and women found at the sanctuary (representing the people making offerings) provided much information about the dress and hairstyles of the period.

Akrotiri, Greece

A cataclysmic volcanic eruption of Thera in 1600 BCE destroyed the Bronze Age port of Akrotiri on the Greek island of Santorini. The tons of volcanic material that buried this important commercial center preserved fragile details that have allowed archaeologists to reconstruct day-to-day life.

STAIRCASE OF STONE
Above is a photograph of the remains of the staircase of a house in Akrotiri. The destructive effects of a volcanic eruption are evident in the crumbling stone. The Thera Foundation continues the important excavation work at Akrotiri started by Professor Spyridon Marinatos in 1967.

THE "FLOTILLA MINIATURE FRIEZE"
In this intricate detail (above right) from the famous and beautiful fresco on a wall in the "West House," we see the town's residents. Note that the ship has a crew but no passengers.

Akrotiri has been inhabited since the fourth millennium BCE, but reached its zenith in the early second millennium BCE (Middle Bronze Age) as one of the Aegean's most important ports. Trading links were established by this time with Cyprus, Anatolia, Syria, and Egypt. The depiction in frescoes of exotic animals such as lions, antelopes, and wild cats suggests that the residents of Akrotiri traveled far, or played host to travelers from exotic locations. At the time of its destruction, the port city would have had thousands of residents.

The site was identified in the late nineteenth century; however, formal excavations were not commenced until 1967 by Professor Spyridon Marinatos. Walking over the site, Marinatos noted that the ground had subsided in places. He realized that those depressions marked where roofs had collapsed under the weight of the tons of ash and pumice that had hidden the city for around 3,500 years. Unfortunately, seven years later Marinatos was killed in a fall at the site.

FROZEN IN TIME
The absence of human remains and valuable objects shows us that the residents of Akrotiri were warned of the coming eruption, probably by a series of severe earthquakes. They fled the town, taking with them their livestock and most valued possessions.

Their sophisticated engineering and artistic skills are eloquently displayed in the extraordinarily well-preserved streets and buildings of their abandoned city. A network of parallel water pipes suggests that the residents of Akrotiri had access to running hot and cold water in their homes. The hot water is likely to have come from springs heated naturally by volcanic processes. Clay pipes carried household waste into stone-lined sewers that ran underneath cobbled streets.

The two-storied "West House" is most impressive. It contained a kitchen, storerooms, and a mill on the lower level. Loom weights found on the first floor indicate weaving activity. The walls of the upper story were adorned with truly beautiful frescoes, including the magnificent "Flotilla Miniature Frieze," which depicts a fleet traveling between ports. The landing-place of the ships is identifiable as the harbor of Akrotiri from its distinctive rocky landscape and multistoried streetscape. Another frieze shows women gathering crocus stamens for saffron, which is still harvested today on the island.

The protective cover of volcanic debris has preserved the outlines of many perished objects. These hollows have allowed archaeologists to take plaster casts of an ornately carved wooden table, beds, and chairs. It has also saved many multistoried buildings from collapse, with some preserved to a height of 26 ft (8 m).

Byblos, Lebanon

LEBANON
Byblos
Beirut

The Lebanese city of Byblos (modern Jbeil, or Gebal in the Old Testament) is claimed by some to be the oldest city in the world. It was an important commercial port from around 3000 BCE to CE 1, but it is best known for its connection to the first alphabet.

ROMAN INFLUENCES
This photograph shows a portico of the rebuilt Roman theater at Byblos. In the first century BCE, the Romans under Pompey took control of Byblos, ruling it from 64 BCE to CE 395.

The first settlement known at Byblos was a small fishing community dating to the Neolithic (about 5000 BCE). However, the first signs of a substantial town having existed on the site cannot be traced beyond the third millennium BCE.

From approximately 1200 to 600 BCE Byblos was a very significant center for the Phoenicians, who were Semitic Canaanite people of the Levant with very strong links to Egypt. The name "Phoenicia" means "purple" in Greek. It was given by the Greeks because the Phoenicians traded a famous and expensive purple dye extracted from murex shellfish.

The prosperity and coastal position of Byblos made centuries of foreign influence and exploitation inevitable. Following the decline of the Phoenicians, Byblos was controlled by Persians, Greeks, the Roman and Byzantine Empires, Arabs, and then Christians when the city fell to Crusader invaders in 1104. Its scale was subsequently diminished, but it remains occupied today.

The earliest example of Phoenician monumental architecture comes from Byblos. The Temple of

Resheph, dedicated to Baalat-Gebal, the city's goddess, was constructed around 2800 BCE, at about the same time that monumental architecture started to appear in Egypt. Byblos and Egypt already had very strong ties at this time. An inscription from the Fourth Dynasty, dating to the reign of the Pharaoh Sneferu (2613–2589 BCE), records that 40 ships laden with Lebanese cedar were sent from Byblos to Egypt. Much later, the Greek philosopher and historian Plutarch retold a myth about the Egyptian goddess Isis visiting Byblos to reclaim the body of her husband-brother Osiris.

A CHALLENGING DIG
The earliest excavators of Byblos were faced with huge challenges. Systematic looting over many centuries had greatly disturbed the site: Crusaders had reused massive blocks of stone from Roman levels in the construction of their castle, damaging other archaeological strata as they moved them. Adding to this confusion, modern residents of Byblos had not only looted stone for their own houses but had conducted clandestine digs in search of valuable artifacts that they could then sell to

THE SARCOPHAGUS OF KING AHIRAM

The oldest discovered complete inscription in the Phoenician alphabet was found at Byblos, engraved on the lid of the sarcophagus of King Ahiram, who was buried by his son Ithobaal. Dating to around 1000 BCE, the inscription is made in an early version of the Phoenician alphabet. The letters spell out a curse against anyone who would disturb the coffin, which was nonetheless taken from its tomb-chamber in 1924, and is today the centerpiece of the collections of the National Museum of Beirut. The alphabet is an early version of the one transmitted to the Greeks. The date of its transmission and adaptation to the Greek language is disputed.

This detail from the bas-relief on the lid of King Ahiram's sarcophagus depicts Phoenicians making offerings to the king.

antiquities dealers. The houses of these villagers were themselves a significant impediment to archaeological excavation, and in 1930 the Lebanese government funded a complete relocation of the village to allow archaeologists easier access to the ancient city.

Nothing was allowed to get in the way of the excavations starting at Byblos in 1921. Not only was the modern village eventually razed but Roman ruins that covered the ancient city were removed and painstakingly reconstructed away from the site. A Roman theater was relocated to a spectacular position overlooking the sea after being moved from its original location (see page 155). Many of these later ruins had already fallen victim to Crusaders, who selected the finest stones and columns from Roman temples for building their castle. The theater today is only one-third of its original size.

BOOKS AND WRITING

The name of Byblos is derived from the Greek word for papyrus (βύβλος, or Bublos). Raw papyrus was imported from Egypt, and exported from Byblos after being processed into scrolls. The word "Bible" derives from the city's name. The city was known by this name from the start of the Iron Age, around 1200 BCE.

The important papyrus trade between Egypt and Greece passed through Phoenician intermediaries at Byblos until around 700 BCE, when a direct trade relationship was established. In exchange for the raw papyrus, Byblos sent its prized cedar to Egypt, where traces have been found in the pyramids.

Papyrus was used by the Greeks as paper after approximately 800 BCE, when they had adopted the Phoenician alphabet, but before this they may have used ropes of papyrus fibers. In *The Odyssey*, Homer refers to a ship's cable made of papyrus.

The antiquarian writer Philo of Byblos (who lived from approximately CE 64 to 141) claims that his city is the oldest in the world, and tells us it was where the Egyptian god Thoth invented writing. The first evidence of writing at Byblos takes the form of an alphabet comprising 22 letters that dates to around 1200 BCE. This alphabet was adopted by the Greeks, and they proceeded to spread it further. Writing had been known throughout the Near East since the fourth millennium BCE in the form of hieroglyphic and cuneiform script; however, the easily understood Phoenician alphabet introduced a new means of communication that was accessible to people other than highly educated scribes.

OUT OF THE ASHES

The Temple of Resheph, burned and rebuilt, is today called the Temple of the Obelisks. Egyptian hieroglyphs were engraved on one of the obelisks erected in honor of the goddess Baalat-Gebal. More than a thousand offerings have been uncovered here, including faience cats, hippopotami, dwarfs, and gold-leafed human figures.

Mycenae, Greece

Heinrich Schliemann's effort to prove the reality of myth has sometimes overshadowed the genuine importance of Mycenae (Mykenai) in the Late Bronze Age Aegean world. His spectacular finds of gold do not prove Homer's legends, but they do confirm the early importance of a city that came to dominate the Aegean.

"MASK OF AGAMEMNON"

We now know that the gold mask Heinrich Schliemann found in Tomb V at Mycenae could not be Agamemnon's mask. Schliemann's golden finds from this ancient city elevated him to the status of "Father of Mycenaen Archaeology."

ACROPOLIS RUINS

In this photograph of the acropolis remains at Mycenae, we can see the ramparts of the city of the Atridae (the "sons of Atreus," who are Agamemnon and Menelaus). The acropolis sits atop a rocky hill.

Mycenae was inhabited as early as 3500 BCE in the Neolithic period. However, building activity in the Middle Bronze Age almost completely removed earlier traces of settlement. The first graves appear around 1800 BCE, and by around 1600 BCE these contained spectacular inlaid daggers, swords, and other weaponry.

Mycenae was such an important center of Greek civilization in the period 1600–1100 BCE that the era is now known as Mycenaean throughout the Aegean. At its peak, its political and economic power extended as far as Athens to the north and Crete to the south.

This ancient city was one of the few Greek centers that rose to prominence during the early second millennium BCE. The abundance of gold, jewelry, weapons, and imported luxuries found in the elite burials of these cities suggests aristocratic warrior classes had risen suddenly from previously egalitarian farming communities.

In the twelfth century BCE a sudden destructive collapse of cities throughout the Mediterranean area saw Mycenae's dominance come to an end. Scholars debate the causes of the end of this period, but it is often attributed to an invasion by the so-called "Sea Peoples" whose identity remains a mystery.

A WALL BUILT BY GIANTS

The spectacular wall of enormous stone blocks around the acropolis was probably built around 1400 BCE. Walls of this type are known as "cyclopean" because later Greeks imagined that they could only have been built by the mythical Cyclopes (Kyklops), a race of giants with an eye in the middle of their forehead.

The most important building within the walls is the palatial complex, which probably had both royal and religious functions. There are other significant public buildings nearby, while workshops as well as houses were constructed outside the acropolis wall. Prominent officials and members of the royal family possibly lived in the palatial complex, with their everyday needs met by the farmers and artisans who worked outside the walls.

THE "MASK OF AGAMEMNON"

"I have gazed upon the face of Agamemnon," wrote Heinrich Schliemann in a telegraph to the king of Greece after opening a spectacular shaft grave. Agamemnon was the legendary king who led the Greek assault on Troy from his kingdom at Mycenae.

The mask that prompted Schliemann's telegraph in 1876 is the most famous artifact recovered from Mycenae. It is still known as the "Mask of Agamemnon" despite now being known to be about three centuries older than the king's supposed reign. The mask was, in fact, one of five masks found in Mycenaean graves, but it is stylistically so different from the others that some scholars still question whether it might be a forgery.

Troy, Turkey

The legend of the Trojan War captured imaginations long before Homer wrote of it in *The Iliad* in the eighth century BCE. Scholars are divided about the historical reality of the war, and whether the site so famously excavated by Heinrich Schliemann is the city of Troy (Troia) known from myth.

The Turkish site that has been identified as Troy is at the modern town of Hisarlik, close to the northwestern coast. It has been connected with Troy since at least the eighth century BCE; however, it is unclear whether it had this name before its associations with the legends.

Ancient Greek sources reported the war as historical, and placed it between 1193 and 1183 BCE. Alexander the Great is said to have made sacrifices at tombs reputedly holding the remains of the Greek war heroes Achilles (Akhilles) and Patroclus (Patroklos) when he visited Anatolia in the fourth century BCE.

Archaeologists today debate the historical reality of the Trojan War. Homer's *The Iliad* was composed around 450 years after the war was said to have been fought, and there is no firm evidence to link Hisarlik with this late account.

NINE CITIES OF TROY

The site was excavated in the 1870s by the German archaeologist Heinrich Schliemann when scientific archaeology was in its infancy. He assumed Homer's Troy would be found at the oldest phase of occupation, and in his enthusiasm to uncover it he destroyed centuries of evidence from the archaeological record. Unfortunately, he dug straight through the level that would have been contemporary with the proposed date of the Trojan War.

There are nine distinct archaeological layers at Troy, dating from the Neolithic (around 3600 BCE) through to around 100 BCE in the Hellenistic period. The twelfth-century BCE level, known as Troy VIIa, contains the city that is commonly associated with the Trojan War, and thought to be described in Homer's *The Iliad*. Tragically, Schliemann largely destroyed this level on his way to uncovering the spectacular remains of Troy II.

Troy VIIa has the appearance of a war-torn city. It was violently destroyed—there is extensive evidence of burning, and human remains were found near bronze arrowheads in the streets. However, there is no concrete evidence to connect this destruction with the Greek campaign of Homer's *The Iliad*.

THE GOLD OF TROY

Schliemann uncovered a magnificent gold hoard, which he named the "Treasure of Priam." It was

unfortunately around 1,000 years too old to be connected to the legend. Some scholars doubt that this spectacular collection of weapons, vessels, and jewelry belonged to the Early Bronze Age level in which it was supposedly found. The Mycenaean character of the workmanship has even led to accusations that Schliemann had the treasure manufactured by local goldsmiths to support his identification of Troy. The treasure remains missing after vanishing from Berlin in 1945.

ROMAN THEATER AT TROY
The Odeon of Troy (a theater made of stone) is part of the ninth and most recently excavated city. Troy IX is the first Roman Troy; the Roman emperors referred to it as *Novum ilium* (the new Troy).

Uluburun Shipwreck, Turkey

In 1984, the challenging underwater excavation of a cedar-hulled shipwreck dating to around 1300 BCE commenced off the southwestern coast of Turkey at Uluburun. After ten years, and 6,613 hours working on the sea floor, archaeologists uncovered a spectacular lost cargo that vastly increased our knowledge of Bronze Age trade.

TREASURES FROM THE DEEP
A diver from the Bodrum Museum of Underwater Archaeology removes a Cypriot juglet from a large storage jar (pithos) aboard the wreck. He and his codiver (the director of the excavation) found 18 pieces of pottery in the pithos.

The Uluburun (Ulu Burun) shipwreck provides direct evidence of maritime trade in copper, tin, and other goods. The cause of the shipwreck is unknown, but it foundered along a rocky part of the Turkish coast that is still perilous for seafarers. The 50 ft (15 m) long wreck was discovered approximately 165 ft (50 m) below the surface by a local sponge diver.

The ship's diverse cargo offers few clues about the journey's origin and destination. There were objects from at least seven different cultures on board: Mycenaean, Canaanite, Cypriot, Egyptian, Kassite, Nubian, and Assyrian. The style of the ship's 24 stone anchors, each weighing as much as 465 lb (210 kg), has led some scholars to suggest that the ship is Syro-Palestinian in origin.

A RICH CARGO

The Uluburun ship sank with around 6.6 tons (6 tonnes) of Cypriot copper on board, mostly in the form of "oxhide ingots," named for their distinctive shape. Valuable ingots of tin were also transported on the ship, presumably intended to be alloyed with the copper to form bronze.

Around 150 ceramic jars of a style originating in the Levant were found to contain varied goods. Some held glass beads, olives, or pomegranates, but most contained terebinth resin, extracted from a type of pistachio tree.

CYPRIOT CERAMICS
These pottery pieces of Cypriot origin were found in one of the immense ceramic storage jars aboard the wreck. Among the bowls and juglets are some oil lamps with pinched nozzles to hold their wicks.

The ancient use of this resin is debated; however, today this precious substance is used as a base for expensive perfumes and in the making of incense.

A large collection of thick glass disks in various shades of blue are the earliest glass ingots yet discovered. Glass is likely to have been a very expensive commodity, possibly restricted to royalty.

The remainder of the cargo included bronze weapons and tools, ivory, tortoise shells,

cylinder seals, scarabs, and ostrich eggshells. Thousands of beads made from amber, agate, carnelian, gold, and other materials were also recovered. Fine gold and silver jewelry was on board, some of it broken or cut up for use as scrap.

LIFE ON BOARD

The fate of the ship's crew is unknown, but personal possessions and supplies found on board give us a glimpse into their lives on this fateful voyage. Different types of nuts, olives, grapes, wine, pomegranates, spices, and grains have been identified from traces inside storage vessels. These may have been consumed by the crew and supplemented by fish caught with the fishing hooks and nets that were also discovered. Bronze razors and oil lamps with blackened nozzles give us an insight into the shipboard routines of the seafarers who most likely perished when the ship and its cargo were lost.

Athenian Agora, Greece

The Athenian Agora was the political, economic, judicial, and social heart of the ancient city. The rise of Athens as a powerful city-state, and her defeats at the swords of various foreign invaders, are captured in the rich archaeological record of this public square in the center of town.

RUNNING WARRIOR
This is a section of the beautifully carved Marathon Stele, which was discovered at the Temple of Hephaestus. The Doric temple was designed by the architect Ictinos, and depicts the exploits of Theseus, the legendary king of Athens, in its friezes and metopes (carved panels).

The word "agora" translates roughly to "marketplace," but this does not convey the importance of the precinct to city life; nor does it reveal the range of activities that were undertaken there. People assembled in the Agora for athletics contests, parades, theater, commerce, politics, as well as judicial activity.

Permanent buildings were constructed long after the Agora had already become a place of public assembly and financial activity. The erection of these buildings simply formalized the activities that were already present, and eventually led to the Agora becoming the focal point of the Greek city.

There is evidence of building on the site of the Agora from as early as around 3000 BCE, but it was only made into a formal public space with the reforms of Solon in the sixth century BCE, when Athens became democratically organized. Around 500 BCE the boundaries of the Agora were marked with inscribed stones.

Early excavations were carried out by the Greek Archaeological Society in 1859. From 1931, The American School of Classical Studies at Athens has been conducting annual excavations. Over this time, more than 400 modern buildings have been demolished to access the ancient site.

A RELIGIOUS CENTER

Today the most prominent building on the site is the Temple of Hephaestus (Hephaistos), known as the "Theseion." This temple was dedicated to Hephaestus, god of fire and metalworking, and Athena, goddess of wisdom and the arts. Construction of the temple started in 449 BCE. It was the religious focal point of the Agora, but there were also many small altars and sanctuaries.

At the center of the Agora was the "Altar of the Twelve Gods," dedicated to the 12 central Greek gods. It was the point from which other cities measured their distance from Athens.

DECLINE AND RECOVERY

The Athenian Agora was substantially damaged in the Persian sack of 480 BCE, but buildings were quickly repaired. Many new structures were erected immediately following the Persian devastation, but the Agora only reached its familiar rectangular shape in the second century BCE.

In 86 BCE an invasion led by the Roman general Lucius Cornelius Sulla again resulted in significant destruction. The Agora was finally deserted in CE 267 following a raid by Herulian Goths. Afterward, stones were taken from the buildings of the Agora to construct the Valerian Wall, which encircled the Acropolis and Agora. The area was residential during Byzantine and later periods, when the Temple of Hephaestus was converted into a Christian church.

AGORA REMAINS
Ruins of the Athenian Agora are seen in the foreground of this photograph. Recent excavations at Section BZ of the Agora site have revealed a series of hydraulic installations, including a closed, round terracotta pipeline dating to the fourth or fifth century CE.

Delphi, Greece

GREECE

Delphi

Athens

Delphi has had strong cultic connections since it was first inhabited around 1400 BCE. Originally it was a seat of worship for Gaia (Gaea), the Earth goddess. A temple to the god Apollo was constructed in Classical times. Most famously, it is the site where the Delphic Oracle shared her wisdom.

MAN OR GOD?

This life-size ivory head with gold headdress dates to the sixth century BCE. Many scholars believe it to be the head of the god Apollo because a matching female ivory head was also found at Delphi. The female is presumed to be his sister, the goddess Artemis.

SANCTUARY RUINS

Here we can see the sanctuary of Athena Pronaia, and the Tholos. Scholars believe that the circular building, the Tholos, was built at the center of the sanctuary between 380 and 360 BCE.

The name Delphi derives from the Greek word meaning "womb," and is probably connected to early worship of Gaia at the site. There is evidence of a small village in the area from around 1400 BCE that was destroyed around 1100 BCE at the end of the Mycenaean period. The settlement that rose from the ruins grew in importance from the eighth century BCE with the establishment of the cult of Apollo. Although the village itself remained small, the sanctuary of Apollo and the Delphic Oracle ensured the site's fame throughout the Greek world. It remained the center of Greek religion until the fourth century BCE.

THE ORACLE AT DELPHI

Ancient Greeks consulted the Oracle at Delphi before they embarked on war, or commenced any other major undertaking. She did not predict the future, but dispensed wisdom about how the Greeks might best proceed in order to avoid failure. In reality, the Oracle had enormous political and social influence, and was instrumental in determining strategies for many military campaigns.

When Greeks established the first overseas colonies in the eighth century BCE, they consulted the Oracle to determine the best sites. They also asked her who should lead the new settlements.

The Oracle was a priestess known as the Pythia, through whom Apollo spoke. The Pythia was always a female more than 50 years of age, and although she was not required to be a virgin, she was obliged to abandon her husband and children after assuming the position. With the growing popularity of the Oracle there were eventually three appointed Pythias at the city of Delphi.

Greeks built handsome treasuries at Delphi to hold votive offerings that commemorated military victories and acknowledged the role of the Oracle in securing them. The best known of these is the heavily restored "Treasury of Athens," which was constructed after the victory at the Battle of Marathon in 490 BCE.

The spectacular riches left as votive offerings in the sanctuaries attracted the attention of numerous invaders and looters. Gauls unsuccessfully attempted to invade in 259 BCE; the Roman general Sulla led an army against Delphi in 86 BCE; the Maidoi ("barbarians" from Thrace) seized offerings in 83 BCE; and the Roman Emperor Nero is said to have stolen 500 statues in 67 BCE. Constantine took many of Delphi's riches to his new capital Constantinople, and soon afterward, by the decree of Emperor Theodosius I in CE 394, the cult of Apollo was abandoned and the sanctuary slipped into ruin.

Olympia, Greece

TEMPLE OF ZEUS
The now-ruined temple was built by Libon, a local architect, of limestone coated with a fine white stucco. The 39 mostly intact lion's heads found at the temple are of varying styles and material.

Today Olympia is most famous as the site of the Olympic Games in Classical times, but to the Greeks it was an important religious and cultural center. It was home to a colossal ivory and gold statue of Zeus that was one of the Seven Wonders of the Ancient World.

Olympia is one of the most important sanctuaries of Ancient Greece. It has been inhabited since the third millennium BCE, but did not become a religious center until Mycenaean times (around 1600–1100 BCE). Votive offerings were left at open-air altars, or hung in trees until the first buildings were erected during the Geometric period (around 900–700 BCE).

Although Zeus was the god of the sanctuary, there was no temple dedicated to him until 457 BCE. Construction of the Temple of Zeus marks the zenith of the life of the sanctuary, and the time when the Olympic Games were most successful. The first stadium was built shortly after the founding of the Temple of Zeus, and from the third century BCE onward the focus at Olympia shifted from religion to athletic competition.

THE WORKSHOP OF PHEIDIAS
Archaeologists were excited to find the remains of a fifth-century BCE sculptor's workshop under a much later Christian basilica. They identified the site as the workshop of Pheidias (Phidias), the sculptor who crafted the monumental gold and ivory statue of Zeus that stood in the temple. The dimensions of the workshop and the temple's inner chamber were almost identical—possibly so the colossal statue could be accommodated during construction.

Among the finds were molds for casting the delicate gold drapery of the statue, tools for carving ivory and gold, and actual fragments of ivory. For many scholars, a modest jug bearing the simple Greek inscription "I belong to Pheidias" confirms this workshop belonged to the famous sculptor.

THE END OF THE SANCTUARY
The decline of the Temple of Zeus is marked by an invasion of Herulian Goths in CE 267. To keep these invaders from the temple, the authorities of the sanctuary destroyed other buildings in the precinct and used the rubble to construct a 12-ft (4-m) high wall around the perimeter. They successfully protected the statue of Zeus from the Goths, but in CE 395, during the reign of Theodosius I, the sculpture was finally carried away to Constantinople, where it was eventually destroyed.

The emperor Theodosius II was responsible for the burning of the sanctuary through his decree of CE 426 that ordered the destruction of all pagan temples. In the sixth century CE a powerful earthquake destroyed what survived this assault, and the site was slowly covered with silt from two nearby rivers. French archaeologists started to uncover Olympia in 1829; however, ongoing excavations were not undertaken until the German Archaeological Institute started regular campaigns in 1875.

The Ancient Olympic Games

The ancient Olympic Games were hosted at Olympia in the Peloponnesian region of Greece. Tradition states the first games were held in 776 BCE. This date is based on a list of Olympic victors composed by Hippias of Elis in the fifth century BCE, but recent scholarship throws its accuracy into question.

Historical sources that describe the earliest games were all composed centuries later. Archaeological evidence suggests a date later than 776 BCE for the start of the competition. A number of wells at Olympia that are thought to have provided water for athletes and spectators cannot be dated earlier than the sixth century BCE. However, scholars believe that these wells were possibly dug at a time when the games had gained greater popularity.

There is evidence for funeral games elsewhere in Greece from as early as the thirteenth century BCE, but there is no archaeological evidence that the games at Olympia were instituted as early as this. They had certainly become popular by the fifth century BCE—it has been calculated that the stadium at Olympia could hold up to 40,000 spectators.

The final ancient Olympic Games were held at Olympia in CE 394, when they were banned by the

Christian emperor Theodosius I. They were revived as the modern Olympics in Athens in 1896.

A LIMITED PROGRAM

The earliest games are described by the ancient historians as comprising a single event—the *stadion* foot race that was contested over a track about 625 ft (190 m) long. According to Hippias, the first winner of this race was Koroibos Elis, a cook. Eventually, more diverse sports were introduced, including wrestling, boxing, and chariot racing. The marathon was never run in the ancient games. Many scholars dispute the simple origins of the games, and argue on the basis of evidence of early statuettes of charioteers at Olympia that the competition always incorporated a diverse range of sports.

From the fifth century CE some writers claim the games of 776 BCE were a revival, rather than the start of the competition, but there is no contemporary support for this assertion. Whether or not the games had an earlier history, it is beyond dispute that many of the sports that formed part of their program were ancient. A fresco from Akrotiri, dating from before 1500 BCE, shows two boys boxing, and there is evidence from the same time of wrestling on Crete.

The evidence of Minoan and Mycenaean sites ends in approximately 1100 BCE. After this time the archaeological evidence of the Olympic Games helps us reconstruct how athletic competition might have

THEODOSIUS I

This is part of a relief on the obelisk of Theodosius I. Here we see the emperor and his courtiers awarding a prize to the winner of a chariot race. This Christian Byzantine emperor banned the Olympic Games because they were pagan. However, chariot racing became enormously popular during the early Byzantine period.

developed in the approximately 300 years that separate the end of the Mycenaean era from the Greek world of Olympia and Delphi.

SPORT AND RELIGION

Athletic competition was not the only focus of the ancient Olympic Games—they were also important religious occasions, and allowed men from throughout the Greek world to gather for social and political interaction.

The ancient games were strongly connected to religion, and particularly to funerary rites. However, at Olympia there is a clear separation between the religious sanctuary of Zeus and the athletic precinct of the site.

Homer does mention that victors in the games were presented with bronze tripods, and many examples of these have been excavated at Olympia in the area of the stadium that date from as early as 1000 BCE. However, some scholars argue that the tripods were votive offerings associated with the sanctuary rather than athletic prizes.

ATHLETIC NUDITY

It was common for Olympic athletes to compete naked. Nudity was so closely connected to athletic pursuits that the word gymnasium derives from the Greek word *gymnos*, meaning naked. The reasons for athletic nudity are not fully understood, but suggestions include safety and aesthetics. Ancient sources describe how an early athlete lost his loincloth during a race and found running without it much easier. Other athletes soon saw his advantage and the tradition was born. Modern scholars suggest that nudity had a cultic explanation, and was closely connected to the religious aspect of the games. Athletes are known to have smeared oil over their bodies from a jar called an *aryballos* (pictured) and later removed it with a bronze spatula called a *strigil*. For wrestlers this may have served to make the skin too slippery to be gripped by opponents. Other athletes may simply have wished to enhance their appearance.

The Parthenon, Greece

The Parthenon is one of the ancient world's most recognizable buildings. It had enormous religious significance to Classical Greece, but is as famous today for its later history. This fifth-century BCE temple towers over Athens from the imposing Acropolis, and maintains its majesty despite centuries of looting and destruction.

AN ANCIENT MARVEL

The majestic Parthenon sits on what some refer to as the "Sacred Rock" of Athens. The earliest evidence of human habitation on the Acropolis dates to the Neolithic period. The Athens Acropolis inspired the remodelers of the acropolis at Pergamon in Turkey.

THE GODDESS ATHENA

The famous ivory and gold statue of Athena by Pheidias (Phidias) was displayed inside the Parthenon. This second-century CE marble copy is currently held in the National Archaeological Museum of Athens.

Construction of the Parthenon was initiated by the Athenian statesman Pericles (Perikles) to replace an earlier temple to Athena (Athene) that was destroyed by Persians in 480 BCE. Work started in 447 BCE, but the temple was not fully built and decorated until 432 BCE. It is thought to have contained more than 13,000 blocks of marble. Today these are white, but scholars believe some blocks may originally have been painted in vivid colors.

It is likely that the name of the Parthenon derives from a huge ivory and gold statue of Athena Parthenos (the virgin) displayed inside. This statue was taken to Constantinople in the fifth century CE, and later destroyed, possibly by thirteenth-century Crusaders.

The Parthenon was used as a treasury, where expensive gifts to the gods were left in thanksgiving by wealthy worshippers.

The history of the Parthenon did not end with the Classical period. It was converted into a Christian church around CE 600, and then into a mosque from 1460 to 1833 when Greece was part of the Ottoman Empire. The Parthenon was almost destroyed in 1687 when invading Venetians bombarded a Turkish ammunition store inside. The sculptures that survived this catastrophe were removed by Lord Elgin between 1801 and 1805 and taken to the British Museum, where they remain on display. The return of the so-called "Elgin Marbles" to Greece remains a controversial issue.

Today, sculptures that remain on site are threatened by acid rain that has already caused some irreversible damage. Many have been removed to the safety of Greek museums and replaced with resin casts.

GODS AND HEROES

Greek myths and legends are retold in the 92 carved panels known as metopes that encircle the Parthenon. On the east side of the building, above the main entrance, Olympic gods and giants battle each other in the so-called "gigantomachy," and the west shows Athenian men in battle with fierce Amazon women. The poorly preserved metopes of the south show Lapiths (a legendary race of early Greeks) battling Centaurs (mythical half-man, half-horse creatures). The barely surviving north metopes appear to present narrative scenes from the Trojan War.

The 525-ft (160-m) long frieze depicts the important religious Panathenaeic Procession. It shows gods, animals, and approximately 360 people. The temple pediments portray two mythological scenes from the life of Athena: the east shows her unusual birth from the head of Zeus, and the west depicts a battle between Athena and Poseidon (Neptune).

Pergamon, Turkey

Pergamon (Pergamum) was the site of one of the world's first hospitals and medical schools. For centuries ailing pilgrims came to be treated by doctors whose inspiration came from Asclepius (Asklepios, Aesculapius), the god of healing. The offerings they left enriched the city—an enduring bastion of Greek culture in Asia Minor.

The ancient city of Pergamon is situated in northwestern Turkey near the modern town of Bergama. It was an important city during the Hellenistic period (323–146 BCE) under the Attalids, whose dynasty lasted from 282 BCE to 129 BCE. The Attalids remodeled Pergamon's acropolis on the acropolis in Athens. The final ruler of the Attalid dynasty, Attalus III, died without an heir, and bequeathed Pergamon to the Romans to prevent a potentially dangerous power vacuum.

The Roman administration did not change the overwhelmingly Hellenistic character of the city, but its independence was effectively gone. Pergamon, along with other cities that formed part of the legacy of Attalus III, was politically reorganized into the Roman province of Asia.

THE ASCLEPION

Outside the city there was a sanctuary of the healer god Asclepius that was established in the fourth century BCE. Associated with this was a hospital and medical school, known as the Asclepion. Pilgrims traveled great distances to bathe in the sanctuary's spring and receive the god's wisdom about how to heal their afflictions. Archaeologists have found many offerings at the sanctuary in the form of terracotta body parts. These probably represent the parts of the body that Asclepius was called on to heal. The spring continued to attract ailing pilgrims up to the second century CE, including Roman emperors such as Hadrian, Marcus Aurelius, and Caracalla.

After the great Egyptian port city of Alexandria, Pergamon boasted the most important library of the ancient world. It is thought to have contained approximately 200,000 scrolls. With the end of papyrus exports from Egypt, the scribes of Pergamon created a new type of paper from fine calf skin— *pergaminus*, or what would later become known as parchment. Income from agriculture, textiles, and silver mining supplemented wealth generated by the parchment trade.

Pergamon is home to a spectacular theater that could seat 15,000 people. The theater's form takes advantage of the natural mountainous landscape. It was built in the mid third century BCE, but was renovated and enlarged during the second century BCE.

A FITTING RESTING PLACE

Pergamon was first excavated in 1878 after the German Carl Humann uncovered part of a beautiful frieze while directing construction of a new railway. The Turkish government granted him permission to conduct excavations for the Berlin Museum. Humann's greatest discovery was the spectacular "Pergamon Altar," which is displayed today in Berlin's Pergamon Museum. Such was Humann's passion for the site that he was buried near the place of the altar's discovery.

GOD OF HEALING

This is a Roman copy of a marble bust of Asclepius, the Greco-Roman god of healing. Legend had it that Asclepius cured the sick in their dreams. This led to a common practice of sleeping in his temples.

ANCIENT ENTERTAINMENT

Pergamon's impressive theater is the steepest Hellenistic theater in the world. Dramas at the theater were performed on a portable wooden stage, which was stored in the lower levels of the terrace.

Ephesus, Turkey

The site of Ephesus (Ephesos) on the western coast of Turkey is renowned as the site of the Temple of Artemis, one of the Seven Wonders of the Ancient World. However, the site's enduring importance for Christians has ensured its ongoing fame long after the destruction of the ancient temple.

LIBRARY OF CELSUS

This spectacular construction faces east to allow users of the library to take full advantage of the morning sunlight. The facade was restored and rebuilt in the 1970s; it had collapsed during an earthquake in the tenth century CE.

Ephesus was officially founded by Greek colonists from Athens, but Mycenaean pottery found on the site attests to much earlier Greek habitation, and there is evidence of settlement on the site pre-dating Greek arrival by more than 3,000 years. Some scholars believe Ephesus is the Hellenized name of Apasa, the capital of the Arzawa kingdom that appears in Hittite historical sources (in the second millenium BCE the Hittites of Anatolia created a vast empire that covered northern Syria and Anatolia). By the first century CE Ephesus might have had as many as 500,000 residents, making it one of the largest cities in the world.

The city was sacked by Goths in CE 263, and Arabs in the eighth century CE. It suffered further damage at the hands of Seljuk Turks in 1090, but by this time the harbor on which it was situated had filled with silt, and the once magnificent city was reduced to the size of a village. This ancient city is located near the modern town of Selcuk.

Ephesus is an important site for Christians. It is where the Apostle Paul is said to have resided when he wrote Corinthians I, and it is also claimed that he lived at Ephesus and died there at the end of the first century CE. A belief that the Virgin Mary spent her last days at Ephesus continues to attract pilgrims.

CELSUS'S LIBRARY

The spectacular two-storied "Celsus's library" was built in the second century CE, and at one time held 12,000 scrolls. It was constructed as a tomb for the Roman governor Celsus, whose grave is located under the ground floor. The four statues in the facade symbolize the four virtues of the deceased: Sophia (wisdom), Arete (character), Ennoia (judgment), and Episteme (knowledge).

THE TEMPLE OF ARTEMIS

From 1863 to 1874 the English railway engineer John Turtle Wood was employed by the British Museum to direct the excavation of the Temple of Artemis (Diana) at Ephesus. This temple, also known as the Artemision, was well known through historical sources as one of the Seven Wonders of the Ancient World.

He found that the remains of this once-spectacular building now lay about 10 ft (3 m) below water, and looting of its marble for building materials over centuries had left few remains. Another short excavation season from 1904 to 1905 was conducted on behalf of the British Museum, this time by David George Hogarth. From 1898 the Austrian Archaeological Institute led regular excavation seasons. These digs continue today.

The Greek traveler Pausanias claimed the Artemision was the largest building of the ancient world. It was built by the Lydian King Croesus in the sixth century BCE, but the remains excavated by Wood and Hogarth date to the late fourth century BCE, when a second temple was rebuilt on the site. Ancient sources describe how a man called Herostratus burned the first temple in an attempt to etch his name in history. The arson is said to have occurred on the night of Alexander the Great's birth in 356 BCE. The writer Plutarch explains that Artemis was too occupied with celebrating this historic event to intervene and save her temple.

The sixth-century temple was built from huge blocks of marble that were transported from a quarry inland near Izmir. These blocks were laid on an ash foundation to stabilize the marshy ground. Extraordinarily, nearly all the roof tiles were made of marble—making a spectacular but extremely heavy roof.

Today only one column of the temple remains on site; the rest have been removed to the British Museum. The bronze statues in the temple were sculpted by some of the most important artists of the day, including Pheidias, who oversaw work on the Parthenon marbles, and sculpted the colossal ivory and gold statue of Zeus at Olympia. The temple primarily had a religious function, but it was also an important marketplace. Pilgrims left rich offerings to Artemis at the temple. Archaeologists have learned that these came from as far away as India.

The temple was destroyed in the fifth century CE; some of its materials were reused to build the nearby Basilica of St. John in the following century.

WOMAN OF GOLD

This gold statue was found in the Temple of Artemis. It dates to the fifth century BCE and was probably one of the numerous offerings left at the temple by pilgrims from far and wide. Also among the gifts were gold and ivory statuettes of Artemis as well as various items of precious jewelry.

THE EPHESIAN ARTEMIS

The Temple of Artemis contained a distinctive cult statue known as the Ephesian Artemis. This was characterized by many breasts that probably symbolized fertility. Artemis was the virgin huntress, and the twin sister of Apollo. The most famous manifestation of the many-breasted goddess dates from Roman times but imitates earlier cult figures. (At Ephesus several amber pendants have been discovered that date to the eighth century BCE; these may have been pectoral attachments of an earlier cult figure.) The Artemis image is likely to be older even than the Hellenistic period, and may have originally represented a different goddess. The enclosure of the goddess's legs in a pillar known as a term is a Near Eastern tradition, and points to the non-Greek origins of the image. She appears on coins minted at Ephesus as well as statues of different sizes.

This intricate marble statue of Artemis is a second-century CE Roman copy of the original cult statue.

Mediterranean Empires

By the last half of the first century BCE, the whole of the Mediterranean Sea and its hinterland lay within the confines of the Roman Empire. This achievement was confidently recognized by many Romans, who referred to the Mediterranean as *mare nostrum*, "our sea."

ALEXANDER IN BATTLE
This section of a Hellenistic marble relief depicts a fearsome Alexander the Great fighting to retain his territory. Dating to the late fourth century BCE, the relief was found at Sidon in modern-day Lebanon.

The development of Roman power in the Mediterranean region emerged in the centuries beforehand often in spectacular fashion, supplanting a number of smaller regional empires in the process. Rome gained its first imperial possessions outside Italy following the victory of Scipio Africanus over Hannibal and the Carthaginians at Zama in North Africa in 201 BCE. Carthage had been the dominant power in the western Mediterranean until its defeat by Rome, at which time Spain came under Roman control. Rome proceeded to establish two provinces in Spain and confined Carthaginian power to North Africa itself.

THE ROMAN EMPIRE EXPANDS

At the same time, Rome also began to intervene in the politics of the eastern Mediterranean empires. This was partly associated with Roman imperialism and partly because some of the major powers in the eastern Mediterranean had taken advantage of Rome's long war with the Carthaginians during the last two decades of the third century BCE. The

ROME AND THE PTOLEMIES

The Ptolemaic Empire of Egypt figured in the complexities of Rome's involvement in the eastern Mediterranean from the early decades of the second century BCE. Egypt had largely remained on good diplomatic terms with the Romans until the fateful alliance between Antony and Cleopatra, which ended in their defeat by Octavian in 31 BCE and the subsequent annexation of Egypt to the Roman Empire.

empires of the eastern Mediterranean comprised a number of Greek (Hellenistic) kingdoms, which emerged after the death of Alexander the Great in 323 BCE. Rome's intervention in the eastern Mediterranean eventually saw it take control of all these kingdoms and empires by 30 BCE.

Rome inflicted a decisive defeat on the Seleucid Empire, which extended from Syria to Babylon, in 190 BCE, curtailing its activities and establishing the mechanism whereby it would intervene on numerous occasions in Seleucid affairs in the future. It did this by backing the interests of the smaller kingdoms of

EXTENT OF THE ROMAN EMPIRE
This map shows just how far Rome's power had expanded by the end of the emperor Trajan's reign in CE 117.

KINGDOM OF NABATAEA

The Urn Tomb is one of three royal tombs carved into the rock face at the capital of Nabataea, Petra (in modern-day Jordan). At the height of Rome's power, the emperor Trajan brought the Nabataeans under Roman control.

Pergamon and Rhodes, which had broken away from the Seleucids in the third century BCE. Whenever the Seleucids threatened these kingdoms, Rome had the pretext to intervene on their behalf. The wealthy and powerful Kingdom of Macedonia came under Roman control in 167 BCE following its defeat by the Roman general Lucius Aemilius Paullus. In 146 BCE Rome finally took control of Carthage itself following the Third Punic War, and in the same year it captured Corinth and southern Greece.

In the middle of the second century BCE a powerful new empire known as the Parthian Empire began to emerge in Iran, eventually taking control of the eastern satrapies of the Seleucid Empire. This, combined with Rome's increasing power in the eastern Mediterranean, marked the beginning of the end for the Seleucid Empire. By the middle of the first century BCE it had been effectively carved up by the Romans, the Parthians, and the smaller kingdoms of Pontus and Armenia based in the area around the Black Sea. The final establishment of Roman domination of the entire Mediterranean came when Octavian (later Augustus) defeated the combined forces of Marc Antony and Cleopatra at Actium before annexing Egypt in 30 BCE.

With the Republic's collapse and the emergence of the imperial system under Augustus and his successors, Rome's domination of the Mediterranean continued and the empire increasingly expanded further north into Europe and also in the Near East. Julius Caesar had famously added much of Gaul to the empire late in the Republican period, and during the reign of the emperor Claudius (CE 41–54) the province of Britannia was added to the empire. The Roman Empire is held to have been at its greatest extent during the emperor Trajan's reign (CE 98–117). Trajan added Dacia (modern Romania and Hungary) to the empire as well as annexing the kingdom of the Nabataeans, with its capital at Petra, to the Roman province of Arabia. Early in the reign of Septimius Severus (CE 193–211), the province of Mesopotamia was established in the area of northern Mesopotamia, and it was probably at this stage that Palmyra was formally incorporated into the province of Syria Phoenice. This took Roman provincial control as far east as it would ever go with part of the province of Mesopotamia located in modern northern Iraq.

THE ROMAN EMPIRE CONTRACTS

The third century CE is seen typically as a period of contraction for the Roman Empire, with large sections of the empire being lost at times to usurpers or foreign invaders. During the final years of the emperor Gallienus (CE 253–268) a great deal of the empire was temporarily out of his control. Almost all of the eastern provinces, including Egypt, had been lost to the revolt of Zenobia of Palmyra while in the north, Gaul and Britain were under the control of the usurper Postumus and his successors in what became known as the Gallic Empire. It was not until the reigns of Aurelian (CE 270–275) and Diocletian (CE 284–305) that a considerable proportion of these territories was returned to the control of the legitimate emperor.

THE EMPEROR CLAUDIUS

This marble bust is currently held in the Museo Capitolino in Rome. During his reign of 13 years, Claudius added the province of Britannia to the already very large Roman Empire.

Tarquinia, Italy

Tarquinia (Tarxuna, Tarquinii in antiquity) is located 47 miles (75 km) northwest of Rome, around 4 miles (6 km) from the Mediterranean coastline. The remains of the ancient city are located on a plateau 2 miles (3 km) to the northeast of the modern town of Tarquinia on the greater part of the Pian di Civita. The closest water source to Tarquinia is the River Marta.

ETRUSCAN PERFUME VASE

This richly colored perfume vase dates to the seventh century BCE. It would probably have belonged to one of the many wealthy citizens of Tarquinia during the time when the city was an important center of trade and commerce.

It seems that Tarquinia was the most important of 12 cities comprising the main urban centers in ancient Etruria, the region to the north of Rome bounded by the Tiber and Arno Rivers. Its inhabitants from the seventh century BCE were the Etruscans, who gave their name to modern Tuscany. Archaeology provides information about the Etruscans' art and lifestyle, and some of their laws and beliefs were described by the later Roman historians; however, their language is still not fully understood. They were great traders and colonists, taking over the Latin town of Rome, whose first Etruscan king was Tarquinius Priscus; he was half-Greek, being the son of a wealthy Corinthian merchant by the name of Demaratus, who is reputed to have come to Tarquinia as a refugee. The Tarquins were the last Roman royal dynasty before the overthrow of Tarquinius Superbus, in 510 BCE. This action resulted in the establishment of the Republic.

A WEALTHY TRADING CENTER

Tarquinia was a city of some significance as early as the seventh century BCE, and its most famous archaeological remains date mostly to the sixth century BCE. Etruria became an important region for the supply of metals including copper, tin, iron, and silver to the Greek and Near Eastern worlds by the seventh century BCE, which is reflected in the story described earlier of the wealthy merchant Demaratus fleeing to Tarquinia from Corinth. The archaeological evidence from Tarquinia shows close links not only with the Greek world, particularly Corinth, but also with Egypt. The cities of Etruria became wealthy and powerful centers of commerce. Tarquinia is thought to have been the most important city in these respects, and it is also considered to have been one of the largest cities in Etruria. The wealth generated at Tarquinia is reflected in the decoration and content of some of the most important tombs to have survived from antiquity.

AN ANCIENT CITY SURROUNDED BY CAPACIOUS CEMETERIES

Excavations carried out at Tarquinia over the past two centuries reveal that there were extensive cemeteries all around this ancient city. The first tomb discovery at Tarquinia was made in 1823, and numerous discoveries continued to be made throughout the nineteenth and twentieth centuries. Pioneering archaeological work performed in the 1950s and 1960s at Tarquinia and other Etruscan sites showed that there were over 2,600 chamber-tombs at Tarquinia, and more have been located since. The most significant Etruscan cemetery at Tarquinia is the Monterozzi cemetery, but many smaller groups of tombs have also been found, particularly to the east of the city.

The best-known tombs from these cemeteries are the painted chamber-tombs that date to the middle of the sixth century BCE. The paintings often depict warriors and other figures including flute players and other musicians as well as dancers and jugglers. The tombs have returned a whole range of important artifacts that show the extraordinary technical and artistic ability of the Etruscans, as well as an array of pottery vessels, large urns, jugs, and bowls that reflect the impact of Greek culture. Numerous metal

PIONEERING ARCHAEOLOGICAL TECHNIQUES

The methods of discovery of the chamber-tombs at Tarquinia and elsewhere in Etruria are of particular interest as they were pioneering and allowed investigation of the tombs with minimal damage. Firstly, aerial photography was used to establish likely locations on the ground under which tombs might be present. Electromagnetometers were then used on the surface in an attempt to detect areas underneath that might represent burial chambers. Finally, exploratory probes through the soil above the chamber-tombs were made as a means of retrieving archaeological samples. These probes were also equipped with small lights and cameras so that pictures of the insides of the tombs could be retrieved. These methods were pioneered by Carlo Lerici at a number of sites beginning in the late 1950s. Initial investigations explored around 20 painted tombs, and many more have been found since. The techniques established by Lerici have since been developed and are now used widely in the field of archaeology.

items have also been discovered, including swords, helmets, fibulae, and lamps. Some items of bronze and gold show intricate metal-working capacity at Tarquinia. In many of the tombs, distinctive pottery urns were discovered; designed to hold the ashes of the owner of the tomb, they reveal that cremation was widely practiced among the Etruscans.

Also found at Tarquinia were extensive burial remains from the culture of the Villanovans, who were the earlier inhabitants and clearly had a considerable impact on the development of Etruscan culture. Despite the growing success of Rome throughout Italy in the fourth century BCE, Tarquinia retained an Etruscan identity. During the Roman period, Etruscan soothsayers were regularly consulted and the most significant non-funerary monument to survive at Tarquinia is a fourth-century BCE temple called the Ara della Regina (The Queen Altar).

PAINTED CHAMBER-TOMB
Inside the Tomb of the Augurs, one of the decorated tombs at Tarquinia, a masked man called Phersu can be seen on the far left dancing; on the right is a man with pointed shoes.

TERRACOTTA HORSES
Dating to the fourth or third century BCE, this statue of two winged horses was found on the steps of the temple Ara della Regina at Tarquinia. The statue is now held in the archaeological museum in the Palazzo Vitelleschi in modern Tarquinia.

Imperial Fora of Rome, Italy

The Imperial Fora in Rome were a central area of Roman political, religious, and legal life for much of the empire's existence. It is important to distinguish between the Imperial Fora and the Roman Forum itself.

ITALY

Imperial Fora — ○ Rome

JULIUS CAESAR

This bust depicts Caesar as a young man. An ambitious Roman general and statesman, Caesar created the first Imperial Forum when he extended the area taken up by the Roman Forum. Julius Caesar was assassinated in 44 BCE.

TRAJAN'S COLUMN

Reliefs on this imposing column illustrate Trajan's victorious campaigns in Dacia. The Basilica Ulpia is in the foreground. The statue atop the column was added in the seventeenth century CE.

The Roman Forum traces its origins to the very beginning of the Roman Republic, while the Imperial Fora adjacent were mostly constructions by individual emperors. The Imperial Fora were designed to promote the individual propaganda programs of the emperors who ordered their construction.

OVERCROWDING LEADS TO EXPANSION

By the middle of the first century BCE, the Roman Forum had become so crowded with buildings and monuments that Julius Caesar extended its area to the northeast, adjacent to where the Senate House stands today. This area was to become the first of the Imperial Fora, the forum of Julius Caesar. Augustus continued much of Caesar's building activities in the Roman Forum and also completed the forum of Julius Caesar before constructing his own purpose-built forum adjacent to it. The emperors Nerva (CE 98) and Trajan

(CE 98–117) also constructed fora in this area. Collectively, these are known as the Imperial Fora. Next to the forum of Nerva is the so-called Temple-Forum of Peace constructed by the emperor Vespasian in CE 75 out of the spoils of the Jewish War. This is not strictly speaking part of the Imperial Fora, but it does demonstrate how the emperors of the first and second centuries CE continued building activity in this area.

Construction on the forum of Julius Caesar began in 54 BCE and, like numerous Julian projects, was completed by Augustus around 29 BCE. The dominating feature of this forum was the Temple of Venus Genetrix from whom Caesar claimed descent via the mythical Trojan hero Aeneas. Perpendicular to the forum of Julius Caesar is the forum of Augustus. Its dominant feature was the temple to Mars Ultor (the Avenger) to whom Octavian (later Augustus) vowed a temple at the battle of Philippi in Macedonia in 42 BCE. This battle saw the deaths of Brutus and Cassius, the leaders of

THE ROMAN FORUM

The area occupied by the Roman Forum was originally a swamp, which by the fifth century BCE was drained and became central to the public life of the city. From the fifth to the third centuries BCE, it was a gathering place for political meetings, public funerals, and also for legal proceedings. As Roman generals won victories throughout the Mediterranean in the second and first centuries BCE, they dedicated temples and other monuments in the Forum as a means of publicly honoring the gods who had supported them in their victories. The Forum was altered considerably by Julius Caesar and Augustus, becoming an important platform for the Julio-Claudian propaganda program. It was also pivotal to the programs of later emperors. Much of what survives in the forum originated in the Julio-Claudian period; however, a major fire in CE 283 meant that many of the monuments and structures in the Forum required reconstruction.

the conspiracy to assassinate Julius Caesar. The forum also contained statues of leading heroes of the Republic together with those of the Julio-Claudian clan. The imagery of the forum of Augustus was designed to link Augustus with the founding of Rome as well as the perpetuation of the Republic, a key element in Augustus's public program.

Next to the forum of Augustus is the smaller forum of Nerva, begun by his predecessor Domitian and inaugurated in CE 97. Like the other fora, it was dominated by a temple, in this case to Minerva, Domitian's favorite goddess. Minerva was the Roman equivalent of Athena and was a favorite of the Roman army.

On the other side of the forum of Augustus is the forum of Trajan, dedicated in CE 112. This considerable undertaking was paid for out of the spoils of Trajan's victory over Dacia in CE 106. The forum was dominated by the Basilica Ulpia, the largest basilica ever constructed in Rome at this stage at 577 by 194 ft (176 by 59 m) and designed to house law courts among other things. The remains of the Basilica Ulpia are confined mostly to some of its large columns, which demonstrate, nonetheless, the impressive size of the structure. In CE 113 a column in honor of Trajan was erected in this forum and it still stands at a height of around 125 ft (38 m). The column illustrates Trajan's victories in Dacia (Romania–Hungary) in graphic detail and provides important evidence for a range of Roman military activities.

MUSSOLINI BUILDS A LINK TO THE PAST

The Imperial Fora have only been partly excavated, particularly in the area between them and the Roman Forum in 1932. In an attempt to connect himself to the greatness and power of ancient Imperial Rome, the Italian dictator Benito Mussolini ordered the construction of a road that runs from the Colosseum between the Imperial Fora and the Roman Forum. The road is known as Via dei Fori Imperiali and was designed for fascist military and political parades linking Mussolini's regime to the Roman emperors. Unfortunately, the road has caused significant damage to the Imperial Fora. Pollution generated by passing traffic has caused damage to the surviving monuments of the Imperial Fora as well as to other monuments in the general area such as the Arch of Septimus Severus in the Roman Forum.

TEMPLE OF VENUS GENETRIX
Julius Caesar's temple to the mother goddess Venus Genetrix was made of solid marble. It had eight columns across the front and eight down each side. The temple housed a rich array of paintings, sculptures, and other works of art.

Pompeii and Herculaneum, Italy

Early in the afternoon of August 24, CE 79, Pliny the Elder, commander of the Roman fleet at Misenum on the Bay of Naples, noticed a strange cloud formation some 19 miles (30 km) to the east. It was later described by his nephew, Pliny the Younger, as resembling an umbrella pine.

Pliny the Elder had just completed a voluminous work in 37 books called *The Natural Histories* and took great interest in this observation. The cloud was, of course, the first significant sign of the eruption of Mt. Vesuvius, which would bury Pompeii and Herculaneum in dramatic fashion. Later in the afternoon, Pliny left by boat to observe the events more closely and to assist a friend who had been caught up in the eruption. Pliny was never seen again.

HOW TWO CITIES WERE BURIED

Volcanologists and archaeologists have undertaken extensive investigations to reconstruct the various phases in which Pompeii and Herculaneum were buried. At Pompeii, approximately 5 miles (8 km) to the south of Vesuvius, white pumice began falling

mid-afternoon and by early evening buildings began to collapse under its weight. By the early hours of the next morning it is thought that the cloud of ash, rocks, and scalding gases had reached a height of over 19 miles (30 km). At the beginning of what is known as the pyroclastic phase, this enormous column collapsed releasing two surges of material in quick succession, completely burying Herculaneum, 3 miles (5 km) to the southwest of Vesuvius, and severely damaging the northern sections of Pompeii. For approximately four hours, while the eruption column built again, there appears to have been a lull in the pumice fall at Pompeii. Soon after daybreak the second column of ash, rocks, and gases collapsed, releasing four devastating pyroclastic surges that wreaked destruction over Pompeii and completely buried what was left. What the pumice had covered

POMPEII CASTS

This dramatic image shows some of the 1,000-plus residents of Pompeii who perished under the volcanic ash of Mt. Vesuvius. The bodies were not preserved but were seen as voids in the solidified ash. These were filled with plaster in the nineteenth century.

was preserved, but what lay above was completely erased by these flows, which are estimated by scholars to have traveled at more than 125 miles per hour (200 km/h) with temperatures greater than 212°F (100°C).

Evidence of tunneling at Pompeii indicates that some who escaped during the first phase of the eruption returned to try and salvage belongings that had been buried or even to find any trapped survivors. Because Herculaneum was buried under 75 ft (23 m) of debris there was no chance of this type of activity succeeding.

WHAT THE EXCAVATIONS HAVE REVEALED

Memories of the buried cities remained in the Campanian region for many centuries, with treasure-hunting taking place on a regular basis; but it was not until the eighteenth century CE that excavations officially got under way at Pompeii and Herculaneum. The state of archaeology at the time meant that this was little more than organized looting, with no proper recordings made until over a century later. Excavations since World War II have been increasingly better organized and more professional. At Pompeii, approximately 80 percent of the town has been excavated and the current focus is on restoration, preservation, and reinterpretation rather than new excavations. At

Herculaneum the remains of the ancient city mostly lie beneath the modern town, meaning that the excavation area has been more limited.

Excavations at Pompeii, together with a few literary references, have allowed a reconstruction of some of the city's history. The city is thought to have been founded in the seventh century BCE and became prosperous during the period of Greek control in southern Italy. There are also clear Etruscan and Samnite influences on the city before it came under Roman control. The street plan was probably established in the third century BCE, with many of the main features of the city having their origins in the second century BCE. The city displays all of the important features of an Italian town including a forum, numerous temples, bath complexes, a theater, stout walls, and a sunken stone amphitheater capable of seating 20,000 people.

The remains at Herculaneum demonstrate that the town was not as large as Pompeii and seems to have functioned as a luxurious resort town. Only about a quarter of the town's estimated area has been excavated; however, this has produced quite a range of important evidence, including the remains of boathouses on the shoreline prior to the eruption. One boathouse contained dozens of skeletons of people attempting to shelter from the effects of the eruption. Because Herculaneum was buried under a much thicker and denser layer of ash, excavation at the site has been more difficult than at Pompeii.

INTRIGUING INSIGHTS INTO ROMAN CULTURE

Pompeii has been the most significant archaeological site for understanding Roman art and architecture up to the time of its destruction. Wall paintings adorn many of the wealthier houses, and some fine mosaics have also been found—the most famous of them is from the House of the Faun depicting the battle between Alexander the Great and Darius III of Persia. Considerable evidence has also been found of the daily life of the city, including over 30 bakeries and flour mills, numerous fulleries, brothels, and domestic houses. Perhaps the best-known discoveries are of human and animal remains, often showing graphic reactions in the moments before their deaths. Some vivid examples include a mother attempting to pro-tect her child, and a dog still chained by its leash. The remains of more than 1,000 human bodies have been found at Pompeii thus far.

HERCULANEUM BATHS

Restoration efforts have helped us understand Herculaneum as it was before the volcanic eruption. Here we see the "warm room" at one of Herculaneum's Roman suburban bath complexes. Bathers would have spent time in a warm bath (tepidarium), a hot bath and "sauna" (caldarium), and a bath for cooling off (frigidarium).

Lugdunum, France

The city of Lugdunum in Gaul, modern Lyon, was founded as a Roman colony in 43 BCE. It quickly became the administrative and religious center of the three Roman provinces in Gaul, and included an office of the imperial mint.

MOTHER GODDESS

Also known as Kybele (the cave dweller), the goddess Cybele was worshipped throughout the Roman Empire. Lugdunum, for example, is well-known for its Temple to Cybele. This fourth-century BCE terracotta bust of Cybele comes from Olynthos in Greece.

The significance of Lugdunum to Rome's northwestern provinces is symbolized in the numerous imperial visits to the city, including three by Augustus and a number by later emperors such as Caligula and Nero. The emperor Claudius (ruled CE 41–54) was born in Lugdunum in 10 BCE, as was Caracalla (ruled CE 211–217) in CE 188, reflecting the importance the city enjoyed over a long period of time.

With a population estimated to be 50,000 by the second century CE, Lugdunum, situated at the confluence of the Rhône and Saône Rivers, was an important port for the shipment of the region's wine and oil production. With the focus increasingly turning to the Rhine frontier in Germany, the importance of Lugdunum began to decrease in the third century CE, but it retained its status as the capital of the reduced province of Lugdunensis Prima throughout the fourth and fifth centuries CE.

IMPRESSIVE ARCHAEOLOGICAL FINDS

The archaeological remains at Lugdunum are impressive and demonstrate considerable imperial patronage in the first and second centuries CE. Among the remains is an amphitheater measuring 420 by 341 ft (128 by 104 m), constructed in CE 19 under the emperor Tiberius. The amphitheater also marked the location where local representatives of the three Gallic provinces met annually to swear allegiance to the Roman emperor. By the middle of

the first century CE the city was supplied with water by four aqueducts. One of these was 46 miles (75 km) in length and it is estimated that around 38,500 tons (35,000 tonnes) of lead was used in the water pipes for the four aqueducts.

Lugdunum was famous for its temples including a Temple to Cybele, a goddess with Babylonian origins, and others to local Gallic gods. The remains of the Temple to Cybele show that its basement measured 164 by 276 ft (50 by 84 m). Worship of Cybele at Lugdunum seems to have been most active from the middle of the second century CE. The competing nature of religious activity at Lugdunum is shown with the emergence of a Christian community there that suffered persecution. The martyrdom of St. Blandina was said by the historian Eusebius to have been carried out in the amphitheater at Lugdunum in CE 177.

The numerous visits by Roman emperors saw Lugdunum receive altars, fountains, and bath complexes among other monuments and structures. The emperor Claudius, for example, dedicated a fountain there in CE 47 in celebration of his victories in what is now Britain. Of particular importance also are the remains of bronze tablets from Lugdunum, recording the speech made by Claudius on the admission of Gauls to the Roman Senate.

SCANT REMAINS OF A ROMAN AMPHITHEATER

The stone inscription below celebrates the dedication of Lugdunum's amphitheater by C. F. Rufus, priest of the imperial cult, in CE 19, after Tiberius had succeeded Augustus as emperor of Rome.

Carthage, Tunisia

It is believed that Carthage was founded as a Phoenician trading colony late in the ninth century BCE. Its importance to trade between the western and eastern Mediterranean is difficult to overestimate, and it came to dominate trade in the western Mediterranean until the latter years of the third century BCE.

FINE MOSAICS
Dating to the fifth century CE, this is part of a series of mosaics depicting buildings on a large agricultural estate in Carthage. This section was discovered in the Master's House.

SYMBOL OF A GREAT CITY
This terracotta head of a man may be linked to the theater or circus at Carthage. The dimensions of the Roman theater, amphitheater, and circus attest to the importance of Carthage in its Roman period.

The emerging power of Rome saw the two empires clash over Sicily, resulting in the First Punic War (264–241 BCE). The Second Punic War (218–201 BCE) saw the defeat of the Carthaginian general Hannibal and Rome's establishment of its first overseas provinces in Spain. Following the Third Punic War (149–146 BCE), the city of Carthage was almost completely destroyed.

The city was revived again during the reign of Augustus (27 BCE–CE 14), becoming a Roman colony. As the capital of the province of Africa, Carthage emerged again as one of the most important cities in the western Mediterranean by the second century CE. Its significance was to continue well into the Late Antique period where it played an important role in the emergence of Christianity in North Africa and throughout the western Mediterranean.

PRE-ROMAN REMAINS
The most significant pre-Roman remains at Carthage are enormous walls of the fifth century BCE, claimed in antiquity to have stretched for more than 19 miles (30 km). Two artificial harbors are thought to date to some time in the third century BCE, one operating for the purposes of trade and the other to house the growing Carthaginian war fleet.

Perhaps the most famous archaeological discovery from Carthage is that of the tophet, an extensive burial ground dating from the late eighth century BCE to the destruction of Carthage in 146 BCE. It holds thousands of urns and graves of children. It has been claimed that these children were sacrificed to the chief gods of Carthage, Baal and Tanit, but this is not proven and many seem to have died of natural causes.

ROMAN REMAINS
Roman Carthage includes all of the features expected of an important city in the Imperial period. The remains of an amphitheater, circus, and theater have been found on the outskirts of the city. In the second century CE, Carthage received a new forum that was said to be the largest outside of Rome itself. The city was also adorned with large imperial bath complexes that were supplied by the longest known Roman aqueduct, stretching for a distance of over 80 miles (130 km). The city's significance to Christianity in the post-Constantinian Roman Empire saw the construction of a number of large churches, many of them built outside the walls. Despite its enormous protective walls, in CE 439 the city fell to the Vandals.

The Technology of War

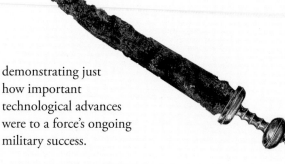

ROMAN DAGGER

This reconstructed Roman dagger represents just one of a range of finely crafted swords and daggers that Roman soldiers would have had at their disposal. Such weaponry would have given the soldiers a great advantage as they fought their enemies.

READY FOR BATTLE

Dating to CE 109, this limestone relief from Romania depicts two Roman soldiers with their shields and spears. Roman soldiers were equipped with an array of very effective weaponry and armor.

Military organization and the development of sophisticated weaponry became the hallmarks of Rome's success as it built its extensive empire from the late Republic through to the Imperial period. Rome's military prowess emerged during the centuries in which its power expanded throughout the Italian peninsula, and when it began to wage war against enemies outside of Italy it was able to achieve some stunning successes.

The high standard had been set by the armies of Alexander the Great and his successors who had shown that military discipline and ingenuity could carry an army an extraordinary distance. The development of the sarissa-armed phalanx in Macedonia under Alexander's father Philip II (356–336 BCE) had revolutionized warfare in the Mediterranean and in the Near East thus demonstrating just how important technological advances were to a force's ongoing military success.

A MOST EFFICIENT AND FRIGHTENING FORCE

The Roman army was a professional standing army that was very well drilled, divided into clearly established units such as legions, possessed a strong command structure, and provided a well-defined career and retirement path for its soldiers. There were clear rules laid down for important activities including the establishment of camps when an army was on the march. The construction of more than 10,000 miles (16,000 km) of roads by the second century CE allowed efficient movement around the empire, particularly to its frontiers where fighting took place regularly. These elements, combined with developments in military technology, made the Roman army into the most efficient and terrifying fighting force the world had yet seen.

By the early Imperial period, Roman armor and weaponry had been through several centuries of development and contributed significantly to the army's ability to achieve success. The classic features of legionary armor by this stage were a bronze helmet with its distinctive plumes, a mail cuirass, a long oval shield, a gladius (sword) with blade up to 19½ in (50 cm) long, and a pilum (javelin). The pilum was particularly well designed because most of the weapon's weight was focused immediately behind the point, giving it a devastating impact. The Roman cavalry increasingly comprised auxiliaries who were equipped with armor and weapons similar to the infantry but modified for the specific needs of fighting on horseback. The discipline of the Roman infantry combined with its development of armor is exemplified in the devising of a technique known as *testudo*. The Latin term for tortoise shell, *testudo* involved a number of soldiers locking their shields together, both above and to the sides, for offensive and defensive purposes.

NEW ARTILLERY

Of enormous importance to the Roman ability to successfully wage war was the development of artillery. Among the more important artillery pieces used by the Romans in the Imperial period were the ballista and the onager. The ballista was a huge

crossbow that fired bolts made of wood and tipped with iron. The ballista came in different sizes and could fire a bolt up to 1,640 ft (500 m). The bolt itself was around 3 ft (0.9 m) long with modern estimates suggesting that it traveled in excess of 112 miles per hour (180 km/h) when first released. The onager was a catapult designed to fire projectiles weighing approximately 155 lb (70 kg). The word onager means wild ass and was used to describe this weapon because it had such a powerful kick. The effect of using a weapon such as the onager was devastating as its projectiles could crash through roofs and walls causing serious damage.

DEFENDING THE EMPIRE

The impressive Trajan's Column in the Imperial Fora, Rome, features intricate carvings of victorious battle scenes. The detail shown here depicts Roman soldiers building fortifications.

BREACHING ENEMY WALLS

The Romans used siege machinery and battering rams to great effect (pictured is an artist's impression of one kind of battering ram). These types of machines had been used much earlier in the Assyrian Empire and also in warfare during the Classical Greek and Hellenistic periods. Ballistae and onagri were particularly useful in sieges, but battering rams were very effective in the final stages of a siege, as they allowed the walls to be breached and the besieged city to be overrun. Battering rams were made of wood with a metal beak attached so as to gouge into the walls of a besieged city. The ram was surrounded by a frame with wheels beneath for easy transport, and coverings were placed on all sides to limit the effect of defensive efforts to destroy it. Other effective methods utilized in sieges were the use of scaling ladders and assault ramps as well as the construction of tunnels under the walls in an effort to destabilize them.

Palmyra, Syria

SYRIA
Palmyra
Damascus

The remains of the oasis city of Palmyra are located in the middle of the Syrian Desert, halfway between the Euphrates River and the coastline of the eastern Mediterranean. Palmyra's strategic location allowed it to build considerable wealth by the first century CE as it levied tariffs on trade passing through it from the Persian Gulf bound for the Roman Empire.

P almyra's wealth from trade was directly linked with the Roman presence in Syria and the Near East, which had been building since the beginning of the second century BCE. The Romans formally gained a territorial presence in the Near East when Pompey established the province of Syria around 65 BCE, and from this time onward Palmyra's importance as a trading go-between began to grow.

MYTHOLOGICAL RELIEF
Discovered at Palmyra, this detail of a first-century CE limestone relief shows Baalshamin with the sun-god. Visitors to Palmyra can see the ruins of the temple of Baalshamin.

TRADE AND INFLUENCE

By the middle of the second century CE Palmyra was the primary destination through which eastern trade bound for the Roman Empire passed. The Palmyrenes actively encouraged the conduct of trade through the city by escorting the camel caravans that bore luxury items from the Persian Gulf up the Euphrates and across the Syrian Desert to the oasis. The escorts were armed and took on the characteristics of a militia designed to protect the vulnerable caravans from plundering by bandits as they made their journeys up the river and across the desert. Inscriptions of the mid-second century CE from Palmyra show that the leaders of these escorts were celebrated in the city and in some cases received impressive public statues.

Evidence has emerged from elsewhere to show that the Palmyrenes influenced trade not only in the Persian Gulf but also around the whole of the Arabian

peninsula and as far east as India. Several Palmyrene tombs have been found on the island of Bahrain, while a Palmyrene tomb dedication has also been found in a cave on the island of Soqotra off the coast of Yemen. Evidence of Palmyrene activity has been found at the

THE TOWER TOMBS OF PALMYRA

Located in the valley behind the main section of the city are the remains of hundreds of tower tombs, which contain magnificent sculptures and, in some cases, paintings. Some tower tombs were so large that they could hold hundreds of bodies. The bodies were preserved using natron, the same embalming material used in mummification in Egypt, before being wrapped in silk and placed in niches in the tower tombs. The niches were then sealed with sculpted busts of the deceased. The earliest datable tower tomb dates to 9 BCE, and a significant majority of them were constructed toward the end of the first century CE and during the second century.

These majestic tower tombs are located in Lamliku in the Valley of the Tombs. They date to the late third century CE.

ports of Berenike and Leuke Kome on the Red Sea and at Coptos, a major trading center on the Nile in Egypt.

A WEALTHY CITY

The striking remains of Palmyra today bear testimony to the wealth of the city in antiquity. The city bears all the hallmarks of a rich city of the Hellenistic and Roman Near East including great temples, colonnaded streets, a theater, an agora, baths, and a Roman army camp. Numerous public inscriptions from the city also survive and provide a unique insight to the city's cultural diversity among other things. Of particular significance at Palmyra are the many tower tombs surrounding the city, which show the exceptional wealth enjoyed by some Palmyrenes and their families.

One of the dominating features at Palmyra today is the Temple of Bel. The most powerful god in the Palmyrene pantheon, Bel equated roughly with Jupiter in the Roman period. The cella of the temple was dedicated in CE 32; the temenos was completed early in the second century CE.

The main colonnaded street, known as the Grand Colonnade, runs on a northwest–southeast axis and begins with an impressive triple-arched entrance. The street was probably completed early in the second

century and runs for around two-thirds of a mile (1.2 km). The columns of the Grand Colonnade contain plinths that held statues of famous Palmyrenes, most of which have now disappeared. Inscriptions in both Greek and Palmyrene are located underneath them and provide the names and deeds of many of the dedicants. The temple of Nabu, a Palmyrene weather god, abuts the colonnade just inside the triple-arched entrance, and not far from it lies the remains of a heavily reconstructed theater.

The most significant surviving temple other than that of Bel is the temple of Baalshamin roughly to the north of the Grand Colonnade. Baalshamin was referred to as "Lord of the Heavens" and his temple was dedicated in CE 131.

To the south of the Grand Colonnade, and at the end of a major intersecting street called the Transverse Colonnade, are the remains of the agora, which was the main marketplace at Palmyra. It seems that tariffs on goods passing through the city were levied and collected at the agora. At the end of the Grand Colonnade and just to the south are the remains of the Camp of Diocletian, a Roman army camp constructed toward the end of the third century CE following a major rebellion by the Palmyrenes 25 years earlier.

TEMPLE OF BEL

Considered the best-preserved ruins at Palmyra, the Temple of Bel features striking Corinthian columns. The temple's temenos (sacred enclosure) measured an amazing 2,207 sq ft (205 sq m).

Early Medieval Europe

The early medieval period in Europe is often interpreted as a time of limited progress and decline following the collapse of the Roman Empire in the west. This is due to reports in the surviving texts written by pro-Roman elites after the event; however, archaeology sometimes tells a different story.

VISIGOTH BELT BUCKLE

The Visigoths (West Goths) were one of several Germanic tribes that challenged Rome's power in western Europe. After taking Spain from the Romans, the Visigoths were overthrown by their relatives, the Ostrogoths (East Goths).

On September 4, CE 476, the last Roman emperor in the west, Romulus Augustulus, abdicated. Rome had faced some serious difficulties in both the west and the east for many decades before this event. In the east the empire continued for almost 1,000 years as the Byzantine Empire, and in the west it fundamentally shaped what was to become medieval Europe.

The challenge Rome faced in its western provinces during the fourth and fifth centuries CE came from migrations beginning in Scandinavia and the Russian Federation. The Ostrogoths, Visigoths, Huns, and the Franks, who were all pushed further west as a result of these migrations, eventually overwhelmed the Roman military and administrative machine. Between the fifth and eighth centuries the Ostrogoths followed by the Lombards took control of Italy, the Visigoths became monarchs in Spain and Portugal, the Saxons ruled England, while the Burgundians and Franks emerged as kings in Gaul and parts of Germany.

THE CENTURIES FOLLOWING THE ROMAN COLLAPSE IN THE WEST

A critical feature of government and society in these kingdoms was Christianity. This religion had been supported by Roman emperors since the long reign of Constantine (CE 306–337), and toward the end of the fourth century it became the official religion of the Roman Empire. From serious conflicts between popes and the monarchs of Europe to the day-to-day existence of serfs and peasants, Christianity was to play a fundamental role in all levels of society.

As a result of the monarchs of the kingdoms of medieval Europe adopting Christianity, the power of the popes and bishops became particularly important. Indeed, in the wake of the collapse of Roman power during the fifth century, bishops came to play an increasingly significant role as local power

THE MOORS IN SOUTHERN SPAIN

An important event in medieval European history was the invasion of southern Spain by the Moors of North Africa in CE 711. Under the leadership of Tariq ibn-Ziyad, the Moors conquered much of Spain and Portugal by CE 720 and established a Caliphate at Cordoba. It was not until the thirteenth century CE that Moorish power was seriously challenged by a coalition of northern Spanish princes, and the Moors remained powerful at Granada until the end of the fifteenth century. An important ramification of the Moorish invasions for Europe was the transmission of Islamic learning and culture. Islamic educational strengths in areas including mathematics were particularly important in this respect. The preservation of Classical Greek texts in Islamic learning saw their reintroduction to Europe. These texts included the important works of Homer and Herodotus, largely unknown in post-Roman Europe. Moorish architecture in southern Spain is renowned for its magnificence, exemplified in the Alhambra at Granada.

A fine example of Moorish architecture, the Mezquita (mosque) in Cordoba features arches of marble, jasper, and granite. Originally built in CE 787, it had almost doubled in size by CE 988.

---

brokers and as ambassadors between regional rulers and kings. Churches and monasteries eventually came to control extensive tracts of land that was essential to food production and taxation. This was central to the development of the feudal system in Europe.

IMPORTANT DEVELOPMENTS IN EARLY MEDIEVAL EUROPE

Some of the significant events in early medieval European history include the formation of the Papal States, the emergence of the Carolingian Empire, the invasion of Spain by the Moors, and also the Norman invasion of England. By the seventh century, the Lombards succeeded in taking control of much of Italy; however, the bishops of Rome, who were now calling themselves popes, became particularly powerful in Rome and across the surrounding territory of Latium. By the end of the eighth century they were the effective rulers of Rome, with the support of the powerful Frankish monarch, Charlemagne. The popes had thus been transformed into European monarchs and this, combined with their supreme religious authority, made them extremely powerful.

In CE 768, Charlemagne succeeded his father Pepin as King of the Franks and by CE 800 had emerged as leader of the first empire in Western Europe since the collapse of the Roman Empire. When Pope Leo III crowned him as Holy Roman Emperor in Rome on Christmas Day, CE 800, Charlemagne controlled modern France and Italy, as well as large parts of Germany. The empire became known as the Carolingian Empire but only remained powerful for the next 90 years until its last ruler, Charles the Fat, died. Charlemagne consciously emulated the emperors of Rome in his drive for empire and even proposed marriage to the Byzantine empress Irene, who shrewdly and tactfully rejected the offer.

THE ASCENT AND DECLINE OF THE ANGLO-SAXON KINGS

The territory of Britain was largely lost to the Roman Empire by CE 420, and eventually the Anglo-Saxons stepped in to fill the power vacuum left by Rome's withdrawal. By the end of the ninth century, the Anglo-Saxon kings, who had become Christian, controlled much of England. Toward the end of the eighth century, Britain experienced the first attacks of the Vikings, and these were to continue for centuries. The attacks were met with varying degrees of resistance. Competition between the Anglo-Saxons and the kingdoms of Scandinavia became increasingly fierce in the tenth century, and in the year 1066 this rivalry contributed to the success of the Normans over the Anglo-Saxons at the Battle of Hastings. The battle was led by William the Conqueror, who hoped to gain personal wealth by controlling England. During the battle, the Anglo-Saxon king, Harold, was killed when he was shot in the eye with an arrow.

Following the Norman invasion, developments that were taking place in England became more closely associated with events that were occurring on the European mainland.

KING CHARLEMAGNE
The medieval king Charlemagne has been represented in countless artworks over the centuries. This 1825 painting by J. P. Scheuren shows the king holding a model of Aachen Cathedral.

Arthurian Archaeology

CAERLEON AMPHITHEATER

Twentieth-century archaeologists revealed that this large grassed area at Caerleon in Wales was once the site of a Roman amphitheater. The excavations were part-funded by the Loyal Knights of the Round Table of America, as many people believed this to be the location of King Arthur's "round table."

KEY ARTHURIAN SITES

The map below identifies some of the significant sites that have been associated with the sixth-century CE legends of King Arthur and the Knights of the Round Table. These tales have entranced children and adults alike for many generations.

The sixth-century CE legend of King Arthur and the Knights of the Round Table is one of the most enduring in Western civilization. Historians are uncertain as to whether Arthur was a real king or a legendary Welsh national figure said to have resisted the advance of the Saxons from England.

A vast array of sites in Wales and England today are claimed to have been associated with the legendary tales and battles of King Arthur and the Knights of the Round Table. Of keen interest are attempts at identifying where Camelot, King Arthur's castle, was located together with his likely birthplace. Other sites of interest from the legend are the locations of Excalibur's Lake, Arthur's burial location, Merlin's prison, and the Holy Grail.

CAMELOT AND ARTHUR'S BIRTHPLACE

An important contender for the location of Camelot is a large hill fort at South Cadbury in Somerset, England. Local legend claims that the hill fort was once Arthur's Camelot, and when excavations took place there in the 1960s the remains of a large Roman fort, which had been refortified after the Romans left Britain, confirmed that a powerful chieftain resided there. Large sections of stone walls were found together with evidence for a wooden hall measuring 63 ft by 34 ft (19 m by 10 m). Dating the fort is reasonably secure, with pottery demonstrating that the refortification probably took place in the sixth century. However, there are particular problems with identifying the fort with Camelot, as it lay within the Kingdom of Dumnonia and was most likely the capital of its kings.

Another important site, often identified as the location of Camelot, is Caerleon in

Wales. Caerleon was originally a Roman fort and housed a legion. The site is famed as the possible location of Arthur's "round table" together with the legendary story of Arthur and one thousand knights sleeping in a cave nearby. What was claimed to be the round table, a large grassed area, was excavated in the 1920s to reveal the remains of a Roman amphitheater. Archaeological investigation has returned only minimal evidence of the area's use as a fortification in the sixth century.

The spectacular ruins of Tintagel Castle in Cornwall have long been associated with Arthur's birthplace. The remains of the castle date to the thirteenth century; however, archaeology at the site has returned evidence for pottery originating in the Mediterranean dating to the sixth century. A number of significant architectural remains are also claimed to date to the sixth century. The archaeological discoveries at Tintagel are particularly interesting for establishing the nature of trade connections between southwest England and Wales in the post-Roman period. A large amount of sixth-century pottery demonstrates that oil from North Africa and wine from Cyprus were among a number of products that were being imported into Britain from the Mediterranean region at this time.

OTHER IMPORTANT SITES CONNECTED TO KING ARTHUR

Also associated with Arthur are Atherston and Glastonbury Abbey, where he is claimed to have been buried. The Chalice Well at Chalice Well Gardens near Glastonbury and the beautiful Rosslyn Chapel near the village of Roslin in Scotland have both been suggested as the locations of the Holy Grail. Dozmary Pool is one contender for the last resting place of Arthur's sword, Excalibur, and Bardsey Island off the Welsh coast is thought by some to be the resting place of the wizard Merlin.

KEY

○ Capital City
○ Other City or Town
◻ Archaeological Site
— International Border

0   100 km
0   100 miles

N

SCOTLAND

Edinburgh
Rosslyn Chapel
STRATHCLYDE
Tweed

SNOWDONIA
Bardsey Island
ENGLAND
Atherston
WALES
Prescelly Mtns
Caerleon
Cardiff   Bath   Salisbury Plain   London
SOMERSET   Chalice Well
Glastonbury   Stonehenge
Cadbury Castle
Tintagel   CORNWALL
Dozmary Pool
Thames
English Channel

REMAINS OF A CASTLE

The ruins of Tintagel Castle, built around CE 1240 by Earl Richard of Cornwall, are popular as a tourist destination. Some people believe the castle was built on the site of King Arthur's birthplace. The castle is also linked to the legendary love story of Tristan and Isolde.

GLASTONBURY ABBEY RUINS

King Arthur and Queen Guinevere are purported to be buried in the grounds of Glastonbury Abbey. The whole Glastonbury area is of great archaeological interest. For example, some excavations have uncovered evidence of pottery of Mediterranean origin.

WHERE DID ARTHUR DIE?

After he was seriously wounded in the Battle of Camlan in CE 537, legend has it that King Arthur was taken to the mysterious Isle of Avalon where he later died. One contender for the location of Avalon is Glastonbury Tor in Somerset, which has returned some interesting archaeological material. Glastonbury Tor today (pictured here) is a hill surrounded by rich farmland; however, before the area was drained in the medieval period, it stood as an island. Excavations on Glastonbury Tor in the 1960s revealed evidence dating to the fifth and sixth centuries CE that may be the remains of an early monastery. The Tor is thought to have been the site of pre-Christian pagan shrines, which were later taken for the establishment of a monastery. The religious significance of the site leads some to think it would be the likely location for Arthur to retire to when injured and preparing for death.

Sutton Hoo, United Kingdom

The archaeological discoveries at Sutton Hoo in Suffolk, England, are among the most important to have been made in the British Isles. They are best known for a burial ship that contained the treasures of an early Anglo-Saxon king, but other important finds have also been made at the site.

Excavations at Sutton Hoo near Woodbridge in Suffolk have taken place at various stages over the past 70 years. On the eve of World War II, an amateur archaeologist made an extraordinary find at the site that would prove to be one of the most important archaeological finds in Great Britain. Prior to this the burial mounds at Sutton Hoo were the subject of treasure-hunting; fortunately the outline of the ship was intact. Once the significance of the discovery became known, a professional team of archaeologists under the direction of Charles Phillips was hired to complete the excavation of the ship and the burial.

BURIAL OF A KING

The buried ship is thought to contain the treasure of King Rædwald, an Anglo-Saxon king of East Anglia who ruled early in the seventh century CE. The burial has been dated to around CE 620 on the basis of numismatic (coin) evidence. This rich find includes the outline of the ship itself measuring 90 ft (27.5 m) in length, the body of the king, weapons, and armor made of gold together with tableware and other implements made of silver. Among the silver vessels was a bowl made in Constantinople around CE 500. A purse found on the body contained nearly 40 gold coins of the Merovingian dynasty dating to approximately CE 620. The style of the burial is clearly Viking; similar examples of ship burials have been discovered throughout Scandinavia and it is thought that the armor from the burial was made in Sweden. When

SILVER AND GOLD ARMOR

This helmet made of precious metals was found among the treasures of King Rædwald at Sutton Hoo. The treasury was discovered on land owned by Mrs. Edith Pretty, who commissioned the 1938 and 1939 excavations at the Sutton Hoo site.

ANGLO-SAXON PURSE LID

A most exquisite example of gold and enamel jewelry, this artifact comes from the seventh-century CE Sutton Hoo treasury. In 2002, the Sutton Hoo site was acquired by the National Trust of England.

the ship was found much of the wood had rotted; however, archaeologists have reconstructed the shape of the ship based on the impressions it has made on the surrounding soil.

While the impressive quality of the objects found in the Sutton Hoo ship burial demonstrate the extraordinary artistic and technical achievements of Scandinavian, Saxon, and Byzantine craftsmen, they also provide us with evidence for the trade and political connections between Anglo-Saxon England and the so-called Norsemen of Sweden, Norway, and Denmark in the seventh century. More excavations conducted at the site by the British Museum in the 1960s and 1970s demonstrated that Sutton Hoo was a complex site of burials from the seventh century. More recently, excavations that have been ongoing since the 1980s have contributed significantly to our knowledge of the history of the site. In excavations conducted in the year 2000, approximately a third of a mile (0.5 km) from the site of the ship, burials were found dating to half a century earlier, illuminating its importance over a period of time.

Oseberg Ship, Norway

Discovered in 1904 in Norway, the Oseberg ship is one of the most important discoveries relating to the Vikings. From the ninth to twelfth centuries CE, the Vikings wreaked havoc on settled populations in northern Europe. The Oseberg ship has helped historians and archaeologists to understand the Vikings' methods.

AN EXCITING FIND
This early photograph shows the Oseberg ship being excavated. The ship was discovered on a farm in the Vestfold region of Norway. The excavation team was led by Professor Gabriel Gustafson from the University Museum of Antiquities, Oslo.

The attacks of the Vikings from Norway, Sweden, and Denmark had a significant impact on Britain and northern Europe for more than 300 years, and their ships were crucial to this. The Oseberg ship is an early example of Viking long boats, which were developed over time to cover long distances at sea. The Gokstad ship (see the following page), built around 60 to 70 years later, demonstrates advances in technology and is much sturdier than the Oseberg ship. Viking boats were highly versatile and could move at lightning speed when required. The Vikings also constructed ships that allowed them to trade and settle colonies in Iceland, Greenland, and briefly in North America.

The Oseberg ship was built around CE 820, and on the basis of dendrochronology it is thought that the burial of which it was a part dates to CE 834. The ship measures approximately 75 ft (23 m) in length. It is 15 ft (4.5 m) wide and was equipped with a mast 30 ft (9 m) in height. The boat could seat 30 oarsmen, and its sail would have had an area of approximately 800 sq ft (75 sq m). These features meant that the ship could make long voyages at sea under sail and very fast attacks on coastal targets using the oarsmen. It has been estimated that the ship could have traveled at speeds of up to 14 knots. The design of the ship includes an impressive prow that makes it ideal for oceangoing voyages. It also has a shallow draft and rudder, meaning that it could be used in coastal estuaries and rivers quite effectively. A noteworthy feature of the ship is its beautiful decoration on the timber of its bow and stern.

UNIQUE VIKING GRAVE GOODS
The ship was a burial, and the skeletons of two females were found in the grave. One was around 70 years of age and the other is thought to have been around twenty-five. Many items were found in the grave, and these items were probably used by the grave's obviously wealthy and powerful owners during their lifetime. Among the items were a four-wheeled cart, a bed, and a very rich find of fabrics and textile tools. Among the fabrics are tapestries and braided silk, demonstrating the Viking capacity for trade over considerable distances. Numerous items made from cloth were also found, including tents and rugs, while the remains of woolen blankets were present as well. Spinning tools and a range of looms were discovered. The textiles from the Oseberg ship are the most important collection of Viking fabrics yet found.

Gokstad Ship, Norway

NORWAY
Oslo
Gokstad

The Gokstad ship burial was discovered and excavated in Norway in 1880. While the burial was not as rich as that of the Oseberg ship, the Gokstad ship is in better condition and demonstrated the developing capacity of the Vikings to build sturdy, oceangoing vessels in the ninth century CE.

The ship burial at Gokstad has been dated to around CE 900, approximately 60 to 70 years after the Oseberg ship was buried. The ship was probably built and used for ten years before the burial, which appears to have been that of a chieftain aged in his 60s at the time of death. The ship is 80 ft (24 m) long and 15 ft (4.5 m) wide. It possessed a detachable rudder so it could be used in shallow inlets and coastal rivers, and it appears that it could accommodate up to 32 oarsmen. Like the Oseberg ship, the sail capacity for the Gokstad ship was considerable with modern estimates approximating it at 1,200 sq ft (112 sq m). With its large sail and numerous oarsmen, the Gokstad ship was capable of long-distance sea travel and rapid advance when close to shore. This was a key feature of Viking ship technology and contributed significantly to the ability of the Vikings to range as far as Britain and northern Europe where they inflicted their devastating raids.

A STURDY VESSEL

The Gokstad ship would have been sturdier than the Oseberg vessel, which was probably used more in coastal journeys. The Gokstad ship was more capable of undertaking long-distance sea travel.

SUITED TO LONG-DISTANCE SEA TRAVEL

The Gokstad ship is much stronger than the Oseberg vessel and demonstrates more clearly how the Vikings developed shipbuilding techniques that allowed their ships to range over larger areas. Indeed, after the discovery of the Gokstad ship in 1880, a full-size replica of it was constructed and sailed from Bergen in Norway to New York before being taken overland to Chicago where it was exhibited as part of the celebrations to mark the World Fair in 1893.

The burial of which the ship was a part is thought to have been robbed before proper excavation work could be carried out. This is because many of the metal items scholars would normally expect to accompany such a burial were missing. The skeleton of a man in his 60s was found inside a wooden burial chamber. Among the burial finds were three smaller boats, 64 painted shields, the remains of bedposts, hunting implements, and a gaming board. Animals also accompanied the burial including dogs and a horse complete with its reins and bridle. The remains of a bird were also found in the burial and have been identified as a peacock.

Novgorod, Russian Federation

RUSSIAN
FEDERATION

Medieval Novgorod is the oldest recorded Slavic city in the Russian Federation, having been founded in CE 859. Eventually it came to dominate a large tract of territory from the Baltic States to the Ural Mountains. Listed today as a UNESCO World Heritage Site, Novgorod is famous for its medieval architecture.

The Russian name Novgorod means "New City," and it was reputedly founded as a defensive stronghold before the majority of the city's buildings were constructed toward the end of the ninth century. Much of what is now known of Novgorod's early history comes from the *Chronicle of Novgorod*, which documents important events in its history from 1016 to 1471. In CE 882 the King of Novgorod, Oleg, captured the city of Kiev and formed the State of Kievan Rus. The city of Novgorod continued to play an important role in the State even though Kiev was the city from which the kings now ruled. It was during the time Novgorod was within Kievan Rus that the Cathedral of St. Sophia was constructed (from 1045 to 1052), and it is the most prominent building in medieval Novgorod today. Novgorod is mentioned in the Norse sagas as the city to which no less than four Viking kings fled during this period when faced with problems at home.

Novgorod remained within Kievan Rus until 1136, at which time a group of merchants formed the Republic of Novgorod, which broke away from the kings in Kiev. It then became a powerful trading State and controlled considerable territory from the Baltic to the Urals. Eventually Novgorod became too populous and began to decline before, in 1478, Ivan III annexed it to Muscovy.

A MAJESTIC CATHEDRAL

Although the Cathedral of St. Sophia in Novgorod has only five domes, it was modeled on the 13-domed St. Sophia Cathedral of Kiev. Since the end of World War II, a great deal of restoration work has been performed on some of Novgorod's churches and frescoes.

FOURTH-CENTURY BCE FIND

Numerous treasures have been unearthed in the Novgorod area, including this gold fish. Although Novgorod is well-known as a rich and powerful medieval city, it has a wealthy archaeological past going back to before the Christian era.

FINE BUILDINGS IN MEDIEVAL NOVGOROD

Novgorod is renowned for its medieval churches with their distinctive rounded roofs and beautiful frescoes. The most famous is the Cathedral of St. Sophia. It occupied a central position in Novgorod and is claimed to be the oldest church in the Russian Federation. Its frescoes date to the middle of the twelfth century and a number of Novgorod's rulers are buried in its crypt. The Kremlin in Novgorod, built in 1433, is claimed to be the oldest palace in the Russian Federation. The city contains a number of churches constructed in the twelfth and thirteenth centuries before and after the establishment of the republic. Unfortunately, the city of Novgorod suffered serious damage during the Nazi occupation that began in August 1941. Many of the city's churches were rifled for treasure, and a number were almost completely destroyed during this time of war.

Since 1945, huge excavations at Novgorod have revealed a wealth of domestic and urban material preserved in waterlogged conditions. These finds give a striking image of the early life of this major city.

Ravenna, Italy

Ravenna occupied an important position in the late Roman, early Byzantine, and early medieval periods. It became the western imperial capital early in the fifth century CE and was the base of the Byzantine presence in Italy from the middle of the sixth century to the middle of the eighth century.

A KING'S MAUSOLEUM

This Renaissance painting is attributed to the Italian artist Giovanni M. Falconetto. It shows a man drinking before Ravenna's Mausoleum of Theodoric. The Gothic leader Theodoric played an important role in the early medieval history of Ravenna.

Ravenna's early history is difficult to reconstruct and it was not until the early fifth century CE that it became an important city. It was at Ravenna, however, that Julius Caesar made his famous decision to cross the Rubicon in 45 BCE. In CE 402, the Roman emperor in the west, Honorius, moved his capital from Rome to Ravenna. By this stage the Roman Empire was ruled by two emperors, Honorius in the west and his brother Arcadius in the east based at Constantinople. For the next 350 years Ravenna would remain a city of importance for a number of reasons. Rome had ceased to be politically and militarily significant by the middle of the third century CE because it was too far from the crucial frontier regions of the Rhine and Danube Rivers. Increasingly cities such as Milan in northern Italy and Trier in Germany became more important to the emperors than Rome. Ravenna had the advantage of being closer to the frontier regions in the Balkans and Germany as well as controlling a major port on the Adriatic where the imperial naval fleet was based.

THE RECONQUEST OF RAVENNA

The collapse of the western empire in CE 476 resulted in the Byzantine emperor Zeno sending a Gothic leader by the name of Theodoric to the west to lead a reconquest. Theodoric succeeded in doing so and established the Ostrogothic kingdom of Italy with its capital at Ravenna. Theodoric and his successors nominally recognized Byzantine authority; however, Zeno's plan in effect failed because Theodoric simply replaced Odoacer, the Gothic general whom he had overthrown. When the Byzantine emperor Justinian attempted to take control of Italy in CE 540 as part of his reconquest of the western provinces, his armies took control of Ravenna. For the next 200 years a Byzantine exarchy was established in the city. This

THEODORIC AND RAVENNA

Theodoric was born around CE 454 and succeeded his father as King of the Ostrogoths when he was eighteen. The Ostrogoths were a Germanic tribe that the Romans had been forced to settle in territory near the Danube River. In CE 488 the Byzantine emperor Zeno sent Theodoric on a mission to the western provinces to reassert Byzantine (Roman) authority. This was partly designed to remove the Ostrogoths as a threat to Constantinople. (Following the deposition of the last western Roman emperor, Romulus Augustulus in CE 476, the Gothic leader Odoacer had repudiated any ties with the court at Constantinople.) After three years of campaigning and a successful siege of Odoacer at Ravenna in CE 493, Theodoric had succeeded in his mission. He based himself at Ravenna; Theodoric paid deference to the Byzantine court but effectively ruled Italy as its king. Theodoric died at Ravenna in CE 526, his mausoleum having been constructed six years before.

BASILICA SAN VITALE
A most significant example of Byzantine architecture, the octagonal Basilica San Vitale is one of the largest of Ravenna's churches. It was commissioned by Bishop Ecclesius and consecrated in CE 548 by Archbishop Maximian.

CHARMING COURT LADIES
This well-known mosaic depicting ladies of the court of Empress Theodora, wife of Justinian, is from the Basilica San Vitale. The Basilica contains some of the most beautiful mosaics in all of Europe.

was to last until the Lombards forced the Byzantines out in CE 752. During the 200 years of Byzantine control of Ravenna a significant number of churches were constructed; they contain some of the finest mosaics from the medieval and Byzantine worlds.

RAVENNA'S CHURCHES AND MAUSOLEA

Ravenna's churches are among the best known across Europe. There are currently eight churches there that are listed as UNESCO World Heritage Sites. Perhaps the most famous is the Basilica San Vitale consecrated in CE 548. Its mosaics are some of the most lavish from antiquity, including stunning depictions of the emperor Justinian with his advisers, and his wife Theodora flanked by her attendants. Another important church is the Basilica di Sant Apollinare Nuovo, which is also a sixth-century CE church and contains a mosaic depicting 26 martyrs walking toward Jesus Christ. Further to these is the Basilica di Sant Apollinare in Classe, which was also constructed in the sixth century CE and contains a mosaic in its apse that is covered with stars and ranks among the finest mosaics at Ravenna.

Ravenna houses some noteworthy tombs and mausolea. The mausoleum of Galla Placidia, who was the half-sister of the emperor Honorius (he reigned from CE 395 to CE 423), is another of Ravenna's important monuments. It was constructed between CE 425 and CE 433 to a cruciform plan and contains the oldest mosaics in the city. The Mausoleum of Theodoric, built in CE 520, was designed to hold the remains of the Ostrogothic king who the emperor Zeno sent to Italy in a vain attempt to reassert Byzantine authority in the west. The mausoleum is made of large blocks of stone and does not employ mortar. The dome of the mausoleum measures 36 ft (11 m) in diameter and in the center of the building is a huge basin made of porphyry, a type of marble that is deep purple in color and usually reserved for royalty. As an indication of Ravenna's ongoing significance in the medieval period, the city also contains the tomb of Dante, who wrote most of *The Divine Comedy* at Ravenna following his exile from Florence. Dante died in Ravenna in 1321 and the tomb was constructed soon after.

Asia

Earliest Peoples of Asia

The oldest evidence for human forebears outside Africa comes from Asia. The best-known sites are those of the fossils popularly referred to as "Peking Man" and "Java Man," and for a time they were considered to be the oldest human ancestors in the world.

THE MIGRATION OF PEOPLES ACROSS ASIA

For a long time it was believed that modern humans developed in Asia and migrated across the world from there. However, evidence has now shown that the first modern people traveled from Africa across the Middle East, toward China and Southeast Asia.

After the publication in 1859 of Darwin's *The Origin of Species*, which suggested that all living things evolved through a process of natural selection over successive generations, European scientists began the search for the joint ancestor of modern apes and humans. It was only natural to turn to the two continents where modern apes were found—Africa and Asia. Some considered tropical Asia the most likely candidate because of its bountiful natural diversity of species of plants and animals, and the fact that several species of apes were found there, particularly the orangutan—Bahasa for "man of the forest"—and gibbons.

"JAVA MAN"

Alfred Russel Wallace, who had written to Charles Darwin with his own version of evolutionary theory in 1858, traveled extensively around the islands of Southeast Asia, and described the "manlike orang-utan," which only inhabited the islands of Sumatra and Borneo. Inspired by this theory, in 1887 a young Dutch scientist named Eugène Dubois gave up a post at Leiden University and sailed to the East Indies as a colonial surgeon, with the specific hope of discovering the "missing link" between the mutual ancestors of apes and humans. Having no luck on Sumatra, he turned his attention to central Java in

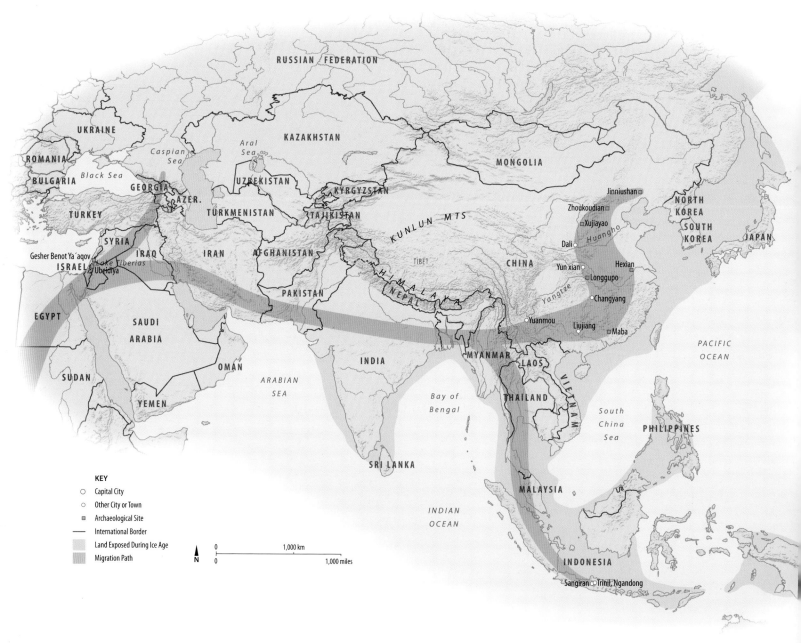

KEY

○ Capital City
○ Other City or Town
▫ Archaeological Site
— International Border
▨ Land Exposed During Ice Age
▨ Migration Path

0   1,000 km
0   1,000 miles

NAMING FOSSILS

In 1940, the German anatomist and physical anthropologist Franz Weidenreich suggested that the Javanese and Chinese fossil forms were not sufficiently diverse to be in a different category from other fossil hominins, and suggested that they be grouped under the same genus as modern humans (*Homo sapiens*) as *Homo erectus*. This is the name by which they are still known. Fossils that were also considered to be of *Homo erectus* type have been found in Africa and Europe, but these days they tend to have different names. In particular, the older African forms are now known as *Homo ergaster*.

Franz Weidenreich (at left) confers with a fellow scientist over the remains of "Peking Man." Weidenreich's insightful scholarship on the subject was widely read and debated.

1891, and, amazingly, on the Solo River at a place called Trinil, he discovered a complete skull cap. It had distinct human aspects, but was more primitive than anything previously known. Dubois also found a thigh bone, which was comparatively modern in appearance, and accordingly he named his discovery *Pithecanthropus erectus*: the ape man that walked upright. On geological grounds, the Dutch scientist estimated the age of this remarkable creature to be approximately 500,000 years old.

"PEKING MAN"

Dubois's discovery, not surprisingly, gave rise to some skepticism, but scientists who were convinced by Darwin's ideas were prepared to accept the finding as a genuine human ancestor. Further discoveries followed some 40 years later at a site near China's capital, then known to the western world as Peking, now Beijing. A cave site called Zhoukoudian was identified in the late 1920s as a place of significant hominin fossils. (The word "hominin" covers all species of humans and their ancestors, and close extinct relatives, including all species of *Homo*, *Australopithecus*, *Paranthropus*, and *Ardipithecus*.) They were initially called *Sinanthropus pekinensis*, or "Chinese man of Peking." These remains were clearly quite similar to, but less primitive than, the Javanese specimens. Thus it appeared in the 1930s that Asia was most likely the cradle of the human species, with an evolutionary line of early human ancestors.

AFRICAN DISCOVERIES

Meanwhile, during the 1920s, Raymond Dart had unearthed fossils of an even older type in South Africa, the Australopithecines, but their acceptance in the scientific community was much slower coming. With the evidence from Olduvai Gorge found by Louis and Mary Leakey in the 1950s and

1960s, it became evident that Africa, not Asia, had the greater claim for the birthplace of the human species.

RECENT RESEARCH

Since the original discoveries, there have been many more Asian sites found with evidence for early hominins. While they contribute a large amount of new knowledge, there are also new complications offered by new evidence, and in some respects the story of the earliest humans in Asia is far from straightforward. This is due to debate over a number of issues, including the dating of sites, as well as how the evidence is to be interpreted.

We would expect the earliest evidence for hominins outside Africa to come from the Middle East, and this can be seen to be the case, at least on one interpretation of the evidence. Finds from Java since the original Dubois discovery, however, can be seen to cast some doubt on this, as also do more recent finds from China. Some very primitive forms from Sangiran in Java hold out the possibility that some older species may have emerged from Africa, and it has even been suggested that *Homo habilis* made it to China. On the other hand, younger fossils from both Java and China, as well as the differences between the original Javanese and Chinese *Homo erectus* remains, show evolutionary development within Asia. Whether that trend leads to an Asian development of modern humans (*Homo sapiens sapiens*) is still strongly debated.

FINDING "PEKING MAN"
Site No. 3 at Zhoukoudian in China, where "Peking Man" was found, held many hominin remains, including some human-like teeth. Zhoukoudian also has a rich geological history.

Ubeidiya, Israel

South of Lake Tiberias in Israel's central Jordan Valley, Ubeidiya is perhaps
the oldest site with evidence for the movement of hominins out of Africa. It is
a deeply layered site with a rich collection of stone artifacts and animal bones,
including those of hominins, dated to 1.5 million years ago.

Since 1959, when farm workers on the local
kibbutz turned up fossil material that they
sent to the Hebrew University in Jerusalem,
the site of Ubeidiya has been the subject of much
archaeological and paleontological research. Major
excavations began in 1960 under the direction of
Moshe Stekelis, and were continued after his death
by Ofer Bar-Yosef and Eitan Tchernov.

The site is dated by a combination of stratigraphic
and paleomagnetic studies to between 1.6 and 1.2
million years ago, very close to the oldest dates for
Homo ergaster (Homo erectus) in Africa. The hominin
fossil remains are scanty, consisting of a few teeth
and cranial fragments. They present problems, one
being that they are too fragmentary to assign to a
particular species. Also, most were not found in the
context of controlled excavation, but loose on the
surface. One incisor however, is said to be securely
assigned to the 1.6 to 1.2 million year time frame,
and is tentatively identified as *Homo ergaster*.

EVIDENCE FOR EARLY HUMAN ACTIVITIES

There is plentiful evidence for a hominin presence
at Ubeidiya, exploiting the resources of what was

once a lake. Large numbers of stone tools include
many of the "hand ax" type, which are found with
Homo ergaster and also at other early *Homo* sites in
Africa and Europe. There is also evidence of meat
exploitation in the form not only of the bones of
large animals, but also of what are clearly hominin
cut-marks on the bones. While some of the meat
may have been scavenged from carcasses, the evidence
suggests active hunting of medium-sized mammals
such as deer and horses.

Another site to the north of Lake Tiberias, named
Gesher Benot Ya'aqov, is somewhat younger, being
dated to *c.* 780,000 years ago. This site expands the
evidence for early hominin activities in the Middle
East, yielding not only stone tools (including hand
axes) and bone remains (including fragments of
hominin), but also some plant remains. Even more
significantly, it includes the earliest known evidence
for the hominin use of fire. It has been suggested that
this site represents a later movement of hominins out
of Africa than Ubeidiya. Be that as it may, the two
sites together demonstrate that *Homo ergaster* was
established in the Middle East from one and a half
million years ago.

ANCIENT BEGINNINGS

The peaceful site of Ubeidiya in
Israel's Jordan Valley, see above,
belies its archaeological and
paleontological significance.
Dated at some 1.5 million years
old, it is one of the oldest hominin
sites outside the African continent.

Zhoukoudian, China

Zhoukoudian (formerly Choukoutien), one of the greatest prehistoric sites in the world, contains a stunning variety of evidence that has been the subject of study for 80 years. It became an important archaeological and paleontological site in 1927, following the identification of "ape man" teeth in an apothecary's shop.

The site is a large limestone cave with a collapsed roof, 31 miles (50 km) southwest of Beijing. Excavations were carried out at the site from 1927 to 1937 by a team of Canadian, Swedish, German, Austrian, American, French, and Chinese scholars.

Several localities at Zhoukoudian have produced archaeological evidence of hominin activity, as well as paleontological evidence of nonhominin fossils, the oldest dating to the Miocene (over seven million years ago) and consisting of fish fossils; the youngest being the Upper Cave, no older than 28,000 years.

HOMO ERECTUS AND ASSOCIATED EVIDENCE

The most productive site at Zhoukoudian was Locality 1, which produced one of the largest collections of *Homo erectus* fossils ever found at one site—with six complete skull caps and other bones representing over 45 individuals, over 6,000 stone artifacts, an extensive collection of animal bones, and some plant remains. The stone tools found at the site are somewhat nondescript, small, flaked items made of a variety of local raw materials, including quite large amounts of quartz. There is also some evidence of fire found within the layers associated with human occupation. The main period of *Homo erectus* occupation has been estimated at between c. 500,000 and 300,000 years ago, mostly between glacial events.

The interpretation of the evidence from Zhoukoudian has been the subject of controversy in recent years. The traditional interpretation was of a cave-dwelling hominin who hunted big game animals and cooked them over fires. This view has been challenged by the suggestion that *Homo erectus* was not such an advanced creature, and the animal bones, and indeed the hominin remains themselves, were the subject of scavenging hyenas, whose remains were also found in the site, and that the evidence for fire was probably due to natural causes.

EARLIER EVIDENCE

There is evidence to suggest the presence of hominins in China earlier than that at Zhoukoudian. A cave site at Longgupo in southern China contains a hominin tooth and some stone artifacts. The tooth is said to have primitive characteristics, which align it with *Homo ergaster* or even *Homo habilis*. The dating of the site is also controversial, one school of thought suggesting the hominin evidence is some 2.4 million years old, another suggesting it is less than one million years old. Other sites that may be up to one million years old have been found in the Nihewan basin in northern China, and at Yuanmou in Yunnan Province in southern China.

Dali, China

Dali is an open-air site in the easternmost part of Shaanxi Province in south-central China. It consists of a deep deposit of silts, sands, and gravels. Near the bottom of this deposit, a hominin skull with intriguing characteristics was found in 1978 by geologist Liu Shuntang.

BIGGER BRAINS

This is a reconstruction of how *Homo erectus* might have looked. One of the distinguishing features of *Homo erectus* is the size of the brain, which was larger than in earlier *Homo* specimens.

The skull is almost complete, although it lacks a lower jaw. The layer in which it was found has been subjected to several forms of dating, and the consensus is that it is about 230,000 years old, perhaps as old as 300,000 years. Nearly 500 stone artifacts were also found at the site. Some of these artifacts have features in common with tools that were found at Zhoukoudian.

WHY IS THIS SKULL SIGNIFICANT?

The Dali skull has been the subject of considerable academic study and debate. It was initially characterized as *Homo erectus*, but many scholars have suggested that it has characteristics more often found in modern humans. It has been accordingly classified as an intermediate form between *Homo erectus* and *Homo sapiens*. This is seen as support for the idea that modern humans evolved from *Homo erectus* in different parts of the world (the "multiregional" hypothesis of human evolution). The contrary view is that modern humans evolved only in Africa and then spread out across the rest of the world (known as the "Out of Africa" hypothesis).

The skull from Dali needs to be seen in relation to other fossil hominins from China, which are younger than the Zhoukoudian Locality 1 *Homo erectus* remains, but which are older than evidence for modern humans *(Homo sapiens sapiens)*. These

STUDYING SKULLS

The Dali skull was found in Liefang Village in Dali County, Shaanxi Province. The skull is rounded and has a small face and prominent forehead. There is much academic debate about whether there is an evolutionary line leading from *Home erectus* to *Homo sapiens*.

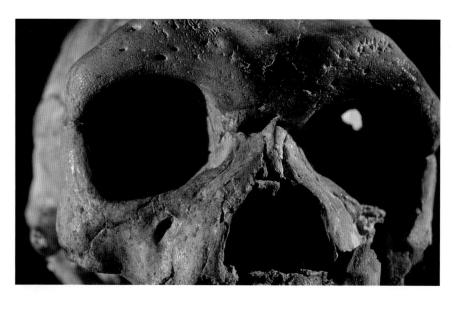

modern humans are generally considered to be much more recent than 100,000 years, and the oldest site in China with *Homo sapiens sapiens* remains is probably Liujiang (Guangxi Zhuang Autonomous Region, south China). It is not a well-dated site, but the human skull seems to be about 70,000 years old.

Other sites with hominin skulls described as being intermediate between *Homo erectus* and *Homo sapiens* are dated to between 400,000 and 120,000 years ago (Yunxian, Hubei Province, north China; Jinniushan, Liaoning Province, north China; Maba, Guangdong Province, south China; Xujiayao, Shaanxi Province, north China). A problem with these fossils is that they have suffered distortion while in the ground (Yunxian and Dali). Another problem for the idea that they represent an evolutionary lineage from *H. erectus* to *H. sapiens* is the discovery of a classic example of *H. erectus* at Hexian (Anhui Province, south-central China), dated to *c.* 150,000–200,000 years ago. If there is indeed an evolutionary line leading from *H. erectus* to *H. sapiens* in China between *c.* 400,000 and 120,000 years ago, there should not be a contemporary example of the ancestral type surviving alongside more evolved types.

Trinil, Indonesia

The site of Trinil is on the Solo River in central Java, where Eugène Dubois unearthed the first example of *Homo erectus* in 1891. In a section of the riverbank, which consisted of soft sandstone and fragments of volcanic rock, he found a skull cap, a femur, and some teeth.

Dubois estimated the age of the deposit containing the skull to be about 500,000 years, but dating old deposits such as these was not a well developed skill in the nineteenth century. Subsequent work in the vicinity has elucidated the context for Dubois's discovery, but there remain many problems with respect to the identification of the fossil species and their antiquity.

RELATED SITES IN CENTRAL JAVA

During the 1930s, further discoveries were made under the aegis of German scientist G. H. R. von Koenigswald at the sites of Sangiran and Ngandong, also on the Solo River, and at other places in the general region. Altogether, the fossil hominins from central Java comprise 21 skulls, 12 jaw fragments, Dubois's femur, as well as many teeth and other fragments; over 50 individuals are represented.

Many of the skulls conform closely with the original find from Trinil, the "classic" *Homo erectus*, but some are very different. Some of the jaws seem to have extremely primitive characteristics, and have been given the not-quite-serious epithet "Meganthropus." It has been suggested that they might represent Australopithecines, which would suggest an extremely early migration out of Africa. Some scientists have suggested that some of the odder examples are in fact apes.

The Ngandong fossils, sometimes known as "Solo man," are seen as more evolved than the classic *Homo erectus* types, and as part of an evolutionary line, in the same way that Dali and similar hominin remains from China are seen as part of a line evolving from *Homo erectus* to *Homo sapiens*.

None of the Javanese hominins has been found in convincing association with stone tools. Since in Africa the presence of stone tools is considered to distinguish members of the genus *Homo* from more primitive forms, this raises problems for the status of the Javanese hominins.

There are problems in dating the fossils because it is not clear exactly where each one was originally found, and it is not necessarily the case that the find location is the original place where the individual died. Because most of the sites are associated with

a riverine setting, it is possible that they could have been redeposited by flooding and other river action. While dates of nearly two million years have been suggested, most scholars seem to be happier with a date of one million years or somewhat less for the Trinil-Sangiran group, and 300,000 years for the Ngandong group.

PUTTING THEIR HEADS TOGETHER FOR SCIENCE

Scientists G. H. R. von Koenigswald (left) and Franz Weidenreich discuss the characteristics of some of the skulls and other fossil remains found in Java.

The Fertile Crescent

About 11,800 years ago the world's first village communities were established, in what is known as the "Neolithic Revolution." After millennia of hunting and gathering, a new strategy had been adopted—people began to live in permanent villages with regular food production. This took place in the Levant, within the modern political units of Israel, Palestine, Jordan, Lebanon, Syria, northern Iraq, and the Euphrates valley of eastern Turkey.

MOTHER GODDESS?
This statuette of a female figure is from a tomb at Tell es-Sawwan in Iraq, and dates to c. 5900 BCE. Some scholars believe that such figurines, both male and female, had ritual significance.

The first phase of the Neolithic period—the Pre-Pottery Neolithic A (9800–8800 BCE)—is characterized by small villages, 0.25–1 acre (0.1–2 ha) in size. People lived, in nuclear families, in rounded and oval structures, each of which contained a cooking area with a hearth and grinding stones. The tools used in daily life were made of flint, limestone, and basalt. The most characteristic flint tools are arrowheads, sickle-blades, and axes. Small quantities of exotic items found there include Anatolian obsidian (volcanic glass), seashells, and green minerals. The few art objects found are female figurines, figurines of birds, and limestone artifacts with geometric incisions. Some scholars believe that the female figures represent a Great Mother Goddess, responsible for the fertility of the lands, animals, and humans. Public activities within settlements were found in a few sites, including at the stone tower of Jericho and a rounded building complete with benches at Jerf el Ahmar. But the most outstanding site yet discovered in the Near East is Göbekli Tepe. This was not a simple village, but a regional cultic center with monumental buildings.

BECOMING MORE ESTABLISHED

The next chronological phase, the Pre-Pottery Neolithic B (c. 8800–6800 BCE), saw larger communities living together. Villages were much bigger in size, sometimes reaching 34 acres (14 ha). The number of known sites increased dramatically and the Neolithic way of life spread into new areas, such as Anatolia, Cyprus, and Southeast Europe. The colonization of the island of Cyprus indicates maritime transportation and the existence of wells there suggests some hydraulic knowledge.

Typical buildings in the Levant were now rectangular, with white floors made of burnt lime plaster painted white or red. Flint, limestone, and basalt remained the main materials for tools. Exotic items like obsidian, seashells, and beads were distributed between the sites, and in the Turkish sites of Çayönü and Aşikli Höyük, items made of native copper were found.

The agglomeration of people in large communities created a new social order. This social stratification is evident in the size of residences and their access to commodities such as burnt lime. There is also an increase in the number of art and cult objects. On

ANCIENT KITCHEN TOOL
Dating to the Neolithic period, this slightly curved mortar and rounded pestle were found in the ancient Palestine region of the Near East. They may have been used to pound wheat grains into flour.

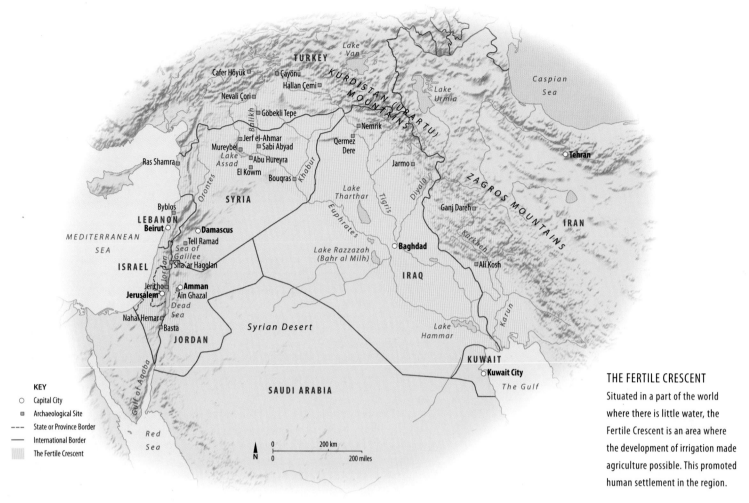

THE FERTILE CRESCENT

Situated in a part of the world where there is little water, the Fertile Crescent is an area where the development of irrigation made agriculture possible. This promoted human settlement in the region.

the household level there were small artifacts, such as human or animal figurines. During this time cattle figurines start to appear in large quantities; rituals around them were probably designed to ensure successful hunting. On the community level there are large-scale, life-size items, like plastered skulls, masks, and large statues. Many of these were found in 'Ain Ghazal, a 34-acre (14-ha) site in Jordan. In the northern Levant impressive stone statues were unearthed at a large cultic building in Nevali Çori. These life-size artifacts suggest that dancing was a main component of religious activity.

DEVELOPED VILLAGE COMMUNITIES

The Pottery Neolithic (c. 6800–5800 BCE), the third chronological phase, was characterized by the introduction of pottery. Many sites seemed to be composed of pits, rather than built structures; archaeologists called this "Retrogression." However, opinions changed when Sha'ar Hagolan was excavated. In this 49-acre (20-ha) site, massive buildings were found located along a network of streets. Flint, limestone, and basalt were still used extensively, but the introduction of pottery opened new horizons in household organization. Pottery vessels stored liquids, grain, and cooked food.

A sophisticated administrative system was developed for the storage and redistribution of various goods. Evidence of this was found at the burnt village of Tell Sabi Abyad, where, in a small room, 209 clay sealings were found, many bearing seal impressions. They were used for sealing containers made of wicker, wood, or pottery.

The general picture is that over time, there was an increased complexity in Neolithic settlements. There were more villages and family dwellings; new building techniques were introduced, water shortages were solved by digging wells, seals and sealings were invented, and complex community rituals developed. The Neolithic way of life spread into Asia, Europe, and Africa. The success of this new economic and social order led to the development of urban cultures and the rise of the state in Mesopotamia and Egypt in the fourth millennium BCE.

BURIAL PRACTICES IN VILLAGE COMMUNITIES

Burial practices changed over time in the Fertile Crescent. In the small villages of the Pre-Pottery Neolithic A period (9800–8800 BCE), adults were commonly buried in a flexed position under the floors of houses. Sometimes the skulls were removed and stored together in another location.

As the size of villages increased during the Pre-Pottery Neolithic B period (c. 8800–6800 BCE), burial practices became more elaborate. The treatment of the individual corpse was much the same, but some of the removed skulls were now plastered or painted and kept in the home for a time. Sometimes, groups of skulls were buried together in pits. Also during this period, there is ritual burial of cultic objects evident for the first time.

Jericho, Israel

Jericho is in the Jordan Valley, near the Dead Sea. In the 1950s Kathleen Kenyon excavated a sequence of four Neolithic phases, one on top of the other: Pre-Pottery Neolithic A, Pre-Pottery Neolithic B, Pottery Neolithic A, and Pottery Neolithic B. This was the first time that such a detailed sequence was recognized in the Near East, and Jericho became the key site for understanding the Neolithic period.

Jericho was a regional center in the Pre-Pottery Neolithic A. This is borne out by a number of discoveries. At 6 acres (2.5 ha), Jericho is the largest known settlement of the period, and nearly ten other smaller sites, such as Netiv Hagdud, Gilgal, Dra', and Zahara a Dra', are known to be one or two days walking distance from Jericho. In addition, large quantities of Anatolian obsidian and green-stone artifacts were imported to Jericho.

THE SECOND NEOLITHIC SETTLEMENT

In the Pre-Pottery Neolithic B period, Jericho was a medium-sized village, with condensed rectangular buildings. The floors were made of lime plaster, sometimes smeared over with branches, and some impressions of rounded mats have been preserved. The flint industry of this phase was characterized by long, elegant blades, which were produced from a special type of flint core, known as "Naviform." Arrowheads and sickle-blades were made from this particular flint core.

Kenyon unearthed a few concentrations of plastered human skulls which were buried in pits. The removal of skulls from dead bodies was noticed already in the Pre-Pottery Neolithic A phase, but in this phase no special treatment took place and the skulls were kept in groups on the floors. Now the skulls received some intensive treatment. They were plastered and sometimes seashells were inserted as "eyes." The skulls are connected with an ancestor cult, which can be connected to the beginning of a sedentary way of life. When the skulls were no longer needed, they were buried in pits. Nowadays plastered skulls are known from a number of Pre-Pottery Neolithic B sites, including Beisamoun, Tell Ramad, 'Ain Ghazal, Kfar HaHoresh, and Tell Aswad.

DOORWAY TO JERICHO
An old archaeological trench at Jericho is now a well-worn pathway. The Jericho site, located to the west of the Jordan River, was one of the first ancient locations in the Near East to be recorded in depth.

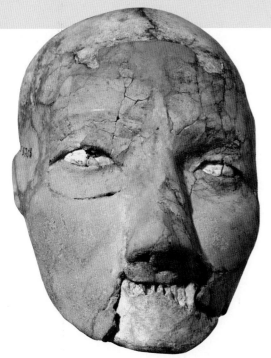

AHEAD OF THE REST
This skull, with the facial features partially reconstructed in plaster, dates
to *c.* 7000 BCE. Shells were often used to represent eyes, and sometimes the
plaster was painted black or red in order to individualize the skulls.

The skulls may represent community elders, both male
and female, and may have been used to justify the
settling of a group in a particular village and its fields.

Jericho is famous for its large plaster statues of
people. These were first uncovered during excavations
conducted by John Garstang in the 1930s. He found
two concentrations of such statues, both inside pits.
Fragments of similar items were also uncovered by
Kenyon, but in a poor state of preservation. The best
examples of such statues are from the excavation of
'Ain Ghazal in Jordan.

At the end of the Pre-Pottery Neolithic B, Jericho
was abandoned for a few hundred years. Only in the
1980s, during the excavations of the Neolithic site of
'Ain Ghazal, did it become apparent that there was
an additional chronological phase—the Pre-Pottery
Neolithic C. Thus, even Jericho did not have a full
sequence of the Neolithic period.

THE LATER NEOLITHIC SETTLEMENTS

In the Pottery Neolithic A, Jericho was probably
used seasonally by nomadic people, as no solid
architecture was found, but rather, many rounded
pits. The pottery of this phase, known as Jericho IX,
is characterized by burnished red or brown lines. In
the same period other cultures flourished in the
southern Levant—the Yarmukian culture to the
north and Nizzanim culture to the west.

The last phase is the Pottery Neolithic B, which
is better classified as Early Chalcolithic. The pottery
is typical of the Wadi Rabah culture, and its main
characteristic is red or black slip and burnished
pottery, complete with various surface manipulation
techniques: incisions, impressions, and punctuations.

THE STONE TOWER OF JERICHO

The most outstanding discovery in Jericho is the stone tower, which was 26 ft (8 m) in
height. Inside it a staircase with 20 steps was constructed. Adjacent to the tower, there
was a stone wall encircling the settlement from the west. Outside this wall was a 16-ft
(5-m) wide trench. Archaeologist Kathleen Kenyon interpreted these elements as
fortifications against enemies and called Jericho the earliest city in the world. Other
interpretations have been suggested over the years—protection from winter floods,
storage centers, or magical devices. In any case, the unique labor-intensive constructions of Jericho, which were not found in any other settlement of that period, required
a sophisticated social organization. The structures emphasize the central role of Jericho
in the settlement pattern of the Pre-Pottery Neolithic A of the southern Levant.

The remains of a wall around the stone tower in Jericho have been dated to around 8000 BCE.
Jericho has been referred to as one of the world's oldest fortified settlements.

In conclusion, the importance of Jericho for the
Neolithic period is twofold. It was the first site in
which a detailed Neolithic sequence was identified by
modern scholars. At Jericho the basic terminology of
the Neolithic period was established (though it has
since been much modified). The methodology used
by Kathleen Kenyon was also of great importance.
She developed, together with Sir Mortimer Wheeler,
an excavation concept that concentrates on digging
very deep sections into archaeological sites. In this
way the history of a site and the dating of the various
architectural units can be closely examined.

In the history of archaeology, Pre-Pottery Neolithic A
Jericho was the first major regional center to be studied,
and indicates a complex settlement pattern already
underway in the first phase of a sedentary way of life.

The Domestication of Plants and Animals

RICH RIVERBANKS

This section of the Euphrates River located in Kurdistan, eastern Turkey, is typical of the type of landscape in which agriculture, and more sedentary settlements, had their beginnings.

The domestication of plants and animals was a major breakthrough in human evolution. Artificial production of food dramatically intensified the carrying capacity of territories and enabled a population growth that hunters and gatherers could never achieve. Domestication was a long process, progressing in stages, that took a few millennia.

THEORIES ON THE BEGINNINGS OF AGRICULTURE

The first intellectual interest in the beginnings of agriculture was raised by Vere Gordon Childe in the 1930s. He created the term "The Neolithic Revolution," and suggested that this was a human response to climatic changes at the end of the last ice age. He suggested that this process took place in oasis environments, where humans, plants, and animals came close to each other, and that the result was the domestication of plants and animals. The first scholar who went into the field in order to excavate a site of an early village community was Robert Braidwood in the late 1940s. According to his theory, the beginnings of agriculture took place in the hilly area that flanks the Fertile Crescent to the north. These mountains are the natural habitat for the wild animals and plants that were later domesticated. So this seemed to be the core area for domestication. Braidwood excavated the site of Jarmo, in Iraqi Kurdistan, which he believed was "the world's earliest village."

Since then many other theories have been suggested as to the beginning of agriculture, which may have been a human response to climatic changes and population pressure. Numerous botanical and zoological studies are being conducted, including examination of archaeological data, observations on the wild species in nature, and even DNA studies.

THE DOMESTICATION PROCESS

Today, after intensive fieldwork in hundreds of sites, we know that domestication of plants and animals took a few millennia to achieve. Already in the Natufian culture, some 14,000 years ago, dogs had been domesticated. The evidence suggests that dogs were used for their hunting skills and for protection.

In the Pre-Pottery Neolithic A, the economy was almost certainly based on hunting wild animals, as well as the cultivation of cereals and legumes. These plants do not bear clear morphological evidence for domestication, and some scholars argue that at this early phase only wild plants were cultivated. From the archaeological records, it is clear that a sedentary lifestyle was in place well before the domestication of edible plants and animals.

In the Pre-Pottery Neolithic B, the agricultural process was well established. Domesticated cereals included emmer wheat, einkorn wheat, and barley; domesticated legumes included lentils, peas, chickpeas, and beans. The herding of sheep and goats was also established. However, in most sites, hunting was

MAN'S BEST FRIEND

These skeletons of a man and his dog, found in Israel, have been dated at more than 12,000 years old. The remains are a poignant reminder of the special relationship humans have had with dogs for thousands of years.

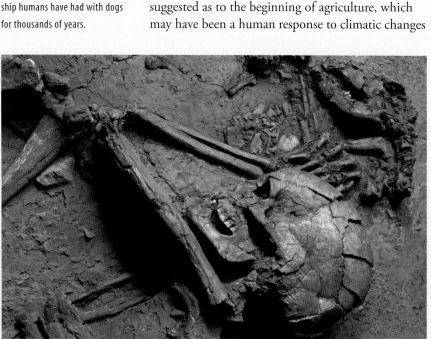

These bronze ax heads date to *c.* 3000 BCE. By that time there had been great advances in metal technology; archaeological evidence shows that there was a movement away from the use of stone tools to tools made of metal, notably copper. This is sometimes called the Chalcolithic period, meaning "copper-stone," as both copper and stone were in use.

THE GRAINS OF LIFE
Emmer wheat was one of the first cereals to be grown in the Fertile Crescent, and it was later used by the Ancient Egyptians to make bread. It is still harvested in some areas of the world today.

still an important source of the community's meat supply. Also, in this period, textiles were being produced. Textiles have been found in large quantities in the Nahal Hemar Cave.

In the Pottery Neolithic period, the domestication process became much more established with the introduction of two new species—cattle and pigs. During this period, the hunting of wild animals decreased drastically. Most of the meat consumed came from animal husbandry. By the end of the Pre-Pottery Neolithic B, the arid zones of the Fertile Crescent underwent a major change. While in the earlier phases they were exploited by Neolithic hunter and gatherer communities, now a new way of life was adopted in the desert. With herds of domesticated sheep and goats, occupation spread into the arid areas and full-time nomadic pastoralism became more common.

THE "SECONDARY PRODUCTS REVOLUTION"

During the Chalcolithic period, further developments took place. These included the domestication of trees, such as the olive and the fig. In what is known as the "Secondary Products Revolution," the exploitation of animals became more intensive, because it included milking, harvesting wool, and using animals to fulfill transportation needs. In the late fifth millennium BCE, the donkey was domesticated as a beast of burden. Domesticated horses are known in the area only since the middle of the second millennium BCE, and the domesticated camel only since the end of the second millennium BCE.

Göbekli Tepe, Turkey

Göbekli Tepe, located in the northern Levant near the modern Turkish city of Sanliurfa, was not only a village, but also a regional cultic center. Monumental structures, built of stone and T-shaped pillars, were constructed over a long period of time. Göbekli Tepe was probably a focus for pilgrimage and religious activities for the Neolithic communities of the northern Levant.

A CAPTIVATING SITE
Many scholars believe that close examination of the archaeological site at Göbekli Tepe will help us to understand the gradual transition from hunter-gatherer societies to farming economies.

Since 1995 Klaus Schmidt of the German Archaeological Institute in Berlin has been excavating Göbekli Tepe, in a site located on top of a limestone hill without any permanent water source nearby. He found monumental architecture with stone walls preserved to heights of 6½–10 ft (2–3 m), and T-shaped stone pillars, 6½–13 ft (2–4 m) tall. Each pillar weighs a few tons.

The pillars are decorated, either with engravings or bas-reliefs, with either various animals or geometric designs. The excellent preservation in the site is the result of the fact that the buildings were partly below ground level, and they were backfilled (probably for ritual reasons) when they fell out of use. Extensive surveys of the surrounding site identified cuttings from which the T-shaped pillars were quarried.

In the upper part of the site at Göbekli Tepe, a complete Pre-Pottery Neolithic B rectangular monumental building was found, with four large pillars still standing. These were decorated with impressive lion figures, portrayed ready to attack, with teeth bared and tails lifted. Representations of humans were also found, including simple floor slab graffiti of naked women, and a limestone statue of a naked male with an erect penis.

THE EARLIEST-BUILT TEMPLES IN THE WORLD

Most of the activity here dates to an earlier phase—the Pre-Pottery Neolithic A. Monumental circular enclosures, with a rounded stone wall, were unearthed here. These have 10 or more T-shaped pillars standing in an inner circle, and two pillars in the structure's center. Various other installations were also cut from one big block of limestone. As at 2006, four such structures have been found.

These constructions are being viewed as open-air courtyards, as no roofs were built over them. The pillars are decorated with animals—boars, foxes, cattle, spiders, snakes, and birds. In many cases the male sex organs were emphasized. Some pillars were decorated with geometric patterns. In addition, many medium-sized limestone statues of animals were found. In the 2006 season, one headless human figure was found on a T-shaped pillar, the first anthropomorphic representation that can be safely related to the early phase at the site.

Sha'ar Hagolan, Israel

Sha'ar Hagolan is a 50-acre (20-ha) site located in the Jordan Valley in northern Israel. This is the largest-known Neolithic site in the Fertile Crescent. The first appearance of courtyard buildings and a street network adds a new chapter in the history of architecture and settlement planning.

Sha'ar Hagolan dates to the Pottery Neolithic period (*c.* 6800–5800 BCE), and is the type site for the Yarmukian culture, which occupied large parts of the Mediterranean climatic zones of Israel, Jordan, and Lebanon. In excavations by Yosef Garfinkel in the 1990s, approximately 3,600 sq yards (3,000 sq m) were uncovered, exposing a well-planned settlement. Dwellings were large courtyard houses, that measured 299–837 sq yards (250–700 sq m) each, composed of between eight and 24 rooms built around an open courtyard. These monumental complexes were used by extended families, unlike the much smaller Pre-Pottery Neolithic buildings, which were used by nuclear families. The courtyard houses are the earliest example of this architectural concept, still used today in the Near East and around the Mediterranean.

The courtyard houses were densely built, abutting each other, along narrow streets. Some streets run from north to south and others run from east to west. Such a street network is not known from other Neolithic sites. Although water could have come from the nearby Yarmuk River, a well was dug inside the settlement to the aquifer level. Was this for security, or for the quality of the well water?

THE ART ASSEMBLAGE

The largest assemblage of prehistoric art ever uncovered in Israel came from Sha'ar Hagolan. Among the more than 300 items are baked clay female figures with wide hips and rolls of fat, seated comfortably and surveying the world through diagonal grooved eyes. The figurines are designed with a wealth of detail and the features are exaggerated, giving them a surrealistic appearance. Another

CHILD-BEARING HIPS

This Neolithic clay-baked female figurine, possibly a Mother Goddess, comes from Sha'ar Hagolan. The site is one of the most important prehistoric centers in Israel.

NEOLITHIC POTTERY

Seen here is a group of Neolithic pottery vessels from Sha'ar Hagolan. Until recently, the remains of the village were covered with olive groves and small ponds. The excavations are being carried out under the guidance of archaeologists from the Hebrew University of Jerusalem.

type of figurine was made from natural limestone river pebbles. With a few incisions, and sometimes by drilling, a schematic human figure was carved on the pebble. These two types represent mainly female figures, possibly the Goddess of Sha'ar Hagolan.

POPULATION PRESSURE AND HUMAN ORGANIZATION

The inhabitants of Sha'ar Hagolan were part of a new mode of life—a few thousand people living together in the same site. Like their neighbors elsewhere in the Fertile Crescent, they developed a new type of architecture—the courtyard building. They reorganized the community in extended families, where a few nuclear families dwelled together around this common courtyard. Only narrow passageways, the street network, were left between the structures, thus increasing the settlement density. Cultic activities were intensified and produced many figurines. The excavations at Sha'ar Hagolan have opened new horizons to our understanding of the later part of the Neolithic period.

Ancient Mesopotamia

Ancient Mesopotamia, "the cradle of civilization," was the birthplace of some of the earliest cities of human history, a sophisticated writing system, complex bureaucracies and literary tradition, and the highly skilled production of artifacts. The Euphrates and Tigris River basins form the backbone of this historical geography: Mesopotamia—literally "land between the rivers" in ancient Greek— the land of cities, agricultural prosperity, scribal culture, and textile production.

Mesopotamian cultures flourished in exceptionally diverse landscapes, from the metal-rich mountains of southeastern Turkey to the Syrian deserts, from the forests of the Levant to the marshes of southern Iraq. Yet, Mesopotamian peoples, from their historical beginnings with urbanization and the emergence of complex societies in the late fourth millennium BCE to the arrival of Alexander the Great in 333 BCE, shared an outstandingly continuous cultural tradition. It is hard to imagine Mesopotamian civilization in isolation from its rich prehistoric cultural heritage, and its legacy in Classical and Islamic civilizations in the Middle East. Yet Mesopotamian archaeology largely focuses on complex societies that populated the regions of the Tigris and Euphrates basins from the late fourth millennium BCE to the late first. The long-term linguistic and cultural continuity across three millennia was maintained by shared memories, identities, and world views. From the very beginning, both Sumerian and Akkadian-speaking populations inhabited the Mesopotamian plains, and the official language of its states alternated between the two for centuries, using the same cuneiform script on clay tablets. Textual documentation on everyday life is abundant, as written documents were highly durable objects. About half a million clay tablets have been recovered in excavations across the region since the mid-nineteenth century. Most remain unpublished and unstudied.

LANDSCAPES OF THE EARLY MESOPOTAMIAN WORLD

The alluvial plains of Lower Mesopotamia (southern Iraq) and the hilly landscapes of Upper Mesopotamia (northern Syria, northern Iraq, southeastern Turkey) offer two distinct environments. The lower Mesopotamian plain is an alluvial landscape laid down by the two rivers. Here, agriculture depends on irrigation. In Upper Mesopotamia, farmers depend on rainfall. In the southern alluvium where the first complex societies of the Near East emerged, the economy depended on irrigation agriculture, which was accomplished through a complex network of irrigation canal systems. As southern Mesopotamia lacked some vital natural resources such as good quality timber, precious and durable stones, and metals, long-distance trade was a significant aspect of Mesopotamian urban economies.

Both landscapes are spotted today with numerous mounds (tells or höyüks) of ancient settlement, formed by multiple layers of occupation and rebuilding with mud-brick.

CITIES, TEMPLES, KINGS: MESOPOTAMIAN CULTURAL HISTORIES

In the second half of the fourth millennium BCE, Uruk and Nippur in the southern alluvium emerged as major ceremonial urban centers. Excavating Uruk's

TIMELINE OF ANCIENT MESOPOTAMIAN HISTORY

Uruk Period	4000–3100 BCE
3500–3100 BCE	Late Uruk Period: urbanization and earliest writing at Uruk (Warka)
Jemdet Nasr Period	3100–2900 BCE
	Beginnings of development of writing and seals
Early Dynastic Period (Early Bronze Age)	2900–2000 BCE
2700–2600 BCE	Tell Asmar statues Construction of Temple Oval at Khafajah
2600–2100 BCE	Royal Tombs of Ur
2334–2193 BCE	Akkadian Empire
c. 2100 BCE	Second Dynasty of Lagash and Gudea
2112–2004 BCE	Third Dynasty of Ur
2112–2095 BCE	Construction of first ziggurat at the time of Ur-Nammu
Middle Bronze Age	2000–1600 BCE
	Old Babylonian Period
Late Bronze Age	1600–1200 BCE
1595 BCE	Sack of Babylon by the Hittites
Iron Age	1200–330 BCE
	Early Iron Age
1200–1175 BCE	Abandonment of major urban centers such as Hattusha and Ugarit
934–611 BCE	Neo-Assyrian Empire
717–705 BCE	Foundation of Khorsabad
612 BCE	Sack of Nineveh by Medes and Babylonians, collapse of the Assyrian Empire
626–539 BCE	Neo-Babylonian kingdom
604–562 BCE	Nebuchadnezzar II's building project at Babylon
550–330 BCE	Achaemenid Empire
334 BCE	Alexander the Great starts his conquest of Persia

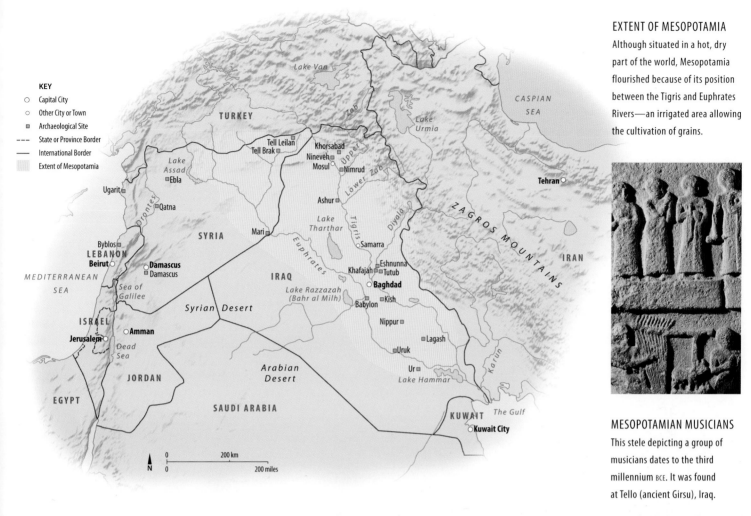

KEY
- ○ Capital City
- ○ Other City or Town
- ◻ Archaeological Site
- --- State or Province Border
- — International Border
- ▨ Extent of Mesopotamia

EXTENT OF MESOPOTAMIA
Although situated in a hot, dry part of the world, Mesopotamia flourished because of its position between the Tigris and Euphrates Rivers—an irrigated area allowing the cultivation of grains.

MESOPOTAMIAN MUSICIANS
This stele depicting a group of musicians dates to the third millennium BCE. It was found at Tello (ancient Girsu), Iraq.

late Chalcolithic levels at the Sanctuary of Inanna, archaeologists came across the evidence of first writing, and also complex administrative tools of exchange such as cylinder seals, monumental architecture with outstanding technologies, and a highly developed visual culture. By the mid-third millennium BCE, the "Early Dynastic Period," southern Mesopotamia was populated with small regional states, with agricultural hinterlands located around an urban center. Among the archaeologically well explored ones, Eshnunna, Nippur, Ur, Lagash, and Tutub stand out as important Early Mesopotamian cities. Two major urban institutions, the temple and the palace, gradually gained power. These were primarily socioeconomic institutions that owned agricultural land and animal flocks, and sponsored craftsmen and merchants.

The short-lived states of the late third millennium BCE, the Akkadian kingdom and the Third Dynasty of Ur, mark the culmination of such sociopolitical development and represent the first territorially ambitious, bureaucratically complex states in Mesopotamia. The Akkadians had an innovative visual culture, elaborate royal ideology, and a massive production of literary and annalistic texts. Nippur became a pan-Mesopotamian cult center in the late third and early second millennia. This role gradually transferred to Babylon in the second and first

millennia, as Babylonian culture came to dominate. The sociopolitical and economic center of gravity shifted to Upper Mesopotamia from the mid-second millennium onward, with Hittite, Mitanni, Assyrian, and Neo-Babylonian empires having their territorial expansions in the Northern Mesopotamian and Anatolian landscapes, the growth of seafaring trade networks in the Mediterranean, and the increasing difficulties in maintaining agricultural production in the southern alluvium.

EPIC RUINS
An Iraqi guide points toward the White Temple, located at the base of the Anu ziggurat, at the archaeological site of Uruk. This was a city known for its ancient king, Gilgamesh, the hero of the famous epic named after him.

Ur, Iraq

IRAQ
Baghdad○

■Ur

The southern Mesopotamian city of Ur, which is associated with the biblical city Ur of the Chaldees—reputed birthplace of Abraham—was an impressive merchant city in the late third to early second millennium BCE, and flourished under the ambitious kings of the Third Dynasty of Ur, who built the first-known ziggurat.

Most of the archaeological work at the site of ancient Ur, known today as Tell al Muqayyar in southern Iraq, was carried out between 1922 and 1934 by Sir Leonard Woolley, and sponsored by the University of Pennsylvania Museum and the British Museum. It became clear that the site was occupied from the Ubaid period (sixth millennium) onward for approximately 5,000 years: we know that Neo-Babylonian kings of the sixth century BCE were restoring prominent buildings at the site.

AN URBAN SPECTACLE: HOUSE OF THE MOON GOD NANNA

The last century of the third millennium (2112–2004 BCE) was probably Ur's most prosperous period. It was the capital of the Third Dynasty of Ur; its rulers built public monuments and maintained urban spaces. The Ur III state was a powerful territorial kingdom with a complex bureaucratic system of provincial administration, taxation, and management of agricultural production and trade, recorded with unprecedented precision on thousands of tablets.

The most outstanding building program was the sanctuary complex of the moon god Nanna, initiated by the first king of the dynasty, Ur-Nammu (2112–2095 BCE) and completed by his son Shulgi (2095–2047 BCE). The sanctuary had its own enclosure wall and included the ceremonial Great Court of Nanna and the earliest archaeologically known ziggurat, built as a three-tiered solid structure of brickwork and measuring 205 ft by 140 ft (62.5 m by 43 m) at its base. Each baked brick was inscribed with Ur-Nammu's name. It was also home to palatial structures, storerooms, and the Giparu, the dwelling of the entu-priestesses, the highest office holders in the temple institution.

THE ROYAL TOMBS OF UR: ARTIFACTS OF COMPLEXITY

Woolley's team also excavated a cemetery, used between 2600 and 2100 BCE, of approximately 2,000 burials. Woolley designated 16 tombs "royal," based

THE AMAZING ZIGGURAT

The ziggurat at Ur was dedicated to the moon god Nanna and was first constructed around 2110 BCE. The restoration work gives us some idea of the grandeur of the original structure.

on the architectural complexity of the burial chambers, the wealth of tomb artifacts, and the evidence for sumptuous funerary rites. Some of the more impressive burials involved groups of individuals, such as musicians, servants, guards, and oxen-yoked carts and drivers, who apparently were sacrificed to accompany the dead in the afterlife. The tomb artifacts are astounding in the technologies of production and diversity of materials used. Queen Puabi's headdress was made of gold, lapis lazuli, and carnelian; the Great Lyre from Tomb 789 featured a gold-sheeted bull's head with an undulating beard in lapis lazuli, and a narrative panel of inlaid shell; a gold vessel in the form of an ostrich egg was inlaid with lapis lazuli, red limestone, and shell. The tombs contained ceremonial vessels, tools, weaponry, inscribed seals, musical instruments, jewelry, and furniture.

85. [90060]
BRICK OF KURIGALZU,
KING OF BABYLON,
RECORDING THE RESTORATION
OF AN ANCIENT TEMPLE OF
NANNAR, THE MOON-GOD,
IN THE CITY OF UR.
FROM
MUKEYYER. [ABOUT
B.C.1400]

AIMING FOR THE MOON

The ancient Brick of Kurigalzu I, king of Babylon, records the restoration of the temple of the moon god Nanna. It was found at Ur, and dates to c. 1400 BCE.

Tell Asmar, Iraq

Tell Asmar, ancient Eshnunna, was a formidable Mesopotamian city of the third to early second millennium BCE, located in the Diyala River valley. The site was excavated by the University of Chicago's Oriental Institute in the 1930s and remains one of our best sources for understanding the complexity of Mesopotamian cities.

Early Mesopotamian literary texts metaphorically refer to cities as the "cattle-pen" *(tùr)* and the "sheep-fold" *(amaš)*, the archetypal enclosures of agricultural people of the southern alluvium.

THE CATTLE-PEN AND THE SHEEP-FOLD: THE EARLY MESOPOTAMIAN CITY

These metaphors for prosperity centered on the king as "shepherd" *(sipa)* who founded cities and exploited landscapes. Cities were laid out by the "precious designs" *(giš-hur)* of their gods, and endowed with "divine powers" *(me).* This complex image of the Mesopotamian city was, however, not formed overnight. Tell Asmar presents a comprehensive image of a densely built urban landscape in the third and early second millennia BCE. Excavations uncovered residential neighborhoods and public buildings including temples, palace complexes, and the city's fortifications.

Eshnunna's urban flourishing coincides with a crucial transition in the history of Mesopotamian cities: the gradual appearance of the temple and the palace as two important, yet rival, socioeconomic institutions. In the Early Dynastic Period, the temple is the more powerful entity. Toward the end of the Early Dynastic Period and during the Akkadian/Ur III periods of the late third millennium BCE, the palace emerges as an equally powerful entity.

ABU TEMPLE CROWD

Early Dynastic Eshnunna was concentrated on the northwestern portion of the Tell Asmar mound, where archaeologists excavated a small temple, dedicated to a local god named Abu, with a long sequence of rebuilding, and some fascinating statues. Excavators determined three different architectural designs—the "Archaic Shrine" of the Early Dynastic I period, the "Square Temple" of the Early Dynastic II period, and the "Single Shrine" of the Early Dynastic III. The "Square Temple" of the mid-third millennium BCE appears to be the most prosperous and extensive phase of the building, with several cult rooms arranged around a central courtyard. One cult room contained a hoard of statues, both female and male, and of varying heights and features, that were carved from veined gypsum. One striking feature is the disproportionately large eyes, inlaid either with black limestone or lapis lazuli. Some scholars believe that prominent families may have dedicated these statues to the temple, the large eyes allowing them intense contact with the divine.

North of the Abu Temple is the North Palace, where evidence for manufacturing activities, including textile production, was found. There was also an elaborate system of drains. In the late third and early second millennia BCE, Eshnunna's urban center moved to the southern sector of the mound where Akkadian, Ur III, and Isin-Larsa kings commissioned many palaces and temples.

The Development of Writing

One of the earliest writing systems of the ancient world was developed in southern Mesopotamia, approximately between 3300 and 2900 BCE. It is widely known as the cuneiform script, written with a reed stylus on soft damp clay tablets, which then either hardened up in Mesopotamia's dry heat or, in rare cases, was baked. The earliest evidence of writing comes from the Late Uruk and Jemdet Nasr Period Levels IVa and III at the site of Uruk (Warka), in the Eanna Precinct (the sanctuary complex dedicated to the goddess Inanna) in the remains of a cultic/administrative building. These earliest documents were composed of pictographic and numerical signs, and appear to be economic documents, testifying to the fact that writing appeared as an administrative, bureaucratic technology in the context of urbanization, increasing social and political complexity, and the appearance of monumental architecture.

KEEPING TALLY

Among the many testaments to everyday life found in Mesopotamia is this Sumerian clay tablet, dating to *c.* 2350 BCE, which lists an account of goats and sheep. It was found at Tello (ancient Girsu), one of the first sites in the region to be extensively excavated.

Stratigraphically the earliest seven tablets come from a structure called Temple C. However, approximately 6,000 tablets were excavated in the Late Uruk and Jemdet Nasr levels in the Sanctuary of Inanna at Uruk, primarily recovered from rubbish dumps or the fills used to create foundations for Level III buildings. This suggests that the practice of using written economic documents quickly spread with the passage of time. Yet the invention of cuneiform script was not a spontaneous invention of the scribes at the Eanna complex. In southern Mesopotamia, since the Neolithic and long before the appearance of tablets, hollow clay balls and clay tokens were used to record and administer economic transactions. Regularly shaped and sometimes incised small lumps of clay (tokens) were deposited in clay spheres that were hollow inside. The outer surfaces were then impressed with cylinder seals.

WEDGE-SHAPED WRITING

Cuneiform means "wedge-shaped"—the triangular tip of the stylus made small triangular signs in combination with lines. The earliest Uruk tablets, also known as "archaic" or "proto-cuneiform" tablets, present a complex system of logographic and numerical-metrological signs. Scholars have pointed out that these logograms or pictograms draw heavily on the pictorial repertoire of representations on seals and other visual media. For instance, the reed bundle that represents Inanna in pictographic writing is also attested extensively on cylinder and stamp seal impressions and alabaster vases. Approximately 900 signs were identified from this earliest phase. The incised iconographically explicit pictograms of the

ROYAL INSCRIPTIONS

This ancient Sumerian stone gate-socket bears an inscription of Ur-Gur, better known as Ur-Nammu (who ruled Ur from 2112 to 2095 BCE). Cuneiform script recorded important political and historical events, as well as daily economic transactions and activities relating to the temples.

archaic tablets were gradually abstracted with the increasingly efficient and dexterous use of the stylus and its multiple combinations of the basic cuneiform mark (a wedge and a line).

COMBINING PICTURES AND NUMBERS

As the archaic tablets from Uruk are entirely pictographic and numerical, they can be a means of incorporating rebus writing, phonetic/syllabic signs, and grammatical affixes; Sumerian is attested as the language of writing in southern Mesopotamia. Among the tablets from Ur dating to around 2800 BCE, traces of Sumerian can be detected. Sumerian cannot be related to any other languages in world history. It was spoken in Mesopotamia until it was restricted to scholarly endeavor from the early second millennium BCE

onward. Cuneiform script was also adopted for writing Akkadian, the commonly used Semitic language of Mesopotamian history.

For both Sumerian and Akkadian, in the script's most complex form and throughout its use in history, cuneiform signs acquired multiple values, used either as syllables or as ideograms that stood for a word. The writing system necessitated a complex combination of both, making the script relatively difficult to follow. Alphabetic writing was not introduced to Mesopotamia until the Iron Age, with Aramaic, which developed out of Phoenician in *c.* 900 BCE. In the Iron Age in northern Syria and Anatolia, a hieroglyphic script was used in writing monumental inscriptions in Luwian by several regional states. Cuneiform was adapted to write both Aramaic and Luwian.

CYLINDER SEALS

Cylinder seals are another ubiquitous invention of Mesopotamian societies in the context of the Late Uruk urbanization, following the more widely known stamp seals. Cylinder-shaped seals were often carved out of hard and precious stones and bore complex pictorial representations (seen at right), which were impressed on clay by means of rolling. They were used to seal vessels, bundles, or doors, in addition to clay tablets or hollow clay balls. Since many of these clay elements used in transactions bear shapes and symbols that can be matched with the earliest pictograms and numerical signs in the earliest Uruk tablets, scholars have argued that they need to be seen as earlier stages in the development of the cuneiform script.

Babylon, Iraq

Babylon has colored Western imaginations, beginning with Herodotus who described it as "different from any other city in the known world." The Hanging Gardens of Babylon became one of the seven wonders in European medieval thought; the biblical account of the Tower of Babel and its "confused tongues" has inspired countless artists.

BABYLON RESPLENDENT

This *c.* 1950 illustration by Mario Larrinaga shows the splendor of the ancient city of Babylon. Two enduring symbols of the city are vividly evoked—the Tower of Babel in the background, and the legendary Hanging Gardens in the foreground.

But what did Babylon look like as a Mesopotamian city? Located on the bank of a branch of the Euphrates, 56 miles (90 km) southwest of Baghdad, Babylon was a vast city of the second and first millennia BCE. Its name is the Greek spelling of the early city's Mesopotamian toponym *babil(a)*, for which Mesopotamians developed a false etymology by reading the name *Bab-ili*, "gate of the gods." Although attested as a town in texts of the late third millennium BCE, Babylon seems to have had its first florescence at the time of Hammurabi (1792–1750 BCE), most prominent of the rulers of the First Dynasty of Babylon. Unfortunately little is known archaeologically of Hammurabi's Babylon due to high levels of groundwater, which did not allow a comprehensive investigation of the Old Babylonian period. Even Hammurabi's famous "law code" stele, which must

have been set up at a public space in Babylon, was not found here, but in Susa, the Elamite capital where it was kept along with other stone monuments taken as booty by the Elamite king Shutruk-Nahhunte around 1155 BCE.

ARCHAEOLOGY OF THE CITY: TINTIR–BABYLON

Most of the archaeological work at Babylon has only exposed the Neo-Babylonian levels of the city, revealing the impressive building programs carried out by the sixth century BCE Babylonian kings Nebuchadnezzar II (604–562 BCE) and Nabonidus (555–539 BCE). The site was explored several times during the nineteenth century, but the most serious archaeological project was by a small German team, led by Robert Koldewey, between 1899 and 1914. They were interested

in a stratigraphic study of the city's architectural remains and a scientific documentation of what was excavated. Although excavated over a century ago, Babylon is extremely well documented.

One other notable corpus of evidence for the city's ancient topography comes from an extensive cuneiform text known as "Tintir–Babylon" which is understood as a scholarly compendium that glorified Babylon as a great ceremonial center, through a detailed description of the city's public monuments. This invaluable source not only tells us names of various neighborhoods, districts, and buildings in the city, but also presents a coherent, albeit politicized, image of the city through the eyes of its inhabitants.

NEBUCHADNEZZAR'S BABYLON: AKITU FESTIVAL AND A CEREMONIAL SPECTACLE

The Neo-Babylonian city was famous for its series of multiple-layered fortifications and spectacular gates. The Euphrates River cut the city into the Eastern and Western halves. There was a large outer city on the Eastern bank, taking the river as part of its fortified enclosure. The Eastern and Western districts of the inner core of Babylon were connected by a bridge southwest of the sanctuary complex of Marduk—the supreme god of the Babylonian pantheon—which was the largest and most spectacular architectural monument of the city in the Iron Age. Nebuchadnezzar II rebuilt the embankments, the moat enveloping the inner city, and the massive outwork structures that made up a complex hydraulic system.

The monuments of the city center seem to have been structured around a spectacular processional street that linked Marduk's sanctuary to the "akitu" house, a cult complex outside the city walls. This processional street became the stage set during the most important annual social event in the city: the akitu festival. Akitu, also known as the "New Year's Festival," was celebrated annually at the time of the spring equinox, and involved a sacred procession of the cult image of Marduk to the akitu house. The event was comparable to Roman triumphal processions. The processional street and the Ishtar Gate through which it passed were decorated with "animals of Marduk" in spectacular wall reliefs composed of glazed molded bricks, representing lions, dragons (*mušhuššu*), and bulls.

The two palaces of the Neo-Babylonian kings were built at the northwestern edge of the citadel and overlooked the Euphrates canal, an architectural tradition well known from Assyrian cities. They were arranged around a series of ceremonial courtyards, also clad with glazed molded brick decorations.

Babylon's architectural landscape in the Iron Age appears as a place of urban spectacle where cultic and political ideologies merged together, with such force that it left a long-lasting imprint in human memory.

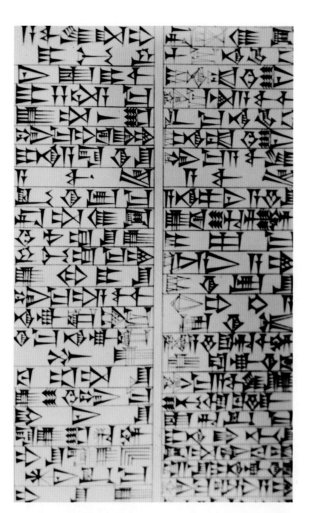

BABYLONIAN LAW

A transcription of the Law Code of Hammurabi, one of the world's earliest-known systems of law. Scholars believe that the law stele would have been placed in a prominent position in the city. It was taken to Susa, Persia, around 1155 BCE.

THE ISHTAR GATE

The Ishtar gate was an enormous baked brick structure rising more than 40 ft (12 m) high. A double gate, it encompassed the whole span of the city's fortifications, and was flanked by monumental towers, enclosure walls of the Southern and Northern Palaces and the Eastern Outworks. Marduk's sanctuary, known as *esagil*, housed the famous ziggurat of Marduk, which inspired the myths about the Tower of Babel. The sanctuary acted as an assembly ground for all Mesopotamian deities during the akitu festival.

The Ishtar Gate, originally built by King Nebuchadnezzar II in c. 575 BCE, was the main entrance to the inner city. The original fragments are in Berlin; this image shows Saddam Hussein's replica.

Khorsabad, Iraq

Ancient Assyrians were ambitious city builders. Throughout the prosperous centuries of the Assyrian Empire (934–611 BCE), they built numerous cities in the Upper Tigris Basin of northern Iraq. The construction of Khorsabad, ancient Dur-Šarrukēn ("Fortress of Sargon"), by King Sargon II (721–705 BCE) was one of the most ambitious building projects of the time.

A planned urban utopia, the city of Khorsabad was built from scratch on virgin soil, with the collaborative effort of craftsmen and workers from all Assyria's provinces.

During the 300 years of Neo-Assyrian rule, the landscapes of Upper Mesopotamia were transformed through the construction and rebuilding of cities, carving of canals, planting of orchards, and marking of territories with rock reliefs. In the making of the "Land of Aššur," these ambitious urban construction projects in the Upper and Middle Tigris Basins were fundamental: Tukulti-Ninurta I's Tulul ul 'Aqar, Aššur-nasir-pal II's Nimrud, Sargon II's Khorsabad, and Sennacherib's Nineveh are the most notable of these, as they each marked the shift of the political and ceremonial center of the empire to new cities.

THE CULTURAL BIOGRAPHY OF A CITY

Khorsabad was founded about 12½ miles (20 km) northeast of Nineveh, on a minor tributary of the Tigris. Started around 717 BCE, the project was unfinished at the time of Sargon's death in 705 BCE, when the Assyrian capital moved again to Nineveh. Archaeologically we know a great deal about Sargon's project, possibly more than any other Assyrian city. There is a wealth of textual sources associated with Sargon specifically about the construction process. Letters between Sargon and building overseers demonstrate the king's involvement with construction details, while suggesting that the city wall and its gates were divided up among craftsmen and builders from provinces across the empire, who were

SET IN STONE

This bas-relief from the palace of King Sargon II in Khorsabad dates to the eighth century BCE. Sargon II extended Assyrian influence and consolidated much of the work of his predecessor, Shalmaneser V.

often responsible for procuring their own materials. The construction was literally a collective enterprise.

The site has been extensively archaeologically explored. Due to its relatively short life (about 100 years), its stratigraphy is straightforward, its architecture well preserved. Nineteenth century colonialist explorations by the French consuls at Mosul (Paul Emile Botta in 1843–1844 and Victor Place in 1852–1854) were mainly directed at recovering wall reliefs and sculptures for the Louvre Museum in Paris. Unfortunately, a large number of stone reliefs from Sargon's palace sank to the bottom of the Tigris River near Qurna while being transported. These reliefs are only known from the drawings of Félix Thomas, Place's draftsman. Excavations of Khorsabad between 1929 and 1935 by the Oriental Institute of the University of Chicago concentrated on Sargon's palatial complex and the main citadel, Palace F, as well as the city's defensive system. The

BUILDING URBAN CENTERS

Construction of each urban center during the Late Assyrian period was a massive and festive undertaking: opening new stone quarries, procuring building materials, bringing in skilled craftsmen and a large labor force, introducing new building technologies, instituting new cult festivals, and finally providing a big feast for all. Assyrian cities are known for their extensive use of cut-stone masonry and wall slabs: palaces, temples, gates, and other public spaces were lined with stone slabs known as orthostats, which were extensively carved with bas-relief representations and royal inscriptions. Stone monuments such as obelisks and steles presented city-dwellers with an ideological version of the society's mythical and political history.

Iraqi Directorate General of Antiquities initiated work there in 1957, excavating the temple of Sebittu.

AN IMPERIAL URBAN LANDSCAPE

The city of Khorsabad was almost square in shape. The overall layout demonstrates a concern for creating large and well-defined public spaces in a systematic way. There were seven evenly placed monumental gates. The citadel was constructed on the northeastern edge of the city and housed Sargon's palace complex, the Nabu Temple, and elite residences. It was a common Assyrian practice to build palace compounds at the edge of the citadel, often overlooking a river or landscape. Palace F, a smaller complex, was also built separately on the southwest citadel wall on a terrace. Archaeologists identify this complex as the state treasury.

The palace complex, which was named *é-gal-gaba-ri-nu-tuku-a* or "palace without rival," and the Nabu Temple were built on a higher level on artificial terraces of rough limestone and mud-brick; they were connected to each other by a corbeled stone bridge. The temple of Nabu, god of writing and wisdom, was an outstanding complex with 45 rooms arranged around five courtyards. The temple's major facade was clad with brightly colored glazed bricks depicting lions, eagles, bulls, and fig trees.

The palace itself was a giant ceremonial, residential, and administrative complex of about 240 rooms, arranged around three large courtyards. The entrance was through three monumental gateways flanked by pairs of colossal human-headed winged bulls, carved out of fine gypsum. The ceremonial courtyards, reception halls, and many other rooms in the palace complex were lined with finely dressed stone slabs beautifully carved with reliefs.

Outside the palace complex, but intricately connected with the palace forecourt, was the southwest sector, a cult complex with three monumental sanctuaries to Sin, Shamash, and Ningal, and smaller shrines to Ea, Adad, and Ninurta. A ziggurat rose to the northwest of the complex. The palace layout illustrates a departure from the earlier more modest-scale Assyrian palatial projects, incorporating administrative, ceremonial, and residential activities into a coherent architectural ensemble.

NIMRUD'S PALACES

An 1853 engraving by James Fergusson, based on information from the English archaeologist Sir Austen Henry Layard, shows the palaces of Ashurbanipal II (883–859 BCE). Layard (1817–1894) was one of the early excavators of the Assyrian site.

WRITING IT ALL DOWN

An Assyrian cuneiform tablet clearly shows the famous wedge-shaped script. Cuneiform was used for about 3,000 years, and was the dominant script throughout Mesopotamia.

The Persian Empire

The Achaemenid Dynasty (550–330 BCE) was the first Persian Empire
that ruled over the Iranian plateau, Caucasus, Central Asia, Indus valley,
Mesopotamia, Levant, Egypt, Nubia, Libya, Cyprus, and modern Turkey—
about 3,089,000 sq miles (8 million sq km) of territory.

According to the old texts, the founder of
this dynasty may have been a local Persian
chieftain called Achaemenes, who led migrant
Persian nomadic tribes that captured Anshan (the
modern province of Fars in Iran), a fertile area in
the ancient Elamite civilization.

CYRUS THE GREAT AND HIS SUCCESSORS

However, Cyrus II the Great (c. 580–529 BCE) was
the true founder and first emperor of the Persian
Imperium. He captured Ecbatana, the capital of the
Median kingdom, in 553 BCE, and in 547 BCE he
conquered Sardis, the capital of the Lydian kingdom
(in modern Turkey). Babylonia and the Chaldean
Empire became part of his realm by 539 BCE.
According to Herodotus, Cyrus the Great then
attacked the Scythians. Tomyris, the queen of the
Massagetae warriors of Scythia, defeated Cyrus's
troops, killed Cyrus, and defiled his corpse.

Cyrus's son, Cambyses II, conquered Egypt, but
was killed in July 525 BCE, and Gaumata, a Persian
priest or magus also known as Smerdis, took the
throne for himself. According to the Behistun
Inscription (see feature box), Gaumata was killed
by members of the royal family, who then installed
Darius I as emperor in 522 BCE. It was during the
reign of Darius I that Persepolis was built. Darius I

DETAIL FIT FOR A KING
A dramatic detail from the Apadana
at Persepolis shows a lion on the
attack. The tomb of Darius I (Darius
the Great), who built Persepolis,
can be found at Naqsh-i Rustam,
situated not far from the city.

THE BEHISTUN INSCRIPTION

The Behistun (Bisotun) Inscription is located on a cliff in
the Kermanshah Province of modern Iran. The inscription,
engraved into the rock, narrates the story of Darius I's
conquests, with the names of the 23 satrapies subject to
him. It explains how Ahuramazda, the great god of all gods,
presented the kingship to Darius. The inscription is written
in three languages—Babylonian, Elamite, and Old Persian.

In 1844, Sir Henry Creswicke Rawlinson copied the cliff's
inscription. By 1857, he had published his deciphered texts.
Yet Rawlinson was not the first European to unlock the
words of the inscription. In the early part of the nine-
teenth century, a German epigraphist, Georg Friedrich
Grotefend, identified the meaning of some of the Old
Persian cuneiform. The site is now an Iranian UNESCO
World Heritage monument.

This gold earring from 600–400 BCE shows the god Ahuramazda,
the personification of goodness, said to have made Darius I king.

managed to expand his empire, invading Greece, but was defeated at the Battle of Marathon in 490 BCE.

PERSIA AFTER DARIUS I

Xerxes I (r. 486–465 BCE), son of Darius I, planned to conquer Greece. Following Xerxes's victory at the Battle of Thermopylae in 480 BCE, the Persians captured Athens. But later that year, the Greeks won the Battle of Salamis and forced Xerxes back to Persia. He left Mardonius in charge of his troops in Greece, but they were defeated in 479 BCE at the Battle of Plataea. A naval defeat at Mycale marked the end of Persian expansion into Europe.

Xerxes I was followed by Artaxerxes I, who reigned from 465–424 BCE, and established Zoroastrianism as the state religion. He was succeeded by his eldest son Xerxes II, who was killed by his brother, Darius II. Darius supported Sparta against Athens in the Peloponnesian War, sending his son Cyrus the Younger to lead some forces. Darius died in Babylon in 404 BCE and was succeeded by his eldest son Artaxerxes II (404–358 BCE). Cyrus the Younger and Artaxerxes II met each other at the Battle of Cunaxa in 401 BCE, where Cyrus was killed.

In 343 BCE Artaxerxes III (r. 358–338 BCE) defeated Sidon and Egypt. He was succeeded by Artaxerxes IV Arses, who was poisoned. Darius III the Codomannus (r. 336–330 BCE) then became king. As a result of the battles against Alexander the Great—the battles of the Granicus River (334 BCE), Dascyleion (334 BCE), Issus (332 BCE), then Gaugamela (331 BCE), Babylon (331 BCE), Susa, Pers, and Ecbatana (330 BCE)—the Persian Empire fell into decline. Darius III was killed by family members in the mountains of modern Afghanistan, and the once great Achaemenid dynasty finally came to an end.

DIGGING UP THE PAST

The archaeology of the Achaemenid dynasty began in the mid-nineteenth century when the British antiquarian William Kenneth Loftus excavated the ruins at Susa in 1851. During the 1880s, French archaeologists Jeanne and Marcel Dieulafoy continued excavations at Susa where they found many Achaemenid artworks such as tiles, pottery, and bas-reliefs.

Later French excavations in Susa in the 1960s and 1970s revealed archaeological traces of the Palace of Artaxerxes II and the statue of Darius the Great, which Egyptian craftsmen had presented at his palace in Susa. This statue now stands in the modern museum of Iran-e Bastan, Tehran. The inscription on the

XERXES GATE AT PERSEPOLIS
Now known as the Xerxes Gate, in Xerxes's time it was called the Gate of All Nations, as all visitors to Persepolis had to pass through it in order to reach the throne room of the king. Stone columns stand on a mud-brick platform. Two stone bulls stand sentinel at the entrance.

statue is written in Egyptian hieroglyphs and lists the subject nations of the Achaemenid Empire under the rule of Darius I.

Excavations at Tepe Hegmataneh, in the modern city of Hamadan, have as yet revealed no Median remains, so some scholars believe that it is possible that Ecbatana is located in the heartland of Azerbaijan, and not in the Zagros highlands.

EXTENT OF THE PERSIAN EMPIRE
During the Achaemenid Dynasty, the Persian Empire spread across much of the Middle East, central Asia, the Indus valley, Mesopotamia, the Levant, northern Africa, Cyprus, and modern Turkey.

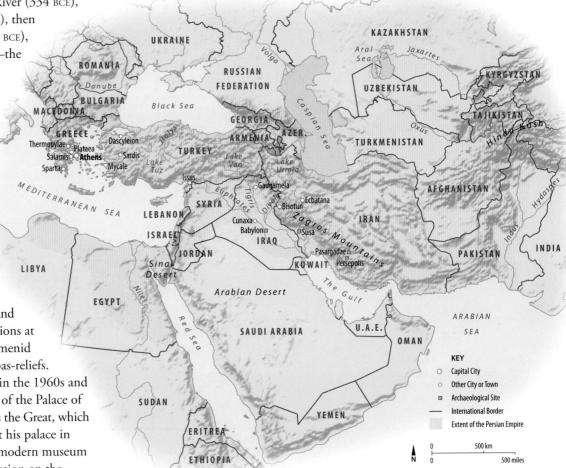

KEY
○ Capital City
○ Other City or Town
□ Archaeological Site
— International Border
▒ Extent of the Persian Empire

0   500 km
0   500 miles

Pasargadae, Iran

The ruins of Pasargadae, an Iranian UNESCO World Heritage Site, stand some 54 miles (87 km) northeast of Persepolis, in modern Iran's Fars Province. The archaeological site covers 400 acres (160 ha) and includes the ruins of the stone mausoleum of Cyrus the Great.

PALATIAL RUINS

The main identifying feature of the Apadana, or audience hall (the ruins are seen below), was the use of many columns. Cyrus is thought to have employed stone-masons from Lydia to construct the city's important buildings.

Other significant ruins found in Pasargadae include the Greek fortification of Tell-i Takht (which literally translates as "mound of royal throne") on top of a nearby hill, the palace of Cyrus the Great, the auditorium palace, some mud-brick fortified walls, the Zindan-i Suleiman (the prison of Solomon), and the Atabaki mosque from the Ilkhanid era (c. 1250–1335). In spite of the fact that E. E. Herzfeld in his 1928 surveys could not positively identify the Marghab Plain as Pasargadae, the British Institute of Persian Studies conducted an excavation project there in 1960. According to the archaeologist David Stronach, if the stone tomb of Pasargadae is indeed the tomb of Cyrus the Great, then Pasargadae is probably the first capital of the Persian kings.

The Elamite cuneiform clay tablets of Persepolis referred to the site as Batrakatash, which, in old Greek, spells the word Pasargad. The Old Persian spelling is Pars Gadeh, or "town of Persians."

BIRTHPLACE OF ACHAEMENID ARCHITECTURE

The first major development in Persian architecture occurred during the Achaemenid Dynasty, and Pasargadae, established and erected by Cyrus the Great, is one of the earliest examples. The mud-brick walls, imposing columns, stone doorways, and walled

gardens are characteristic of this "archaic" period. Some scholars refer to Pasargadae as "the birthplace of Achaemenid architecture."

The gardens of the site provide one of the earliest known examples of the Persian style of landscape architecture known as "chahar bagh," a design based on four sections separated by paths or water features.

Cyrus the Great is thought to have commenced construction in 546 BCE, following his victory in Lydia, but his death meant that building was not completed, and it appears that Susa became the capital of the Persian Empire after Cyrus's death. Pasargadae was, however, retained as an important Persian town, even after Darius I ordered the construction of Persepolis.

Generally speaking, the art and architecture found at Pasargadae exemplify the Persian synthesis of various traditions, drawing on precedents from Elam, Babylon, Assyria, and Lydia. One bas-relief shows a praying winged man who is dressed as an Elamite but whose crown is Egyptian, displaying the different influences on artisans. Some scholars regard the figure in this relief as Cyrus the Great.

In the development of Achaemenid architecture, Pasargadae paved the way for the eminent city of Persepolis. Archaeologically there is a local prototype to Pasargadae which has been reported in Borazjan, about 124 miles (200 km) from the coast of the Persian Gulf. The architectural style of Borazjan, both in columned halls and stone carving using ashlar masonry, is very similar to Pasargadae, although less developed. For instance, there is no trace of the Neo-Assyrian style of bas-reliefs in Borazjan, which are visible in Pasargadae as decorative motifs.

THE TOMB OF CYRUS THE GREAT

The most significant monument in Pasargadae is certainly the stone tomb of Cyrus the Great. The

tomb has six broad steps leading to the burial chamber, which is 6½ ft (2 m) high, 6½ ft (2 m) wide and 10 ft (3 m) deep and has a low and narrow entrance. Arriannus, writing in the second century CE, recorded that Alexander the Great found an inscription on the tomb. No trace of any such inscription survives today, so there is considerable disagreement as to the exact wording of the text. According to the Greek historian and geographer Strabo, the text said, "O man! I am Cyrus the Great, who gave the Persians an empire, and was king of Asia. Grudge me not therefore this monument."

According to some classicists, the style of the tomb shows that it has strong connections with the Lydian tombs of Anatolia. In fact, some scholars believe that Cyrus may have brought Lydian stonemasons to Pasargadae to construct his mausoleum. In particular, the tomb at Pasargadae has almost exactly the same dimensions as the tomb of Alyattes II, father of the Lydian King Croesus. The stone tomb of Tash Kuleh in modern Turkey is probably a prototype of Cyrus's tomb in Pasargadae; however, another similar stone tomb is reported by Iranian archaeologist Ali Akbar Sarafraz, on the plain of Bozpar, south of the Marghab Plain and close to the shores of the Persian Gulf.

THE TOMB OF CYRUS
Resembling the imposing construction of a ziggurat, the tomb of Cyrus the Great at Pasargadae once housed the remains of the founder of the Persian Empire.

SOLOMON'S TOWER

A significant feature of Pasargadae is the Zindan-i Suleiman, a collapsed high stone tower that is very similar to the Kaabeh-i Zartosht (Cube of Zoroaster) in Naqsh-i Rustam near Persepolis. The function of this building is unclear, as is the building in Naqsh-i Rustam, but it is possible that it was a fire temple, used by Zoroastrians, as well as a tomb. In general it resembles the Urartian stone architecture of some fire temples in Azerbaijan and eastern Anatolia.

Prior to Stonach's excavations in the 1960s, Qashqai peoples, the native Turkic-language people of Fars Province, regarded the site as the property of Solomon the king, because of its huge masonry.

A COMBINATION OF STYLES
This bas-relief of a four-winged door guardian was found on a door in Pasargadae. The wings are in the Assyrian style, the headdress is Egyptian, and the clothing is borrowed from the Elamite culture.

Persepolis, Iran

The archaeological site of Persepolis stands about 49 miles (70 km) north-east of the modern city of Shiraz, in Fars Province, Iran, and is one of Iran's UNESCO World Heritage Sites. In Old Persian, the city was known as Parsa, which means "city of Persians." Persepolis is the Greek translation of the name.

Persepolis is an incomplete complex of buildings and palaces, construction of which began in 518 BCE during Darius I's reign (522–486 BCE). One possible reason why the project was never finished is the invasion of Alexander the Great in 331 BCE. The site includes the ruins of the Apadana (an audience hall with 36 columns), Tachar (the private palace of Darius I, which is in the Egyptian style), Hadish (the private palace of Xerxes I), the Talar-i Takht (the throne hall, also called the 100-columned hall), the Darvazeh-i Mellal (the Gate of all Nations), the Khazaneh (the royal treasury), the palace of Artaxerxes III, and the rock-cut tombs of kings.

The dominant feature of Persepolis is the terrace, which measures 150,000 sq yards (125,000 sq m). It is partly cut out of a mountain, with one side set against the mountain of Kuh-e Rahmet. The rest of the site is man-made. It typifies the classic period of Achaemenid architecture, seen in its monuments and the royal tombs at Naqsh-i Rustam, both of which were initiated by Darius I and which remained practically unchanged for two centuries.

EXCAVATING ACHAEMENID HISTORY

German archaeologist Ernest E. Herzfeld believed that Cyrus the Great chose the site of Persepolis, but Darius I was the one who built both the terrace and some of Persepolis's more impressive buildings, such as the Apadana Palace, the Tripylon (the three-gated council hall), and the imperial Treasury. Building continued until the attack by Alexander the Great and his army. Herzfeld's excavations at Persepolis on behalf of the Oriental Institute of Chicago University began in 1931, and his discoveries of the ruins of incomplete palaces of Achaemenid kings helped to reveal more about the culture and customs of Achaemenid times.

Another archaeologist from the same institute, Erich F. Schmidt, followed up on Herzfeld's excavations in 1933 and discovered bas-reliefs of Achaemenid satraps in the staircase of the Apadana auditorium and more than 33,300 Neo-Elamite and Aramaic clay tablets, now housed in the Oriental Institute of Chicago University. Schmidt was also successful in excavating Naqsh-i Rustam and Istak-har where he found other important architectural remains of the Persian Empire.

Herzfeld felt that Persepolis was constructed for symbolic and ceremonial reasons—important religious and cultural events were celebrated there—and that the site represented the supremacy of the Achaemenid Empire.

STAIRWAY TO THE TOP

In 518 BCE, construction began on a wide, double, symmetrical stairway to provide access to the top of the terrace at Persepolis. At 65 ft (20 m) above the ground, the intention was that this would be the only entrance to the terrace. Situated on the western side of the Great Wall, behind the palace of Darius the Great, the "Persepolis stairway" has more than 100 steps, which are wide and deep enough to accommodate men riding horses. The walls at the side of the stairway are engraved with bas-reliefs.

This beautifully carved limestone relief of a Persian nobleman is part of a frieze adorning the walls of the Apadana staircase. It is dated to c. 465 BCE.

THE GLORY OF THE ACHAEMENID DYNASTY
It is easy to imagine the grandeur of Persian court life from this view of Persepolis taken in 1971. The 100-columned hall is in the foreground; behind it is the main audience hall of Darius. In the background, tents have have been erected to celebrate the 2,500th anniversary of the Persian Empire.

MAJESTIC MONUMENTS
Columns are the primary characteristic of the architecture of Persepolis, and gray limestone was used extensively for construction. According to the Greek historian Diodorus Siculus, writing in the first century BCE, Persepolis had three walls with ramparts, all with towers whose prime function was to protect soldiers defending the site. Diodorus reports that the walls ranged from 23 ft (7 m) to about 88 ft (27 m) high, but there are no remains left, so archaeologists are unable to verify whether this information is correct.

Darius's sumptuous palace, the Apadana, or audience hall, was used for all the king's official business. Construction began in 518 BCE and took 30 years to complete. The square-shaped grand hall had 72 columns, of which 13 remain. The columns are 62 ft (19 m) high, and the tops are decorated with sculptures of bulls, eagles, and lions.

Talar-i Takht (the throne hall or 100-columned hall) is next to the Apadana, and is the second largest building on the terrace. Archaeologists believe that Xerxes I began the building, which was finished by his son Artaxerxes I. It was a large hall designed for receiving

guests and foreign visitors; some scholars believe that this is where the king met with his military commanders. The eight stone doorways are decorated with scenes of the king fighting demons, or on his throne.

Behind Persepolis are three rock-cut tombs in the hillside, the facades decorated with bas reliefs, but these belong to later kings (fourth century BCE). Darius I and his three successors chose the cliffs of Naqsh-i Rustam in which to cut out their tombs.

ROYAL NECROPOLIS
The tombs of Xerxes I and Darius I are carved out of the rock face at Naqsh-i Rustam. Artaxerxes I and Darius II are also buried in the rock-cut mausoleum. The Sassanid reliefs, which decorate the lower part of the tomb, were added later.

Susa, Iran

Susa was founded in about 5500 BCE. It became the capital of the Elamite Empire in about 3200 BCE, and later an important city of the Persian Empire. Located about 124 miles (200 km) east of the Karun River in the Khuzestan Province of modern Iran, it is a very important archaeological site for a number of civilizations.

Susa was the capital of the Elamite Empire until Cyrus the Great took it for the Achaemenids in 539 BCE. Darius I moved the capital there from Pasargadae. There are a large number of remains of the Achaemenid Dynasty at Susa, such as the palaces of Darius I and Artaxerxes II, but archaeologists have also found significant Elamite traces at the site. The tomb of the prophet Daniel, important to Persian Jews, is also reported to be in Susa.

It is not clear why Cyrus chose Susa as a site for his fortress. It had a favorable position on the route from Elam to Mesopotamia and Anatolia, and it may have functioned as an important depot on the trade route between the Persian Gulf and the areas around the Caspian Sea. The protective wall he built has been discovered to be considerably higher than the encircling wall of the unknown "proto-Elamites."

Alexander the Great entered Susa in 331 BCE, when the Achaemenid Dynasty was on the verge of collapse and the Persian satrap Abulites surrendered the city to him. Alexander is said to have found gold and silver and large quantities of purple dye there, and there were reports that he needed 10,000 camels and 20,000 donkeys to carry away these treasures.

PERSIA AND THE "FRENCH MONOPOLY"

The first excavations at Susa were conducted by W. K. Loftus in 1851. British archaeological work in Persia was usually small-scale. At major sites, such as Persepolis and Susa, it focused on clearing sculptures and retrieving plans.

These investigations represented a developmental stage beyond the seventeenth- and eighteenth-century antiquarian tradition of observation and recording of standing remains, which was championed by early European travelers to Iran. A tablet unearthed in 1854 by Henry Austin Layard in Nineveh reveals Ashurbanipal as an avenger, seeking retribution for

TILE WORKS AT SUSA

The Achaemenid palaces of Susa are famous for their tile works. The tiles are fired glazed bricks in green, yellow, and brown. Some showed the king with his bodyguards. Among the best-known tile works from the Achaemenid Empire are the "10,000 Immortals," the king's guard found at both Susa and Persepolis—they stand, dignified and alert, ever ready to protect the Empire's interests.

The four courtyards of the Apadana (audience hall) contain panels of brightly colored glazed bricks adorning the walls. These panels depict guardsmen, lions, griffins, and sphinxes. The guards wear richly patterned Persian dress, grasp an upright spear in both hands, and carry bows and quivers. Some of the stairways were also decorated with glazed brick panels. The Apadana had elaborate stone columns topped with capitals in the form of two bulls back to back. The site was used by rulers throughout the Achaemenid period. Artaxerxes I performed restoration work on the Apadana and also built himself a palace elsewhere at the site.

This beautiful glazed brick relief of a griffin, a fabulous mythical winged beast with the body of a lion, and a popular image in Persian art, is from Susa, Iran.

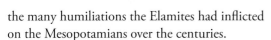

the many humiliations the Elamites had inflicted on the Mesopotamians over the centuries.

In the 1880s, Jeanne Henriette Dieulafoy and her husband, Marcel, both French archaeologists with a particular interest in Persia, directed the excavations at Susa for the Louvre Museum in Paris. In his book *The Acropolis of Susa*, published in 1890, Marcel Dieulafoy describes the four mounds that were found at Susa. The first is a citadel; the second one, to the east, was identified as the location of the palace of Darius I. It is known that Darius I undertook a lot of construction work at Susa and built his first major palace there. The third mound, to the south, contained the royal Elamite city; the fourth mound revealed some of the poorer dwellings. According to the inscriptions of Darius I, the stone pillars used on the building of his palace in Susa were brought from Abiradu, a village in Elam, not far from Susa.

The finest pottery was found in the lowest strata and was from the Chalcolithic era. Above the early strata were remains of Elamite and early Babylonian civilizations. In the upper portions of the mounds, Elamite, Achaemenid, Hellenistic, Parthian, and Sassanid remains were found.

In 1895, French archaeologist Jacques de Morgan convinced French officials in Tehran to press for a French monopoly on any archaeological research there. He continued excavations on the Acropolis a couple of years later, uncovering three important artifacts: the obelisk of the Akkadian king Manishtusu, the stele of his successor Naram-Sin that dates to around 2250 BCE, and the famous code of Hammurabi of Babylon, which dates to c. 1790 BCE. The French maintained their archaeological monopoly from 1895 until 1927, and continued to work until the 1970s.

Nomadic States of Central Asia

If a group of riders mounted their horses and set off eastward from Warsaw, apart from negotiating forest and farmland as they began their journey, and finding their way across some major rivers, there would be very little to impede their progress until they reached Siberia.

STEPPE TREASURES

The lives of nomads were inextricably linked with their horses, so it is not surprising that the horse was a popular decorative motif. This gold and pearl Sarmatian earring dates to the first century CE.

Thousands and thousands of miles of open steppe would lie before them, over which they could ride unhindered, finding grazing for their horses and usually a stream or pool where they might water them. This vast grassland became the native home of numerous mounted herding tribes.

THE RICH HISTORY OF THE STEPPES

From time to time natural disasters or the rise of charismatic leaders caused the tribes to move, sometimes in search of conquest, sometimes simply to find fresh pastures. In either case, this often led to conflict and to serious threats to the settled peoples living on the edges of the steppes. This history brings us names that cast a long shadow of fear down the ages: Attila the Hun, the Mongol hordes, Timur (Tamurlane). While these ogres color the popular image of the Eurasian steppes, the real story is more complex and richer in history, innovations, and artistic traditions. Up until around 2000 BCE the Eurasian steppes were inhabited by a diverse population of hunters, stockbreeders, and farmers, each group having its own distinct cultural markers. In the period from 2000 to 1500 BCE there was a marked shift toward less

TIMUR THE GREAT

One of the last great nomadic leaders, the Turko-Mongol military commander Timur (c. CE 1336–1405) conquered much of western and central Asia. Founder of the Timurid Dynasty, he claimed kinship with Genghis Khan.

varied lifestyles as the peoples of the steppes rapidly adopted similar customs and traditions across wide areas. East of the Ural Mountains lived one distinct cluster of groups named by archaeologists the Andronovo complex. Contemporary sites to the west of the Urals are associated with the Timber-Grave or Srubnaya culture.

This cultural shift heralded the opening up of the Eurasian steppes and with it the need for transport. It was here that some of the world's most significant transport ideas were developed. First, wheeled carts, and then chariots, facilitated movement across large distances. The people who traveled in them were mainly nomadic or seminomadic herders.

Where conditions permitted, they were more settled and practiced small-scale agriculture. By around 1400 BCE the combination of advances in metal technology, along with quality horse breeding and improved stock husbandry, had provided suitable foundations for the development of very large and powerful nomadic groups. Horse riding was first developed as a widespread practical skill on the Eurasian steppes and this period saw the full-scale appearance of mounted pastoral nomadism, which was also marked by the beautiful artistic tradition known as the Animal Style.

A MELTING POT

These tribes and tribal confederacies had the means to conquer new lands and soon they began to appear in the historical records as threats to the settled and civilized world. The Scythians occupied the Central Asian and southern Siberian steppes, but moved westward, eventually ending up along the shores

THE GREAT SILK ROAD

The history of Central Asia is by no means only one of nomadic invasion. One of the features it was most famous for was the great Silk Road. Not a single road, it was a complex, intertwined network of trade routes that threaded their way across deserts and mountains, through the bazaars of the great oasis cities of Kashgar, Samarkand, and Bukhara, bringing silks from China to an ever-hungry Roman market. Many other goods traveled along the same routes: jade, amber and gemstones, fruits and other produce, fabrics, and handicrafts. The Silk Road linked east to west for the first time in history, opening up the potential for much greater imperial expansion in years to come.

Camels follow the Silk Road through sand dunes. Running between China and the Mediterranean, it is arguably the world's most famous trade route.

of the Black Sea where they came into contact with the Greeks, who had settled in towns on the western coast around the delta of the Danube River. The Scythians were one part of a vast pool of nomadic peoples spread across the Eurasian steppes. The linguistic and cultural ties show that there were fairly close relationships between all of them. The tribes to the east were well known to the Persians who referred to them as Saka. Some Saka lands and even the nomads themselves were incorporated into the Persian Achaemenid Empire.

By the fourth century BCE a new people, the Sarmatians, moved into Scythian territory. By the first century BCE they were known as far as the Danube River basin, and the names of individual Sarmatian tribes appear in the works of Roman writers. By the late first century CE new tribes had

moved in and mixed with the Sarmatian population. From this period onward, the historical sources document the tribes as Alans. Written records indicate that the Sarmato-Alans continued to occupy the northern Black Sea steppes until the appearance of the Huns in the late fourth century CE.

The Huns formed the first wave of a flood of Turkic-speaking peoples from the east who blended with other steppe peoples to give the region the complex ethnic character it possesses today. At the end of the seventh century CE came the Arab conquest. Later the Mongols added to the population mix, followed finally by the Russians from the late nineteenth century onward.

SARMATIAN SKILLS
This Sarmatian first century CE silver cup with a horse-shaped handle is another fine work of art paying homage to the horse.

The Land of Cities, Russian Federation

The Land of Cities lies in the southeastern part of the Ural Mountains, where a remarkable group of early fortified settlements has been located. This enigmatic cluster of sites has attracted much attention because of its discovery in a land known best for its nomadic peoples. Russian archaeologists have named these sites the Sintashta-Petrovka culture.

The sites are dated to a short period around 2000 to 1600 BCE and are characterized by their fortifications and extensive evidence for metalworking. They are distributed approximately 12–18 miles (20–30 km) apart and appear to have controlled their own individual territories. Despite their highly unusual features, they remained long unrecognized because they were so markedly different from the classic Bronze Age Andronovo culture of the eastern steppes.

THE SINTASHTA-PETROVKA CULTURE

The significance of the Sintashta-Petrovka sites lies in the early cultural development of the Eurasian steppes. While farming villages first developed in western Asia around 8000–7000 BCE, the earliest stockbreeding in Eurasia was only introduced from the Danube and the Caucasus into the Ukraine and southern Russia around 5000 BCE. It then took another 2,000 years to spread across the Urals into the eastern steppes where people living there relied on wild resources until around 3000 BCE. Along with stockbreeding came increasing demands for mobility as herders sought fresh pasture for their flocks. The earliest wheeled vehicles appeared west of the Caspian Sea around 2900 BCE. These were slow, solid-wheeled wagons, probably drawn by oxen. The importance of these as combined transport and housing is indicated by their presence in burials.

The later nomads of the steppes were well known for their horsemanship, but the earliest date for the domestication of the horse is a hotly debated topic. Burials associated with the Sintashta-Petrovka sites dated around 2000 BCE provide the first solid evidence for horse domestication and for the use of horses to draw chariots, although taming of horses probably occurred several hundred years before. The Sintashta chariots were light vehicles with two spoked wheels. The invention of the chariot revolutionized warfare. Warriors could attack at great speed and fire a bow while simultaneously charging the enemy. The horse-drawn chariot, though, is less maneuverable than a mounted rider, but it was not until about 1,000 years later that mounted pastoral nomadism emerged in its classic form on the Eurasian steppes, and with it the ability of tribes to muster a vast army of cavalry with ease.

The fortified settlements of the Sintashta-Petrovka culture were located along the rivers. The best-known site is Arkaim, which has been extensively excavated.

LANGUAGE AND ARCHAEOLOGY

The Sintashta-Petrovka sites are linked to the question of Indo-Iranian migrations. It is well known that the ancestral languages of the main European languages spoken today are derived from peoples who spread across Eurasia several thousand years ago. When the Land of Cities became very well publicized, it was speculated that this may have been the imagined Indo-Iranian homeland. But language cannot be directly associated with cultural markers—the two spread separately by different means and a direct link with the Sintashta-Petrovka culture has been dismissed. However, archaeologists now generally accept that the people who lived in these cities were predominantly Indo-Iranian speakers.

A clay tablet shows Ural-Altaic text, dating to 786–764 BCE. Although not of Indo-Iranian origin, this language is the ancestor of many central Asian languages and also of Finnish and Hungarian.

SCYTHIAN HORSES
These gold horses were found in a Scythian tomb at Arzhan. The craftsmanship and use of precious metals suggest that this was a royal grave. The graves of horses also contained gold decorations.

It was some 215,000 sq ft (20,000 sq m) in size with a central square surrounded by two concentric circles of houses. A street separated the two rings of houses, and the outer row of houses backed onto the innermost of two circular fortification walls. The external wall was built of rammed earth, supported by a timber frame and faced with sun-dried mud bricks. An outer ditch completed the defenses. The main entrance to the site was to the west. The homes were rectangular in shape with storage pits, open hearths, wells, and even metal smelting furnaces. The nearby site of Sintashta, from which the culture derives its name, was less well preserved but shared many similarities in form.

BURIAL SITES

Cemeteries are associated with the sites. The burials were placed in deep pits dug into the ground and reinforced by timber or stones. The dead were buried singly or collectively, together with pottery, and bronze and stone artifacts. Cattle, sheep, horses, and dogs were sacrificed and buried both with humans and in separate graves. Several of the burials contained chariots, placed with the lower half of the wheels sunk into the ground. It is only because of this practice that it is possible to reconstruct them. The wood has long since rotted away but the impressions left by the spoked wheels give vital clues enabling archaeologists to reconstruct the original design of the vehicles. Once filled in, the graves were covered by a

kurgan, a stone or earthen mound commonly used to mark graves on the Eurasian steppes.

Archaeologists have found it difficult to explain the purpose of these sites and many different interpretations have been suggested. It is possible that they performed varied functions including administration, ceremony, and protection and production of the precious metals that were so much needed by the steppe nomads.

GOLDEN WARRIORS
This gold plaque from the fifth to the third century BCE shows a horseman, wielding a spear, attacking a warrior. It was found in the Ukraine and is another treasure from the Scythian period.

The Stone Statues of the Steppes, Russian Federation

The Altai Mountains rise to 4,500 ft (1,372 m) above sea level on the southern fringes of Siberia. To the west lie the vast Eurasian grasslands; to the east, the Gobi Desert. Despite their remote location, the high mountain valleys have sheltered a wide range of nomadic cultures through the ages, while the rocky terrain provided them with materials to record their passing.

DEER STONE
These memorial stelae or
grave markers feature stylized
representations of deer, and are
often made of granite. They are
commonly about 3 ft (0.9 m) high.

Among the most famous remains are stone monoliths, most often erected as grave markers or memorial stelae. The earliest of these are often referred to as Deer Stones, because of the stylized deer that feature on many examples. The stones are narrow slabs, placed upright in the ground, in groups or singly, and are usually found in association with graves or ritual locations. The term Deer Stones is misleading as the stones are probably anthropomorphic in shape, that is, representing stylized human figures, and not all of them have animals depicted on them, deer or otherwise.

STYLIZED STONES

The stones vary in size from 3–10 ft (0.9–3 m) high. A "belt" carved around the stone, with weapons hanging down from it, indicates their anthropomorphic shape. The figures generally face east, and three diagonal lines at the top appear to represent features. Some have rounded earrings carved on the upper sides, and the head is defined by a necklace. Some scholars offer an alternative interpretation of the images, seeing them not as human figures, but suggesting instead that the three sections of the

images represent the sky, with the sun and the moon; the world of the living, indicated by animals such as the deer; and the world of the dead, with tools and weapons. The carvings of deer on many of these stones are executed in a stylized, elegantly curving form with elongated bodies and backswept antlers stretching in waves along the stone. The deer depicted are elk, *Cervus elaphus*, a massive animal with huge antlers. Only the male develops antlers, and it is always the male shown on the carvings.

The Deer Stones date from *c.* 1000 to 700 BCE, the period of mounted pastoral nomadism on the steppes, but the tradition has earlier roots right back into the Bronze Age, with simpler versions of the anthropomorphic stelae, occasionally with depictions of animals. Forward in time, the tradition continued up to the time of the Turks, between the sixth and eighth centuries CE. These are shorter and more rounded standing stones, with clearly recognizable but highly stylized human features. They are shown generally holding a cup or bowl with their right arm raised across their chest. Some show warriors holding weapons in their left hand. These fascinating stones are known locally as Balbals.

Pazyryk Tombs, Russian Federation

Pazyryk is a glacier-cut hanging valley high in the Altai Mountains at the point where the Russian Federation, Mongolia, and China intersect. Thanks to a most unusual set of climatic conditions, the area has a remarkable collection of over 700 burial mounds preserved almost intact by ice, together with all the trappings that accompanied the deceased to the grave.

A lthough the Pazyryk valley has a cold climate, the soils of the valley are not frozen all year, yet the tombs themselves are permanently sealed in ice. The reason for this is a unique micro-climate created through the method of construction of the tombs. At the bottom of a shaft about 13 ft (4 m) deep was a log chamber some 540 sq ft (50 sq m) in size. The upper part of the shaft was filled with layers of logs and large rocks and was covered by an earthen mound sealed with a layer of stones. The uppermost stone layer acted to insulate the shaft, encouraging the development of ice below the mound but inhibiting defrosting in warmer conditions. Added to this was the fact that most of the tombs had been robbed in antiquity, only a short time after burial. The robber pits permitted the entry of rainwater, which then froze. As the soil collapsed in over the robber pit, the ice hardened and remained firm for thousands of years.

SKIN ART

In the center of these tattoos on the upper arm of a 60-year-old man, buried at Pazyryk, c. 300 BCE, is a mythical horned animal somersaulting. Above it is a long-tailed feline with bared fangs.

ARCHAEOLOGICAL TOMB TREASURES

The graves date to about 450–250 BCE and were constructed by forest-dwellers who were contemporaries of the Saka of the east Eurasian steppes and the great Scythian tribes around the Black Sea. Many of the bodies were embalmed and tattooed with designs of mythical beasts. The tattoos were created using soot pricked into the skin by sharp needles, creating a blue color. The graves contained sweat tents and bronze cauldrons with stones and burnt cannabis seeds. The Greek historian Herodotus vividly describes how the Scythians delighted in the fumes given off by hemp seeds as part of a funerary rite. Horses were buried both in the graves and in separate tombs of their own. Their manes were cropped and their tails plaited with a leather strap faced with gold, while the harness and saddles were richly decorated with leather and gold ornaments.

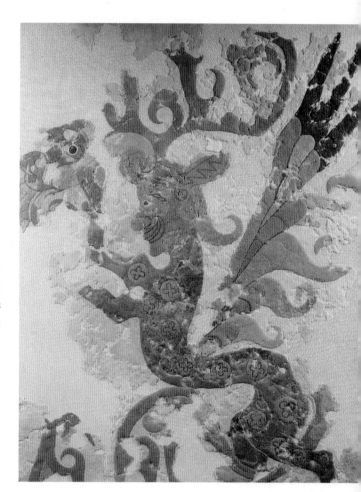

FANTASTIC THREADS

Among the significant finds in the Altai Mountains are fabrics that have survived the passage of time, such as this piece of felt depicting a mythical animal, which dates to the third to second centuries BCE.

The textiles recovered from the graves are especially remarkable. They show a wealth of design and technique involving animal, plant, and abstract motifs created in embroidery, appliqué, weaving, beading, and gold leaf. In one grave was a pile carpet which, to judge by its designs, was imported from the Iranian region, while a finely embroidered silk drape had been brought from China. It is clear from this, and from other finds such as coriander seeds and Chinese bronze mirrors, that the ancient inhabitants of the Altai Mountains had wide trading links with other peoples across and beyond the steppes.

The Mongols

The Mongol Empire was the greatest empire that Asia has ever seen—stretching at its height from China to central Europe. The power of the Mongols was forged by their harsh land, a land in which they were constantly on the move, their only protection a felt tent, their lives dependent on their horses.

Mongolia's 1 million sq miles (2.6 million sq km) are divided between the nation-state of Mongolia, and the Inner Mongolia Autonomous Region of China. Archaeological investigations have shown that there was some urbanism in the second century BCE, when the Xiongnu (eastern Huns) defeated the Han. Several steppe peoples conquered northern China: the Xianbei (ruling as the Northern Wei Dynasty, CE 386–534), the Khitan (Liao Dynasty, CE 907–1125), and the Danxiang (Western Xia state, CE 1032–1227). Their skills in warfare, when combined with the Chinese knowledge of administration, enabled the Mongols not only to conquer but also to govern one of the largest empires the world had ever known.

THE GREAT GENGHIS KHAN

The Secret History of the Mongols tells how Timujin, son of a minor chieftain, and an outcast after the death of his father, became a tribal leader himself. The Chinese sought him as an ally against the Tatars, and as his success grew he eventually became Khan of the Mongols. In 1206, Timujin, then about 40, convened a khuriltai tribal assembly at Aurug, about 150 miles (24 km) east of Ulaanbaatar; 13 earth platforms in this 100-acre (40-ha) site are thought to be the remains of the palace where he proclaimed himself Genghis Khan (emperor of emperors). He structured the tribes into a vast army with units made up of a mixture of clans, so that no clan loyalty could develop to threaten his rule. To hold together his new nation, he found new enemies to fight, new peoples to conquer, and embarked on a series of campaigns against China's Jin Dynasty. He defeated the Xia and besieged the Jin emperor at Beijing (then Zhongdu) but was bought off by tribute and marriage alliances. Mongol lands now bordered those of the Khwarezm Shah who controlled a large part of Central Asia, including the rich oasis cities of Samarkand and Bukhara.

In 1218 the Khwarezm Shah, very seriously underestimating his opponent, killed a Mongol ambassador, unleashing the greatest flood of

MONGOL HORSEMEN

This thirteenth-century CE Japanese scroll, attributed to Tosa Nagataka, depicts Mongol horsemen on the attack. Mongol warriors were skilled riders, learning horsemanship at an early age. They used bows and arrows as well as spears in battle.

EXTENT OF THE MONGOL EMPIRE

At its peak, the Mongol Empire stretched more than 12 million sq miles (31 million sq km) from China into central Europe.

KEY
○ Capital City
○ Other City or Town
▪ Archaeological Site
— International Border
░ Extent of the Mongol Empire

0 — 1,000 km
0 — 1,000 miles
N

SITE OF AN ANCIENT CITY

A solitary stone tortoise marks the ancient site of Karakorum, the capital of the great Mongol Empire established by Ogadei, son of Genghis Khan. Ogadei also reestablished Karakorum as a major city on the Great Silk Road. The stones on the tortoise's back have been dropped there by passersby, as a tribute to the glory days of the past.

devastation the East had ever seen. The Mongols pursued the Khwarezm Shah to the shores of the Caspian Sea, then continued through Azerbaijan into Georgia, and around the western Caspian into Russia. Genghis himself turned south, fired the city of Bukhara and took Samarkand. He then pursued Jalal al-Din, the Shah's son, south through Persia into Afghanistan, then into Pakistan and across the Indus River. In 1227 Genghis died during a victorious siege against the Western Xia in modern Ningxia. All living beings encountered by the funeral procession were sacrificed to serve him in the afterlife; then herds of horses were driven over the gravesite to conceal it. Genghis Khan is still revered in Mongolia.

NEW MONGOL STATES

Genghis Khan had divided his empire among his three older sons: the eldest was given the Caspian Sea area, or Khanate of the Golden Horde, the second was given central Asia and modern Xinjiang. The third, Ogadei, was elected great Khan in 1229. He established a Mongol capital at Karakorum and the Mongol Empire expanded into Russia and eastern Europe. Westward expansion was halted by Ogadei's death in 1241. The Golden Horde's greatest ruler, Timur (Tamerlane, c. 1336–1404) conquered most of southwestern Asia. Babur (the Tiger, 1483–1530) invaded northern India, creating the Mughal Empire.

Excavations at Karakorum in the 1940s revealed the town was a small rectangle, with tiled buildings, coinage, and stores of metal tools. The Mongols' most lasting physical monument is Beijing—then named Dadu, the great capital—which was remodeled by Kublai Khan. The Tibetan Buddhist Baita "white pagoda," built in 1279, still stands there.

KUBLAI KHAN

The Empire of the Great Khan in China was marked by the magnificent reign of Kublai Khan that lasted from 1264 until 1294. Grandson of Genghis Khan, Kublai defeated the Song dynasty. Kublai created the fabled Xanadu—Shangdu, the upper capital—now the Summer Palace at Chengde, a World Heritage site. Both places were described by admiring foreigners: Marco Polo in the 1270s and Ibn Battuta in the 1340s–1350s. China remained in Mongol hands until 1368, when the first Ming emperor was installed in power. Kublai and his Yuan-dynasty descendants centralized foreign trade, setting up export industries for silk, tea, and "china" ceramics with state-run factories and a merchant navy.

A FEAST AT KARAKORUM

This sixteenth-century CE Mughal image from the court of Akbar the Great shows Mangu Khan, brother of Kublai Khan, hosting a feast in his tent-palace at Karakorum.

The Indus Civilization

Although taking its name from the river flowing from the Himalayas to the Arabian Sea, the Indus Civilization stretched as far north as Shortugai in northern Afghanistan, east to the Ganges-Yamuna doab (land between rivers), south as far as Surat on India's west coast, and west along the north shore of the Arabian Sea.

Dating from 2600–1900 BCE, the Indus Civilization encompassed an area of over 193,000 sq miles (500,000 sq km) and is characterized by a uniform script, a system of weights and measures, craft specialization, and planned urban centers. The discovery of Neolithic communities in Baluchistan, to the west of the Indus, that demonstrate cultural and occupational continuity for several millennia leading up to the Indus Civilization have helped to dispel concepts of diffusion regarding its origins. Yet, the Indus Civilization differs from many contemporary Bronze Age civilizations through its lack of hereditary elites and a class-based society, and the absence of a highly visible army.

PRIEST-KINGS AND PAUPERS: RANK AND VALUE IN THE INDUS CIVILIZATION

Traditionally, the Indus Civilization was seen as a state-level society ruled over by an autocratic priest-king, who dominated the society from the twin capitals of Mohenjo-Daro and Harappa. This rigid social structure was supposed rather than proved, and recently archaeologists have begun to question the validity of such an interpretation. Archaeological indicators of elites—lavish residences, accumulations of great wealth, opulent burials, monumental

WHERE DID POWER LIE?

One of the most striking elements of the Indus Civilization has been the inability of archaeologists to identify any evidence of weaponry or a standing army, leading to confusion surrounding the method by which elites maintained such a widespread and uniform society. In the absence of any means of physical coercion, some scholars have suggested that power may have resided in the hands of ascetics, who suppressed public displays of wealth differentiations, and competition between individuals and cities alike. However, it is also possible that depictions of elites, battles, and deities were confined to perishable materials such as textile or bark cloth, which is why there is no evidence of them.

architecture, and any depictions of themselves—are all conspicuously absent from Indus sites.

Indeed, there is very little visible evidence of any kind of authority, either religious or secular. Instead, scholars have suggested that the cities of the Indus Civilization were ruled over by conglomerate groups of traders, landowners, and ritual specialists. These groups may have extended their control over a number of cities, or joined with other ruling groups to form alliances for trade and defense. The poor archaeological visibility of any elite groups is not indicative of their absence, but suggests that they played a very different role from elites within other

INDUS SPEARHEADS

These copper spearheads and other implements from the Indus Civilization are kept in the National Museum of New Delhi, India. It is possible that items such as these were manufactured in one major center and then distributed throughout the region.

Bronze Age civilizations. It has been suggested that wealth and power were not concentrated within urban centers, but rather, were measured in terms of cattle numbers and agricultural land. Such a notion is certainly in keeping with much of modern South Asia, as well as many other communities residing in marginal climatic regions.

CONQUEST AND CATASTROPHE: THE COLLAPSE OF THE INDUS CIVILIZATION

The beginning of the second millennium BCE witnessed the end of the Indus Civilization, characterized by the abandonment of numerous social and cultural elements including their urban centers, the use of the Indus script, the standardization of artifacts, weights and measures, and long-distance trade. The widespread cultural homogeneity was replaced by a series of regional stylistic groups, often reflecting communities that existed before the emergence of the Indus Civilization itself. So sudden was this end, that early archaeologists attributed it to invading Indo-Aryan people from the north (see page 245), a theory that has since been widely refuted in academic circles. Many scholars have since proposed alternative explanations—ranging from flooding, earthquakes, land overuse, and diminishing rainfall, to shifting trade routes and political allegiances in Mesopotamia.

However, while the core cities and regions of the Indus Valley underwent this collapse, its peripheries flourished. The valleys to the north of the Indus witnessed the emergence of the Gandharan Grave culture, characterized by rich megalithic pit burials. In Baluchistan to the west, sites such as Mundigak and Pirak expanded in size and engaged in the construction of monumental buildings, maintaining trade links with western India, the Ganges-Yamuna doab, and the Arabian Gulf.

In western India itself, we see an increase in the number of settlements, a result of people adopting a more pastoral lifestyle. To the east, a number of sites stretching from the Indus Valley to the Ganges demonstrate continuity in occupation through to the Early Historic period. As such, it appears that while the core regions of the Indus Civilization were collapsing, the peripheries were flourishing in the absence of a centralizing authority.

Our understanding of the Indus Civilization has developed dramatically over the last 20 years or so, and it is slowly becoming apparent that it was a society that contradicted itself in many ways: where urban centers relied upon pastoral communities, armies were supplanted by ascetics, and where elites actively sought to hide their own positions of power. However, until the Indus script is deciphered (see pages 244–245), we are unlikely to fully understand this ancient civilization.

FAMILY HEIRLOOM

This brooch made of silver, gold, and steatite, estimated to be 2,000–2,500 years old, was found at the excavated site of Harappa in Pakistan, and is now housed in the National Museum in Karachi.

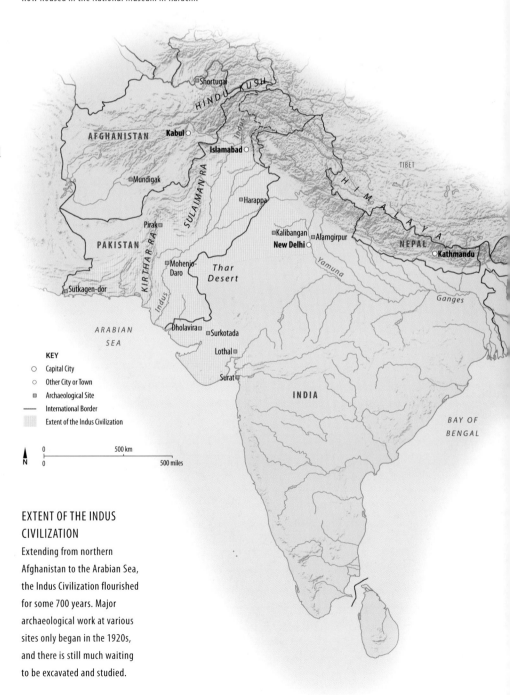

EXTENT OF THE INDUS CIVILIZATION

Extending from northern Afghanistan to the Arabian Sea, the Indus Civilization flourished for some 700 years. Major archaeological work at various sites only began in the 1920s, and there is still much waiting to be excavated and studied.

KEY
○ Capital City
○ Other City or Town
▫ Archaeological Site
— International Border
▨ Extent of the Indus Civilization

0   500 km
0   500 miles

Mohenjo-Daro, Pakistan

Located on the floodplains of the Indus River, Mohenjo-Daro in Pakistan is the largest and most spectacular site of the Indus Civilization. Its "citadel" or "acropolis" rises 40 ft (12 m) above the modern plains, with a series of monumental structures sitting atop a massive man-made platform.

Located on this citadel were the "Great Bath," "College of Priests," and the "Granary," and it was believed to be the home of the ruling elite of the Indus Civilization. To the east of the citadel lies the Lower Town—the densely populated habitation area of the city, with cardinally oriented streets and a mixture of houses, shops, and workshops. Structures in the Lower Town were constructed using standardized sun-dried bricks (following the 1:2:4 ratio found throughout the Indus), and consist of a series of rooms organized around a central courtyard.

INDUS CRAFTSMANSHIP

This terracotta vase, decorated with a painting of a goat, is from Mohenjo-Daro and is dated to c. 2000 BCE. Workshops, including potters' kilns, were found at the site. Terracotta was also used to make figurines and jewelry.

THE CITADEL MOUND

A testament to Indus architectural skills, the Great Bath complex is over 200 ft (60 m) long, the bath itself being 40 ft by 23 ft (12 m by 7 m) and 8 ft (2.4 m) deep. Water for the bath was supplied by a deep well on the citadel, while an intricate well and drainage system ensured a continual flow of clean water. The Great Bath complex was built from fired, as opposed to sun-dried, bricks, and the bonding was so intricate that the gap between courses was less than 1/16 in (1 mm). Its inner wall was coated with a layer of bitumen to render it impermeable.

Located right next to the Great Bath is a second large structure called the Granary, although its actual function is still debated, much like the College. Many archaeologists have suggested that some form of water worship took place on the citadel, as evidenced by the Great Bath—especially when one considers that the vast majority of houses in the Lower Town contained their own private bathing platforms, supplied by a network comprising hundreds of wells across the city.

STREETS AHEAD OF THE OTHERS

A section of the ruins at Mohenjo-Daro, looking toward the citadel. The settlement had a well-planned layout, based on a grid of streets, and boasted an advanced drainage system. Mohenjo-Daro is widely considered to be one of the most significant early cities in south Asia.

The Great Bath did not play a functional role in hygiene, but the vast investment in its construction assures us its purpose was of utmost importance to the inhabitants of Mohenjo-Daro.

The role of the citadel is still unknown. While most scholars assume that it housed the elites of the Indus Civilization, there is very little artifactual differentiation from the Lower Town. Additionally, the greatest concentrations of wealth are to be found within the smallest rooms of the Lower Town. As yet only 10 percent of the Lower Town has been excavated, much of the remainder lying beneath several feet of alluvium. In the areas that have been excavated, the lowest levels lie below the water table, preventing us from truly understanding the origins of this metropolis.

Harappa, Pakistan

The first Indus city to be discovered by archaeologists was Harappa, which is located 354 miles (570 km) to the northeast of Mohenjo-Daro, close to an old course of Ravi, one of the major tributaries of the majestic Indus River.

Earlier excavations exposed the city's plan, but recent American and Pakistani teams have reconstructed the site's sequence and suggest that the site was first occupied in the fourth millennium BCE—almost a millennium before it achieved city status.

BRONZE AGE TOWN PLANNING

For many years, archaeologists assumed that all Indus cities and towns shared a similar imposed plan, that of a "citadel" mound in the west and a "lower town" to the east. However, it is now becoming clearer that while a range of different sized sites do possess such features, such as the 495-acre (200-ha) site of Mohenjo-Daro and the 49-acre (20-ha) site of Kalibangan in Rajasthan, many do not. The plan of 370-acre (150-ha) Harappa, for example, has been revised and is now thought to comprise four walled mounds centered on a central depression, which its

excavators have suggested may be a reservoir. Excavations have also demonstrated that this dispersed pattern was already in place before the Indus cultural and urban convergence began in the middle of the third millennium BCE. Similar antiquity of plan has been found at Kalibangan where archaeologists have identified the presence of a walled compound below the citadel mound of the Bronze Age city. However, there appear to be no similarities or antecedents for the plan of the city of Dholavira in the Indian region of Kutch. Located on a small island, it consists of a nested series of walled rectangular compounds surrounding a square "castle" at its highest point. Western India also has some "factory-forts," which appear to be isolated but planned compounds, located to exploit semi-precious stone deposits.

This diversity is also found within the use of building materials as many of the cities utilize mud-brick but some, notably those close to suitable sources, utilized stone blocks, as at Surkotada in Kutch and within Dholavira. Sandstone blocks were used for houses and drains at the latter, with wooden pillars supported on polished circular bases. Some other suggested differences may be due to different archaeological interpretation as groups of mud-brick podiums at Mohenjo-Daro and Lothal have been interpreted as granary foundations, while a similar function has been attributed to very different structures at Harappa. However, uniformity of house plan throughout the civilization is undeniable, with a limited number of variants identified within excavated quarters. Most houses appear to comprise a single courtyard surrounded by ranges of rooms on one, two, three, or four sides with a notable absence of large elite complexes. This uniformity within urban areas is reinforced by evidence of craft activities, suggesting that the function of most units was undifferentiated and that crafts were conducted throughout the cities rather than being clustered in bazaars.

The Mystery of the Indus Texts

Despite examples having first been published in 1873, the Indus script has defied attempts by generations of scholars to decipher it. Since that time, the corpus of known artifacts, seals, and sealings bearing the Indus script has grown to over 2,700 examples recovered from sites in the broad region defined by the Persian Gulf and the Indus, Oxus, and Euphrates Rivers.

The Indus script has been found on a variety of objects ranging from steatite seals, metal axes, and vessels, to terracotta bangles and clay sealings, and appears to comprise between 170 and 220 simple signs and between 170 and 200 composite signs. One of the most striking features of the script is that it is frequently displayed on seals in association with the depictions of animals, some of which are endemic to South Asia, such as cattle and rhinoceroses, but some of which must be mythical. Some scholars have suggested that the different animals represent the totems of competing lineages within the civilization, but it is quite possible that they represent deities themselves. Other scenes appear to be more narrative in nature and may depict ritual activities, and some seals are thought to contain the images of cult figures, some of whom survived into modern times as Hindu gods.

GENERAL AGREEMENT ON SCRIPT FEATURES

Despite the failure of scholars to decipher the Indus script, there are a number of agreed general features. The first of these is that most scholars agree that the Indus script was written from right to left as indicated by the cramping of many examples in the left margins. The second is that most scholars would agree that simple downward slashes represent single units and that semicircles represent units of ten. Thirdly, most scholars would agree that the script represented a mixture of word-signs and phonetic

SEARCHING FOR ANSWERS

The ruins at Harappa (seen above) and Mohenjo-Daro yielded many artifacts containing Indus script, such as seals and vessels. Until scholars are able to decipher the script, many secrets of this fascinating civilization will remain hidden to us.

FLYING HIGH

Despite the obstacles to a successful decipherment of the Indus script, a number of scholars have proposed readings of individual signs and even collections of signs. For example, the Finnish academic Asko Parpola assumed that some signs were pictograms but that they were also homophones—that is, words pronounced the same but having different meanings. As Parpola assumed that the Indus script represented a Dravidian language, he suggested that the "fish" sign could be read as the Dravidian word for fish, "min." He then assumed that the sign was also a homophone and that as "min" also meant star or planet in Dravidian, the Indus "fish" sign represented a star or planet. Other scholars have argued that the "fish" sign represents fish, and that it occurs so frequently because the text refers to the allocation of fish rations. Such confusion is suitably illustrated by various decipherments of the "jar" sign, which is the most commonly occurring sign in the Indus script and whose readings include "a vessel dedicated to a god or gods," "a vessel," "the western cardinal direction," "the sound sa," "the third person singular honorific," "a ship," "a title of respect commonly added to proper names, whether human or divine," "a bird," "an eagle," "cow's head," and even the verb "to fly"!

MAKING A GOOD IMPRESSION

The Indus script is shown on these two seals, which also feature animals—a rhinoceros (above) and a zebu bull (right). The script has been inscribed in reverse, so that it will be clear after it has made an impression. The use of such powerful animals on seals may indicate high social status.

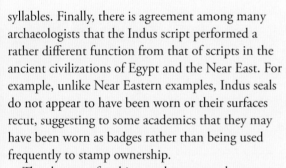

syllables. Finally, there is agreement among many archaeologists that the Indus script performed a rather different function from that of scripts in the ancient civilizations of Egypt and the Near East. For example, unlike Near Eastern examples, Indus seals do not appear to have been worn or their surfaces recut, suggesting to some academics that they may have been worn as badges rather than being used frequently to stamp ownership.

The absence of archives and any texts that are longer than a string of 26 signs is also rather puzzling, and scholars have suggested that longer texts may have been written on perishable materials such as birch bark or even cloth.

DISAGREEMENT ON OTHER MATTERS

In contrast, there is no real scholarly consensus as to the language that is depicted in the Indus script. One of the earliest interpretations was that the script depicted a Dravidian language, and that such Dravidian-speaking communities had been almost entirely replaced by an invasion of Indo-Aryan speakers at the end of the Indus Civilization in *c.* 1900 BCE. As noted above, however, the causes of the collapse have been reassessed by scholars. It is thought that the script may represent an early Indian language, or Proto-Elamite or an Austro-Asiatic, Sino-Tibetan, or even now-extinct languages.

Until such time as much longer inscriptions or bilingual inscriptions are discovered in the region, the enduring mystery of the Indus script is going to continue to fascinate and challenge amateur and professional decipherers alike.

USING ANIMAL MOTIFS

This steatite seal depicting an elephant beneath Indus lettering was found at Mohenjo-Daro and dates to 2500–2000 BCE. There is speculation among academics as to whether the elephant may have been domesticated at the time. Some of the other animals found on Indus seals include crocodiles and buffalo, as well as mythical creatures such as unicorns.

Early Chinese Dynasties

From the early second millennium to the third century BCE, a period that corresponds approximately to China's Bronze Age, three dynasties (Xia, Shang, and Zhou) flourished in succession in north-central China's Yellow River valley and environs. Beyond this area, Bronze Age cultures developed in the Yangtze River Valley in the south (Xingang) and southwest (Sanxingdui).

China's Bronze Age civilization developed out of a variety of regional Late Neolithic cultures that are sometimes collectively described as the Longshan horizon (c. 3000–2000 BCE).

LATE NEOLITHIC AND XIA

Some of the traits that characterize the culture of the Bronze Age dynasties, such as city building, jade working, bone divination, and ancestor worship, appear already as significant traits of the Chinese late Neolithic. According to historical accounts, the first dynasty to dominate the region of the middle Yellow River valley was Xia (traditionally 2100–1700 BCE). Several archaeologists in China believe that the Erlitou culture (c. 1950–1600 BCE), which follows the Longshan horizon in parts of Henan and Shaanxi Provinces, corresponds to the domains of the Xia Dynasty and that the remains of the Erlitou site (Yanshi, Henan) belong to this dynasty's last capital, Zhenxun. The Erlitou site, a large ensemble of palatial and other remains, was discovered in the 1950s when the area was surveyed following some literary accounts that described the location of Xia's Zhenxun. Repeated excavations of the Erlitou area from the 1960s to more recent times have brought to light two large palace foundations, evidence of an emerging bronze metallurgy, as well as ritual jades and ornaments. Aside from a few undecipherable signs carved on some pottery, at Erlitou there is no evidence of writing, a fact which renders difficult the confirmation of the existence of the Xia Dynasty.

THE SHANG DYNASTY

The Shang, who appear to have been eastern neighbors of the Xia, established their rule probably between 1600 and 1550 BCE by replacing their predecessors as the dominant political force in the middle Yellow River and surrounding areas. Various Shang sites (capitals, large settlements, and burial grounds) have been excavated. The best-known city sites are at Yanshi, Zhengzhou, Panglongcheng, and Anyang. These settlements are characterized by the remains of palatial structures, ritual and sacrificial areas, burials, and in some cases defensive walls, and by the presence in fairly large numbers of ceramic artifacts, ceremonial jades, and bronzes (mostly vessels and musical instruments, but also weapons). The Shang are well-known for their mastery of bronze metallurgy, which they employed to manufacture vessels and implements for the ritual libations offered to royal ancestors. During these worship ceremonies Shang kings and ritual specialists carried

RITUAL VESSELS
This pair of bronze tripod food vessels, known as *ding*, are from the Shang Dynasty. These ritual food vessels were often placed in tombs as offerings for the dead. They may have been used in burial rituals of the time.

CAN YOU FEEL IT IN YOUR BONES?
Dating to the fourteenth to thirteenth centuries BCE, this fragment of a bovine shoulder blade bears a divinatory inscription, warding off danger. It is from the Shang Dynasty. Oracle bones provided divination lists for kings and queens.

FINDING BURIAL SITES
In 2006, construction work on a water diversion project in the Yunxian County of Hubei Province unearthed an ancient tomb. Archaeologists are now painstakingly excavating the area for relics that will shed new light on China's rich archaeological heritage.

out divinations by burning ox shoulder bones and turtle plastrons. While pyroscapulimancy (burning shoulder bones) was practiced also in the Neolithic, the bones began to be inscribed only in the late Shang. Oracle bone inscriptions are one of the earliest forms of writing in China (the other being bronze inscriptions).

THE ZHOU DYNASTY
Originally a subject population in the western part of the Shang domain (the Zhouyuan, where their

ancestral temples remained for centuries), the Zhou overthrew the Shang in 1046 BCE and ruled for almost 800 years. The long rule of the Zhou is divided into Western Zhou (1046–770 BCE), when the capital was in the west near present-day Xi'an, and Eastern Zhou (770–256 BCE), when the capital was moved east following nomad attacks on the western territories. After the conquest, the Zhou state was organized in a feudal system with relatives or former allies of the Zhou kings being given titles to control parcels of the royal domain. Finds of hoards of bronze vessels with lengthy inscriptions, such as those of Zhuang-bai in the Zhouyuan, which record investment ceremonies and family histories, suggest that ritual bronzes played a significant function in the Zhou feudal system. The Eastern Zhou Period, which is traditionally divided into the Spring and Autumn Period and Warring States Period, witnessed the progressive disintegration of the Zhou feudal system and the growth of regional state cultures that eventually annihilated the Zhou Dynasty.

Much of the material evidence that has been excavated at late Zhou archaeological sites, such as the burial place of Count Yi of Zeng at Leigudun (Hubei), or the tomb of the King of Zhongshan at Shijiazhuan (Hebei) confirm the regionalization of both power and Zhou culture.

BRONZE RITUAL VESSELS

Based on their shape, ritual vessels are classified as food, wine, or water containers. Some food vessels (like the *ding* tripod or the *xian* steamer) were used for cooking offerings, others for serving ritual meals. Likewise, some wine containers like the *jue* pitcher were employed to heat grain wine, while others, like the *gu* goblet, were used to serve it. Water vessels were probably for rinsing implements. While the earliest vessels are plain, those of the Shang are decorated with the *taotie* face, sometimes called "ogre mask," and occasionally carry short inscriptions. With the Zhou, bronzes exhibited longer inscriptions and decorations ranging from bird designs to abstract patterns and narrative panels. Bronzes were made by piece-mold casting, a technique that required creating a prototype of the object to be cast, pressing clay molds on the outside and inside of the model, discarding the model, and finally filling the molds with molten bronze.

Zhengzhou, China

The Shang city at Zhengzhou (Zhengzhou Shang Cheng) is a large, walled site situated below the modern city of Zhengzhou in Henan Province. The settlement, excavated in the early 1950s, is thought to be an early Shang capital, possibly either the famed Bo or Ao that are mentioned in historic sources.

The Zhengzhou site consists of the walled city, originally occupied by the Shang kings and the aristocracy, and its surroundings, which were home to the larger population. From the stratigraphic point of view, archaeologists have identified two Shang phases which account for the occupation of Zhengzhou somewhere between 1500 and 1300 BCE. The earliest stratum, lower Erligang, corresponds to the period of construction of the city walls and its most significant remains, the following one, upper Erligang, is contemporaneous with the later use of the site.

THE WALLED CITY

Zhengzhou's walls take a roughly rectangular shape with a perimeter reaching almost 4 miles (7 km). The sloping walls, made of pounded earth layers (hangtu), were originally of a massive width—measuring between 105 ft (32 m) and 72 ft (22 m) at the base and 35 ft (10 m) at the summit. Today, they are mostly underground, but in the areas where they are still visible they stand at a height of 16 ft (5 m). The enclosure is interrupted by a number of gaps, which are probably the remnants of the city gates.

Within the walls are the remains of temples and ritual areas as well as of what were once royal and aristocratic palaces. Over 20 pounded earth platform-foundations are concentrated in an elevated section in the northeastern quarters of the city. One of these is remarkably large (213 ft by 44 ft [65 m by 13.5 m]) and was subdivided into nine separate rooms and a corridor. Another, denominated Palace n. 16, measures 102 ft by 125 ft (31 m by 38 m). While some of these foundations may have been dwellings, others were probably temples or ritual structures, as in their vicinity there is evidence of human and animal sacrifice. From one pit alone, archaeologists have retrieved the skulls of nearly 100 young men. Some of these skulls were sawn in half and otherwise worked, perhaps to manufacture ritual objects of human bone. The skeletons of 92 sacrificed dogs were discovered in nearby pits. Sacrifices of enslaved prisoners and animals (usually dogs, pigs, oxen, and sheep) were a fundamental part of the rituals in honor of Shang gods and royal ancestors.

In addition to these larger remains, some houses have been discovered in the northeastern and northwestern corners of the city, as well as in the central area, and a few simple burials, possibly belonging to commoners, have been identified along the inside of the city walls. Still, there is a good portion of Zhengzhou that remains unexcavated as it lies below the modern city.

SACRIFICIAL SKULLS

These skeletons are part of an archaeological display of a Shang Dynasty Period sacrificial site, located at the Henan Provincial Research Institute and Archaeological Field Station, Zhengzhou. Human sacrifice was possibly used as a means to consecrate a temple's foundations.

BEYOND THE WALLS

In the vicinity of the walled enclosure, the larger Zhengzhou site includes cemeteries, commoners' houses, workshops, and other remains. Four burial grounds have been discovered on three sides of the city (one on the west, one on the south, and two on the east). Overall these tombs are not particularly large or lavish and clearly do not belong to the kings that ruled at Zhengzhou. The richest of these, Tomb n. 3 at Baijiazhuang, is a moderate-sized burial site furnished with nine ritual bronzes, two jades, and few other artifacts: too little for a king.

Several areas dedicated to craft productions surround the city, suggesting that at Zhengzhou there was specialized large-scale production of luxury goods, probably under government control. These work areas range from bone workshops (north), to pottery workshop and kilns (east), to bronze foundries (north and south of the city).

Bronze played an important role at Zhengzhou. Three large hoards of bronzes buried in pits have also been excavated outside the Zhengzhou walls. The largest at Nanshuncheng Street yielded nine ritual vessels and three weapons. Another at Duling included two very large square *ding* tripods. Further away, about 12 miles (20 km) northwest of the walled city, one palace complex with sacrificial evidence has been discovered at Xiashuangqiao.

YELLOW RIVER HISTORY
The second-longest river in China, the Yellow River is often referred to as the cradle of ancient Chinese culture. The city of Zhengzhou, birthplace of the Shang Dynasty, sits just south of the river.

BEAUTIFUL BRONZE
This rounded, bronze ritual vessel, a *pou*, was probably used for wine. It is 10⅝ in (27 cm) high and has the typical Shang *taotie* ogre mask with bulging eyes, a nose, and horns on either side.

IDENTIFYING AN ANCIENT CAPITAL

Archaeological evidence indicates that Zhengzhou was an early Shang city which predated Yin, the last Shang capital at Anyang, and was in use for hundreds of years. Its large size suggests that it was probably a capital. However, to this day archaeologists and historians are unsure of the exact identity of the Zhengzhou remains. According to some, Zhengzhou could be the ancient Bo, the first Shang capital established by the Shang founder, King Tang. Others think it may instead be Ao (or Xiao), the second Shang capital, which was founded by King Zhongding. Records support the second theory, because Ao and not Bo is said to have been in the Zhengzhou area. However, historic sources say that Ao was the capital for only 26 years, too few years compared with the long occupation of the Zhengzhou site, which seems to be more in line with the 183 years of occupation at Bo.

Anyang, China

A large area near modern Anyang in Henan Province is the location of the ruins of Yin (Yinxu), the Shang Dynasty's last capital. Yinxu was known for centuries as a historic Shang center. Antique bronzes have been excavated there since at least the eleventh century CE, and inscribed divination bones were retrieved in the late nineteenth century.

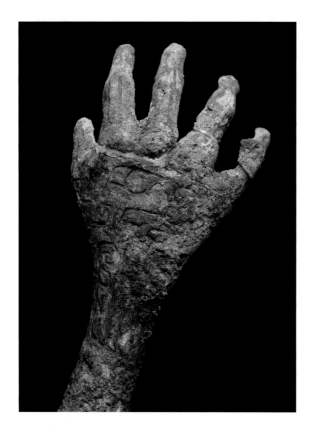

HAND OF DESTINY

The Shang Dynasty is known for its bronze works, many of which had ritual functions. No one knows what significance this bronze hand had. It was found in the tomb of a Shang officer at Anyang.

In fact, it was to investigate oracle bones that the Anyang excavations began in 1928. The ruins of Yin are found north of the Yellow River straddling the Huan River. According to traditional records, Yin was the ritual–political center of the Shang Dynasty for 12 kings who ruled for about 250 years from *c.* 1300 to 1050 BCE.

THE ARCHAEOLOGICAL SITE

Excavated inscriptions on oracular bones confirm the presence at Yin of the last nine of these kings (from Wuding to Dixin), and archaeologists have identified four phases of occupation of the site: Yinxu I–IV. The site is very extensive (*c.* 11½ sq miles [30 sq km]), and most of it appears to have been outside the recently discovered defensive walls that date to the earliest phase. This suggests that the Shang may have conceived of this city more as a uniting ritual center rather than a political capital with definite borders. Nonetheless, at Yinxu there is a very clear center (the Anyang core) with ritual centers and cemeteries, and a periphery made up of numerous contemporaneous

sites spread in the surroundings. The two key parts of the Anyang core are the Xiaotun palatial site south of the Huan River and the Xibeigang royal cemetery north of the river.

XIAOTUN PALATIAL SITE

In the vicinity of the modern Xiaotun village, an elevated area surrounded on two sides by a moat and defended on the remaining sides by the Huan River contains over 50 palace or temple foundations as well as large deposits of oracle bones, human sacrifices, and workshops. The buildings appear to have been arranged into three groups known as Group A (north), Group B (west), and Group C (south). The northern group of palaces (Group A) may have been primarily a residential zone, as there is no evidence of ritual activities. The remaining two palatial zones are instead interspersed with sacrificial burials of animals, humans, and even chariots, an indication that ceremonies were performed there.

Southwest of the palatial area, just outside the moat, is the tomb of Fuhao (Lady Hao). This is a small tomb with no ramps, but it is the only undisturbed aristocratic burial of Anyang. At the bottom of the burial pit was the lacquered funerary chamber within which were nestled the wooden coffins. The pit held a number of sacrificial victims: 16 persons (four males, two females, two children, plus eight people of undetermined sex and age) and six dogs followed Fuhao in death. The offerings were lavish including 460 bronze vessels, bells and weapons, as well as jades, cowrie shells, pottery, bone, ivory, and stone objects. Fuhao's tomb is dated to Yinxu phase II, which corresponds to the reign of King Wuding. This is consistent because Fuhao is thought to have been one of Wuding's wives. Her name, inscribed on vessels and weapons retrieved from the burial, is also mentioned in oracle bone texts. In divination records the king inquired about Fuhao's pregnancy, in others there is evidence that she was in charge of military operations and rituals.

THE ROYAL CEMETERY AT XIBEIGANG

The Xibeigang cemetery is located across the river from the Xiaotun palatial area and to the north of the modern villages of Houjiazhuan and

Wuguangcun. Here there are 11 extremely large tombs oriented north–south and arranged in two clusters. On the west side are seven burials and an unfinished pit, while to the east there are four burials and one pit. Eight tombs have access ramps on four sides and appear cross-shaped, while three have only one or two ramps. The burials range in length from 65½ to 260 ft (20 m to 80 m), with the shaft reaching a depth of 32 ft to 50 ft (10 m to 15 m).

Surrounding the large tombs there are over 1,400 sacrificial victims—some formally buried, others brutally killed. While all these tombs have been looted long ago and it is difficult to identify their owners, the number, size, shape, and large sacrifices of these burials suggest that they belonged to the kings and queens that ruled at Anyang. One of these (No. 1001) could be King Wuding's tomb, while one of the unfinished pits may have been meant for Zhouxin, the last Shang king.

SHANG RELIGION AND BONE DIVINATION

Shang religion centered on the cult of ancestors, nature deities (river and mountain gods), and Shangdi or God in High. Evidence of these cults is found in records of bone divinations performed for the Shang royal house. Divination, which involved burning ox shoulder bones or turtle plastrons in order to read the cracks provoked by the heat, was necessary to communicate with ancestors or deities and understand their needs or wishes. Divinations also provided information on future events, such as weather, hunting, or battles. Bronze vessels and musical instruments were important ritual tools: the libations requested by ancestors or deities were served in special bronze containers while chime bells provided the ceremonial music.

Oracle bones, such as this turtle shell and ox bone, were used by royalty to divine the future. The inscriptions on oracle bones embody the earliest forms of writing in China.

Sanxingdui, China

Sanxingdui, a Neolithic and Bronze Age settlement in China's southwestern Sichuan Province, first came to archaeologists' attention in 1929 when a farmer accidentally unearthed some ancient jades. It was excavated more extensively from the 1980s onward after two sacrificial pits filled with bronzes, jades, and elephant tusks were discovered.

The Sanxingdui site spans an area between 4½–6½ sq miles (12–17 sq km) with remains dating from the Neolithic to the Bronze Age (c. 2800–1000 BCE). The most significant finds relate to the Bronze Age and comprise a large walled city and two sacrificial pits.

The city walls, made of compressed earth, enclose an area of 1½ miles (2½ km) and at present stand at 13 ft (4 m) high. Their foundations are massive, ranging in width from 65–130 ft (20–40 m). The city's construction and occupation (c. 1700–1000 BCE) appears to have been roughly contemporaneous with the period of the Shang Dynasty in northern China, and the cities share some characteristics. Within this enclosure, in addition to the sacrificial pits, bronze, jade, gold, and stone objects were discovered as well as an elevated north–south axis and a number of building foundations.

SACRIFICIAL PITS

Along the north–south elevated central axis of the walled city were several sacrificial pits. Two significant ones were discovered in 1986. Pit 1 contained about 300 items: elephant tusks, gold, jades, stone objects, pottery, and bronzes (including vessels and heads of statues). These offerings appear to have been burned, thrown in the pit, and ritually buried. Pit 2 is a similar but more lavish sacrificial receptacle. In it were found over 400 objects, which, like those in Pit 1, had been burned before transfer. As well as 60 elephant tusks and numerous jades, shells, and smaller objects, the most impressive find was a number of large bronze sculptures. These include a life-size statue of a standing man (possibly a ritual specialist), 41 heads that may originally have been attached to wooden bodies, 15 masklike objects (some of massive proportions and with protruding eyes), as well as a spirit tree, an auspicious plant decorated with birds and dragons.

Some of the objects excavated from these pits are similar to those produced in association with Shang culture (for instance some jades and bronze vessels), others (like the large statuary) are radically different. Since at Sanxingdui there is no evidence of writing that could explain the significance of these objects, the cults with which they were associated are not entirely clear. Nonetheless, material remains suggest that the rituals and beliefs of Sanxingdui were different from those documented in Shang Dynasty contexts. It thus appears that Sanxingdui was the center of an independent Bronze Age culture, which had contacts with the Yellow River valley, but maintained unique ritual and artistic traits.

ALL EYES!

This gilded bronze head, with its large, protruding eyes, was found at Sanxingdui and was probably a totem to a god or king. The bronzes found at Sanxingdui are among the most outstanding bronzes unearthed in China.

HISTORY REMEMBERED

A man rides past a tablet marking the ancient ruins of Sanxingdui in Guanghan City, Sichuan Province. Archaeologists have been working on the site for almost 80 years, yet the civilization that lived there remains largely unknown.

Zhouyuan, China

The Zhouyuan, Plain of Zhou, is in the counties of Qishan and Fufeng (Shaanxi Province) and has a high concentration of predynastic and early dynastic Zhou remains. In the twelfth to eleventh century BCE, before they overthrew the Shang, this was the political center of the Zhou people; later it remained their ritual heart. Here were palaces, temples, large aristocratic tombs, and royal workshops.

BURROWING INTO THE PAST
Laborers work at the excavation site of a Zhou Dynasty tomb (below right) in Qishan. Large-scale excavation work has been carried out in the Zhouyuan area since the 1950s.

FINAL RESTING PLACE
These human remains and some pottery vessels were unearthed in 2006 from a tomb found during construction of public works at Zhouyuan. The ancient relics are believed to belong to the Chu Kingdom during the Spring and Autumn Period and Warring States Period (770–221 BCE).

While scientific excavations only began at the site in the 1950s, Zhouyuan has long been known as a source of ancient bronzes. Several, like the famed Mao Gong Ding, were excavated during the last dynasty (Qing, 1644–1911), others were retrieved recently. Most significant is the Zhuangbai hoard, which consists of 103 Western Zhou ritual bronzes belonging to the aristocratic Wei family. Seventy-three of these bronzes are inscribed, and one of them, the Shi Qiang *Pan*, carries a 284-character text recounting the historical relations between the Wei family and members of the Zhou monarchy.

THE FENGCHU PALACE AT QISHAN

At Fengchu (Qishan county) archaeologists have brought to light the pounded earth foundation of a walled compound attributable to the predynastic Zhou. The rectangular pillared structure was organized symmetrically along a central axis. It was fully enclosed by buildings and covered corridors. These structures had thatched and tiled roofs, plastered walls and floors, and even a drainage system. To the east of the compound were the remains of walls and to its west another foundation that may have been residential. Access to the interior of the compound was gained through a central gate that led to the front courtyard and the main hall, places where investiture ceremonies and ancestral rites took place. From the main hall a covered passageway led to the rear yards and halls that were probably used for more private activities such as dressing and cooking.

The ritual significance of the compound is made clear by both its structure, which fits the descriptions of Zhou ritual halls found in classic texts, and the discovery below the palace foundations of 17,000 oracle bones. Close to 300 of these bones were inscribed and document the ceremonies performed by the Zhou aristocracy in accordance with the rules of Shang ritualism.

FUFENG: THE ZHAOCHENG COMPLEX AND THE LIJIA FOUNDRY

A ceremonial complex datable to the mid- to late Zhou Period was unearthed at Zhaocheng in Fufeng county. The Zhaocheng complex featured numerous ritual halls, including one that stood on an elevated platform. Postholes filled with stones indicate that massive pillars were used to support a heavy and possibly double-eaved roof. Also at Fufeng, near the village of Lijia, archaeologists have recently excavated evidence of a large bronze workshop, including thousands of pottery molds used to make Western Zhou ritual bronzes.

The First Empires of China

The first empires of China were the Qin and Han Dynasties, which existed from 221 BCE to CE 220. They were characterized by developed agriculture; a centralized system of government; large palaces, cities, and mausoleums; overseas and domestic trading; and highly skillful craftsmanship.

TOMB ARTIFACTS

During the Han Dynasty, it was common to include items from everyday life in tombs. This was based on the belief that there was life after death, so the deceased was provided with items to remind him of his daily life. This model bullock and cart is one such item.

SYMMETRY IN CURRENCY

Han Dynasty coins: Ban Liang (left) and Wu Zhu (right), from 206 BCE–CE 220. Liang was a unit of weight. The square hole in the center of the round coin represents the earth surrounded by the heavens.

The founder of the Qin Dynasty was Ying Zheng (also called Zhao Zheng), a powerful king from northwestern China. His capital was Xianyang, which was located a few miles north of modern-day Xi'an City, Shaanxi Province. Ying Zheng succeeded to the throne of the Qin Kingdom in 247 BCE at the age of thirteen.

THE FIRST EMPEROR

From 230 to 221 BCE Ying Zheng launched a series of military campaigns, conquered all the other states, and unified China. He declared himself "The First Emperor of the Qin Dynasty" (Qin Shi Huang Di) in 221 BCE at Xianyang. During his reign he established a centralized political system, which became the dominant system for the next 2,000 years, and unified the written language, coinage, and measurements. He also connected and further constructed the defensive walls built by the previous kingdoms in northern China, and forced thousands of laborers to build his mausoleum.

The Qin Dynasty, however, was short-lived. Ying Zheng died in 210 BCE, and was succeeded by his son Huhai, who was not a capable ruler. After Ying Zheng's death, the empire he had built was racked with unrest. There were widespread revolts—mainly because of accumulated social resentments toward brutal government policies. The Qin Dynasty collapsed in 206 BCE. Its capital Xianyang and the mausoleum of the First Emperor were ransacked, looted, and burned.

TIMELINE OF CHINESE HISTORY

Time	Dynasties	Important Events
2070–1600 BCE	Xia	Beginning of the Bronze Age and Chinese civilization in the Yellow River Valley.
1600–1046 BCE	Shang	Written Chinese developed in the Yellow River Valley.
1046–771 BCE	Western Zhou	Further development of states in the Yellow River Valley and institutionalized social hierarchy.
770–221 BCE	Eastern Zhou	Development toward feudalism.
722–481 BCE	Spring and Autumn Period	Decentralized power and the emergence of many states and different religions: Confucianism, Taoism, Legalism, Mohism etc.
403–221 BCE	Warring States Period	Continuous battles among seven prominent states. Construction of defensive walls by several states. Occurrence of iron casting.
221–206 BCE	Qin	Unification of China.
206 BCE–CE 23	Western Han	Confucianism established as a ruling philosophy and ideology and remained so until the Qing Dynasty. Trading between the West and China via the "Silk Road." Formation of the "Han" ethnic group and "Han" culture.
CE 25–220	Eastern Han	Buddhism introduced into China.
CE 220–280	Three Kingdoms	Dissolution of the centralized system. Development of porcelain, operas, and novels.
CE 265–316	Western Jin	Beginning of a turbulent epoch until CE 618.
CE 304–439	Sixteen Kingdoms	
CE 317–420	Eastern Jin	Beginning of powerful family politics.
CE 420–581	Southern and Northern Dynasty	
CE 581–618	Sui	Reunification of China.
CE 618–907	Tang	Prosperous period with blooming craftsmanship, trade, arts, and poetry etc.
CE 907–960	Five dynasties and ten kingdoms	Unstable period with continuous warfare.
CE 907–1125	Liao	Founded by Khitan in northeast China.
CE 960–1279	Song	Flourishing of ceramic manufacturing and trading. Occurrence of China's antiquarianism (Jinshi Xue).
CE 1032–1227	Western Xia	Founded by the Tangut tribes in northeast China.
CE 1115–1234	Jin	Founded by the Jurchen in northeast China.
CE 1279–1368	Yuan	This dynasty established by the Mongols.
CE 1368–1644	Ming	Increase in maritime trading.
CE 1644–1911	Qing	This dynasty established by the Manchu ethnic group.
CE 1911–	Republic of China	End of dynasties and imperial China.

DANCING FOR JOY
This Han Dynasty statuette depicts an entertainer, dancing and playing a musical instrument. The Han period, with its patronage of literature and the arts, is considered one the greatest periods in Chinese history.

THE HAN DYNASTY

There were continuous wars among different rebel leaders between 206 and 202 BCE, but eventually Liu Bang was victorious. Liu established the Han Dynasty and built a new capital Chang'an, which is almost 2 miles (3 km) northwest of Xi'an City. Intensive archaeological works have been carried out since the 1950s to examine both the size and structures of Chang'an. Today, the remains of the city walls and the palace foundations are still visible.

The Han Dynasty was mainly a centralized state, although in the beginning there were still some local kingdoms. However, the fourth emperor Liu Che (also called Emperor Wu) launched several military campaigns to destroy these local polities and enforce the centralized system. The Han Dynasty emperors declared Confucianism to be the state philosophy, established a system to nominate educated men to be government officials, and encouraged trading between the West and China (the "Silk Road").

Continuous military campaigns against the Xiongnu and other nomadic groups, and demand from the ruling class led to heavy taxation. Peasants lost their lands, which led to intensified conflict between different social groups, and, eventually, a number of uprisings in the first century CE. In CE 9 a government official, Wang Mang, seized the throne and ruled until CE 24, when he was overthrown by Liu Xiu, who restored the Han Dynasty.

EASTERN AND WESTERN DYNASTIES

Chang'an was burned to the ground during continuous wars in the first century CE, and Liu Xiu chose Luoyang, in modern-day Henan Province, as his capital. Because the previous capital Chang'an was west of Luoyang, the previous Han Dynasty is called the Western Han Dynasty, and the Han Dynasty established by Liu Xiu in CE 25 is called the Eastern Han Dynasty.

Terracotta Army, Xi'an, China

The terracotta army consists of more than 8,000 life-size terracotta warriors and horses dating back 2,200 years, which were discovered in three pits 1 mile (1.5 km) west of the Mausoleum of the First Emperor of the Qin Dynasty near present-day Xi'an in Shaanxi Province. These sculptures provide important information for our understanding of Qin culture.

In 1974, while digging a well, villagers of Lintong County in Shaanxi Province found broken terracotta pieces. Local archaeologists were informed, and excavations conducted the same year revealed terracotta warriors from a huge pit measuring 755 ft (230 m) long and 203 ft (62 m) wide, containing wooden chariots, terracotta warriors and horses, and tens of thousands of bronze weapons including arrows and arrowheads, bows, swords, halberds, and spearheads. This pit, Pit No. 1, has become the primary exhibition of the Qin Terracotta Army Museum established in 1979.

Further archaeological excavations have been carried out since 1974. To date, three pits have been discovered. Pit No. 1 is the largest. North of it, Pit No. 2 is about 407 ft (124 m) long and 320 ft (98 m) wide, and contains more than 1,400 chariots, terracotta horses, and warriors. To the west is the smallest pit, Pit No. 3 measuring 95 ft (28.8 m) long and 80 ft (24.5 m) wide, and containing one chariot, 70 warriors and horses, and 34 bronze weapons.

A FORMIDABLE COLLECTION USING TECHNOLOGICAL KNOW-HOW

The terracotta army is important archaeological evidence and helps us to understand the military organization and armament of the Qin Dynasty. The three pits together imitate a formidable Qin army. More than 6,000 infantry, 116 cavalrymen, and over 50 chariots in Pit No. 1 form a huge corps ready to fight, with 204 soldiers as vanguard, 50 chariots, and 4,000 foot soldiers being the primary force, flanked by the left and right divisions, and protected by the rear guards. Each division is led by a higher ranked officer.

Pit No. 2 consists of four corps. The first consists of 120 bowmen. The second consists of 64 chariots, each associated with four terracotta horses and three

LIFE-LIKE FACES AND FEATURES

The attention to detail is breathtaking. Even after more than 2,000 years, this warrior's face is full of life. This clearly suggests that each warrior was sculpted individually, and not cast in molds.

GETTING THE POINT

This bronze arrowhead was found buried in one of the vaults, and is now on display at the Qin Museum in Xi'an, China. All of the weapons found in the three pits are real weapons, not mere models. Most are made of bronze.

warriors. The third corps includes 19 chariots, each with four horses and three warriors, and 264 foot soldiers. The fourth corps is made up of six chariots and 108 cavalrymen.

Pit No. 3 contains a chariot in the center with four warriors and four horses. The chariot is flanked by two rows of a total of 64 armed foot soldiers. Doorframes and bronze door handles were found nearby, indicating that there must have been some sort of shelter enclosing the chariot and its warriors. So this chariot may symbolize army headquarters.

Apparently, the terracotta army imitates the powerful and efficient war machine of the First Emperor of the Qin Dynasty, who unified China through military campaigns. Meanwhile, tens of thousands of bronze weapons found in the three pits also demonstrate contemporaneous technologies. When discovered, the bronze weapons were still shining after being buried for more than 2,000 years. Scientific analysis revealed that these weapons were covered with a coat of oxidized chromium, preventing corrosion. The fact that hundreds of crossbow parts measure exactly the same suggests a standardized manufacturing.

AN ARTISTIC COLLECTION AND MORE

However, the terracotta army is not just an imitation of a war machine. The sculptures of the warriors and horses also manifest a realistic artistic style, and very skillful craftsmanship. Not one warrior of the whole army is identical to another. Each has a detailed facial expression, gesture, hairstyle, and uniform, the latter two also indicating the warrior's rank. Even the details of the shoe soles of kneeling bowmen were not neglected. Many warriors were originally covered by lacquer and paintings, although the decorations deteriorated after excavation. The horses were also life-size and lifelike, some with detailed terracotta saddles and halters.

The terracotta army and other burial pits, as well as the Mausoleum of the First Emperor of the Qin Dynasty, were declared World Heritage Sites by UNESCO in 1987, and have become one of the major tourist attractions of China.

AN ARMY FOR THE EMPEROR IN HIS AFTERLIFE

Why did the First Emperor of the Qin Dynasty expend such a huge amount of labor and materials to produce this terracotta army, along with other items such as bronze carriages and bronze sculptures of birds and animals, that were found in other pits enclosing the Mausoleum of the Emperor himself? According to Chinese archives, the Qin people believed that people had the same needs in the afterlife, so when a person died, he should be buried with items similar to those he used when alive. In reality, however, only the rich and the powerful could furnish their tombs with such items, and the more powerful the person was, the more items he would need. The First Emperor of the Qin Dynasty spent more than 30 years building his own mausoleum and pits to bury items for his own afterlife, and this included the terracotta army. This army illustrates the Qin Dynasty's command of technology and its capacity for planning.

PERFECT FORMATION
The terracotta army is one of the most significant archaeological finds of the twentieth century. The warriors and horses are about the same size as real men and horses, so it is hardly surprising that it took the emperor over 30 years to prepare his tomb.

Chinese Tomb Treasures

Tens of thousands of tombs dated to the Qin and Han Dynasties have been discovered since the 1950s in China. Although the imperial mausoleums of the Han Dynasty have been looted—either in ancient times or more recently—several undisturbed tombs of local kings and nobles have been discovered and excavated, yielding many treasures.

TREASURES FROM THE GRAVE

The tomb treasures of the Qin and Han periods mainly consist of jade, bronze, gold, silver, lacquer, silk, and ceramic items, although it is hard to find well-preserved silk garments.

Jade items are probably the most impressive tomb treasures of this period. Although the use of jade as grave goods extended back to at least 8,200 years ago in China, it was the First Empires period that saw an unprecedented development of jade craftsmanship and popularity. Jade was used for ornaments, daily vessels, ritual implements, and even burial suits tailored for nobles and emperors.

Bronze vessels are also important tomb treasures, the most beautiful coming, not surprisingly, from tombs of nobles and royals. Bronze craftsmanship was very delicate and lavish. Some bronze vessels were gilded, while others were inlaid with gems, gold and silver, or with very fine incisions. New implements, such as bronze lamps and incense burners, also became popular during the Han Dynasty. Bronze figurines of humans, horses, and chariots were created to imitate their living counterparts—these were only buried with the dead of the ruling class.

Gold and silver items are other tomb treasures, most of them body ornaments, although some were

THE APEX OF CRAFTSMANSHIP
This bronze censer was found in the tomb of Queen Dou Wan in Mancheng. A man sitting on a monster's back holds a cosmic mountain in his hand. This beautiful artifact measures little more than 13 inches (34 cm) high.

WEALTH FROM THE GRAVE
The interior of a Han Dynasty tomb has brick-vaulted chambers sealed by stone doorways, which are ornately carved with images of auspicious animals, including fish, dragons, and phoenixes.

used for seals, containers, and other items. Gold and silver were also used to decorate and strengthen lacquer and bronze vessels.

Lacquer items are another of the significant tomb treasures. Thousands of lacquer vessels, tables, boxes, musical instruments, and even coffins, have been found in the Qin and Han tombs. Lacquer is a tough, glossy varnish derived from *lac*, the resin of the tree *Rhus vernitecera*, which grows widely in the Chinese mountains. The *lac* has to be boiled and filtered. It is then painted on wood, in many layers—sometimes up to 300 layers were used. There were government workshops in southern China.

TOMB TREASURES, CULTURE, AND SOCIETY OF THE FIRST EMPIRES

The richness of tomb treasures in China is the result of the custom of burying the dead with everything that they may need in their afterlife. This custom was inspired by the long lasting Confucian virtue of filial piety, traditional ancestor worship, and the human desire to confirm and exhibit their social and economic status. During the Qin and Han Dynasties, the quantity and quality of grave goods were often determined by the political and social rank of the deceased.

Tomb treasures also triggered treasure hunting in China, an activity that can be traced back at least to the Bronze Age. For example, the Mausoleum of the First Emperor of the Qin Dynasty was ransacked shortly after the emperor's burial. Looting remains a significant issue in China today. According to the virtue of filial piety and ancestor worship, the dead should be laid to rest in peace, along with the items they need. Ironically, the tomb treasures seem to have caused continuous disturbance to the dead.

JADE AS A TOMB TREASURE

Jade manufacturing reached its heyday in the Qin and Han Dynasties, and was one of the most commonly found tomb treasures. A mausoleum of a local king dated to 122 BCE was discovered in Guangzhou (Canton), Guangdong Province in 1983. Hundreds of jade items have been discovered, including a burial suit, seals, containers, and ornaments, such as the jade pendant in the shape of a phoenix, at right.

One beautiful item found in a tomb is a jade cup in the shape of a rhinoceros horn. Legend has it that rhinoceros horn will disintegrate immediately if it comes into contact with poisonous materials, thus protecting the user from harm. The cup's owner, the second king of the Nanyue Kingdom founded in South China from 204 to 111 BCE, was continuously pressured by the Han emperors in the Yellow River Valley to give up his autonomy. The Nanyue Kingdom was conquered by Emperor Wu of the Han Dynasty in 111 BCE.

The Great Wall, China

Described as one of the world's Seven Wonders, the Great Wall is an extremely impressive piece of architecture constructed from the seventh century BCE to the seventeenth century CE. Beginning from Jiayuguan in northwest China, it stretches for more than 4,160 miles (6,700 km) before reaching its eastern end, Shanhaiguan, at the coast of the East Sea.

THE GREAT WALL OF CHINA

One of the greatest feats of engineering the world has ever seen, the Great Wall of China runs for thousands of miles, winding across a rich and varied landscape. It has survived thousands of years of warfare as well as the effects of tourism and climate change.

According to the archives, the earliest defensive wall was constructed in the Chu Kingdom of the Yangtze River Valley in 656 BCE to ward off the Qin army. Several other states in north and northwest China followed suit in order to protect themselves. However, it was the First Emperor of the Qin Dynasty who launched a massive construction program after unifying China in 221 BCE. Separate walls built by the previous Yan, Zhao, and Qin kingdoms during the Warring States Period were linked and restored, and more sections were added. When this construction was completed, the defensive wall stretched for more than 3,100 miles (5,000 km) from western to eastern China, or more than 10,000 Chinese "li" (a Chinese measurement of length equal to about one-third of a mile [0.5 km]), thus obtaining its current Chinese name—"Long Wall of Ten Thousand Li."

THE GREAT WALL AS ARCHITECTURE

The building of the Great Wall of China followed a consistent master plan. The wall itself consists of the inner and outer wall, with openings for lookouts and for shooting, platforms, watch towers, buttresses, and fortified cities at locations of strategic importance. Whether the wall was on a plain or higher ground, the construction suited the local terrain. At lower elevations, the Great Wall could measure 23–26 ft (7–8 m) high and about 13 ft (4 m) thick, whereas on steep mountains or areas of less importance, the wall is lower and relatively thinner in order to save on human resources and materials. The drainage system was designed to discharge rainwater and also to prevent the wall foundation from erosion. When crossing river valleys, channels were engineered and dug to discharge floodwaters.

The public image of the Great Wall today is of the monument of brick and stone, constructed during the Ming Dynasty. However, the Great Wall of the Qin and Han Dynasties in northwest China is made mainly from tamped earth, covered in tiles to protect it against rainwater.

Only a small proportion of the Great Wall built during the Qin Dynasty survives. The remains vary in height from 8 ft (2.4 m) to 23 ft (7 m), with a thickness of about 6½ ft (2 m). In hilly areas, the Qin Great Wall was built on mountain ridges and cliffs to utilize the latter as foundations. On plains, deep trenches were dug to build the wall. Lookout platforms were constructed at intervals of 722–750 ft (220–230 m) on the plains, but at intervals of only 262–330 ft (80–100 m) in mountainous areas, to facilitate better observation. When the enemy came into view, fires were lit at lookouts to inform the neighboring garrisons, who would then follow suit. It is clear that building the Great Wall—a massive yet integrated defensive system using local materials and employing different designs in a number of environments and different periods—is truly a magnificent example of human creativity.

KEY
○ Capital City
○ Other City or Town
▣ Archaeological Site
— International Border
--- Provincial Border
▪▪▪▪ Great Wall

FOLLOWING IN HISTORY'S FOOTSTEPS

Hikers climb a section of the Great Wall (below), which is China's major tourist attaction. But the Wall, resembling a huge winding dragon (right), is more than just history—it has become deeply ingrained in the Chinese psyche, symbolizing the country's continuity and longevity.

THE GREAT WALL AS A SYMBOL OF ANCIENT CIVILIZATIONS IN CHINA

Chinese civilization has been primarily founded on agriculture, which began at least 8,500 years ago in the Yellow River Valley, and almost 9,000 years ago in the Yangtze River Valley. This agricultural civilization was sedentary, requiring land and water resources, but the ruling class also wanted luxurious items from other countries. In addition, nomadic tribes in Inner Mongolia, northwest and northeast China, from the prehistoric epoch onward also needed land and water resources for their livestock, cereals, pottery production, and other goods produced in agricultural societies. The needs of agricultural and nomadic societies, from at least the Bronze Age to the Qing Dynasty, were largely satisfied through both trading and warfare occurring mainly at China's northern frontier. Social structures, values, and lifestyles differed significantly between agricultural and nomadic societies. So the Great Wall was a necessary defense system for China's agricultural civilization, and was built and constantly rebuilt from the Qin to the Ming Dynasties.

The First Emperor of the Qin Dynasty not only launched the first massive construction of the Great Wall. By unifying the territory from the Yellow River Valley to South China, and standardizing written language, public roads, measurement, and coinage, the First Emperor also laid solid foundations for a centralized state and a society based primarily on farming. The Great Wall protected this development.

A DANGEROUS CONSTRUCTION

Over the last 2,000 years, tens of thousands of people have died along the Great Wall—either in construction accidents, or as victims of warfare. Many legends, stories, and poems have been created by different peoples living around the Great Wall. Some of them are sad, others are heroic, others are romantic. The Great Wall is not only a tangible heritage item testifying to architectural genius and associated with important historical persons and events, it is also a carrier of the intangible heritage of different cultures and civilizations inside and outside present China. For these reasons it was inscribed as a World Heritage Site by UNESCO in 1987.

Changsha Han Tombs, China

The Changsha Han tombs are located at Mawangdui, 3 miles (5 km) east of the present Changsha City, Hunan Province. The three tombs date from the second century BCE. Tomb No. 1 contained the body of Lady Xin, a woman of about 50 years old; her husband, the First Marquis of Dai, was buried in Tomb No. 2; one of their sons was buried in Tomb No. 3.

RICH FABRICS UNEARTHED

This brocade banner was found in Tomb No. 1. The painting is very lightweight, in keeping with the ancient descriptions of textiles as being as "light as a mist." Even after 2,000 years, the colors have the power to evoke the splendor of an era long past.

The tombs were discovered in the 1950s and excavated from 1972 to 1974. All three tombs followed a contemporaneous burial practice of the local Chu culture, which was to bury the dead, then backfill the tomb pits with charcoal and white sticky clay, and then to cover the tomb with earth. The charcoal and clay protected organic materials from deterioration and oxidization. The woman's body in Tomb No. 1 was so well preserved after 2,000 years that an autopsy could be carried out to find out the cause of her death.

TREASURES DISCOVERED

The tombs had not been disturbed before excavation, so all the grave goods, including the organic items, were well preserved. Treasures discovered in the three tombs included silk garments and textiles, silk paintings, hundreds of lacquer items, jade and wood utensils, musical instruments, and more than 30 Chinese archives written on silk or bamboo and wooden sticks, many of which had been unknown to us. Large quantities of food and drink were also discovered. These archaeological data illustrate the material culture, beliefs, and burial customs common in the Yangtze River Valley in the Western Han Dynasty. Textiles are the most impressive items found in these tombs. The body in Tomb No. 1 had been wrapped in 22 silk garments. One of them is a silk gown measuring a little over 4 ft (1.2 m) long and weighing just 1.7 oz (49 g). Many other silk textiles were found in Tomb Nos. 2 and 3, including gauze, brocade, and plain weaves, some of them dyed with cinnabar, others embroidered or printed. It is very rare that silk textiles from over 2,000 years ago have been found preserved. The textiles found in the Changsha Han tombs provide invaluable data for studying textile techniques in ancient China.

Among the 500 or so lacquer items found in the three Changsha tombs are cups, bowls, plates, chess sets, dressing boxes, screens, and small tables. Most of these items had been decorated with colorful paintings or incisions. The coffins of the tombs had also been covered with layers of lacquer and colorful paintings of a dragon, phoenix, birds, and deer, as

PRECIOUS LACQUERWARE

Some 500 items of lacquerware such as this bowl were found in the three tombs at Mawangdui. The artifacts discovered in the Changsha Han tombs are clearly those of an aristocratic family.

well as other imaginary animals. While the lacquer items demonstrate a highly developed craftsmanship in the Western Han Dynasty, the paintings on the coffins and on the T-shaped silk banners covering the coffins illustrate the spiritual beliefs and religion of the local Chu culture.

Mancheng Han Tombs, China

The Mancheng Han tombs are the burial sites of King Liu Sheng of the Zhongshan Kingdom, who died in 113 BCE, and his wife, Queen Dou Wan, who died slightly later. Both tombs were found on a small hill, Ling Hill, near the present Mancheng County, Hebei Province.

IMPERIAL BRONZE

Bronze vessels have been found in abundance in Chinese tombs of the Qin and Han periods. This is a particularly lovely bronze lamp being held by a woman who would have been part of the imperial court. It was found at Mancheng in Hebei Province. The craftsmanship, a hallmark of the period, is impeccable.

The two royal tombs were discovered by members of the Chinese army in 1968, while involved in a military construction project. They had set explosives in Ling Hill, unearthing the tomb channels of King Liu Sheng, and reported their finding to archaeologists. Excavation of the king's tomb was soon carried out. Later, the nearby queen's tomb was also discovered. Both royal tombs were constructed from deep channels dug into the hill; the entrance was then sealed with molten iron. Both tombs consist of six chambers, and the dead king and queen were each laid in the central chamber of their own mausoleum.

MAJOR DISCOVERIES

The tombs had not been disturbed, and more than 4,200 items have been found, from ceramics, bronze, iron, gold, silver, jade, lacquer, textiles, and coins, to sculptures of chariots and human figurines. Although the quantity of ceramics outnumbered the rest of the grave goods, it is the bronze, gold, and jade items that attract the most attention.

The bronze items unearthed include lamps, incense burners, and pots. Many were extremely well crafted and inlaid with gold and silver. One of the most eye-catching items is a beautiful lamp with inscribed scripts of "Changxin Palace," which was a palace of the mother of the Han emperor. This lamp is in the shape of a young, kneeling woman holding a lamp in her hand, with one of her sleeves acting as the chimney for smoke. The lamp base can be rotated, and there is a door to control the amount of light shed. Based on the scripts, this item might have been given by the emperor's mother to her granddaughter, Dou Wan.

Jade items found in the tombs include ornaments and seals, but the most noteworthy items are the two burial suits for the king and queen. The king's jade suit was made using 2,488 pieces of jade, each of them cut, pierced, and polished, then sewn together with gold thread that weighs 2½ lbs (1100 g).

The queen's jade suit is made of 2,160 pieces of jade sewn together with gold thread weighing 1½ lbs (700 g). Each jade suit was individually tailored for its wearer, with different pieces of jade made to suit different body lengths and structures. According to Chinese documents, jade suits were very fashionable in the Western Han Dynasty, because people believed that jade had properties that could preserve the body forever.

CLOTHES TO DIE FOR

The jade funeral suit of Queen Dou Wan, sewn together with golden thread, is one of the best artifacts of the period. It was a common practice to bury husbands and wives in separate graves in the same burial area.

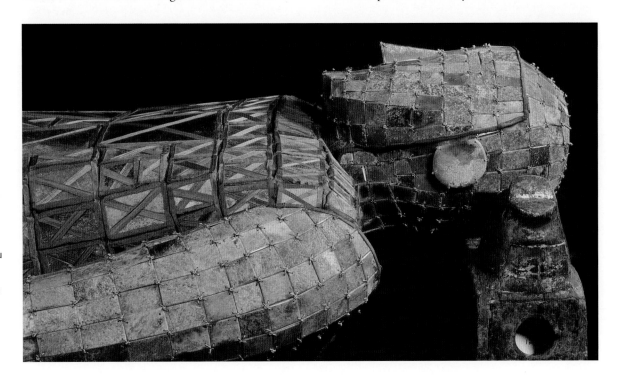

Japan

There are thousands of excavations across the Japanese archipelago, from Paleolithic base camps and kill sites to villages of Holocene Jomon foragers, regional centers of Yayoi-period chieftains supported by paddy rice cultivation, the great tombs of the early paramount rulers of the first Japanese state, and the palaces, cities, and temples of the historic periods.

At various times during the Pleistocene, land bridges joined Japanese islands to the east Asian mainland. Paleolithic occupation began before 30,000 years ago, and the earliest inhabitants of the archipelago hunted game with stone tools. The refitting of stone tools, cores, and flakes from sites such as Suzuki and Sunagawa show that many sites were reused over long periods. Waterlogged Paleolithic sites such as Lake Nojiri in Nagano and Tomizawa in Sendai show evidence of changed climate conditions. The land bridges joining Kyushu to the Korean Peninsula and Hokkaido to Sakhalin and eastern Siberia were submerged, and the archipelago separated from the mainland.

FORAGERS, COLLECTORS, AND THE BEGINNING OF RICE CULTIVATION

Temperate forests supported communities of foragers and collectors who lived on nuts, fish, deer, and wild boar. These people lived in relatively sedentary village communities comprising a number of pit dwellings, often arranged in a circle around a central space, in which graves were sometimes located. Storage pits and rubbish dumps were located around the outside. These foragers made distinctive earthenware vessels decorated with elaborate designs, often applied with twisted plant fibers, leaving cord marks. This is called Jomon, also the name of the period.

By about 500 BCE, as evidenced by sites such as Itazuke, rice cultivation was introduced to northern Kyushu from the Korean Peninsula. A new pottery style, named Yayoi, after the location in Tokyo where it was first identified in 1888, is also evident, as is metallurgy, silkworm raising, and weaving.

By the first century CE there was contact with China, as we learn from Chinese chronicles. As is often the case with protohistorical accounts of this sort, it is not easy to identify where these places were, such as the land of Yamatai, ruled over by Queen Himiko, named in the *Wei Zhi*. However, she probably ruled in the Kansai region, and may be buried under the great mound of Hashihaka, one of the best large ditch-enclosed settlements, with watchtowers, palisades, and dwellings, discovered at Yoshinogari in Kyushu.

TOMBS OF THE KOFUN PERIOD

Hashihaka is one of the earliest of the great mounded tombs, known as *kofun*. These tombs give their name to this period in which the first state-level society emerged, with its center in the Kinai region in the vicinity of modern-day Osaka and Nara. The spectacular, massive keyhole-shaped tombs were constructed in the fifth century CE. The largest probably

TIMELINE OF JAPANESE HISTORY

Time	Period	Important Events
Before 30,000 years ago		First human occupation of Japanese archipelago.
c.13,500–c. 9200 BCE	Incipient Jomon	First evidence for pottery manufacture (at Odai Yamamoto, Aomori Prefecture).
c. 9200–c. 5300 BCE	Initial Jomon	Large quantities of pottery, settled village life develops. First lacquer being made.
c. 5300–c. 3500 BCE	Early Jomon	Marine transgression associated with warmest period of Holocene. Occupation of Sannai Maruyama begins.
c. 3500–c. 2500 BCE	Middle Jomon	Highest population densities of Jomon period reached, especially in Central Honshu.
c. 2500–c. 1200 BCE	Late Jomon	Slight climatic deterioration. More settlements in lower wetlands. Increase in ritual artifacts and facilities. Increasing social complexity.
c. 1200–c. 500 BCE	Final Jomon	Relatively standardized pottery style (Obora). Distinctive "goggle-eyed" ceramic figurines.
c. 500 BCE–c. CE 300	Yayoi period	
c. 500 BCE–c. 100 BCE	Early Yayoi	Rice farming and metallurgy introduced to northern Kyushu from East Asian continent.
c. 100 BCE–c. CE 100	Middle Yayoi	Increased contacts with East Asian continent.
c. CE 100–300	Late Yayoi	Large burial mounds constructed. Increasing conflict and warfare.
c. CE 300–700	Kofun period	
c. CE 300–400	Early Kofun	Keyhole-shaped tombs constructed.
c. CE 400–500	Middle Kofun	Largest tombs built (such as tomb designated to Emperor Nintoku).
c. CE 500–700	Late Kofun	Tomb building appears, but keyhole-shaped tombs stop being built after c. CE 600. Human haniwa figures become popular in eastern Honshu. Buddhism arrives in mid-sixth century. Asuka region in Nara basin becomes center for Yamato rulers. Fujiwara Palace and capital constructed in CE 694, first Chinese style city; regional administrative centers established.
CE 710–794	Nara period	Nara established as capital in CE 710. First histories of Japan written (*Kojiki* CE 712 and *Nihon Shoki* CE 720). Capital moved to Nagaoka in CE 784.
CE 794–1192	Heian period	Capital at Heian (Kyoto).
CE 1192–1603	Medieval period	
CE 1603–1868	Early Modern period	

THE HEALING TOUCH

Divine beings on the pedestal of the Yakushi Nyorai, the Buddha of medicine and healing (at right). This bronze relief dates to the early eighth century CE and was found at Nara, Japan.

TEMPLE ELEGANCE

Construction on the Yakushi-ji temple at Nara, Japan began in the late seventh century CE. The symmetrical layout is a hallmark of Japanese architecture, and the multitiered pagodas functioned primarily as religious buildings, although they were also occasionally used as watchtowers. A UNESCO World Heritage site, Nara attracts thousands of visitors each year.

houses the remains of Emperor Nintoku, whose predecessors established a hegemony over other regional chiefs, bringing most of western Japan under the control of the single Yamato ruler.

CHINESE INFLUENCES

In the sixth century CE, increased contacts with the East Asian continent brought Buddhism to Japan. Intensification of links with China and Korea resulted in the adoption of the Chinese language and writing system, taxation, the codification of laws based on Chinese models, embodied in the Taiko reforms of 645, and the construction of the palaces and capital areas, at Fujiwara and Nara, using Chinese-style architecture.

More of the country was ruled by elites who owed allegiance to the Yamato court. In Gunma Prefecture in central Honshu, volcanic debris from an eruption of Mt. Haruna in the mid-sixth century covered an elite residential compound at Mitsudera, surrounded by a stone-lined moat, and a farmstead at Kuroimine, with horse paddocks and seedling beds.

A PRINCELY PARADE

This illustration on paper dates to the late seventh century CE. It depicts Prince Shotoku Taishi (CE 574–622), a ruler from the Yamato Period, accompanied by his two sons, Yamashiro Oe and Ekuri.

Sannai Maruyama, Japan

In the mid-1990s, the largest Jomon settlement yet discovered was excavated at Sannai Maruyama, in the southern part of Aomori city at the northern tip of Honshu, the largest island in the Japanese archipelago. Sannai Maruyama was a major regional center that was occupied, at various levels of intensity, from about 5,900–4,400 years ago, according to calibrated radiocarbon dates.

CHILDREN'S BURIAL POTS

When children died, their remains were placed in pots such as this one, which were intentionally broken, or that were made without a bottom. The remains were then interred within the residential area, often between houses.

FROM PILLAR TO POST

The remains of a huge pillar-supported structure were found at Sannai Maruyama, Japan. The six pillars are believed to have supported a large rectangular "long house," so called because it was usually about 35 ft (10 m) in length.

Over 700 pit buildings were discovered, including several large buildings, perhaps occupied by several family groups during particular seasons. Many scholars believe that between 40 and 50, and on occasion as many as 100, pit houses were occupied at any one time, suggesting a population of between 200 and 500. Some of the deceased were buried in graves arranged in two lines on either side of a possible processional way, creating a linear cemetery stretching away from the settlement area. Some children who died were buried in urns amid the houses.

MIDDEN WEALTH

A series of structures whose floors were probably raised off the ground were found in the center of the main excavation area, one of which had particularly large postholes in the bases; six massive chestnut posts set in large postholes were discovered. This may have been a tower, a large roofed building, or a setting of posts with calendrical significance. Large midden deposits were found, containing large quantities of pottery shards and—where waterlogged conditions permitted—the survival of some organic remains important for understanding the subsistence economy.

The artifact assemblage is extraordinarily rich. In addition to thousands of pottery shards, some 1,500 figurines and figurine fragments were recovered. The well-preserved organic remains are evidence for what is usually lost from most Jomon sites, including elaborate basketry, lacquerware, and textiles. Especially notable was a carefully woven basketry bag containing walnut remains.

There are also many objects made of obsidian, jadeite, and amber, which must have been brought there from afar, suggesting that the site operated as a trading center. Animal bones suggest that the Sannai Maruyama diet relied on smaller animals such as rabbit and flying squirrel, presenting a different image from other Jomon settlements, where larger species such as wild boar and sika deer were favored. Fish and sharks were also eaten. A wide variety of plants were utilized, including chestnuts and walnuts, as well as soft fruits including elderberry, mulberry, and wild grapes, perhaps indicating the brewing and fermentation of fruit wines.

Pollen analysis suggests that chestnut trees may have been intentionally managed, and DNA analysis of chestnuts indicates an unusually low genetic diversity, which is interpreted as positive evidence for domestication. Other possible cultivated plants include bottle gourd, burdock, beans, and barnyard millet. These rich floral and faunal remains have led archaeologists to believe that the site was occupied year round, although more detailed analysis of remains from different phases in the site's occupational history suggests that people may have spent particular seasons in different locations.

Nara, Japan

The capital of Japan moved from Fujiwara to Heijo (later known as Nara) in CE 710. Measuring 2¾ miles (5½ km) east–west and 3½ miles (4½ km) north–south, this Chinese-style city was home to up to 100,000 people, and boasted palaces, temples, boulevards, markets, and residences for elites and commoners, distinguished in terms of both location and scale.

The Palace (Heijo-kyu), a walled compound accessed through 12 gates, sat in the northern part of the city. The palace compound contained the emperor's private quarters, and important state buildings, notably the Great Supreme Hall, a State Halls Compound, offices, and workshops, along with gardens and ponds. Each year archaeologists excavate parts of the palace site, and some key buildings have been reconstructed in the original locations, preserving the actual archaeological remains beneath protective layers of earth.

ARCHAEOLOGICAL AND HISTORICAL RECORDS

The city was laid out on a rectangular grid oriented north–south, and divided into the Left Capital and the Right Capital by the main thoroughfare, the Scarlet Phoenix Avenue. The grid comprised a series of blocks, further divided into individual plots. Archaeological evidence is complemented by early historical sources, notably the *Kojiki* and *Nihon Shoki* (which were written in CE 712 and CE 720 respectively) and information gleaned from over 150,000 wooden tags, called *mokkan* in Japanese, which bear ink-brush writing. These tablets are divided into four types: official correspondence and records; shipping labels for tribute such as salt and silk; inventories of stored goods; and miscellaneous, including writing practice and graffiti. Details of everyday life come from archaeological excavations, which have uncovered residential compounds, markets, temples, streets and drains, buildings, and even toilets. Parasites preserved in these deposits reveal that sickness and plague were commonplace.

THE TODAIJI TEMPLE

The most famous Nara temple is Todaiji, best known for its enormous bronze statue of the Buddha, completed in CE 752—at over 52 ft (16 m) high, it is one of the largest cast objects of antiquity, housed in one of the largest wooden buildings ever constructed.

A DUSTING OFF
The Great Buddha at the Todaiji Temple in Nara is cleaned annually. The "traditional dusting" of the Diabutsu is usually performed by Buddhist monks and volunteers. Since it was first constructed, the Great Buddha has undergone numerous restorations.

Excavations in 1988 uncovered the pit in which this great figure was cast. The Buddha Hall and the Great Buddha itself have been restored and repaired over the centuries. Todaiji was at the center of a network of temples that were built across the country in each province in conjunction with the regional administrative centers through which Japan was ruled.

The treasure house of Todaiji is the Shosoin. This building, whose floor was raised about 10 ft (3 m) above the ground by 40 large wooden pillars, was constructed from Japanese cypress. It contains over 10,000 treasures accumulated by Emperor Shomu (r. CE 724–749). Many of these objects, including musical instruments, furniture, glassware, masks, and screens, testify to close contacts with China and the Silk Road, and are evidence of the broad ties Nara rulers had with other parts of Asia.

DRAMATIC MASKS
This mask, worn in Gigaku dance drama, dates to the so-called Nara period, CE 710–794, and is made from lacquered wood. The art of Gigaku may have been brought to Japan from Korea. Many masks have been found at the Nara site.

The Development of Pottery in East Asia

Fragments of the earliest dated ceramic container in the world were discovered in 1999 at Odai Yamamoto at the northern tip of Honshu, the largest island in the Japanese archipelago. Carbonized accretions, believed to be the remains of a broth, on these 30 or so fragments were tested using Accelerated Mass Spectrometer radiocarbon dating. Once calibrated to take into account changes in the amounts of radioactive carbon isotopes in the atmosphere over time, they dated to 16,500 BP.

These fascinating fragments were associated with an assemblage of stone tools including partly polished stone axes and long knife blades. Elsewhere in the Japanese archipelago, pottery shards dating to well before 10,000 BCE were discovered associated with microliths. There were clusters of these sites, in particular in central Honshu along the upper reaches of the Shinano River, and in southern Kyushu.

In China, pottery was being made from around 9000 BCE. Shards from the Xianrendong Cave in Jiangsi Province are reported as comprising both fine and coarse wares, with crushed white quartzite used as temper. Equally early shards are known from the Amur River region in the Russian Far East. By about 9000 BCE, pottery was being made in relatively large quantities in the Japanese archipelago, as people started to live in stable village communities such as Uenohara in southern Kyushu, and Hanamiyama near the modern-day city of Yokohama. These early inhabitants of the Japanese archipelago gained their subsistence through fishing, gathering, and hunting, living on the wild food resources that were available to them in the natural environment.

DECORATING POTS

From early on, they decorated their pots, which were hand-built using coils or slabs of clay and fired in bonfires, with the impressions of twisted plant fibers, giving the name Jomon (Japanese for cord-marked) to the period during which they were made. Jomon foragers came to use ceramics to make a range of artifacts, including elaborate figurines and ear ornaments. They made ceramic vessels in a number of forms, including deep jars for cooking and later storage, shallow bowls for serving, and spouted vessels for liquids.

JOMON ARTISTRY

These two striking items are from the Jomon tradition. The pottery jar at right dates to the Middle Jomon Period (*c.* 3500–2500 BCE) and was probably used for storing food. The female figurine at the far right is from the end of the Late Jomon Period (*c.* 1200 BCE). Called *dogu*, these figurines tend to have squat, compact bodies and small arms.

THE YAYOI TRADITION

In the Japanese archipelago, the arrival of rice agriculture in the middle of the first millennium BCE heralded the end of the long-lived Jomon tradition, and a new form of pottery, named after the location in Yayoi-cho in Tokyo where it was first discovered, spread through the archipelago. Yayoi pottery was decorated with a new range of motifs, seemingly less elaborate than its Jomon forebears. Spectacular developments included the construction of large earthenware funerary urns, often found in cemeteries of linear burials. A number of Yayoi pots, in particular from sites such as Karako-Kagi near modern-day Nara, bear incised drawings relating to Yayoi religious beliefs. The pot shown above with a stand and a lid dates to the Middle Yayoi period. Its simple, functional shape contrasts with the decorative style of the Jomon.

STRAIGHT FROM THE HORSE'S MOUTH

This terracotta *haniwa* horse is from the Late Kofun period (*c.* CE 500–700). *Haniwa* were clay sculptures arranged in and around Japanese graves. These tomb offerings took many forms: animals such as horses and birds were popular subjects for sculpture, as were figurines of humans.

In China, potters of the Chinese Neolithic painted their vessels, and the polychrome vessels of the Yangshao culture, found at agricultural villages such as Banpo on the Yellow River, bear distinctive abstract and representational designs. High fired ceramics of the Longshan tradition of the Late Neolithic in China owed something to the development of metalworking technology, and produced exquisite black burnished vessels, the "eggshell" wares that expressed the prestige of the newly emerging elite consumers in society. Some of these Chinese Neolithic pots bear what are thought to be potters' marks, the forebears of the Chinese ideographic writing system, which was eventually to spread throughout East Asia. Clay was sometimes used in its unfired state, for example to create the remarkable statue of a goddess from Niuheliang in northeastern China.

DEVELOPING TECHNOLOGIES

Ceramic technology in early imperial China reached new heights—the First Emperor was buried with thousands of terracotta warriors, whose bodies were modeled in molded clay, their heads and faces individualized. During the Han Dynasty in China, stoneware started to be produced, fired at high temperatures (up to 2,372°F [1,300°C]). Elites in the Han Empire lined the walls of their tombs with bricks and roofed their buildings with ceramic tiles. Stoneware technology became highly developed on the Korean Peninsula, and the technology was imported by the Japanese in the Kofun period. They then produced distinctive gray stoneware vessels, known in Japan as Sue ware, in large quantities in specialist kilns for use in the funerary rites at the *kofun,* or great mounded tombs in which the ruling classes were now buried. With the earliest known ceramic containers in the world, and the remarkable diversity of pottery forms (containers, figurines, bricks, and tiles) and the range of types (earthenwares, stonewares, and porcelains), East Asian ceramics represent a major and innovative set of pottery traditions dating from earliest times through to the modern day.

Southeast Asia

Southeast Asia, home of the spectacular temple ruins of Angkor, Bagan, and Champa, and the enigmatic polities of the Indonesian archipelago, is only beginning to be understood by archaeologists. While some of these sites are well known, we know little of the societies that built them and even less of the societies that preceded them.

The early centuries of the first millennium CE saw the florescence of several complex societies from modern Myanmar to the shores of Vietnam and through the Indonesian islands.

Mainland and insular Southeast Asia now incorporates Myanmar, Laos, Thailand, Malaysia, Cambodia, Vietnam, Borneo, and Indonesia: a large area of considerable cultural and linguistic diversity. The languages of Southeast Asia fall into three main families: Thai, Austroasiatic, and Austronesian. The Thai group originated in southern China and has expanded southward over the last 1,000 years or so into what is today Thailand. Prior to the arrival of Thai speakers, the area was probably occupied by speakers of the Austroasiatic language group, specifically Mon and Khmer speakers.

Austronesian languages are found throughout Malaysia as well as in Vietnam. Khmer speakers dominate Cambodia, and modern Vietnam is now occupied by Viet speakers, but previously the Cham language had a strong foothold there. Languages belonging to the Burmese, Karen, and Mon families are spoken in Myanmar and western Thailand, and the islands of the Indonesian archipelago are home to the speakers of Austronesian languages, with the exception of the Papuan languages.

EARLY SOUTHEAST ASIA

The earliest human inhabitants of Southeast Asia were hunter-gatherers who adapted to life in different ecological niches including the interior, uplands, and coastal areas. The former were likely more mobile than the latter. The earliest peoples are classified as

AIMING HIGH

This detail of archers on a bas-relief sculpture of Bayon warriors at Angkor, Cambodia, dates to the late twelfth to early thirteenth centuries CE. Bayon was the official temple of King Jayavarman VII.

PHUM SNAY, CAMBODIA

Little is known of Cambodia's prehistoric past, but in the year 2000 a new site was discovered that shed some light on this remote period. The site of Phum Snay was discovered during road construction, and the remains of hundreds of people were found beneath a modern village. The site was heavily damaged by looting, but excavations there by Cambodian and international experts led to the recovery of 2,000-year-old burials. Locals reported that some of the graves contained skeletons wearing helmets. Although this was not confirmed during the excavation, there was a strong indication that a martial people were buried at the site. Many of the men bore epaulets made of clay with iron buffalo horns attached to them, and most were buried with large iron swords, daggers, and caches of arrowheads. The skeletons were well preserved, and it was noted that a significant number of the dead had had their secondary incisors removed during their lifetime, a practice that seems to have been widely followed in Cambodia's ancient past.

RESTORING THE PAST

The ruins at Angkor Wat in Cambodia are constantly being restored and maintained. Here, experts are carrying out conservation work on a statue of Vishnu, who is one of the major Hindu deities.

SOUTHEAST ASIA

Southeast Asia has a rich and multifaceted political, social, economic, and cultural history. Archaeologists are only just beginning to learn more about the people and societies that make up this fascinating part of the world.

belonging to the "Hoabinhian culture," a term used to describe cultures that used a broadly similar tool kit of roughly chipped stone implements.

Rice agriculture was ushered in during the Neolithic, beginning around 3000 to 2500 BCE. The archaeological and linguistic evidence suggests that agriculture originated in southern China and entered Southeast Asia via the river valleys. It then moved from island to island throughout Indonesia.

THE BRONZE AGE

The Bronze Age of Southeast Asia is poorly understood, but it appears that the technology was introduced to the region from around 1500 BCE. Bronze Age settlements are likely to have been autonomous villages of no more than 500 people in which status was quite flexible. The majority of Bronze Age cemeteries in Thailand do not offer definitive social divisions demarcated by wealth or symbols, and there is scant evidence of elite control of resources or craft production.

THE IRON AGE

Social stress may have increased during the Iron Age as the inclusion of weaponry in burials is more common. Settlement size appears to have increased in some areas, as did site density. A greater number of grave goods are included in burials as well as a wider variety of artifacts. Exotic items, including glass and semiprecious stone beads, are common, as well as metal artifacts. It appears on present evidence that there was a shift from unranked social organization c. 500 BCE to that which may have been more stratified and enduring.

EARLY POLITIES OF SOUTHEAST ASIA

The early first millennium CE witnessed the development of much more complex societies in Southeast Asia. In the Mekong Delta, an apparent protostate began to develop. This society was well known to the Chinese, who called it Funan. Another polity, known as Chenla and based in central Cambodia, eventually subsumed Funan. On the coast of Vietnam, Linyi was engaged in trade with China, and this culture may have evolved into the group of principalities known as Champa. In Myanmar, the Pyu dominated central Burma and coexisted with the Mon in the south until the rise of the Burmans who came to dominate. Malaysia saw the rise of several small but powerful cities that eventually came under the control of Srivijaya, an Indonesian power, and briefly the Cola of India. The early polities were influenced by the infiltration of Indian culture. Most embraced the Hindu and Buddhist religions, incorporating their own indigenous beliefs to form a unique culture, one that would produce some of the world's most beautiful art, literature, theater, and advanced water technology.

KEY
- ○ Capital City
- ▫ Archaeological Site
- — International Border
- Dai Viet Kingdom
- Champa Kingdom
- Bagan Kingdom
- Khmer Kingdom
- Srivijaya Kingdom

0   500 km
N
0   500 miles

Bagan, Myanmar (Burma)

MYANMAR
(BURMA)
■ Bagan

Yangôn
(Rangoon)

Bagan, located on the eastern banks of the Irrawaddy River in central Myanmar (Burma), is a beautiful place and of considerable archaeological interest. The city was originally known as Arimaddanapura and served as the capital of several kingdoms. The ancient ruins cover an area of about 16 sq miles (41 sq km).

Most of the structures at Bagan are Buddhist foundations built between CE 1000 and 1200, but the city was established in the late ninth century and was abandoned and reoccupied through the centuries. Bagan represents the capital of a people known as the Bamar, from which the country formerly derived its name. Although their origins are debated, it has been suggested that this ethnic group slowly infiltrated Myanmar from China, eventually overwhelming or integrating with the Pyu populations that were already established there. The Pyu dominated Central Myanmar from the second to the ninth century CE, leaving behind traces of enormous fortified urban sites, hydraulic works, and religious foundations from the modern cities of Pyay in the south to Schwebo in the north.

In CE 1057 King Anawrahtha of Bagan embarked on a campaign to subjugate the Mon kingdom of southern Myanmar. He captured the Mon capital of Thaton and brought many Mon artists, intellectuals, monks, and holy scriptures back to Bagan. Therevada Buddhism was established as the state religion of Anawrahtha's kingdom. From this point on the Burmese dominated Myanmar, and this hegemony was consolidated by succeeding rulers.

By the mid-thirteenth century the kingdom of Bagan was under threat from the Mongol peoples who had swept through most of the region. In an attempt to avoid a Mongol invasion the Burmese king, Narathihapate (r. 1254–1287), led a pre-emptive strike into Yunan, China, to confront the Mongol army. The Burmese force was routed and the Mongols swept into Myanmar, easily subjugating Bagan's territories. In 1289 the Mongols installed a puppet-king on the throne, and the kingdom never recovered its former greatness.

BRICK STRUCTURES

Today Bagan represents one of Myanmar's most important heritage sites and is home to hundreds of brick temples. Many of these temples have undergone restoration with little understanding of their original form. There are over 2,000 brick structures scattered over the 16-sq-mile (41-sq-km) site of Bagan. Most of the structures at the site are of two types, the stupa or zedi and the temple or pahto. Zedi are bell-shaped structures which are said to hold religious relics. The temples come in various forms, some employing barrel vault architecture and others being massive square structures known as pahto.

Bagan has weathered centuries of war and looting, and a massive reconstruction program threatens the integrity of the complex, but the remains on the banks of the Irrawaddy continue to captivate visitors.

SEEKING ENLIGHTENMENT
The Thatbyinnyu temple in Bagan takes its name from "Thatbyinnyutanyan," which means the "omniscience of the Buddha." This beautiful white temple dates from the mid-twelfth century CE.

Angkor, Cambodia

The archaeological site, known today as Angkor, was home to a number of capitals of the Khmer empire from the ninth century through to the fifteenth century CE. The city is located on the shores of the Tonlé Sap, a huge lake in the center of Cambodia.

The foundation of Angkor is traditionally dated to CE 802 when King Jayavarman II established his capital in the region. Succeeding kings kept the capital city in the region through to the mid-fifteenth century CE.

KHMER TEMPLES

The best-known and largest temple at the site, Angkor Wat, was built between CE 1112 and 1150 by King Suryavarman II and is dedicated to the Hindu god Vishnu. Angkor was a very large, low-density urban center. Tradition has it that the capital was abandoned after an attack by neighboring armies from Thailand, but evidence is mounting that the city may have been in decline due to environmental degradation and the deterioration of the complex hydraulic system, which fed canals and reservoirs.

Each ruler of the Khmer Empire erected a state temple at the capital, which had varied names. One of the earliest names was Yasodharapura, named for the monarch who established a city around a small mountain, Phnom Bakheng. Most of the kings of Angkor worshipped Hindu deities, and the majority of temples are dedicated to the god Shiva. Many of the temples are constructed as microcosms of the Hindu conception of the universe, with Mt. Meru represented by the central tower, the walls around

the temple signifying the surrounding mountains, and the moats representing the cosmic ocean. The historic temples of Angkor are heavily decorated with narrative relief, much of it depicting the epic tales of the *Ramayana* and *Mahabharata* as well as significant events in Cambodian history, primarily battles with the neighboring Cham.

REBUILDING THE CAPITAL

King Jayavarman VII purportedly rebuilt the Khmer capital after the sack of the city by the Cham in CE 1177. Jayavarman is a notable monarch, as he changed the state religion from Hindu to Mahayana Buddhism. This energetic ruler constructed hundreds of temples and public monuments, and he fortified his capital with a massive surrounding wall. Entry to Angkor Thom is through five gates—each with four, gigantic, enigmatic faces thought to represent Jayavarman as the bodhisattva. Angkor Thom is centered upon the state temple, the Bayon, decorated, once again, with these sculpted faces.

Angkor was abandoned in the fifteenth century CE and was largely overgrown by the jungle, although the temple of Angkor Wat remained in use as a Buddhist temple. The hundreds of ruins were at last brought to the world's attention in the early twentieth century by a group of French archaeologists and scientists.

NATURE HITS BACK!

Not quite swallowed up by the greedy jungle, the Buddhist temple of Ta Phrom, which was built during the reign of King Jayavarman VII, has fallen prey to rampant tree roots.

A LIFE IN PICTURES

Beside a tiled wooden house, an older woman cooks rice and fish-skewers over a portable ceramic hearth. A younger woman picks fruit, and a child plays with a buffalo. All wear short skirts and heavy earrings. Archaeology confirms the details of daily life shown on the Bayon.

Champa, Vietnam

Champa is the name of a poorly understood polity or group of principalities that at one time dominated coastal Vietnam. During its height, Champa was a formidable military and maritime power in Southeast Asia. The remains of this polity, which at one time rivaled Angkor, are found all along the coast of Vietnam.

VIETNAM
Hanoi

Champa

Champa dominated south and central Vietnam from the seventh century through to the fifteenth century CE, but its origins are not clearly understood. It is possible Champa developed from an earlier polity called Linyi that existed from the late second century CE. Vietnamese archaeologists have suggested that Champa may have its roots even further back in the Sa Huynh culture established in Vietnam since at least the first century BCE.

A TRADING AND CULTURAL CENTER

Champa grew in prominence as the trade between India and China flourished. The people spoke an Austronesian language belonging to the same family as those spoken in Malaysia, Indonesia, and many Pacific Islands. The Cham people adopted Indic ideas and religions, creating polities that were highly influenced by Hindu ideals. It seems unlikely that Champa was a unified polity, but rather a number of coastal principalities linked by ethnicity, language, and perhaps royal ties. The Cham fought at various times with the Khmer, the Vietnamese peoples to the north, the Chinese, and the Mongols.

Champa had several important centers and the remains of many of their religious monuments still stand today. The earliest structures date to the late fourth century CE, and the Cham continued to erect brick sanctuaries until the fifteenth century. The most famous site is My Son, a collection of mostly Hindu foundations in the Thu Bon Valley. It is thought that one of the Cham capitals was located close to My Son at Trà Kiêu.

SHIFTS IN POWER

There appear to have been some significant political changes during the mid-eighth century CE. Power seems to have been centered around Nha Trang, where the sanctuary of Po Nagar is located. Later, power shifted further south to Panduranga. During the late ninth century CE the Cham embraced Mahayana Buddhism, erecting temples at Dông Duong and Rôn as well as adding sanctuaries at My Son. The capital was established at Indrapura (present-day Quang Nam Province) in CE 875.

The Cham were militarily active in the twelfth century CE, battling the Viet ethnic groups in the interior. They captured the Khmer capital at Angkor in 1177. The Khmer threw off this foreign yoke in 1181 and occupied Champa for nearly 40 years. The Cham regained their independence only to weather Mongol occupation and further warfare with the Viet and Khmer. Cham dominance of Vietnam finally waned in 1471 with the capture of the capital, Vijaya, by the Viet.

INDIAN FLAVORS
An important religious and spiritual center for the Cham people, the design and decoration of the temples at My Son show some Indian influence. Sanskrit was the sacred language.

CHAM ARCHITECTURE
The Champa temple at the archaeological site of My Son was listed as a World Cultural Heritage Site by UNESCO in 1999. Archaeologists are still trying to determine exactly how these remarkable brick structures were constructed.

Borobudur, Indonesia

In 1814 a Dutch engineer, H. C. Cornelius, was led by local people to a massive temple in central Java, so overgrown and buried in volcanic ash that it looked like a natural hill. The temple turned out to be a ninth-century CE Mahayana Buddhist construction called Borobudur located near Yogyakarta, in central Java, Indonesia.

The temple comprises nine levels, the top three of which are circular and those below square. Richly decorated, the temple also has hundreds of images of the Buddha stoically surveying the surrounding jungle.

THE ROAD TO ENLIGHTENMENT

Many scholars believe that the temple was a place of pilgrimage in which devotees would begin at the bottom, from the eastern side, circumambulating the structure and symbolically passing through Kamad-hatu, Rupadhatu, and Arupadhatu respectively—the world of desire, the world of forms, and finally, at the top of the monument, into the world of formlessness. All along this journey are illustrated Buddhist reliefs in nearly 1,500 panels. These reliefs tell of episodes in the Buddha's life, from his birth as a noble to his attainment of Nirvana, as well as illustrating past lives and the notion of karma. Borobudur is famed for its cross-legged Buddha statues inside latticed stupas that sit on the square platforms of the monument. The entire structure is capped with a large stupa about 115 ft (35 m) above the base of the monument.

It is unclear who built the monument but it has been stylistically dated to *c.* CE 800 and may have been built under the Sailendra dynasty of Java. The

Sailendra oversaw the construction of both Hindu and Buddhist monuments on Java including the nearby Shaivite temple of Prambanan. Prambanan is the largest Hindu temple complex in Indonesia comprising eight main shrines and over 200 surrounding candi (temples).

The monument is built on a natural hill and it resembles a stupa more than a traditional Buddhist temple. Viewed from above it is recognizable as having the shape of a mandala, a geometric design representing the universe. It is estimated that almost 2 million cubic feet (55,000 m³) of stone was used in the construction of Borobudur.

Borobudur appears to have been abandoned sometime around the fifteenth century. In the ensuing centuries Islam made significant inroads in the Indonesian archipelago, and many Buddhist and Hindu monuments lost their significance. It is, however, possible that the area around Borobudur was abandoned due to volcanic activity in the area.

Although Borobudur is one of the major tourist attractions in Indonesia, Buddhists continue to revere the temple as a holy place and thousands of pilgrims come to the site for religious purposes especially during Vesak. On this day Buddhists gather together to celebrate the birth, death, and enlightenment of the Buddha.

AT ONE WITH THE UNIVERSE
The stupas are the most striking feature of the largest Buddhist temple in the world at Borobudur. Built *c.* CE 778–856, it is a sacred place of mystery and imagination. It is difficult to believe that such a monumental structure was so covered by ash that it remained unseen for centuries.

Indonesian Hobbits

CAVE OF DISCOVERY

The cave of Liang Bua is the site of the amazing discovery of humans referred to as "Indonesian hobbits" because of their small size. The term "hobbit," essentially a small version of a human, comes from the fantasy novels of English writer J. R. R. Tolkien. Whether the remains found will be classified as a new human species is yet to be determined.

A remarkable discovery was made in 2003 on the Indonesian island of Flores by a joint team of Australian and Indonesian paleoanthropologists, who were searching for evidence of early *Homo sapiens* migration from Asia into Australia—a new species in the human family tree, *Homo floresiensis*.

In a cave known as Liang Bua, the researchers encountered the remains of very small people. The first individual to be uncovered was labeled LB1. Partial remains of a further seven skeletons have since been uncovered and have been dated to between 38,000 and 13,000 years BP. That some of the remains date so recently is of enormous scientific interest because it means that these small people lived contemporaneously to modern humans.

SMALL ISLAND, SMALL PEOPLE

The researchers argue that the remains represent a new species of human, based on the small size of the body and the reduced cranial capacity or brain size of the first skeleton they uncovered. Other features also seem to distinguish the skeleton from a modern human, including the dental morphology, recessed chin, and the morphology of the forearms. The *H. floresiensis* remains are similar in many regards to the remains of *Homo erectus* found in Indonesia. *H. erectus* remains have been dated to nearly two million years upward and there may indeed be a relationship between the two, although *H. erectus* remains have not yet been discovered on Flores. Their diminutive stature may be the result of environmental factors— dwarf species may result if there are limited resources in a location such as a small island. This hypothesis has come to be known as the "island dwarfing" theory. Flores is also home to dwarf stegadons (prehistoric mammoths) and elephants so the effect may have been universal on the island.

It appears that *H. floresiensis* may have manufactured stone tools, as several were found with the remains. These tools, similar to those made by humans of the Upper Paleolithic period, were undersized and seemed to be made for use specifically by smaller people. The cave also bore evidence for the use of fire and cooking.

Local folklore on Flores contains references to small people called the Ebu Gogo who inhabited the forest. It is thought that *H. floresiensis* may have existed in other parts of Flores into the historic period. If this is true, there was a long period of coexistence on Flores as it has been inhabited for at least 35,000 years by modern *H. sapiens*. How *H. floresiensis* got to the island is not clearly understood.

THE LITTLE LADY OF FLORES

The most complete skeleton found has been dubbed "Flo" or the "Little Lady of Flores," as it represents a female who was about 30 years of age at death. Flo stood about 3½ ft (1 m), well below the range for normal human adult height and even shorter than the smallest known people, the African Pygmies, Andaman islanders, and Twa peoples, who range between 4½ ft (1.3 m) and 4 ft 11 in (1.5 m). Flo is thought to have weighed about 55 lb (25 kg), which is far smaller than any other human group known and even smaller than the human ancestors, *Homo erectus* and the Australopithecines. The cranial capacity of the Flores skeletons is limited as well, LB1 being only 23 in³ (380 cm³), similar in size to the Australopithecines.

Flores remained an island even during the lowest sea levels of the last glaciation, so they would have had to cross open ocean to get there. The people of Liang Bua may have died out due to a volcanic eruption around 13,000 BP, as other fauna seem to disappear at the same time.

A NEW HUMAN SPECIES?

Whether *H. floresiensis* represents a new species has yet to be confirmed. Some scholars feel that the individuals had microcephaly, an illness that causes sufferers to have a small brain, or that perhaps they were pygmy humans. Some feel that the remains may be a subspecies of *H. sapiens*. Recent research has determined that the remains are unlikely to represent pygmies but did find indications of possible microcephaly. The original discoverers contend that there is little indication that the individuals were diseased, and also that several specimens, all of diminutive size, were found. The bone from the site has not fossilized, and there is a possibility that some mitochondrial DNA may be recovered to shed further light on the origins of these unusual people and perhaps resolve the debate surrounding the proclamation of a new species of humans.

BONES OF CONTENTION?

Some of the remarkable finds on the Indonesian island of Flores include stone tools, stegadon teeth, and the bones of the Liang Bua hobbits (see below). The site is of interest not only to archaeologists, but also to paleoanthropologists, who are hoping that the discovery will shed new light on the origin of the human species.

NOT JUST A FAIRY TALE

Two members of the joint Indonesian-Australian excavation team examine the area around where the legendary Ebu Gogo are said to have lived. The discovery of the bones of a smaller race of people may mean that researchers will turn to local folklore for hints about these amazing hominids.

The Americas

Earliest Peoples of the Americas

Two million years ago, humankind's hominid ancestors began to expand their geographic range out of southern and eastern Africa in a process that ultimately brought their *Homo sapiens* descendants to America, the last major landmass to be populated. Arriving at, and colonizing, the Americas represents a significant but not extraordinary chapter in human prehistory—just another step in a long evolutionary journey.

HISTORY IN THE MAKING
In this 1927 photograph taken at the Folsom bison quarry site in New Mexico, United States, Barnum Brown and Carl Schwachheim study a Folsom point in situ. The chipped stone spear points found at Folsom have been dated to around 10,000 years ago.

SHORT, SHARP, AND TO THE POINT
These Native American arrowheads were found across the western United States. Used to hunt prey and as weapons of war, early arrowheads were made from a variety of different materials, depending on the resources available to the person creating the points.

Each significant advance in this journey occurred when these beings were biologically and culturally equal to the biological and geographic opportunities and challenges of a new territory. These last steps occurred within the last 50,000 years, after fully modern humans had evolved. Most of tropical and temperate Africa, Europe, and Asia were peopled long before that time, and Australia was colonized by 50,000 BP. Between 50,000 and 30,000 BP, humans with sophisticated cultural equipment were pressing into the colder latitudes of northern Eurasia and had developed watercraft capable of near-shore maritime travel. Ocean margins were becoming part of the human niche. Glacial conditions advanced southward from the Arctic between 25,000 BP and 18,000 BP, and then retreated by 11,000 BP, greatly affecting plants, animals, and humans in the Northern Hemisphere. Global climatic changes, some occurring rapidly, drastically altered geographic ranges, the composition of biotic communities, and the viabilities of most species.

By the time the Americas were colonized, humans were biologically and culturally adapted to the vast temperate and tropical areas of the Northern Hemisphere. Human technology had by this time overcome harsh arctic and subarctic marine and terrestrial environments, and humans had tapped the extraordinarily rich circumpolar marine resources of fish, sea mammals, birds, and land mammals. Some species of fish, sea mammals, and birds occurred in staggering numbers, posing irresistible challenges to human ingenuity.

THE "CLOVIS FIRST THEORY"
The peopling of the Americas has been the subject of anthropological and archaeological research for some 100 years, and over that time has given rise to much acrimonious debate and many misadventures. By the 1940s, the majority view held that during the

HUNTERS, GATHERERS, AND EARLY FARMERS

Foraging remained the dominant means of subsistence in significant regions of South and North America at least until the coming of Europeans. Some subsistence foragers relied heavily on plants, as at Danger Cave, Utah, United States (see page 288), while others exploited large animals, as at Head-Smashed-In, Alberta, Canada (see page 289). In South America, foraging prevailed with or without minor food production except in the Andes and Pacific coastal zone, where potatoes, beans, maize (corn), and other crops facilitated the rise of complex societies. Horticultural and agricultural societies flourished in Central America, and in southwestern and southeastern North America.

last glacial period, around 11,000 BP, when sea levels were lowered as a result of the amount of water locked up in the ice sheets, specialized big-game hunters migrated out of Siberia, crossed a land bridge (known as "Beringia") that was exposed between the Chukchi and Bering seas, walked down a narrow, ice-free corridor through the ice sheets of Canada, and emerged south of the ice sheets onto the Northern Great Plains. There they encountered enormous herds of mammoths, mastodons, bison, horses, and other animals that had evolved in the absence of humans and were, therefore, easy prey.

Several finds of large, fluted spear points made from chipped stone, dating to around 13,500 years ago, led archaeologists to theorize that these points represented the characteristic technology of these first Americans. This style of spear point soon became known as Clovis, named for the town in New Mexico where the first specimens were found. "Clovis culture" came to represent the founding population of the Americas. Clovis and other people spread to the southern tip of South America in fewer than 700 years, and they may have brought about the extinction of many Late Pleistocene animals. Distinctive Clovis artifacts and sites are found across almost all of North America south of the ice sheets, and south into Belize, Costa Rica, Panama, and the northernmost part of Venezuela.

Contemporary with Clovis in North America are cultures employing non-fluted Plainview/Goshen and Great Basin Stemmed styles of projectile points. In South America, large, fluted, Fish Tailed-style points may overlap in time with Clovis.

PUSHING BACK THE FRONTIERS

In more recent years, dissatisfaction with the "Clovis First Theory" has grown. Compelling evidence of earlier human occupations has been found at such sites as Monte Verde in Chile (14,500 BP), Meadowcroft Rockshelter in Pennsylvania (14,000 BP), and Cactus Hill in Virginia (17,000 BP), and has come to be widely accepted. It is unclear when people first arrived in the Western Hemisphere and who they were. It seems likely that they were Upper Paleolithic people adapted to far northern latitudes and that they had boats. They may have been centered on the eastern fringe of Asia and the North Pacific, or the western edge of Europe and the North Atlantic, or both.

The very early people in the Americas, including the Clovis people, were foragers who subsisted by hunting and gathering a variety of resources. The Monte Verdeans and the Clovis people hunted large game among other prey, but they were not specialized big-game hunters. Later groups living in the

AT HOME IN MONTE VERDE
Encompassing sand, gravel, and wood, this hut foundation at Monte Verde in Chile is shaped like a wishbone. Just outside the entryway, in the lower right-hand corner of the photograph, a square chunk of ancient meat can be seen.

Plains of North America did specialize in big-game hunting. Following on from these early foragers and big-game hunters, a long succession of regionally differentiated archaeological traditions emerged. In some areas, favorable niches supported populations who remained foragers until they came into contact with Europeans, whereas in others population growth soon exceeded the natural resource base, leading to the rise of food production.

Artistic expression is abundantly represented in American prehistory in the form of pictographs and petroglyphs on rock surfaces, and portable carvings, engravings, and paintings made on stone or bone. Examples of engraved or pecked artifacts range from Clovis-age engraved stones to petroglyphs extending over a long time span.

A LONG ARTISTIC TRADITION
Newspaper Rock State Historical Monument in Utah, United States, protects a wealth of petroglyphs that may be at least 2,000 years old. Petroglyphs are notoriously difficult to date, but some of the earliest examples found in the Americas are thought to be around 13,000 years old.

Monte Verde, Chile

Monte Verde is an open campsite along the banks of Chinchihuapi Creek in the Central Valley of southern Chile, between the Andes Mountains and the Pacific coastline. The site called Monte Verde II was occupied, for perhaps a year, some 14,500 years ago. This places it among the small number of sites in the Americas generally accepted as being more than 13,500 years old.

Monte Verde II is the most completely studied and reported of ancient sites in the Americas, and it also has the widest acceptance of its antiquity. Situated at 42° south latitude, the region today is a cool-temperate rain forest, which is not greatly different from how it would have been when prehistoric people occupied the area. The excavation and analysis of the site, plus the publication of the team's many findings, took 20 years (1977–1997). The work engaged more than 40 investigators, led by Professor Tom D. Dillehay.

An earlier layer of the site, Monte Verde I, yielded 26 stone artifacts associated with three small fireplaces that have been radiocarbon dated to at least 33,000 years ago. Unfortunately, Monte Verde I has provided far less material for interpretation than Monte Verde II, and its great age is more challenging to reconcile with known human prehistory. For this reason, its place in American archaeology is far less secure than that of the Monte Verde II site.

A REMARKABLY INTACT EARLY CAMPSITE

Chile's Central Valley is filled with glacial moraine and outwash gravels that readily shift during the region's frequent earthquakes. This evidently occurred at the time people were living at the site. Remarkably complete remains of their camp were found resting on a sandy creek bank and covered with a layer of peat, indicating that an abrupt but slight change in the gradient of the creek caused the camp to be flooded. The peat layer preserved a wealth of those perishable items that archaeologists rarely find, including wood, leaves, roots, tubers, fruit, fibers, bone, and even meat and skin. From this unusually rich trove of evidence, a great deal was learned of the way people were living in southern Chile 1,000 years before the time of Clovis culture, long thought to have been the earliest in the Western Hemisphere. Monte Verde II has been instrumental in bringing about a fundamental rethinking of the peopling of the Americas.

Cultural features at Monte Verde II include a rectilinear array of timbers interpreted as remnants of the infrastructure of some 12 skin-covered, wooden residential shelters. Nearby, the earthen base of a smaller, horse-shoe-shaped hut was found, which was believed to have served a more specialized purpose. On the same well-defined living surface were numerous hearths, pits, postholes, human footprints, and miscellaneous stained areas.

In and around these features, excavators recovered 800 stone objects, 250 pieces of bone, more than 500 large items of wood (timbers, limbs, and pieces), several hundred small items of wood (burned and unburned chunks, slivers, and flecks), more than 20,000 plant specimens, 38 pieces of animal meat and hide, 33 pieces of fiber cordage, and 11 impressions of cordage in clay.

ANCIENT LLAMA SKIN

Paleollama remains were found at the Monte Verde II site in the form of pieces of leather (seen below) and bones. This prehistoric ancestor of the modern-day llama formed a stable part of the diet of the early South Americans who occupied Monte Verde.

A RARE INSIGHT INTO PREHISTORY

The well-preserved assemblage found at Monte Verde in Chile affords a remarkable glimpse into human foraging behavior very early in the archaeological record of the Western Hemisphere. Monte Verde II occupants had such a thorough knowledge of their surroundings that it is clear that they had been in the region for decades or centuries. Without the cultural features and perishable evidence that have survived there, largely thanks to this prehistoric campsite having been buried in peat, only a small handful of recognizable stone artifacts would have survived—which informs us as to how impoverished and nearly invisible most of the early American archaeological record must be.

CHINCHIHUAPI CREEK

The Monte Verde site looks as pristine as the day the archaeologists arrived—this is a concerted move by the original excavators to deter looters and amateur diggers from disturbing this important location in their search for the ancient campsite and its valuable artifacts.

Stones were mostly used in natural or minimally modified states. Most stones are small and were selected from local gravels, but a few are exotic stones that variously came from the coastal range, Pacific beach gravels, or the Andes Mountains. In addition to the stone tools, excavators also found spheroids, grooved spheroids, a polished stone perforator, fragments of three slender bifacial points, a large biface, a core, and flakes.

AT HOME IN THEIR ENVIRONMENT

Bones, primarily of an estimated six mastodons, along with chunks of preserved animal meat and bits of proboscidean hide, indicate that people hunted and also used bone and hide for tools, shelter, and possibly other purposes. At least one bone has been identified as paleollama, and others as belonging to amphibians, reptiles, birds, or unidentifiable mammals. Wood was used as fuel, and to make utilitarian items such as spears, handles, and food-processing basins.

Diverse edible, medicinal, and otherwise useful plants have been identified among the large number of botanical specimens found at the site. Plants show that the site was occupied during all seasons of the year and that its occupants obtained plants nearby in the bogs and forest, from salt marshes and coastal dunes 35 miles (55 km) away on the Pacific coast, and from higher elevations in the Andes some 25 miles (40 km) distant. At least 28 species of food plants—including wild potatoes—have been identified, along with at least 10 medicinal plant species. Noteworthy among the potatoes is one previously unknown species. Numerous additional species with multiple uses were documented as providing food, fuel, construction material, and tools for the Monte Verdeans.

CAST IN CLAY FOREVER

The soft clay soil of Monte Verde allowed three human footprints to be preserved for posterity; one of these impressions is clearly seen above. Archaeologists believe that at least one of the footprints was made by a child.

A TIMEWORN TOOL

Fragments of mastodon tusk were used as tools by the early Monte Verdeans. Related to mammoths and modern elephants, mastodons are a now-extinct elephant-like animal that existed throughout much of the world during the Miocene and Pleistocene.

Meadowcroft Rockshelter, United States

Meadowcroft Rockshelter is a stratified site underneath a sandstone overhang in southwestern Pennsylvania. In 1975, pre-Clovis ages for cultural evidence in Stratum II were published, initiating an intense, 30-year controversy. Today, however, Meadowcroft is widely accepted as having pre-Clovis archaeological evidence that is at least 14,000 years old, and perhaps older.

PREHISTORIC SHELTER

Albert Miller rediscovered Meadowcroft Rockshelter in 1955. Subsequent excavations at the site unearthed an abundance of artifacts and organic remains, including ceramics and Paleoindian tools, plus early forms of corn and squash.

Intensive investigations from 1973 to 1979, led by Dr. James Adovasio, exposed 13 ft (4 m) of deposits accumulated in the shelter over the last 30,000-plus years. Degradation of the shelter ceiling and sheet wash from further up the slope introduced sand, silt, and sandstone blocks to the shelter. The excavators meticulously followed natural strata and microstrata, identifying 11 well-defined stratigraphic units, I through XI, from the base upward. These are well dated via 52 radiocarbon assays. The overall archaeological sequence, the quality and quantity of the cultural evidence, and the number of radiocarbon dates from Meadowcroft are among the best for any single site in northeastern North America—facts that have been overshadowed by the disputed pre-Clovis dates from Stratum II.

THE EVIDENCE IN DISPUTE

Stratum I is a natural sediment that lacks any cultural evidence; radiocarbon dates taken at the top of the stratum cluster around 30,000 BP. Stratum II is sand and silt and includes four layers of roof blocks. This stratum is documented in the following sequence: lower IIa silt/sand; minor spall layer; middle IIa silt/sand; minor spall layer; upper IIa silt/sand; major roof spall layer; and IIb silt/sand. Hearths, burned areas, and chipped stone artifacts from lower Stratum IIa and middle Stratum IIa constitute the early and bitterly disputed cultural evidence. Chipped stone items include a nonfluted projectile point, small prismatic blades, and other items, some of which are made of nonlocal kinds of stone. Some bone and plant materials were also recovered from lower and middle Stratum IIa.

Overlying Stratum II are prehistoric Strata III to X—dated from *c.* 3,000 BP to an estimated 600 BP and containing late Archaic to very late Woodland cultural remains—and early historic Stratum XI, with a radiocarbon date of CE 1775, which contains a number of Euro-American artifacts.

The archaeological sequence, environmental context, and radiocarbon dates obtained from Stratum IIb through to Stratum XI are not disputed by scholars. The cultural evidence derived from lower and middle Stratum IIa were challenged on the grounds that the radiocarbon samples had been contaminated by coal particles or soluble, coal-derived organic compounds, or that younger artifacts had become mixed with the older organic remains in that particular stratum. Critics initially questioned the sparse animal and plant evidence from Stratum IIa, which indicated cool-temperate environmental conditions during late glacial times, when the southern edge of the ice sheet was only 25 miles (40 km) away, but corroborative evidence from the surrounding region has dispelled this concern. Today, Meadowcroft's pre-Clovis evidence is widely accepted as being at least 14,000 years old, and perhaps older.

Thanks to its solid evidence and Dr. Adovasio's staunch advocacy of the site, the Meadowcroft Rockshelter has contributed greatly to a paradigm shift away from Clovis as the first archaeologically known culture in the Americas.

Clovis, United States

Two archaeological discoveries in New Mexico, near Folsom in 1926–1927 and near Clovis in 1933–1936, were among the earliest in America to bring forth scientifically acceptable evidence of human artifacts in direct association with bones of extinct Pleistocene animals. The effect of this was to almost triple the estimated duration of human presence in the Western Hemisphere, from less than 4,000 years to more than 10,000 years.

At Folsom were found small, fluted spear points (named "Folsom"), which were used to kill a single herd of bison, the bones of which had been noticed eroding from the side of an arroyo (gully). Clovis proved to be a more complex and informative kind of site, discovered as a result of fossil animal bones being exposed by extensive gravel quarrying. At Clovis, familiar Folsom points were found with bison bones, but larger fluted points (named "Clovis") were also found in association with mammoth bones in deeper and older deposits. This established their relative ages. The earliest investigations at Clovis were by E. B. Howard and J. L. Cotter. Numerous excavations by various investigators took place intermittently over the next 70 years.

CRAFTED FROM FLINT

A Folsom point is shown in situ, in a muddy soil matrix. Since the discovery of the original Folsom point at the New Mexico site, this style of point has been found throughout North America.

THE FIRST EVIDENCE OF CLOVIS CULTURE

The Clovis site is located on the semiarid margin of the Southern Plains, and consists of a spring-fed intermittent pond. For at least the last 15,000 years this pond overflowed into Blackwater Draw during very wet intervals; in less wet times it was an isolated pond, and during extreme drought conditions it remained dry and subject to wind deflation. Animals and humans both frequented the locality in wetter times, when it was an oasis. Stratified layers of pond and wind deposits separated by wind-scoured unconformities (erosional breaks in the deposits) contain a long sequence of Paleoindian and Archaic artifacts dating to between *c.* 13,000 BP and 2,000 BP. Numerous wells were dug by hand in the floor of the pond during the prolonged dry interval of the middle Holocene period (*c.* 6,000–4,000 BP).

A CLOVIS POINT QUARTET

Clovis spear points have a groove at their base that archaeologists believe was used to securely fasten the points onto short shafts, which were in turn attached to longer and heavier spear shafts. The spears were thrown using an *atlatl*.

As the "type site" or definitive site of so-called Clovis culture, Clovis has contributed a number of significant finds. Several episodes of mammoth hunting and butchering have been documented at Clovis. The first unequivocal evidence of Clovis beveled-base bone spear points was recovered there. One of the first two caches of stone tools attributable to the Clovis period was found at the site; this cache also produced the first evidence indicating that Clovis artisans produced prismatic stone blades. An early Paleoindian engraved stone is reported from the site, and a wide variety of stone cutting and scraping tools have been documented in Clovis deposits at the site.

Since the Clovis site was so well stratified and seemed to contain evidence for all of the early archaeological periods in the region, it gained special status as the referent Paleoindian cultural-historical site. When no earlier cultural manifestations were found in strata below Clovis artifacts at Clovis (or any other site) in the 40 years following the initial work, the view that Clovis artifacts represented the first human presence in the Americas virtually became dogma.

Native American Petroglyphs

Petroglyphs—art rendered on stone surfaces by pecking and incising—are a worldwide phenomenon. In Europe, dated examples go back at least 30,000 years. The origins of petroglyphs in the Americas are poorly understood and hotly debated, because of the inherent difficulty of dating this art form. In stylistic terms, however, it has long been felt that pit and groove petroglyphs represent one of the earliest traditions in the Americas.

Unless petroglyphs contain time-diagnostic images, it is very difficult to date them since the scorings lack organic constituents that can be radiocarbon dated by conventional means, and the scored rock surfaces generally weather at unknowable rates. Recent efforts to date decorated rock surfaces via cation ratio or AMS radiocarbon dating are problematic and controversial. In the Americas, early examples of petroglyphs are characterized by small hemispheric percussion cupules and abraded grooves. Cupules are one of the world's oldest rock art traditions, and have been interpreted as such in North and South America as well. The tradition continues for thousands of years worldwide, so the style itself does not necessarily signify a particular age.

AN ANCIENT ROCK ART TRADITION

Petroglyphs in the Coso Range in California and Grapevine Canyon in Nevada, and at the Mud Portage site in Ontario, are of this style and may be of Late Pleistocene (13,000–12,000 BP) or Early Holocene (12,000–10,000 BP) age. Roughly pecked animal glyphs in Wyoming's Black Hills have also been interpreted as Paleoindian in origin. Found along with the pecked cupules in Grapevine Canyon are geometric petroglyphs of grids, herringbones, and paired parallel lines similar to those found on engraved stones known to be of Clovis age from the Gault site in Texas and the Clovis site in New Mexico. These geometric patterns on both portable objects and rock surfaces may be among the earliest forms of art worldwide. In spite of these indirect suggestions of antiquity, petroglyphs on rock surfaces cannot be dated by the currently available archaeological dating techniques.

Several petroglyph and pictograph (rock painting) sites on the Colorado Plateau of southeastern Utah depict animals strongly resembling mammoths. Since mammoths were extinct in the area by approximately 13,000 years ago, these images are strongly suggestive of Paleoindian artwork, but some authorities question the authenticity of the art or the identification of the animals depicted, or both.

In South America, the primary claims for Pleistocene-age art have been for rock paintings. Simple pecked petroglyphs are often overlooked or ignored in favor of figurative art, but both pecked cupules and linear engravings have been found in Bolivia and Argentina. One site in Argentina, Estancia Los Toldos, has evidence of petroglyphs in association with Fell's Cave Fish Tailed projectile points thought to be of late Pleistocene/Early Holocene age.

PETROGLYPHS, PICTOGRAPHS, AND GEOGLYPHS

Petroglyphs, pictographs, and geoglyphs (large-scale images scored on the landscape, also known as "intaglios,") are the oldest and most widespread art form in the Americas. The rock art images are often in one of three categories: human or human-like figures (anthromorphs); animal or animal representations (zoomorphs); and shapes, objects, and symbols (geomorphs). Distinctive design characteristics and techniques used at various times and by different peoples

WHAT DOES ROCK ART MEAN?

There is considerable controversy as to what rock art means. While most researchers agree that not all rock art would have been done for the same reason, interpretations of particular images at sites throughout the world vary widely.

Images are open to a wide range of meanings. They might commemorate a specific event, form part of a religious ritual, act as signs or messages, signify "I was here," be graffiti, or simply be art for art's sake. While some images can be directly interpreted via some reference to a known event or via a contextual association, the meaning of most rock art can only be guessed at—and for that reason rock art will continue to pique our curiosity and intrigue us as to its purpose and meaning.

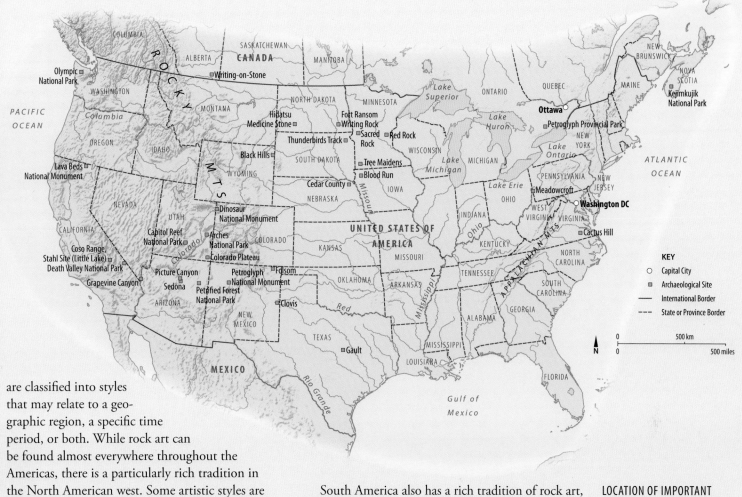

are classified into styles that may relate to a geographic region, a specific time period, or both. While rock art can be found almost everywhere throughout the Americas, there is a particularly rich tradition in the North American west. Some artistic styles are readily recognizable and have been the subject of popular photography books, such as the rock art of the Lower Pecos, Pueblos, and Big Horn Basin. This style of rock art flowers in the Archaic period (8,000–1,000 BP) and continues through to the historic period with memorable images depicting both peaceful and violent European contact.

South America also has a rich tradition of rock art, although research has focused more on the art of later civilizations such as Tihuanaco, Chavín, and Incas. While Chile, Bolivia, and Colombia have impressive rock art, the most famous site is the Nazca Lines in southwest Peru. Covering more than 190 sq miles (500 sq km), these geoglyphs were formed by removing rocks and scraping the ground to reveal lighter soils.

LOCATION OF IMPORTANT PETROGLYPH SITES

Petroglyphs in a variety of styles are located throughout North America, but there is a clustering of sites in the southwest of the United States, where the earliest signs of human occupation are found.

DOODLE OR DESIGN?

Native American petroglyph images can range from birds, animals, and humans to abstract or geometric designs. The imagery may have a literal meaning, or the significance may rely on spiritual or cultural knowledge that has been lost through time. The unusual images seen here are from the Three Rivers Petroglyph site in the Tularosa Basin of New Mexico.

Danger Cave, United States

Near the end of the last Glaciation, *c.* 13,000 BP, the level of the Great Salt Lake dropped below the elevation of the floor of a cave in Utah known as Danger Cave, and the cave was never again flooded. Human occupation began shortly afterward and continued intermittently until CE 1400. Because the cave remained almost perfectly dry, many ordinarily perishable kinds of materials were preserved.

MOUNTAIN HIDEAWAY

Danger Cave is located less than 2 miles (3.2 km) from the town of Wendover, Utah. Other caves in the area, such as Jukebox and Raven Caves, were searched by archaeologist Jesse Jennings before he discovered the wealth of material in Danger Cave.

Danger Cave is a large chamber with an opening overlooking the western shore of the Great Salt Lake in the Great Basin of western North America. Once viewed as inhospitable, the Great Basin has produced an archaeological record showing that humans have long exploited areas of the basin rich in natural resources. This record has stimulated important and far-reaching theories of human adaptation.

Jesse Jennings of the University of Utah carried out the major excavation of Danger Cave from 1949 to 1953, but there have since been numerous additional excavations. For interpretive purposes, Jennings combined the hundreds of depositional layers into five major natural stratigraphic layers. Beneath these layers were exposed lake sediments, beach gravels and sands, and dune sands, reflecting the dropping level of the Great Salt Lake during the last Glaciation. Traces of the earliest human presence in the cave were found below the dune sands and dated to *c.* 12,100 BP. Deposits containing the record of human occupations

were concentrated close to the cave entrance and reached a total thickness of more than 10 ft (3 m). By 1,000 BP, the entrance to the cave interior was essentially blocked by the accumulated deposits.

BEYOND THE "WESTERN ARCHAIC"

Danger Cave and similar sites formed the basis of Jennings's "Desert Culture" concept, which was soon revised and renamed the "Western Archaic." These cultural-historical constructs greatly oversimplified Great Basin prehistory. Many caves in the region afforded refuge from the cold, and extensive patches of aquatic resources near springs and stream mouths sustained near-permanent human occupations throughout most of prehistory. These lake-margin habitats supported prolific communities of plants, birds, fish, and terrestrial animals. The steep mountain ranges dotting and surrounding the nearly flat-bottomed basin store and release snow and rainfall water into the basin, and during periods when the lake level is high, the extent of productive aquatic, lake-margin habitats is reduced to a narrow band at the toe of the mountains. At times of lowered lake levels, the basin habitats expand geometrically—a drop in lake levels of just a few feet exposes hundreds of square miles of former lake beds. Very low lake levels, reduced runoff, and lowered aquifer levels in very dry intervals clearly diminish the carrying capacity of the region.

At the same time that groups in some areas were settled near lake margin habitats with plentiful resources, groups in other areas would have had to forage farther afield for the kinds of plants and animals that were adapted to living in dry or desert conditions. Relatively late in the prehistoric record, upland patches of pinyon pine nuts and mountain game formed an important part of the diet of Great Basin peoples, and this pattern continued into historic times.

Head-Smashed-In, Canada

Kill sites of Pleistocene animals date from very early in the human history of the Americas, and include proboscidean remains found at Taima Taima in Venezuela and at the Clovis site in New Mexico. Examples dating to the Holocene period, almost exclusively of bison, are dotted across the Great Plains of North America. Head-Smashed-In, in southern Alberta, Canada, is a prime example of one hunting technique: bison jumping.

BUFFALO KILL SITE
Seen from the air, Head-Smashed-In is a most impressive site. As well as man-made barriers, hunters would use the natural topographic features of the area such as hills and depressions to guide the buffalo toward the jump.

Evidence that people engaged in big-game hunting—especially of bison—over a long time span is found widely in North America. This evidence includes kill sites with the skeletal remains of anywhere from one to hundreds of individual animals found where they were slain, either in a single event or over many repeated events. To take bison by the jump technique, hunters working in sizable groups stealthily maneuvered around a herd of bison and then caused them to stampede toward an unseen, abrupt drop in the landscape. To guide the animals toward the desired drop, hunters often erected drive lanes in the form of closely spaced stone piles. These may have supported brush or some other perishable, creating the visual impression of a barrier to the rushing herd. Essential to this technique are suitable topography—including a cliff and adequate approaches—sufficient grazing to attract enough animals for the exercise to be worthwhile, suitable cover to allow the hunters to move in on the animals and initiate the drive, and a means to easily access the dead and wounded animals at the base of the jump.

PREHISTORIC BONE BEDS

Head-Smashed-In, one of several jump sites found along a large sandstone cliff in the Porcupine Hills, manifests all of these requirements. The gathering area is a well-watered basin 15 sq miles (40 sq km) in extent, with abundant grazing. Thousands of stone piles bounding drive lanes that are more than 9 miles (14 km) long connect the basin to the cliff. At the base of the cliff, degradation of the cliff as well as accumulated wind-blown dust have buried bison bones from innumerable jump events in stratified layers totalling more than 36 ft (11 m) in thickness. Among the bones are found stone knives and choppers, many chips from resharpening stone tools, and hundreds of stone dart and arrow points. These points are diagnostic of successive archaeological time periods and, along with radiocarbon dating, attest to use of the locality beginning at least 5,700 years ago and lasting into historic times.

Located near the bone beds is an open area where the bison products were processed. Activities in this

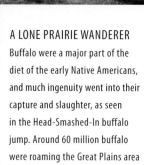

A LONE PRAIRIE WANDERER
Buffalo were a major part of the diet of the early Native Americans, and much ingenuity went into their capture and slaughter, as seen in the Head-Smashed-In buffalo jump. Around 60 million buffalo were roaming the Great Plains area at the time of European contact.

campsite would have included tasks such as retooling weapons, scraping hides, drying meat, rendering fat, and making pemmican.

Head-Smashed-In has been designated a World Heritage Site by UNESCO in recognition of its outstanding preservation and its status as a communal bison-hunting site. Its comprehensive interpretive center informs thousands of visitors each year.

Ancestral Pueblo

The magnificent sites of Keet Seel, Mesa Verde, and Chaco Canyon are among the best-known Indian ruins in the American Southwest. They flourished between CE 900 and 1300. For many years they lay steeped in mystery. Who built them? Where did these people go? We now know the answers to those questions.

Once thought to be members of a vanished civilization, the builders of Cliff Palace (c. 1250) at Mesa Verde and Pueblo Bonito (c. 1075) at Chaco Canyon are now known to be direct ancestors of the modern-day Pueblo Indians of Arizona and New Mexico. These ancient people are known as Anasazi, a word borrowed from the Navajo Indian language, though they have only a distant connection with the Navajo. To honor their Pueblo history, archaeologists now refer to them by the term "Ancestral Pueblo;" but the name Anasazi retains the mystery and excitement of the early archaeological finds in the Southwest. Anasazi: Why did they leave? Where did they go?

PIT-HOUSE TO "GREAT HOUSE"
Pueblo architecture developed from pit-houses to free-standing stone structures with adjoining rooms. From CE 850 to 1150, "Great Houses," massive houses featuring fine sandstone masonry, were built at Chaco Canyon. Pueblo Bonito (seen here) was one of the first.

SOLVING THE MYSTERY
Pueblo peoples are deeply embedded in the history of the Southwest—they have been there from "time immemorial," as many Indians would say. For archaeologists, Pueblo history comes into focus around the year CE 500, during the period called "Basketmaker III." The architecture and the pottery of Basketmaker times began a sequence that can clearly be followed all the way to present-day

Pueblos. Basketmaker villages, however, did not look like Taos or Hopi: those modern pueblos are compact, terraced, apartment-like buildings or tight, multi-family blocks of so-called row-houses. Basketmaker settlements, in contrast, were loose clusters of three to five pit-houses, each of which housed a family. A pit-house was built by digging a flat-floored, straight-sided hole perhaps 4 ft (1.2 m) deep by 14 ft (4 m) in diameter. A timber post-and-beam framework was then erected within the hole; the timbers were covered with mats or brush, and soil from the pit was layered over the top, creating a sturdy, well-insulated home.

Pit-houses were the preferred house form for many decades before "pueblos"—free-standing structures of stone with adjoining rooms—appeared during the "Pueblo I" period (CE 750–900). Initially, pueblos were not houses but were built for storage; families continued to live in pit-houses. Pueblo architecture developed over three centuries. Rough stone walls were superseded by the kind of fine sandstone masonry for which the sites of Mesa Verde and Chaco Canyon are justly famous. As pueblos

TIMELINE OF ANCESTRAL PUEBLO ("ANASAZI") HISTORY

Basketmaker II	**1200 BCE–CE 500**
	Shallow pit-houses; maize (corn) becomes the staple crop
Basketmaker III	**CE 500–750**
	Deep pit-houses, pottery, bow and arrow
c. CE 500	Short-lived, large pit-house villages at Chaco Canyon (Shabikeschee)
Pueblo I	**CE 750–900**
	Black-on-white painted pottery, short-lived large towns
c. CE 800	First Great Houses in the Mesa Verde area
c. CE 850–900	First Great Houses at Chaco Canyon
c. CE 900	Mesa Verde region largely abandoned (repopulated in CE 1000)
Pueblo II	**CE 900–1150**
	Most of the Anasazi area incorporated into a region centered on Chaco Canyon; development of black-on-white pottery and sandstone masonry pueblos
c. 1020–1100	Chaco rises to regional prominence
c. 1100	Aztec Ruins begins (construction continues through to 1280)
c. 1130	Chaco ends
Pueblo III	**1150–1300**
	Large towns, violence; the Four Corners area is abandoned
c. 1200	Large pueblos in the Mesa Verde region; cliff dwellings at Mesa Verde, Keet Seel, and throughout the Four Corners area
c. 1250	Large groups begin to leave the Four Corners area
c. 1275–1300	"Great Drought"; the Four Corners area is finally abandoned
Pueblo IV	**1300–1450 (and subsequent Spanish contact)**
	Reorganization into modern Pueblos
c. 1300–1350	People resettle in the Rio Grande, Acoma, Zuni, and Hopi areas
1540	Vasquez de Coronado leads the first Spanish army into the Southwest
1600	Pueblo region is colonized by the Spanish

became increasingly prominent, more household activities moved into the aboveground rooms, and pit-houses shrank in size but not in importance. Pit-houses eventually became "kivas," the underground ceremonial chambers still used by modern-day Pueblo ritual organizations.

For 500 years, from CE 800 to 1300, a typical house consisted of a pueblo of six to eight rooms built in front of a pit-house (often called a kiva, perhaps prematurely). The pit-house continued to be the focus of family activities. An important development in the history of Pueblo architecture occurred in the period known as Pueblo I (CE 750–900), when people started to join together their six-rooms-and-a-kiva dwellings, building them side by side. Lines or "streets" of conjoined houses appear in Pueblo I villages, clear precursors of later pueblo forms.

PUEBLO POLITIES

The line of development from Basketmaker pit-house to modern-day pueblo is not straight or direct. Pueblo prehistory was marked by incidents and events as many and varied as those of any people, anywhere. Migrations from an old village to a new site were common, even constant (see page 296). Against this backdrop, more permanent political systems came and went, perhaps first during Pueblo I and certainly by Pueblo II (CE 900–1150) at Chaco Canyon (see page 294). For a century or more, Chaco Canyon served as the capital of a vast region; but this did not last. With Chaco's fall (*c.* 1130), new centers rose: to the north in the Mesa Verde region (Pueblo III, *c.* 1150–1300); and, later, far to the south at Casas Grandes, in northernmost Mexico (Pueblo IV, 1300–1450). The ruins of

the northern center can be seen at Aztec Ruins National Monument in New Mexico, and Casas Grandes (also known as Paquimé) lies about 60 miles (100 km) southwest of El Paso, Texas.

The Pueblo IV period (*c.* 1300 to 1450) was when "Anasazi" became "Pueblo." The architectural forms, pottery styles, and social institutions that archaeologists recognize as distinctly Puebloan were now unmistakable. The old family home of Pueblo I, II, and III—six rooms and a kiva—lost the kiva. The home's six rooms were restacked into apartments in much larger blocks of contiguous houses, and instead of every home having a kiva, each village had only one, and towns two or three. By this time, kivas housed men's ceremonial societies. Pueblo IV pueblos looked very like modern-day Taos or Hopi. After Pueblo IV, the connections through to modern Pueblo peoples are clear. We know a great deal about the history of Pueblos after *c.* 1450, both from Pueblo traditions and from archaeological research.

PUEBLO "BASEMENTS"

As families moved out of pit-houses into aboveground stone structures—the precursors of modern-day pueblos—pit-houses became "kivas," the underground ceremonial chambers still used by Pueblo ritual organizations. This sun-lit kiva is at Mesa Verde.

HUMAN EFFIGY

This ceramic effigy dates to the Pueblo II period (CE 900–1150). It is coated with a clay slip, which is a runny mixture of clay and water, often white or cream in color, that is used to coat the surface before firing.

Mesa Verde, United States

Mesa Verde is the name of a landform, a national park, and a region. The Mesa Verde is a 200-sq-mile (50-sq-km) tableland cut by deep, parallel canyons. Alcoves in the sandstone canyons contain hundreds of cliff dwellings, large and small. Cliff Palace, in Cliff Canyon, is the largest, with an astonishing 220 rooms and 23 kivas.

Most of Mesa Verde's cliff dwellings are included in Mesa Verde National Park. Mesa Verde also refers to a larger archaeological region, characterized by architecture and pottery similar to that found in the park, stretching 150 miles (240 km) across southern Colorado and southeastern Utah. Over that vast area, tens of thousands of ruins represent farmsteads, villages, and towns dating mainly from CE 800 to 1300.

Mesa Verde is best known for its cliff dwellings. The largest, Cliff Palace, was built between 1200 and 1280 and abandoned by 1300. More than two dozen village-sized cliff dwellings (and over 500 smaller alcove sites) are found in other canyons of Mesa Verde. The masons who worked in the sheltered alcoves were masters of their craft. Seven centuries after they were built, the mud-mortared walls still stand two or even three stories tall.

The cliff dwellings were built by ancestors of the Pueblo Indians. In recent times, Ute Indians lived around Mesa Verde. Both tribes knew of the cliff dwellings, but the wider American community only learned about these magnificent sites in 1888, when they were discovered by a local rancher, Richard Wetherill. When Wetherill first entered the cliff dwellings, he found many baskets, sandals, pots, and other objects left by people he called "Anasazi." The quality of these artifacts and the dramatic cliff settings of the architecture—enhanced by the romance attached to abandoned cities—made Mesa Verde famous.

MESA VERDE TOWNS

Towns many times larger than Cliff Palace were built in the plains northeast of the park. Because those sites were not protected by alcoves, they have fallen into ruin. There were at least 15 such towns (many in canyons of the Ancients National Monument); the largest has 1,200 rooms and 200 kivas. Archaeological investigations suggest violent times, with remnants of surrounding walls and towers and also evidence of battles. Large towns arose for the same reason that villages moved into cliff alcoves: defense.

From about 1250, sizable groups of people began leaving the troubled region and were received by the towns that became Hopi, Zuni, Acoma, Zia, Laguna, and the many Pueblo towns of the Rio Grande in New Mexico. By 1300, the Mesa Verde region was empty. The "mystery of the Anasazi" is no mystery to modern Pueblo people: the villagers of ancient Mesa Verde were ancestors of modern Pueblos.

MASTER MASONS

This village of adobe brick houses, one of many in Mesa Verde National Park, was built into a cliff recess by ancestors of modern-day Pueblo Indians. It is a testament to the craft of these ancient masons that walls of two and even three stories still stand.

NATURAL PROTECTION
Built in huge natural alcoves in the red sandstone of the Tsegi canyon system, Keet Seel is the best-preserved large cliff dwelling in the Southwest. Many original roofs remain intact, and fragile *jacale* walls still survive. The village of Keet Seel housed 125–150 people.

Keet Seel, United States

One of three large cliff dwellings at Navajo National Monument, near Kayenta, Arizona, Keet Seel is the best-preserved large cliff dwelling in the Southwest. Its remote location and the generations of Navajo Indians who lived in its canyon spared Keet Seel the damage suffered by many cliff dwellings elswehere.

A NEW "CENTER PLACE"
Contemporary with the village of Keet Seel, which comprised more than 150 rooms and six kivas, Betatakin cliff dwelling has some 100 rooms and only one or two kivas. It was built in *c.* 1275–1277, when an entire clan or village relocated here.

The village of Keet Seel comprised more than 150 rooms and a half-dozen kivas, housing between 125 and 150 people. The village grew gradually. Construction started *c.* 1250; there was a burst of building between 1272 and 1275; and small-scale construction continued until *c.* 1286. The village was abandoned less than a generation later, by 1300. Keet Seel's history contrasts with that of the contemporary Betatakin cliff dwelling—also in Navajo National Monument, some 6 miles (10 km) from Keet Seel. With some 100 rooms and only one or two kivas, Betatakin was constructed mostly in a single event around 1275 to 1277, when an entire clan or village relocated to the site.

The cliff dwellings were built in huge natural alcoves in the red sandstone of the Tsegi canyon system. The western half of Keet Seel was built directly on the floor of its alcove. In the eastern half of the alcove, the bedrock floor sloped too sharply to act as a base, so a massive 175-ft (53-m) long terrace had to be built for this purpose. The terrace was first walled up with stout sandstone masonry and then filled in, basket by basket, with sand from the canyon bottom. The terrace provided a stable foundation for half the town's families. The alcove sheltered the buildings from rain and snow, and consequently many original roofs remain intact and fragile *jacale* walls still survive. (*Jacales* are made of lines of thin, upright posts to which rough mats were secured, the whole then being plastered with mud.) The generations of Navajo Indians who lived in Chaco canyon never lived in its cave. When Richard Wetherill found the ruins in 1895, they contained baskets, sandals, and bowls and jars of the characteristic "polychrome" pottery, with designs in red, black, and white on an orange background.

NATIVE TRADITIONS
Keet Seel and Betatakin are well known to Navajo and Hopi Indian peoples. Navajo people still live in the canyons around Navajo National Monument. In their language, Keet Seel means "shattered house" and Betatakin means "house on a rock ledge." They have many stories about these Anasazi places. Hopi Pueblo Indians, 60 miles (100 km) to the south, remember them differently; for Hopis, Kawestima (Keet Seel) and Talastima (Betatakin) were built by Hisatsinom (Hopi ancestor) clans that later migrated to the Hopi mesas. These clans endure in Hopi towns: members of the Fire, Flute, and Bighorn Sheep Clans came from Kawestima/Keet Seel.

Chaco Canyon, United States

Chaco Culture National Historical Park, in northwestern New Mexico, preserves a regional center that flourished from CE 850 to 1130. A dozen "Great Houses"—huge buildings, built with extraordinary sandstone masonry—are Chaco's principal feature. There is little water, and there are few trees. The lack of resources in and around the canyon explains what happened there.

SKILLED WORKERS

Finds of ancient tools like this Anasazi stone ax, with its original handle still intact, make the achievements of the people who lived in this often harsh environment in pre-Columbian times seem even more remarkable.

Chaco Canyon itself is not spectacular. Sandstone cliffs 100 ft (30 m) tall flank a barren valley bottom less than a mile (1.6 km) wide; the canyon runs some 9 miles (14 km) through the park. Summers are hot and dry, winters brutally cold.

GREAT HOUSES

Beginning in about CE 850, the people of Chaco Canyon began to build "Great Houses"—originally, massive versions of the typical homes of that time. A normal home consisted of a small, six-room building and a kiva. The largest Great Houses, Pueblo Bonito and Chetro Ketl, had up to 800 rooms and scores of kivas. An entire normal house might fit into the largest room at Pueblo Bonito, one of the first Great Houses. Originally, there were three Great Houses, but from 1020 the pace of construction rose dramatically in a century-long "building boom." By 1130, when construction ceased, Chaco Canyon comprised six large and eight smaller Great Houses, and hundreds of normal homes.

Some Great Houses were built over many decades, others over much shorter periods. All had ground plans of startlingly geometric regularity: there are ovals, half-circles, and rectangles, along with other carefully calculated layouts, often astronomically aligned. The scale of the buildings, and their geometric formality, suggest that they were designed by individuals acting as architects. The work would have to have been planned and organized by people filling the role of construction foremen. Hundreds of thousands of wood beams, for example, were cut and brought from forests 40 miles (65 km) or more away. Specialist masons supervised quarrying and the shaping and laying up of walls 3½ ft (1 m) thick and four stories tall. To carry out this work, large labor forces had to be recruited, organized, and directed.

AN ANCIENT CAPITAL

What were Great Houses? Early excavators thought they were pueblos: compact, apartment-like farming communities, like modern Pueblo towns. If Pueblo Bonito was indeed a pueblo, it would have housed at least 500 people. Recent work suggests that only a fraction of the many rooms were actually occupied. Pueblo Alto, for example, had 100 rooms, but only a half-dozen resident families. The "extra" rooms were storage, administrative, or ritual facilities, or temporary quarters. Several Great Houses may not have been houses but rather warehouses or empty monuments built to commemorate or to impress.

The people who lived in Great Houses had many precious things brought to the canyon: turquoise, shell from both the Pacific and Atlantic coasts, and objects and animals from the contemporary civilizations of Mesoamerica. Much of the pottery found at Chaco was not made there. It was imported

BUILT TO IMPRESS?

Pueblo Bonito was one of Chaco Canyon's first "Great Houses." This complex could have housed 500 people or more, but the evidence suggests that only a small proportion of the rooms were actually occupied.

from 50 miles (80 km) or more away. Some (and perhaps most) of the maize found at Chaco Great Houses was grown in outlying communities and brought to Chaco Canyon for regional festivals, and to feed the elites who lived there year-round.

The central area of Chaco Canyon—3 or 4 sq miles (8 or 10 sq km) around Pueblo Bonito—formed a complex of Great Houses, roads, earth-filled mounds, and other monuments. This central core was planned almost as an urban "cityscape," aligned on a prominent north–south axis. At its peak, from 1075 to 1100, perhaps 3,000 people lived at Chaco—the size of a small Mesoamerican city.

Chaco's rise and fall reflect local Southwestern histories and environments set within a much larger continental context—the great cities and states of Mesoamerica, of which Chaco's rulers were clearly aware. The lords of Chaco probably had contact with Mesoamerican kings. Chaco's story was played out again at other, very distant sites. When construction ended at Chaco, a second monumental center, Aztec Ruins National Monument, 60 miles (95 km) to the north, began to take shape. Aztec Ruins was contemporary with Mesa Verde (see page 292). It never achieved Chaco's power or importance, and when the Mesa Verde region was abandoned between 1275 and 1300, Aztec Ruins, too, was left empty.

When Richard Wetherill began excavations at Chaco in 1900, the canyon was home to many Navajo Indian families, who told of an ancient ruler at Chaco who enslaved all the people of the region. Chaco Canyon is remembered, more directly, in traditional histories of modern-day Pueblo Indian towns. It was a great yet terrible place where Pueblo people learned important lessons about how to live. Pueblos today do not have kings, but they had rulers at Chaco Canyon. Pueblos chose to avoid elite rulers thereafter, and succeeded in doing so—until European colonists arrived almost five centuries after Chaco's fall.

PRECISION BUILDING

A clifftop view shows the D-shaped ruins of Pueblo Bonito. The ground plans of Chaco's "Great Houses" are startlingly geometric, and include ovals, half-circles, rectangles, and other carefully calculated layouts.

CANYON CULTURE

The tall cliffs of Chaco Canyon flank a barren valley bottom that is less than a mile (1.6 km) wide. Nothing about the environment explains the extraordinary regional center that flourished in the canyon from CE 850 to 1130.

CHACO'S REGION

Great Houses were not limited to Chaco Canyon: more than 200 smaller versions, with similarly geometric layouts and constructed in the same way, dot the Anasazi region. Those distant Great Houses (called "outliers") mark the border of a region about the size of Ireland, of which Chaco Canyon was the center and, probably, the capital. Roadlike monuments—30 ft (9 m) wide and arrow-straight—radiate outward from Chaco to the outliers like the spokes of a wheel. These were not roads in the modern sense: many were discontinuous, disappearing in the long reaches between Chaco Canyon and the outlying Great House communities. Elaborate stairs and ramps show that people walked on roads, but Chaco "roads" were not a transportation network. Chaco was a capital for Ancestral Pueblo (Anasazi) people, but its power may have been as much ritual as political.

Where Did the Anasazi Go?

The mystery of the Anasazi: Where did they go? Why did they leave? Those questions intrigued early archaeologists, such as Richard Wetherill, the rancher who between 1888 and 1900 discovered Mesa Verde and Keet Seel, and undertook the first excavations at Chaco Canyon. The local Indians—Ute or Navajo—stated that their people had not built those magnificent structures (although they had much to say about the ancient ones). Wetherill modified the Navajo word *anaasa'zi'*, meaning "enemy ancestors" or "alien ancestors," to refer to the people of Mesa Verde and Chaco Canyon—whoever they were.

THE "MYSTERY OF THE ANASAZI"

The romance of vanished civilizations appealed to Americans and Europeans. The "mystery of the Anasazi," often referred to in travel books and adventure stories, remains a favorite theme of tourism in the "Four Corners" country—the adjacent corners of Arizona, Colorado, New Mexico, and Utah. If you ask Indians living in one of 20 modern pueblos (from Hopi to the Rio Grande) about the "mystery of the Anasazi," they will most likely say that there is no mystery: the Anasazi were Pueblo ancestors who migrated from the Four Corners to where Pueblo towns stand today. Indeed, Pueblos prefer to use names from their own languages instead of the Navajo name "Anasazi." Hopi people, for example, call their ancestors *hisatsinom* (meaning "the ancients"). Since there are several different Pueblo languages, archaeologists use the less elegant phrase "Ancestral Pueblo."

WHY DID THEY LEAVE?

Archaeologists and Indians agree that there is in fact no "mystery." But the real story is no less compelling than the myth. Around 1250, there were tens of thousands of Pueblo people living around the Four Corners; by 1300, they were gone. We know where they went. "Why did they leave?" remains a valid question.

Archaeologists postulated one good reason: drought from *c.* 1275 to 1300. (We can estimate rainfall by decoding tree-rings in the roof beams of ruins.) The Four Corners region was only marginally suited to growing maize (corn), the Pueblo staple then and now. Rainfall was usually sufficient, but from 1275 to 1300 drought made farming difficult. Archaeologists thought that Pueblo people were driven out of the Four Corners when their crops failed.

We now know that people started leaving the area as early as 1225, long before the drought. And recent computer analysis tells us that even during the drought about a third of the population could have stayed in place; there was no practical need for *everyone* to leave. Yet everyone did leave.

WHERE DID THEY GO?

Pueblo people preserve migration stories, long and elaborate oral histories of their wanderings through the Southwest. In those stories, people left a village and moved to a new location for many reasons, including drought (certainly), sickness, and other natural events, but also for reasons we would call spiritual or political. Such things as impieties, social misconduct, or violence might trigger a movement. Migration stories encompass the lessons people learned at each village along the way, and explain how and why traditional Pueblos live as they do today. They also reflect the importance of movement itself. As Tessie Naranjo from Santa Clara Pueblo said: "People have moved from place to place and have joined and separated again throughout our past, and we have incorporated it into our songs, stories, and myths because we must continually remember that, without movement, there is no life."

NATURAL PROGRESSION
Pueblo people of today, like this man standing in front of adobe houses in Taos, New Mexico, find nothing extraordinary in the "disappearance" of their ancestors, the Anasazi, from places like Chaco Canyon. Pueblo people have wandered through the Southwest since "time immemorial," and have a philosophy of movement.

CLIFFTOP DEFENSE

"Where did they go?" The people of New Mexico's Acoma Pueblo (far left) trace their origins to the inhabitants of ruins to the west and north. Acoma Pueblo was built on top of a 357-ft (109-m) sandstone mesa, probably in the twelfth century CE, for defense against raiders, and lays claim to being the oldest continuously inhabited city in the United States.

TEMPORARY TOWNS

These cliff dwellings at Bandelier National Monument in New Mexico (left) are a fraction of the several thousand dwellings Ancestral Pueblo people built among the mesas and canyons of this region between 1250 and 1450. Most of these towns were inhabited for only a few generations before people moved on once more.

Archaeology registers these stories as the movement of people away from the north—a place of increasing violence and disruption in the thirteenth century. Between 1250 and 1450, clans and villages moved to very large towns near today's Pueblos. These sites include Poshuingue Ruins and Bandelier National Monument in New Mexico; and Homolovi Ruins State Park in Arizona. Those towns were quite large—several much larger than Pueblo Bonito—but most were inhabited for only two or three generations. The migrations were not yet over.

Pueblo migration stories are quite specific about the last few centuries before European colonization. Each Pueblo (and often each clan) has its own history of finding the "center place"—locations to which they were directed by portents and signs during long migrations. Pueblo people know where they came from ("where did they go?"), and the findings of archaeology support their traditions. The answer to "Why did they leave?" requires an answer that includes drought, political strife, and a basic philosophy of movement.

FARMING THE FLOODPLAIN

Homolovi Ruins State Park in northern Arizona preserves the ruins of a fourteenth-century CE Anasazi settlement. Here, Ancestral Pueblo people stopped to farm the rich floodplain of the Colorado River before continuing on their way to join people already living on the mesas—the people today known as the Hopi.

Early Mesoamerican Cultures

As a cultural region, Mesoamerica extends north to the southern fringes of the great deserts in northern Mexico and south to parts of modern-day El Salvador and Honduras. The "Mesoamerican civilization" that emerges after 1500 BCE is the full expression of the agricultural and village life, religions and cosmology, which distinguished the cultures of this area for 3,000 years.

The period in Mesoamerican archaeology known as the Formative (or pre-Classic), extending from 1500 BCE to CE 200, saw dramatic changes in social and political organization, beginning with the first chiefdoms and ending with the first states and the beginning of the Classic period, which lasts until CE 700 in non-Maya Mesoamerica. Early in the Formative period, the characteristics that define Mesoamerica as a unified cultural area crystallize: the sacred calendar of 260 days and the solar calendar of 365 days; the ball game (more important ceremonially than as a sport, the losing team or team's captain being sacrificed); auto-sacrifice (blood offered from body parts such as the ear, tongue, or penis) and human sacrifice (usually through heart extraction or decapitation), which repaid a primordial blood debt; hieroglyphic writing; a complex assortment of deities; advanced astronomical and mathematical knowledge; pyramidal architecture, which served as the base for important public structures and temples; urban centers laid out according to sacred cosmic principles and alignments; and an extraordinarily rich religion and cosmology.

DOMESTICATION OF PLANTS AND ANIMALS

The archaeological evidence indicates that people were living in Mesoamerica from *c.* 10,000 BCE. These early people depended on hunting big-game

CEREMONIAL BALL GAME
Located in the northeast corner of the Main Plaza, the ball court at Monte Albán in Oaxaca, Mexico, exhibits the typical "I" shape. The earliest version of this ball court was built after 200 BCE, as the ceremonial core of the Zapotec city evolved to the plan that is visible today.

CHIEFS AS "AGGRANDIZERS"

Archaeologist John Clark presents a model that the earliest chiefdoms in Mesoamerica emerged through generosity. In these early villages, individuals whom Clark calls "aggrandizers"—probably male—sought an enhanced status for themselves. Through their hard work, and that of their families, they accumulated great surpluses. They started to acquire exotic goods from more distant regions, and became patrons both of local craftspeople who could create special products, including exquisite pottery, and of farmers who domesticated plants to be served on special occasions. In order to attract more followers, these competitive aggrandizers invited prospective supporters to feasts, where luxury items were displayed and given as gifts. Since most people could not return such gifts in kind, they repaid the "aggrandizer" by their labor and by performing other social tasks. Perhaps the most interesting twist in Clark's model is that rather than leading to chiefdoms, population increase was a result of such strategies to attract followers; chiefdoms themselves were probably an unanticipated outcome. Similar processes probably influenced the development of social complexity on the Gulf Coast.

animals, but by 7000 BCE a warming trend caused many of the large herd animals to migrate to other areas. People responded by diversifying their diet to incorporate the remaining animals and more wild plants, some of which would ultimately be domesticated and form the basic diet of all Mesoamerican peoples until the invasion of Spanish conquistadors in the sixteenth century.

Mesoamerican peoples relied on maize (corn), beans, squash, and chili peppers. Each of these vegetables went through a unique process of experimentation as people domesticated them, changing them from their wild forms to make them more productive. Some of the earliest plants domesticated (some as early as 8000 BCE) were the bottle gourd—used as a container before clay pottery was developed—and the squash. Maize was probably domesticated in the fifth millennium BCE, with early dates from both the Gulf Coast of Tabasco and Guilá

Naquitz cave in the Valley of Oaxaca. The transition to agriculture occurred gradually and at different times across Mesoamerica; each region used different combinations of plants, although there was substantial sharing of information among groups and between regions. The only significant domesticated animals were the dog and the turkey, both used for food; no large animals (suitable for labor) were ever domesticated.

Domestication also had substantially different impacts in different regions. In the highlands, some scholars suggest that the wild ancestor of maize, *teosinte* (a wild grass), was domesticated in the Balsas River drainage area of western Mexico, although the exact ancestor of maize, and where it was first domesticated, remain the subject of a lively debate. Years of research in caves and rock shelters by Richard MacNeish had suggested that maize had been domesticated in the Tehuacán Valley; it now appears that the earliest maize cobs from his excavations represent a domesticated plant that was introduced into this dry region. In the Central and Southern Highlands of Mexico, people's reliance on wild plants and animals gradually gave way to a reliance on agriculture as maize in particular became

more productive and dependable, allowing people to settle in villages by 2000 BCE. In the lowlands of the Gulf Coast and along the Pacific Coast (around the border between modern-day Mexico and Guatemala), people had settled in villages before agriculture was developed to any degree, relying on maritime and riverine products and the wild plants and animals found in these bountiful areas. Indeed, the research of John Clark and his colleagues into the so-called Mokaya people of the Soconusco region suggests that maize initially played a minor role in their diet, being used primarily to make a maize-beer.

THE RISE OF CHIEFDOMS

Excavations at sites such as Paso de la Amada, in the Soconusco region of coastal Chiapas, date the rise of chiefdoms in Mesoamerica to *c.* 1600 BCE. Chiefs' residences/public structures (including the earliest documented ball court in Mesoamerica) were located on mounds, and as structures were modified or new structures were built on the same mound over time, these were oriented the same way.

ORIGINS OF AGRICULTURE
It was previously thought that maize was first domesticated in Mesoamerica in the Tehuacán Valley, but in fact the earliest cobs found here represent an already domesticated plant that was introduced. This diorama depicts men cultivating maize in the Tehuacán Valley *c.* 3400 BCE.

FUNERARY OFFERINGS
Grayware urns like this one from the facade of Tomb 104 at Monte Albán in Oaxaca, Mexico—often showing an elite person dressed as a deity—epitomize Zapotec funerary offerings.

EXTENT OF MESOAMERICA
As a cultural region, Mesoamerica extends north to the southern fringes of the great deserts in northern Mexico and south to parts of modern-day El Salvador and Honduras.

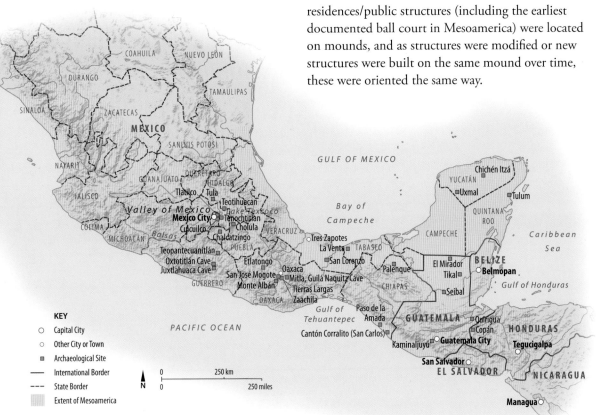

KEY
○ Capital City
○ Other City or Town
■ Archaeological Site
— International Border
--- State Border
▨ Extent of Mesoamerica

0   250 km
0   250 miles
N

San José Mogote and Etlatongo, Mexico

Excavations of two villages in adjacent highland valleys in the state of Oaxaca—San José Mogote in the Valley of Oaxaca (associated with the Zapotecs) and Etlatongo in the Nochixtlán Valley (associated with the Mixtecs)—have provided insights into the changes that took place in early societies in this part of the world leading up to the development of the first chiefdoms in the southern highlands of Mesoamerica.

BUILDING ON THE PAST

This photograph shows the view from Mound 1, the Early Formative public area at Etlatongo, looking north to the Classic and post-Classic site on the hill. Constructed on an elevated site, the mound was expanded during successive periods of occupation.

BEYOND THE GRAVE

This anthromorphic incense brazier excavated from Structure 26 at San José Mogote dates to between 700 BCE and 500 BCE. It was found in an apparent storage unit in what has been interpreted as an elite residence, and was used to communicate with ancestors.

The research of archaeologists such as Kent Flannery and Marcus Winter has shown that before 1200 BCE small villages dotted the Valley of Oaxaca. Villages such as Tierras Largas averaged 2.5–7 acres (1–3 ha) in size and housed 4–12 families. Even then, San José Mogote was larger than other villages. After 1200 BCE, both San José Mogote and Etlatongo expanded to some 50 acres (20 ha), becoming the only sites of this size in their valleys.

Until *c.* 1200 BCE, most people lived in small houses of some 13 ft by 20 ft (4 m by 6 m), with walls made of wattle-and-daub, thatched roofs, and earth or sand floors. Families buried their deceased kin under or close to the house, and stored food and surplus items in nearby storage pits. At San José Mogote, there is evidence of public space before 1200 BCE; small structures on platforms, largely lacking domestic debris, may have been meeting places for males of the community. At both villages, some families—the leaders—lived in slightly better-made houses, and also ate more meat, as evidenced by deer bones. But there was no fundamental chasm in social status; differences lay along a continuum.

FROM VILLAGE TO CHIEFDOM

Chiefdoms emerged in response to social changes and external factors. Social changes are thought to include those suggested by the "aggrandizer model" and the fact that emerging elites tied themselves to

powerful ancestors. The importance of ancestors is a basic part of Oaxacan culture. External factors include contact with other groups and access to exotic and luxury items, such as fancy pottery (both local and imported, Olmec-style pottery), stingray spines (for auto-sacrificial rituals), and *Spondylus* and pearl oyster shells. Emerging elites at San José Mogote concentrated labor and organized specialized craft production of objects such as magnetite mirrors, further enhancing their status relative to others. San José Mogote and Etlatongo became large, central villages. Each administered the civic-ceremonial affairs of the villages in its surrounding valley and had spaces where public rituals took place.

Olmec-style pottery and figurines found in excavations indicate a connection with a larger pan-regional cult related to the Olmec religion. This served the interests of leaders both in Oaxaca and on the Gulf Coast, linking emergent religion and cosmology with developing exchange networks.

With the rise of Monte Albán in 500 BCE (see page 305), San José Mogote became an administrative center for that city. A carved stone found in San José Mogote, known as Monument 3, shows a sacrificed captive with two glyphs representing his name in the 260-day calendar. While some date it to 700 BCE, seeing it as one of the earliest examples of writing in Mesoamerica, others link it to Monte Albán's "Danzantes" sculptures, created some 200 years later.

Olmec Colossal Heads, Mexico

In 1862, in the course of oil-drilling operations, the first colossal head emerged from the jungles of the Gulf Coast, bringing to light the Olmec civilization. While some features that define Mesoamerica, such as the ball game, originated before the rise of Olmec civilization *c.* 1200 BCE, the Olmecs synthesized and expressed this vast mosaic of elements in a way and on a scale not seen before.

Museum curators had identified a disparate assemblage of objects in a certain style as Olmec before the colossal heads were linked with Gulf Coast Olmec culture, primarily by Matthew Stirling in the 1930s. Olmec culture has two major phases: San Lorenzo (1200–900 BCE) and La Venta (800–500 BCE). Both sites are located in the tropical lowlands of the Gulf Coast; while they overlap, their apogees were far apart.

Some archaeologists consider San Lorenzo to be Mesoamerica's first city. Ann Cyphers documented that it extends over 1,200 acres (500 ha), dwarfing all contemporaneous sites. San Lorenzo had a more complex socio-political organization than places such as San José Mogote. Elites at San Lorenzo lived in the "Red Palace," a structure with columns and drains made from basalt—a raw material that had to be floated and dragged some 40 miles (60 km). They took control of the hinterland and established administrative sites—marked by the appearance of monumental art—at important places along nearby rivers.

The colossal stone heads symbolize the great power held by Olmec rulers. These multi-ton heads appear shortly after the ascendance of San Lorenzo, and along with basalt "altars"—actually, thrones on which Olmec rulers sat—they manifest control over labor. Each head has different facial features and headgear, and portrays an Olmec leader. After the decline of San Lorenzo *c.* 900 BCE, colossal heads were created in successive Gulf Coast regional centers: ten heads come from San Lorenzo, four from La Venta, two from Tres Zapotes, and one from an undocumented site.

ICONOGRAPHY AND INTERACTION

The Olmecs developed an art style that is remarkably naturalistic in its three-dimensional depiction of both humans and fantastic creatures, such as the so-called were-jaguar. Olmec iconography abstracts aspects of Olmec religion and cosmology. During the San Lorenzo Olmec, pottery in this style appears at sites throughout Mesoamerica.

A debate centers on the Olmecs' impact on contemporaneous cultures. Some view the Olmec as one of many similar chiefdoms, with no priority in creating and disseminating these symbols. However, discoveries related to the San Lorenzo rulers' power contradict this view. Others see the Olmec as playing a central role. Analysis of Olmec-style pots from San Lorenzo, San José Mogote, and Etlatongo reveal that the two Oaxacan sites made local versions of such pottery and also imported it from San Lorenzo, but not from each other. San Lorenzo generally did not import such pottery, suggesting that it originated there. Olmec influence varied in different regions. While in Oaxaca it appears limited, the Mokaya chiefdoms in Soconusco were fundamentally trans-formed through Olmec contact; political power moved from Paso de la Amada to Cantón Corralito.

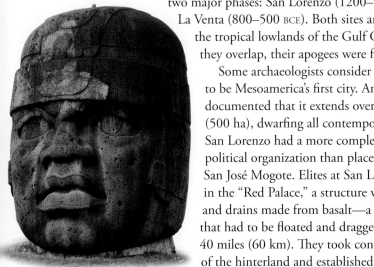

SAN LORENZO GIANT
Colossal Head 1 at San Lorenzo, Veracruz, stands nearly 10 ft (3 m) tall. At San Lorenzo, the multi-ton basalt heads may have been displayed in rows in the city center. Despite speculation about an African influence on Olmec culture, the heads show typical indigenous features.

LA VENTA GIANT
Colossal Head 1 at La Venta, Tabasco, stands nearly 8 ft (2.4 m) tall. This head is squatter than the San Lorenzo heads, and is prognathic in profile. La Venta heads may have faced outward from the site's ceremonial center.

Teotihuacan, Mexico

So important was Teotihuacan that its impact lingered with the Aztecs for nearly a millennium after its demise; it was the place where the deities gathered to begin the Fifth Sun—our current earth, sun, and moon. The word Teotihuacan is Aztec, and means "place of the gods." In its heyday, between CE 100 and 650, Teotihuacan became one of the largest cities ever to have existed in the prehispanic New World.

Teotihuacan is located in a side valley in the northern part of the Valley of Mexico. The origins of the city can be traced back at least to 200 BCE. While springs and nearby obsidian sources would have influenced the city's location, Teotihuacan owed its success in part to the misfortune of a competitor, Cuicuilco, located in the southern part of the Valley of Mexico. Known primarily for its ceremonial center dominated by a huge, circular pyramid, Cuicuilco was abandoned c. CE 100 when the nearby Xictli volcano erupted.

PYRAMIDS, TEMPLES, AND A SACRED CAVE

Teotihuacan stands out for its size, its planning, and its impact on the entire Valley of Mexico; many of the valley's substantial settlements and their inhabitants relocated to Teotihuacan, which swelled to between 100,000 to 200,000 people. Unlike other Mesoamerican cities, which had a cosmologically oriented core (see Monte Albán, page 305), all structures at Teotihuacan share the same urban grid and sacred orientation of just over 15° east of true north. The city ultimately extended over 8 sq miles (20 sq km) and was filled with densely packed apartments,

palaces, and public structures. Two major roads divided the city into quarters; the main north–south avenue of the city, the Avenue of the Dead, extends 2 miles (3 km) to the north and ends at the massive Pyramid of the Moon, positioned to reflect a sacred mountain in the distance. To the east of the Avenue of the Dead is one of the largest structures in the prehispanic New World—the Pyramid of the Sun. Rising nearly 250 ft (75 m), this massive structure— essentially a core of 1.6 million cu yd (1.2 million cu m) of sun-dried brick and rubble with a cut-stone facade—was placed over an already sacred cave. We know from the Aztecs that caves were seen as symbolic wombs for the ancestors; the location of this cave guided the placement of the Pyramid of the Sun and the overall orientation of Teotihuacan.

The Temple of Quetzalcoatl, probably built by the third century CE, is constructed in the typical *talud-tablero* style found throughout the city, with a combination of sloping *(talud)* and vertical *(tablero)* panels. Quetzalcoatl, the Feathered Serpent, appears both as serpent heads projecting from the staircase balustrade and as serpent bodies undulating across the facade, interspersed with Fire Serpent heads

QUETZALCOATL EMERGES

A head representing Quetzalcoatl, the Feathered Serpent, protrudes from the balustrade of the Temple of Quetzalcoatl. This important Mesoamerican deity was worshipped before Teotihuacan was founded and continued to be worshipped by the Aztecs.

and effigy seashells. The whole facade may represent opposing forces interacting at the moment of the earth's creation. While it had long been thought that Teotihuacan was a peaceful theocracy, excavations at this structure by Rubén Cabrera Castro, Saburo Sugiyama, and George Cowgill in the late 1980s and early 1990s uncovered burials of some 260 warriors and females who had been sacrificed as offerings, generally in groups based on numbers in the sacred 260-day calendar. As further evidence of Teotihuacan's long-overlooked martial aspect, many of the warriors wore necklaces made of human jaws.

In addition to the massive ceremonial architecture, large apartment complexes covered much of the city and housed the vast majority of its residents. Differences in room size, quality of construction, and distance from the Avenue of the Dead reflect the inhabitants' social status. Apartment compounds feature a series of courtyards, around which rooms—interspersed with temples—were densely packed.

Palaces are more spacious and better built. Many apartments and palaces feature brilliant polychrome murals, often consisting of repeated scenes and images, almost like ancient wallpaper.

A COSMOPOLITAN CITY

This cosmopolitan city encompassed neighborhoods of people from other regions of Mesoamerica, such as the "Oaxaca barrio," where people made and used pottery in the style of Monte Albán. While long-distance trade and exchange featured prominently in Teotihuacan's success, its impact outside the Valley of Mexico remains unclear. Figures that look distinctly Central Mexican appear on several Maya monuments, and Classic Mayan texts from cities such as Tikal refer to foreigners who may have been involved in the intrigues relating to a particular dynasty's or ruler's succession, but evidence of major influence in terms of material culture and architecture is limited to sites such as Kaminaljuyu in Guatemala. A "special relationship" existed between Teotihuacan and Monte Albán (see page 305).

TEMPLE SACRIFICES

This assemblage of skeletal fragments and jewelry was found with sacrificed individuals under the Temple of Quetzalcoatl. Some sacrificed warriors wore necklaces made of human, animal, and imitation teeth, further decorated with human—and other—jaws.

SACRED SITE

Shown below is the heart of Teotihuacan, as viewed from the northernmost point—the Pyramid of the Moon—south along the Avenue of the Dead. More than 2,000 apartment complexes lie at various distances from this main thoroughfare; the large building is the Pyramid of the Sun.

THE GREAT GODDESS OF TEPANTITLA

Probably the most famous example of Teotihuacan's murals was found in an apartment complex called Tepantitla. Several of a series of murals feature a figure often referred to as the Great Goddess, who, flanked by priests/attendants, presides over a magical landscape that may represent features in the surrounding valley. Most murals at Teotihuacan show supernatural figures. Humans, when shown, are in profile and generally lack specific features, and so cannot be linked to historic personages. Deities also feature heavily in the limited corpus of sculpture art from Teotihuacan, which features blocky images of deities who continued to be worshipped by later Central Mexican cultures such as the Aztecs.

Chalcatzingo, Mexico

MEXICO
Mexico City
Chalcatzingo

Established near an important highland trade corridor, Chalcatzingo, in eastern Morelos, is situated where three igneous intrusions tower above the surrounding Amatzinac Valley. A rich corpus of reliefs, dating from 700 BCE to 500 BCE, epitomize the changing local and external political relationships during this final period of Olmec influence in Mesoamerica.

BRINGER OF RAIN
Monument 1 from Chalcatzingo, often referred to as "El Rey," depicts an individual (who could be male or female) seen in profile and seated within a cave, from which vegetation sprouts and smoke billows. Raindrops fall from clouds onto the exterior of the symbolic cave.

Some 100 years after the decline of San Lorenzo c. 900 BCE, the site of La Venta, with its elaborate ceremonial district—defined by a huge, 110-ft (34-m) high earthen pyramid and a world of subterranean offerings (such as mosaic pavements buried shortly after they were created)—rose to prominence on the Gulf Coast, ushering in the second major phase of Olmec culture and interaction, centering on relationships with sites along vital trade and exchange corridors. The Olmec-style monumental art at such sites appears to be designed to cement alliances and trade routes rather than to foster religion and cosmology.

SACRED SPACES AND POLITICAL ALLIANCES

One site outside the Gulf Coast that displays Olmec art yet retains its local identity—with no evidence of having been an Olmec colony—is the highland center of Chalcatzingo. On the surfaces of what must have been sacred mountains, as well as in other public spaces throughout the site's civic-ceremonial core, Olmec-style bas-reliefs dating to after 700 BCE exhibit themes of rulership, alliances, and possible intimidation, suggesting that local leaders participated in exchange with the Olmecs but may not have accepted many associated ideas of religion and ideology. The most famous carving, Monument 1, shows an individual seated within a cave. Iconography incised on the cave suggests that it represents the mouth of the earth monster, who belches smoke and steam—a frequent motif in Mesoamerican rulership images, caves being considered portals to the underworld. The ruler is shown as the intermediary who interacts with sacred forces to bring rain and other events necessary to survival. The figure holds a ceremonial bar and wears a headdress exhibiting raindrops. Identical raindrops fall from clouds above the cave.

Imagery at other Chalcatzingo sites variously shows individuals brandishing clubs, and strange

felines attacking humans. A stela depicts a woman who may have cemented, through marriage, an alliance between Chalcatzingo and its allies. A unique monument is a local version of the famous "altars" (actually thrones) at San Lorenzo and La Venta, which comprises numerous stones depicting a mosaic face. David Grove, who has directed much of the research at Chalcatzingo, suggests that Olmec artists from the Gulf Coast may have created the art at the site, but that the Olmecs did not politically dominate Chalcatzingo.

As important sites rose throughout Mesoamerica before 500 BCE, Olmec influence declined in the region. The final major Olmec site, Tres Zapotes (c. 300 BCE–CE 200), seems to have had little impact outside its hinterland, but produced one of the earliest Mesoamerican monuments bearing a date; it converts to 32 BCE.

Monte Albán, Mexico

Located on a ridge in the middle of the Valley of Oaxaca, Monte Albán was established *c.* 500 BCE and became the seat of the powerful Zapotec civilization. Shortly after it was founded, Monte Albán became the center of an expansive state, the limits of which are still debated. The city was heavily occupied for more than a millennium, until CE 700, and may have had a population of up to 20,000 people.

CEREMONIAL CORE

The Main Plaza covers an area of 8 acres (3 ha). The Zapotecs modified the architecture to achieve bilateral symmetry on the east and west sides of the plaza. The southernmost building in the center of the plaza is Building J.

EXQUISITE FINDS

This gold mask of the god Xipe Totec was found in Tomb 7. Initially from the Classic period, this tomb was reused in the post-Classic, and is filled with exquisite objects made from gold, rock crystal, and other precious stones.

The Zapotecs, based in the Valley of Oaxaca, had a cosmology and religion devoted to ancestor worship. Deceased lords, venerated in elaborate tombs, became "Cloud People," and their living descendants drew legitimacy from this connection. Beginning in 1931, Mexican archaeologist Alfonso Caso established the general chronology and evolution of the city. While its origin is still debated, its location on a prominent hilltop in the valley center suggests that the city had a defensive function and may have been a response to perceived threats within and outside the Valley of Oaxaca.

In contrast to Teotihuacan (see page 302), only the ceremonial core of Monte Albán has a special orientation; most of the population lived on terraces along the hillsides. The core of the site features the Main Plaza, a flat expanse with a series of public structures on all sides and, in the center, the major temple (Building H) and Building J, an unusual arrowhead-shaped building. The main acropolis did not begin to take shape until after 200 BCE. Most elites lived in compounds to the north and built elaborate tombs that were reused for generations.

THE "DANZANTES" SCULPTURES

When Monte Albán was founded, a series of carved stones, often known as "Danzantes" ("dancers"), was erected in the southwest corner of the site core. These low-relief sculptures feature not dancers, as once thought, but a series of naked and mutilated men—most representing prisoners perhaps sacrificed, or enemy soldiers killed, in the founding of Monte Albán—along with Zapotec writing. Later sculptures also feature writing, but in different contexts. The sculptures on Building J slabs appear to show conquered or tribute-paying provinces, while later sculptures celebrate the lineage of named rulers. Visitors depicted as being from Teotihuacan appear on several sculptures after CE 300, suggesting a special relationship between the two cities. Marcus Winter has excavated a possible Teotihuacan barrio on the edge of the North Platform, finding pottery and a stone figure that suggest the presence of visitors from Central Mexico, who may have supervised the production of mica tiles used at Teotihuacan.

Zapotec artists created elaborate gray ceramic urns decorated with figures wearing deity masks, often included in burials. They also painted murals, but only, it seems, in tombs, unlike at Teotihuacan. While the reasons for this great city's collapse after CE 700 remain unclear, Zapotec culture continued to thrive in a series of smaller city-states, such as Zaachila and Mitla, while after its collapse Monte Albán continued to receive burials of both Zapotecs and Mixtecs. One of Caso's discoveries was a fabulous burial known as Tomb 7, packed with gold ornaments, turquoise-covered skulls, and vessels carved from rock crystal and alabaster.

The Maya

Deep within the tropical forests of southeast Mexico and northern Central America lie the ruins of one of America's most spectacular civilizations: the ancient Maya. For nearly 2,000 years, the Maya built hundreds of impressive cities, developed sophisticated systems of hieroglyphic writing and calendars, and created spectacular art and architecture.

The publication in the 1840s of *Incidents of Travel in Yucatan and Central America* by John Lloyd Stephens and Frederick Catherwood marked the beginning of the West's long fascination with the ancient Maya civilization. Images of ruined cities and broken sculptures reclaimed by the jungle captured the imagination of their contemporaries and launched an era of exploration during which many ancient sites were discovered. For more than a century, the Maya have been the subject of intensive archaeological and epigraphic research.

ORIGINS OF MAYA CIVILIZATION

The Maya region encompasses southeast Mexico (the states of Yucatán, Quintana Roo, Campeche, Chiapas, and parts of Tabasco), Guatemala, and Belize, and the western parts of Honduras and El Salvador. The coastal and highland areas were the first to be colonized by the people called the Maya, from *c.* 2000 BCE. By *c.* 1000 BCE, sedentary populations were established in the interior lowlands, and by *c.* 500 BCE the population of the central lowlands had increased rapidly and had developed more complex social and political systems. A few early villages, like Nakbé and El Mirador in northern Guatemala, had grown in size and regional influence, becoming the first civic-ceremonial centers.

By CE 250, a new social order had emerged—one centered on divine kingship. Maya rulers claimed ties to the supernatural and acted as intermediaries between the earthly and the supernatural domains. Believing themselves to be ordained to maintain the natural and social order, including agricultural fertility and the rhythmic cycles of time (as measured by solar, lunar, sacred, and other calendars), rulers performed rituals of self-sacrifice, including bloodletting—blood was the ultimate sacred offering to the gods—and presided over public ceremonies. Commoners supported the lavish lifestyle of kings and nobles through tribute obligations.

Between CE 100 and 200, for unknown reasons, many of the spectacular centers that had flourished during the Late pre-Classic, such as El Mirador, suddenly declined. Other sites survived and thrived. This is a common pattern in the sequence of Maya civilization. El Mirador's collapse left a power vacuum that led to the emergence of two of the most powerful Classic Maya states: Tikal and Calakmul.

THE CLASSIC PERIOD AND BEYOND

During the Classic Period (CE 250–800), hundreds of lowland Maya ceremonial centers flourished, many becoming the capitals of powerful kingdoms ruled by divine kings. Despite the vast territory the Maya occupied—an area of 125,000 sq miles

TIMELINE OF LOWLAND MAYA HISTORY

Pre-Classic Period	2000 BCE–CE 250
c. 2000 BCE	Earliest lowland Maya villages along east coast
c. 1000 BCE	Colonization of interior lowlands
c. 600 BCE	Nakbé is earliest site with monumental construction
400 BCE–CE 100	El Mirador dominates central lowlands
c. 100 BCE	Oldest mural paintings at San Bartolo, Guatemala
c. CE 90	Tikal's ruling dynasty is established with founder Yax Ehb' Xook
c. CE 150	El Mirador is abandoned
Early Classic Period	CE 250–600
CE 292	Earliest Long Count date in lowlands, recorded in Tikal's Stela 29
CE 378	Under Teotihuacan's influence, Tikal's dominance begins
CE 426	Copán's ruling dynasty established with founder K'inich Yax K'uk Mo'
CE 431	Palenque's ruling dynasty established with founder K'uk Balam I
CE 562	Defeat of Tikal by Caracol under the auspices of Calakmul; Calakmul dominates central lowlands until *c.* CE 695
Late Classic Period	CE 600–800
CE 615	Pakal the Great (K'inich Janaab' Pakal I) begins his rule at Palenque
CE 682	Ruler Hasaw Chan K'awil I begins revitalization of Tikal
CE 695	Tikal defeats Calakmul
CE 738	Quirigua defeats Copán; Copán ruler is captured and sacrificed
Terminal Classic	CE 800–900/1100
CE 800–900	Collapse of Classic polities in central and southern lowlands
CE 909	Last inscription with a Long Count date in the Maya area, recorded at Toniná
CE 800–1000	Many new polities arise in Puuc area of northern lowlands (western Yucatán)
Post-Classic	CE 900/1100–1525
1100	Fall of Chichén Itzá
c. 1200	Mayapán is founded; dominates northern lowlands
c. 1200	Tulum is founded
c. 1450	Fall of Mayapán
1502–1525	First Spanish contact with the Maya

The region over which the ancient Maya ruled encompassed southeast Mexico, Guatemala, and Belize, and the western parts of Honduras and El Salvador.

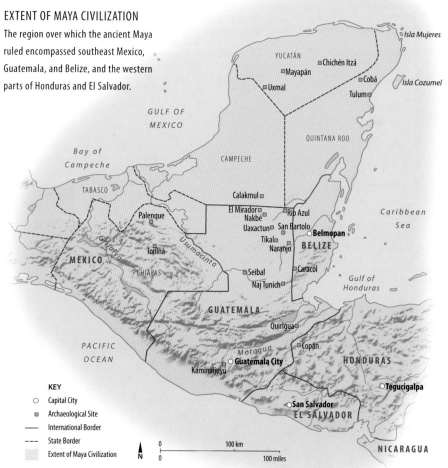

JOURNEY FROM THE UNDERWORLD
This detail from a 2,000-year-old mural in San Bartolo, Guatemala, depicts the corn god's journey from the underworld to Earth. This painting is the oldest known Maya mural that has survived intact.

(324,000 sq km)—these polities were never unified under a single government, ruler, or emperor. Rather, the Classic Maya political landscape comprised kingdoms with varying degrees of autonomy that competed for alliances, influence, and resources.

During this period, Maya rulers went to great lengths to document their lives and the fortunes of their kingdoms. Historical and mythological events were recorded in hieroglyphic texts inscribed on various media: free-standing monuments (stelae), architectural embellishments, pottery, and artifacts made of jade, wood, and bone.

In the Maya lowlands, the Late Classic was in general a period of population growth and prosperity, but it was also marked by conflict, with increasing competition between elites. Many cities and towns were established, and most achieved their maximum size. The most outstanding works of Maya art were produced in this period. Within this environment, struggles over land, water, food, and other limited resources accelerated. Over time, the landscape underwent profound changes. In the central and southern Maya lowlands, a period of radical social transformation ensued. Fragile sociopolitical systems, inter-polity competition and warfare, and environmental degradation are all thought to have played a role. Many aspects of Classic-period elite culture came to an end, and construction was halted at most lowland Classic Maya centers. These centers were abandoned between CE 800 and 900.

RECLAIMED BY THE JUNGLE
It is easy to imagine the astonishment of early explorers who stumbled upon an ancient city covered by jungle—here, the ancient Maya city of Tikal, in Guatemala. In the foreground is the Northern Acropolis, as seen from Temple I.

Tikal, Guatemala

Tikal was the capital of one of the largest and most prominent Classic Maya kingdoms. Through conquest, alliances, and trade networks, Tikal successfully spread its influence throughout the Maya lowlands. At the height of its power, Tikal's territory covered 950 sq miles (2,500 sq km), with an estimated population of 360,000.

Tikal is located in northern Guatemala's Department of El Petén, near the modern-day town of Flores. The ruins of this extraordinary city were first reported in 1848 by members of a Guatemalan expedition led by Modesto Mendez and Ambrosio Tut. Not long after news of its existence spread to the outside world, a series of scholars visited Tikal to photograph and record the site's spectacular art, hieroglyphic inscriptions, and monumental architecture.

In 1955, the University Museum at the University of Pennsylvania initiated the Tikal Project, the first full-scale, long-term archaeological investigation at the site. For the next 15 years the Tikal Project employed more than 100 archaeologists and other specialists to survey and map Tikal's urban core and surrounding settlement and to excavate and restore buildings associated with all levels of society, from the humblest household to the site's most monumental structures. Among the latter are Temples I and II, which delineate the Great Plaza; the North Acropolis, a royal necropolis composed of more than 100 superimposed temples; and the Central Acropolis, one of the most impressive palace complexes ever investigated in the Maya area. Since 1979, the Guatemalan government has sponsored excavations and preservation efforts at Tikal.

THE RISE OF TIKAL

Tikal originated as a small farming village c. 600 BCE. By the Late pre-Classic period, a significant ceremonial precinct had been constructed near the western edge of Tikal. Inscriptions from a later period listing what appears to be a complete dynasty suggest that a royal dynasty was well established in Tikal by the first century CE. By the beginning of the Early Classic, Tikal began to expand its regional influence, taking advantage of the political and economic vacuum created by the decline of El Mirador. Through conquests, Tikal incorporated other major centers into its domain, including Uaxactun, Naranjo, and Rio Azul. Tikal's royal elite established political alliances with noble families in other cities by engaging in strategic marriages. Tikal also controlled

TEMPLE OF THE GIANT JAGUAR

Temple I, also known as the Temple of the Giant Jaguar, consists of a stepped pyramid rising some 144 ft (44 m) surmounted by a temple. It is the mortuary shrine of the ruler Hasaw Chan K'awil, who was inaugurated in CE 682.

ANCIENT MAYA HIEROGLYPHIC INSCRIPTIONS

The Maya developed one of the most sophisticated writing systems in the Americas. During the Classic period, Maya rulers commissioned monuments commemorating their lives and important events in the histories of their kingdoms. By one recent estimate, there are at least 15,000 such inscriptions, most of them dating to the Late Classic period (CE 600–800). Maya hieroglyphs were carved in stone or wood; modeled on stucco on building facades, stairways, and roofs; and painted on the walls of rooms, tombs, and caves. Texts were often combined with artistic images, and many included detailed calendrical notations. Hieroglyphic narratives encompass a variety of themes: important battles or rituals; the courtly life of nobles; major events in the life of a ruler, such as birth, marriage, ascension to the throne, and death; and references to royal or mythical ancestors.

This detail is from a stela carved with hieroglyphs and a calendar found at the Palace of Palenque, Mexico. The stela bears a date equating to CE 644.

long-distance trade networks, the source of exotic and prestigious goods as well as new ideas and cultural innovations. During the Early Classic, various cultural practices that began at Tikal started to spread throughout the Maya area, including the making of beautiful polychrome ceramics, architectural innovations, and the practice of erecting intricately carved, commemorative stelae.

Archaeological evidence indicates that from CE 378 until *c.* CE 550 Tikal was influenced by the great Central Mexican metropolis of Teotihuacan. Although the nature of this influence remains unclear, various lines of evidence suggest that Tikal's initial military expansion took place with assistance from Teotihuacan.

CHALLENGES TO TIKAL'S SUPREMACY

As Tikal's regional power and influence increased, a number of strong rival polities emerged. By the middle of the sixth century CE, Tikal's economic prosperity and political domination were at an end. Epigraphic and archaeological evidence suggests that this was due to a military defeat by the kingdom of Caracol, far to the east in present-day Belize, in CE 562. Caracol had been assisted or sponsored by an even more powerful polity centered in the city of Calakmul, to the north in present-day Campeche, Mexico.

Following this defeat, Tikal's rulers did not erect inscribed monuments or sponsor major construction projects for nearly a century. Tikal's territory also contracted as subordinate settlements began to break away. Many Early Classic monuments at Tikal and throughout the surrounding El Petén region were partially destroyed or desecrated.

These events triggered a major geopolitical reorganization in the Maya lowlands. Other polities emerged and competed for regional dominance.

Tikal did recover, however. Although it never regained its supreme position in the Maya lowlands, the city underwent a spectacular Late Classic renaissance. This began in CE 682 with the inauguration of a new king, Hasaw Chan K'awil, who initiated an impressive building program. The buildings erected in this period include Temple I (his mortuary shrine), Temple II, and Temple 33 in the North Acropolis (his father's mortuary shrine).

The Central Acropolis palace complex, where he resided, was expanded. Together these structures comprise the Great Plaza, which became the city's focal point during the Late Classic. Tikal's renaissance was aided by Hasaw's military conquests, particularly the defeat of Calakmul in CE 695.

Hasaw's successors continued to revitalize the city. Nevertheless, Tikal began a steady decline around CE 800. Inscriptions at the site end abruptly in the year CE 869, after which time the city and surrounding region were abandoned.

ANCIENT ALTAR

The altar and stela (above left) date from the Late Classic period (CE 600–800). Identified as altar 10 and stela 22, they are located in Tikal's Q double pyramid. Only a small proportion of Tikal's structures have been excavated; they are numbered sequentially.

TLALOC THE RAIN GOD

The lid of this painted vessel from the Early Classic period (CE 250–600) at Tikal bears an image of Tlaloc the rain god, who was particularly important for the growing of maize. He is commonly depicted as a blue being with goggle eyes and fangs.

Copán, Honduras

Copán is one of the best-known Maya sites, having been the focus of long-term archaeological and epigraphic research. It was the capital of a large polity that dominated the southeastern Maya region during the Classic period. Copán is notable for the abundance and quality of its monuments, its hieroglyphic inscriptions, and its architectural sculpture.

COPÁN'S HIEROGLYPHIC STAIRWAY

The Hieroglyphic Stairway, which includes Copán's most spectacular monuments, adorns the east side of Structure 10L-26, which is adjacent to the Ball Court. The stairway comprises 62 steps, each 10 m (33 ft) wide. A large figure sits at the midpoint of every twelfth step, each figure apparently representing a major ruler in Copán's dynasty. More than 2,200 sculpted glyphs appear on the faces of the steps. The longest of all Maya hieroglyphic texts, it provides an unprecedented record of Copán's dynastic history. Commissioned by Copán's fifteenth ruler, Smoke Shell, and dedicated in CE 756, it was meant to revitalize the city after a devastating defeat by the neighboring city of Quirigua.

Archaeologists measure the ruin of the Hieroglyphic Stairway, the longest Maya text known.

Copán is located in the middle of the Copán Valley, in western Honduras, just across the border from Guatemala. Although the ruins of Copán had been known since the sixteenth century, it was the description of the site published in the 1840s by John Lloyd Stephens and his traveling companion Frederick Catherwood that brought Copán to the attention of the outside world. By 1935, the Carnegie Institution of Washington had begun a large-scale program of excavating and restoring major buildings in the Principal Group at Copán that lasted for over a decade. Since 1975, there have been intensive excavations at the site core, as well as numerous investigations of nearby settlements and the surrounding environment.

ANATOMY OF A CLASSIC MAYA CITY

Copán's Principal Group, the core of the Classic-period capital, extends over 44 acres (18 ha). The Ball Court, the Court of the Hieroglyphic Stairway, and the Great Plaza—the setting of most of Copán's magnificent carved monuments—are located in the low-lying northern half. The elevated southern half includes the Acropolis, a massive royal complex built around two enclosed plazas known as the East and West Courts. Surrounding the Principal Group are several important elite residential zones, including the Cemetery Group, the more elaborate Sepulturas Group, and the North Group.

Deep tunneling within the Acropolis has revealed a sequence of construction spanning more than 500 years. Excavations have revealed small earth and cobble structures dating to the initial occupation of the site between the first and second centuries CE; adobe and masonry platforms dating to the founding of Copán's dynasty at the beginning of the fifth century CE; a series of lavishly decorated shrines with brightly painted stucco facades built during the sixth century CE; and the monumental structures visible today—including Structure 10L-16, the highest point on the Acropolis—built during the last two centuries of the Late Classic period.

The Copán Valley is one of the most fertile and resource-rich valleys in Central America. The Maya quarried nearby outcrops of volcanic tuff to obtain stone for building facades and sculptures at the site.

The high quality of this stone is one reason why Copán's sculptures are in a remarkably good state of preservation. Copán was also strategically situated in respect to trade networks, which gave it access to important raw materials such as jade and obsidian, and was at the intersection of two distinct culture areas: the southeast frontier of the Maya area and the Intermediate Area of Central America.

THE HISTORY OF COPÁN

Before the arrival of the Maya, the Copán Valley had been settled for more than 2,000 years. Excavations at Copán have revealed that the site was occupied for at least 300 years before Copán's dynasty was founded in CE 426. Various lines of evidence suggest that the kingdom of Tikal played a role in this. Analyses of the skeletal remains of the dynastic founder K'inich Yax K'uk Mo', whose tomb was located deep within the Acropolis, indicate that he may have come from the Tikal region. Inscriptions on later monuments suggest that the dynasty K'inich Yax K'uk Mo' founded comprised 16 kings, who between them ruled Copán for nearly 400 years. Two spectacular monuments record Copán's dynastic history: the Hieroglyphic Stairway of Structure 10L-26, dedicated by the fifteenth ruler in CE 756, and Altar Q, a square monument with beautifully carved portraits of all 16 Copán kings on its four sides, dedicated by the sixteenth ruler in CE 775.

Relatively little is known about Copán in the Early Classic period, as most of the remains from this time lie deeply buried beneath constructions of the Late Classic period. By the beginning of the Late

Classic, Copán's kingdom had reached its zenith under the long and prosperous reign of Smoke Imix, the twelfth ruler (CE 628–695). His successor, 18 Rabbit, continued the construction of the Copán Acropolis and renovated the Great Plaza, which became the setting for monuments he commissioned.

During the reign of 18 Rabbit, Copán suffered a disastrous defeat. With the aid of the powerful Calakmul kingdom, the previously subordinate city of Quirigua waged a successful war against Copán. 18 Rabbit was captured and sacrificed, and Copán's power was severely weakened. Following the defeat, Copán's elites adopted a new political strategy. They sponsored the construction of a *popol na* ("mat house," or council house), a building in which lineage leaders or representatives of the polity's major subdivisions gathered to discuss the kingdom's affairs. This power-sharing strategy represented a major break from the earlier political tradition under which Copán's divine ruler enjoyed absolute power.

By the time the fifteenth ruler, Smoke Shell (K'ak' Yipyaj Chan K'awiil), ascended to the throne, in CE 749, a short-lived recovery was underway. In an attempt to restore the kingdom's prestige, Smoke Shell commissioned the Hieroglyphic Stairway. His successor, Yax Pasaj Chan Yoaat, commissioned the construction of many buildings and monuments, including Altar Q. The last dated monument at Copán is Altar L, which is dated CE 822. It was never finished. Copán was abandoned and its valley depopulated by the end of the ninth century CE.

BRUTAL BALL GAME

Copán's Ball Court is situated within the Great Plaza. The Mesoamerican ball game was more important ceremonially than as a sport. It was played with a large, solid rubber ball. The losing team or team's captain was sacrificed.

FIRST TO LAST

The square monument known as Altar Q was dedicated in CE 775 by the sixteenth ruler, Yax Pasaj Chan Yoaat. Its four sides bear beautifully carved portraits of all 16 of Copán's kings. The West Side, shown here, depicts the first two and the last two kings of Copán.

Palenque, Mexico

MEXICO

Mexico City ○
Palenque ▫

Located among the vivid green rolling hills that mark the northern edge of the Chiapas highlands of Mexico, Palenque is one of the most beautiful of the Classic Maya cities. Palenque was the capital of the kingdom of B'aakal (Bone), which during the Late Classic became a major power in the western Maya lowlands.

Palenque has been known since the eighteenth century, and since then a succession of explorers has visited the site to document its remarkable art and architecture. One of the earliest reports, published in 1822, records the findings of Antonio del Rio, a Spanish artillery captain who explored the site in 1787. After John Lloyd Stephens and Frederick Catherwood visited the site in the mid-nineteenth century, Palenque became the most studied of Maya cities—with investigations carried out by William Dupaix, Frédéric Waldeck, Désiré Charnay, and Alfred Maudslay, the last of whom created an invaluable photographic record of the site.

Early in the twentieth century, the Mexican government began an ongoing program of investigation, conservation, and restoration at Palenque. Since the 1990s, a number of structures at the site have been excavated, and a survey and mapping program has further documented the extent and density of ancient settlement within the city.

ART AND INSCRIPTIONS

Palenque's uniquely rich historical records led to major breakthroughs in the decipherment of ancient Maya hieroglyphic inscriptions during the 1970s. Pioneering epigraphic studies by Floyd Lounsbury, David Kelley, Linda Schele, Merle Green Robertson, and Peter Mathews, which focused on texts from Palenque, yielded a deeper understanding of Maya cosmology and dynastic history. Palenque's rulers left an abundant corpus of Late Classic inscriptions—accompanied by iconography and richly symbolic artistic portraits of historic personages—that reveal how myth and history were often woven together for political purposes. Many of Palenque's texts explicitly refer to creation mythology as well as to details of dynastic succession, providing insights into the supernatural basis of Maya royal authority. Unlike contemporary Classic period rulers at other sites, who memorialized themselves on free-standing monuments (stelae), Palenque's rulers chose to be portrayed on panels carved in low relief or modeled in plaster and painted with bright colors. These panels were placed on the walls of buildings, some on interior walls, which has contributed to their remarkable state of preservation.

PALENQUE'S GREAT KINGS AND QUEENS

Palenque's dynasty was founded in CE 431. In contrast to most Classic-period dynasties, which leave no record of female rulers, the Palenque dynasty included at least one queen who reigned in her own right, Lady Yohl Ik. She remained in power for nearly 20 years, from CE 583 to CE 604, and possessed all the royal titles of her male counterparts. Another female ruler, Lady Sak K'uk, may have acted as regent for her son

PAKAL THE GREAT'S MAGNIFICENT TOMB

In the early 1950s, archaeologist Alberto Ruz Lhuillier discovered Pakal the Great's spectacular tomb deep within the Temple of the Inscriptions. It took nearly three years for him and his team to clear rubble from the stairway descending to the tomb. Then, finally, they reached the large burial chamber, its walls decorated with nine figures modeled in stucco representing the nine lords of the Maya underworld.

Pakal's skeleton lay within a massive limestone sarcophagus, the sides of which were carved with portraits of Pakal's royal ancestors. Pakal's remains were covered with lavish offerings, including jade beads and a beautiful jade mosaic mask. The magnificent low-relief carving on the sarcophagus lid—Pakal emerging from the jaws of the underworld, the World Tree sprouting behind him—is a masterpiece of Classic Maya art.

This jade mosaic mask, now housed at Mexico's National Museum of Anthropology, was one of the lavish offerings that accompanied Pakal to the Maya underworld.

Janaab' Pakal I until he was old enough to take over the throne. He was inaugurated at the age of twelve.

Janaab' Pakal I—also known simply as Pakal—became Palenque's greatest ruler. During his reign of 67 years, from CE 615 until his death in CE 683, Palenque emerged as a major regional power in the western Maya lowlands. Pakal commissioned the construction of many buildings at Palenque, including portions of the famous Palace. The Palace comprises a series of long galleries arranged around several interior courtyards, all built on a 33-ft (10-m) high platform that covered nearly 2.5 acres (1 ha). Most of the buildings were decorated with beautiful carved stone panels and stucco reliefs. Its four-story tower, which contains an inner staircase, is an architectural innovation unique to Palenque. The Palace was the residence of several generations of Palenque's ruling families, who repeatedly remodeled and expanded the complex.

The most outstanding building constructed during Pakal's reign was the Temple of the Inscriptions, a terraced platform rising some 80 ft (25 m) that supported a temple with five doorways. This was Pakal's mortuary shrine. Lengthy inscriptions carved on wall panels recorded the dynastic history of

Palenque up until the ascension to the throne of Pakal's son, Kan Balam II.

By c. CE 750, Palenque's power had waned. The last record of a Palenque king comes from a pottery vessel found at the site that dates his inauguration to CE 799. Thereafter, Palenque's inscriptions fall silent.

SUPERNATURAL ENCOUNTER
Glyphs and stucco tablets in the temples and palaces at Palenque immortalize the ancestry and accomplishments of its rulers. This detail is from a relief carving on the throne in Temple XXI showing Pakal's heir, Kan Balam II, before a supernatural being.

MONUMENTS FOR KINGS
The beautiful city of Palenque is a Classic Maya city. Its monuments include (clockwise from top center) the Temple of the Inscriptions (the mortuary shrine of Pakal the Great); the Palace, with its four-story tower; the Ball Court; the Temple of the Sun; and the Temple of the Foliated Cross.

Naj Tunich Cave, Guatemala

Naj Tunich is the most extensive cave system known to have been used by the ancient Maya for ritual purposes. The cave consists of an intricate system of passages some 2 miles (3.2 km) in length and contains the largest corpus of Maya cave art and hieroglyphic inscriptions ever found. Naj Tunich was used continuously from the Late pre-Classic period through to the Late Classic.

Naj Tunich means "stone house" in the Mopan Maya language. The cave is located in Guatemala, in the foothills of the Maya mountains. It was discovered in 1980 by Bernabe Pop. In 1981, James Brady and Andrea Stone and their colleagues initiated formal archaeological investigations within the cave. Despite concerted efforts to protect it, Naj Tunich was vandalized in 1989, when nearly two-thirds of its most significant paintings and inscriptions were destroyed.

ENTRANCE TO THE WATERY UNDERWORLD

Epigraphic and archaeological evidence indicates that Naj Tunich was a major pilgrimage site. For the Maya, caves were sacred spaces, entrances to the watery underworld—a realm inhabited by powerful supernatural beings, particularly those responsible for rain and fertility. Water from caves was considered to be the purest, and the most fitting for use in rituals.

The entrance to Naj Tunich leads into an enormous chamber. Along the eastern side of this chamber, the Maya modified a natural rise to create a two-tiered structure known as the Balcony, which has yielded the greatest concentration of artifacts anywhere in the cave, as well as seven masonry structures interpreted as tombs. Artifacts include pottery, obsidian blades, shell pendants, and carved jade objects, and there are also remains of burials, including possible evidence of child sacrifice. The chamber could have accommodated a large audience and probably served as a site for public ceremonies.

Beginning at the entrance chamber, the Main Passage passes through a flowstone pool fed by a spring and continues northward for some 110 yards (300 m) before branching off to the west. On the walls of the Western Passage is found the largest concentration of paintings and inscriptions in the cave. The North Passage (an extension of the Main Passage) leads into a maze of tunnels, where remains of ceremonial offerings have been found, as well as altars and drawings.

More than 90 individual drawings and petroglyphs, including more than 40 texts, have been documented on the cave's surfaces. The drawings are diverse in subject, and include scenes of bloodletting and other rituals, musicians, ball players, and a rare scene of sexual intercourse. Both the drawings and the hieroglyphic texts are rendered in a beautiful cursive style reminiscent of that found in the few surviving pre-Columbian Maya books.

Although inscribed dates indicate that the cave's texts and drawings were created primarily during the Late Classic, other evidence suggests that the cave was continuously in use since the Late pre-Classic.

Chichén Itzá, Mexico

Chichén Itzá was one of the largest and most powerful of the ancient Maya cities, the capital of a kingdom that dominated the northern lowlands of Yucatán during the Terminal Classic period. In its heyday, Chichén Itzá's political, commercial, and religious influence extended well beyond the Maya area.

JEWELED JAGUAR

This jaguar throne, made from painted limestone and inlaid with flint and jade, was found inside El Castillo. The jaguar was an important symbol for the Maya, as for other Mesoamerican cultures.

FEATHERED SERPENT

Seen here from the Temple of the Warriors, El Castillo—also known as the Pyramid of K'uk'ulkan (the Feathered Serpent)—is Chichén Itzá's largest temple. Elevated on a massive terraced platform, it has a stairway on each of its four sides.

At its peak, Chichén Itzá extended over an area of at least 2 sq miles (5 sq km). The southern part of the site, known as Old Chichén, includes a concentration of buildings constructed with the mosaic-decorated facades characteristic of the Puuc architectural style of western Yucatán. The buildings in the northern part of the site are grouped on a low platform and are dominated by the impressive structure named El Castillo—the site's largest temple, elevated on a massive platform with nine terraces and a stairway on each of its four sides. To the north of the Castillo are two small platforms and a *tzompantli*—a "skull rack" in Nahuatl—used to display trophy heads from sacrifice and warfare. To the west of El Castillo is the Great Ball Court, the largest in Mesoamerica, and to the east lie the Temple of the Warriors and the Court of the Thousand Columns. The colonnaded buildings of the latter were originally topped by beam-and-mortar roofs and may have served as council halls.

A small causeway extending northward from El Castillo leads to the Sacred Cenote, a large natural sinkhole. Until the Spanish conquest, people made pilgrimages to the Sacred Cenote from all parts of the Maya area and beyond. When the cenote was dredged, jadeite, gold, pottery, human remains, and heirlooms from periods before Chichén's peak were discovered.

THE RISE OF CHICHÉN ITZÁ

Chichén Itzá was founded *c.* CE 800. It grew and expanded rapidly, and within a century of its founding had brought most of the northern Maya lowlands under its hegemony. At the height of its power, Chichén Itzá probably controlled the largest and most populous state in Maya history.

Chichén Itzá's success in maintaining such a vast domain was probably due to its economic prosperity, its novel political system, and a new religious ideology. Chichén Itzá assumed control of the production and trade of key commodities like salt, cotton, and cacao. At the time of the Spanish conquest, political authority was based on a relatively decentralized arrangement known as *multepal* (shared rule). *Multepal* involved a supreme council made up of the leaders of the most prominent lineages, whose members helped to administer the territorial subdivisions within the polity. In addition, a new religion based on the pan-Mesoamerican cult of the Feathered Serpent (known as K'uk'ulkan to the Maya and as Quetzalcoatl in Central Mexico) facilitated commerce and communication throughout Mesoamerica. Chichén Itzá's apogee as the political and commercial capital of Yucatán ended *c.* 1050. Major construction ceased, and by 1100 the city had lost the majority of its population.

Tulum, Mexico

Situated on striking bluffs overlooking the Caribbean on the northeast coast of Yucatán, Tulum was an important post-Classic port and trading center. The site, which is protected by a massive wall on three of its sides, contains some of the best-preserved Late post-Classic architectural remains and the finest examples of mural painting in the region.

Tulum was occupied from *c.* 1200 until probably the time of Spanish contact. It appears to have been sighted by an expedition led by Juan de Grijalva in 1518, during one of the earliest Spanish reconnaissance voyages along the Yucatán peninsula. In the mid-nineteenth century, American adventurer-diplomat John Lloyd Stephens visited the site, and his traveling companion Frederick Catherwood produced the first illustrations of some of its architecture. It was not until 1924, however, that Samuel Lothrop initiated more systematic archaeological investigations at Tulum, generating the first map of the site and recording details of its architecture. William Sanders also examined Tulum as part of a study of regional settlement patterns along the eastern Yucatán coast, publishing his findings in 1960. In the early 1970s, Arthur Miller carried out archaeological and art historical investigations, focusing on the famous mural paintings at Tulum and neighboring coastal sites. In recent decades, a number of Mexican-led projects have continued investigations at Tulum, while taking steps to preserve and manage the site.

TULUM AND THE COASTAL TRADE NETWORK

During the post-Classic period (1100–1525), Maya populations throughout most of the northern lowlands of Yucatán reached their maximum size. New settlements were established along the Caribbean coast from Quintana Roo to northern Belize, and also on islands off the mainland, such as Cozumel Island and Isla Mujeres. This demographic expansion was mostly contemporaneous with the rise of Mayapán, the dominant political capital in northern Yucatán from *c.* 1200 to 1450, although it continued until the Spanish conquest.

The unprecedented prosperity of the east coast of Yucatán during the post-Classic was due primarily to the expansion of coastal commerce. The eastern part of Yucatán was a major center for the production of honey, beeswax, and ceramics—goods that were transported via sea routes that circled the peninsula. The various ports that were established along the coast served as important storage, transportation, and distribution nodes in this thriving network.

Tulum was one such node in the coastal trade network. It was strategically located on a rocky outcrop adjacent to the sea, directly across from a break in the barrier reef that runs along the east coast of Yucatán. Archaeological evidence indicates that Tulum was occupied primarily during the Late post-Classic, beginning *c.* 1200. It may have been founded as a port and trading center associated with the capital of Mayapán.

COASTAL COMMERCE

During the post-Classic, honey, beeswax, and ceramics produced on the prosperous east coast of Yucatán were transported via sea routes that circled the peninsula. Strategically located on a rocky outcrop on the northeast coast, Tulum was a vital node in this thriving coastal trade network.

ARCHITECTURE AND MURAL ART

The civic-ceremonial precinct at Tulum covers some 15 acres (a little over 6 ha). This area is bounded on the north, west, and south sides by a massive masonry wall more than half a mile (1 km) long, 20 ft (6 m) thick, and 10–16 ft (3–5 m) high, with a walkway and parapets along its length. The wall has five narrow entryways and two small structures at its corners, interpreted as watchtowers. The east side is naturally protected by the 40-ft (12-m) high cliffs that rise up from the sea. A narrow gap in the cliff forms a small inlet that was probably used as a landing beach for Maya trading canoes.

Within Tulum's defensive wall lies the civic-ceremonial core of the site: a group of structures that include colonnaded palaces with beam-and-mortar roofs and temple-shrines elevated on masonry platforms. The most imposing structure at Tulum is the Castillo (Structure 1), consisting of a platform 25 ft (7.5 m) in height that supports a small, two-room temple accessible on its western side. The temple's doorway is supported by Feathered Serpent columns reminiscent of columns found at Chichén Itzá. The Castillo platform was built over and incorporated an earlier palace. To the north of the Castillo is Structure 5, also known as the Temple of the Diving God. On the interior of its east wall are the remains of a magnificent mural executed in the Mixteca–Puebla style that originated in highland Mexico but is also found at Mayapán and other coastal sites. Such artwork testifies to a widespread sharing of ideas throughout Mesoamerica during the post-Classic period. The Temple of the Frescoes (Structure 16) has a similar mural on the inner wall of its lower gallery, while its exterior facade is decorated with stucco reliefs, including depictions of the so-called "diving god"—identified as Xux Ek, a deity associated with the planet Venus.

BIRDS ON THE WING

The murals found in various buildings at Tulum—this one, depicting birds, is on the wall of an elite house—are exceptionally fine, and include examples of the Mixteca–Puebla style that originated in highland Mexico.

COAST GUARD

Tulum was bounded on three sides by a massive masonry wall with a walkway and parapets along its length. Two small structures at its corners, one of which is seen here, were most likely watchtowers. The town's east side is naturally protected by high cliffs.

ORIGINS OF COASTAL TRADE DURING THE POST-CLASSIC

Many of the socioeconomic and political changes that characterized the post-Classic period resulted from a shift in the nature of commerce that was initiated by Chontal Maya groups from the Tabasco coast, who became very successful coastal traders. As Classic Maya polities in the central and southern lowlands declined in the ninth century CE, so too did the long-established overland trade routes and the demand for prestige goods that the lavish lifestyle of the Maya elite had once sustained. Merchants took control of critical resources, such as salt and honey, and also traded in a range of utilitarian goods that were produced in bulk and were more efficiently transported by large, ocean-going canoes. Ports and trading colonies were established along a vibrant coastal trade route that extended from the Tabasco region on the Gulf of Mexico, around the Yucatán Peninsula, to the Gulf of Honduras—thereby linking most of Mesoamerica.

The Aztecs

Aztec civilization was one of the most extraordinary in recorded history. The pattern of urban life was in many ways advanced: the Aztecs had impressive roads, canals, aqueducts, and temples, along with extensive commerce and a middle class of professional traders supplying towns with goods and food. The nobility lived in fine houses and had a taste for art and poetry.

But no people were more warlike, and Aztec aggression against adjacent states made them numerous bitter enemies. Deeply religious, the Aztecs appeased their many gods by practicing human sacrifice on an almost unimaginable scale. Because the internal supply of sacrificial victims could not keep pace with demand, they terrorized their neighbors and seized men, women, and children. The hostility these raids provoked contributed to their downfall in 1521.

Geographically, the Aztec Empire stretched from the Pacific Ocean to the Gulf of Mexico— from the land of the Zapotecs in the south to coastal Veracruz and Tabasco in the north. Within this sizable area lived a number of conquered peoples, including the Mixtecs, Totonacs, and Tlaxcalans. Both the northern and southern coastlines had hot tropical lowlands that were ideal for habitation. But it was above 6,560 ft (2,000 m), in the high cool Central Valley of Mexico, that the Aztecs chose to build their breathtaking capital city, Tenochtitlan.

AZTEC CALENDAR STONE

Now the centerpiece of Mexico's National Museum of Anthropology, the huge Calendar Stone (or Sun Stone) measures 12 ft (3.5 m) across and weighs 26.5 tons (24 tonnes). There are indications that the basalt surface was originally painted.

THE RISE OF AZTEC CIVILIZATION

People had been living in the Central Valley of Mexico for a long time: archaeology tells us that maize cultivation began 9,000 years ago. The true rise of a distinctive civilization, however, occurred only within the last 2,000 years. Between CE 150 and 650 the metropolis of Teotihuacan grew to 150,000 inhabitants, making it one of the largest cities in the world before it was destroyed by fire. Later, the Toltec city of Tula was an important urban center between CE 950 and 1150. Next, seven northern tribes migrated southward from a semi-mythical place called Aztlan (the origin of the name Aztec), and after the arrival of a group of people called the Mexica in CE 1250, a number of unstable and continuously warring Aztec city-states arose. All shared a common culture. All spoke Nahuatl. All embraced the cult of the feathered serpent, the god Quetzalcoatl, and built tall step pyramids where human sacrifice took place.

THE IMPERIAL SYSTEM

In 1428, three previously warring city-states— Tenochtitlan, Texcoco, and Tlacopan—buried their differences and formed the Triple Alliance. This became the strong and stable heart of the Aztec Empire, and the first goal of the Alliance was to subordinate all the other city-states in the Central Valley. Tributary provinces were defined and demarcated, and the tribute itself (textiles, quetzal feathers, strings of jade, cochineal, gold dust) was collected directly by imperial tribute collectors. This prevented local tribal chiefs getting their hands on it.

The Alliance was highly successful. By the time the Spanish arrived in 1519, the Aztecs had more people in more cities than anyone else in the Americas— although the Incas in South America had a larger empire geographically. The Aztecs ruled indirectly, with local authorities being allowed to administer subject populations without interference as long as

TIMELINE OF AZTEC HISTORY

Chronology	Events
CE 100–650	Classic period of Teotihuacan, major center in Mesoamerica and one of the largest cities in the world at the time.
CE 750–950	Period of warring city-states that included Xochicalco, Cacaxtla, and Teotenango.
CE 950–1150	Nahuatl-speaking Toltecs establish their city of Tula.
CE 1200–1250	The Aztlan migrations. Several Nahuatl-speaking tribes move down from the north into the Central Valley, the Mexica being the last to arrive.
CE 1250–1350	Growth of Aztec city-states under petty kings called *tlatoque*. Consolidation of a common Aztec regional culture.
CE 1325	Founding of Tenochtitlan on a swampy island in Lake Texcoco.
CE 1325–1428	The Mexica develop highly productive raised fields on swampy land *(chinampas)*, and build a system of dikes and canals to keep the brackish Lake Texcoco water away from the fresh water of Lakes Chalco and Xochimilco.
CE 1391–1415	Reign of Huitzilihuitl. Successful marriage alliances formed between Mexica and adjacent states.
CE 1428–1521	Empire of the Triple Alliance. Motecuhzoma I (Montezuma) reigns for 28 years from 1440, beginning construction of the Great Temple of Tenochtitlan and issuing a new legal code. Invasion by Hernán Cortés, and the overthrow of the Aztec Empire by the Spanish.

the supply of tribute was guaranteed. In theory the Aztec emperor reigned supreme over all his conquered lands. In reality, however, the central government was weak—the provinces were ruled more by threats and intimidation.

One motive for imperial expansion was strategic: smaller city-states were brought into the empire as allies for collective security—not as sources of tribute. Despite all their efforts, the Aztecs were never able to militarily subdue the powerful Tlascalans to the east of the Central Valley, or the Tarascans to the west and north. Alliances with minor states along the frontier, which were able to provide military forces, helped secure the Aztec Empire against major enemies.

TRADE AND MARKETS

Another motive for imperial expansion was purely economic: groups of adjacent city-states that had been conquered were organized as tributary provinces. Annual quotas required by the Triple Alliance were set, the amounts due were recorded on manuscripts, and a complete record of what was demanded and what was received was stored in the capital cities of the Alliance.

But unlike the Incas, who had a kind of centrally directed command economy, the provisioning of Aztec cities was more market-driven. Places where buyers and sellers met and traded were a striking feature of all major Aztec centers. The Spanish con-quistador Hernán Cortés wrote of Tlatelolco, a sister city of Tenochtitlan, that:

> The city has many open squares in which markets are continuously held and the general business of buying and selling proceeds. One square in par-ticular is twice as big as that of Salamanca and completely surrounded by arcades where there are daily more than sixty thousand folk buying and selling. Every kind of merchandise such as may be met with in every land is for sale there, whether of food and victuals, or ornaments of gold and silver, or lead, brass, copper, tin, precious stones, bones, shells, snails, and feathers…

Everything made or grown anywhere in the Aztec Empire was available in the Tlatelolco market. Organ-ized into guilds with hereditary membership, the merchants, or *pochteca*, had a lower status than the nobility, but a higher status than Aztec commoners. Like prosperous middle classes elsewhere, many became richer than the nobility as a result of the success of their trading enterprises.

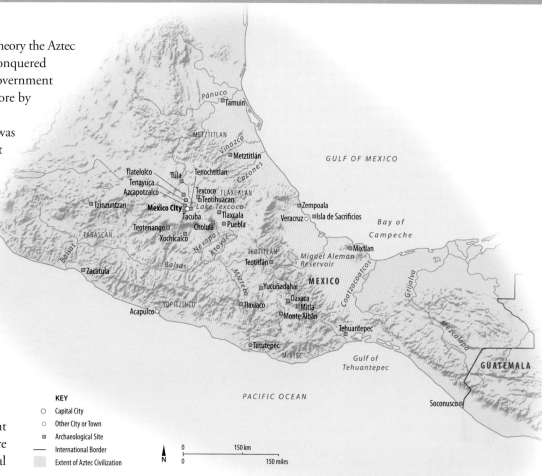

KEY
○ Capital City
○ Other City or Town
▫ Archaeological Site
— International Border
▫ Extent of Aztec Civilization

N
0 ——— 150 km
0 ——— 150 miles

EXTENT OF AZTEC CIVILIZATION

The Aztecs ruled a region in the southeast of modern-day Mexico, from the Pacific Ocean to the Gulf of Mexico. Numerous cities developed within the empire, leaving a rich archaeological record.

VIBRANT MARKET IN TLAXCALA

As seen in this mural by Mexican artist Desiderio Hernández Xochitiotzin (1922–), the Tlaxcala market was a typical Aztec trading place—a busy location with buyers and sellers from throughout the empire.

Tenochtitlan, Mexico

On February 21, 1978, electricians working in the heart of Mexico City uncovered a huge round stone with unusual carvings on it. Some 10½ ft (3.2 m) across, it represented the dismembered body of the Aztec goddess Coyolxauhqui. The area where it was discovered, near the Metropolitan Cathedral and the large square known as the Zocalo, was formerly the site of the Great Temple (el Templo Mayor, as the Spanish called it) in the capital city of the Aztecs, Tenochtitlan.

EAGLE-EYED CARETAKER
Discovered in 1981, the sacred building known as the House of the Eagles or the Palace of the Eagle Warriors features two striking eagle heads, one on either side of the staircase leading to the temple's platform.

TEMPLO MAYOR FROM THE AIR
Most Mexico City inhabitants of today go about their daily business oblivious to the archaeological treasure they have in their midst. However, the Templo Mayor Project has been running since 1978, and continues to unearth a wealth of artifacts from this site every year.

Not since the discovery in 1790 of the Aztec Calendar Stone (also known as the Sun Stone) had there been such an important find. Acting quickly, the president of Mexico ordered a systematic excavation of the site under the direction of archaeologist Eduardo Matos Moctezuma, and in the course of this work 7,000 objects were found—effigies of deities, ritual masks, sacrificial knives, jade beads, and the skeletal remains of human sacrifices. An altar with more than 240 carved stone skulls, and a writhing sculptured serpent measuring 20 ft (6 m) in length, were among the most spectacular finds. More recently, during excavations at the Great Temple in the year 2000, archaeologists made another important discovery. Inside an offering to the Aztec rain god, Tlaloc, they found a rare pre-Columbian piece of textile.

AZTEC ARCHITECTURE

At the time of the Spanish Conquest, Tenochtitlan—with its towering Great Temple rising 200 ft (60 m)—was an awesome sight. The city was built on an island in Lake Texcoco, linked by straight and level causeways to the markets of Tlatelolco in the north, Tlacopan to the west, and Coyoacan to the south. Even the narrow southern causeway was described by Hernán Cortés as being "as broad as two lances and very stoutly made such that eight horsemen could ride along it abreast." In addition, there was a massive barrier known as Nezahualcoyotl's Dike. This separated the brackish water of Lake Texcoco from the fresh water of Lakes Xochimilco and Chalco, making possible the unusual system of lake agriculture called *chinampas*. A variety of watercraft plied the lakes—big flat-bottomed barges with elaborate awnings transported the nobility, while small canoes carried farm produce to the markets at Tlatelolco.

Excavations at Chiconautla, near Lake Texcoco, show that the housing of the nobility was spacious. Patios were encircled by colonnaded rooms. Floors were of white stucco or cement, while wooden columns that rested on stone blocks supported the roofs. According to Franciscan missionary Bernardino de Sahagún, the house of a rich Aztec official would contain an anteroom, an audience chamber, dining and reception rooms, separate quarters for men and women, storerooms, a kitchen, and a servants' hall. But this was nothing compared to Motecuhzoma Xocoyotzin's (Montezuma II's) palace of 300 rooms, with zoos and aviaries attached. In the words of one Spanish chronicler, "I walked till I was tired, and never saw the whole of it."

Cholula, Mexico

Situated in the Valley of Puebla, beyond the destructive volcanoes and some 87 miles (140 km) from modern-day Mexico City, Cholula was for many years the religious capital of highland Mexico, and a pre-Columbian place of pilgrimage. In 1910, during the construction of an asylum for the mentally ill, a huge earth mound within the city precincts was excavated, and it was found to contain the Great Pyramid of Tepanapa—one of the largest step pyramids ever built.

Measuring over 1,310 ft (400 m) on each side, it covers 25 acres (10 ha) and rises to a height of 181 ft (55 m). A colonial church now stands on top of the mound. Excavation of the step pyramid began in 1931 under the direction of José Reygadas Vérti. Ignacio Marquina was the next archaeologist to work at the site, with the overall excavation being conducted on behalf of the Instituto Nacional de Antropología e Historia. Archaeological investigation at the site continues today.

A COMPLICATED COMPLEX

The step pyramid at Cholula is perhaps better described as a huge temple-pyramid complex, since it contains a variety of interrelated structures that appear to have been built over a period of many years. Dedicated at some stage to the Aztec god Quetzalcoatl, construction began in the second century BCE and continued to the early sixteenth century CE. Early in the Christian era the architectural style and ornamental motifs of both Classic Teotihuacan culture and El Tajin became evident. This influence can be seen in what is called the *talud-tablero* structure of Cholula's pyramidal platforms. More dramatic and pleasing to the eye than the sheer walls of Egyptian pyramids, these had sloping sections called *taluds* alternating with vertical rectilinear panels called *tableros*. The proportion of the sloping to the vertical panels, which themselves contain a recessed feature, is roughly 2:1. Archaeologists have reconstructed one side of the lower part of the Great Pyramid and excavated about 5 miles (8 km) of tunnels that visitors to the site are free to explore.

The attitude of the Cholulan people to the Aztecs was uneasy and ambivalent. The Aztecs in the Central Valley were just over the hills from the Valley of Puebla—far too close for comfort. A subject people who were desperate to break away and exercise their independence, the Cholulans at various times formed an alliance with the Tlaxcalans. A curious ceremonial combat, called "the war of flowers," regularly took place between the forces of the Aztec Triple Alliance and those of the Cholulans and Tlaxcalans. Intended mainly to secure sacrificial victims, this was fought only until each side had obtained a satisfactory number of captives: then it was called off.

Cholulan pottery was spectacular. The Aztec emperor Motecuhzoma Xocoyotzin (Montezuma II) refused to eat from any other plates. Glazed, and in a variety of colors, the pottery developed some time in the twelfth century under the influence of the Mixtec culture to the south, and was one of the outstanding ceramic achievements of pre-Columbian civilization.

A HINT OF WHAT LIES BENEATH
In deference to the church (Iglesia de Nuestra Señora de los Remedios) built by the Spanish in 1594 on top of the Cholula mound, the Great Pyramid has not been fully excavated. Visitors can only guess at the sheer size of the construction as they wander around the site.

Human Sacrifice

Visitors to Mexico find the stairs of some step pyramids too steep to climb. But this steep ascent to the scaffold had a purpose. After victims were sacrificed on the altar at the top, their cadavers were tipped over the edge and went tumbling down, spilling blood as they fell. This highly visible spilling of blood was a central feature of Aztec life—no culture spilled more. Estimates of the total number of people sacrificed each year vary widely, but it is likely that around 20,000 people died annually in the capital city of Tenochtitlan, and there were thousands of other temples and sacrificial events elsewhere.

REASON FOR THE BLOODSHED

It is important to understand why Aztec sacrifice was performed. According to the creation myth of the Mexica, the gods had given their own blood to create mankind. For this gift of life, humanity was eternally in debt to the gods—a debt requiring regular offerings of human blood in return. Blood was also linked to fertility in Mesoamerican religion, and everyone was expected to give blood at some point in their lives. Usually it was to secure the growth of crops and the birth of children, and was obtained by piercing the tongue, thigh, arm, chest, or genitals. But the most important and spectacular ceremonial blood offering took place at the top of step pyramids. Four priests grasped a captive by the hands and legs and stretched the person out between them, while a fifth cut out

ON THE WINGS OF AN EAGLE
A stone *cuauhxicalli* (which literally means "eagle gourd vessel") was used by the Aztec priests to make offerings to the gods, and was often shaped like an eagle or jaguar. A cavity held the most prized offering—the still-warm heart moments after it had been cut out of the body.

the heart. Later, down on the ground, another priest cut off the head for mounting on a nearby skull rack.

All early Spanish observers recalled seeing racks filled with skulls, known as *tzompantli*, alongside the step pyramids. The one next to the Great Temple of Tenochtitlan was estimated to contain over 100,000 skulls. Modern excavations of the site conducted by Eduardo Matos Moctezuma have revealed a sacrificial altar with an ornamental decoration of more than 240 carved stone skulls arranged in rows, as described by Hernán Cortés's soldiers. It is significant that thousands of skulls, when excavated, include the upper vertebra still attached. This shows that the victim's head was cut off at the time of death. During recent excavations at the site of the Great Temple, the sacrificial stone described by the Franciscan priest Motolinia, who was there at the time of the conquest, was found just where he said it was: "above the steps and before the altar of the idols." The same recent archaeological project found an offering to Tlaloc of 42 skulls and bones of children.

VISIONS OF DEATH

Death and dismemberment were fearsome subjects often seen in Aztec art. The huge carved disk of the Aztec goddess Coyolxauhqui found in 1978 shows her with severed arms and legs. The colossal statue of the goddess Coatlicue is festooned with hearts, human entrails, skulls, and limbs. On the Calendar Stone (or Sun Stone) from Tenochtitlan, the face of the sun god Tonatiuh is flanked by claws holding human hearts. The sculptures of the god Xipe Totec are especially striking. After being sacrificed, the victim was flayed and a priest then wore the fresh human skin, neatly tied at the back. Several stone images of Xipe Totec show the victim's skin covering the wearer in this way.

Was cannibalism an important feature of Aztec sacrifice? The limbs of many cadavers were certainly eaten, especially by the nobility. But the theory that the consumption of human flesh was necessary to provide protein for dietary reasons—as argued by Michael Harner and Marvin Harris—is not generally accepted. Although there was little meat in the average Aztec diet, maize complemented by beans provided an adequate protein source, as it still does for many people in Mexico today.

A WORLDWIDE PHENOMENON

Human sacrifice has been practiced all over the world. It was a conspicuous feature of Bronze Age Chinese civilizations 3,000 years ago, and it was found among the Polynesian cultures of the Pacific just 200 years ago. The Skidi Pawnee of Nebraska (United States) tortured and sacrificed human captives until at least 1834, and human sacrifice was still being practiced in Dahomey in western Africa until the middle of the nineteenth century.

Sometimes victims were buried alive, as servants of the deceased were in China; sometimes they were put in a shallow grave and apparently left to die of cold, as in Peru; and sometimes their fate was to be publicly despatched, as among the Aztecs (seen in the 1579 illustration at right). The explanation given by those who practice human sacrifice has usually been much the same: since human life is the most valuable thing we have, sacrificing a life is the most valuable offering we can make to gods and kings.

MACABRE WALL DECORATION
The Aztecs exhibited the skulls of their sacrificial victims in racks called *tzompantli*. Although none of these gruesome displays survive today, reliefs covered with stucco that once formed the northern section of the Templo Mayor site depict quite graphically the rows of skulls that would once have stared out from the *tzompantli*.

The Incas

The Incas ruled the largest empire to develop in the Americas before the arrival of Europeans. Their realm was called Tawantinsuyu ("The Four Quarters United") in the native Quechua language, and it was a region of great environmental and cultural diversity. Inca provinces included coastal deserts, tropical rain forests, and high mountain valleys and grasslands rising up toward the towering peaks of the Andes Mountains.

In present-day terms, the Inca Empire extended from northern Ecuador/southern Colombia to central Chile and northwestern Argentina. The people living in these places had diverse cultures, and the Incas developed a range of strategies and policies to incorporate them into their empire and govern them.

THE RISE OF INCA CIVILIZATION

The Inca Empire has its origins in the region surrounding the city of Cuzco, in Peru. The site that would become Cuzco was settled some time after CE 1000, and the settlement grew into a city over time. By 1200–1300, the Incas had established a system of centralized government and had begun to extend their rule over neighboring groups, incorporating them through alliances, military conquest, and intimidation. By 1400, the Incas controlled the Cuzco region and had begun to conquer more distant areas, starting their campaign in the mountain areas of the Andes and eventually extending it to the Pacific coast, conquering such wealthy states and empires as the Chimú and the Chincha. By 1532, they had extended their territory as far north as southern Colombia, and as far south as central Chile. They had a strong, battle-hardened army, which they used both to push Inca frontiers outward and to suppress provincial rebellions.

RULING AN EMPIRE

On the Pacific coast, the Incas often left local rulers in charge but posted their own administrators at important sites. In the highlands, they took a more direct role in administration, developing new agricultural lands, building roads, and establishing new cities for the administrative hierarchy they put in place. Local populations were reorganized into decimal units (households of ten or a multiple of ten), with a local official (curaca) to oversee each level, and many populations were forcibly resettled in other parts of the empire. In the Cuzco region, the royal Inca families controlled most of the best farmland. They were served by yanacona, or retainers, members of subject populations who had to leave their homelands permanently to serve Inca nobles or the state religion. Some groups were required to send colonists to Cuzco to provide temporary labor, and

ANCIENT CAPITAL

This copperplate engraving of Cuzco, the capital of the mighty Inca Empire, dates from 1594. It appeared in *Civitates Orbis Terrarum*, a six-volume city atlas published in Cologne between 1572 and 1617 and edited by German cleric Georgius Braun.

TIMELINE OF INCA HISTORY

Chronology	Events
c. 1200	Cuzco begins to grow into a city as Inca state government develops
c. 1300–1400	The Incas form alliances and use military conquest to extend their territory locally
c. 1400	First imperial campaigns begin in the central Andean highlands
1438	Traditional accession date for the ruler Pachacuti Inca Yupanqui, often credited with forging Inca imperial order
1471	Traditional accession date for the ruler Topa Inca Yupanqui, who started to consolidate Inca rule in many highland regions
1493	Traditional accession date for the ruler Huayna Capac
c. 1525	Huayna Capac dies in Quito, leaving his son Huascar to rule in Cuzco, while another son, Atahuallpa, commands the army in the north
c. 1530	Disputes between Atahuallpa and Huascar lead to civil war
1532	Atahuallpa's generals defeat Huascar; Spaniards under Francisco Pizarro capture Atahuallpa at Cajamarca
1536	Manco Inca (Atahuallpa's successor) rebels against Spanish rule and nearly takes back Cuzco; he retreats to the jungle and founds a kingdom in Vilcabamba
1572	Spaniards capture and execute Tupac Amaru, the last Inca ruler in Vilcabamba

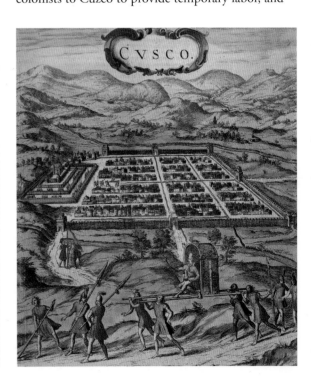

CVSCO.

WOMB OF THE WORLD

These ruins on the Island of the Sun, in Lake Titicaca, are the remnants of the Temple of the Sun God. Highland groups believed that a deity known as Viracocha created the universe on the islands in Lake Titicaca, and they made ritual pilgrimages there.

FUNERARY RITES

The complex known as Machu Picchu was built as a royal estate and has some of the finest and best-preserved Inca architecture known today. Seen here are the stone ruins of the prison quarter, with its necropolis.

others to provide specialists to carry out skilled work, such as masonry, cloth production, and salt-making.

CHILDREN OF THE SUN

The Incas used religion to explain their right to rule over the Andes region and also to help them incorporate new groups into their empire. Their principal deity was the sun; one of the Inca ruler's titles was *intip churin* ("Son of the Sun"). The sun was vital for growing maize, the most important state crop, but the Incas invested other natural forces with supernatural powers as well, including the Moon (associated with women), the ocean, and thunder and lightning. Special temples in Cuzco and elsewhere were dedicated to these forces. In Cuzco, Inca royals carried out important rituals and sacrifices to the Sun, whereas local people made simple offerings to Pachamama, the Earth Mother, to ensure the fertility necessary to grow their crops.

In some regions within the Inca Empire, people worshipped important mountains or sacred objects called *huacas*. The Incas tended to be tolerant of local religious beliefs and practices, and often supported local pilgrimage centers and shrines. The Inca ruler would often send sacrificial animals, maize, and other offerings to be used in important local ceremonies. On the Pacific coast and in the Lake Titicaca area, people worshipped beings they believed had created the universe. The Incas extended their patronage to the coastal shrine of Pachacamac, and developed an elaborate pilgrimage system on the sacred islands in Lake Titicaca, where highland groups believed a deity known as Viracocha had created the universe.

It was important that people be pure when carrying out religious celebrations, so the Incas of Cuzco would prepare themselves by fasting or giving

up chili peppers and salt. For some important rituals, the city of Cuzco was ritually cleansed, and foreigners, sick people, and those with deformed earlobes (from wearing large earspools) were forced to leave. Most Inca religious events involved some sort of sacrifice to the sun deity or to other natural forces. This might consist of offerings of food and drink, or of more valuable items such as cloth, marine shells, and coca-leaf. Animals were sacrificed in important rituals, usually llamas and guinea pigs.

Human sacrifice was practiced only in relatively few ritual contexts. In the *capacocha* ritual, girls and boys were sent from the provinces to Cuzco to be purified and were then returned to be buried alive or left on mountaintops to die. Mountaintop sacrifices of children took place mainly in the southern parts of the empire (northern Chile and northwestern Argentina), where religious patronage of important mountains was a significant element of Inca provincial power.

EXTENT OF INCA CIVILIZATION

The Incas ruled the largest empire to develop in the Americas before the arrival of Europeans. In present-day terms, it extended from northern Ecuador/southern Colombia to central Chile and northwestern Argentina.

Cuzco, Peru

Once the Inca capital, Cuzco is one of the oldest continuously occupied cities in the Americas. Nearly a million tourists visit the city each year to surround themselves with the splendor of ancient times—sleeping in Spanish Colonial buildings converted to luxury hotels, and eating in restaurants whose walls were once part of the palaces of Inca emperors.

A CITY TRANSFORMED

This painting shows the dramatic transformation the ancient Inca capital underwent following the arrival of the Spaniards in 1534. The colonial city was built around and on top of Inca monuments and houses.

A walk around Cuzco today shows how the modern city is built around and on top of the colonial city founded by Spaniards from Francisco Pizarro's expedition in 1534—which itself was created around the monuments and houses of the most important city in the Inca Empire. Inca walls still stand throughout the city; carefully cut squared blocks (ashlar masonry) were used for houses and compound walls, and large, skillfully shaped polygonal stones supported domestic terraces and the foundations of monumental buildings.

Even though archaeologists can see traces of Inca architecture in Cuzco today, it has been difficult to conduct large-scale excavations in the modern city, especially in places where important colonial monuments might be disturbed. Because of this, scholars rely heavily on early Spanish descriptions of the Inca capital that were written by men who arrived in the city in the early 1530s.

THE CENTER OF THE INCA UNIVERSE

The first Spaniards to see Cuzco describe the Inca capital as a rich city, filled with palaces and the houses of elites, including both the Inca nobility and important lords from across the empire. Cuzco was the center of the Inca universe, and its civic heart was a plaza called the Haucaypata, an open space where the four principal highways to the provinces converged. The city had exclusive places—some military decisions and ceremonies took place in the royal palaces built around the plaza, and the nearby Coricancha temple ("Golden Enclosure"), the most important Inca temple to the sun, was the place where important ritual circuits out of the city began—but the Haucaypata was a place where the Inca nobles gathered for festivals, and where ceremonies to unite the Inca rulers with their subjects were carried out. This plaza was used for judgment, for the solar observations on which the Inca calendar was based, and for initiation rituals. Another nearby plaza called Kusipata ("Joyful Terrace") was designated as a space where goods could be bartered at certain times.

SACRED SITE

The Dominican Priory and Church of Santo Domingo were built on top of the Coricancha temple. A major earthquake in 1950 severely damaged the church (since restored), but the Inca architecture held up. The Coricancha's granite walls were exposed, as were many Inca walls throughout the city.

HOUSE OF THE CHOSEN WOMEN

The walls of the *acllahuasi* complex in Cuzco still stand. An *acllahuasi* was a restricted compound where girls were trained in textile production and the production of ritual food and drink. The most noble and skilled girls were sent to Cuzco for more specialized training.

AT HOME WITH THE INCA

Inca emperors built themselves palaces near the Haucaypata, as well as country estates like Machu Picchu (see page 328) in the surrounding region. Spanish descriptions of Inca palaces tell us that these were elaborate complexes, with ornate entryways either painted or decorated with fine masonry. Entry to the emperor's palace was highly restricted, and only high officials and noble Incas could pass through the imposing palace gates to enter the complex within. A visitor would have encountered small plazas, where feasts could be held or warriors could gather, and if permitted to enter even further, would have seen the living quarters of the royal family. Some writers say that noble boys from the provinces were housed in the ruler's palace, where they were educated in Inca customs and kept under close supervision to ensure their parents' cooperation.

Inca rulers were not the only people living in sumptuous houses in Cuzco. Provincial nobles and royal officials were also required to maintain homes in the capital and to reside there for part of the year. Each ruler built his own palace, and after his death his descendants continued to live in his palace.

SUPERNATURAL ENCOUNTERS

A visitor to Cuzco would have seen people from across the Inca Empire in the city, and on special occasions might have glimpsed the Inca himself on a dais in the Haucaypata. Opportunities to see the living emperor were not just encounters with the mightiest ruler that South America had ever seen— they were also opportunities to see supernatural beings. The Sapa Inca (the "Peerless Lord" or "Unique Lord") was often accompanied in public by images of the most important supernatural beings in the Inca state religion—the Sun, the Moon, and Thunder—as well as by the mummies of his deceased male and female ancestors. Royal ancestors held a special place in the Inca religion and were believed to possess special powers. The Sapa Inca even consulted them on matters of state. Cuzco was the site of some of the most important Inca temples, paramount among them the Cori-cancha. The city also had an *acllahuasi* complex, which was a place where female specialists gave religious instruction to young women and trained them in the production of ritual food and drink and of fine cloth (see page 330).

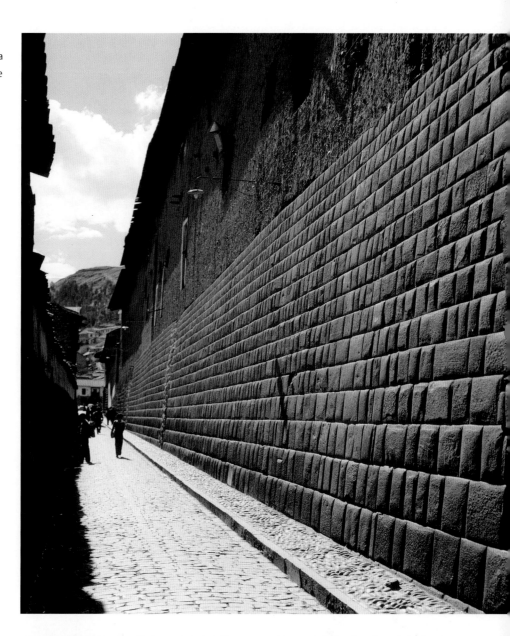

DAILY LIFE IN THE INCA CAPITAL

Cuzco was not just a city for royalty and religious festivals. Commoners lived in the outer neighborhoods, and Cuzco's population included people from across the empire. The ruler initiated a range of urban development projects, such as paving streets and planning house sites, to make the city orderly and accessible. Canals were built to bring water to the city and carry away waste. Storage buildings were built on the outskirts of the city and were stocked with staple foods, such as maize and potatoes, as well as tools for state projects and exotic goods used to produce fancy craft items for gifts and offerings. Artisans made up part of the population of the city, some of them resettled from cities like Chan Chan after the Incas conquered the northern coast.

Artifacts like this painted wooden vessel depicting a llama hunter were used as gifts and offerings.

Machu Picchu, Peru

PERU

Lima○   ☐Machu
              Picchu

With its exotic location and its merging of natural and man-made beauty, Machu Picchu has captured scholarly and spiritual imaginations for almost a century. Perched on an almost inaccessible ridge some 2,600 ft (800 m) above the Urubamba River, which thunders from high in the Andes Mountains toward the jungles of the Amazon Basin, the complex known as Machu Picchu has some of the finest and best-preserved Inca architecture known today.

The rediscovery of Machu Picchu early in the twentieth century stimulated modern studies of Inca archaeology and history. For people everywhere, Machu Picchu has become the symbol of the Inca Empire and is the image that comes immediately to mind in connection with the Incas.

REDISCOVERY OF THE SITE

In 1911, members of the Yale Peruvian Expedition set out for South America. Their goal was to traverse a cross-section of Peru along the 73rd meridian, a route that would pass through unknown territories where the Incas were said to have established a final refuge called Vitcos after the Spaniards invaded their empire in the 1530s. The group's leader was Hiram Bingham, a young explorer who organized the expedition after a previous visit to the Cuzco region had stimulated interest in the Incas. In July 1911, Bingham traveled from Cuzco to Ollantaytambo, and then descended the Urubamba Valley. In a hamlet called Mandor Pampa, a local muleteer named Melchor Arteaga told the expedition of

some remarkable ruins at Machu Picchu. He guided them there on July 24, 1911. Bingham was overwhelmed by the fine architecture at the site, and returned in 1912 to conduct excavations that represent some of the most extensive archaeological studies of Inca civilization carried out in the early twentieth century. Since then, the site has been cleared and restored, but its remoteness and exotic look have captivated the imagination of millions of visitors, many of whom travel to the site on foot via the Inca road through the mountains.

ROYAL ESTATES

Machu Picchu was a royal estate of the ninth Inca, Pachacuti Inca Yupanqui. When the Incas started to extend their territory beyond the Cuzco Valley, their rulers began to use the labor service they required of their growing number of subjects to develop new farmlands and to build palaces in Cuzco and the surrounding countryside. The sixth ruler was the first to engage in this practice, building a series of new irrigation canals and agricultural terraces in the

ROYAL RESIDENCE

Machu Picchu was a royal estate of the ninth Inca, Pachacuti Inca Yupanqui. The ruins of the royal quarter are seen here, overlooking the prison quarter. The Incas were masters of drystone construction, where stones are set in place with no mortar to bind them.

TAXING LABOR

The Incas did not use coins, and their economy ran without significant reliance on the buying and selling of goods in the marketplace. People in provincial areas paid taxes in the form of labor rather than goods or money, and many provinces were organized into decimal administration units that were responsible for a wide range of tasks, including guard duty, agricultural work, and carrying harvests from state fields to storage facilities. Some provincial groups were required to send temporary colonists (mitimacona) to work in other parts of the empire, including the Cuzco region. The area around the capital also had large numbers of special retainers (yanacona) and individuals who specialized in different kinds of food production or the making of fancy craft goods used for gifts and offerings. Inca nobles at Machu Picchu would have been served by these retainers and specialists, who worked directly for the Inca emperor and his family.

Cuzco Valley near a place called Larapa, where his country residence was constructed. By the reign of the eighth Inca, rulers had multiple estates in the Cuzco Valley and the neighboring Sacred Valley—areas where large maize crops could be grown to support the army, as well as the royal family and its servants. As the Incas conquered groups outside the Cuzco region, rulers began to develop estates in the hot jungle lands near Cuzco, in areas where the coca-leaf could be cultivated. Machu Picchu was built on an Inca road into this coca-producing region, and its location would have allowed the Incas to monitor traffic along the floor of the valley below.

As a royal property, Machu Picchu was an exclusive and restricted place. Entrance to the main architectural compounds is highly controlled, and the open plaza spaces are of a modest size. The site would have housed no more than 1,000 people or so, and the gabled stone structures are of a high quality throughout. The terraces that surround housing and religious buildings are integrated into the natural boulders and outcrops of the landscape, creating a visually arresting effect that would have been even more impressive when they were sown with crops or decorative plants. Fountains throughout the site provide the sight and sound of water. Several buildings were used for religious purposes. Excavations by Bingham and later by Peruvian archaeologists have revealed considerable evidence of the daily life of Inca nobles and their servants.

CONSTRUCTION AT MACHU PICCHU

While Inca commoners lived in small houses made from mud-brick or other perishable materials, the Inca elite had impressive palaces and houses built from finely worked stone. Machu Picchu has some of the finest examples of Inca stonework, as well as evidence of how it was worked—usually only with stone tools. The quarry used to build the complex still contains stones that were in the process of being broken from rock outcrops. Once removed, stones were pecked into shape—to form either ashlar blocks or polygonal shapes—and transported to the structures where they were to be placed. Polygonal blocks were worked so that all angles fitted precisely with those of neighboring stones, and the finest constructions were built without the use of mortar.

SPIRITUAL SPECTACLE

Perched on an almost inaccessible ridge high above the Urubamba River amid a landscape of spectacular beauty, Machu Picchu is the best-known symbol of the Inca Empire. It continues to capture the imagination of scholars and travelers alike.

SOLAR CALENDAR

This structure is known as the Intihutuna, which literally means "for tying the sun." As the winter solstice approached and the sun seemed to disappear more each day, a priest may have conducted a ceremony here to tie the sun to the stone and prevent it from disappearing entirely.

Inca Textiles

MASTERS OF THEIR CRAFT

In Inca times, most local people wore a rough cloth made of llama wool or maguey, while specialists produced fancy textiles—like this woven bag in a medley of colors and designs—using cotton and the soft wool of the alpaca or wild vicuña. Yet other specialists gathered the wool and dyes used to produce cloth in a wide spectrum of colors.

Cloth was one of the most important of the goods produced in the Inca Empire. People from different regions wore distinctive outfits and hats to distinguish themselves from their neighbors, and the Incas required the people in many of their provinces to weave cloth every year as part of the labor service they were obliged to give the empire.

Colonial period documents tell us that most commoners wove *abasca*, cloth made of llama wool or maguey fiber, while specialist weavers produced fancy textiles using cotton and the soft wool of the alpaca or wild vicuña. A male textile specialist was called a *cumbicamayoc*. The Incas set up small groups of cloth specialists in the towns near their capital, Cuzco, and in the provinces. Other kinds of specialists were required to collect the wool and prepare the dyes that were used to produce cloth of many different colors.

SPECIALIST SPINNERS AND WEAVERS

Female textile specialists were called *mamacona*. They received formal training in Cuzco or one of several provincial cities through a state institution called the *acllahuasi*. The *acllahuasi* was a restricted compound where selected girls were trained to spin wool, weave cloth, and prepare food and drink for state festivals and religious events. Girls lived in the provincial *acllahuasi* for several years, learning these skills and receiving religious instruction. After this initiation, the most noble and skilled girls were sent to the *acllahuasi* in Cuzco, where they learned more delicate weaving techniques and were initiated into important religious rites. They were then either assigned by the emperor to religious cults or married to important men in Inca imperial society.

Spanish documents tell us a good deal about how the Incas herded animals for their wool and how artisans living in communities throughout the highlands wove cloth. Although cloth is seldom well preserved in the highlands, archaeologists have identified weaving tools during excavations of the houses of local people near Cuzco and in mountain villages. Archaeologists working at Huánuco Pampa, an Inca provincial capital in the central Andean highlands, have also identified an *acllahuasi*.

KNOTTY NARRATIVES: WRITING HISTORY WITHOUT DOCUMENTS

Unlike many early civilizations, the Incas did not use a form of writing to record events in their history and to keep records of everyday activities. Instead they used a device known as the *quipu*, consisting of a set of knotted cords—which were tied and untied as required—to keep track of tribute payments, population counts, and the contents of storage buildings. The *quipu* also served another very important purpose. In the hands of special practitioners, it was used to record selected deeds of the Inca emperors. Archaeologists and art historians have yet to identify and decode a *quipu* that records this kind of valuable information, and our knowledge of the Inca past comes from documents written by Spaniards and native Andeans in the first century following the Spanish Conquest (c. 1532–1653), as well as from the work of archaeologists.

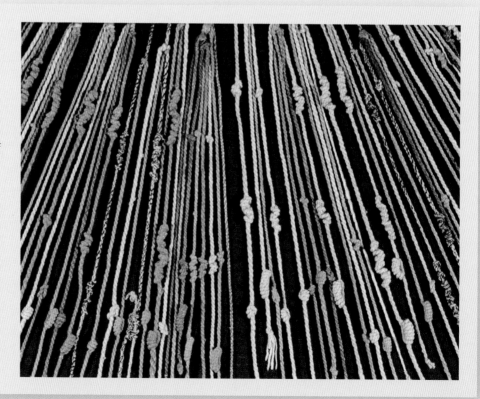

Excavations there yielded many spindle whorls (for spinning wool into yarn) and weaving tools.

Along the Pacific coast, desert conditions have led to finds of extraordinarily well-preserved textiles and other remains at some sites. Museum collections around the world hold remarkable examples of Inca textiles, most of which come from coastal tombs that were looted. While these are valuable pieces of art, we have no way of knowing the cultural context within which each was produced, used, and discarded or buried. It is only when graves or other sites are excavated completely by professionals that we can gain an insight into the social meanings of Inca textiles.

THE *QUIPU:* AN EARLY RECORDING DEVICE

During the Spanish Conquest and the decades of wars that followed it, Europeans often took food and other supplies from Inca storehouses located at provincial cities and way stations along the royal highway. Spaniards noted that whenever they did so, Inca officials brought out a set of knotted cords called a *quipu,* which they used to record the contents of the storehouses. The keeper of the *quipu,* called a *quipucamayoc,* would variously untie and tie knots to record the items that had been removed.

The *quipu* was a very important device made up of cords of cotton and wool in a wide range of colors. The people who used it were specially trained to record and decode information by this method. Inca administrators and provincial record-keepers kept parallel records of births and deaths, tribute payments, ritual cycles, and such things as the number of llamas and alpacas in a province's herds. Scholars have learned to decode the numerical information in the *quipu,* but no one has yet succeeded in decoding the other information that these devices hold.

FROZEN IN TIME

This 500-year-old mummy of a teenage Inca girl, her clothing intact and holding ritual objects, was found near the summit of Nevado Ampato in Peru in 1996. She was killed by a powerful blow to the head, perhaps in a ritual sacrifice to appease Inca gods.

THE DAY'S SUPPLY

Like other Andean peoples, the Incas chewed coca-leaves as a food source, to lessen hunger and pain, and to boost energy on long journeys by foot through the mountains. Traditionally, people carried a woven pouch to hold their day's supply. This coca-leaf bag, fringed and featuring a llama pattern, dates to 1440–1534.

Ollantaytambo, Peru

PERU

Lima○   Ollantaytambo ■

A PLANNED ECONOMY

The Inca Empire shifted the focus of agricultural work to the production of large surpluses of foods (especially maize and potatoes) that could be stored; they often resettled populations in new locations—such as Ollantaytambo—to provide labor for these endeavors.

Ollantaytambo is an Inca town located in the Urubamba Valley, about 30 miles (50 km) from the city of Cuzco. Once the royal estate of Pachacuti Inca Yupanqui (who reigned from *c.* 1438 to *c.* 1471), it tells us a great deal about how the Incas expanded and controlled their empire, which eventually encompassed the Andes region from Ecuador to Chile.

When the Incas began to extend their power throughout the Cuzco region in the fourteenth and early fifteenth centuries CE, they allied themselves with the people living in a place called Tambo. After some years of peaceful interaction, the Tambos resisted Inca territorial expansion and were conquered by the Inca king Pachacuti Inca Yupanqui, who took Tambo lands as one of his personal estates.

AN AGRICULTURAL REVOLUTION

Pachacuti Inca Yupanqui is the Inca king most often credited with forging Inca imperial order. After conquering the Tambos, the Incas used labor tribute to terrace the bottom of the Urubamba Valley and to build irrigation canals to water highly productive

fields of maize, the state's most important crop. They also constructed a town in the valley to support these activities. Ollantaytambo was designed and built in a trapezoidal form, with a regular grid plan and blocks of rectangular houses laid out around a courtyard. Storage buildings were constructed on the hillsides, so that the valley's occupants could see the abundance of food the empire produced.

At its height, Ollantaytambo would have had a population of 1,000 or so, made up of local Tambo people and a variety of different groups. Inca people settled in the town, some of them related to the royal family who owned the estate. Retainers (*yanacona*) were required to administer and support the royal estate. There is evidence that people from the central highland provinces were relocated there as well.

Land improvement and the economic shift to maize production were strategies that had been promoted throughout the growing Inca Empire for a century or more. The Incas shifted the focus of agricultural work to the production of foods that could be stored in large quantities (especially maize and potatoes), and they often required provincial populations to resettle in new locations. Food surpluses fed armies and helped to maintain administrative centers, as well as the way stations along the 25,000 miles (40,000 km) of roads that the Incas built throughout their vast empire. Relocation served a dual purpose.

RESETTLING AN UNEASY EMPIRE

The Incas were a major force in changing settlement patterns throughout the Andes, resettling conquered peoples to sustain their maize economy and to quash opposition to their rule. Troublesome provincial groups were often resettled near the capital, and some were put into service as retainers for the royal family. Particularly resistant groups, like the Chachapoyas of north Peru and the Cañaris of Ecuador, were forcibly scattered throughout the empire and were also required to provide men (often accompanied by their family) to serve in long-term military campaigns. At the same time, Inca groups from the Cuzco region were sent from their homes to colonize provincial areas and to serve in the empire's expanding administrative network.

These policies had the effect of putting large amounts of land around Cuzco into the hands of the royal families, who then required many retainers to support their lifestyle.

A ROYAL RETREAT

As a royal estate, Ollantaytambo had its share of grand architecture. The remains of a complex built at the foot of the Halancoma mountain, to the west of the planned town, still stand. Consisting of several small residential clusters and a finely constructed

THE COLUMBIAN EXCHANGE

When Spanish conquistadors came in contact with the Inca Empire in 1532, they were initially at a loss to describe the plants and animals of the Inca world. They wrote back to Spain about Inca "sheep," meaning the Andean relatives of the camel—the llama, which was used for carrying burdens and also provided meat and wool, and the alpaca, which was raised for its soft wool. Guinea pigs (cuy), which could be found scurrying around any Inca kitchen—until they became part of a special meal, that is—were called "rabbits." Although Spaniards were familiar with maize (as food and beer) from their explorations in the Caribbean and Mexico, they had never seen potatoes or quinoa before, foods that were important parts of the Inca diet. Europeans eventually learned the Quechua names for these things, often adapting them for their own use, as American plants and animals were taken back to Europe and incorporated into European economies and cuisines.

Llamas have long been used in Peru to provide wool and meat, and as beasts of burden.

temple complex, it includes many fine examples of stonework. The temple, thought to have been dedicated to the Sun, was not completed, and several of the cyclopean blocks destined for its walls still lie where they were left in the process of being hauled up the mountainside. Along the valley floor, rock outcrops have been carved and modified in various ways, and canals bring water to fountains that would have given pleasure to the Inca royals who lived here.

The planned town of Ollantaytambo was restored in the 1980s. Local people now live in Inca house blocks, with water rushing through Inca canals.

THE INCAS AFTER THE CONQUEST

After the Spaniards arrived in the Cuzco region in 1534, Ollantaytambo continued to be an important town. Manco Inca, the native ruler whom the Spaniards installed as their puppet-ruler, invested labor tribute in this and other royal Inca estates. When he led the Incas in an uprising in 1536, Manco Inca planned his campaign from Ollantaytambo. He fortified the site and withstood an attack by Spanish cavalry before abandoning the Inca heartland and retreating to the jungles of Vilcabamba.

SKILLED LABOR

The Inca ruins at Ollantaytambo show the massive stones that were quarried, dressed, and hauled into place to build the town. The Incas used labor tribute to carry out such work, and to construct the agricultural terraces and irrigation canals needed to grow maize.

Chan Chan, Peru

At the time of the Spanish Conquest, Chan Chan may have been the largest city in South America. It had been the capital of the Chimú Empire, a powerful coastal civilization conquered by the Incas toward the end of the 1400s, and the city continued to be an important center in Inca times.

At its largest, Chan Chan occupied some 8 sq miles (20 sq km) and had a population estimated to have numbered in the tens of thousands. Archaeologists mapped the remains of the city in the 1970s and have carried out excavations throughout the city.

THE REALM OF THE CHIMÚ

The Chimú Empire developed in the Moche Valley, in northern Peru, the birthplace of the first Andean state, founded by the Moche culture (*c.* CE 100–800). Chan Chan was founded *c.* CE 900 on vacant lands near the irrigated fields of the valley's floodplain, and grew into a city over time. It grew rapidly between 1100 and 1200 and between 1300 and 1470, periods corresponding to the rise of the Chimú Empire, which controlled some 300 miles (500 km) of the Pacific coast by the time of the Inca invasion. The

Chimú established control over the Moche Valley and a few valleys to the north and south between CE 900 and 1200, developing large-scale systems of irrigation canals and agricultural terracing, and building roads and defensive sites to link and protect their growing empire. After 1200, the Chimú took control of the coastal states centered in the Lambayeque and Casma Valleys, and were continuing on their path of territorial expansion when they were conquered by the Incas toward the end of the 1400s.

PYRAMIDS AND PALACES IN DOWNTOWN CHAN CHAN

The center of Chan Chan—an area of some 2 sq miles (6 sq km)—was dominated by five low pyramids and ten palace complexes called *ciudadelas* (Spanish for little cities). These complexes were built at different times and are thought to have housed the noblest

CENTER OF POWER

Ruins of adobe walls are all that is left of the once powerful city of Chan Chan. The city center was dominated by five low pyramids and ten palace complexes called *ciudadelas*. Chan Chan is inscribed on the World Heritage List.

families of the Chimú capital. Each is thought to have been built by a particular ruler or dynasty.

Earlier *ciudadelas* are smaller than later ones, which typically consist of a rectangular compound enclosed by a thick adobe wall up to 30 ft (9 m) in height. Entry to the *ciudadelas* was highly restricted. As well as the living spaces of their elite occupants, the *ciudadelas* comprised areas for administrative activities and storage, and truncated mortuary pyramids of a style known to have been used for Chimú royalty. The elaborate friezes on many of the buildings and the rich burials that have been found within some of the mortuary pyramids also attest to the elite nature of the *ciudadelas*.

Several of these complexes also have dozens of U-shaped structures called *audiencias* in Spanish. These structures are laid out in association with plaza spaces, and are thought to have been used by state bureaucrats for everyday administrative activities. The *ciudadelas* were homes for kings, but many of the most important political and economic activities of the Chimú Empire are thought to have taken place inside them.

Archaeologists have also identified some 35 walled compounds representing smaller elite residences in Chan Chan. Of varying sizes and constructed of varying materials, they have a range of additional features, including storage buildings, courtyard spaces, and wells. These features and the enclosing wall clearly distinguish them from the remains of houses occupied by commoners. Such houses are found throughout the city. Many of these dwellings appear to have been built at a late stage in the city's occupation, perhaps reflecting an administrative shift out of the palace that occurred as the Incas came to control the coastal region.

ARTISANS, BUREAUCRATS, AND RETAINERS

Most of Chan Chan's residents lived in and around the city center in modest dwellings made of cane or wattle-and-daub. These commoners numbered 20,000 or so, and most likely included temporary laborers, traders, and servants of the royal families. Archaeological investigations have identified that many of the city's humbler residents were artisans who produced the fine craft goods—cloth, metal, featherwork, and shell objects—used by nobles to display their status. Commoners lived in residential wards that may have been organized on the basis of kinship or occupational specialization.

FEEDING THE CHIMÚ CAPITAL

Chan Chan's populace was largely fed by farming and fishing communities in the surrounding area. Because the city is located in the desert, the Chimú government put major resources into building irrigation canals and managing agricultural

production. The cold coastal waters of the Pacific Ocean were home to a wide range of marine life, including large schools of anchovies and sardines. Chimú administrators may have managed the work of local fishing and farming communities, and state bureaucrats are thought to have managed the state food stores on which nobles, priests, and artisans living in the city relied. However, excavations in rural fishing and farming communities, and at Chan Chan itself, suggest that the common folk were relatively self-sufficient in obtaining their own food and did not rely solely on fish and maize. Fruits like the lúcuma and the guanábana were also important parts of a fairly diverse diet.

RAINBOW TEMPLE

The structure known as the Rainbow Temple (Huaca del Arco Iris) or the Dragon Temple (Huaca del Dragón) has high-relief, rainbow-shaped friezes with a central motif that some have interpreted to be that of a dragon. The outer walls have reliefs of snakes and strange lizards.

CHAN CHAN IN INCA TIMES

In Inca times, Chan Chan continued to be an important city, although some of its artisans were sent to Cuzco to produce fancy metal and other goods that the Inca nobility could variously wear, give to loyal subjects, and use in the state religion. The Chimú ruling family held less power under the Incas, although local nobles appear to have continued to play an important role in the state government. Agricultural production appears to have shifted from the Moche Valley to the nearby Chicama Valley, and the Incas built a road system along the coast, along with roads linking the coastal highway with important highland centers, and also some new administrative sites, to maintain an indirect imperial presence along this part of the coast.

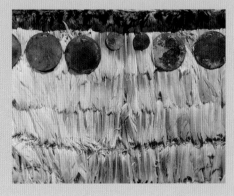

Dating from Chimú times, this colorful fragment of fabric featuring feathers and bronze plaques may have been part of a noble's cape.

Other Cultures of the Americas

The ancient Americas teemed with people, from desert nomads to sophisticated urban dwellers. Rigorous archaeological research has been carried out in the New World for only a century, and so a full picture of ancient cultures is only slowly emerging. Nevertheless, the number of important and fascinating sites and significant places so far known is enough to fill many pages.

The Incas in the fifteenth and sixteenth centuries CE proved to be the last representatives of thousands of years of cultural processes in western South America. They were the last great "horizon"—a unique period of time when people throughout great areas of Peru shared common practices and ideas.

PERUVIAN PERTURBATIONS

ERODED BY TIME

The Pyramid of the Sun (Huaca del Sol) was the capital of the early Moche Empire, in northern Peru. Originally more than 100 ft (30 m) high, and built of more than a million adobe bricks, this great pyramid complex has been worn down by weather and looters.

The earliest such time was the Early Horizon (c. 700 BCE–0), when the magnificent highland site of Chavín de Huantar appears to have synthesized centuries of earlier developments into a powerful cult combining highland, coastal, and tropical forest religious motifs that spread throughout Peru.

Eventually, for uncertain reasons, Chavín collapsed, and in the subsequent Early Intermediate Period (0–CE 650), regionally based cultures, some

of which were quite widespread, emerged. Two on the coast are perhaps the best known: the Nazca, in the south, and the Moche, in the north. Among their many accomplishments, the Nazca made many of the famous Nazca Lines; the Moche are known for their large adobe pyramid complexes. One of these, Sipán, yielded the richest and most informative elite burial ever found in the New World.

The Moche and Nazca cultures and other contemporary cultures underwent radical transformation during the eighth century. This time, the dramatic changes were due at least partly to the rise of two powerful cultures: Tiwanaku, a great civic-ceremonial complex east of Lake Titicaca, in Bolivia, and Huari, another urbanlike center, in the south-central highlands of Peru. With their widespread influences, the era of Tiwanaku and Huari is termed the Middle

ANCIENT METROPOLIS

The Kalasasaya Platform is one of the ceremonial buildings in the core area of the huge urban center of Tiwanaku, in Bolivia. Now in ruins, it was probably a great stone-faced structure with temples on top. The humanoid figure seen through the opening originally stood in the plaza.

Horizon (*c.* CE 650–1000); this is followed by another period of regionalism, known as the Late Intermediate Period (*c.* CE 1000–1450), and finally by the rise of Inca imperialism.

OTHER HORIZONS

Like Peru, ancient Mesoamerica experienced periods of widespread common cultural patterns (Olmec, Teotihuacan) punctuated by periods of regionalism. Elsewhere in the Americas, where research has perhaps not been as intense or sustained, similar patterns have emerged.

The Intermediate Area is one of the least known yet one of the most important cultural areas of the ancient New World. Indeed, the fact that arguably the richest set of gold tombs ever found in the New World (but perhaps second to Sipán) was excavated at Sitio Conte, Panama, before World War II is hardly known outside of a small group of specialists. Awkward not only in name, the Intermediate Area includes the eastern parts of El Salvador and Honduras, stretches through southern Central America, and encompasses most of Colombia and parts of Ecuador. As in Mesoamerica and the Central Andes, there was probably great internal variation in this area, but it also displays many commonalities, such as the predominance of Chibchan languages, the shared physical characteristics of its populations, and common material cultures, especially distinctive styles of gold metallurgy and stone sculpture.

In the Eastern Woodlands of the United States, a mortuary cult known as Hopewell was practiced throughout a great area, from southern Ohio to at least Wisconsin, from *c.* CE 250 to 500. Later, however, the great ceremonial and residential complex of Cahokia rose to prominence in Illinois,

near the Mississippi River, across from the modern-day city of St. Louis.

Large architectural complexes of stone-built masonry are not well known from the Intermediate Area, and the tropical forest hides much of what was built. In a few areas, however, impressive architecture is known, such as at Buritaca (*c.* CE 800–1600) in Colombia, a Tairona residential and ceremonial complex covering 35 acres (14 ha) on top of a mountain. One of the most accessible of such sites for visitors, although it is still poorly known, is Guayabo de Turrialba in Costa Rica. Its complex of cobble-built mounds, patios, fountains, roads, and house platforms follows a distinctively Southern Central American architectural form. While Guayabo is the largest ceremonial center known in this area, several more are known and many more are likely to be discovered.

There is much research to be done throughout the New World. Considering that serious archaeological study of the past is, debatably, little more than a century old, and that the American past goes back to at least 15,000 BCE, we have only just begun to learn of its many cultures.

FABULOUS BURIAL FINDS

This large gold plaque, 8–10 in (20–25 cm) in diameter, was one of eight discovered in elite burials at Sitio Conte, in Panama. Ornately decorated in high relief, most of the plaques show saurian-human and avian-human figures. Five were found in one burial, No. 11.

THE MISSISSIPPIAN MOUND BUILDERS

The site of Cahokia, in Illinois, near modern-day St. Louis, still boasts the largest pyramid-mound north of Mexico (see page 345). In ancient times, it drew a vast number of people and an equally vast amount of resources to its complex of mounds, temples, plazas, and other ritual centers. Cahokia ushered in the so-called Mississippian phenomenon. The site itself prospered from *c.* 1000 to 1250. After that time, construction at the center halted, and new, smaller, complexes arose farther south—Etowah in Georgia, Moundville in Alabama, and Spiro in Oklahoma being among the most prominent.

Chavín de Huantar, Peru

Perched high on the eastern slopes of the Andes, the ceremonial center of Chavín de Huantar was a spectacular cult center that drew upon religious traditions and exotic goods from all three of Peru's major environmental zones: the coastal desert, the Andes mountains, and the tropical forest. Some consider it to be the origin of Andean civilization.

Large ceremonial complexes were built in Peru perhaps as early as 2500 BCE. By 1800 BCE, architectural complexes exhibit regional styles, and this pattern continued in the Initial Period, starting *c.* 1500 BCE, when ceramics and weaving were adopted. Starting at about 1000 BCE, Chavín de Huantar appears to have synthesized centuries of trends in religious cults and created a new cult. Located on the high eastern Andean slopes, on a river leading to the Amazon but also on an important pass to the east, Chavín was ideally located to draw both pilgrims and resources to its cult center. It began as a small settlement with a single temple. Between 500 and 200 BCE, however, Chavín grew into a great ceremonial complex surrounded by a large, citylike community.

MAN OR BEAST?
A series of sculpted stone heads attached to the facade of the Old Temple were intended to represent the shamanistic transformation of human to beast.

THE FANGED GOD IN THE LABYRINTH

Even in its early phase, Chavín was impressive. The "Old Temple" was a U-shaped structure 330 ft (100 m) on its longest side and 230 ft (70 m) deep. Built of fieldstone slabs and mortar, the exterior walls exhibited large carved stone heads in ecstatic states of shamanistic transformation from human to beast. Between the two arms of the "U," a sunken Circular Plaza was faced with fine stones carved with a parade of marching deities. Inside the Old Temple a warren of passageways led to galleries that may have contained storerooms and, perhaps, the cells of religious mystics.

On an axis with the center of the Circular Plaza, the tunnels of the labyrinth intersect to form a cross. In the center of the cross stands the Lanzón, one of the most ancient cult statues known to be in its original setting. It is a 15-ft (4.5-m) high stone monolith with the image of a fanged god engraved on its sides. This image may be the temple's principal deity, as it is also seen on other carvings. The design of the chamber in which it stands in the labyrinth includes a hidden chamber, where a priest may have

made oracular statements to pilgrims fortunate enough to be given the privilege of entering the temple's most holy of holies.

THROUGH THE BLACK AND WHITE PORTAL

The New Temple is associated with the expansion of the Chavín community, who lived outside the sacred precinct in a town with more than 2,000 inhabitants—quite large for its time. The temple complex more than doubled in size. The southern arm of the U of the Old Temple was expanded, and the axis of the complex was now oriented to the entry of this section, known as the New Temple. The entry was a dramatic portal built of black stone, with a carved female bird deity column on one side and a white male bird deity column on the other. A grand, square, sunken plaza was aligned with this entry more than 330 ft (100 m) away, below a series of large, successively lower patios and impressive granite and limestone stairways.

Although there were other impressive ceremonial sites in the Andes, Chavín de Huantar appears to have had a special role in reinterpreting old traditions and packaging them as a new religious cult that spread throughout much of Peru. The period of influence, *c.* 700 BCE–0, is known as the Early Horizon. Cult centers that fused local traditions with Chavín influence developed in central and northern Peru in particular, while communities in more distant regions, such as those on

A NEW CULT CENTER

The ruins of the New Temple still stand at Chavín de Huantar. This spectacular cult center perched high in the Andes seems to have synthesized centuries of trends in religious cults into a new cult that drew large numbers of pilgrims.

AWE-INSPIRING MYSTERIES

The stone carving style of Chavín is one of its most appealing features today, as it probably was in the past. In addition to the Lanzón, a number of other carvings are known, although their original locations are often uncertain. Among the most notable is the Tello Obelisk, which portrays a mythological caiman sprouting various plants from its body, suggesting that it may depict an origins myth. The spectacular Raimondi Stone shows the "Staff God," whose headdress "reads" as a series of nested monster faces when viewed upside-down. The use of such visual tricks is a key element in Chavín art and was probably designed to mystify and to inspire awe in religious pilgrims who visited the site.

Viewed upside-down, the headdress of the "Staff God" comprises a series of nested monster faces.

the south coast, may have been influenced less directly by the Chavín cult.

As it spread its cult outward, Chavín was rewarded with a pouring-in of many kinds of goods, most likely gifts from pilgrims or tributes from dependent centers. These included a number of styles of ceramics from different parts of Peru, rare shells from the warm waters off Ecuador, and valuable obsidian and cinnabar from the southern highlands.

Chavín seems to have grown in times of peace, but between 200 and 1 BCE its trajectory wavered and the city then went into a decline. Its collapse may have been sudden, and was perhaps due to a combination of factors, including environmental stress. When Chavín fell, there was a period of great instability for at least two centuries.

The Nazca Lines, Peru

On the Pampa de Nazca, a plain on the south coast of Peru, a palimpsest of engravings in the dry desert crisscross one another in multiple layers like the scratches of ice skates on a frozen pond. Straight lines, trapezoids, truncated triangles, rectangles, concentric rays, spirals, and a host of plant and animal forms feature in the most enigmatic of ancient America's archaeological sites.

Some 80 miles (50 km) from the Pacific Ocean, several seasonal river channels, or *quebradas*, form to produce the Rio Grande de Nazca. Despite the fact that measurable rainfall occurs only once every several years, the region has hosted human settlement from the time of early fisher-gatherers at the end of the last Ice Age through the Inca occupation to the present day. But of the many archaeological remains in the dry coastal desert, none has attracted more attention than the ground drawings, or geoglyphs, found on the high, dry plain above the *quebradas*.

Although the lines were certainly known to local people, scholarly and public knowledge of them is relatively recent. The first publication about the geoglyphs appeared in 1927, thanks to the work of Julio C. Tello, one of Peru's greatest archaeologists. Since then, many scholars and visitors have been fascinated by the lines. Among them, German-born Maria Reiche spent four decades studying, publicizing, and safeguarding the site. At the other extreme, the astounding accuracy of the markings has inspired fanciful interpretations, such as writer Erich von Däniken's sensational claims that the lines served as landing strips for alien astronauts.

LINES, RAYS, GEOMETRICS, AND BIOMORPHS

The pampa is a triangular-shaped area of 85 sq miles (220 sq km) bounded by the Rio Grande de Nazca, the Ingenio River, and the Andean foothills. The most common markings on the desert surface are straight lines, followed by geometric forms. Biomorphic forms are the least common, and consist of animals—mostly birds and fish, but also a monkey, a spider, and a killer whale—and a few plants. There are approximately 800 miles (300 km) of straight lines, some 12 miles (20 km) or more in length; about 300 geometrical figures; and three dozen biomorphs.

Lines commonly radiate from a central node, often a hill, and the rays often lead to irrigated oases located off the pampa itself. Among the geometric designs, trapezoids or truncated triangles are common, often measuring 130 ft by 1,300 ft (40 m by 400 m). Their axes often parallel the courses of *quebrada* channels, and the thin ends of about

FANCIFUL FIGURES

The Nazca lines are perhaps best known to many people through the sensational claims of writer Erich von Däniken, who interpreted geoglyphs like this as "proof" that the lines served as landing strips for alien astronauts.

WHO WALKED THE SACRED SPIRALS?

While lines and geometric figures may have been tied to fertility rituals associated with irrigation waters, other features appear to have played different ceremonial roles. A person can walk along the path of the outline of the animals and never step in the same place twice. This presumed ceremonial role is even more dramatically in evidence in the spirals, which take a person from the outside to the center and back again in a single line, much like medieval and contemporary church labyrinths.

Some of the Nazca geoglyphs may have been tied to fertility rituals that were associated with irrigation waters, others to unknown ceremonies.

two-thirds of them point upstream. Although the fact that most of the figures are on flat land has led to speculation that the lines could only have been seen in their entirety from the air, these links to natural features strongly indicate that the lines are associated with water and fertility, and were therefore of both practical and symbolic import.

The orientations of lines and trapezoids to water sources suggest that these markings were tied to rituals. A comparison has been made to the *ceque* system of the Inca city of Cuzco: a series of imaginary lines radiating from the center of the city outward to connect ceremonial structures, sacred geography, and important points in the irrigation system. The Nazca lines seem mostly to be oriented to important water sources, but, like the *ceque* lines, they also could have been pilgrimage routes that cut across the landscape. Research has not supported early ideas that the main purpose of the geoglyphs was linked to astronomical observations, although

some of them may have been connected to astronomical events associated with the annual arrival of the all-important irrigation waters.

THE KEY TO TWO MYSTERIES

The key to solving two of the "mysteries" that surround the geoglyphs—how they were made and who made them—was twofold. First, the lines are easily made by raking away the dark surface soil to reveal lighter materials underneath. Lines and even spirals can be made with simple tools such as wooden stakes, some of which have been found still in place. Second, ceramic shards have been found in association with some of the lines. The designs on the shards match the style of some of the figural geoglyphs, indicating that they were made by people of the Nazca Culture, *c.* 200 BCE–CE 600. It is likely that many other people also made lines, however, producing the dense layering of lines and adding to the "mystery" of these remarkable traces of the past.

FLIGHT OF THE CONDOR

This huge, 440-ft (135-m) long condor is among the relatively few biomorphic drawings on the desert surface of the pampa. Most of these depict birds and fish, but there is also a monkey, a spider, and a killer whale. Some figures, like this condor, can only be seen in their entirety from the air.

Sipán, Peru

The Huaca Rajada de Sipán in the Lambayeque Valley is neither the largest nor the most impressive site of the Moche culture of Peru's north coast. In 1987, however, Peruvian archaeologist Walter Alva found the New World's most spectacular royal burial at Sipán.

Walter Alva was alerted to the fact that looters were uncovering treasures in an adobe platform at a *huaca* (ancient adobe structure) complex near the town of Sipán. After looting was stopped, Alva initiated the first scientific investigation of a high-ranking burial in the New World as his team began the work of uncovering a number of elaborately buried Moche rulers accompanied by retainers and offerings.

The burials were found in a low side platform made of adobe bricks next to the much larger Huaca Rajada, which once had been a brightly painted ceremonial center. The elaborate burials in the low platform were probably the remains of priests who had once served the temple or lords who had been brought there to be buried in state.

ULLUCHU MAN

This mysterious figure was found below the mask of a warrior-priest in one of the tombs at Sipán. It was once mounted on a fabric banner covered with gilded metal plates. Traces of an ancient fruit called the ulluchu were found on the banner—hence the nickname Ulluchu Man.

SPECTACULAR IN DEATH

The tomb of the Lord of Sipán has been reconstructed in its original location. This is the richest and most informative elite burial ever found in the New World. The lord was buried in a wooden coffin, accompanied by other burials. His body was richly adorned with symbols of wealth and status.

THE LORD OF SIPÁN

Three major interments were found. The most elaborate, known as the Lord of Sipán, included more than 1,000 pottery vessels, a "guardian" with his feet cut off, and a main chamber containing the buried lord and six other individuals. The Lord of Sipán had been in a wooden coffin and had been adorned with headdresses, earspools, necklaces, rattles, knives, and ceremonial implements of gold and gold-copper alloys. Two men, three young women, and a young child, as well as plates of food, a sacrificed dog, and two sacrificed llamas, were placed around the Lord at some time around CE 290.

Tomb 2 is similar, with a central lord buried with fine offerings and five other burials. Tomb 3, known as "Old Lord," is an older burial dating to around CE 100. He was buried with a large quantity of metal objects but not with other people.

MOCHE LORDS AND *HUACAS*

At its height, *c.* CE 400, Moche culture extended for more than 300 miles (500 km) along the north coast of Peru, with *huaca* complexes situated in almost every valley. Political alliances may have linked valleys at various times, while at other times lords ruled over the agricultural communities of a single valley from their brightly painted *huacas*—which were centers of religious ceremony, including celebrations in remembrance of the dead that included drinking and feasting.

Moche society was highly ranked, and included specialists of various kinds and an elite warrior corps. The taking of prisoners for ceremonial sacrifice is frequently shown on ceramics and in vibrantly painted temple wall friezes. Moche craftsmen produced some of the most exquisite jewelry in the New World. Semiprecious stones were brought from long distances, as were *Spondylus princeps* shells from Ecuadorian waters.

After six or seven centuries of dominance, Moche culture underwent a radical transformation in the eighth century. Environmental disasters, demographic pressures, class conflicts, and external influences are all considered to be possible causes of Moche's demise.

Guayabo de Turrialba, Costa Rica

Poorly known compared to the great civilizations to the north and south, the ancient cultures of the Intermediate Area, between Mesoamerica and the Andes, were nevertheless highly sophisticated. Guayabo de Turrialba, in modern Costa Rica, represents the elaborate ceremonial complexes developed by the ancient people of the region.

Constructed *c.* CE 700–1300, Guayabo consists of a series of tombs, mounds, aqueducts, and pools built of river cobbles and connected by walkways and plazas. Stone statues were placed in prominent locations, and petroglyphs and offertory receptacles were carved into some of the cobbles. The core area of monumental architecture investigated by Costa Rican archaeologists since the 1890s consists of approximately 4.5 acres (2 ha), but it is likely that the residential area surrounding it was double or more in size.

LANDSCAPE BY DESIGN

The monumental complex at Guayabo follows the topography. Small creeks were channeled into pools that may have been sources of delight as well as serving a practical purpose. Four main sectors of the site appear to have been defined by controlled water sources. Breaking with this architectural flow, a 26-ft (8-m) wide causeway runs from two square platforms to Mound I, the largest at the site, 90 ft (28 m) in diameter and 9 ft (2.7 m) in height. On clear days, the cone of Turrialba Volcano appears to rise above Mound I as one walks toward it on the causeway. In the other direction, a stairway descends to a smaller causeway some 6–10 ft (2–3 m) wide leading to two mounds roughly half a mile (1 km) to the southeast of the site. In ancient times, paths such as these may have extended all the way to distant site complexes.

The long causeways connecting sites and the location of such centers in relatively vulnerable locales suggest that the era in which Guayabo was built may have been a time of relative peace. These communities were very likely bound by ties of marriage and trade. New value systems were emerging, with gold jewelry replacing the previous emphasis on jade and other semiprecious stones as wealth and status items. Powerful families very likely held sway as chiefly rulers, but important rituals based on honoring the dead may have distributed power widely among specialists in various religious rituals.

The network of trade, rituals, and feasting that sustained communities such as Guayabo and, on the Pacific side, Rivas may have arisen as a result of changes in trade routes and disruptions of power centers in Mesoamerica and the Andes. Between 1300 and 1400, a realignment of such forces appears to have caused the collapse of this system and the abandonment of Guayabo and similar sites.

TRADE AND RITUALS

The excavated site of Guayabo de Turrialba is seen here from the air. This ceremonial complex may have developed in response to changes in trade routes and disruptions of power centers in Mesoamerica and the Andes.

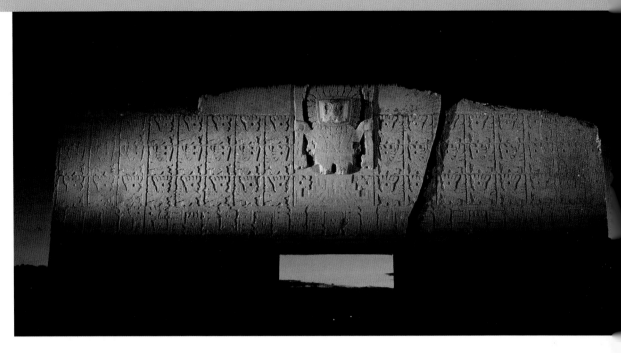

GATEWAY OF THE SUN

The structure known as the Gateway of the Sun (Puerta del Sol) is located at the northwest corner of the Kalasasaya Platform. It is believed to be associated with the sun god, and may have been used as a calendar. The surface seen here has bas-relief designs and a sculpture of a deity.

Tiwanaku, Bolivia

By the time the Inca Empire emerged in the 1400s, the greatness of Tiwanaku had faded from memory to myth. The importance of the culture represented by this vast site on the Bolivian altiplano can, however, be measured by the fact that the Incas saw Tiwanaku as the place of their sacred origins.

For a thousand years, the vast urban center of Tiwanaku held sway over the Titicaca Basin and the south-central Andean region. Beginning around 200 BCE, the Tiwanaku adapted earlier traditions and constructed a ceremonial center that grew into a huge urban complex. At its apogee, around CE 500, it occupied more than 2 sq miles (5 sq km).

The city core, encircled by a moat, housed ceremonial buildings and elite residences. It was constructed on a north–south/east–west grid, and the most important temples were oriented to distant mountains and celestial events.

The most striking features at Tiwanaku are the large, finely made stone structures and monumental sculptures, including the Kalasasaya Platform and Semi-Subterranean Temple, and the Akapana. The former includes a rectangular, sunken, stone-faced court with carved human heads projecting from it. In the plaza was one of the largest pre-Columbian stone sculptures known: the Bennett Monolith— a humanoid figure more than 20 ft (6 m) high. The adjacent Kalasasaya was probably a great stone-faced structure with temples on top that was later dismantled. Southward, the Akapana consisted of seven earth-filled platforms stacked one on top of the other in the shape of a stepped triangle. It may have been a man-made replica of sacred mountains, complete with miniature rivers coursing through

stone-lined tunnels and canals. Many other structures remain to be investigated at the site.

RAISED FIELDS AND CAMELID CARAVANS

The cold and arid Bolivian altiplano was made productive through a grand system of terraced fields, which extended the growing season for highland crops such as quinoa, potatoes, and other tubers. Tiwanaku's wealth and influence also relied on llama caravans transporting goods to and from distant regions, while alpacas produced high-quality wool for textiles. Indeed, Tiwanaku-style textiles are among the most vibrant and skillfully made fabrics of the ancient New World. Skilled craftsmanship is also in evidence in beautiful ceramics, metalwork, woodcarving, and other arts.

While architecture, ceremony, and trade supported Tiwanaku's power, the nature of its hegemony is uncertain. Warrior themes are not commonly found in Tiwanaku, although war may still have occurred. Tiwanaku's influence mostly spread southward. The Wari culture, which came slightly later and was based at an urban complex in Peru, dominated most of that region. Wari appears to have borrowed from Tiwanaku, although the relationship between the two remains unclear. So, too, the cause of Tiwanaku's end is uncertain; a century-long drought may have contributed to its demise in the eleventh century CE.

STONE GIANT

This humanoid figure is known as the Bennett Monolith after anthropologist Wendell Bennett, who carried out excavations at Tiwanaku in the 1930s. Standing more than 20 ft (6 m) high, it is one of the largest pre-Columbian stone sculptures known.

Cahokia, United States

It was the greatest metropolis of its time and place, with nothing comparable to it north of Mexico. In its heyday, from CE 1050 to 1200, more than 120 earthen mounds, houses, and other features extended over an area of 3 sq miles (8 sq km) in this, the greatest site of Mississippian culture.

Cahokia ■ Washington DC
UNITED STATES

No contemporary site in the Eastern Woodlands approaches the size of Cahokia or the number of its flat-topped pyramids and other earthen features. Situated near the confluence of great rivers, Cahokia received precious goods and products, most likely via trade and tribute. Archaeologists consistently find a plaza and wooden, pole-and-thatch residences associated with most pyramids. Storehouses, marker posts, compounds, and conical or rectanguloid burial mounds also filled the urban space. Bastioned palisades were erected, and at least one "woodhenge"—a circle of large, wooden posts—tracked celestial events.

At the summit of each pyramid was a community leader's house and/or a mortuary crypt. The pyramid, plaza, other mounds, and residences most likely comprised the basic social unit. At its height, the site was probably occupied by thousands of people. And Cahokia was part of a greater metropolitan area that included large sites across the river, where modern St. Louis now stands (with 26 pyramids); East St. Louis, to the south (50 pyramids); and many others.

GRAND MOUNDS AND ELABORATE BURIALS

At least nine large plaza groups occupying 22 acres (9 ha) are known. At the site core, the 46-acre (19-ha) Grand Plaza was surrounded by large mounds in a formal setting. To the north lies Monks Mound, covering 17 acres (7 ha) and rising 98 ft (30 m). Monks Mound, like others, probably grew in stages and changed over time from a burial mound to a platform temple-chiefly residence. Presumably, an important person lived at its summit, but the nature and degree of the power held remain unclear.

Power is clearly in evidence in Mound 72, one of the few major structures to have been extensively excavated. Relatively small, it nevertheless held eight mortuary tombs or platforms, which merged together over time to form the mound's final shape. The burials included high-status men—one of whom was interred with a falcon-shaped, shell-beaded cape— and groups of people accompanied by mica crystals, copper tubes, beads, and distinctive arrows, probably brought from distant regions. Groups of executed men and women suggest that people were sacrificed to accompany high-status individuals in the under-world—a sign of the Cahokians' power over local and foreign underlings.

By 1400, Cahokia had been abandoned. Other mound centers had risen farther south—Etowah, in Georgia; Moundville, in Alabama; and Spiro, in Oklahoma. The reasons for Cahokia's rise and fall, and who the modern descendants of Cahokians are, remain to be investigated.

SITE OF POWER

Cahokia lies in the fertile valley of the Mississippi River just south of the confluence of the Missouri, Illinois, and Mississippi Rivers. Monks Mound (seen here) is the largest mound in North America. Like other mounds, it probably changed its role over time from a burial mound to a platform temple-chiefly residence.

Australia and
the Pacific

Australian Aborigines

Archaeology provides a dynamic picture of Aboriginal colonization and settlement of Australia. In the process of colonizing the continent, Aboriginal people needed to weather extreme environmental changes, including the arid conditions of the Last Glacial Maximum (LGM) around 18,000 BP, as well as the environmental changes wrought by a significant rise in sea levels some 10,000 years ago.

The indigenous colonization of Australia provides some of the earliest evidence for the emergence of fully human behavior, and is proof of a major technological achievement, a first for humankind: the ability to build and navigate boats capable of crossing open sea between Indonesia and Australia. Moreover, this first colonization of the Australian region is highly significant for arguments about language origins and modern human behavior.

Apart from this, Australia has some of the earliest examples of elaborate burial practices in the world, including the first recorded cremation at Lake Mungo in New South Wales. Personal ornamentation, cranial deformation, and meaningful rock art are further aspects of complex symbolic behaviors.

THE FIRST AUSTRALIANS

The initial colonizers of Australia were *Homo sapiens sapiens,* and the current archaeological consensus is that they came from Asia, rather than Africa or America. The origins debate is complicated, however, by the discovery of morphologically distinctive people that are either robust or gracile. The robust group contains individuals from Kow Swamp and Cohuna in Victoria, while the gracile group contains individuals from Lake Mungo in New South Wales and Keilor in Victoria. Arguments continue as to whether these represent the arrival of two different colonizing groups or one morphologically variable group.

The most recent evaluations of radiocarbon dates for sites of human occupation suggest that people were living throughout Australia by 42,000–48,000 years ago. However, it is likely that colonization of the continent occurred slightly earlier than this, when sea levels in the region were at their lowest, at around 53,000 years BP. On their arrival, the colonists are most likely to have used their maritime economies and skills to focus on the coast as well as inland

waterways. By 30,000 BP, humans had traveled from the far north of Australia to the very tip of southern Tasmania and inhabited all but the most extreme of the country's environmental zones.

THE IMPORTANCE OF TRADE

For more than 40,000 years before the arrival of Europeans, Australian Aborigines mined the land for commodities such as quality stone for ax blades and ocher for ceremonies and art. Quarries such as at Koonalda Cave in South Australia were not only valuable resources but also the locations for gatherings that involved trade, ceremonies, and initiations. Valuable items formed part of a regional or interregional trade and exchange network, as was the case for ocher from northwestern South Australia and stone ax blanks from the Mount Isa–Cloncurry area. Pearlshell from the Kimberley region in Western Australia was transported as far as southern Australia, while the Kaurareg group in the Torres Strait had trade relations with both Cape York and the Fly River in Papua New Guinea.

INNOVATIONS AND ADAPTATIONS

While early European observers who visited the Australian continent naively saw an unchanging people in an unchanging land, the archaeology of the indigenous past shows several thresholds of substantial change occurring over the past 50,000 years. One of the most notable of these changes took place around 2,000–5,000 years ago, with an "intensification" involving refinements in existing technologies, increasing site use and site formation, and the exploitation of a range of new food resources. New technologies were invented in different parts of the country, often related to the more effective exploitation of seasonal foods. In some places, this involved the building of permanent stone structures such as the eel traps at Toolondo in Victoria. In central Australia, grindstones were used for the first time to process seeds into flour.

At some time during the sixteenth and seventeenth centuries, fishermen from Indonesia called Macassans began to visit the northern coastline of Australia. The Indonesians were seasonal visitors who came to harvest trepang (also known as bêche-de-mer). During the seventeenth and eighteenth centuries European explorers visited Australia's shores, but, unlike the Macassans, the Europeans were unable to establish amicable relationships with the Aboriginal people they encountered. While their visits initially appear to have had little impact on the Aboriginal people, the consequences for the health and social structure of the indigenous population were dire.

AN ANCIENT CULTURE

Like these men, photographed in the late nineteenth century, many indigenous Australians choose to maintain a traditional way of life. Techniques for living off the land, religious rituals, and other age-old facets of life are still passed down from generation to generation.

STONE TOOL TRADITION

In the past, Aboriginal tools have been made from readily available materials such as bone, teeth, wood, and stone. Flaked stone tools, like those seen below, make up most of the archaeological record in Australia because they survive the longest.

TIMELINE OF AUSTRALIAN ABORIGINAL HISTORY

Chronology	Events
c. 60,000 years ago	Major sea crossing of at least 55 miles (90 km) from Indonesia to the Australian continent.
60,000–40,000 years ago	Deliberate cremation and ocher burials occurring at Lake Mungo (New South Wales). Occupation of Malakunanja II site (Northern Territory).
40,000–35,000 years ago	Shell beads at Mimbi (Western Australia), traded from the coast. Human predation of megafauna at Devil's Lair (Western Australia).
35,000–30,000 years ago	Cone-shell beads made at Mandu Mandu (Western Australia).
30,000–25,000 years ago	Rock art made at Walkunder Arch Cave (Queensland).
25,000–20,000 years ago	Ground-edged axes made and used in northern Australia.
20,000–15,000 years ago	Settlement of the east coast with artifacts identified at Kenniff Cave (Queensland).
15,000–10,000 years ago	Bone beads made at Devil's Lair (Western Australia). Artificial cranial deformation practiced at Kow Swamp (Victoria).
10,000–5,000 years ago	Beginning of the Holocene. People at Roonka (South Australia) buried with bone necklaces and pendants. Wooden boomerangs preserved at Wyrie Swamp (South Australia).
5,000–400 years ago	Three-stage cultural sequence at Devon Downs (South Australia).
c. 350 years ago	First contact between Aboriginal people and Europeans.
c. 220 years ago	British colonization of Australia.
1967	Aboriginal people recognized as citizens of the Commonwealth of Australia.

Lake Mungo, Australia

Lake Mungo is an extinct lake in the semiarid country of southwestern New South Wales. It is important for its long-term paleoenvironmental data, archaeological evidence, ancestral remains (human burials), and 20,000-year-old human footprints. It is not strictly "a site"; the material comes from the shores of Mungo and other nearby lakes, and results from the whole period of human occupation of Australia.

Lake Mungo is one of a series of lakes that have been dry for the last 15,000 years, but which were often full during the Pleistocene. Sands, silts, and clays, coming from the lakes under different water regimes, built up dunes on their eastern shores. Dating these dunes shows when the lakes were dry or held water, and their stratigraphy allows distant archaeological materials to be linked up.

A HOST OF HUMAN BURIALS

Lake Mungo is best known for its ancestral remains, especially WLH1 and WLH3, discovered in the early 1970s. These and all other remains are of *Homo sapiens*, who were very similar to modern Aboriginal people.

WLH1 is the cremation of a slender young woman. After burning, the bones were gathered together, smashed, and placed in a pit, perhaps with some shells and red ocher. WLH3 is an extended burial of a man, lying on his back with his hands clasped over the pubic area. Pink ocher powder, probably from 125 miles (200 km) away, was scattered over the corpse. The man was about 50 years old, suffered from osteoarthritis of his right elbow—perhaps from throwing spears—and had lost his two lower canine teeth when young, probably deliberately knocked out as part of a ritual. His molar teeth were worn in a way that suggests he used them to strip plant fiber for making nets or baskets.

These two burials were originally dated to between 20,000 and 30,000 years old, with WLH3 being the older. Recently, definitive optical luminescence dating has shown that the overlying and underlying quartz sands date to 38,000 and 42,000 years respectively, so that both of the burials are now believed to be about 40,000 years old.

More than 150 other burials have been recorded at Lake Mungo. Some have been described but, in accordance with the wishes of the Aboriginal groups that manage the Willandra World Heritage Area in which Lake Mungo lies, very few have been dated and many reburied or left to decay.

The importance of the remains at Lake Mungo lies in the fact that they constitute one of the largest collections of Pleistocene human remains in the world; the WLH1 cremation is a very early example of this thoroughly modern human behavior.

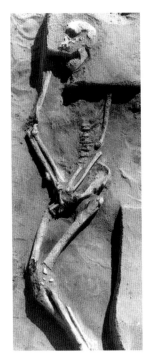

MIGHTY MUNGO MAN
The skeleton of an ancient man was discovered in the Lake Mungo region in 1974 by Jim Bowler. Known in scientific circles as WLH3 or Lake Mungo 3, there has been much debate over the years as to the exact age of the remains.

FOOTPRINTS FROM THE PAST

Only a few years ago, 124 human footprints were found (with hundreds more discovered since then). The footprints occur over 7,535 sq ft (700 sq m) of silty clay hardpan between two extinct lakes near Mungo. When they were made, the ground was soft and a bit muddy, so people walking on it sank in a little and made tracks that were subsequently preserved. Dates on the sands above and below the tracks are 19,000 and 23,000 years respectively. Interestingly, 76 of the prints occur as 8 trackways, made by men, adolescents, and children. Calculations based on the foot sizes show that one of the men was at least 6 ft (185 cm) tall, while the form of the footprints and the space between them show that all were running or trotting. These tracks are direct evidence that people then were similar in stature and physique to modern Aboriginal people.

Pleistocene human footprints near Lake Mungo were discovered by members of the local indigenous population.

A LONG-DESERTED LAND
The scattered mounds and tall pinnacles that line the foreshore of Lake Mungo are the remains of a huge sand dune. Although now arid, this region was once part of a system of freshwater lakes linked by Willandra Creek. When the lakes in the area were full, Aboriginal people lived here in large numbers.

EARLY INDIGENOUS KITCHEN
In 2005, Professor Steve Webb from Bond University in Queensland visited Mungo National Park, and discovered a small series of animal bones in an area that was possibly used for cooking. This fireplace has been dated to between 19,000 and 23,000 years old.

LIFE AT LAKE MUNGO

The evidence of peoples' lives at Lake Mungo consists of hearths, ovens, stone and bone tools, and food remains. While hearths appear simply as layers of ash and charcoal, ovens are depressions with ash, charcoal, and some food remains, above which are fist-sized lumps of clay, used as heat retainers to cook the food. The food remains may include animals such as wallaby, wombat, and native cat, as well as emu eggshell, fish, and shellfish. Variations in the contents show that meals were sometimes restricted to shellfish, or could contain a broader menu.

The mammal remains are all from species that are still living in the area today—there are no remains of extinct giant animals. The fish are mostly golden perch, many of them similarly sized. Capture by nets has been suggested, as this technique was used recently by Aboriginal people, but the natural cycle of perch behavior may have sometimes resulted in

fish of a certain size being the only ones present. Other fish were more likely caught by spearing. The shellfish are all freshwater mussels: small piles come from single meals but larger middens indicate more people or longer stays. The various animal remains combine to show people could have camped in the area at any time of the year, and frequently obtained food from all surrounding areas.

The stone artifacts discovered in the Lake Mungo area are similar to those found throughout Australia in the Pleistocene. Originally described as the "core tool and scraper tradition," it is now clear that sharp-edged flakes were the most commonly used tool, with blunt-edged, heavier lumps of rock being used for roughing out tools or chopping bones. Stone quarries occur on the western side of Lake Mungo, which means that stone for artifacts made near the WLH3 cremation was carried 8⅔ miles (14 km) or more before being flaked.

ENTER THE DEVIL'S LAIR
The Devil's Lair site was systematically excavated from
1972 to 1973 and produced
evidence of human occupation,
as well as the remains of more
than 30 different animal species.

Devil's Lair, Australia

Devil's Lair is located 3 miles (5 km) from the sea on the eastern side of the Leeuwin–Naturaliste ridge in Western Australia. This single-chamber limestone cave has a sandy floor roughly 660 ft (200 m) square. The former entrance to the cave is low, and the interior would have been extremely dark. Based on the stalactites that continue to grow from the roof, it is also likely to have been damp.

Excavations at Devil's Lair made in the 1970s confirmed human occupation of the site from at least 31,000 BP, at which stage the entrance had been widened to allow human access. One of the oldest dates came from charcoal collected in situ from a small, undisturbed hearth that was directly associated with burnt bone and quartz artifacts. The Devil's Lair site has important implications for the model of indigenous colonization of Australia.

The current model for colonization assumes that people arrived through the north coast of Australia and migrated south; the antiquity of Devil's Lair suggests that people moved quickly across the continent.

Archaeologists argue that, once established, the Devil's Lair cave was occupied by small family groups and/or infrequent hunting parties. Part of this argument is based on the fact that the excavations revealed a surprisingly low artifact density over a long time period. In addition, a seasonal pattern for human visitation has been argued based on the discovery of emu egg shells in Pleistocene deposits, as the breeding cycle of the emu means that these eggs would only be available during the winter months.

JEWELRY FROM NATURE
One of the most interesting finds at the Devil's Lair site was a trio of beads made from macropod bone. This shows that the indigenous inhabitants of the cave were not simply concerned with the day-to-day needs of survival—they also valued personal ornamentation.

TREASURE TROVE OF ARTIFACTS

The enclosed nature of the Devil's Lair cave and the alkaline soil both provided good preservation of a long cultural sequence. The bones found are predominantly from land-based animals such as large marsupials, which were the preferred prey. Hunters targeted both wet and dry habitats, and the variety of animals in the assemblage suggests human predation. This was confirmed by the existence of Pleistocene hearths and fire-pits, which were excavated in the same context as burnt bone and quartz plus fossiliferous chert artifacts.

The range of artifacts recovered from the Devil's Lair assemblage includes three ground-bone beads dated to between 19,000 and 12,700 BP, when the cave was a den for scavengers such as the Tasmanian devil. Devil's Lair is important because it is one of the earliest examples of the technology used in the production of bone beads in Aboriginal Australia, and of the development of personal ornamentation in Aboriginal societies. Between 12,000 and 6,500 BP, the entrance was obstructed by rubble and the deposit was sealed within. The cave did not reopen until 300 BP, when a new opening was created after the roof collapsed at the back of the cave.

Kow Swamp, Australia

In the late 1960s and early 1970s, excavations at Kow Swamp, located in central-northern Victoria, uncovered an extensive series of burials. The individuals whose remains were excavated had rugged physical features—very different to modern indigenous Australian populations—with thick cranial vault bones, well-developed muscle attachment sites, and prominent brow ridges.

These excavations challenged theories about the origins of indigenous Australians—in particular, whether there were one, two, or more colonizing groups, and where these groups may have come from. The skeletons also provided some of the earliest evidence of artificial cranial deformation, a practice undertaken to enhance the aesthetic "look" of the body, like tattoos or other forms of body ornamentation.

TWO CONTRASTING INTERPRETATIONS

The intriguing notion of two morphologically distinct colonizing populations was first put forward by Alan Thorne, who argued that the physical differences were so great that each must have had a different point of origin: the "robust" group were descendants of *Homo erectus* from Java in Indonesia, while the "gracile" group were originally a north Asian *Homo erectus* population. Kow Swamp and excavations at other sites such as Cohuna in Victoria contained robust individuals, while sites like Lake Mungo in New South Wales and Keilor in Victoria contained more gracile individuals.

In an apparent reversal of normal evolutionary trends, which tend to move from rugged to gracile, the robust individuals from Kow Swamp, dated to around 10,000–13,000 BP, were much younger than the gracile-looking people from Lake Mungo, who were dated to at least 40,000 BP and perhaps earlier. Thorne argued that the "archaic" robust people arrived first, followed by the morphologically more "modern" gracile group, and that the people from Kow Swamp constituted a relict population that retained a high proportion of the original population's physical features.

Others, however, have disputed these interpretations. Peter Brown, in particular, contends that the morphological range in both the robust and gracile groups lies within the normal range of variation exhibited by any single human population. He argues that the gracile population consists of a single individual, Lake Mungo 1 (or WLH1), and that the individuals known as Keilor and Lake Mungo 3 (or WLH3) actually share terminal Pleistocene traits of relatively great size and robustness. In opposition to Thorne's notion of two colonizing populations, Brown's position supports the notion of a single widely varied founding population, whose descendants included people from both Kow Swamp and Lake Mungo.

IMPACT ON MODERN ABORIGINES

The importance of Kow Swamp lies not only with the scientific information gleaned from the skeletons, and the origins debate that arose from this, but also with the significance these remains have for their descendants. The Kow Swamp remains also played an important role in debates concerning the repatriation of human remains to Aboriginal communities. Through this debate, Australian archaeologists discovered how Aboriginal people view these remains: for indigenous people they are not inert, scientific specimens, but ancestors whose spirit is linked to the bones. Australian archaeologists came to understand and support this position, and in 1990 the Kow Swamp skeletons were returned to the Aboriginal people of Echuca for reburial.

SUNSET ACROSS THE SWAMP
Kow Swamp is one of the most important archaeological sites in Australia for Aboriginal history. Between 1968 and 1972, Alan Thorne excavated in the region and identified the remains of 22 individual skeletons.

Cuddie Springs, Australia

Cuddie Springs is the only site in Australia where many bones of extinct giant animals and large numbers of stone artifacts have been found together. It is thus the focus of the question of how these animals died out. Were they killed off by people, or a natural and inevitable process?

ANCIENT STONE ARTIFACT
Found at Cuddie Springs, this sandstone grinding rock is around 30,000 years old. It is thought to be the oldest grinding stone in the world, some 20,000 years older than Northern Hemisphere specimens.

UNEARTHING THE PAST
Megafauna bones were first discovered at Cuddie Springs as long ago as the 1870s, but it wasn't until the 1990s that researchers uncovered evidence of human occupation of the site.

The site is an ephemeral lake in the semiarid inland of northern New South Wales. Many bones of large, now-extinct animals, most notably macropods (kangaroos), diprotodons (wombat-like marsupials weighing up to 3.3 tons [3 tonnes]), and the bird *Genyornis* are found down to 20 ft (6 m). Stone artifacts are found in two layers (6A and 6B), about 5 ft (1.6 m) below the surface. They are sealed in by an unbroken stony layer. Under them is a consolidated land surface. Radiocarbon and luminescence dates show both layers are around 30,000–35,000 years old. However, all attempts to directly date the animals' bones have failed.

The bones in layers 6A and 6B are not found in articulation. This shows that the animals did not die through being trapped in mud, nor did people kill them on the spot. The excavators claim that a few bones show traces of burning, or of being cut with sharp-edged stones. Rare earth element analysis shows that the bones were not derived from other layers, and 6A and 6B are different assemblages. Bone surfaces are not flaky, showing they were not long exposed before burial.

The stone artifacts are clearly intermingled with the bones. Microscopic wear on the edges of some, and residue still adhering to these edges, show that they had been used in some cases for butchering animals—though not which kind of animal.

THE WIDER CONTEXT
Cuddie Springs is important because it is unique. In other, older archaeological sites (such as Devil's Lair and Lake Mungo) there are no bones of extinct animals; all animals are those that are present today. A handful of other sites with extinct animal bones have dates or rare artifacts that suggest use during human times, but none provide good evidence. If large animals were still living when people arrived in Australia, we would expect these animals to have been hunted and their bones to appear in many archaeological sites. They don't.

The late date of Cuddie Springs is a challenge to the major model of animal extinction, which states that it is a rapidly occurring event caused by humans hunting the animals. This model, which is based on the extinction of the moa bird in New Zealand, has been commonly applied to Australia and the Americas. There is data that supports some extinctions occurring when people arrived in Australia over 40,000 years ago. If the model is right, something is wrong with Cuddie Springs.

The archaeologists who worked at Cuddie Springs, not surprisingly, believe that their site is correctly dated and interpreted. They note the site contains only a few species of extinct animals, and suggest that these may have been among the last examples still alive to be hunted by people.

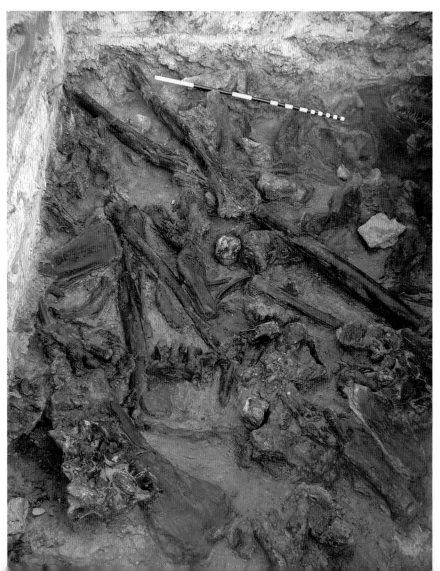

ISOLATED IMAGERY
The Punda Art Site near Newman in the Pilbara region of Western Australia boasts a prolific array of engravings on a remote hillside. The images represent various aspects of Aboriginal life in the area, including animals, water, boomerangs, and people.

Pilbara Petroglyphs, Australia

Pilbara   AUSTRALIA

○Canberra

Located in the arid northwest of Western Australia, the Pilbara remains at the forefront of current political and academic debate in Australia. Home to one of the largest concentrations of rock engravings in the world, it is also the location of some of Australia's largest companies, including the North West Shelf Gas Project, Pilbara Iron, and Dampier Salt. This cohabitation of rock art and industry has been uneasy.

RICH ARTISTIC LEGACY
While much of the rock art in the Pilbara is strongly defined and easily recognizable, there are many examples that have suffered from years of natural erosion, and are now so faint that it takes a trained eye to see the images.

It has been alleged that within the last 50 years around 20 percent of the total rock engravings of the Pilbara have been destroyed, with a further 12 percent in imminent danger of being lost forever. A minimal estimate by the government of Western Australia suggests that there are currently around 3,690 rock art sites in this region. In many cases these rock art sites stretch for a number of miles and often involve in excess of 4,000 engravings.

Particular concentrations of rock art are located on the Burrup Peninsula near Dampier, where figurative engravings have been carved into dolerite and fine-grained granitic rocks. Similar engravings are also found on many of the rocky islands known today as the Dampier Archipelago, with Dolphin and Angel Islands containing particular concentrations of art. Inland, large numbers of sites are found in close proximity to water sources such as the upper catchments of the Yule and Shaw Rivers and also along the De Grey River. It has been suggested that these were all either sites of former base camps or areas favored for hunting and fishing.

WINDOW ON AN ANCIENT WORLD
Within the Pilbara there are significant differences in engraving style and content, however, there are regions (such as the coastal Pilbara) where comparisons have been made. Friezes range in size from about 4 in (10 cm) to 8 ft (2.4 m), and frequently involve distinctive human figures engraved in profile and often engaged in scenes such as hunting, fighting, dancing, and lovemaking. Some figures are depicted naturally, while others are drawn with antenna-like projections from their heads, protruding muzzles, or exaggerated genitals, hands, and feet. Often these anthropomorphs appear to float within the rock art frieze with legs pointing in all directions. Other engravings such as animal tracks, birds, eggs, and land and marine mammals appear to reflect hunting and fishing activities. There are also depictions of the now extinct Tasmanian tiger or thylacine.

Although colonization of the Pilbara is known to have occurred over 20,000 years ago, the antiquity of the engravings remains in question. While the extensive superimposition of rock engravings suggests a great antiquity, radiocarbon dates from associated sites do not date back any further than 4,500 BP, and it is known that this artistic tradition continued until the pastoralist incursion into the area in the late nineteenth century. However, limited excavations have been conducted in this area, so it may be that older dates will emerge from future work.

Aboriginal Rock Art

STARTLING REGIONAL MOTIFS
These unusual pecked rock engravings in the Northern Territory are now protected by the N'Dhala Gorge Nature Park. The anthropomorphs feature rayed headdresses, and may represent mythological, ancestral, or Dreamtime figures.

Australian Aboriginal rock art provides some of the earliest examples of humanity developing an aesthetic and symbolic sense. Aboriginal people first colonized the Australian continent around 50,000 years ago, and Aboriginal people today inherit one of the oldest rock art traditions in the world.

While it is notoriously difficult to date rock art because the art does not usually contain materials that can be radiocarbon dated, excavations at some sites have revealed fragments of rock art in datable deposits, allowing us to speculate on the antiquity of Australian Aboriginal rock art. The oldest date for rock engravings is 13,000 BP, at Early Man Shelter in Cape York, Queensland, while the oldest painted rock fragment, dated to around 40,000 BP, was excavated from a site at Carpenter's Gap, Western Australia. Striated pigments were dated to around 50,000 years ago at Malakunanja II in the Northern Territory, but it is uncertain whether these pigments were used to produce rock art, body art, or some other form of art.

A SENSE OF PLACE

Aboriginal rock art sites are often a focus of the unique power that emanates from the Dreaming. They do not comprise silent and inert illustrations of mythological pasts, but images that have direct and potent relevance to the present. Australian Aboriginal rock art has its genesis in the Dreaming, the creation era during which ancestral beings traveled throughout the land, creating its topographic features through their actions and finally "sitting down" in one place to become an important part of that place forever.

In areas such as southern Arnhem Land, Aboriginal people construct their social identities partly through the rock art created at these places. An integral part of the process of growing up is learning about relationships to place and to country. As people move through their lands not only do they learn about relationships between place and ancestors, they also learn about themselves and their particular rights and responsibilities to land.

While the majority of rock art was created for a public audience, the production of certain forms of rock art can be linked to Aboriginal ceremonies. In Aboriginal societies, visual and performing arts contributed to the development of unique artistic traditions, each with regional variations. Such arts encompassed rock art and body designs, as well as dance, music, and song.

EVER-WATCHFUL WANDJINA
Wandjina figures are found throughout the Kimberley region of Western Australia. They are often very large, some measuring over 20 ft (6 m) in height, and are typically painted in black, red, or yellow lines over a white background.

FRAGILE SANDSTONE STENCILS
A treasure trove of red ocher stencil art has been found in Carnarvon National Park in southeastern Queensland. Boomerangs, hands and arms, kangaroo legs, nets, and carrying dishes are among the many stunning images in the area.

TYPES OF ABORIGINAL ROCK ART

There is enormous diversity in the kinds of rock art that exist throughout Australia. In the Sydney region of New South Wales there are rock engravings of fish and sea animals, as well as painted rock art. In Tasmania much of the art is engraved in geometric circles and lines, but there are also rock paintings of Pleistocene age. There are many geometric and animal track engravings in the center of Australia, part of an Australia-wide style that is known as the Panaramitee. In Cape York, Queensland, the most recent rock art encompasses figurative paintings of people and animals. In the Kimberley region of Western Australia, there are distinctive Wandjina figures, paintings of the ancestors who lived at that place and whose spirits still reside there. Hand stencils, which signify a person's relationship to a particular place, are found throughout Australia.

Rock art has not stayed the same through time. For example, the Gwion Gwion/Bradshaw tradition of the Kimberley was augmented by Wandjina figures in the more recent past. Likewise, the Mimi paintings of Arnhem Land were augmented by "X-ray" images in later times. Archaeologists think that new rock art styles were developed around 5,000 years ago, possibly related to an increase in territoriality, itself tied to an increase in population. This regionalization of rock art styles is particularly evident in the Kimberley and Arnhem Land areas of northern Australia. Occurring during the Holocene, the regionalization provides important evidence for major developments in Aboriginal land use and the emergence of corporate land-owning groups.

WHY STUDY ROCK ART?

The study of rock art is one of the most fascinating areas of archaeology, as art is crucial to our understanding of what it means to be human. All societies produce art. But art is not just something that is beautiful or of religious significance, it also communicates information about societies as whole entities and about the behaviors of individuals within those societies. The archaeological study of rock art is one of the most direct ways of accessing the beliefs and social structures of past indigenous societies.

Lake Condah, Australia

The shortfinned eel *(Anguilla australis)* aquaculture system engineered by the Gunditjmara Aboriginal people at Lake Condah in southwestern Victoria confounds European representations of traditional Aboriginal societies as hunter-gatherers. In 1841, Protector of Aborigines George Augustus Robinson first recorded these "earthworks," and stated that they "resembl[ed] the works of civilized man but ... on inspection I found [them] to be the work of the Aboriginal natives, purposefully constructed for catching eels."

While subsequent European farming activities over the past 150 years have destroyed some eeling facilities and associated sites, considerable parts of the eeling landscape remain intact, especially across rugged basaltic lava fields known locally as "stony rises." With the eruption of Mt. Eccles 30,000 years ago, lava flows radically altered drainage patterns to create a resource-rich wetland landscape of forested rises, swampy lowlands, creeks, and Lake Condah. According to Gunditjmara cosmology, this volcanic landscape is an expression of the Dreamtime being known as Budj Bim—his forehead is Mt. Eccles, and the scoria cones are his teeth.

Hundreds of facilities to harvest eels and other fish have been recorded along the 25-mile (40-km) lava flow to reveal an eeling landscape. All sites are walled structures up to 3½ ft (1 m) high, made by piling up blocks of lava by hand. They include races (walls to channel and redirect water flow that in some cases are over 165 ft [50 m] in length), canals (excavated ditches to channel water flow that in some cases are over 1,000 ft [300 m] in length), traps (funnel-shaped walls with a central gap to accommodate a woven basket), and dams (to block off natural depressions and create artificial ponds to hold and rear eels). In conjunction with similar archaeological evidence of Aboriginal people in southwestern Victoria excavating canals over 3,280 ft (1,000 m) long to extend eels into swamps beyond their natural range, it is clear that the Gunditjmara and their neighbors practiced eel aquaculture.

EFFECTIVE EEL CATCHER
Aboriginal inhabitants of Lake Condah made this long, funneled eel trap from woven reeds or grasses in 1910. Knowledge about how to catch and keep eels has been passed on from generation to generation, and these techniques are still being used today.

HOW DID THE EELING SYSTEM WORK?

Determining how eeling sites functioned is limited by the disruption of natural water flows and annual flooding cycles by European swamp drainage to create agricultural lands. Facilities were designed to accommodate the spring migration of juvenile eels up local waterways from the ocean, local maturation of eels to adulthood, and the autumn migration of

PROTECTION FOR THE FUTURE

Many archaeological sites in the Lake Condah region are within the Budj Bim National Heritage Landscape, which was inscribed on the Australian National Heritage List in 2004. Management of this unique area is controlled and coordinated by the Gunditjmara traditional owners through key organizations such as the Winda Mara Aboriginal Corporation. An important Gunditjmara management goal is restoration of natural water regimes to Lake Condah to reactivate the ancestral eeling landscape.

highly nutritious fat adult eels returning to the sea some 10 to 20 years later. Orientation of traps reveals that eeling could occur as water levels rose and fell. Virtual three-dimensional reconstructions of sites and associated topographies using geographical information systems (GIS) allow simulation of different water flows and water levels to reveal how traps and channels located hundreds of feet apart formed an integrated eeling system that operated on a landscape scale during different seasons of the year. Gunditjmara eeling involved family and clan-owned facilities and would have accommodated the resource needs of considerable numbers of people throughout the year. The complex levels of interclan social and political organization required to operate and manage this landscape may explain the occurrence of intergroup gatherings and the unique ethnographic evidence for hereditary leaders ("chiefs") in this region of Aboriginal Australia.

The scale of eeling operations is matched by the associated domestic sites. On elevated areas, adjacent to many fish traps, are circular walled houses 7–10 ft (2–3 m) in diameter and up to 3½ ft (1 m) high. These site clusters are consistent with permanent occupation of the region made possible by rich wetlands with perennial water, a wide range of reliable plant foods, and eel aquaculture. Year-long availability of food was enhanced by the storage of eels preserved by smoking. Archaeological evidence of eel storage and preservation includes stone-walled eel cache structures and eel smoking trees with microscopic traces of eel fats in charcoal-rich sediments within hollow trunk bases. Gunditjmara manipulation and mastery of freshwater hydrology and fish ecology, productivity, and preservation regularized environments such that continuous food supplies and permanent settlement were possible.

HOW OLD IS THE LAKE CONDAH SITE?

Few scientific insights are available on the antiquity and long-term development of eeling facilities. Coring of Lake Condah sediments suggests that water levels were sufficiently high enough for traps to operate only within the past 2,000 years. Limited excavation of channels and a dam structure have produced dates within the past 500 years. Indirect evidence suggests major elaboration of the eeling system during the past 3,000 years in association with major increases in the scale and complexity of Aboriginal use of the region, as revealed by excavation of nearby rock shelters, shell middens, and oven-mound sites. Gunditjmara beliefs hold that eel aquaculture has a much older antiquity.

During the Eumeralla War of the colonial frontier era, the Gunditjmara people used the "stony rises" as a refuge from the British invaders, and it is likely that the use of some eeling facilities increased accordingly. This view is consistent with the establishment of new settlements, as revealed by the excavation of stone houses containing "contact" materials (such as clay tobacco pipes and flaked bottle glass tools). The Gunditjmara continue to use stone-walled traps and baskets to capture eels today.

CONDAH CONSERVATION
Dr. Peter Coutts, Director of the Victorian Archaeological Survey, checks the remains of an Aboriginal hunting hide at Lake Condah in 1982. Efforts to preserve this area have been going on for decades, and the Lake Condah region is now protected by the Budj Bim National Heritage Landscape.

AN ABORIGINAL VILLAGE?
The Gunditjmara people built around 700 circular stone houses in the Lake Condah area. Visible remains show that separate groups of up to 16 huts existed on the 31-mile (50-km) Tyrendarra lava flow, which originated from the Mt. Eccles volcano in prehistory.

Nullarbor Caves, Australia

The Nullarbor Plain is a vast limestone plateau that runs along the south coast of Western Australia and extends up to the Great Victorian Desert. It is some 100,000 sq miles (260,000 sq km) of generally flat bedrock. The name Nullarbor comes from the Latin *nullis arbor* or "no tree," reflecting the aridity of the region. Today the annual rainfall is a low 6–10 in (150–250 mm), and resources have probably always been minimal.

YAWNING DESERT CHASM
Limestone caves such as Koonalda offered Aboriginal travelers in southern Australia a cool respite from the searing heat of the bleak Nullarbor Plain above. The subterranean lake may have also been a source of fresh water for the indigenous nomads.

Nonetheless, about 60 cultural sites have been identified throughout the Nullarbor region, most of which are found in caves dotting the limestone ridge. The most famous of these is Koonalda Cave, which lies at the western edge of South Australia, and only about 31 miles (50 km) from the ocean. The cave is a craterlike sinkhole that lies around 200 ft (60 m) below the surface of the plain and stretches at least 820 ft (250 m) horizontally, culminating in a subterranean lake. Two large passages extend from the northwestern side of the sinkhole—one leading to wall markings and the other to underground lakes, the furthest of which lies 1,970 ft (600 m) from the cave entrance and 300 ft (90 m) below the surface of the plain.

Archaeological investigations of Koonalda began in 1956 and identified this as an important stopping point for Aboriginal people traveling through this arid landscape. Described by one archaeologist as an awesome gothic chamber, it has been argued that the primary function of Koonalda Cave was mining, as flint nodules were removed along the length of its corridor. Artifacts made from this flint have been excavated inside this cave alongside torches that may have been used to give light to miners.

THE ROCK ART OF KOONALDA

One of the most remarkable rock art discoveries in Australia is the presence of Pleistocene wall markings deep inside Koonalda Cave, far below the Nullarbor

Plain. In total darkness, and as far as 850 ft (260 m) inside the cave, a large number of graphic markings were found on the walls. In some areas of the cave the walls are soft and easily carved, and many of these walls have been decorated with finger-marked geometric lines, which run parallel to one another. These markings appear to cluster around the cracks and imperfections found in the rock surface.

The Northwest Passage of Koonalda Cave is garnished with markings leading to the upper chamber, which is thought to have been used for ritual purposes. The majority of the wall markings in this passageway are "finger flutings," which are made by drawing the fingers across the soft limestone surfaces. In most cases three or four fingers were held close together and drawn down the wall, resulting in a clear trail of parallel lines. Some large, flat wall surfaces are completely covered with crisscrossing sets of parallel finger markings. Often, at the beginning of the wall marking, the fingers were spread slightly, but as the hand was dragged down the wall, the fingers drew closer together, and the lines are closely bunched. The repeated engravings are thought to represent repeat visitations to the site, with miners adding to their existing marks. Similar markings are found in other limestone areas in Victoria, Western Australia, and southeastern South Australia.

Koonalda Cave was abandoned by Aboriginal miners nearly 19,000 years ago. One reason for this may have been a massive rock fall within the upper chamber at that time. Radiocarbon dates from well-stratified hearths excavated in this cave range from 22,000 to 15,000 BP. These dates have been used to argue convincingly for an antiquity of around 20,000 years for the finger flutings.

Local missionaries and government officials mentioned the cave in passing throughout the 1900s, and most acknowledged that it was an important stopping place for indigenous people traveling across the bleak Nullarbor region. Such rock holes are natural storage places for rainwater, utilized for drinking water, and five similar rock holes lie within a radius of 15 miles (24 km) of Koonalda Cave.

OTHER CAVES OF THE NULLARBOR

Since the 1960s many other caves of varying sizes have been explored in this region, including Warbla and Abracurrie. Local Aboriginal people reported that the caves on the eastern side of the Nullarbor were inhabited by Ganba (a Dreaming snake), whose breathing could be heard in the rushing water of the subterranean rivers and lakes. For the most part these caves do not appear to have been occupied by humans, despite containing a large quantity of animal bones (including extinct megafauna).

Caves on the western side of the Nullarbor, such as Allens Cave, however, have clear human signatures. Allens Cave dates back to around 20,000 years, and stone fragments have been controversially thermo-luminescence dated back to 40,000 BP. If this date is correct, it marks the earliest human occupation of the arid zone in Australia. The terminal Pleistocene site of Madura Cave represents an environmental shift away from arid scrubland to coastal woodland at this time. This site produced the oldest reliable radiocarbon dates for the Australian dingo, which has been dated to 3,450±95 BP.

PRIMEVAL PREDATOR

In 2002, cavers exploring the Nullarbor region came across a cavern that held the complete skeleton of a giant marsupial lion, *Thylacoleo carnifex*, lying where it had perished hundreds of thousands of years before.

BOUND TO DIE IN THE DARK

Paleontologist Dr. John Long studies the remains of an extinct giant kangaroo, found in the depths of a Nullarbor Plain cave. Many large kangaroos met their end here; if they landed on one of the small openings that dot the landscape, they were unable to stop themselves from falling through to the cave below.

A HARSH LANDSCAPE FOR HUMANS

The arid limestone plain of the Nullarbor has always been a marginal habitat for humans. The excavations of Pleistocene deposits in the region suggest that human populations were small and arguably highly mobile. Increasing artifact densities in Holocene deposits suggest that sites began to be used with accelerating frequency from 4,000 years ago, but they were never used with the same intensity as sites in other regions of Australia.

Ubirr Rock, Australia

Located in the East Alligator region of Kakadu National Park in the Northern Territory, Ubirr Rock contains some of the most important examples of Aboriginal rock art in Australia. Ubirr consists of a group of rock outcrops and natural overhanging shelters that contain an assemblage of Aboriginal rock paintings, some of which are many thousands of years old. The art depicts creation ancestors, spirit figures, and animals, as well as events such as first contact with Indonesian trepang harvesters and British colonizers.

A VISUAL HISTORY
The Main Gallery of Ubirr contains images painted by Aboriginal visitors who used the overhanging rock as a shelter. Some images pay tribute to the animals that were hunted for food, to ensure abundant resources in the future.

Ubirr Rock is located in the homeland of the Gagudju indigenous people, whose culture is rich in social complexity, spirituality, and has a high level of social sophistication. The rock art at Ubirr connects storytelling, myths, rituals, and sorcery. The artists symbolically describe the Dreaming/creation stories, their beliefs, their history, and their spirituality in their art. The strong and enduring relationship between the ancestral beings, the landscape (including the surfaces of Ubirr Rock), and every living creature establishes the creative source of the art. Side by side, and sometimes superimposed on one another, are ancient seminaturalistic representations, along with symbolic stylizations of mythological figures. In addition, there are fascinating "X-ray" pictures that show the internal structure and organs of local animals and fish including barramundis, crocodiles,

and turtles. There are three main art assemblages at Ubirr: Main Gallery, Namarrgarn Sisters Gallery, and Rainbow Serpent Gallery.

THE MARVELS OF THE MAIN GALLERY

The Main Gallery contains many examples of the famous Aboriginal style called "X-ray" art, as well as paintings of European males with their hands on their hips like bosses, and Mimi spirit figures that are so thin they can live in the cracks of the rocks. The Mimi came out at night and painted figures, including self-portraits, on high and inaccessible rock surfaces. The local explanation is that the Mimi spirits painted the pictures themselves by bringing the rock down to ground level and then replacing the rock when they had finished. The Mimi self-portraits remind people of the spirits' presence, and the art's inaccessibility tells of their unnatural abilities.

The northern end of the Main Gallery holds a painting of a thylacine, or Tasmanian tiger, which has been extinct in that locale for some 2,000 years.

KAKADU NATIONAL PARK

Comprising around 7,700 sq miles (20,000 sq km), Kakadu National Park is a place of outstanding beauty, great antiquity, and seasonal diversity. Aboriginal people have lived in this region for more than 50,000 years, and it has two distinct seasons: "the wet" and "the dry." The land teems with wildlife in "the wet" and wears a dusty coat in "the dry." The ecological features are reflected in much of the region's rock art, such as that found at Ubirr Rock. In 1984, Kakadu National Park was placed on the World Heritage List for its natural and cultural value.

The Anbangbang Gallery is one of Kakadu's most visited rock art sites.

This painting indicates the age of some of the artwork. Pieces of striated ocher at the nearby site of Malakunanja II were thermoluminescence dated to around 50,000 BP, suggesting that art was produced in this area at around this time.

MEET THE NAMARRGARN SISTERS, REPTILIAN TRICKSTERS

The Namarrgarn sisters are the primary figures in the Namarrgarn Sisters Gallery. The gallery's story is that the two sisters spent a great deal of time playing and talking together and were good friends. They are depicted with pieces of string, which they can throw down from the stars. The sisters can then climb down the string and make people sick. In the Dreamtime the sisters were also able to change into crocodiles and frighten creatures by creeping up on them. They often played this trick on each other and on people.

The Namarrgarn sisters are represented as crocodiles, evident by the lumps behind their eyes. These lumps represent their cunning ability to detect prey above and below the water. The story of the sisters is told to children to warn them about crocodiles and to explain why they are so dangerous. This tale is part of a series of stories that are intended to warn people of the dangers within the landscape. The stories are also, possibly, a device for social control.

THE REMARKABLE ROCK ART OF THE RAINBOW SERPENT GALLERY

The Rainbow Serpent Gallery is the most sacred of the three main sites at Ubirr, and is traditionally a women-only site. This is a reflection of the Rainbow Serpent as creator, because she "sang" the rocks, plants, and animals into being as she traveled across the land. Ubirr is one of several places visited by the Rainbow Serpent during her Dreaming travels across the top end of Australia. As she passed through Ubirr, she painted her image on the rock to remind the Aboriginal people of her presence.

In the region of Ubirr Rock, the Rainbow Serpent is known as Garranga'rreli. In her human body she is named Birriwilk, and as such she traveled with another woman searching for sweet lily roots. The path of her travels is a special song-line that is sacred to Aboriginal people. The story of the Rainbow Serpent Gallery is that a mother once ignored her child's crying for sweet lily roots. The child's incessant crying attracted the Rainbow Serpent, who wound herself around the people, killing and eating them, including the child. The moral of the parable is that crying children should always be looked after.

The stories, paintings, and features at Ubirr Rock are powerful images that are interlinked as parables, which reinforce the ancient moral and legal codes of the Gagudju people. These stories remind people that spiritual life and the law are inseparable.

UBIRR DONS A DUSKY CLOAK
As with much of the sandstone in the region, the rays of the setting-sun serve to enhance the colors of Ubirr. The oldest rock art at Ubirr, from the Pre-Estuarine Period, features warm ocher pigments that reflect the color of the landscape.

PLACE OF QUIET REFLECTION
From the top of the escarpment at Ubirr Rock, modern-day visitors can enjoy the same 360-degree panoramic view of the surrounding floodplains, Arnhem Land, and dark patches of rain forest that ancient Aborigines enjoyed.

The Melanesians

The term "Melanesia" was defined in the early nineteenth century by the French explorer Dumont d'Urville, and it literally means "black islands" or "dark islands." It is made up of the main island of New Guinea and the archipelagos to the east: Bismarck Archipelago, the Solomon Islands, New Caledonia, Vanuatu, and Fiji.

REMARKABLE FIND IN FIJI

In 2002, a 2,900-year-old skeleton was found at Naitabale in Central Fiji. Named Mana, meaning "truth," the skeleton is that of a woman, whose ancestors are believed to have come from the Solomon Islands.

PIECES OF HISTORY

Lapita pottery is the archaeological signature of the movement of peoples out of Near Oceania and the colonization of Remote Oceania for the first time. Over 500 different motifs have been distinguished on Lapita pottery.

FIRST MELANESIAN SOCIETIES

These early societies were remarkable for a number of reasons. Firstly, as New Guinea was never joined to Southeast Asia, and New Britain and New Ireland were never joined together or joined to mainland New Guinea, colonization required exceptional feats of prehistoric seafaring. Secondly, there is evidence of environmental management by either fire and/or physical clearance. The presence of waisted blades at the early sites of Nombe, Kosipe, and the Huon Peninsula suggests Pleistocene forest clearance in both highland and lowland environments.

Thirdly, there is clear evidence of long-distance interactions between New Ireland and New Britain occurring 20,000 years ago. Obsidian sourced to outcrops in western New Britain is found in sites on southern New Ireland (Matenbek), a distance of some 220 miles (350 km). Fourthly, from around 9,000 years ago when global temperatures rose, there is evidence for agriculture from the highlands of New Guinea. Crops including bananas, sugar cane, other types of canes, tubers, breadfruit, taro, and yams were domesticated in New Guinea and are thought to have been grown at Kuk.

The spread of agriculture outside of mainland New Guinea occurred much later—about 3,000 years ago—and is associated with the colonization of Remote Oceania for the first time. The unique archaeological signature of this expansion is a particular form of highly decorated pottery called Lapita. These colonizing populations not only introduced agriculture into Remote Oceania, but also animals and birds from Southeast Asia such as the chicken, dog, and pig.

MELANESIA IN THE LAST 2,000 YEARS

This period of time is marked by a number of changes in the archaeological records suggestive of continuing interaction between communities, and eventually strong regionalization and diversity within the region in the last millennium. By 2,000 years ago, pottery ceases to be made in New Britain and New Ireland, but continues to be made in Manus, the Solomons, Vanuatu, New Caledonia,

I n biogeographical terms, the area can be divided into two: Near and Remote Oceania. Near Oceania incorporates mainland New Guinea, the Bismarck Archipelago, and the Solomon Islands, and forms a chain of intervisible islands where the next island can either be seen from the last, or at least be seen when at sea but not out of sight of the last island. Beyond the Solomon Islands lies Remote Oceania, where the islands are not intervisible.

The divide between Near and Remote Oceania is a cultural boundary for Pleistocene explorers. Near Oceania was first occupied at least 40,000 years ago, and probably earlier. Evidence for this early occupation is not only found on the Huon Peninsula of mainland Papua New Guinea, but also in the Bismarck Archipelago site of Buang Merabak on New Ireland. By 30,000 years ago both the highlands of Papua New Guinea and the North Solomons were colonized. By 20,000 years ago the island of Manus, located 250 miles (400 km) north of New Guinea, was colonized. On the island of Guadalcanal, situated in the Solomons, evidence shows that the first occupation is much later, at around 6,000 years ago.

MELANESIAN FAUNA

The further east one progresses in Melanesia, the less varied the fauna becomes. For instance, while New Guinea has five species of wallaby, two anteaters, plus a number of phalangers (possums) and tree kangaroos, the Bismarck Archipelago has no anteaters, only two phalangers, and one wallaby. Of the 265 birds found on the New Guinea coast opposite New Britain, only 80 are found on New Britain itself. Further to the east, there is even less diversity. Within Remote Oceania the only land animals are two large rats; no major land mammals crossed this 220-mile (350-km) divide.

EVIDENCE OF EARLY PEOPLE
Initial research at Buang Merabak cave in New Ireland determined that it was first occupied 32,000 years ago (further studies of the cave deposits may see this date change). These early hunter-gatherers ate bats and shellfish while occupying the cave.

and Fiji. At that time, changes to the pottery style are seen from Manus and Buka to New Caledonia and Vanuatu. Gone are the bowls and stands, jars, and globular pots with everted rims, and present are the incurving or inverted vessels, with complex incision, appliqué, and punctation not seen before. In Fiji similar pottery appears much later, and is dated to just over 800 years ago.

Two major developments occurred in the last 500 years in this region. The first was the appearance of the classic trading networks that are cited in most anthropology texts. The second had a far-reaching impact on New Guinea: the introduction of the sweet potato. This plant was imported from South America, although the mechanism of introduction is still unknown. Theories suggest that it was either brought to New Guinea as a by-product of sixteenth-century Spanish exploration, or perhaps even earlier by Polynesians who had returned from long voyages to South America. Its introduction had a great impact on the highlands region, where it soon replaced taro as the staple in many areas. It is a more versatile crop than taro, as it can be grown at higher altitudes and in poorer soils, plus it requires less time to mature. Unlike taro, it provides food for pigs without the need to be cooked. The introduction of the sweet potato led to intensification in agricultural production, an increase in pig husbandry, and also to the major structural changes within highland societies that were observed at the time of European contact.

MELANESIAN ARCHAEOLOGICAL SITES

The artifacts and organic remains unearthed by archaeologists at these sites reveal much about the migration of people through Melanesia, and the cultures that flourished throughout the islands.

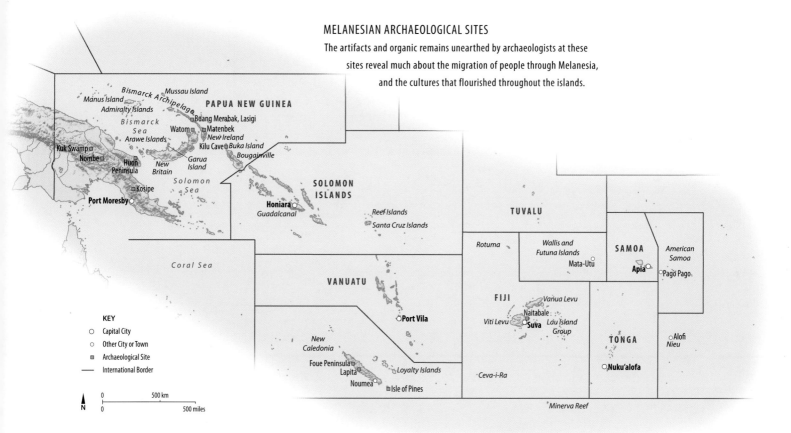

KEY
○ Capital City
○ Other City or Town
▣ Archaeological Site
— International Border

Huon Peninsula, Papua New Guinea

Jutting out from the east coast of Papua New Guinea, the Huon Peninsula has an imposing coastline made up of raised terraces climbing hundreds of feet out of the sea. It was on one of these raised terraces that remnants of peoples who occupied this coastline 40,000 years ago were found.

In 1980 Les Groube, a lecturer at the University of Papua New Guinea, led a team of students on a field trip to the Huon Peninsula. Alerted to the antiquity of the Peninsula by Professor John Chappell, a geomorphologist from the Australian National University, Groube and his students located over 100 surface finds of waisted axes in an area called Fortification Point, below Bobongara Hill. These tools were found in terraces 260–660 ft (80–200 m) above sea level. A number of subsequent field trips undertaken by Groube and his students from the University of Papua New Guinea have taken place, which have shed more light on the history of the Huon Peninsula's occupation.

The location and dating of the raised terraces is of importance. These were once coastal sites, and finding comparable 40,000-year-old coastal occupation sites is difficult as many would have been destroyed by rising sea levels. Secondly, Groube's attention was focused on these terraces because John Chappell had already dated a nearby raised reef using 230TH/234U (thorium/uranium) methods to 48,000 years.

THE EXCAVATIONS

Groube and his team conducted many archaeological excavations along and into the bank of a stream (Jo's Creek) that cut into the terraces, exposing a number of stratigraphic units. Artifacts including waisted axes were found in situ within a tephra (layer of volcanic ash) that was dated by thermoluminescence to around 40,000 years in age. The underlying coral is dated to between 50,000 and 60,000 years old. The waisted stone tools are large and unifacial (flaked on one surface). In weight they average just below 4½ lb (2 kg), with the largest one over 5½ lb (2.6 kg). They are 4–9 in (10–22 cm) in length.

Waisted axes have been found in other archaeological sites in Papua New Guinea as well as in Australia; however, these finds from the Huon Peninsula are the earliest. Groube speculated about their use, noting that the nature of the raw material made it impossible for them to be sharpened, thus they were probably not used as fine chopping tools. The waist, however, does suggest hafting onto a wooden handle. Groube argued that they were probably used for forest clearance such as ring barking and/or root removal, in thinning pandanus strands to enable fruit ripening, or in the processing of sago.

The Huon Peninsula provides a unique glimpse into the lives of these earliest of settlers in the Pacific region. More waits to be unearthed in the area by future teams of archaeologists.

MISTY MOUNTAIN TERRACES
The Huon Peninsula rises some 13,000 ft (4,000 m) from sea level to the Saruwaged, Rawlinson, and Cromwell Ranges. The lower section along the coastline forms horizontal ridges on which early inhabitants were able to live.

Kosipe, Papua New Guinea

PAPUA NEW GUINEA
Kosipe
Port
Moresby

The Kosipe Valley contains some of the oldest remains left by Melanesian ancestors, dating back to 35,000 years ago. Located about 84 miles (135 km) north of Port Moresby, it sits 6,560 ft (2,000 m) above sea level and provides a unique glimpse into peoples' adaptability during the late Pleistocene era.

HIGH-ALTITUDE HABITATION
Due to the scatter of fireplaces, organic remains, and stone tools in the area, archaeologists believe that Kosipe was not a permanent settlement—but it was used as a site of seasonal encampment, possibly related to the availability of food sources.

The archaeological site is located in the grounds of the Kosipe Sacre Coeur Mission, on a ridge overlooking the Kosipe Valley. Evidence of prehistoric occupation was brought to light in the 1960s by the Catholic fathers of the mission, who found waisted stone axes while digging church foundations. A young PhD student looking for a suitable project, Peter White, was made aware of the finds, and he subsequently excavated Kosipe over two seasons during the mid- to late 1960s.

The location is basically a hillside surface scatter of stone tools overlying a well-stratified site. The tools (in association with carbon) are sandwiched between volcanic tephras from Mt. Lamington, located 87 miles (140 km) away. White radiocarbon dated charcoal found with the earliest occupation to 26,000 years ago, making this (at the time) the oldest evidence of people in New Guinea. Published in 1970, the results of these excavations showed that people may have traveled to this high-altitude area in search of mountain pandanus. The waisted stone tools, similar to those found at the late Pleistocene sites of Nombe and on the Huon Peninsula, could have been used for forest clearance or pandanus harvesting.

THE AGE OF KOSIPE REVISITED
Professor Geoff Hope, a paleobotanist, visited the Kosipe Valley in 1970. He took a number of pollen cores from the valley floor and demonstrated that forest clearance had occurred some 30,000 years ago, with an increase in the use of a technique that involved firing the vegetation. Hope returned in 2005, this time with Professor Glenn Summerhayes from Otago University in New Zealand. Summerhayes and his team reexcavated the Kosipe site, and they discovered that human occupation in this region extended to 35,000 years ago.

Of importance was the identification by Dr. Andy Fairbairn (from the University of Queensland in Australia) of pandanus seeds using a Scanning Electron

LAYER UPON LAYER
Excavations at Kosipe show clear stratification of the site. When Peter White first worked here, he excavated over 506 sq ft (47 sq m), discovering deposits down to about 32–40 in (80–100 cm).

Microscope, in the levels dated to 30,000 radiocarbon years. These were found in the same levels as the waisted stone tools. It must be remembered that during the late Pleistocene the temperature at Kosipe was up to 5 degrees colder than today, with the site situated close to the highest point of tree growth, and within sight of snow-topped mountains. This was a harsh place, yet people who had just colonized New Guinea adapted to the colder climates as they searched for pandanus.

The archaeological site at Kosipe is significant as it provides important evidence to show that early modern humans not only adapted their behavior to suit new environments, but also used and deliberately managed the landscape by fire. This is some of the earliest evidence in the world of modern peoples changing their landscapes.

Kilu Cave, Papua New Guinea

The earliest evidence of people in the North Solomons area is found within Kilu Cave. Located near Malasang Village on southeast Buka Island, it is a large cave with two chambers. The outer chamber is over 100 ft (30 m) wide and 55 ft (17 m) deep. The inner chamber is wet, with water covering the cave floor.

The Kilu Cave site was surveyed and excavated during 1987 by Steve Wickler as part of his PhD fieldwork. Wickler excavated a 10 × 3 ft (3 × 1 m) trench within Kilu to a depth of just over 7 ft (2 m). Cultural materials including fish, reptile, and mammal bones, shells, and stone tools were found throughout. Most of the stone tools were small unretouched flakes made from quartz, chert, volcanic rock, and calcite.

The site has two main phases of occupation, with the first dating to between 29,000 and 20,000 years ago. As well as a suggestion of sporadic use of the site, there is unique evidence for the subsistence strategies of the early population. The faunal remains suggest that a major part of the diet was made up of reptiles, rats, bats, and fish. Both pelagic (open-sea) and inshore fish remains were found, suggesting that a variety of fishing techniques were used. Shell remains are made up mostly of gastropods and the nerite species.

Kilu Cave is important as it also provides evidence for the use of aroids such as taro or yams some 29,000 years ago. This is based on the identification of small starch grains, cellulosic plant tissue, and crystalline raphides found on stone tools. If substantiated by scientific analysis, this is the earliest evidence of the use of root vegetables in the world.

THE SECOND OCCUPATION

There is a hiatus in occupation of around 10,000 years at Kilu that Wickler thinks may be related to the drop in sea level of 430 ft (130 m) during the height of the Last Glacial Maximum. Occupation resumes by 10,000 years ago, and this second phase continues to 5,000 years ago. During this second phase there is evidence for a more intense use of the site, with an increase in the density of midden material. Many of the animal and fish species eaten in the Pleistocene continue to be exploited into the Holocene, but there are two major additions to the diet. The first is phalanger (possum), which is not endemic to the area. The second is the bivalve *Polymesoda coaxans*. As this bivalve lives in the muddy floors of mangrove swamps, changes in the environment occurring with sea-level rises are evident.

The upper level of Kilu is disturbed, with the top 12 in (30 cm) containing evidence of Buka-style pottery known to be late second millennium BP in age, along with pottery from much later contexts and artifacts from World War II.

ISLAND LIFE IN MELANESIA

Buka and Bougainville Islands are separated by the very narrow Buka Passage. Although geographically part of the Solomons, these two islands are politically part of Papua New Guinea. Kilu Cave is the earliest occupied site in this region.

FOOD FOR THOUGHT

Kilu Cave is located 165 ft (50 m) in from the sea, at the base of a 115-ft (35-m) high limestone cliff. As well as evidence of root vegetables playing a part in the diet of the early occupiers, wild canarium and coconut palm (*Cocos nucifera*) have also been identified.

Kuk Swamp, Papua New Guinea

Located at 5,400 ft (1,650 m) above sea level in the highlands of Papua New Guinea, Kuk Swamp provides some of the earliest evidence of agriculture in the world. The site was part of the Kuk Tea Plantation excavations just outside the town of Mt. Hagen in the upper Wahgi Valley.

The site first came to prominence in the 1970s, when drainage ditches were being cut into the swampy valley floor to make the area suitable for an agriculture research station. Excavations were undertaken over a number of decades by Professor Jack Golson, of the Australian National University. As well as wooden implements, the major features of the Kuk excavation are prehistoric water channels that were dug to control swamp conditions.

THE SIX PHASES OF KUK

Golson placed the Kuk channels into a chronological sequence of six phases using the volcanic ash found in the drainage fill. The top five phases are situated above a gray clay layer, while the oldest lies below it. Phase One dates from 9,000 years ago and is made up of hollows and gutters, as well as stake holes. It is the earliest proof of agriculture in New Guinea, based on geomorphologic (erosion) and structural (water control measures) evidence. Phase Two dates from 6,000 to 5,000 years ago and overlies the gray clay, suggesting major forest clearance related to agricultural intensification. This phase has evidence of structures and channels in swampland gardens that suggest taro cultivation. Raised beds for other crops are also present.

Phase Three lasts from 4,000 to 2,500 years ago and consists of a network of channels to drain water from agricultural areas. This is followed in Phase Four by a grid-like system of elaborate field ditches that drained a larger area. Phases Five and Six date from the last 400 years and have extensive drainage systems indicating sweet potato cultivation. The earliest evidence for major forest clearance elsewhere is in the Baliem Valley, over 2,000 years later than at Kuk.

THE DOMESTICATION OF CROPS

Why did agriculture develop 9,000 years ago? It was impossible before then because of the colder climatic conditions. The warmer conditions during the early Holocene allowed the movement of the crops from the tropical lowlands to the highland region, whether carried by trade or with population movements. At these lower and mid-altitudes many indigenous vegetable, nut, and fruit species were exploited in a hunter-gatherer economy, leading to domestication.

Thirty years ago, it was assumed that most of the domesticated crops (yams, taro, and bananas) were of Southeast Asian origin. It is now clear that *Australimusa* banana, sugar cane, tubers *(Pueraria lobata),* and breadfruit were domesticated in New Guinea. Some aroids were independently domesticated in New Guinea and in Asia, notably taro and the *Eumusa* banana. This evidence places New Guinea as one of the earliest centers of agriculture.

WAHGI WILDERNESS

Kuk Swamp is located in the Wahgi Valley, one of the largest inter-montane valleys in the Papua New Guinean highlands. Although it is an important site, and was nominated for the World Heritage List in 2006, Kuk Swamp forms only a small section of the North Wahgi wetlands.

Lapita, New Caledonia

NEW CALEDONIA
Lapita
Noumea

The name "Lapita" was coined by archaeologists E. W. Gifford and Richard Shutler when excavating in New Caledonia in the 1950s. They recognized that the ancient, finely decorated pottery found in New Caledonia was similar to other examples found from Papua New Guinea to Samoa, and was archaeological evidence for the movement of colonizing peoples through Near Oceania and out to Remote Oceania.

In 1910 Maurice Piroutet, a geologist working on the Foue Peninsula of New Caledonia, found examples of pottery with intricate, stamped designs. These finds went unrecognized for just over 40 years until August 1952, when Gifford and Shutler, two American archaeologists, arrived on the west coast of New Caledonia. They excavated at what they called Site 13, and found impressed pottery. Gifford noted that it was similar to sherds he had found in both Tonga and Fiji, and also to pottery dug up 50 years earlier from Watom in New Britain. He even recognized similar pottery collected from the Isle of Pines (Ile des Pins) on the south coast of New Caledonia. Gifford sent charcoal from Site 13 to Willard Libby, to have it analyzed using his new technique called radiocarbon dating. To their surprise a date for the pottery of nearly 3,000 years ago was returned. They named the pottery Lapita, after a nearby village.

It should be noted that Lapita pottery is more than just stamped pottery. Although it is most often characterized by complex dentate-stamping, half of the assemblages are plain, with a third of the vessels characterized by other forms of decoration including incision, fingernail impression, and appliqué. Vessel forms include bowls and stands, jars, and globular pots with everted rims.

CERAMICS THAT TELL A STORY

The variety of stamped motifs and their structured arrangement on Lapita pottery was not purely for decorative purposes—each pattern and its positioning had a meaning. The designs were incised or stamped into the wet clay before the pot was fired.

PIGS AND POTS

As well as a large number of pottery sherds, archaeologists have unearthed organic remains such as pig bones from the Lapita site in New Caledonia. These finds reveal much about the diet of the people of the time.

THE MARCH OF LAPITA ACROSS MELANESIA

The spread of Lapita pottery across the western Pacific took over 500 years. From the first appearance in the Bismarck Archipelago at 3,400–3,300 years ago, it was taken to the Reef Islands and Santa Cruz by 3,100 years ago, to Vanuatu and New Caledonia by 3,000 years ago, to Fiji by 2,900 years ago, and eventually to Tonga and then Samoa in Polynesia by at least 2,800 years ago. The people who made it are thought to be Austronesian speakers, socially related groups that managed to keep strong communication ties during the colonization phase.

Identical types of pottery spread over thousands of miles was originally thought to have been a product of regular trade and exchange between the various Austronesian groups; however, we now know that most of these pots were produced on the islands from where they were recovered. The dentate-stamped pottery indicates continual interaction between these early colonizer groups, as the later Bismarck Archipelago pottery assemblages are similar to those from Fiji, Tonga, and Samoa. This suggests not only continued relationships, but also a shared motif history. The motifs were not meaningless, decorative scribbles; they were social and ideological signifiers that conveyed vital information, fostered group identity, and maintained social boundaries.

THE OBSIDIAN TRAIL

There is archaeological evidence for the movement of important resources such as obsidian from sources in New Britain and the Admiralty Islands out into Remote Oceania, reaching as far as the Lau Island group of Fiji and island chains in between. The obsidian was not heavily reduced, which is expected of scarce resources. This has led many archaeologists to argue that obsidian was considered a prestige good, and its appearance in Remote Oceania was a by-product of not only the initial colonization of the area but also of the continued interaction between these far-flung outposts.

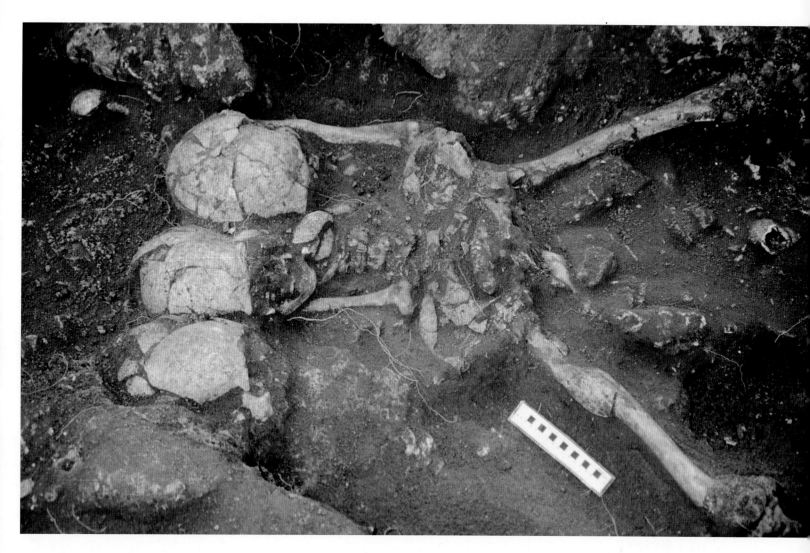

THE END OF LAPITA POTTERY

Dentate-stamped pottery was relatively short lived within Remote Oceania, dropping out after a few generations. However, plain ware and other forms of decoration continued, in addition to new incised patterns and motifs. Vessel forms also remained the same until the end of the third millennium BP. In cultural terms, the abandonment of dentate pottery indicates the social transformation occurring within these Austronesian societies, as well as the beginning of the regionalization of this area. Thus, the disappearance of dentate-stamped motifs equates to changing social boundaries, as these visual social markers are no longer needed or relevant.

In Vanuatu such a transformation is seen when Arapus and Ponamla ware appears 2,800 years ago. In New Caledonia it can be seen in a number of assemblages where Podtanean ware—the plain and paddle-impressed non-dentate component of Lapita assemblages—continues after dentate drops out and is joined by Puen ware and other incised types. In Fiji it can be seen in the Sigatoka plain phase, which also contained paddle-impressed ware.

Lapita dentate-stamped pottery had a longer duration within the Bismarck Archipelago, where it lasted over a thousand years. Late Lapita pottery dated to

between 2,500 and 2,000 years ago has been recorded from the Arawe Islands in southwest New Britain, Garua Island on the north coast of west New Britain, Watom in east New Britain, and Lasigi in New Ireland. Late Lapita pottery at these sites contains not only dentate-stamped motifs but also a continuation of plain ware, incised and relief decoration, and fingernail impressions.

In contrast to Remote Oceania, the longevity of dentate-stamped pottery in the Bismarck Archipelago as a form of signifier or marker of social boundaries was no doubt related to the vastly different social conditions faced by the Austronesian communities of this region, where they had to share the land with inhabitants whose ancestry went back 40,000 years. This possible conflict between peoples led to the reinforcement of the demarcation of social boundaries, reflected in the continued use and importance of dentate-stamped pottery.

A FACE FROM THE PAST
Although best known for pottery featuring geometric patterns, Lapita potters occasionally used anthropomorphic designs. This example, found on the seabed off Boduna Island in Papua New Guinea's west New Britain region, clearly shows a molded face.

ANCIENT BURIALS
In 2004, an excavation in Vanuatu unearthed 13 headless skeletons dated to around 3,000 years ago. The man seen above was buried with three skulls sitting on his chest, and was found to have a healed thigh fracture.

Polynesian Peoples

The name "Polynesia" refers to the islands in the Pacific Ocean that fall within what is called the "Polynesian Triangle," the extents of which are defined by Hawaii in the north, New Zealand in the southwest, and Easter Island in the southeast. Within this area, two major subdivisions exist: West and East Polynesia.

A EUROPEAN PERSPECTIVE
British explorer Captain James Cook (1728–1779) made three voyages around the world, and visited several islands in Polynesia including New Zealand. He was killed by indigenous people in Hawaii during his third voyage.

SACRIFICE IN THE SOCIETIES
Ancient Polynesians in Tahiti made sacrifices to their deified ancestors *(tiki)* on stone altars *(ahu)*. Many of these sites were damaged or destroyed during the 1800s when Christianity came to the islands, and are now being restored.

West Polynesia includes the archipelagos of Tonga, Samoa, Fiji (which is also considered to be part of Melanesia), and some smaller islands. East Polynesia includes New Zealand, Hawaii, the Societies, the Cooks, the Australs, the Marquesas, the Tuamotus, the Gambiers, the Pitcairn Island group, and Easter Island. While widely dispersed, Polynesians share many genetic, linguistic, and cultural similarities. There are 36 documented Polynesian languages, which form a branch of the Austronesian language family, the most widely dispersed language family in the world. Captain James Cook, who discovered many of the islands of Polynesia for the Western world, noted the numerous similarities in his journals, and was amazed that the Polynesians had reached so many islands over such a vast ocean.

THE MIGRATION OF THE POLYNESIANS

Polynesia was the last region of the world to be settled by humans, and the Polynesians themselves were arguably the greatest seafarers ever. They navigated their great double-hulled voyaging canoes over vast distances using the sun, stars, currents, birds, and winds as their guides. Beginning in around 1500 BCE, groups of Austronesian seafarers began to spread throughout Melanesia from islands to the west. These people brought their own language, a distinct dentate-stamped pottery tradition, some Southeast Asian crops (including taro, banana,

breadfruit, yam, and sugar cane), and domesticated animals and birds such as pig, dog, and chicken; the rats that accompanied the travelers on their canoes may have been stowaways.

These travelers touched upon the northern coast of New Guinea, and they continued on southeast through Melanesia to the islands of Vanuatu and New Caledonia. They crossed into what is now known as West Polynesia by around 1000 BCE. They were able to travel further than any previous Pacific population perhaps due to superior canoe technology, but the real reason for their journeys of exploration will never be known for certain.

THE EAST POLYNESIA MYSTERY

From here the archaeological evidence becomes controversial, for the most reliable radiocarbon dates place the earliest settlements in East Polynesia in the late first millennium CE, and most date from around CE 1200–1300. At this point, however, the material culture is quite distinct from that of contemporaneous West Polynesian sites, suggesting that there is a gap in the archaeological record of several centuries. While pottery making gradually declined in West Polynesia, it appears to have been dropped altogether in East Polynesia; no pottery-making site has yet been found there, despite a handful of sherds, probably imports.

By around CE 1000, Polynesian people had settled virtually every island in East Polynesia. The presence of the South American sweet potato throughout East

ISLANDS OF DISTINCTION

Polynesian islands are geologically very diverse. They include vast continental temperate islands, tropical and temperate volcanic islands of various sizes and elevations, and coral atolls. The islands vary considerably in terms of arable land and marine resources. Important raw materials such as basalt for adzes and pearlshell for fishhooks are also unevenly distributed, which led to a disparity in the development of Polynesian cultures. The islands of Polynesia are known and studied throughout the world because of their isolation, in which independent social evolution occurred as humans interacted with their environments.

Polynesia in prehistory is generally taken as proof that at some point Polynesians reached the continent and brought it back with them. Currently, no one particular island or archipelago is a candidate for being the earliest settled. Radiocarbon dates taken from all the earliest sites are virtually identical. These sites are characterized by a distinct array of artifacts, including stone adzes that differ from what we know existed in West Polynesia; a large variety of one-piece pearlshell fishhooks and harpoon heads; and ornaments made from whale teeth, bone, and pearlshell. These colonization-phase sites are also recognizable by a relative abundance of land- and seabird bone and fishbone, with fewer domesticated animal species. Archaeologists believe that early settlers were able to exploit readily available protein sources as they gradually expanded agricultural activities. When local protein resources began to diminish after several generations, domestic animal populations were increased to compensate.

The period of time from CE 1000 to 1450 is generally known as the Archaic Period, during which similar artifacts were made and used throughout the East Polynesia region. Today this homogeneity is attributed to exchange via long-distance voyaging, when settlers would try to obtain and transport as many necessities as possible from their original homes and elsewhere in Polynesia. Archaeologists note a distinct drop in the appearance of exotic goods around CE 1450, and believe that interaction gradually declined as the various populations became more self-sufficient.

POLYNESIA AFTER THE ARCHAIC PERIOD

In the centuries that followed, up until extended European contact in the late eighteenth century, the islands of Polynesia became diverse; languages and material culture became distinct from archipelago to archipelago. Monumental architecture flourished, such as the rectangular stone platforms (*marae*) for religious ceremonies. Warfare also intensified, sometimes resulting in the construction of fortifications. Importantly, the sociopolitical situation had changed dramatically. Some island groups with the most abundant resources, such as Hawaii and Tahiti, became very complex chiefdoms. Others, such as the impoverished atolls of the Tuamotus and other more marginal areas, did not "evolve" into complex entities.

POLYNESIAN PLATFORMS

Stone platforms (*marae*), such as this one on the island of Hiva Oa in the Marquesas, are found throughout Polynesia. Some of these sites also feature enormous stone statues.

MORE THAN JUST A TOOL

Made from black argillite, Poutamawhiria is a *c.* fifteenth-century CE sacred adze that is believed to have been taken to Taranaki in New Zealand in the ancestral Tokomaru canoe of the Te Atiawa people. Lost for 400 years, the adze was found again in 1921.

The Spread of Peoples Through Oceania

OLD MEN OF THE SEA

In July 2005, archaeologists announced their discovery of 16 skeletons at Bourewa in Fiji. Dated to around 3,000 years BP, the human remains provide clear evidence for the first settlement of the Fijian archipelago by the seafaring Austronesians.

The peopling of the vast Polynesian region was the last chapter in the history of the colonization of the Pacific Ocean, a process that began around 40,000 years ago. Despite the fact that during the Pleistocene epoch sea levels were as much as 330 ft (100 m) lower than they are today, the spread of peoples through Oceania still involved quite amazing feats of seafaring.

Sumatra, Java, and Borneo, and what would become many of their surrounding islands, were joined to mainland Southeast Asia; geologists call this ancient landmass Sunda. Over 60 miles (100 km) away, New Guinea, Australia, and Tasmania were joined together in the landmass known as Sahul. Between Sunda and Sahul lay the islands of Wallacea, including Timor, Sulawesi, and Flores, among others.

Anatomically modern *Homo sapiens* were well established in Southeast Asia by at least 70,000 BP (and probably earlier). Shortly after this time, they began making the world's first true open-sea voyages. Archaeological sites in Australia date the colonization of Sahul to roughly 50,000 BP. The crossing from Sunda to Sahul probably involved island-hopping through Wallacea, which was also likely settled at around the same time. Dates from the earliest known sites in New Guinea begin at about 38,000 BP, with nearly contemporaneous

ones in New Britain and New Ireland, and in the Solomon Islands shortly thereafter. To the north, the Philippines were also settled at least around the same time, and possibly earlier. By 30,000 BP the Pleistocene colonization of Near Oceania was complete; it would be another 28,000 years before humans ventured into Remote Oceania.

THE INTREPID AUSTRONESIANS

The group of people who spread into Remote Oceania are known as the Austronesians, in other words, the speakers of an ancestral Austronesian language. Austronesian is recognized as the second-largest language family in the world, and it probably originated in southern China. The Austronesians grew a variety of crops such as foxtail millet, rice, and sugar cane, and they had domesticated pig, dog, chicken, and possibly water buffalo. They made some form of watercraft (possibly with sails), as well as pottery and stone adzes. Such groups are known in Taiwan between 4000 and 3000 BCE. Austronesians had spread into the Philippines and Indonesia around 2500 BCE. (By around CE 500 Austronesians had colonized Madagascar.)

In their initial spread throughout the islands of Southeast Asia, the Austronesians added to their wide array of cultigens, picking up taro, banana, coconut, yam, sago, and breadfruit. By this time their boats, probably canoes, were equipped with sails. The Austronesians then spread in all directions within a few centuries: northeast into the Marianas Islands, and southeast through Melanesia. This latter group of migrants used a distinctive dentate-stamped pottery known as Lapita ware.

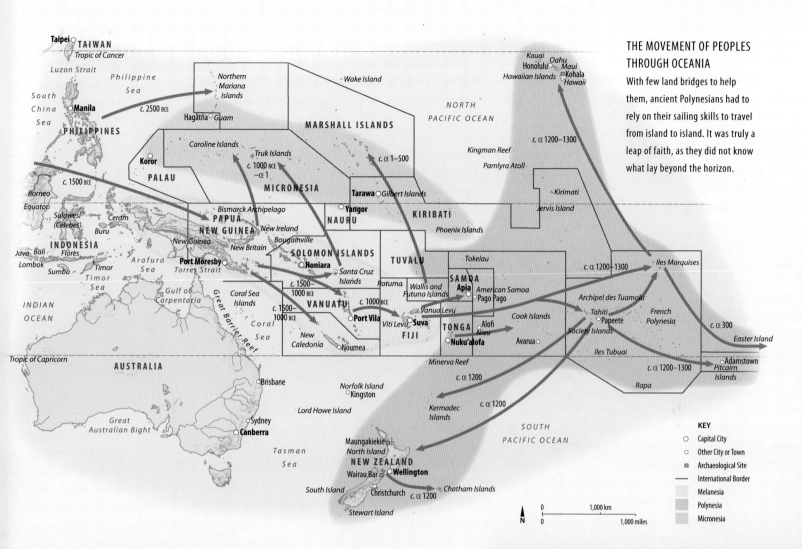

THE MOVEMENT OF PEOPLES THROUGH OCEANIA

With few land bridges to help them, ancient Polynesians had to rely on their sailing skills to travel from island to island. It was truly a leap of faith, as they did not know what lay beyond the horizon.

KEY

○ Capital City
○ Other City or Town
▢ Archaeological Site
— International Border
Melanesia
Polynesia
Micronesia

VOYAGES INTO THE UNKNOWN

From around 1400 to 900 BCE, the Austronesians touched upon the coast of New Guinea, went south through the Solomons, and finally made their way into Remote Oceania. They were the first humans to do so, reaching Vanuatu, New Caledonia, and West Polynesia around 1000 BCE. Foxtail millet and rice had long since been dropped from the cultigen kit before the Austronesians spread through the islands of Melanesia, and farmers concentrated on root and tuber crops. In the meantime, other Austronesian groups settled in southern Micronesia by around 2,000 years ago.

Finally, toward the end of the first millennium CE, their descendants, whom we now call Polynesians, set forth into East Polynesia, a region that no human had ever set eyes on before. Like their ancestors, they moved swiftly, so rapidly that radiocarbon dates can tell us nothing about which islands in East Polynesia were settled first. They spread to virtually every remaining island in the eastern Pacific, with New Zealand probably the last region to be settled, in around CE 1200. It would be almost another four centuries before Europeans ventured so far, seeking trade routes to the East Indies.

MARITIME MARVELS

Not long after they had colonized Southeast Asia, *Homo sapiens* bravely set sail on sea voyages, probably on simple bamboo rafts. Throughout Near Oceania (New Guinea, the Bismarck Archipelago, and the Solomons), the islands are relatively close to one another, being often intervisible, and are therefore accessible by means of simple watercraft without the need for more sophisticated sailing technology. In Remote Oceania, which includes all the islands to the east of Near Oceania, the islands are far more dispersed and require much longer voyages and more complex vessels to reach them. By the time the descendants of the Austronesians ventured into East Polynesia, they had developed great double-hulled canoes in which to make their extraordinary voyages.

ANCIENT VOYAGE RECORDS?

The wall of a rock shelter in New Zealand's Kaingaroa Forest is decorated with ancient petroglyphs depicting canoes at sea. Thought to be around 700 years old, the images may show the great migrations that brought the ancestors of the Maori to New Zealand. At the base of the wall is a discarded Maori canoe.

Kohala, Hawaii, United States

Kohala, whose boundaries have existed for centuries, is the northernmost district of Hawaii Island, and it is subdivided into North and South Kohala. Because of the large amount of contract archaeology on the island—and on the west coast in particular—a great deal of literature exists on the archaeology of the region, which contains virtually every type of Hawaiian archaeological site.

Kohala is home to some of the most impressive architecture in Hawaii and was also the birthplace of King Kamehameha I. North Kohala is an area of great ongoing archaeological interest, because in prehistory it was one of the largest dryland field systems (primarily sweet potato with some dryland taro) in Polynesia. South Kohala, on the other hand, was comparatively barren and desolate except for some coconut groves along the coast. The land is harsh, rough, volcanic terrain with little potential for agriculture. Nevertheless, South Kohala was home to numerous small villages and contains many features of archaeological significance.

THE ARCHAEOLOGY OF NORTH KOHALA

Now dormant, Kohala Mountain is the oldest of Hawaii's numerous volcanoes and forms the narrow northern peak of the island. Located around Kohala Mountain, which has both a leeward and a windward coast, North Kohala is geologically distinct from the rest of the island. In prehistory North Kohala was an area of immense agricultural importance. Being geologically older, the soils of North Kohala were well developed and consequently very fertile.

From the coast, the land ascends gradually into gently sloping hillsides that are cut by streams. Archibald Menzies, surgeon and naturalist on George Vancouver's voyages in the late eighteenth century, described the land as being bare of trees and bushes, and divided into a number of small fields. Based on the number of houses on the coast, he noted that it was the most densely populated district on the island.

The *ahupua'a* (an ancient Hawaiian land unit designation for a narrow strip of land stretching from the coast to the mountains) of Lapakahi has been particularly well studied. The leeward Kohala Field System, as it is known, has been extensively mapped. Though no longer in use as farmland, the Kohala Field System contains an intricate grid network of low stone wall formations that served many functions: field boundaries, windbreaks, animal enclosures, shelters, and habitations.

Beginning at least in the fifteenth century CE, Hawaiians living on the coast began cultivating the land, probably through casual slash-and-burn agriculture. Over the following centuries, to support

REVERED STATESMAN AND LAWGIVER
King Kamehameha I (*c.* 1758–1819) united the Hawaiian Islands and proclaimed the Kingdom of Hawaii in 1810. Many of the archaeological sites in Kohala date back to the time of his rule, such as the Pu'ukohola *heiau* (temple) and the *alaloa* trail, also known as the "King's Highway."

NORTH KOHALA FROM THE AIR
Remnants of the original stone walls built by the Hawaiians can be seen when the lush green landscape of North Kohala is viewed from above. Modern housing developments and large cattle ranches are encroaching on this area, making preservation of the stone walls difficult.

their increasing population, Hawaiians gradually intensified agricultural productivity. They first began permanently designating field boundaries, then increasingly subdivided them into smaller and smaller parcels as the population grew. The labor that went into keeping the land productive also increased, necessitating crop rotation and additional mulching, with more and more walls needed to offset erosion. Eventually people who once lived on the coast moved upland on a semipermanent basis.

In contrast to the dryland fields of the leeward coast, the windward coast of North Kohala is home to some of the most intensive wetland-irrigated agricultural zones on the island, not to mention the spectacular scenery. (Waipi'o Valley in particular is one of the island's most popular tourist destinations.) The valleys are deeply incised, lush, and rugged, containing abundant waterfalls. While significant initial work was involved in terracing portions of the land for wetland taro cultivation, the crop is more productive than any dryland one and also uses far less additional labor to maintain.

THE ARCHAEOLOGY OF SOUTH KOHALA

The extremely inhospitable terrain of South Kohala resembles a bleak moonscape, and consists of both jagged 'a'ā and rippling pāhoehoe lava flows. Sites of archaeological interest include late prehistoric fishing villages, which contain large fishponds that were

constructed to trap and breed fish populations for easy harvesting. While fishing was the mainstay, very limited dryland agriculture was made possible by the construction of walls that served to divert precious floodwater onto alluvial basins.

The lava flows that cover the land contain countless lava tubes that were used in prehistory as burial caves, habitation caves, refuge caves, and rock shelters. One of the most famous burial caves, called Forbes' Cave, contained a canoe burial and an immense cache of wooden images of Hawaiian deities and other fine objects. (The question of the repatriation of these objects has been a subject of controversy for years.) It is worth noting that under current law, any cave that contains at least one burial is virtually off-limits in terms of removing any artifacts.

Refuge caves, which litter the districts of Kona and South Kohala, are often heavily modified lava tubes. The natural entrances were made narrower by the addition of boulders, while defensive walls and fortifications were added to the interior for extra protection. The more elaborate refuge caves were mainly for chiefs and their families if the tides of war turned against them. The harsh terrain of South Kohala also contains some of the largest petroglyph fields in the archipelago, some containing thousands of glyphs.

CURIOUS ROCK CARVINGS
Puako Petroglyph Archaeological Preserve protects thousands of carvings etched into volcanic rock. The age of the ki'i pohaku (petroglyphs) is unknown, but the style developed from stick figures to people with triangular torsos. Rock carvings featuring cattle and horses were made after European contact.

TEMPLE OF WAR

South Kohala's primary seaport is the town of Kawaihae. Although it later became important for European shipping, during prehistoric times it was only a small village. Its most significant feature is the war heiau (temple) Pu'ukohola, which King Kamehameha I built in 1790–1791 and upon which he sacrificed his cousin and rival chief Keoua. Another historic archaeological site of significance is also nearby, namely the homestead of Englishman John Young, who assisted Kamehameha in extending his dominion.

Easter Island, Chile

Easter Island was discovered for the Western world by the Dutch captain Jacob Roggeveen on Easter Sunday (April 5), 1722, hence its popular name; the local name of the island is Rapa Nui. It is one of the most isolated inhabited islands in the world, located 2,240 miles (3,600 km) west of the Chilean coast and 1,290 miles (2,075 km) east of its nearest island neighbor, Pitcairn.

Easter Island is a small volcanic island in the Pacific Ocean, with a landmass of approximately 63 sq miles (163 sq km). It is formed from three volcanoes (Poike, Rano Kau, and Terevaka), giving it a flat triangular shape. It is a relatively low island, with a maximum elevation of 1,675 ft (510 m) above sea level. Easter Island is primarily famous for its monumental stone heads *(moai),* and has attracted more international archaeological attention than any other island in East Polynesia.

THE ARRIVAL OF THE POLYNESIANS

Polynesians were the first humans to reach Easter Island, arriving in around the twelfth century CE, which makes its settlement contemporaneous with most other East Polynesian islands. While we cannot know for certain from which islands the colonizers came, linguistic evidence and experimental voyaging suggest the Gambier Islands or possibly the Marquesas (Iles Marquises) in French Polynesia. Given Easter Island's isolation, it is likely that the island was colonized in only a single episode, with probably little or no further communication with any other islands.

While the Polynesian settlers brought the pig, dog, and chicken to most of the islands they colonized, only the chicken made it to Easter Island. It is possible that the other animals either died on board the canoes during the relatively long voyage or they were unable to maintain a population on the island.

At first, the Polynesians on Easter Island subsisted much as they did elsewhere, with slash-and-burn agriculture, fishing, and hunting local land- and seabird populations. The latter activity resulted in the depletion of bird populations and the extirpation of species. Easter Island is hot and humid, the soil has poor drainage, and there are no permanent streams (only lakes in the volcanic craters). The island's waters are not rich in fish, and the climate is generally too severe for taro, yam, breadfruit, and coconut, which made sweet potato the mainstay. As the population grew, more land had to be cleared for agriculture, usually by burning.

Easter Island possesses few trees, and palynological evidence has demonstrated that it was once forested by the Chilean palm, which no longer exists on the island. It is likely that forest clearance was largely

AHU TONGARIKI REBORN

In 1960, a tidal wave destroyed the *ahu* (stone platform), washing the 15 heavy *moai* of Tongariki inland. Under the watchful eye of Chilean archaeologist Claudio Cristino, a dedicated team spent five years in the early 1990s restoring *Ahu* Tongariki to its former glory.

BIRDMEN OF EASTER ISLAND

According to tradition, in the late seventeenth century CE a group of warriors known as *matatoa* invented a cult based on the relatively minor god Make-make. This Birdman cult centered on an annual competition in which selected young men represented their clans. The object was to swim to the nearby islet Motu Nui, collect the season's first egg of the sooty tern, and return with it intact. In this contest the men braved shark-infested water, rough seas, and climbs over very rugged terrain. The prize was that the winner's clan would take total control of the island and its resources for the entire year—a powerful incentive.

Birdman petroglyphs on the rim of the Ranu Kau crater overlook the islets of Motu Nui, Motu Iti, and Motu Kao Kao.

responsible for this. The Polynesian-introduced rat *(Rattus exulans)* may also have contributed to the disappearance of the palm by eating its nuts. The island's fragile ecosystem eventually yielded, and diminishing forest cover resulted in severe erosion. The lack of timber also prevented the construction of decent canoes for fishing and voyaging; the ones the first Europeans saw were all small and crude, made of stitched-together planks.

THE MYSTERIOUS *MOAI*

The construction of the island's famous *moai* is commonly thought to have contributed to the island's deforestation, as timber would have been needed to some extent in order to quarry and move the statues (some up to 6 miles [10 km] away). Most were carved from the soft volcanic tuff at the Rano Raraku quarry, and range in height from a modest 3½ ft (1 m) to a monumental 36 ft (11 m). At one time over 200 standing *moai* adorned the island's ceremonial platforms *(ahu).* In total, approximately 900 have been documented, 400 of which are still in and around the quarry (one unfinished example would have stood 65 ft [20 m] high on completion); additional survey will probably increase the number. The presence of unfinished *moai* suggests that the quarry was abruptly abandoned by the Polynesians in late prehistory.

The extent to which the Easter Islanders carried statue carving is indeed without parallel in East Polynesia and remains one of the world's most popular archaeological "mysteries." Another "mystery" associated with Easter Island is a handful of wooden tablets on which is carved a strange written script known as *rongorongo.* This semipictographic script has defied all attempts at decipherment, and is generally considered to have been invented after the islanders had come into contact with European writing.

Human activity on the island took its toll by around the seventeenth century CE. Food shortages probably brought about increased warfare, possibly made deadlier by the invention of crude obsidian spearheads call *mata'a*. Rats were increasingly used as food, and it is possible that cannibalism intensified. Civil strife also led to the toppling of the *moai* in such a way as to snap the head off at the neck in a symbolic decapitation.

SILENT SENTINELS
The *moai* probably represent revered ancestral chiefs. Originally, the heads were crowned with a topknot carved from red tuff (volcanic rock), and the eyes featured inlays of white coral.

Wairau Bar, New Zealand

NEW ZEALAND
Wairau Bar □ ○Wellington

Wairau Bar is an archaeological site of great importance due to the type of cultural artifacts and number of moa bones found there. Located in the north of the South Island of New Zealand, it is called Wairau Bar because it is a bar (i.e., a bank) of gravel formed where the Wairau and Opawa Rivers meet and enter the ocean.

DEATH OF A SPECIES
Extinct for around 700 years, the giant moa was a victim of vigorous human hunting. Investigations at Wairau Bar have determined that some 8,000 moa were killed by early hunters in this region.

QUESTIONS TO BE ANSWERED
Recent research at Wairau Bar, seen here from above, suggests that some people buried here may have been born elsewhere in Polynesia. Analysis of elements in the remains will determine the deceased's diet, and perhaps their origins.

The early settlers of New Zealand hunted the giant flightless moa birds in the area and buried their dead there as well. Consequently, the site is extremely rich in moa bone and intact human burials accompanied by grave goods. A 13-year-old boy named Jim Eyles discovered the site in 1939. In 1942, while still a schoolboy, he assisted Roger Duff of the Canterbury Museum in excavating the site, a project that lasted several years. Duff's book on the subject, *The Moa-Hunter Period of Maori Culture* (1950), is still considered a classic in archaeological literature. Additional archaeologists have worked on the site in the decades since Duff's excavations.

SIGNIFICANT FINDS AT WAIRAU
There are three burial areas and additional habitation and occupation areas. The burials were accompanied

by an unparalleled array of Archaic (*c.* CE 1000–1450) East Polynesian artifacts. No site anywhere else has yet yielded so many. These artifacts include complete necklaces of both real and imitation whale tooth pendants, necklaces of whale-ivory reels, intact moa eggs, and a full complement of Archaic adze types. (Duff's still-used classification system of Polynesian adzes was largely based on the Wairau Bar assemblage.)

Typical East Polynesian sites rarely yield many ornaments, which are extremely uncommon outside of burials; when examples of ornaments are located, only individual units are usually found. Finished adzes are mostly found broken, as are many of the preforms. Therefore the importance of the Wairau Bar assemblage is understandable. Sites throughout East Polynesia have yielded almost identical artifacts, albeit in much smaller quantities, pointing to a largely homogeneous and unique East Polynesian culture that was quite distinct from its West Polynesian predecessor.

The site's stratigraphy is shallow, with cultural remains lying mostly around 12–16 in (30–40 cm) below the surface of the ground. The burials may represent several generations, with the earliest being accompanied by the most Archaic grave goods, which become scarcer in the later burials. The presence of mortuary objects suggests a differentiation in the status of those buried, with the richer graves possibly representing the chiefly class. Radiocarbon dates on human and moa bone and moa eggshell point to a relatively narrow time span from the late thirteenth to the late fourteenth century CE. These dates are perfectly consistent with other Archaic period sites throughout East Polynesia, corresponding to the similarity in material culture. The narrow range of dates and shallow stratigraphy both suggest that the site was occupied for around 20 years, possibly as a permanent but short-term base camp. Moa were plentiful and easily hunted, which resulted in their extinction within one to two hundred years of human arrival in New Zealand.

Maungakiekie, New Zealand

Maungakiekie, located in Cornwall Park, Auckland, is a pre-European Maori fortified settlement *(pa)* built on a 597-ft (182-m) high volcanic cone. More commonly known as One Tree Hill, its Maori name means "mountain of the vine." Maungakiekie is the largest and most extensively terraced volcanic cone *pa* in the Auckland region and one of the largest in all New Zealand.

The village covers approximately 111 acres (45 ha) and contains over 250 extant terraces. The site was probably first occupied by at least the fifteenth century CE. According to Maori tradition, in the 1700s Maungakiekie was the principal *pa* of the Te Wai o Hua tribe, headed by the region's paramount chief, Kiwi Tamaki, who united the tribes of Auckland. The site's strategic location on an isthmus between two key harbors allowed Kiwi Tamaki to exact tribute from travelers passing north and south.

In its heyday, Maungakiekie probably had a population of at least 3,000 people, and possibly as many as 7,000. The cone's rich volcanic soils provided excellent terrain for agriculture, parts of which can still be seen today in the form of field boundaries. The principal crop was sweet potato (also known as kumara), supplemented by taro and gourds. Maungakiekie's location near the sea also provided marine resources; middens on the site include large quantities and varieties of both fish and shellfish.

ANATOMY OF THE *PA*

Maungakiekie comprises an elaborate series of terraces, ditches, and banks, dug into the slopes of the cone itself. The construction of the *pa* would have entailed a great deal of cooperative manual labor. The terraces served as level surfaces on which a variety of different structures were built and rebuilt over time. On some of the terraces, pits for storing sweet potatoes were dug. Postholes indicate that houses dotted the site, and hearths, earth ovens, and middens suggest food-preparation areas. A series of wooden palisades would have surrounded the hill. Together with the ditches and banks, the palisades would have provided Maungakiekie with formidable defenses, including four strong points located on the higher ledges of the crater rim.

Construction of a memorial obelisk in 1940 to Sir John Logan Campbell, who owned the land in the nineteenth century, revealed and destroyed traces of the summit's original occupation area. Usually reserved for the chiefly family, the summit of Maungakiekie covered approximately 5,380 sq ft (500 sq m) and contained hearths as well as postholes for palisades, houses, and storage areas. Human remains have also been found at various places around the site. Like most *pa,* Maungakiekie was abandoned by the early nineteenth century, and when first observed by Europeans, it was already densely grown over. European farming activities in the nineteenth century have also left archaeological traces, notably lengths of drystone walls.

CLEVER COMMUNICATION

Maungakiekie is one of 48 volcanic craters and cones in the Tamaki (Auckland) region. It is believed that the Maori would send signals from the top of Maungakiekie to residents of other *pa* in the area.

REFERENCE

Guide to Sites by Country

The archaeological sites with individual entries in this book are listed below, under the name of the country in which they are located. The diamond symbol (♦) after the name of the site indicates that it is World Heritage Listed; if the site is within a region that is World Heritage Listed, the name of the region is given in brackets.

AUSTRALIA
Cuddie Springs *see page 354*
Devil's Lair *see page 352*
Kow Swamp *see page 353*
Lake Condah *see pages 358–359*
Lake Mungo♦ (part of Willandra Lakes Region) *see pages 350–351*
Nullarbor Caves *see pages 360–361*
Pilbara Petroglyphs *see page 355*
Ubirr Rock♦ (part of Kakadu National Park) *see pages 362–363*

AUSTRIA
Venus of Willendorf *see page 131*

BOLIVIA
Tiwanaku♦ *see page 344*

BULGARIA
Varna *see page 136*

CAMBODIA
Angkor♦ *see page 273*

CANADA
Head-Smashed-In♦ *see page 289*

CHILE
Easter Island♦ *see pages 378–379*
Monte Verde *see pages 282–283*

CHINA
Anyang♦ (part of Yin Xu) *see pages 250–251*
Changsha Han Tombs *see page 262*
Dali *see page 204*
The Great Wall♦ *see pages 260–261*
Mancheng Han Tombs *see page 263*
Sanxingdui *see page 252*
Terracotta Army, Xi'an♦ *see pages 256–257*
Zhengzhou *see pages 248–249*
Zhoukoudian♦ *see page 203*
Zhouyuan *see page 253*

COSTA RICA
Guayabo de Turrialba *see page 343*

CZECH REPUBLIC
Dolní Věstonice *see page 130*

DEMOCRATIC REPUBLIC OF THE CONGO
Matupi Cave♦ *see page 81*

EGYPT
Abydos *see page 88*
Deir el-Medina *see pages 90–91*
Giza Pyramids♦ (part of Memphis and its Necropolis) *see page 89*
Rosetta Stone, Rosetta *see page 99*
Saqqara *see pages 86–87*
Tanis *see page 98*
Tell el-Amarna *see page 97*
Tutankhamun's Tomb♦ (part of Ancient Thebes and its Necropolis) *see pages 92–93*
Valley of the Kings♦ (part of Ancient Thebes and its Necropolis) *see page 96*

ETHIOPIA
Axum♦ *see page 105*
Lucy Skeleton, Hadar♦ (part of the Lower Valley of the Awash) *see page 65*

FRANCE
Bougon *see page 144*
Carnac *see page 152*
Cro-Magnon Rock Shelter♦ (part of Prehistoric Sites and Decorated Caves of the Vézère Valley) *see page 118*
La Ferrassie♦ (part of Prehistoric Sites and Decorated Caves of the Vézère Valley) *see page 120*
Lascaux Cave♦ (part of Prehistoric Sites and Decorated Caves of the Vézère Valley) *see page 127*
Lugdunum♦ (part of the Historic Site of Lyons) *see page 182*

GERMANY
Feldhofer Grotto *see page 121*

GREECE
Akrotiri *see page 159*
Athenian Agora *see page 165*
Delphi♦ *see page 166*
Knossos *see page 157*
Mycenae♦ *see page 162*
Olympia♦ *see page 167*
Palaikastro *see page 158*
The Parthenon♦ (part of Acropolis, Athens) *see page 170*

GUATEMALA
Naj Tunich Cave *see page 314*
Tikal♦ *see pages 308–309*

HONDURAS
Copán♦ *see pages 310–311*

INDONESIA
Borobudur♦ *see page 275*
Trinil *see page 205*

IRAN
Pasargadae♦ *see pages 226–227*
Persepolis♦ *see pages 228–229*
Susa *see pages 230–231*

IRAQ
Babylon *see pages 220–221*
Khorsabad *see pages 222–223*
Tell Asmar *see page 217*
Ur *see page 216*

IRELAND
Hill of Tara *see page 145*
Newgrange♦ (part of the Archaeological Ensemble of the Bend of the Boyne) *see pages 146–147*

ISRAEL
Jericho *see pages 208–209*
Sha'ar Hagolan *see page 213*
Ubeidiya *see page 202*

ITALY
The Iceman *see page 137*
Imperial Fora of Rome♦ *see pages 178–179*
Pompeii♦ and Herculaneum♦ *see pages 180–181*
Ravenna♦ *see pages 196–197*
Tarquinia♦ *see pages 176–177*

JAPAN
Nara♦ *see page 267*
Sannai Maruyama *see page 266*

KENYA
Enkapune ya Muto *see page 73*
Olorgesailie *see pages 70–71*
Turkana Boy, Lake Turkana♦ *see page 67*

LEBANON
Byblos♦ *see pages 160–161*

MALI
Jenne-jeno♦ *see page 112*

MALTA
Temples of Tarxien♦ *see page 156*

MEXICO
Chalcatzingo *see page 304*
Chichén Itzá♦ *see page 315*
Cholula *see page 321*
Monte Albán♦ *see page 305*
Olmec Colossal Heads *see page 301*
Palenque♦ *see pages 312–313*
San José Mogote and Etlatongo *see page 300*
Tenochtitlan♦ *see page 320*
Teotihuacan♦ *see pages 302–303*
Tulum *see pages 316–317*

MYANMAR (BURMA)
Bagan *see page 272*

NAMIBIA
Apollo 11 Cave *see page 80*

NEW CALEDONIA
Lapita *see pages 370–371*

NEW ZEALAND
Maungakiekie *see page 381*
Wairau Bar *see page 380*

NIGERIA
Nok *see page 108*

NORWAY
Gokstad Ship *see page 194*
Oseberg Ship *see page 193*

PAKISTAN
Harappa *see page 243*
Mohenjo-Daro♦ *see page 242*

PAPUA NEW GUINEA
Huon Peninsula *see page 366*
Kilu Cave *see page 368*
Kosipe *see page 367*
Kuk Swamp *see page 369*

PERU
Chan Chan♦ *see pages 334–335*
Chavín de Huantar♦ *see pages 338–339*
Cuzco♦ *see pages 326–327*
Machu Picchu♦ *see pages 328–329*
The Nazca Lines♦ *see pages 340–341*
Ollantaytambo *see pages 332–333*
Sipán *see page 342*

PORTUGAL
Côa Valley Petroglyphs♦ *see page 126*
Lagar Velho *see page 125*

RUSSIAN FEDERATION
The Land of Cities *see pages 234–235*
Novgorod♦ *see page 195*
Pazyryk Tombs *see page 237*
The Stone Statues of the Steppes♦ (part of the Golden Mountains of Altai) *see page 236*

SERBIA AND MONTENEGRO
Lepenski Vir *see page 133*

SOUTH AFRICA
Klasies River *see page 72*
Lydenburg *see page 113*
Taung Child, Norlim♦ (part of Fossil Hominid Sites of Sterkfontein, Swartkrans, Kromdraai, and Environs) *see page 66*

SPAIN
Altamira Cave Paintings♦ *see page 119*
Atapuerca♦ *see page 124*

SUDAN
Kerma *see pages 102–103*
Napata♦ and Meroe♦ *see page 104*

SWITZERLAND
Swiss Lake Dwellings *see page 141*

SYRIA
Palmyra♦ *see pages 186–187*

TANZANIA
Laetoli *see page 64*
Olduvai Gorge *see pages 82–83*

TUNISIA
Carthage♦ *see page 183*

TURKEY
Çatal Hüyük *see pages 134–135*
Ephesus *see pages 172–173*
Göbekli Tepe *see page 212*
Pergamon *see page 171*
Troy♦ *see page 163*
Uluburun Shipwreck *see page 164*

UKRAINE
Mezhirich *see page 132*

UNITED KINGDOM
Avebury♦ and Stonehenge♦ *see pages 148–149*
Bush Barrow♦ (part of Stonehenge, Avebury, and Associated Sites) *see page 153*
Skara Brae♦ (part of the Heart of Neolithic Orkney) *see page 140*
Sutton Hoo *see page 192*

UNITED STATES
Cahokia♦ *see page 345*
Chaco Canyon♦ *see pages 294–295*
Clovis *see page 285*
Danger Cave *see page 288*
Keet Seel *see page 293*
Kohala *see pages 376–377*
Meadowcroft Rockshelter *see page 284*
Mesa Verde♦ *see page 292*

VIETNAM
Champa♦ (partly covered by My Son Sanctuary) *see page 274*

ZIMBABWE
Great Zimbabwe♦ *see page 109*

Further Reading

INTRODUCTION

Baillie, M. G. L. *A Slice Through Time: Dendrochronology and Precision Dating.* Routledge: London, 1995.

Chapman, Henry. *Landscape Archaeology and GIS.* Tempus Publishing Limited: Stroud, 2006.

Chippindale, Christopher and George H. Nash. *The Figured Landscapes of Rock-Art.* Cambridge University Press: Cambridge, 2004.

Chippindale, Christopher and Paul S. Taçon. *The Archaeology of Rock-Art.* Cambridge University Press: Cambridge, 1998.

Daniel, Glyn. *The Origins and Growth of Archaeology.* Penguin Books: Harmondsworth, 1967.

Daniel, Glyn. *A Short History of Archaeology.* Thames and Hudson: London, 1981.

Delgado, James P. *Encyclopedia of Underwater and Maritime Archaeology.* Yale University Press: New Haven, 1998.

Fagan, Brian M. (ed.). *The Oxford Companion to Archaeology.* Oxford University Press: New York, 1996.

Finkelstein, Israel and Neil A. Silberman. *The Bible Unearthed: Archaeology's New Vision of Ancient Israel and the Origin of its Sacred Texts.* Free Press: New York, 2002.

Gilchrist, Roberta. *Gender and Archaeology: Contesting the Past.* Routledge: London, 1999.

Hodder, Ian and Scott Hutson. *Reading the Past: Current Approaches to Interpretation in Archaeology*, 3rd edn. Cambridge University Press: Cambridge, 2003.

Johnson, Matthew. *Archaeological Theory: An Introduction.* Blackwell Publishers: Malden and Oxford, 1999.

Nash, George H. and Christopher Chippindale. *European Landscapes of Rock-Art.* Routledge: London, 2002.

Peregrine, Peter N., Carol R. Ember, and Melvin Ember. *Archaeology: Original Readings in Method and Practice.* Prentice Hall: New Jersey, 2001.

Price, T. Douglas. *Principles of Archaeology.* McGraw-Hill Publishing: Boston, 2006.

Renfrew, Colin and Paul G. Bahn. *Archaeology: Theories, Methods, and Practice.* Thames and Hudson: New York, 1991.

Renfrew, Colin and Paul G. Bahn. *Archaeology: Theories, Methods, and Practice*, 4th edn. Thames and Hudson: New York, 2004.

Renfrew, Colin and Paul G. Bahn. *The Cambridge Illustrated History of Archaeology.* Cambridge University Press: Cambridge, 1996.

Schnapp, Alain. *The Discovery of the Past.* British Museum Press: London, 1996.

Taylor, R. E. *Radiocarbon Dating: An Archaeological Perspective.* Academic Press: Orlando, 1987.

Thomas, D. H. and R. L. Kelly. *Archaeology.* Thomas Wadsworth: Belmont, 2005.

Whitley, D. S. *An Introduction to Rock Art Research.* Left Coast Press Inc: Walnut Creek, 2006.

Whitley, David S. (ed.). *Handbook of Rock Art Research.* AltaMira Press: Walnut Creek, 2001.

Whitley, David S. (ed.). *Reader in Archaeological Theory: Post-processual and Cognitive Approaches.* Routledge: London, 1998.

AFRICA

Alemseged, Z., F. Spoor, W. H. Kimbel, D. Geraads, D. Reed, and J. G. Wynn. "A Juvenile Early Hominin Skeleton from Dikika, Ethiopia." *Nature* 443(7108), 2006, pp296–301.

Ambrose, S. H. "Chronology of the Later Stone Age and Food Production in East Africa." *Journal of Archaeological Science* 25(4), 1998, pp377–392.

Ambrose, S. H. "Late Pleistocene Human Population Bottlenecks, Volcanic Winter, and Differentiation of Modern Humans." *Journal of Human Evolution* 34(6), 1998, pp623–651.

Brain, C. K. *The Hunters or the Hunted? An Introduction to African Cave Taphonomy.* University of Chicago Press: Chicago, 1981.

Breunig, P. "New Studies on the Nok Culture of Central Nigeria." *Journal of African Archaeology* 3(2), 2005, pp283–290.

Cann, R. L., M. Stoneking, and A. C. Wilson. "Mitochondrial DNA and Human Evolution." *Nature* 325(6099), 1987, pp31–36.

Childs, T. S. and D. Killick. "Indigenous African Metallurgy: Nature and Culture." *Annual Review of Anthropology* 22, 1993, pp317–37.

Connah, G. *Forgotten Africa: An Introduction to its Archaeology.* Routledge: London and New York, 2004.

Dart, R. A. "*Australopithecus africanus*: The Man-ape of South Africa." *Nature* 115(2884), 1925, pp195–199.

de Barros, P. "Societal Repercussions on the Rise of Large-scale Iron Production: A West African Example." *African Archaeological Review* 6, 1988, pp91–113.

Deacon, H. J. and S. Wurz. "A Late Pleistocene Archive of Life at the Coast, Klasies River" in A. Stahl (ed.), *African Archaeology: A Critical Introduction.* Blackwell Publishing: Malden, 2005, pp130–149.

Edwards, David N. *The Nubian Past: An Archaeology of the Sudan.* Routledge: London and New York, 2004.

Fontein, Joost. *The Silence of Great Zimbabwe: Contested Landscapes and the Power of Heritage.* UCL Press: London, 2005.

Gagneux, P., C. Wills, U. Gerlof, D. Tautz, P. A. Morin, C. Boesch, B. Fruth, G. Hohmann, O. A. Ryder, and D. S. Woodruff. "Mitochondrial Sequences Show Diverse Evolutionary Histories of African Hominoids." *Proceedings of the National Academy of Sciences* 96(9), 1999, pp5077–5082.

Garlake, Peter S. *Early Art and Architecture of Africa.* Oxford University Press: Oxford, 2002.

Haaland, Randi and Peter Shinnie (eds.). *African Iron Working: Ancient and Traditional.* Norwegian University Press: Oslo, 1981.

Henshilwood, C. S. and C. W. Marean. "The Origin of Modern Human Behavior." *Current Anthropology* 44(5), 2003, pp627–651.

Herbert, Eugenia. W. *Iron, Gender, and Power: Rituals of Transformation in African Societies.* Indiana University Press: Bloomington, 1994.

Huffman, Thomas N. *Snakes and Crocodiles: Power and Symbolism in Ancient Zimbabwe.* Witwatersrand University Press: Johannesburg, 1996.

Isaac, Barbara (ed.). *The Archaeology of Human Origins: Papers by Glynn Isaac.* Cambridge University Press: Cambridge, 1989.

Isaac, Glynn Llywelyn. *Olorgesailie: Archaeological Studies of a Middle Pleistocene Lake Basin in Kenya.* University of Chicago Press: Chicago, 1977.

Johanson, D. C. and T. White. "A Systematic Assessment of Early African Hominids." *Science* 203(4378), 1979, pp321–330.

Johanson, D. C., T. White, and Y. Coppens. "A New Species of the Genus *Australopithecus* (Primates: Hominidae) from the Pliocene of Eastern Africa." *Kirtlandia* 28, 1978, pp1–14.

Kemp, Barry J. *Ancient Egypt: Anatomy of a Civilization.* Routledge: London and New York, 2006.

Klein, R. G. "The Archaeology of Modern Human Origins." *Evolutionary Anthropology* 1(1), 1992, pp5–14.

Leakey, M. D. *Olduvai Gorge III: Excavations in Beds I and II 1960–1963.* Cambridge University Press: Cambridge, 1971.

Leakey, M. D. and R. L. Hay. "Pliocene Footprints in the Laetolil Beds at Laetoli, Northern Tanzania." *Nature* 278(5702), 1979, pp317–323.

Lovejoy, O. "The Origin of Man." *Science* 211(4480), 1981, pp341–350.

Manley, Bill. *The Penguin Historical Atlas of Ancient Egypt.* Penguin Books: London and New York, 1996.

McBrearty, S. and A. S. Brooks. "The Revolution That Wasn't: A New Interpretation of the Origin of Modern Human Behavior." *Journal of Human Evolution* 39(5), 2000, pp453–563.

McHenry, H. "The First Bipeds: A Comparison of the *A. afarensis* and *A. africanus* Postcranium and Implications for the Evolution of Bipedalism." *Journal of Human Evolution* 15(3), 1986, pp177–191.

McIntosh, Roderick J. *Ancient Middle Niger: Urbanism and the Self-organizing Landscape.* Cambridge University Press: Cambridge, 2005.

McIntosh, Roderick J. *The Peoples of the Middle Niger: The Island of Gold.* Blackwell Publishing: Malden, 1998.

McIntosh, Susan K. (ed.). *Beyond Chiefdoms: Pathways to Complexity in Africa.* Cambridge University Press, Cambridge, 1999.

McIntosh, Susan K. "Changing Perceptions of West Africa's Past: Archaeological Research Since 1988." *Journal of Archaeological Research* 2(92), 1994, pp165–98.

McIntosh, Susan K. and R. J. McIntosh. "The Early City in Africa: Toward an Understanding." *The African Archaeological Review* 2, 1984, pp302–319.

Miller, D. "Indigenous Copper Mining and Smelting in Pre-colonial Southern Africa" in Paul T. Craddock and Janet Lang (eds.), *Mining and Metal Production Through the Ages.* British Museum Press: London, 2003, pp101–110.

Miller, D. E. and N. J. van der Merwe. "Early Metal Working in Sub Saharan Africa." *Journal of African History* 35, 1994, pp1–36.

Ndoro, W. "Your Monument Our Shrine: The Preservation of Great Zimbabwe." *Studies in African Archaeology* 19. Department of Archaeology and Ancient History, Uppsala University: Uppsala, 2001.

Payne, Malcolm (ed.). *Face Value: Old Heads in Modern Masks: A Visual, Archaeological and Historical Reading of the Lydenburg Heads*. Axeage Private Press: Cape Town, 1993.

Phillipson, David W. *African Archaeology*, 3rd edn. Cambridge University Press: Cambridge, 2005.

Phillipson, David W. *Ancient Ethiopia: Aksum, Its Antecedents and Successors*. British Museum Press: London, 1998.

Pikirayi, Innocent. *The Zimbabwe Culture: Origins and Decline in Southern Zambezian States*. AltaMira Press: Walnut Creek, 2001.

Potts, R. "Olorgesailie: New Excavations and Findings in Early and Middle Pleistocene Contexts, Southern Kenya Rift Valley." *Journal of Human Evolution* 18(5), 1989, pp477–484.

Potts, R., A. K. Behrensmeyer, A. Deino, P. Ditchfield, and J. Clark. "Small Mid-Pleistocene Hominin Associated with East African Acheulean Technology." *Science* 305(5680), 2004, pp75–78.

Schick, Kathy and Nicholas Toth. *Making Silent Stones Speak*. Simon and Schuster: New York, 1993.

Schulz, Regine and Matthias Seidel (eds.). *Egypt: The World of the Pharaohs*. Könemann: Cologne, 1998.

Shaw, T. "The Nok Sculptures of Nigeria." *Scientific American* 244(2), 1981, pp154–166.

Shaw, T., P. J. J. Sinclair, B. Andah, and A. Okpoko (eds.). *The Archaeology of Africa: Food, Metals and Towns*. Routledge: London and New York, 1993.

Singer, Ronald and John Wymer. *The Middle Stone Age at Klasies River Mouth in South Africa*. University of Chicago Press: Chicago, 1982.

Stringer, Chris B. and Robin McKie. *African Exodus: The Origins of Modern Humanity*. Jonathan Cape: London, 1996.

van der Merwe, N. J. "The Advent of Iron in Africa" in Theodore A. Wertime and James D. Muhly (eds.), *The Coming of the Age of Iron*. Yale University Press: New Haven, 1980, pp463–506.

Walker, Alan and Richard E. F. Leakey (eds.). *The Nariokotome Homo erectus Skeleton*. Harvard University Press: Cambridge, 1993.

White, T. D. and G. Suwa. "Hominid Footprints at Laetoli: Facts and Interpretations." *American Journal of Physical Anthropology* 72(4), 1987, pp485–514.

Willoughby, Pamela R. *The Evolution of Modern Humans in Africa: A Comprehensive Guide*. AltaMira Press: Lanham, 2007.

EUROPE

Ashbee, P. *The Bronze Age Round Barrow in Britain: An Introduction to the Study of the Funerary Practice and Culture of the British and Irish Single-grave People of the Second Millennium B.C.* Phoenix House: London, 1960.

Bahn, Paul G. and J. Vertut. *Journey Through the Ice Age*. Weidenfeld and Nicolson: London, 1997.

Bailey, Douglass. *Balkan Prehistory: Exclusion, Incorporation and Identity*. Routledge: London, 2000.

Bailloud, G. et al. *Carnac. Les premières architectures de pierre*. CNRS Editions: Paris, 1995.

Bhreathnach, Edel. (ed.). *The Kingship and Landscape of Tara*. Four Courts Press for The Discovery Programme: Dublin, 2005.

Bradley, Richard. *Altering the Earth. The Origins of Monuments in Britain and Continental Europe* (Monograph Series Number 8). Society of Antiquaries of Scotland: Edinburgh, 1993.

Bradley, Richard. *The Significance of Monuments: On the Shaping of Human Experience in Neolithic and Bronze Age Europe*. Routledge: London, 1998.

Burl, Aubrey. *Prehistoric Avebury*. Yale University Press: New Haven and London, 1979.

Burl, Aubrey. *The Stone Circles of Britain, Ireland and Brittany*. Yale University Press: New Haven and London, 2000.

Burl, Aubrey. *The Stone Circles of the British Isles*. Yale University Press: New Haven and London, 1976.

Cameron, David and Colin Groves. *Bones, Stones and Molecules: "Out of Africa" and Human Origins*, Elsevier Academic Press: Burlington, 2004.

Chamberlain, A. and M. Parker Pearson. *Earthly Remains: The History and Science of Preserved Human Bodies*. The British Museum: London, 2001.

Chapman, J. *The Oxford Companion to Archaeology*. Oxford University Press: Oxford, 1996.

Chippindale, Christopher. *Stonehenge Complete*, new and expanded edn. Thames and Hudson: London, 2004.

Clarke, D. and P. Maguire. *Skara Brae: Northern Europe's Best Preserved Neolithic Village*. Historic Scotland: Edinburgh, 2000.

Cunliffe, Barry. (ed.). *The Oxford Illustrated History of Prehistoric Europe*. Oxford University Press: Oxford, 2001.

Darvill, Timothy. *Stonehenge: The Biography of a Landscape*. Tempus Publishing Limited: Stroud, 2006.

Eogan, George. *Knowth and the Passage-tombs of Ireland*. Thames and Hudson: London, 1986.

Gibson, Alex. *Stonehenge and Timber Circles*. Tempus Publishing Limited: Stroud, 1998.

Hodder, Ian. *The Leopard's Tale: Revealing the Mysteries of Çatalhöyük*. Thames and Hudson: London, 2006.

Ivanov, Ivan and Maya Avramova. *Varna Necropolis: The Dawn of European Civilization*. Agat'o Publishing: Sofia, 2000.

Kinnes, I. et al. "Bush Barrow Gold." *Antiquity* 62, 1988, pp24–39.

Lister, Adrian and Paul G. Bahn. *Mammoths*. Boxtree: London, 1994.

Menotti, Francesco (ed.). *Living on the Lake in Prehistoric Europe: 150 Years of Lake-dwelling Research*. Routledge: London, 2004.

Midgley, M. S. *The Monumental Cemeteries of Prehistoric Europe*. Tempus Publishing Limited: Stroud, 2005.

Mohen, J. P. and C. Scarre. *Les tumulus de Bougon. Complexe mégalithique du Ve au IIIe millénaire*. Editions Errance: Paris, 2002.

North, John D. *Stonehenge: Neolithic Man and the Cosmos*. HarperCollins Publishers: London, 1996.

O'Kelly, Michael J. *Newgrange: Archaeology, Art and Legend*. Thames and Hudson: London, 1982.

Pollard, Joshua and Andrew Reynolds. *Avebury: Biography of a Landscape*. Tempus Publishing Limited: Stroud, 2002.

Ritchie, Anna. *Neolithic Orkney in its European Context*. McDonald Institute for Archaeological Research: Cambridge, 2000.

Roebroeks, W., M. Mussi, J. Svoboda, and K. Fennema (eds.). *Hunters of the Golden Age*. University of Leiden: Leiden, 2000.

Scarre, Chris. (ed.). *The Human Past: World Prehistory and the Development of Human Societies*. Thames and Hudson: London, 2005.

Scarre, Chris. (ed.). *Monuments and Landscape in Atlantic Europe: Perception and Society During the Neolithic and Early Bronze Age*. Routledge: London, 2002.

Soffer, Olga. *The Upper Paleolithic of the Central Russian Plain*. Academic Press: Orlando, 1985.

Spindler, Konrad. *The Man in the Ice: The Preserved Body of a Neolithic Man Reveals the Secrets of the Stone Age*. Weidenfeld and Nicolson: London, 1994.

Srejovic, Dragoslav. *Europe's First Monumental Sculpture: New Discoveries at Lepenski Vir*. Thames and Hudson: London, 1972.

Stringer, Chris and Peter Andrews. *The Complete World of Human Evolution*. Thames and Hudson: London, 2005.

Svoboda, J., V. Lozek, and E. Vlcek (eds.). *Hunters Between East and West*. Plenum Press: London, 1996.

Tattersall, Ian and Jeffrey Schwartz. *Extinct Humans*. Westview Press: Boulder, 2000.

Turner, R. and R. Scaife (eds.). *Bog Bodies: New Discoveries and New Perspectives*. The British Museum: London, 1995.

ASIA

Akkermans, Peter M. M. G. and Glenn M. Schwartz. *The Archaeology of Syria: From Complex Hunter-Gatherers to Early Urban Societies (c. 16,000–300 BC)*. Cambridge University Press: Cambridge, 2003.

Albenda, Pauline. *The Palace of Sargon, King of Assyria: Monumental Wall Reliefs at Dur-Sharrukin, from Original Drawings Made at the Time of their Discovery in 1843–1844 by Botta and Flandin*. Editions Recherche sur les Civilisations: Paris, 1986.

Bacus, Elisabeth, Ian Glover, et al. "Uncovering Southeast Asia's Past." *Selected Papers from the 10th International Conference of the European Association of Southeast Asian Archaeologists*. University of Singapore Press: Singapore, 2006.

Bagley, Robert et al (ed.). *Ancient Sichuan: Treasures from a Lost Civilization*. Seattle Art Museum: Seattle and Princeton University Press: New Jersey, 2001.

Barnes, Gina Lee. *China, Korea and Japan: The Rise of Civilisation in East Asia*, 2nd edn. Thames and Hudson: London, c. 1993.

Barnes, Gina Lee. *State Formation in Japan: Emergence of a 4th-Century Ruling Elite*. Routledge: London and New York, 2007.

Bar-Yosef, O. "The Neolithic Period" in Amnon Ben-Tor (ed.), *The Archaeology of Ancient Israel*. Yale University Press: New Haven, 1992, pp10–39.

Bar-Yosef, O. and A. Belfer-Cohen. "The Origins of Sedentism and Farming Communities in the Levant." *Journal of World Prehistory* 3, 1989, pp447–498.

Black, Jeremy A. "The New Year Ceremonies in Ancient Babylon: 'Taking Bel by the hand' and a Cultic Picnic." *Religion* 11, 1981, pp39–59.

Bottéro, Jean. *Mesopotamia: Writing, Reasoning and the Gods.* University of Chicago Press: Chicago, 1992.

Bottéro, Jean. *Religion in Ancient Mesopotamia.* University of Chicago Press: Chicago, 2001.

Caubet, Annie (ed.). *Khorsabad, Le Palais de Sargon II, Roi d'Assyrie. Actes du Colloque Organisé au Musée de Louvre par le Service Culturel les 21 et 22 Janvier 1994.* La Documentation Français: Paris, 1995.

Chang, Kwang-chih. *The Archaeology of Ancient China.* Yale University Press: New Haven, 1989.

Chang, Kwang-chih, Xu Pingfang, Lu Liancheng, et al. *The Formation of Chinese Civilization: An Archaeological Perspective.* Yale University Press: New Haven, 2005.

Chavalas, Mark (ed.). *The Ancient Near East: Historical Sources in Translation.* Blackwell Publishing: Malden and Oxford, 2006.

Cheng, Dalin. *Peregrinations Along the Great Wall.* Commercial Press Limited: Hong Kong, 1987.

Cohen, Andrew C. *Death Rituals, Ideology, and the Development of Early Mesopotamian Kingship: Toward a New Understanding of Iraq's Royal Cemetery of Ur.* Brill Academic Publishers: Leiden and Boston, c. 2005.

Cooper, Jerrold S. "Babylonian Beginnings: The Origin of the Cuneiform Writing System in Comparative Perspective" in Stephen D. Houston (ed.). *The First Writing: Script Invention as History and Process.* Cambridge University Press: Cambridge, 2004, pp71–99.

Curtis, John. *Ancient Iran: Introductory Guide.* British Museum Press: London, 2000.

Curtis, John and Nigel Tallis (eds.). *Forgotten Empire: The World of Achaemenid Persia.* British Museum Press: London, 2005.

Delougaz, Pinhas and Seton Lloyd. *Pre-Sargonid Temples in the Diyala Region.* Oriental Institute of the University of Chicago: Chicago, 1942.

Delougaz, Pinhas, Harold D. Hill, and Seton Lloyd. *Private Houses and Graves in the Diyala Region.* Oriental Institute of the University of Chicago: Chicago, 1967.

Delougaz, Pinhas, Harold D. Hill, and T. Jacobsen. *Old Babylonian Public Buildings in the Diyala Region.* Oriental Institute of the University of Chicago: Chicago, 1990.

Flannery, K. V. "The Origins of the Village as a Settlement Type in Mesoamerica and the Near East" in Ucko, Peter J., Ruth Tringham, and G. W. Dimbleby (eds.). *Man, Settlement and Urbanism.* Duckworth: London, 1972, pp23–53.

Frankfort, Henri, Seton Lloyd, and Thorkild Jacobsen. *The Gimilsin Temple and the Palace of the Rulers at Tell Asmar.* Oriental Institute of the University of Chicago: Chicago, 1940.

Fuchs, Andreas. *Die Inschriften Sargons II aus Khorsabad.* Cuvillier Verlag: Göttingen, 1994.

Garfinkel, Yosef. *Dancing at the Dawn of Agriculture.* University of Texas Press: Austin, 2003.

Garfinkel, Yosef. *The Goddess of Sha'ar Hagolan: Excavations at a Neolithic Site in Israel.* Israel Exploration Society: Jerusalem, 2004.

George, Andrew R. "Babylon Revisited: Archaeology and Philology in Harness." *Antiquity* 67, 1993, pp734–746.

George, Andrew R. *Babylonian Topographical Texts.* Departement Oriëntalistiek: Leuven, 1992.

George, Andrew R. "Bonds of the Lands: Babylon, the Cosmic Capital" in Bruch Wandel and G. Wilhelm (eds.), *Die Orientalische Stadt: Kontinuität.* SDV Saarbrücker Druckerei und Verlag: Saarbrücken, 1997, pp125–145.

Glassner, Jean-Jacques. *The Invention of Cuneiform: Writing in Sumer.* Johns Hopkins University Press: Baltimore, 2003.

Glover, Ian and Peter Bellwood (eds.). *Southeast Asia from Prehistory to History.* RoutledgeCurzon: London and New York, 2004.

Habu, Junko. *Ancient Jomon of Japan.* Cambridge University Press: Cambridge, 2004.

Higham, Charles. *The Civilisation of Angkor.* University of California Press: Berkeley, 2002.

Higham, Charles. *Early Cultures of Mainland Southeast Asia.* River Books: Bangkok, 2002.

Kenyon, Kathleen M. *Digging Up Jericho: The Results of the Jericho Excavations 1952–1956.* E. Benn: London, 1957.

Kobayashi, Tatsuo. *Jomon Reflections.* Oxbow Books: Oxford, 2004.

Kuhrt, Amélie. *The Ancient Near East: c.3000–330 B.C.*, 2 vols. Routledge: London and New York, 1995.

Kuhrt, Amélie. "The Palace(s) of Babylon" in Inge Nielsen (ed.), *The Royal Palace Institution in the First Millennium B.C.: Regional Development and Cultural Interchange Between East and West.* Monographs of the Danish Institute at Athens: Athens, 2001, pp77–94.

Loewe, Michael and Edward L. Shaughnessy (eds.). *The Cambridge History of Ancient China: From the Origins of Civilization to 221 B.C.* Cambridge University Press: Cambridge, 1999.

Loud, G. and C. B. Altman. "Khorsabad, Part II: The Citadel and the Town." *Oriental Institute Publications* 40. University of Chicago: Chicago, 1938.

Loud, G., H. Frankfort, and T. Jacobsen. "Khorsabad, Part I: Excavations in the Palace and at a City Gate." *Oriental Institute Publications* 38. University of Chicago: Chicago, 1936.

Maisels, Charles K. *The Emergence of Civilization: From Hunting and Gathering to Agriculture, Cities, and the State in the Near East.* Routledge: London and New York, 1990.

Matthews, Roger. *The Archaeology of Mesopotamia: Theories and Approaches.* Routledge: London and New York, 2003.

Meyers, Eric M. (ed.). *The Oxford Encyclopedia of Archaeology in the Near East,* 5 vols. Oxford University Press: New York, 1997.

Mizoguchi, Koji. *An Archaeological History of Japan: 30,000 B.C.–A.D. 700.* University of Pennsylvania Press: Philadelphia, 2003.

Morton, W. Scott. *China: Its History and Culture,* 4th edn. McGraw-Hill Publishing: New York, 2005.

O'Reilly, Dougald. *Early Civilizations of Southeast Asia.* AltaMira Press: Lanham, 2006.

Pollock, Susan. *Ancient Mesopotamia: The Eden That Never Was.* Cambridge University Press: Cambridge, 1999.

Pollock, Susan. "Of Priestesses, Princes and Poor Relations: The Dead in the Royal Cemetery of Ur." *Cambridge Archaeological Journal* 1, 1991, pp171–189.

Pollock, Susan and Reinhard Bernbeck. *Archaeologies of the Middle East: Critical Perspectives.* Blackwell Publishing: Malden and Oxford, 2005.

Postgate, J. Nicholas. *Early Mesopotamia: Society and Economy at the Dawn of History.* Routledge: London and New York, 1992.

Redman, Charles L. *The Rise of Civilization: From Early Farmers to Urban Society in the Ancient Near East.* W. H. Freeman: San Francisco, 1978.

Roaf, Michael. *Cultural Atlas of Mesopotamia and the Ancient Near East.* Equinox: Oxford, 1990.

Sasson, Jack M. (ed.). *Civilizations of the Ancient Near East,* 4 vols. Scribner: New York, 1995.

Schmandt-Besserat, Denise. *Before Writing.* University of Texas Press: Austin, 1992.

Schmidt, Klaus. *Sie bauten die ersten Tempel.* C. H. Beck: München, 2006.

Snell, Daniel C. *A Companion to the Ancient Near East.* Blackwell Publishing: Malden and Oxford, 2005.

Talai, Hassan. *The Archaeology and Art of Iran in the First Millennium B.C.* Samt Publications: Tehran, 1995.

Tsuboi, Kiyotari and Tanaka Migaku. *The Historic City of Nara.* UNESCO Centre for East Asian Cultural Studies: Tokyo and Paris, 1991.

Van de Mieroop, Marc. *The Ancient Mesopotamian City.* Oxford University Press: Oxford, 1997.

Van de Mieroop, Marc. *A History of the Ancient Near East: c.3000–323 B.C.* Blackwell Publishing: Malden, 2004.

Van de Mieroop, Marc. "Reading Babylon." *AJA* 107.2, 2003, pp257–275.

Whitfield, Roderick and Wang Tao (eds.). *Exploring China's Past: New Discoveries and Studies in Archaeology and Art.* Saffron: London, 1999.

Woolley, Leonard and P. R. S. Moorey. *Ur "of the Chaldees": A Revised and Updated Edition of Sir Leonard Woolley's Excavations at Ur.* Cornell University Press: New York, 1982.

Yang, Xiaoneng (ed.). *The Golden Age of Chinese Archaeology: Celebrated Discoveries from the People's Republic of China.* National Gallery of Art: Washington with the Nelson-Atkins Museum of Art: Kansas City and Yale University Press: New Haven, 1999.

Yang, Xiaoneng (ed.). *New Perspectives on China's Past: Chinese Archaeology in the Twentieth Century.* Yale University Press: New Haven with the Nelson-Atkins Museum of Art: Kansas City, 2004.

Zettler, Richard L. and Lee Horne (eds.). *Treasures from the Royal Tombs of Ur.* Museum of Archaeology and Anthropology, University of Pennsylvania: Philadelphia, 1998.

THE AMERICAS

Bauer, Brian S. *Ancient Cuzco: Heartland of the Inca.* University of Texas Press: Austin, 2004.

Berdan, Frances F. *The Aztecs of Central Mexico: An Imperial Society,* 2nd edn. Thomson-Wadsworth: Belmont, 2005.

Berlo, Janet (ed.). *Art, Ideology and the City of Teotihuacan.* Dumbarton Oaks: Washington DC, c. 1992.

Berrin, Kathleen and Esther Pasztory (eds.). *Teotihuacan: Art from the City of the Gods.* Thames and Hudson: New York and the Fine Arts Museum of San Francisco: San Francisco, 1994.

Blomster, Jeffrey. *Etlatongo: Social Complexity, Interaction and Village Life in the Mixteca Alta of Oaxaca, Mexico*. Thomson Wadsworth: Belmont, 2004.

Burger, Richard L. and Lucy C. Salazar (eds.). *Machu Picchu: Unveiling the Mystery of the Incas*. Yale University Press: New Haven, 2004.

Coe, Michael D. and Rex Koontz. *Mexico: From the Olmecs to the Aztecs*, 5th edition. Thames and Hudson: New York, 2002.

Cortés, Hernán. *Letters from Mexico*. Translated by Anthony Pagden. Yale University Press: New Haven, 2001.

Covey, R. Alan. *How the Incas Built Their Heartland: State Formation and the Innovation of Imperial Strategies in the Sacred Valley, Peru*. University of Michigan Press: Ann Arbor, 2006.

D'Altroy, Terence N. *The Incas*. Blackwell Publishing: Malden, 2002.

Davies, Nigel. *The Aztecs: A History*. University of Oklahoma: Norman, 1973.

Díaz del Castillo, Bernal. *The Conquest of New Spain*. Translated by J. M. Cohen. Penguin: New York, 1963.

Diehl, Richard A. *The Olmecs: America's First Civilization*. Thames and Hudson: London, 2004.

Durán, Fray Diego. *Book of the Gods and Rites and The Ancient Calendar*. Translated by Fernando Horcasitas and Doris Heyden. University of Oklahoma Press: Norman, 1971.

Evans, Susan. *Ancient Mexico and Central America: Archaeology and Culture History*. Thames and Hudson: London, 2004.

Fagan, Brian M. *From Black Land to Fifth Sun: the Science of Sacred Sites*. Addison-Wesley: Reading, 1988.

Fash, William L. *Scribes, Warriors, and Kings: The City of Copán and the Ancient Maya*. Thames and Hudson: New York, 1991.

Flannery, Kent (ed.). *The Early Mesoamerican Village*. Academic Press: New York, 1976.

Flannery, Kent and Joyce Marcus (eds.). *The Cloud People*. Academic Press: New York, 1983.

Grove, David (ed.). *Ancient Chalcatzingo*. University of Texas Press: Austin, 1987.

Harrison, Peter D. *The Lords of Tikal: Rulers of an Ancient Maya City*. Thames and Hudson: New York, 1999.

Lekson, Stephen H. (ed.). *The Archaeology of Chaco Canyon: An Eleventh Century Pueblo Regional Center*. SAR Press: Santa Fe, 2006.

López Luján, Leonardo. *The Offerings of the Templo Mayor of Tenochtitlan*, revised edn. Translated by Bernard R. Ortiz de Montellano and Thelma Ortiz de Montellano. University of New Mexico Press: Albuquerque, 2005.

Martin, Simon and Nikolai Grube. *Chronicle of the Maya Kings and Queens: Deciphering the Dynasties of the Ancient Maya*. Thames and Hudson: London and New York, 2000.

Matos Moctezuma, Eduardo. *The Great Temple of the Aztecs: Treasures of Tenochtitlan*. Thames and Hudson: London, 1988.

Moseley, Michael E. and Kent C. Day (eds.). *Chan Chan: Andean Desert City*. University of New Mexico Press: Albuquerque, 1982.

Noble, David Grant (ed.). *Houses Beneath the Rock: The Anasazi of Canyon de Chelly and Navajo National Monument*. Ancient City Press: Santa Fe, 1992.

Noble, David Grant (ed.). *In Search of Chaco: New Approaches to an Archaeological Enigma*. SAR Press: Santa Fe, 2004.

Noble, David Grant (ed.). *The Mesa Verde World: Explorations in Ancestral Pueblo Archaeology*. SAR Press: Santa Fe, 2006.

Protzen, Jean-Pierre. *Inca Architecture and Construction at Ollantaytambo*. Oxford University Press: New York, 1993.

Schele, Linda and Peter Mathews. *The Code of Kings: The Language of Seven Sacred Maya Temples and Tombs*. Scribner: New York, 1998.

Sharer, Robert J. and Loa P. Traxler. *The Ancient Maya*, 6th edition. Stanford University Press: Stanford, 2006.

Smith, Michael E. *The Aztecs*, 2nd edn. Blackwell Publishers: Oxford, 2003.

Stone, Andrea J. *Images from the Underworld: Naj Tunich and the Tradition of Maya Cave Painting*. University of Texas Press: Austin, 1995.

Varien, Mark D. and Richard H. Wilshusen (eds.). *Seeking the Center Place: Archaeology and Ancient Communities in the Mesa Verde Region*. University of Utah Press: Salt Lake City, 2002.

Viele, Catherine W. *Navajo National Monument*. Southwest Parks and Monuments Association: Tucson, 1993.

Von Hagen, Victor Wolfgang. *The Ancient Sun Kingdoms of the Americas: Aztec, Maya, Inca*. Thames and Hudson: London, 1962.

Winter, Marcus. *Oaxaca: The Archaeological Record*, 2nd edition. Carteles-Editores: Oaxaca, 1992.

AUSTRALIA AND THE PACIFIC

Bahn, Paul G. and J. Flenley. *The Enigmas of Easter Island: Island on the Edge*. Oxford University Press: New York, 2003.

Bellwood, Peter. *Man's Conquest of the Pacific: The Prehistory of Southeast Asia and Oceania*. Oxford University Press: Oxford, 1979.

Bellwood, Peter. *The Polynesians: Prehistory of an Island People*, revised edn. Thames and Hudson: London, 1987.

Blainey, Geoffrey. *Triumph of the Nomads*. Sun Books: Melbourne, 1996.

Bowler, J. M. *Lake Mungo: Window to Australia's Past*, CD-ROM. University of Melbourne: Parkville, 2002.

Builth, H. "Gunditjmara Environmental Management: The Development of a Fisher-Gatherer-Hunter Society in Temperate Australia" in C. Grier, J. Kim, and J. Uchiyama (eds.), *Beyond Affluent Foragers: Rethinking Hunter-Gatherer Complexity*. Oxbow Books: Oxford, 2006, pp4–23.

Duff, Roger. *The Moa-Hunter Period of Maori Culture*. R. E. Owen, Government Printer: Wellington, 1956.

Field, J. H. "Tramping Through the Pleistocene: Does Taphonomy Matter at Cuddie Springs?" *Australian Archaeology* 63, 2006, pp9–20.

Flood, Josephine. *Archaeology of the Dreamtime: The Story of Prehistoric Australia and Its People*. J. B. Publishing: Marleston, 2004.

Horton, David. (ed.). *The Encyclopaedia of Aboriginal Australia*, 2 vols. Aboriginal Studies Press: Canberra, 1994.

Kirch, Patrick V. *The Evolution of the Polynesian Chiefdoms*. Cambridge University Press: Cambridge, 1984.

Kirch, Patrick V. *Feathered Gods and Fishhooks: An Introduction to Hawaiian Archaeology and Prehistory*. University of Hawaii Press: Honolulu, 1995.

Kirch, Patrick V. *The Lapita Peoples: Ancestors of the Oceanic World*. Blackwell Publishers: Oxford, 1997.

Kirch, Patrick V. *On the Road of the Winds: An Archaeological History of the Pacific Islands Before European Contact*. University of California Press: Berkeley, 2000.

Lourandos, Harry. *Continent of Hunter-Gatherers: New Perspectives in Australian Prehistory*. Cambridge University Press: Cambridge, 1997.

Mulvaney, Derek J. and Johan Kamminga. *The Prehistory of Australia*. Allen and Unwin: Sydney, 1999.

Sharp, Andrew. *The Discovery of the Pacific Islands*, Clarendon Press: Oxford, 1960.

Spriggs, Matthew. *The Island Melanesians*, Blackwell Publishers: Oxford, 1997.

Wroe, S. and J. Field. "A Review of the Evidence for a Human Role in the Extinction of Australian Megafauna and an Alternative Explanation." *Quaternary Science Reviews In Press*, 2006.

Glossary

Acheulean The Lower Paleolithic "industry," starting about 1.6 million years ago.

Adze A woodworking tool of stone or metal, similar to an ax, but hafted so that the blade faces downward (see Hafted).

Agora A civic center and market area of ancient Greek cities.

Antiquarianism The practice of collecting old documents and artifacts as part of a general interest in the past.

Apadana The large hall where Persian kings held audience, receiving various ambassadors, officials, and supplicants.

Archaeobotany The study of plant remains recovered in archaeological excavations. This enables archaeologists to learn about past environments.

Archaeological feature An item or structure discovered during a surface survey or an archaeological excavation.

Artifact A term meaning "deliberately made," which describes any object made, modified, or moved by humans. This can include landscapes, fixed structures, temporary structures (for example, a hearth), burials, and portable items.

Assemblage Any collection of artifacts found together within one archaeological feature.

Aurignacian The Upper Paleolithic "industry," starting from about 30,000 BCE.

Australopithecine A term meaning "southern apes," which refers to an early hominid whose fossils have so far been discovered only on the African continent.

Australopithecus (A.) The Australopithecine family (genus); species are often named after their place of discovery (e.g., *A. afarensis* from Afar, Ethiopia; *A. africanus* from southern Africa).

Australopithecus boisei Also known as *Paranthropus boisei*, this is the name of the hominid fossil found at Olduvai Gorge in Tanzania in 1959, then known as *Zinjanthropus boisei*.

Austronesian A term meaning "southern islands," which refers to a large family of languages that developed probably in southern China and Southeast Asia and whose speakers settled as far south as Indonesia, as far west as Madagascar, and as far east as Easter Island (Chile).

BCE A term meaning "before the Common Era"; it is a secular form of dating that replaces the Christian form BC (before Christ).

Biface/Bifacial A piece of stone, often a natural pebble, which has been worked from both sides to create sharp chopping edges; these are sometimes called hand axes, as they can be held in the hand, without a haft (see Hafted); they are typical of the Lower Paleolithic.

Bloomery A process of extracting iron from ore and refining it at high heat in a charcoal-fired hearth. Archaeologically, bloomeries are visible as fire-hardened clay hollows, typically surrounded by slag left over from the smelting process. The iron forms a spongy mass at the bottom of the hearth, which can then be hammered by the smith into the finished metal.

Bodhisattva A term in Buddhism, which refers to a person who has attained enlightenment but delays going to nirvana in order to help others reach enlightenment.

Bos primigenius A term meaning "first-born ox," referring to a species of wild cattle called the aurochs, which is now extinct; the likely ancestor of the cattle that was domesticated from the ninth millennium BCE.

BP A term meaning "before the present" (i.e., before the year CE 1950); an abbreviation used in expressing dates, such as those derived from radiocarbon dating and other methods. The year CE 1950 was chosen because that was when radiocarbon dating was invented.

Breccia A natural conglomerate of angular rocks cemented together by finer material.

Burin A small tool with a sharp edge at the top, used for engraving or other fine work.

c. See Circa.

Candi The Javanese name for Hindu and Buddhist temples.

Canopic jar An Egyptian stone or pottery container used to store the internal organs removed from a corpse before it was mummified.

CE A term meaning "Common Era"; it is a secular form of dating that replaces the Christian form AD (*anno Domini*, in the year of our Lord).

Cella The enclosed main room of a Greek or Roman temple, usually housing the statue of the deity.

Chamber-tomb A burial place built aboveground, usually as a flat-topped stone structure high enough for mourners to stand in; it is often used for multiple burials and often covered by a mound.

Châtelperronian The Upper Paleolithic "industry," starting c. 35,000 BCE.

Chert A flintlike form of quartz, used for making sharp-edged implements.

Chronometric dating A term meaning "time measure," it is a dating system that relies on laboratory methods, rather than on stratigraphy or stylistic analysis. Techniques include counting radioisotopes, such as radiocarbon, or the ratio of minerals to gases (e.g., thorium/argon), as well as luminescence and dendrochronology (see Dendrochronology, Luminescence, and Radiocarbon dating).

Circa A term meaning "at, in, or approximately" when used with dates; it is abbreviated c.

Cist A Neolithic or Bronze Age "box" tomb made by lining a small pit with stone slabs.

Coprolite Fossil dung; very useful for examining the diet of animals and humans.

Cranial vault The top of the skull (cranium).

Cro-Magnon A subset of *Homo sapiens*, whose fossils have been found primarily in Europe, from c. 40,000 BCE.

Cross-dating A method of dating from culture to culture, or site to site, by establishing connections between artifacts or environmental factors.

Cultigen A domesticated plant not known in a wild form.

Cuneiform script A writing system, composed of wedge-shaped characters, developed in Mesopotamia and used for many different languages; it was often written on soft clay tablets, which were then hardened in dry heat or, in rare cases, baked into a permanent ceramic.

Cursus A term derived from Latin meaning "racecourse," it is the name given to long rectangular earthen enclosures, created in the Neolithic probably for ceremonial gatherings. Well-known examples are near Stonehenge in England and Tara in Ireland.

Cyclopean A style of building, using unusually large stones. The Cyclops were giants in Greek mythology.

Deme A term derived from Greek meaning "the people"; they were voting citizens in ancient Athens; the word "democracy" (rule of the people) is derived from it.

Demotic script Everyday script for ordinary documents, particularly used in Egypt, where it was different from the "hieratic" sacred script used for religious texts.

Dendrochronology A method of relative dating that analyzes the rings formed within a tree each year that it grows; as the weather is never quite the same, the rings vary slightly each year and can be compared to those from other trees. In this way it is possible in some regions to establish a time scale extending back 9,000 years.

Dentate-stamped A term meaning "tooth-stamped," which refers to the decorative marks made by pressing an object with notches or teethlike serrations, such as a comb, into soft material, such as clay.

Denticulate A stone flake with notched edges.

Diffusionism A theory that there were only one or two centers of invention (of domesticating plants, for instance, or writing, or mummification), and that all knowledge spread from these centers; it denied the possibility of independent invention.

Dilettante Somebody who "delights in" a study, but may approach it in an amateur fashion.

Discoid A stone that has been hand-flaked into the shape of a flat circle.

Dolmen A term meaning "stone table" in Breton; usually refers to aboveground megalithic structures consisting of several vertically set stones with one or more flat stones balanced on top of them.

Ecotone A transitional zone between two adjacent plant and animal communities, containing species of each zone, as well as its own species.

Epigraphic Pertaining to an engraved description.

Ethnoarchaeology The study of contemporary societies that focuses on their lifestyle and material culture (buildings, clothing, craft techniques, food production, burial customs, etc.).

Everted Turned outward.

Exarchy A system of governing a social unit or geographical area from outside the unit or area.

Extirpation A term meaning "taking out the root"; the total removal of something.

Faience Powdered quartz formed into a paste then shaped in a mould and baked, which gave it a glossy surface. In Egypt it was often painted blue or green with copper-based pigments and was used like a semiprecious stone.

Felid An animal of the cat family (*Felidae*).

Flake A piece of stone, struck off a larger piece to make a sharp blade or scraper.

Geoglyph A term meaning "earth sign"; large symbols or designs made by manipulating surface land features (e.g., the Nazca Lines located in Peru).

Glaciation The spread of ice over the ground surface during a very cold period.

Gravettian The Upper Paleolithic "industry," from about 25,000 BCE.

Hafted To mount or set in a handle, which is usually made of wood.

Hematite A term meaning "blood stone"; iron oxide, also known as ocher; widespread in nature and used by itself or as a coloring by many human communities.

Henge A circular earthen enclosure that was built throughout Britain and Ireland in the Neolithic period.

Hermeneutics The study of meaning, or interpretation, especially in written documents.

Hieroglyph A term meaning "sacred sign"; a character in a system of writing used for religious purposes, especially in Ancient Egypt.

Holocene The present geological period, starting with the end of the Pleistocene ice ages about 10,000 years ago.

Hominid A member of the family of present humans and their ancestors, which is bipedal with a large brain; the oldest-known fossils are about 3.5 million years old.

Hominin A member of the total family of humans, including their earliest ancestors, defined by having an upright posture and walking on their hind legs (bipedalism); the earliest fossils are about 7 million years old.

Hominoidea A biological classification called a superfamily, which includes not only all forms of humans (the hominidae family, with its subdivisions of hominids and hominins), but also apes (the pongidae family).

Homo **(H.)** A term meaning "human"; the human genus; fossil species have descriptive names, for example, *H. erectus* (standing human); *H. ergaster* (human the worker); *H. floresiensis* (human from Flores, Indonesia); *H. habilis* (able human); and *H. heidelbergensis* (human from Heidelberg, Germany).

Homo neanderthalensis See Neanderthals.

Homo sapiens A term meaning "knowledgeable human"; the modern human species.

Homogeneity A term meaning "same kind"; uniformity in structure or composition.

Höyük/Hüyük The Turkish word for a high artificial mound, often created from the build-up of archaeological remains of cities or villages one on top of the other.

Humanist A scholar whose principal interest is in people rather than in religion or nature.

Interstratified A term meaning "between the layers" of a stratigraphy (see Stratigraphy).

Iron Age A time when iron was the most commonly used material for making tools and weapons, superseding bronze and stone.

Jomon period The earliest culture of Japan, from about 13,500 BCE.

Kouros The idealized image of a youth, as represented in Ancient Greek statues (plural: kouroi).

Kurgan The local name for a burial mound in the Caucasus, Ukraine, and southern Russia.

Laterite Iron-rich clay that is quite soft when quarried but hardens with exposure to the air; used in tropical countries for making building blocks or road surfaces.

Levallois technique A Lower Paleolithic "industry," which extends into the Middle Paleolithic; this toolmaking technique consists of preparing a stone core, from which blades or other implements can be flaked off.

Loess soil A loose wind-blown dust that can be fertile when irrigated. Much of the loess comes from soil that was ground up by ice movements during the last glaciation and was deposited in dense layers close to the edge of the retreating ice caps.

Lozenge A diamond shape or rhombus.

Luminescence A method of dating objects from which sunlight has been excluded; when they are reexposed, electrons that had been trapped release energy in the form of light (luminescence), which can then be measured; the method is useful for dating certain types of sites, such as buried cave floors.

Magdalenian The Upper Paleolithic "industry," from about 15,000 BCE.

Magnetite A glossy, dark-colored iron oxide, which is strongly magnetic.

Magus A Persian priest, diviner, or prophet; the word "magic" is derived from it.

Mandible The jawbone, especially of the lower jaw.

Massif The backbone of a mountain range.

Mastaba A rectangular Egyptian tomb of the Old Kingdom; the tomb was underground with a chapel above it at ground level; the first mastabas were built of mud-brick; later they were made of stone.

Menhir A term meaning "standing stone" in Breton; it is a long boulder, which is not worked but has been set upright and can stand alone or be formed into circles or alignments with other boulders, presumably for ritual purposes.

Metope A decorative square stone panel at the top of the facade of Greek temples; it is sometimes carved with images.

Microenvironment Environmental conditions within a confined space (e.g., a cave, underground site, burial mound, or underwater wreck), which make this space different from its surroundings.

Microlith A term meaning "small stone"; a sharp little flake mounted singly or in groups to make arrowheads or sawlike tools.

Microwear The study of the edge of stone tools to determine what they were used for (e.g., cutting leather, wood, or plants).

Midden A term meaning "garbage heap"; refers to a mound of food and other debris left at a habitation site or along the coast (e.g., shell-midden).

Miocene A geological period (the fourth epoch of the Tertiary), sometimes called the age of mammals, when there was some evolution of primates; it occurred from 23 to 5 million years ago.

Mitochondrial DNA DNA that is transmitted through the mother.

Mousterian The Middle Paleolithic "industry," associated with Neanderthal fossils; from about 75,000 years ago.

Natron A naturally occurring salt used to mummify bodies in Ancient Egypt.

Naviform Boat-shaped.

Neanderthals Fossil species of *Homo heidelbergensis* and *Homo neanderthalensis;* they lived in Europe and western Asia until around 27,000 years ago.

Neolithic A lifestyle and material culture associated with farming as it developed in different parts of the world; typically it implies the use of permanent habitations (farms and villages), gardens, and field systems.

Nome An administrative district of Ancient Egypt; there were 42 in all.

Obelisk A tall pillar of worked stone with carved inscriptions or reliefs on all four sides.

Obsidian Hard volcanic glass, often black, which can be flaked to produce a sharp edge.

Ocher See Hematite.

Oldowan The Lower Paleolithic "industry"; it is the earliest known, associated with Australopithecine fossils at Olduvai Gorge, Kenya, and started about 2 million years ago.

Orthostat A large upright slab of stone, often used to support a horizontal lintel, or as walling.

Paleoindian The earliest human settlers in the Americas, during the Pleistocene.

Paleolithic A term meaning "old stone"; the time during which human beings evolved and developed distinctive artifact types. It is roughly divided into: Early or Lower Paleolithic, from earliest times (1.8 million years ago) to *c.* 75,000 BCE; Middle Paleolithic, from *c.* 75,000 BCE to *c.* 40,000 BCE; and Later or Upper Paleolithic, from *c.* 40,000 BCE to *c.* 10,000 BCE. The dates are tentative.

Paleolithic "industry" The name applied to types of stone implements made according to a consistent pattern or style; the various styles can be tied into stratigraphic layers. They are usually named after the places where they were first identified, many of them in France (e.g., Acheulean from St. Acheul, Levallois from Levallois, and Magdalenian from La Madeleine).

Paleomagnetic studies Using variations in the Earth's magnetic field to establish relative dating.

Paleopathology The study of disease in the past, by examining human skeletons and mummified bodies.

Paleosol Old or buried soil, as exposed by archaeological excavation.

Palynology Also known as pollen analysis, this is a method of studying past environments by counting the pollen from grasses, trees, and other plants; this gives a good indication of what the vegetation was like in any given area and whether the plants were wild or cultivated.

Parietal Art decoration on the walls of a natural cave or artificial structure.

Passage grave A tomb in which the burial chamber is entered by a separate passage, rather than an opening directly onto the outside.

Patina A surface film of greenish color that develops on bronze, or the gloss that repeated rubbing often imparts onto some wooden or stone surfaces.

Pelagic A term meaning "open sea."

Peregrination Travel, usually with a spiritual purpose (e.g., to visit sacred places or shrines).

Perigordian An Upper Paleolithic "industry," which overlaps with the Aurignacian about 40,000 to 20,000 years ago.

Petroglyph A term meaning "stone sign"; a symbol or representation on natural rock, usually carved or pecked with a sharp stone tool.

Pharaonic A term derived from *per-aa* meaning "royal palace" in Ancient Egyptian, and used to refer to the kings or the periods during which they ruled.

Phenomenology A philosophical approach concentrating on the study of the direct experience of "being in the world"; it has a bearing on approaches to material culture.

Pictograph A term meaning "image writing"; it is a form of writing which used pictures of objects as signs for them; Egyptian hieroglyphs are pictographic, so perhaps is the Indus Valley script; it is sometimes used to refer to rock painting.

Pithecanthropus erectus A term meaning "standing ape-man"; the early name for the *Homo erectus* (Java Man) fossil found at Trinil, Indonesia, in 1891.

Pithos A large ceramic jar used in the ancient Mediterranean world for storing olives, grain, oil, and other foodstuffs (plural: pithoi).

Pleistocene A recent geological period (Quaternary), which includes the ice ages; modern humans *(Homo sapiens)* developed during this time (1.6 million years ago to 10,000 years ago) and spread across much of the planet.

Potsherd A fragment of ceramic from broken pots; millions have been found in archaeological excavations around the world, as ceramics are almost indestructible.

Prehistoric A term meaning "before history"; the time period prior to the use of written documentation (literacy) in any given region—some literate societies might, nonetheless, be described as "prehistoric" because we cannot read their language (e.g., Minoan Crete, the Indus Valley).

Processualism A theoretical approach that sought to devise general laws of behavior (processes) which could be applied to the archaeological record; it has been criticized for denying individual agency.

Protohistoric A term meaning "just before history"; the period when some written documentation is available close to, but not in any given region; the adjacent information can be used, with caution, to study the nonliterate region (e.g., information about "barbarians" from Greek and Roman sources).

Provenance/Provenience The place that an artifact has certainly come from (e.g., an excavation site); ancient objects of uncertain provenance, bought in a market, for example, have limited value as objects of study.

Ptolemy A Greek term meaning "warlike," which refers to the dynasty of Greek-speaking kings—beginning with Ptolemy I Soter—whose dynasty came to rule Egypt, Cyrene, Palestine, and Phoenicia in the aftermath of Alexander the Great's death in 323 BCE; Ptolemaic control of Palestine was effectively lost to the Seleucids by around 200 BCE; Ptolemaic kings continued to rule Egypt until it was annexed by Rome in 30 BCE.

Pyramid A standing structure with a square base and equal triangular sides tapering to a point (called the apex).

Pyroscapulimancy A term meaning "fire-shoulder bone-divination," which refers to reading the cracks in shoulder bones that have been heated in a fire in order to make prophecies about the future; this method was commonly used during the Shang Dynasty in China. The prophecies were actually written on the cracked bones, for record purposes; this is not only the earliest-known form of Chinese writing, but also a useful insight into life at the time.

Quartz A mineral form of silica (sand) with six-sided crystals, sometimes used as ornaments.

Quartzite A rock consisting mostly of quartz; useful for making sharp-edged stone tools.

Radiocarbon assay Obtaining and testing samples for radiocarbon dating.

Radiocarbon dating A method of dating by counting how much of the radioactive isotope carbon 14 (C14) remains in an organism that has died; as all living things take in carbon from the atmosphere, when they die, they cease to absorb it, and the carbon starts to decay; C14 emits radiation that can be measured and gives an approximate time of the death of the organism.

Raphide A needle-shaped crystal of calcium compounds formed within a plant; it survives after the soft tissue has decayed and can give information about past environments.

Relative dating Establishing a time-sequence of objects through stratigraphic, technical, or stylistic analysis. For instance, object A is below object B in the stratigraphy and should therefore be earlier, or object B has some technical improvement over object A and should therefore be later.

Sarcophagus A term meaning "flesh eater"; a coffin made of stone, clay, wood, or metal (plural: sarcophagi).

Sarsen The local name for a very hard natural conglomerate stone found in the region of Avebury, England, and used to build the great stone circles at Stonehenge.

Satrapy A province of the ancient Persian Empire; its governor was called a satrap.

Savanna Grassland with scattered tree cover, found normally in tropical or semitropical regions.

Scarab An Egyptian seal or amulet (good-luck charm) in the shape of a dung beetle, usually made of stone; the flat underside is often carved with an image, or a name.

Schist A rock that flakes easily and can be cut into flat plates or tiles.

Seleucid A Greek term denoting the dynasty name of Seleucus I Nicator, a distinguished general of Alexander the Great, whose dynasty came to rule Asia Minor, Syria, Mesopotamia, and Iran to the borders of India in the aftermath of Alexander's death in 323 BCE; the Seleucids effectively gained control of Palestine by c. 200 BCE, which they ruled until the Maccabean revolt.

Semiotics The study of signs and symbols.

Seriation A method of analyzing artifacts that compares their shapes and tries to place them in a sequence of development whereby similar shapes/styles are assumed to be of a similar age.

Shabti A figurine placed in an Egyptian tomb to act as a servant for the dead person.

Shard/Sherd A fragment of glass or ceramic (see Potsherd).

Silcrete Hard stone used like flint and chert for making flaked tools; particularly used in Australia and southern Africa.

Sinanthropus pekinensis A term meaning "Chinese human of Peking"; "Peking man" is a *Homo erectus* fossil found at Zhoukoudian near Beijing in the 1920s. The location is now a UNESCO World Heritage site.

"Slash-and-burn" A method of agriculture whereby fields are carved out of woodland by burning, with the wood-ash enriching the soil; fields are cultivated only for a couple of seasons, after which new areas are cleared.

Slip (applied to clay) A thin coating of clay diluted by water so that it flows over the surface of an earthenware pot; on baking this gives a slightly glossy surface; the slip can be darker or paler than the clay used to make the pot.

Smelting Extracting metals from the ore by heating it at sufficiently high temperatures for the metal to melt into liquid form.

Smithing Working metal into shape, often by heating it until it is soft and then hammering it on an anvil.

Soil matrix The soil in an archaeological deposit, in which the artifacts are embedded.

Solutrean The Upper Paleolithic "industry," from about 20,000 BCE.

Staff A long stick used as a support when walking, carried as a symbol of power, or utilized as a weapon (plural: staffs or staves).

Stave A long, flat piece of wood used to make the side of a boat or barrel.

Steatite A "soapstone" or a glossy stone, which is quite soft and easy to carve.

Stela/Stele A stone or pillar placed upright, usually worked to be quite flat; it can be decorated with images, or inscribed with text; often used as a marker for an important place (plural: stelae).

Step pyramid A standing structure with a square base and equal sides, made up of successively smaller levels, one on top of the other, tapering to a flat top.

Stone Age The time during which the implements that have survived were made of stone (lithic) rather than of metal; as it covers most of human existence, it has traditionally been subdivided into Paleolithic (Old), Mesolithic (Middle), and Neolithic (New) ages.

Stratigraphy A term meaning "writing the layers," it involves studying the various deposits in an archaeological site; normally the bottom layers would be earlier (older) than the ones on top.

Stupa A Buddhist shrine that is in the shape of a burial mound.

Tel/Tell A term meaning "mound" in Arabic; *te'l* in Hebrew; tell names are often applied to archaeological sites where there has been a successive build up of layers, creating an artificial mound.

Temenos A sacred area around a Greek temple; any sacred enclosure.

Tephra A layer of volcanic ash and debris.

Term A pillar used as a boundary stone.

Terracotta A term meaning "cooked earth"; earthenware or clay baked at relatively low temperatures to make a cheap ceramic; usually red or black in color.

Testudo A term meaning "tortoise shell"; a Roman military formation, in which a group of foot-soldiers placed a wall of body-shields above their heads and around the group.

Thermoluminescence Similar to luminescence, except that this method measures the heat that is emitted by the release of the trapped electrons (see Luminescence).

Tophet The childrens' burial place in Carthage; it is believed to be sacred to the god Baal and the goddess Tanit.

Torc An ornamental neck-ring without a fastening; typically the ends of the open ring (terminals) are highly decorated.

Trilithon A "three-stone" arrangement of two vertical stones with one horizontal stone above them, as seen at Stonehenge, England.

Tufa/Tuff A porous rock made up of volcanic ash which has solidified on cooling; it is light and easy to carve.

Tumulus An earthen mound built over a tomb.

Unifacial A stone tool worked on one side only.

Uraeus The cobra-diadem (crown in the shape of a snake) worn by the kings and queens of Ancient Egypt.

Viscera Entrails or inner organs.

Waisted A shape that narrows at its center, like the human waist.

Wessex A term traditionally used by archaeologists to describe the Bronze Age throughout southern England, as represented by the area that roughly corresponds to the historic West Saxon kingdom of Wessex.

Ziggurat An Assyrian term meaning "temple tower" or "mountain peak," which refers to stepped pyramidlike structures erected as shrines for Mesopotamian deities.

Zinjanthropus boisei See *Australopithecus boisei*.

Zoroastrianism A religion of ancient Persia, preached by the prophet Zoroaster, who lived in the seventh or sixth century BCE.

Index

Plain numbers indicate references in the body text. *Italicized* numbers indicate references in image captions or maps, while **bold** numbers indicate references in feature boxes.

Picture Credits

The Publisher would like to thank the following picture libraries and other copyright owners for permission to reproduce their images. Every attempt has been made to obtain permission for use of all images from the copyright owners, however, if any errors or omissions have occurred Global Book Publishing would be pleased to hear from copyright owners.

Key: (t) top of page; (b) bottom of page; (l) left side of page; (r) right side of page; (c) center of page.

AAP Image: 203(tr); AFP PHOTO/Clay Bryce/WA Museum/HO, 361(tr), 364(tl); AFP PHOTO/HO/ANU, 371(tr); AFP PHOTO/University of the South Pacific, 374(t); AP, 276(t), 277(b), 277(t); AP Photo/Peter David Josek, 137(br); AP Photo/Saedi Press, 93(b); The Australian Museum, 371(b); Perth West Australian/John Mokrzycki, 361(tl).

akg-images: 102(b), 113(r); Peter Connolly, 184(tr), 185(b); Hess Landesmuseum, 116(tr); Erich Lessing, 133(bl), 184(bl); Joseph Martin, 192(bl); Sambraus, 148(tr); Juergen Sorges, 64(c), 150(tr); Ullstein-Schlemmer, 126(r).

Ancient Art & Architecture Collection: 119(bl); 121(tr), 123(b), 132(b), 158(b), 209(tr), 223(b); M. Andrews, 136(bl); C.M. Dixon, 145(tr), 168(tr), 237(l), 245(tl), 245(tr); R. Kawk, 254(b); B. Norman, 216(r); Ronald Sheridan, 218(t), 219(b); Uniphoto Press, 255(t), 263(t).

The Art Archive: 18(t), 21(br), 26(b), 178(b), 265(br), 265(tr), 267(l), 268(l), 269(tr), 313(b), 119(t), 242(bl), 242(tr), 188(tl); Agora Museum Athens/ Dagli Orti, 155(br); Archaeological Museum Amman Jordan/Dagli Orti, 209(tl); Archaeological Museum Beirut/Dagli Orti, 160(b); Archaeological Museum Delphi/Dagli Orti, 166(tr); Archaeological Museum Istanbul/Dagli Orti, 174(tl); Archaeological Museum Lima/Dagli Orti, 331(b), 339(cr); Archaeological Museum Lima/Mireille Vautier, 330(b); Archaeological Museum Naples/Dagli Orti (A), 19(b); Archaeological Museum Tarquinia/ Dagli Orti, 176(c), 177(b); Archaeological Museum Tikal Guatemala/Dagli Orti, 309(c); Archaeological Museum Venice/Dagli Orti (A), 171(t); Bardo Museum Tunis/Dagli Orti, 183(cr), 183(t); Biblioteca Nacional Madrid/Dagli Orti, 323(t), 324(br); Biblioteca Nazionale Marciana Venice/Dagli Orti (A), 54–55; Bibliothèque des Arts Décoratifs Paris/Dagli Orti, 12–13, 21(t), 22(t); British Museum, 20(t); British Museum/Dagli Orti, 223(t), 228(c), 231(t), 99(r); British Museum/Eileen Tweedy, 47(b), 192(tr); Château du Grand-Pressigny/Dagli Orti, 122(l); Manuel Cohen, 186(bl); Stephanie Colasanti, 175(t), 382–383, 38(t), 40(bl), 208(t), 275(t); Culver Pictures, 349(tr), 92(b); Dagli Orti, 20–21(b), 48(b), 101(b), 147(t), 156(bl), 181(t), 299(cr), 30(r), 37(t), 50(tr), 76(b), 86(t), 87(b), 114–115, 162(bl), 165(br), 166(bl), 168(bl), 179(r), 210–211, 227(b), 229(t), 272(b), 301(bl), 302(bl), 307(br), 308(b), 309(tl), 311(t), 315(b), 315(t), 317(c), 320(b), 320(tl), 322(t), 323(b), 325(c), 325(tl), 326(b), 327(t), 328(b), 335(t), 338–339(c), 338(cl), 88(bl), 96(r), 101(tl), 141(r), 147(bl), 159(tl), 160(t), 161(t), 167(t), 169(t), 170(t), 171(b), 187(t), 229(b), 372(b), 91(br), 197(tl), 134(l), 225(t), 172(b), 309(tr); Egyptian Museum Cairo/Dagli Orti, 93(t), 60–61, 98(l); Egyptian Museum Turin/Dagli Orti, 91(tr); Egyptian Museum Turin/Jacqueline Hyde, 14(tr); Ephesus Archaeological Museum Selcuk Turkey/Dagli Orti, 173(bc); Ephesus Museum Turkey/Dagli Orti, 173(tr); Ethnographic Museum Vinnica Ukraine/ Dagli Orti, 232(t), 233(b); Etruscan Necropolis Tarquinia/Dagli Orti, 177(t); Genius of China Exhibition, 258(t), 263(br); Hebei Province Museum/Laurie Platt Winfrey, 249(b); Herklion Museum/Dagli Orti, 157(tr); Hermitage Museum Saint Petersburg/Dagli Orti, 235(b), 234(b), 237(r); Historical Museum Sofia/Dagli Orti, 136(t); Jarrold Publishing, 191(tr); Christopher Lay, 271(t); Luxor Museum, Egypt/Dagli Orti, 97(t); Mohammed Khalil Museum Cairo/Dagli Orti, 86(b); Moravian Museum Brno/Dagli Orti, 128(t); Musée Boucher de Perthes Abbeville/Dagli Orti, 211(tr); Musée de la Civilisation Gallo-Romaine Lyons/Dagli Orti, 182(b); Musée des Antiquités St. Germain en Laye/Dagli Orti, 35(t); Musée du Louvre Paris/Dagli Orti, 16(b), 84(tr), 94–95(b), 169(b), 218(b), 224(br), 95(l), 99(bl), 186(tr), 230(b), 231(b), 215(tr); Musée du Quai Branly Paris/Dagli Orti, 108(bl); Musée Guimet Paris/Dagli Orti, 247(tr); Museo Capitolino Rome/Dagli Orti, 175(br); Museo de las Culturas Oaxaca/Dagli Orti, 300(bl), 305(bl); Museo del Oro Lima/Dagli Orti, 335(b); Museo del Templo Mayor Mexico/Dagli Orti, 322(b); Museo della Civilta Romana Rome/Dagli Orti (A), 178(t); Museo di Antropologia ed Etnografia Turin/Dagli Orti, 82(tr), 74(t), 120(l); Museo Franz Mayer Mexico/Dagli Orti, 17(b); Museum of Anatolian Civilisations Ankara/Dagli Orti, 135(t); Museum of Anatolian Civilisations

Ankara/Dagli Orti, 135(b); Museum of London, 14(b); National Anthropological Museum Mexico/Dagli Orti, 29(l), 65(bl), 312(bl), 318(t); National Archaeological Museum Athens/Dagli Orti, 50(l), 162(tr), 170(b), 159(tr), 165(tc); National Museum Bucharest/Dagli Orti (A), 185(t); National Museum Karachi/Dagli Orti (A), 241(t), 245(b); National Science Academy Kiev/Dagli Orti (A), 195(bl); Navy Historical Service Vincennes France/Dagli Orti, 16(t); Palazzo Arco Mantua Italy/Dagli Orti, 196(b); Palenque Site Museum Chiapas/Dagli Orti, 313(t); Polyghiros Museum Greece/Dagli Orti (A), 182(t); Private Collection Paris/Dagli Orti, 238(t); San Apollinare in Classe Ravenna/Dagli Orti, 197(tr); Shandong Provincial Museum/Laurie Platt Winfrey, 251(t); Southwest Museum Pasadena/Laurie Platt Winfrey, 291(b); Staatliche Sammlung Ägyptischer Kunst Munich/Dagli Orti, 100(tr); Stadtmuseum Aachen/Dagli Orti (A), 189(t); Eileen Tweedy, 17(t); University Museum Cuzco/Mireille Vautier, 327(b); Mireille Vautier, 46(tr), 198–199, 326(t), 332(t), 273(b), 278–279, 292(b), 311(bl), 317(t), 319(b), 329(b), 329(t), 334(b), 273(t); Xalapa Museum Veracruz Mexico/Dagli Orti, 301(tl).

Bridget Ayling: 366(b).

Dr. Jeffrey Blomster: 300(t).

The Bridgeman Art Library/Lauros/Giraudon: 144(t).

Andrew Collins: 212(b).

Corbis Australia: 22(b), 36(c), 41(tl), 41(tr), 43(b), 44(t), 46(bl), 53(b), 53(t), 62(b), 63(tl), 63(tr), 64(b), 66(b), 66(tr), 73(b), 77(br), 77(t), 78(t), 82(b), 83(tr), 94(l), 103(t), 105(b), 106(br), 118(bl), 122(tr), 124(t), 125(bl), 127(tr), 129(t), 133(r), 137(bl), 139(t), 140(b), 140(t), 142(b), 143(t), 151(t), 152(t), 155(t), 157(bl), 163, 180(b), 190(t), 191(tl), 194(b), 201(cr), 201(t), 204(tr), 205(r), 206(b), 206(tl), 226(b), 236(bl), 239(tl), 240(t), 243(b), 246(b), 248(bl), 249(t), 256(l), 259(t), 261(l), 262(l), 262(r), 265(tl), 268(r), 269(tl), 270(c), 274(b), 274(c), 285(b), 294(t), 297(br), 297(tr), 298(b), 299(t), 305(t), 321(t), 336(b), 337(c), 337(t), 340(bl), 340(br), 341(t), 345(b), 350(l), 350(r), 351(cr), 369(b), 376(b).

The Cultural Properties Protection Division, Aomori Prefectural Board of Education: 266(b), 266(c).

Denver Museum of Nature & Science: All Rights Reserved, Image Archives, 280(tl), 285(t).

Department of the Environment and Water Resources, Australia: Photograph taken by John Baker, 359(b).

Professor Tom Dillehay: 281(t), 282(b), 283(b), 283(tr).

Dr. Judith Field: 354(b), 354(t).

Focus New Zealand Photo Library: 381(r).

Foundation for the Advancement of Mesoamerican Studies, Inc.: Photograph by Linda Schele, © David Schele, courtesy, www.famsi.org, 304(t).

Getty Images: 294–295(b); AFP/Stringer, 65(br); Altrendo Travel, 290(b); Stephen Alvarez, 314(t), 331(t); Maurice Ambler/Stringer, 51(b); Richard Ashworth, 25(t); Jose Azel, 81(t); Bruno Barbier, 221(b); Joseph Baylor Roberts, 295(tr), 344(t); Nathan Benn, 342(tl); Milos Bicanski/Stringer, 42(t); Ira Block, 5(c), 68(t), 72(c), 293(t), 330(t), 353(b); Anders Blomqvist, 148(bl); Cris Bouroncle, 51(t); Robert Caputo, 104(c); China Photos/Stringer, 15(t), 246–247, 253(bl); Richard A. Cooke III, 316(b); Joe Cornish, 2–3(c); Marco Di Lauro/Stringer, 96(bl); Jerry Driendl, 257(t); Alistair Duncan, 43(t);

Acknowledgments

The Publisher would like to thank the Proofreader, Bradley Wood, and the Art Director's Assistant, Paula Kelly, for their assistance with this book, as well as Lynn Lewis and John Mapps for their help during the conceptualization process prior to production. Special thanks go to Debbie Argue and Mandy Mottram from the Australian National University in Canberra for their expert guidance.

CAPTIONS FOR PRELIMINARY PAGES, OPENERS, AND COVER

PAGE 1 Petroglyph, Pu'ukohola Heiau National Historic Site, Hawaii, United States

PAGES 2–3 Megalithic menhir alignments of Ménec in Brittany, France

PAGE 5 Cemetery excavation at Puruchuco-Huaquerones, Peru

PAGES 8–9 Sulamani Temple at Bagan, Myanmar

PAGE 10 Byzantine-era carving on the wall of a cave at Kibbutz Tzuba, near Jerusalem, Israel

PAGES 12–13 Engraving of archaeological work at Nimrud by Sir Austen Henry Layard (1817–1894)

PAGES 54–55 Illustration from the *Nautical Atlas* (1554) by Giorgio Sideri

PAGES 60–61 Hieroglyphic inscription from the black granite topstone of the pyramid of Amenemhat III

PAGES 114–115 Plaster cast of a victim of the Mt. Vesuvius eruption, Pompeii, Italy

PAGES 198–199 Sitting Dhyani Buddha at Borobudur, Indonesia

PAGES 278–279 Agricultural terraces at Machu Picchu, Peru

PAGES 346–347 The Anbangbang Gallery at Kakadu National Park, Northern Territory, Australia

PAGES 382–383 Carved stone pots at Knossos on the island of Crete, Greece

FRONT COVER Two-thousand-year-old skeleton with ceremonial flint knife from Remedello Sotto cemetery in Italy

SPINE The gold mask of Tutankhamun

BACK COVER (LEFT TO RIGHT) *Moai* statue from Easter Island, Chile; Assyrian relief; Machu Picchu, Peru; detail from the throne of Tutankhamun; Italian krater from the fourth century BCE

Produced by Global Book Publishing
Level 8, 15 Orion Road
Lane Cove, NSW 2066, Australia
Ph: (612) 9425 5800   Fax: (612) 9425 5804
Email: rightsmanager@globalpub.com.au

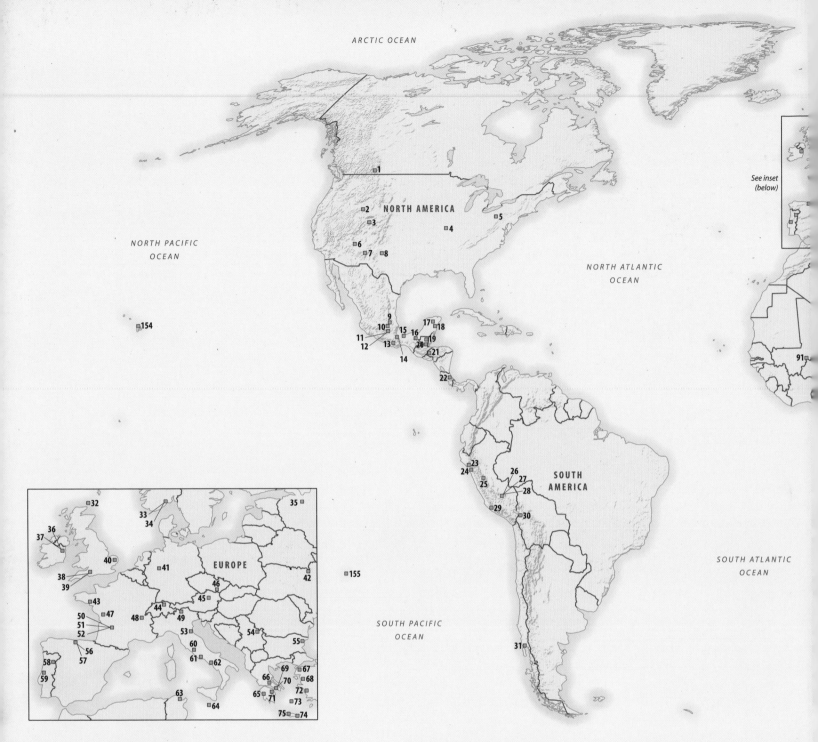

Key to Archaeological Sites